May 23, 1970

In Loving Memory

To my Dad, Edwin August Doehler, for his tremendous support,
unconditional love, and most of all for "REALLY LISTENING"
to me
no matter what I had to say!

FOREWORD

by G. Byron Kallam, M.D.

BUTTER BUSTERS THE COOKBOOK was originally written four years ago following the introduction of the National Cholesterol Education Program guidelines. It was noted by professionals that individuals who adhered to strict low-fat and low-cholesterol diets not only lowered their cholesterol levels, but lost significant amounts of weight, too. If exercise and weight training were added to their dietary lifestyle changes, this weight loss was even more profound and permanent. Since that time, there have been an explosion of books expounding on this fact.

photo by Gittings®

Medical evidence has now documented that dietary and exercise efforts have a pronounced effect on heart disease. Individuals with established heart disease have demonstrated reversal of the cholesterol blockages in the vessels (coronary arteries) that supply the heart muscle. This number of heart attacks, as well as the deaths from heart disease, has been lowered as a result.

The benefits of lowering cholesterol on vessel blockage has extended beyond reversing the mechanical blockage. There are several chemical substances in the walls of vessels that actually cause the blood vessel to narrow even further in a "high cholesterol environment." By lowering blood cholesterol these chemicals resume their normal function which allow the vessel to relax and more blood to flow to the heart muscle. This, in part, explains the observed effect that certain individuals can improve their heart disease without diminishing the size of the blockage.

I'M LISTENING! is a further extension of Pam Mycoskie's first cookbook, but written in a different style. It is organized in topic fashion, but interspersed with answers to many questions which she has encountered since her first publication. There is detailed information about low fat food preparation and eating along with an extensive narrative about exercise. There are innumerable suggestions on ways to change eating lifestyles in order to ultimately lose and maintain a healthy weight and fitness state. This involves not only the selection of proper foods, but preparation at home and eating out. The new food label is dismantled and explained in detail.

The name brand low fat shopping section lists countless items that are commercially available on the shelves of the grocery store. A directory of companies with their 800 numbers is included in order to locate the new products that you may have heard about or even seen elsewhere but cannot find in your city. Best of all, there are numerous new and delicious recipes that are all low fat and use all the low fat cooking tricks.

There is no doubt that diet and exercise play a major role in many diseases that we see and treat as physicians. This includes not only heart disease, but hypertension, diabetes, many types of cancers and obesity. These may be, in part, directly the result of poor dietary and lifestyle choices, but fortunately can be changed with better selection and some effort on our part.

A chapter on the preventive aspects of nutrition has been included that extends beyond cholesterol and heart disease. Many medical diseases have multiple factors that may play a role in their causation and ultimate treatment. Proper nutrition and exercise are two such factors. This section discusses in detail current information regarding antioxidants, one of the newest rages in preventive medicine. Additionally, current information about the dietary relationship to other diseases such as cancer, diabetes, high blood pressure, osteoporosis, headaches and eating disorders has been included.

Preventive medicine is much akin to every day issues. If your parent handed you a set of keys to a brand new car at the age of 16 and said "son, (or daughter) this car has to last you the rest of your life." No doubt each of us would have cared for that automobile differently. Our bodies, in a sense, are no different than the auto that has to last a lifetime. It, fortunately, is more tolerant of abuse, but nevertheless will function better if fed right and exercised properly. In our car, we would certainly be more likely to use high octane fuel, have the oil changed regularly and start and stop in a more gradual fashion if it had to last us a lifetime.

It is hoped that you will find this book an exciting beginning or extension of a healthy lifestyle of eating and exercising which will serve you well for many years to come. Health does not come in a pill, but in a significant part from the lifestyle choices that we make.

Byron Kallam mo

Highly respected in his field, Dr. Kallam has twelve patient information publications in circulation, and received the American College of Obstetrics and Gynecology-Mead Johnson "Patient Education Award for Cholesterol."

June 1, 1963
The Doehler family moves from Kansas City to Arlington, Texas.
Pam: age 14 (about Paige's age)   Tom: age 18 (about Blake's age)
Mom: age 45 (My age)   Dad: age 49

December 24, 1976
Dad, Pam, Blake, and Mom

August 1, 1977
Blake, Dad, and Gretchen

Pam lives in Arlington, Texas with her husband of twenty-five years, Mike. They have three very active children who provide a host of sports to follow. Blake is 19 and a freshman at Southern Methodist University. Along with his studies, Blake is busy as a member of the tennis team. Paige, 15, a sophomore at Martin High School, is also active in sports as a member of a select volleyball team, and the school tennis and volleyball teams. Tyler, 11, is a sixth grader at Dunn Elementary School. Tyler plays football (even after breaking his leg doing so last year) and ice hockey. Does this tell you something about Tyler's personality? The whole family enjoys skiing (Mike and Pam) and snowboarding (Paige, Blake, and Tyler) as well as scuba diving (except Pam who is afraid of sharks). Mike is an orthopedic surgeon and serves as the Medical Director of the Texas Ranger's Baseball Team. He, more than anything, enjoys golf whenever he can fit it into his busy schedule. Pam, in her spare time (if she ever finds any) enjoys working out, reading, travelling, rock climbing, and especially snow skiing. Most of Pam and Mike's spare time is spent shuffling kids to their activities and cheering them on in their various sports. The Mycoskies are certainly a busy bunch and insist their family vacations are what they enjoy the most. This is very important to each family member and something everyone manages to work into THEIR schedule.

Madearis Studio ©

Hi! I would like to personally thank each of you for purchasing I'M LISTENING! As a result of your many letters, I found the need for a book such as this. I've tried my best to answer all YOUR questions, and hope that the reader's letters I've included will prove inspirational to each of you. I truly believe in my heart that my work is what God planned for my life. I feel quite blessed to have been given the opportunity to provide information to people who are searching for answers. Thank you for giving me the desire to learn so much (more than I ever would have) as a result of your questions and letters. I hope you find "the answer" YOU are looking for and will enjoy reading the book half as much as I enjoyed writing it.

Good Luck!
Pam

I have found, through my experience in research, a vast difference of opinion concerning information on the same subject. I read constantly. I acquire information from many sources. Since opinions differ (including my own), I have tried to give you, the reader, the most accurate information possible. The information in this book is not intended to take the place of any medical advice. It simply reflects my opinion on studies, research, and experience regarding healthy eating and physical fitness. The information I provide is accurate to the best of my knowledge. My advice to each of you is:

Take what you want and leave the rest!

ATTENTION READERS:

If you don't find the answer to your question in this book, please write to me at the following address:

Pam Mycoskic
Butter Busters Publishing, Inc.
P.O. Box 150562
Arlington, Texas 76015

With more questions *I'M STILL LISTENING!* could also become a reality! If you would like your favorite recipe de-fatted, include it with your letter and PERMISSION TO BE REPRINTED. Who knows, it COULD end up in one of my future cookbooks, along with your full name and hometown (of course) as credit.

The author does not directly or indirectly dispense medical advice or prescribe the use of diet as a form of treatment for sickness without medical approval. Nutritionalists and other experts in the field of health and nutrition all have different opinions concerning ideas and suggestions. It is only the intent of the author to offer health information to be used IN CONJUNCTION WITH THE ADVICE OF YOUR PHYSICIAN!! If you do choose to use this information without your doctor's approval, you are prescribing for yourself. This is your constitutional right, but you must realize that the author assumes no responsibility for your actions.

NOTE: In most cases the reader's letters were printed in their exact words. For this reason their punctuation was not edited. Please keep this in mind as you read the book.

TABLE OF CONTENTS

THANK YOU FOR BEING MY FRIENDS!!

Top Row:
Char Doehler, Me, Michael Hadwin, Debbie and Roy Madearis, Jenna Bristow, Sharon Krassney, Me, Pam Hicks

Second Row:
Tyler, Blake, Paige, Me, Pennye and Brad Wilemon, Char Doehler, Dell and Clay Ellis, Me, Vicki and Steve Barnett, Valinda and Byron Kallam, and Mike, Mike and Cheryl McWithey, Me, Mike

Third Row:
Me, Debbie Stier Gumin, Me, Larry Kirshbaum, Mike, Me, Mel Parker, Me

Bottom Row:
Stephanie Christian, Ken Hicks, Tanya Spruill, Suzanne Green and Me, Zulema Rivas and Me

After traveling across the country meeting literally hundreds of people with all kinds of questions, and receiving more than a thousand letters over the past two years, I felt there was a need for this book. The questions you asked led to the long, exciting "labor of love" that ultimately resulted in it's birth.

Since many of you contributed to the growth and development of my work by planting seeds of thought in my mind, I thank you. By taking the time out of your busy schedules to come and meet me while I was on the *BUTTER BUSTERS* Book Tour, and writing the letters that inspired me to learn more information in order to answer your questions, this book is my gift to you. It is YOUR letters, by the way, that serve as my constant reminder just how THIRSTY YOU ARE for information, and your kind words that keep sending me back to the well-of-knowledge to QUENCH YOUR THIRST! Nothing makes me feel better than knowing my book has made a difference in someone's life. Since THAT was the reason *BUTTER BUSTERS THE COOKBOOK* was written in the first place, I don't have to tell you why I'm constantly looking for more answers. Your questions stimulated me to search (and in some cases research) until I learned enough to provide you with an accurate explanation. You have helped me grow and learn way beyond my own expectations and I thank each of you for that gift.

To my dear friend, typesetter, and computer tutor, Ken Hicks, I OWE YOU!! With the patience of Job, you have overlooked my compulsive behavior and everything else about me that MUST "drive you crazy." Thanks for always greeting me with a kind word and warm smile (even if you do grit your teeth after I leave). You have performed the job of deciphering my scribbles and notes when even I couldn't read what I had written. Most of all, thanks for the "late night answers" to my dumb computer questions, and staying on the phone with me until "I got it!" My thanks to Ken's wife, Pam, who helped out with the typesetting and saved us all a lot of time and energy!

I thank Mel Parker for his persistence and support. Had he not taken the time to make that trip to Texas to meet me in April 1993, your letters WOULD HAVE STILL BEEN ANSWERED, but only pasted in my scrapbook, instead of being published here for everyone to read and hopefully benefit from, too.

I include Sharon Krassney (Mel's assistant) in my gratitude for always listening, providing positive feed-back, and locating Mel when I really needed him. Sometimes he was on the road and it wasn't as easy as you might think. What a pleasant, cheerful voice she has, and a real sweetheart to all that know her!

A sincere thanks to Larry Kirshbaum who encouraged me, and shared my excitement with other book related ventures. It all resulted from that Spring day in Texas when you cared enough to ask. I look forward to a long working relationship with Warner Books thanks to you. Larry, I appreciate your faith, trust and for believing in me from the very beginning!

My heartfelt appreciation is certainly extended to Debbie Stier Gumin of Warner Books Publicity. What a time consuming job she had coordinating every detail of my life while touring across the country. Debbie endured many late night phone calls while I was on the road. More than once I realized there was a two hour time difference, after I had already dialed her home phone number. She was ALWAYS interested "in my day" no matter how busy or tired she was when I called. What a dear friend she became and one I will always treasure.

Suzanne Green, formerly of Warner Books Special Sales, took me under her wing, offered me positive reinforcement, and accompanied me when I appeared on THE JOAN RIVERS SHOW (not once but twice). Never leaving my side, she always made sure I had what I needed, and even insisted on carrying it for me! Thanks for your smile and friendship! I miss your voice and wish you continued success!!

You won't find Anna Maria Piluso's picture in the collage, but that is only because I've never met her. Anna Maria, of Warner Books Trade Production, is my long distance telephone friend who worked countless hours coordinating all the photo scans and proofreading. She served as the liaison between myself and everyone at Warner Books involved in this massive project. I sincerely thank Anna Maria for all the time, attention, and dedication she put into her work to make everything turn out "just right." I can't wait to meet her "in person" so I can see what a real Angel looks like!

I would like to especially thank Debbie and Roy Madearis and their assistant, Jenna Bristow, who spent two days photographing me for this book. I can't believe how patient they were (even when I changed my mind and/or clothes 3 different times for one shot)! Madearis Studio has been photographing our family since Blake was four (the last 15 years) and have helped us capture our children "at their best" through various photos and portraits over the years. I STILL carry pictures in my wallet today that Madearis Studio made of Blake (when he was four), Paige (at three), and Tyler (at age two) taken many years ago. They are the most patient people I know (in that business). Thanks for making me look good (even when I didn't). Your wonderful attitude and great ideas contributed greatly to the photographs in this book. (By the way, I love the vegetable shot, Debbie!)

Mike McWithey, my business manager and good friend, deserves a HUGE thank you for putting up with my requests and never saying "no" even when I deserved it. He always has the will and finds the way no matter what I ask. An example of his dedication came near my deadline to send this manuscript to Warner Books. Time was running out and we still didn't have the photos scanned into the text. Mike graciously lent me three of his employees to finish the book. As you read through the text you will quickly notice what a tremendous job that was! Stephanie Christian worked day and night over a weekend to help me out. Tanya Spruill and Michael Hadwin were a great help, too. Have you ever noticed when God shuts a door, He always opens a window? Mike's personal interest along with his great business sense have proven a tremendous contribution to the success of my ventures. I must also thank Cheryl, Mike's sweet wife who shares so many hours of Mike's time and energy with me, and never complains.

To Vicki and Steve Barnett, Pennye and Brad Wilemon, Valinda and Byron Kallam, and Dell and Clay Ellis (who were all in my dedication of *BUTTER BUSTERS*) I appreciate your continued love and support.

I would like to thank a very special friend, Zulema Rivas. She does not speak English nor do I speak Spanish. Through the miracle of computers, I now own a program that translates English to Spanish and vice versa. Zulema is one of the most thoughtful and considerate people I know. She was a tremendous help in deciding which recipes would ultimately end up in this book for my readers to enjoy, as my "official taster." I love you, Zulema, more than Spanish or English words can say! You are a blessing to our whole family and an example of what true friendship really is! I don't know very many people who would sit and watch me on T.V. for an hour not understanding a word I said, but "telling me" I did a great job with a positive nod, sincere smile, and a warm hug! It's amazing how we can communicate without speaking each other's language. I guess it goes to show that love, respect, and understanding really do come from the heart! Maybe some day my books will be translated into Spanish so you can use them for cooking, as you read the words you watched me type. Until then, you can read THIS page and know how much I appreciate your friendship! Zulema, YOU ARE THE GREATEST!

Quisiera agradecir una amiga muy especial, Zulema Rivas. Aunque ella no habla Inglés ni hablo yo Español, hemos encontrado muchas maneras de comunicarnos. Por el gran aranza de tecnología. Nos podemos comunicar por un programa de la computadora que traduce Inglés a Español y vice versa. No conozco mucha gente tan simpática como ella. Ella ha sido una ayudante muy importante. Le llamé mi "probador oficial" porque asistía en probar y elegir las recetas que ultimamente pusimos en el libro para que tengan Uds. las mejores recetas. Te amo, Zulema, más de lo pueden decir las palabras en Inglés o Español. Has sido una bendición para nuestra familia y un ejemplo de lo que es una verdadera amistad. Son muy pocas las personas que se pueden sentar al frente de la televisor observarme por una hora sin poder entender mi idioma y despues, decirme que había hecho un buen trabajo por un cabeceo positivo, una sonrisa sincera y un abrazo fuerte. Es increíble como nos comunicamos sin hablar nuestros propios idiomas. Supongo que estas acciones demuestran que amor, respeto y entendimiento realmente vienen del corazón. Quizás algún día mis libros estarán traducidos en Español para que los uses. Y también puedes recordar los días cuando estos libros fueron escritos. Hasta que estos libros vayan a ser traducidos en Español, puedas leer esta página y sepas lo mucho que aprecio su amistad. Zulema - eres la mejor!

A special thanks goes to Mom for simply "asking" for my help. I never push what I believe on anyone (even family) so I waited patiently until "she was ready." It took a high cholesterol reading to finally convince her, but since then she has managed to drop over fifty pounds and decrease her cholesterol. With her low-fat eating and regular aerobic exercise, she has become the perfect example of the low-fat lifestyle at the tender age of 75. Because she had the courage to "ask," there is no doubt she has added years to her life, but more importantly she has added "life" to her years!

To Mike, my dear, sweet, and patient husband of twenty-five years. I thank you more than all the rice in China (a personal joke)! Not only did you read hundreds of letters helping me choose the selections (as we went through all five scrapbooks together) that ended up here, you proof-read my work, and served as a tremendous source of encouragement. Thanks for putting up with my late night working, compulsive behavior, and loving me in spite of it all! You believed in me once again and thought this book was a great idea, but most importantly you told me so!!!

Thank you Paige and Tyler, two of my three kids, for excusing my tardiness on more than one occasion, when picking you up from school of wherever else you might have been. I appreciate your patience and understanding knowing I was probably "on a roll" working on this very book, had lost track of time, and didn't say a word when I drove into the parking lot and you were the only kid still waiting for their Mom to show up. Thank you for loving me in spite of my worst fault, being late!! I'm really working on getting better!! I promise!!

I must especially thank Blake, my oldest son, for he was the one who helped me find my way back to the main highway of life when I became side-tracked and scared on the lonely dirt road of fear!! (This story will be explained in _BUTTER BUSTERS TOO! THE ULTIMATE COOKBOOK_.)

Last, but certainly not least, I graciously thank OUR HEAVENLY FATHER, THE LORD GOD. For when I reached in my heart to answer YOUR questions, He was ALWAYS THERE with wisdom and guidance telling me what to say. I TAKE NO CREDIT!! I certainly realize that I am just along for the ride and appreciate the opportunity and blessing of being used as His mode of transportation. Allowing me to drive this car of dreams as He navigates the way, has given me a tremendous amount of hope, courage and most of all RELIEF, just knowing that HE is the one carrying the map and leading the way!

Madearis Studio ©

I thank each of you for your contributions, and ask only one favor in return. PLEASE, DON'T EVER STOP ASKING because I promise that I AM HERE FOR YOU, and believe me, I'M LISTENING!!

Love,
Pam

TO MY EARTH ANGELS

Laura and James Reeves

Carolyn and Morris Kiker

   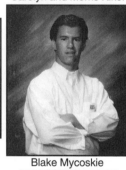   

| Jill
Humbracht | Sharon
Krassney | Sally
Mycoskie | Blake Mycoskie | Janet
Selders | Edita
Kaye | Paula
Owen |

Glenn Williams

Nina Burgett

Pam and Ken Hicks

TO MY EARTH ANGELS

You guide me along on Life's Bumpy Road,
You've loved me, not judged me
You're Worth More than Gold!

You support me through the tough times
You listen, Oh So Well!
You have always been there waiting
And Caught Me When I Fell!

I can share my feelings with you
And you understand, I know!
I confide in you through trust
It's To You I bare my Soul!

I want to thank each one of you,
For your generous gifts of love!
I feel you all were sent to me
By God from Up Above!

For you have been my patient friends,
You've never looked away
You led me down the Spiritual road,
I Travel on Today!

My Guardian Angels Right Here on Earth
Thanks For All You Do
I Speak Directly From My Heart,
I Love Each One Of YOU!!

I Honor and Thank Each of You for Your Special Friendship!

Nina Burgett, Carolyn and Morris Kiker, Laura and James Reeves, Jill Humbracht, Pam and Ken Hicks, Sharon Krassney, Sally Mycoskie, Janet Selders, Paula Owen, Edita Kaye, and my son, Blake, who TAUGHT ME how to "Really Listen" to God. A special thanks goes to Glenn Williams, who ministered to Blake, which in turn started the miraculous chain-of-events that ultimately influenced our whole family.

Thank you ALL for "LISTENING" to me!!!

Madearls Studio ©

To Jennifer who cared enough to ask...

I'd like to tell you one of the main reasons I decided to write this book. Although there are several, one stands out above the rest. In December 1993, shortly before Christmas, I received a very special gift that meant a great deal to me. Jennifer Ellis, one of my best friend's 17 year old daughter, asked if she could interview me for a project that she was working on for school. Her name might sound familiar because it was her family (The Clay Ellis family) that I mentioned in the dedication of *BUTTER BUSTERS THE COOKBOOK*. They were the unbiased tasters that tried many of my recipes as I compiled the book. Her Mom, Dell called the next day to see if I had time and wouldn't mind answering Jennifer's questions. I said that I would be glad to help and it sounded like fun. At that time, I had no idea what the interview was about. When I received the long list of questions I realized that I had been "especially chosen" for this interview. The topic was "What Adult Do I Most Admire And Why?" I couldn't believe my eyes. What an honor to think that a 17 year old girl picked me out of all the adults she knew (and admired me) because of what I had done with my life. I'll never forget that day. Because of Jennifer, and her request, I decided there were a lot of questions that deserved answers. She was the push I needed to put together this book for you, my readers, so you might also receive the answers to *your* questions. *I'M LISTENING!* (because of *your* many kind letters) has been written by **you and me —together!**

...and by the way Jennifer, thanks for asking!!

I'd like to share some of Jennifer's thought provoking questions along with my answers from the interview. It might help give you some insight as to why I wrote the book, how I wrote the book, and some of the ways it has affected my friends, family, and myself.

BUTTER BUSTERS THE COOKBOOK saved my heart (literally) and changed my life (dramatically)!! Learn more about how and why in *BUTTER BUSTERS TOO! THE ULTIMATE COOKBOOK*.

Jennifer: Why did you decide to write *BUTTER BUSTERS*?

Pam: After many years of depriving myself of food, excessive exercise to stay slim, and always being on some kind of diet, I was really tired of living that way. In March 1990 my cholesterol was found to be 242. This is considered borderline high. Since my brother, Tom, had died at the age of 19 from a heart related illness, I was scared. It was suggested by my physician that I try cutting the fat in my diet initially and see if my cholesterol would come down. In six months my cholesterol dropped almost 100 points to 146. I was excited about this but still concerned with my erratic eating habits and excessive exercise. After attending *Shape* Magazine Camp in Malibu, California, I felt that I finally had the answer to my problem. It was August 1990. I had just been re-tested and had lowered my cholesterol to 146. After spending one week at the camp learning why dieting makes you fat, all about metabolic rate, and how you can eat a lot more food if you eat low-fat, my questions were answered. I had eaten 3-5 smaller meals a day, exercised aerobically, and came home from the trip about six pounds lighter. I had never consumed that much food in my life. It was also at this time that I felt the need to do something positive with my life. I had gained a better self-image while away at camp. I came home with a courage and belief in myself that I had never felt before. I was driven to do something to help other people that might just make a difference. It had taken me 25 years to discover something so simple. I wanted to teach others what I had learned so they might not have to go through what I did to find happiness. On September 1, 1990 I began writing the book. I published the book myself in March, 1992. Writing and publishing the book is quite a story in itself. As a matter of fact the whole story will be told in *BUTTER BUSTERS TOO! THE ULTIMATE COOKBOOK*.

Jennifer: What kind of training did you have that helped you in writing the book?

Pam: That is a funny question. I really didn't have any training to write a book at all. I must say that I have always enjoyed writing essays and short stories. Creative writing and poetry came easy for me in school. I was in Florida when I began the text of the book. I had started cooking and developing recipes in September, but it wasn't until March 1991, almost six months later, that I wrote my story and the beginning of the book. I guess you could say I wrote the book from my heart and some people say I write just like I talk. It's funny because a lot of people have told me that they have enjoyed that part of the book as much as the recipes. My readers have told me when they bought the book and started reading my story they couldn't put it down and go to sleep, because they found it so interesting. Many readers say they can identify with my story. That makes me feel really good. I think my book proves that you don't necessarily have to have a lot of credentials and training in writing to tell a story that people will enjoy reading.

Jennifer: How did you get started? Did you just sit down at a word processor and the words appear like magic?

Pam: I got started by cooking four hours a day about five days a week beginning in September 1990. I continued this schedule for about one year. I was cooking a lot. As far as writing the book, I began the text in Florida while on vacation. I had, of course, been recording my recipes as I developed them. I had also written the "Modifying Recipes" section and a lot of the cholesterol information. My research and reading began even before March 1990 when I first started changing my eating habits and learned through trial and error to modify my recipes to low-fat. I had been interested and involved in exercise and fitness most of my adult life as well. I have a dear friend, Dr. Byron Kallam, who happened to be in Florida while we were there in March 1991. After completing my cholesterol section, I gave it to Byron to read over and offer his suggestions. Dr. Kallam specializes in O.B.-GYN, but is an expert in cholesterol related disease. As a matter of fact he has received the American College of Obstetrics and Gynecology-Mead Johnson "Patient Education Award for Cholesterol." He also has seven patient information publications in circulation. He was very helpful in critiquing my cholesterol section of the book. I really enjoyed learning more from such a gracious expert.

As a matter of fact, that is how I obtained a lot of information. Through reading, classes, workshops, and clinics I gathered all kinds of information that I put into easy-to-understand common language for my readers to enjoy. *Shape* Camp was a major contributing factor to my education and experience that led to the book. As far as the words appearing like magic- they didn't really, but in a sense they almost did. I sat down in front of the word processor and basically told my story and how it affected my life. Once you start writing an experience that you have actually lived, it is really quite easy to come up with the words.

Jennifer: When did you realize that the book was a success?

Pam: We initially printed 5,000 copies. I can remember loading some of the books in the back of my suburban and transporting them to a mini warehouse in Arlington. The majority were stored at River Oaks Printing in Ft. Worth. I can remember thinking if I ever sell these 5,000 books to my friends and my family and their friends and their families, it will be a miracle. The most amazing thing was that they sold in three weeks, and we ran out of books. We next printed 10,000 books and they sold in three weeks. Next we printed 20,000, then

40,000, then 70,000, 120,000, 125,000, etc. We ended up printing and selling 450,000 in a year and four months. I felt the book was a success when we ran out three weeks after it was first printed. I kind of thought it was a fluke and would soon be over and my life would go back to the way it was before. When we continued to print more and more books, and still run out every time, I guess this was when it REALLY OCCURRED to me the book might actually be successful. But, when I started receiving letters from readers telling me how my book was changing their lives, was when I knew the book had done what I had set out to do- help other people! IT WAS AT THIS TIME, I FELT IN MY HEART, THE BOOK WAS (IN FACT) A SUCCESS!!

Jennifer: Has the book ever interfered with your family life and if so, how did you handle it?

Pam: I have to say, yes it has. After about the third printing, and newspaper, television, and radio exposure, people started recognizing me when I was out in public. When we were out eating as a family folks came up to our table asking me if I was the "Butter Busters Lady?" It also happened in the grocery store, movie theater, and even at the kid's schools. At first the kids thought it was really neat that people came up to us and recognized me in public. IT GOT OLD REALLY FAST! It was especially bad when I was at the kid's sporting events or their school and people asked me questions about the book when I was trying to watch their games or whatever they were doing that I was there to watch. They started to resent the attention I was getting because it was taking me away from watching them. Kids are kids and they were very used to me giving them my undivided attention. Before I wrote the book, my family was my whole life. This is kind of hard to say. I didn't have a lot of other interests. The book has given me a new identity. I'm no longer just my husband's wife and my kid's Mom. I realized after the book was published, for the first time in my life, people were actually interested in what I had to say. This has been great for my self-image, but the kids are having a little trouble understanding the new interest people have in their Mom. To them, I am just Mom. Don't get me wrong, that is the way I want it to be. I don't want them to think I am any different than I have ever been as far as my interest in them. I would just like them to try and understand I do have a life other than the role of chauffeur, cook, cheer-leader, and housekeeper. I try to steer away from conversations about the book as much as I can when I am attending the kid's activities. This isn't easy to do at times, but I do the best that I can.

Jennifer: You have become quite a celebrity, especially in Arlington. How has it affected you personally?

Pam: I don't really think of myself as any kind of celebrity. In fact, it still surprises me when people come up and recognize me from the book, have seen me on T.V., or heard me on the radio. The most important thing to me is that my friends and family realize that I will never change on the inside no matter what happens with my career. I love my work, and feel that it has helped and influenced a great many people, but I will do my best to balance my priorities and never lose sight of the most important people in my life, my family!

I have had the opportunity to meet a lot of people I probably never would have, had it not been for the book. I've had the opportunity to meet a lot of celebrities because I have appeared on shows with them. It's always exciting to meet these people, but I would never include myself as "one of them." I will always consider myself A WIFE AND MOTHER WHO HAPPENED TO WRITE A BOOK that has helped people, and this is the way it will always be.

Jennifer: Young women today can look to you as an example of a woman who has it all, with success in your relationships AND success in the business world. How did you do it?

Pam: Thank you for the compliment, Jennifer. I feel my success in the business world is a direct result of my ability to deal with and get along well with people. I feel if you have a fairly good track record in getting along with people, it will help you in every aspect of your life. Another contributing factor to my business success (although it sometimes drives me and my family crazy) is my compulsive personality and perfectionism. I don't delegate well because I know if I do the job myself and it falls, I have no one to blame but myself. My husband thinks that I am too compulsive, and I have to agree with him to a certain extent. When I receive a letter from a reader with a question, I usually sit down that evening, answer it, and mail the next day. If I get ten letters in one day, I allow myself two days to answer them. My husband thinks it would be just fine to handle my correspondence once a week. I don't agree. I feel like a person writes because they are anxious for a reply before they can continue with what the question is about. For that reason, I feel the need to answer all questions as quickly as possible. As I said, this behavior can tend to drive everyone a little crazy. I honestly feel a little compulsive behavior can be found within the personality of most successful people. I have always enjoyed people and feel I relate well with others. Most people find me easy to talk to, and I get along with most everyone I meet. I have been told by my readers they can relate to me because of my honesty and straight-forward personality. I consider this a great compliment. I am very conscious of other people's feelings, and have always tried to live my life by the Golden Rule, "Do unto others as you would have them do unto you." I feel consideration is the most important thing in any relationship, and I try to approach everyone I meet with this attitude.

My success in the business world has been what I consider, a fluke (so to speak). If you would have asked me when I was twenty, no, even if you would have asked me when I was thirty, "What are you going to do with your life?" my answer would have never been in one million years that I was going to have some kind of career in writing or have some kind of success in the business world. I just wasn't interested in that at all. I worked after college and up until I had my first child, but I was not interested in working once I become a full-time mother with my three children. I was perfectly happy being a stay-at-home Mom.

Believe me, my intention in life was not to write a book or become any kind of business person with a career. I didn't plan any of this. I wrote the book because I felt the need to share the information I had learned with others. When I wrote the book, I never considered what might happen after they sold. I was so focused on writing and getting it finished, that the response or result of my work never entered my mind. The whole process kind of developed and evolved out of necessity. I learned a lot about the printing process because I took an active part by publishing the book myself. Once the books were printed I learned by trial and error how to market and distribute myself, because I had no role model and, as I mentioned before, I don't delegate responsibility very well. I used my own common sense and (luckily) good judgment regarding getting the book into the right people's hands. An example of this was the wonderful article Beverly Bundy, of the *Ft. Worth Star Telegram,* wrote about me when the book first came out. She wrote a very positive piece that was syndicated all over the country which stirred up a lot of interest and resulted in the sale of thousands of books. Most of all, I attribute my success in the business world to LUCK and even more than that, to GOD'S WILL. By luck, I mean the right people liked it enough to tell others, so the book sold by word of mouth. By God's Will, I mean in my heart I am sure this is what God wants me to do with my life. I feel very blessed that He has chosen me as a courier to deliver this message to help other people change their lives for the better. Believe me, I am not that smart. It's true that I study and read everything I can get my hands on regarding health and fitness, but when it comes to going out and speaking to the people, there is no doubt in my mind that He is there with me every step of the way. It really takes a lot of the pressure off of me. People ask me all the time if I get nervous when I do T.V. shows or interviews. I tell them no, because I never feel like I am alone.

I try to educate myself with the pertinent information so I have the tools necessary to provide me with the right answers, but I leave the way it's delivered up to God! He hasn't let me down with a loss for words yet. Sometimes what comes out of my mouth even surprises me. For this reason I feel very secure and confident in my work because of my faith and trust in God.

Jennifer: You started your career as an author at age 40, did this late start help or hinder you?

Pam: I have to say it definitely helped me. At 40 I finally grew up and matured enough to really be interested in learning. Before that, I attended school and classes as a duty, rather than a pleasure. At forty, I finally found a subject I was interested in (health and fitness) and now I can't get enough. I read constantly and I am genuinely interested in all the new information I can get my hands on. I could have never done something like this when my children were small (nor did I have the desire). I think this had a lot to do with it. I was ready (my kids were all in school) to do something that might make a difference and possibly help people. It took caring enough about myself to want to try and change. At forty I started liking myself for the first time, and felt I could make a positive contribution. I was forced to change my eating habits to lower my cholesterol at forty. Up until then I thought I was invincible. I thought heart disease and cholesterol problems were a result of bad hereditary luck or happened to the overweight out-of-shape couch potatoes that didn't take care of themselves. Boy, was I stupid. When my cholesterol turned up high, this was probably the best thing that ever happened to me for many reasons. My attitude changed dramatically because I was forced to change. I felt so lucky when I figured out that I could control my cholesterol through a low-fat diet, that I couldn't wait to spread the good news. When I finally figured out that diets didn't work and you can eat a lot of food and not gain weight (if you eat low-fat), I was even more anxious to share my new-found knowledge. I think forty was the perfect time to begin a career because I had spent most of my adult life taking care of everyone else (as a lot of mothers tend to do). This all came at a really good time in my life, a time that I needed to feel good about myself. I needed to do something.... How do I say this? I don't want to say it the wrong way.

I had to do something, kind of to prove to myself that I could do and be more than just a wife and mother. I don't mean to say that it isn't a very wonderful feeling to be a wife and mother. As a matter of fact, when people asked me what I did for a living, I was always quick and proud to reply, "I'm the best mother there is, and I'm proud of it!" I felt that I did a good job and I really was a great mother. I hope I'm still doing a good job, but I must admit it isn't as easy to get to every single activity in your children's lives when you have a full-time career, too. I have so much more respect for working mothers than I ever did before this all happened and I found myself in this most difficult situation!! However, I wanted an identity of my own and a sense that I could really do something that mattered outside of my own family situation. I wasn't out searching for something. It wasn't like, oh, here I am at this point in my life and I need something to do. It wasn't that at all. It just really evolved and grew. I had no idea anything like this would happen. It has helped me understand myself a little better. To tell you the truth, I feel like I really have a lot more to offer my children than before I worked. I don't mind asking for their help, even though I USED TO DO EVERYTHING FOR THEM myself. I think they appreciate the fact I NEED THEM just as much as they need me. This has made us all understand, respect and admire each other in a new exciting way!

Jennifer: I know physical fitness is a very important part of your life. How do you find the time in your busy schedule for regular workouts?

Pam: That's really easy, because it goes right up there on the top of my priority list. I feel that physical fitness has to be that way. You know, you can find every excuse in the world not to workout...you don't have time, you're too tired, you don't want to have to take another shower and clean up again, you don't look good in a leotard, you don't have a place to work out, you don't like to sweat, you don't have good shoes, the weather is bad, you have a luncheon date, you're having a bad day, you don't have anyone to watch the kids, you're sore from your last workout, you have a headache (or PMS)....OH PLEASE... I mean we can all find a million and one excuses not to work out. I know because I've used them, too!!! I have always needed my workout as a stress release.

Oh, I do it for my heart and health, weight control, and to help prevent osteoporosis, too, but the bottom line is that exercise for me is the best form of mental balance I've come across so far. I need that outlet. I need that physical and mental outlet. I feel better when I work out. I find when I don't workout that I am tired and sluggish. Besides that, I get VERY IRRITABLE when I don't get to workout. Just ask my children and husband if you don't believe me. It's amazing how a good workout energizes me. When I work out I feel refreshed and happy with myself. It may sound crazy to some of you, but it is a little gift I give myself. I really do think of it that way. This is MY TIME! I turn on the answering machine, read, meditate, pray, and generally plan my day. When I am in the middle of writing a column, letter, or even a book, great inspiration and ideas have come to me when I was on the Stairmaster climbing away. I think it's because I let my mind wander. I always keep a pen and paper handy next to my water bottle and cassette player (the other two necessities of my workout). If I have a choice, I workout early in the day. I like to get it out of the way, otherwise things come up and I find myself struggling to work it in. It's not that I don't want to, there are just more demands on my time as the day progresses (especially once 3:30 rolls around and the kids are out of school). Sometimes you do have to re-arrange your schedule. Life isn't perfect. I might have an early morning meeting or appointment and I have to workout at 5:00 or even late at night. The point is if you at least schedule it and try to stay halfway consistent, nine times out of ten, you will work it in and most likely it will become a habit you enjoy. It's obvious why you will find exercise high on my priority list. It makes me feel better inside and out, gives me the tools physically and mentally to deal with stress, and is the only undemanding time of the day that I give myself.

Jennifer: If you had two weeks left to live, what would you do and why?

Pam: Oh Jennifer, this is heavy!! I think, this might sound really strange, but I would take my family and go to Europe. I feel that is one thing in my life I really still want to do that I haven't done yet. I want to see Europe. Of course two weeks probably wouldn't give me much time.

I would want to take my family and I would want to get away from everything and just spend two weeks with them traveling, enjoying their company, and gradually saying good bye, I guess. That's a tough question. I don't know why I said Europe, but I do know why I said I would want to be with my family. It's because they are the most important thing in my life and always will be.

Jennifer: If you had one wish, what would it be and why?

Pam: That's even harder, Jennifer. My wish would be that no matter where my career takes me or how it affects my life, I will never change my values or priorities. No matter what has happened so far (and a lot has happened), I feel like I still have my feet on the ground. I try to keep my priorities in order. My family is ranked #1. If you took away everything else in my life... all the materialistic things (which are fun, enjoyable and nice) ... the extras ... that's all OK, but my one wish would be that I would have my family and that I would never really change, because I feel like I know where I'm going, I know where I have been, and I know where I want to be...and that's pretty much where I am right now. If I can just stay this way and keep things in perspective, then I feel like I will have done what I set out to do with my life.

Jennifer: If you could change one thing in your life, what would it be?

Pam: That's easy. More time in the day! But you know Jennifer, that really is my biggest problem and the one thing I would like to change in my life. I tend to fill every minute and can't stand to waste time. Sometimes I really carry it too far. My compulsive personality tends to get in the way. I have been so blessed with everything around me, I really have. Rather than me having time to do more, I would like to make myself slow down, and TAKE THE TIME to appreciate the life I have. I need to stop and smell the roses (so to speak) rather than be in such a hurry to plant more flowers. You see, "my garden of life" really is quite beautiful just the the way it is. I THANK GOD EVERY DAY for the all the blessings He has bestowed upon my family. That is the ONE THING I always take the time to do!!

Well Jennifer, now you have it, the untold story (until now) of Pam Mycoskie. I hope I gave you the answers you wanted to hear. Your questions really made me stop and think about some things that I had never thought about before. Your questions inspired me to follow my heart, and in doing so, gave me the push I needed to write this book.

I really appreciate you selecting me as your role model. I feel very honored, very proud, and most of all very touched that I was considered in a group of people you respected and chosen BY YOU to be placed in such a prestigious position.

Like Forrest Gump's mother told him, "Life is like a box of chocolates, you never know what you're going to get." This couldn't be more true. However, I feel very blessed with the box of chocolates I was given. Every piece I sample tastes better than the one before, as does my life and what I have experienced. Every time I remove the wrapper on a piece of chocolate, and take the risk of trying something new, tasting what God has in store for me, I realize just how much I really do love surprises!!

Madearis Studio ©

Thank you for allowing me to share my box of chocolates with you, Jennifer, and for THE GIFT YOU GAVE ME by asking!!

Monte Borders ©

Jennifer Ellis
May   1995

Jennifer graduated from The Oakridge School in Arlington, Texas in May, 1995 with a long list of honors. She was a member of the National Honor Society, Foreign Language Club, and Infinity Club. A beautiful girl, Jennifer refuses to sit on the sidelines and watch others participate in sports. As captain of the varsity basketball team, she lead her school to 2nd place in state. She was honored as Most Valuable Player and selected to First Team All City. She will attend Brigham Young University in the fall of 1995. I've had the opportunity to get to know Jennifer quite well over the past fifteen years, and have watched her grow into a bright, kind, sensitive, and determined young woman. There is no doubt that Jennifer will attain the many goals she has set for herself, for she is most definitely a participant in life, not a spectator.

YOU CAN LEARN A LOT BY LISTENING!

Did you know that you are actually forced to learn if you really listen to what people have to say? I'm not just talking about information they happen to give you. What I am really talking about is the questions people ask. How many times have you had a conversation with another person when they didn't ask you some kind of question before they stopped talking? See, I just did it to you! As you probably know, when someone asks you a question your response is called an answer. Do you know the most effec-

Talk Radio in Houston January 1994

tive way to answer a question? With accurate information, that's how! Sometimes we know the answer right away as a result of past experience. If we don't know the answer, what

Atlanta Talk Radio   February 1994

do we do then? Most people do what they can to find it, right? So, like I said, LISTENING FORCES US TO LEARN!

This book is a result of me listening to your questions and learning so I could give you the answers. You forced me to learn more about a subject (in some cases) than I ever would have, had you not written to me and asked. For this I thank each of you for encouraging me to listen (and therefore learn) and answer (so I could inform) all your thought provoking questions!

FIRST THINGS FIRST!

I will answer the #1 most popular asked question right now, before you even have a chance to ask again.

You: Pam, when are you going to write another cookbook?

Me: As a matter of fact I am currently in the process of writing two books. *THE BUTTER BUSTERS COOKNOTES for KIDS IN THE KITCHEN* is due out soon with *BUTTER BUSTERS TOO! THE ULTIMATE COOKBOOK* to follow.

WARNER BOOKS CAME TO TEXAS AND FOUND ME!

Now that we have the #1 MOST POPULAR ASKED QUESTION out of the way, I would like to tell you WHY I decided to write this book. After self-publishing *BUTTER BUSTERS THE*

Paige filling mail orders.

COOKBOOK in March 1992, and learning a lot in the process, I was approached by Warner Books in April 1993. They had found my book in Texas while attending a wholesale book show. They inquired about me while visiting a Taylor's Book Store in Ft. Worth after finding *BUTTER BUSTERS* in the #1 Bestseller Slot. The manager told them I was a local woman who lived in Arlington with her husband and three kids. He explained I had written the book after dramatically lowering my cholesterol (242 to 146 in six months) by simply cutting the fat in my diet. He

also let them know that I had self-published the book and managed to sell more than

300,000 copies in less than six months. This must have sparked their interest, because they called me from New York the next week and made an offer to purchase publishing rights to *BUTTER BUSTERS THE COOKBOOK*. I told them that I was very flattered and thank you very much, but I was really enjoying doing it myself. I had, at this time, sold over 400,000 copies in less than a year. They called back THE NEXT DAY and doubled the offer. I again told them thank you, but it was not a money issue. *BUTTER BUSTERS* was a "labor of love." With the

The Butter Busters office (my dining room)

concern of my brother's heart-related death at the age of nineteen in 1965, along with my own scare of a high cholesterol at age 40 in 1990, I had found myself "driven" to write the

Tyler helps, too!

book. I told them I never wrote the book to make money, it had turned into a family venture, and we were all having a lot of fun with it. They next asked if they could at least come to Texas and meet me. I didn't want to be rude, so I said "yes, that would be fine, but my husband and I are going snow skiing next week, and my son, Tyler, has an ice hockey tournament the following weekend so the earliest you can come is a week from next Tuesday." They said, "Fine, we will be there." I hung up the phone not believing what I had heard. They didn't give up. I could just picture in my mind what they must be like. I figured they were a bunch of stuffy, forceful New York Slick Willies that couldn't take "No" for an answer and were very used to getting their own way. I was so busy traveling the next couple of weeks, I really didn't give the upcoming meeting with Warner Books much thought.

MEL PARKER COMES TO TEXAS!

The folks at Warner Books made a very wise choice when they sent Mel Parker as their representative to Texas. He was one of the nicest men I had ever met (definitely not stuffy). He was kind, personable, interested in me as a wife and mother (not just about my book), funny, smart, and basically a very pleasant person. I immediately took a liking to him (that is a Texas phrase by the way). After a nice long conversation and wonderful dinner he finally popped the big question. Mel Parker asked me, "Pam, tell me, why did you REALLY write BUTTER BUSTERS anyway?" I thought about this for several minutes before I answered (remember you always learn by listening). I learned something about myself as I was sitting in the restaurant that evening in April. When I really searched my heart (for I knew that was where I would find the answer), I told him my honest reply. "Mel, I wrote this book to simply teach others what I had learned." He didn't say a word for about two

Pam and Mel Parker

minutes. He just looked at me with this great big smile on his face, knowing that I had given him the answer he wanted to hear. He replied by saying, "Pam, you have done a really good job getting your book out all by yourself. As a matter of fact you have done an UNBELIEVABLE job getting your book out! However, THIS is where Warner Books can help you deliver your message (so to speak). With our publicity and sales force, a National Book Tour, full page ad in PEOPLE MAGAZINE, and other National media exposure, think how many lives you could REALLY touch!"

THEY WANTED TO HELP ME "SPREAD THE WORD!"

I must have sat there five minutes without saying a word. It was true I had sent my book to "Good Morning America," "Regis and Kathi Lee," "The Home Show," "Oprah," etc. and had never even received one reply that my book and personal letter had been delivered. Even though they were sent by certified mail and SOMEONE had signed for them, my time and effort were not acknowledged. I know how busy those folks are with the thousands of books and letters received weekly, but I almost feel there should be a staff within every organization to handle such matters. In most cases the materials never reach the person they are sent to. I've been told most end up on a shelf in a mail room or filed away never to be looked at again. I realized then that a small publisher like myself, even though I had sold MORE BOOKS than MOST that graced The New York Times Bestseller List, needed A BIG NAME PUBLISHER behind me to get noticed in the "real publishing world." I have to tell you this was not an ego decision like it might sound as I relay the story. It was instead the practical solution to the problem I had dealt with all along. I considered the idea that Mel Parker from New York City might just have a point. To REALLY teach others what I had learned on a national level would require the assistance of someone much bigger then "little ole me" down in Arlington, Texas. He didn't try to push me in any way, but only asked if my husband and I would consider coming to New York to meet the staff at Warner Books and let them "show us their stuff." Mike and I told him we would discuss it between ourselves and my business manager, Mike McWithey, would call him with an answer within a week.

A BASEBALL SIGNED BY NOLAN RYAN MEANT MIKE LIKED HIM TOO!
My husband really liked him, too. As a matter of fact after we left the restaurant Mike insisted we all stop by his office before Mike McWithey took Mel back to his hotel. I had no idea what my husband had in mind. As we sat out in the parking lot, Mike ran into his office and came back a few minutes later with something that made Mel's eyes light up even more than when I gave him "the answer he wanted to hear" in the restaurant. Mike brought him a baseball signed by Nolan Ryan. My husband is the Medical Director for The Texas Rangers Baseball Team to explain why he had an autographed ball at his office. PLEASE don't call him asking for one, however. Mike really hates to impose on Nolan by asking for an "autographed anything." He is quite aware of the MANY REQUESTS and demands placed on Nolan constantly, and would rather not take advantage of their friendship. Because of Mike's consideration, his own personal collection is really quite small. That was my BIG CLUE that HE MUST REALLY LIKE MEL in order to part with one of his beloved treasures. I guess during dinner when I had excused myself to go to the ladies room, the subject of baseball, The Texas Rangers, and Nolan Ryan must have come up. There was no doubt in my mind that Mike REALLY liked Mel Parker from New York City!

A TRIP TO THE BIG APPLE!
Since our anniversary was coming up in May, and the folks at Warner Books really wanted

us to come New York, we decided to make the trip for our twenty-third anniversary and mix business with pleasure. Mike and I had only been to New York one other time, in October 1989 to celebrate my 40th Birthday. I hadn't wanted one of those "everyone wears black and makes jokes about how you are over the hill parties." I had, instead, requested a trip to the "City of My Dreams," New York. We enjoyed ourselves so much the first time, that we couldn't wait to go back for another visit.

Mike McWithey, Pam and husband Mike
New York May, 1993

THE FOLKS AT WARNER BOOKS ARE SPECIAL!

They held a luncheon in my honor at The Time Warner Building and I was able to meet several more of the (couldn't be nicer) folks from Warner Books. Larry Kirshbaum, the president of the company, was even at the meeting. I couldn't have asked for a warmer reception. It didn't take me five minutes to realize these people were going to become my

Mike, Pam, Mel, and Larry

friends. I knew immediately (before they even had a chance to ask) that my answer would be YES! It had nothing to do with the long list of "things" they planned on doing to promote my book. I could tell they spoke from the heart and were SINCERE. They wanted TO HELP ME "spread the word." They were good people and I knew I could trust them with "my baby" (as Larry put it), *BUTTER BUSTERS*. We had a wonderful time in New York and went home with a long detailed contract to read over.

A DECISION I WILL NEVER REGRET!

After a few weeks of ironing out details, I officially signed on the dotted line June 25, 1993. It was a decision I will never regret and one that gave me the opportunity to experience something very special with my son Blake, that literally changed my life. Try to "hold that thought" when the answers to your questions will be revealed in *BUTTER BUSTERS TOO! THE ULTIMATE COOKBOOK*. Before turning my book over to Warner Books, I had managed to sell 450,000 copies of *BUTTER BUSTERS* on my own. After joining forces with Warner, revising my book to the updated 7th edition, and traveling to twenty-three cities in

Pam signs with Warner Books
June 25, 1993

4½ weeks on a National Book Tour, we were able to "spread the word" on a much greater scale. After selling 700,000 copies (of the new 7th edition) in less than twelve months, the number of books quickly surpassed the 1 million mark!! There was no doubt in my mind that the folks at Warner Books knew what they were talking about. I had trusted them with "my baby" and TOGETHER WE DID MAKE IT HAPPEN!! They supported and believed in me, and for those reasons earned my dedication, respect, and heartfelt gratitude.

WHY AND HOW I WROTE THIS BOOK

THIS BOOK IS ABOUT YOUR QUESTIONS AND MY ANSWERS!

Even before I signed with Warner Books, I had received hundreds of letters and phone calls from people all over the country. Everyone wanted more information. There were questions about recipe make-overs, new products, substitutions, exercise and fitness, how to figure individual fat grams, cholesterol and heart disease information, etc., etc. You name it and I have been asked.

IT WAS YOUR LETTERS THAT GAVE ME THE IDEA TO WRITE I'M LISTENING!

A couple of weeks ago as I sat at my desk answering mail, I glanced at my watch surprised to see it was 2:00 A.M. My family had gone to bed hours before. After receiving eight letters that day, I knew they must be answered for the next day there would be more. Four of the eight contained the very same questions. While answering the last letter, the idea of writing this book came to me. I wanted to give my readers the information they deserved but was finding it more and more difficult to do so on a daily basis. I've always felt if someone made the effort and took the time to write, they deserved an answer with the best information I could provide. Because of the great number of books in print, writing letters had grown to a full time job. I was finding it more and more difficult to answer the letters as QUICKLY as I had in the beginning. This REALLY bothered me because there just wasn't enough time in the day to take care of my correspondence, work on *KIDS IN THE KITCHEN, BUTTER BUSTERS TOO! THE ULTIMATE COOKBOOK*, keep up with my three DEMANDING children (with their hectic schedules) and have any time or energy left for my VERY PATIENT DEAR HUSBAND, MIKE. For these reasons, I decided THERE WAS A NEED for a book such as this. Because so many of the same questions were asked over and over again, I felt the book was an obvious solution.

KNOWLEDGE IS MY GIFT TO EACH OF YOU!

I've always believed we never really possess love, until we give it away. Like love, what good is knowledge if you keep it within yourself? There is no greater gift, than "giving of yourself." For this reason, I want to share my gift of knowledge, through *I'M LISTENING*,  with each of you! I hope you will enjoy reading the book, knowing you are contributing to the salvation of my marriage (just kidding). Hopefully my other books will be finished and in your hands in the near future. Please try and be patient, knowing I am cooking and writing as fast as I can to bring you the books YOU EXPECT AND DESERVE! I PROMISE THEY WILL BE WORTH THE WEIGHT (no pun intended)!!

..In the kitchen and loving it! *Pam*

P.S. If I could only cook and write as fast as I CAN TALK, we would REALLY have it made, now wouldn't we? Don't answer that!

UP FRONT
AND PERSONAL

THE AMERICAN DREAM CAN HAPPEN TO YOU!!!
(If you have the courage and desire to make it happen!)

I'm including this essay because it answers a lot of the questions you have asked me. Maybe it will help each of you understand me a little better and some of my reasons for writing THIS book:

February 1995

I'm here to let you know that the American Dream really can come true! I am living proof. Let me introduce myself. My name is Pam Mycoskie. I am the forty-five year old mother of three children (Blake-19, Paige-15, and Tyler-11), and have been married to Mike (my high school sweetheart) for 25 years.

Tyler, Blake, Paige, Mike, and Pam
December 1994

After my first child was born in 1976, I became a typical stay-at-home Mom. I was perfectly happy taking care of my home and raising my children. In March 1990 my cholesterol profile was taken (for the first time) at my yearly OB-GYN exam and was found to be 242. I wasn't overweight, didn't smoke, exercised, and thought I was a healthy specimen. When I received the test results I was quite alarmed. You see, my bother Tom died in 1965 of heart disease at the age of nineteen.

He was playing intramural fraternity football at TCU, caught a pass in warm-up, collapsed, and was unconscious. This was before anyone knew about CPR. Mouth-to-mouth was attempted by one of his fraternity brothers to no avail. He was then rushed to the hospital for open heart surgery, but they never could revive him. My parents requested an autopsy. The report read: "Cause of death- unknown, a cardiac arrest." You can't imagine what this did to my parents. Tom had never been ill, so it came as a shock to all of us. When I received the high cholesterol reading, I was really scared. I thought there might be some kind of hereditary heart disease that ran in my family. My physician suggested I first try lowering my cholesterol by cutting the fat in my diet. In March 1990 very few people read labels. Most people didn't even know what cholesterol was (nor did they care). There weren't a lot of low-fat products on the market. Everyone, myself included, was

Tom Doehler, my brother
September 1965

UP FRONT AND PERSONAL

***SHAPE* FITNESS WEEK**
MALIBU, CALIFORNIA   AUGUST 1990

concerned with calories, not fat. I started reading labels, changing all my favorite recipes to low-fat, and learning everything I could about the different kinds of fats and cholesterol containing products. After six months I managed to bring my cholesterol down almost 100 points BY JUST CUTTING THE FAT in my diet. It went from 242 to 146. Boy, was I ever relieved to find I didn't have hereditary heart disease and I COULD CONTROL MY CHOLESTEROL THROUGH MY LOW-FAT DIET.

It was about that time (August 1990), I attended *SHAPE* Camp (a week of fitness seminars and activities conducted by *SHAPE* Magazine) in Malibu, California. Even though I had remained thin most of my adult life, my eating habits were terrible. I under-ate and over-exercised to control my weight. I was always on some kind of diet and, to tell you the truth, I was miserable and tired of living that way. At *SHAPE* Camp I learned all about metabolic rate, why dieting makes you fat, and yo-yo dieting. I decided to give the control of my terrible eating habits to them by following whatever they said to do. After all, 25 years of my way wasn't working too well. I ate more food that one week than I had ever consumed in my life (aside from my three pregnancies), exercised aerobically, and came home about six pounds lighter. I also came home with a new, improved self-image. During my week at *SHAPE* Camp I learned a lot about myself. It was the first time I met Barbara Harris, the Editor in Chief of *SHAPE*, and felt the pages of the magazine "come to life" before my very eyes. The more she talked, the more I realized she REALLY WAS the kind, caring woman I had imagined all those months I had read her personal note in the "Shapescene" section of the magazine. It was obvious she really cared about all of us, and, after her inspirational talk, I felt for the first time I really could do something with my life. She had planted the seed of hope and desire to become the best I could be, and fertilized me with the tools to start growing. I grew and blossomed a little more each day at camp, and when I got back to Texas I felt I had grown into a flower ready to plant my very own garden. I had never experienced so much support in my life. Everyone on the staff was encouraging and it was obvious the counselors were "hand picked" from the best crop available. By the end of the week there was a closeness among us that I had never experienced. We REALLY CARED about each other. As a matter of fact, I have remained in contact and still write to several girls I met in Malibu five years ago.

I went back to Texas with "a new lease on life" and a mission to accomplish! I was excited and ready to begin! I knew that I wanted to do "something" to make a difference, but what? Several people had previously suggested I write a low-fat cookbook. They had tasted my modified recipes and thought the food tasted great. (At that time there really weren't any TRULY low-fat cookbooks on the market.) Until then, I had never taken their suggestions seriously. After all, I was "just a Mom" with no training in the field of writing. After much thought and consideration however, I decided (with God's help) maybe I COULD write a very simple (easy to understand) cookbook with regular food recipes. I had studied a great deal (when I lowered my cholesterol) and felt my tips and suggestions might help others change their eating habits, too. My main objective was to do the footwork and make the book easy to understand and follow for anyone and everyone. Thanks to *SHAPE* Camp, I had the self-confidence to pursue my dream. I felt with God behind the project along with His constant direction, I just might be able to write a book after all.

I began my venture in late August 1990 with much excitement and dedication. I cooked 4-5 hours a day, five days a week, for nine months. I worked late many nights at my word processor entering my recipes and ideas. There just wasn't enough time in the day to do it all! At 3:00 every afternoon, I took off my cook's hat and became a full-time wife and Mom once again. I was very focused on the book, but I

Pam and Tyler work on recipes 1991

still had the responsibility and desire to take care of my family. My husband helped out a great deal by getting the children off to school, thus allowing me some much-needed rest before I start-

Tyler, Briana Sundberg, and Paige Florida Spring Training March 1991

ed all over with the same routine the next day in the kitchen. I wrote most of the intro-duction and text of the book while in Florida

Blake with pitcher Jeff Russell Florida 1991

during four weeks of baseball Spring Training in March 1991. (My husband is the team physician for The Texas Rangers, so I find myself in Florida every year on a beautiful island off the coast of Port Charlotte.) I found the solitude and beauty of my surroundings on the island quite inspira-tional.

I finished writing the book in a little over one year. I decided to publish it myself because I didn't want anything changed or removed from my original text. I didn't really think a big publisher would be interested anyway. I never wrote the book with the intention to make money, so that was not a contributing factor when I planned how the book would be printed. I didn't want to cut any corners. I wanted the book to be usable, durable, and affordable. These were my primary concerns. I began my search for a printer that could handle the job.

After shopping around for a several days, I decided on a small husband/wife printing company for all the WRONG REASONS. I felt sorry for them. The woman was obese and the office was pitiful. It was very small and kind of dirty. Actually two words come to mind when describing their office, "a dive." It was obvious they didn't have a lot of business, OR money. However, they were really nice, told me they thought my book was wonderful, and promised they would do a great job. In other words, they believed in me! They told me they could print my book just the way I wanted (including laminated tabs, a plastic cover, GBC printed binding, and 70# paper). They told me MY WAY would be expensive because the books would have to be put together by hand. I told them that was OK, because the quality of the book was very important to me. I promptly went to the bank and applied for a loan. I was told the only way the bank would loan me that much money would be if my husband co-signed the papers. You see, I had no credit references. I had worked before I had children but was "just a wife and mother." That was what THEY told me anyway. My husband, Mike, was happy to co-sign. He was so proud of me and what I had accomplished. He didn't want to interfere or try to control my decision. As a matter of fact he never met the printers I had hired. He wanted it to be "my deal." This is one time I wish he would have intervened. You see, the printers took my money and spent it, went bankrupt, and I ended up losing $30,000.00. They never had any intention of printing my book. They "saw me coming" and took advantage of the situation. It was a tough lesson to learn. I had trusted them with "my baby" and the whole experience just about destroyed me. I can only compare it to an unwanted abortion. I felt as if I'd been robbed of my precious possession that I had conceived, nurtured, and developed before it even had the chance to be born (or printed). I had given this project over two years of my life and they took it away from me. I couldn't do a thing about it (or so I thought). It's a long story and I don't have the time or room to tell it here. (It could actually be a book in itself!) As a matter of fact, the "whole story" will be told in *BUTTER BUSTERS TOO! THE ULTIMATE COOKBOOK*.

Before I lost the money, the printer went bankrupt, and I went into self-induced solitary confinement and depression, I had the opportunity to return to *SHAPE* Camp (this time in Destin, Florida) and share my experience of writing the book with my peers and friends. (This all happened before the disaster hit in January 1992 when the printers locked me out of their office and stopped taking my phone calls.)

Going back a bit to October 1991, after the book was finished, typeset, and ready for production, I returned to *SHAPE* Camp with six sample copies to share with the girls. Even though it wasn't printed yet, I had photo-copied the pages myself and my printer had laminated a few covers so I could show everyone at camp what I had accomplished over the past year.

I'll never forget that first night when Barbara Harris had me up on stage to tell my story. That was only the second time I had ever seen Barbara, but admired and respected her so much. She had been such an influence in my life, and now she had given me the opportunity to share my story with the other women. I had actually finished what I set out to do by writing the book. She watched and listened like a proud parent as I spoke to the group that evening. I could see the pride in her eyes as if one of "her children" had pleased her. I was also proud, but more than that, thankful that God had used me in a way that might actually benefit others. I felt so blessed that I had been especially chosen by Him to deliver the message and teach other people what I had learned. I knew that I owed the glory to Him, but I couldn't help but enjoy the moment and satisfaction knowing together "we" had accomplished the job. I made a personal commitment to God that night. He had given me the knowledge, dedication and will to write the book. Barbara had given me the confidence, desire, and courage.

With these gifts, I had accomplished a feat, I would never have considered possible in my lifetime. When I climbed into bed that night, I made a promise in my prayers that I would devote my work and life to accomplish whatever HE wanted me to do. I asked Him to show me the way and I would

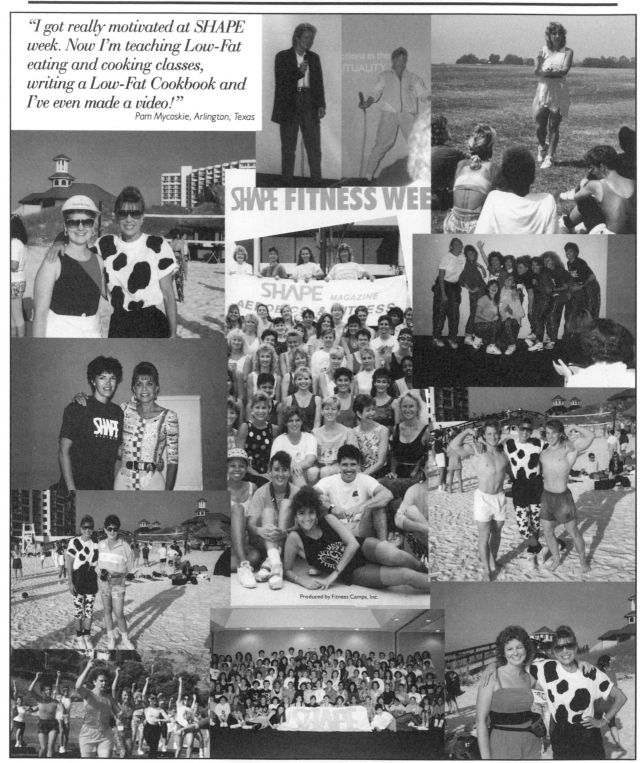

"I got really motivated at SHAPE week. Now I'm teaching Low-Fat eating and cooking classes, writing a Low-Fat Cookbook and I've even made a video!"

Pam Mycoskie, Arlington, Texas

SHAPE FITNESS WEEK
SANDESTIN, FLORIDA NOVEMBER 1991

follow, knowing He would never let me get lost in the process. I knew the road might not be an easy one, but I was committed and trusted HIM. Whatever it took, I was willing to give.

Later in the week, I had the opportunity to have dinner with Barbara, and, for the first time, I REALLY got to know her. I discovered within the first few minutes she was a very unique and special person. I had never met anyone in her position that took such a genuine personal interest in a "regular person" like myself. She made me feel special, and I'll never forget how she turned my life around by giving me the courage and confidence to pursue my dreams. Before I attended *SHAPE* CAMP IN AUGUST 1990, I had lacked self-confidence and the courage to take a risk. Barbara gave me encouragement from the first time we met, but more than that, made ME believe that I DID HAVE SOMETHING TO OFFER!

BACK TO THE STORY:
After the bankruptcy and several days spent in severe depression and isolation, my husband, Mike, tried to get me "to snap out of it." He was quick to remind me I had given two years of my life to something I believed in, and INSISTED we go back to the bank and get another loan. I wasn't really sure I could handle another set-back. To tell you the truth, I was ready to chunk the manuscript in the trash (at this point), and try to get back to some kind of normal life.

Bob Machos and Pam
River Oaks Printing Ft. Worth

I had a great recommendation for another printer (River Oaks Printing) in Ft. Worth, Texas, and after much coaxing from my husband, we went to meet them together. I didn't want to make anymore decisions on my own! After meeting with the owner, Bob Machos, Mike and I BOTH agreed that they could do the job. We really liked Bob as soon as we met him and felt we really could trust him with the project. We were right! They printed 5,000 books in about three weeks.

The River Oaks "Family" delivers I remember storing part of them in our mini-warehouse thinking it would be a miracle if I ever (in the next ten years) sold those books. They were gone in three weeks. In fact, we ran out before we realized that we needed to print again. I had sent books to radio stations, newspapers, magazines, and anyone else I could think of that might want to review it.

Hot off the press and into my car
March 15, 1992

**Ft. Worth Star Telegram
April 1992**

The food editor of *The Ft. Worth Star Telegram*, Beverly Bundy, wrote a really nice story about me and my book with a huge color picture of my face on the front page of the "Life Section" of the newspaper. The article was syndicated all over the country and the word spread quickly.

News 4 Texas did a story on me that ended up running five times on T.V. over a three day period. They even featured the story on the weekend special. That is how we ran out of books so quickly. We then printed 10,000 and they sold in four weeks. We next printed 20,000, then 40,000, then 50,000, then 70,000, then 125,000, etc. I ended up selling 450,000 on my own in one year and four months. I had a large mail order business, as well as bookstores, and price clubs. I was selling 5,000 books a month to Sam's Club alone. I managed to learn a great deal about the printing business as well as distributors, advertising, and marketing without a bit of education or experience in any of those areas. I guess you could say I was a self-taught woman!!

In April 1993 Warner Books found me in Texas while they were in town for a wholesale book show. They found my book in the #1 Best-Seller Spot and inquired about me in a Taylor's Bookstore. They went back to New York and called me the next week with an offer to purchase publishing rights to my book. I told them, "Thank you, but I really am enjoying doing it myself."

They called back the next day and doubled their offer. I couldn't believe these people. It appeared they weren't going to give up no matter what I said. They asked if they could come to Texas to meet me. I had to put them off for a couple of weeks, because my husband and I were going skiing, and the following week my youngest son, Tyler, had an ice hockey tournament. I'm sure they thought I was playing hard to get, but that wasn't the case at all. Two weeks later they flew

Taylor's Bookstore #1 Bestseller   April 1993

to Dallas and we had dinner together. As soon as I met them I knew they were sincere. I really liked them a lot. They cared about me as a person and they were interested in my life (outside the book), and asked about my children. Everyone knows the way to a woman's heart is to ask about her kids! They invited Mike and me to New York to meet the rest of the Warner staff. After spending a week in "the city," we decided to go with them. I had sold a lot of books on my own, but knew I could never reach all the people (who really needed my book) as a small publisher.

Warner Books sent me on a 24 city national tour in January and February. I appeared on the Joan River's Show "Can We Shop?" twice (March and May) and sold 7,000 books in two ten minute segments. I was on "The Ricki Lake Show," "The 700 Club," and all the local news and talk shows across the country while on tour. I also did a lot of "talk radio." I really enjoyed the tour because it allowed me to get out there with the people and meet several I had previously written in response to their letters.

Butter Busters and Warner Books join forces for 24 city national book tour.   January, 1994

We now have well over ONE MILLION BOOKS in print. I keep thinking that I'm going to wake up, because this dream is just too unbelievable to be true! I often wonder how it all happened. I thank God every day for the opportunity He has given me to serve Him in such a wonderful way.

***SHAPE* magazine   January 1995**

SHAPE magazine honored me in their January 1995 issue by including an article about the success of *BUTTER BUSTERS* and the book tour.

Madearis Studio ©

UP FRONT AND PERSONAL

BUTTER BUSTERS BOOK TOUR
JANUARY - FEBRUARY 1994

BUTTER BUSTERS BOOK TOUR
JANUARY - FEBRUARY 1994

UP FRONT AND PERSONAL

I feel my work is also a tribute to my brother, Tom. Because of him, I have read and learned so much about cholesterol and heart disease and have been able to pass on important information that has influenced many people and even saved lives (so I've been told).

I've also written a *BUTTER BUSTERS* Low-Fat Guidebook and produced three videos. Warner Books and Warner Music backed an infomercial I appear in to introduce "The Butter Busters Low-Fat System." We filmed the infomercial in L.A. during December.

INFOMERCIAL FILMING
LOS ANGELES DECEMBER 1994

I signed a contract with Alpine Lace Products to serve as their National Spokesperson for the next two years. The contract in no way limits me from promoting and using competitive products. I feel that is part of my appeal. I try to inform the consumer of ALL THE CHOICES and recommend products from many different manufacturers. They said that would be no problem and why they wanted me in the first place (because of my honesty). I will be traveling all over the country speaking to organizations such as "The American Dietetic Association" and "The American Heart Association" representing Alpine Lace Products.

As a result of the book, I was contracted to write three columns for *FITNESS* Magazine. The column was called "Fat Busters." I completed my commitment of the three columns, but chose not to renew the contract due to my other projects and lack of time.

I have started a Newsletter (as a result of several hundred requests from my readers). I love writing a regular newsletter because it enables me to get all the current and updated information to my readers between book publications.

Pam's first *Fitness* column July 1994

I feel this whole story is a MIRACLE and has certainly changed my life! The AMERICAN DREAM REALLY CAN COME TRUE! If you believe in your heart that you can accomplish your goal, no matter how impossible it may seem (and don't give up), your dream can become a reality! I know because I have lived the experience! The success of the book has surprised no one more than me. When I wrote the book I did it for one reason. I simply wanted to teach others what I had learned. People ask me all the time, "Why does YOUR book sell so well when there are a million other low-fat cookbooks out there, too?" My answer is always the same, "The food is GOOD!!" (I also feel this is what God intended for me to do with my life.) My book sells "by word of mouth" and does so because it REALLY DOES help people lose weight and control their cholesterol.

Char before

One of the most wonderful things that happened as a result of the book, was the 50 pound weight loss of my seventy-five year old Mom, Char Doehler, who had always been extremely overweight. She managed to drop her cholesterol to a safe level and incorporate aerobic exercise into her life as well. I dedicated my BUTTER BUSTERS LOW-FAT SYSTEM to her, for she is a walking example of what I teach.

I'm in the process of writing two more books. My next book The *BUTTER BUSTERS COOKNOTES for KIDS IN THE KITCHEN* will be out in late 1995 or early 1996. It will contain over 200 pages of "geared toward kids" information including the many facets and benefits of a low-fat diet in conjunction with aerobic exercise. The book includes over 100 quick and easy kid tested (and in some cases prepared in my kitchen by kids) recipes with preparation instructions kids can understand and follow. I've included a "Kids Shopping Guide" and a complete "Fast Food Restaurant Guide." You will find information concerning diseases (such as eating disorders in children). Watch for this "fun for the whole family" cookbook.

Char after

BUTTER BUSTERS TOO! THE ULTIMATE COOKBOOK will be in the bookstores sometime in 1997 (hopefully) or as soon as I recover from writing and touring the country to promote *I'M LISTENING!* and *KIDS IN THE KITCHEN.*

Official kid testers..................

As you can see, I'm staying quite busy, but love what I do and feel my work REALLY IS helping people. From the phone calls and letters I receive daily, I've been told that I have made a difference in the lives of many people. Hearing from my readers keeps me motivated and encouraged to continue with my work. I feel so blessed by the opportunity I've been given by God to help change the lives of others in a positive way! The American Dream really can come true! If you believe in your heart, follow God's lead, and don't give up, IT CAN HAPPEN TO YOU, TOO!!

................and tasters

Busting Butter*...........*a family project!!

Your Basic American Dreamer,

Pam Mycoskie

"I trust in the Lord with all my heart, and I lean not unto my own understanding" (Proverbs 3:5). "In all my ways I acknowledge Him and He directs my path" (Proverbs 3:6). "I will do all things through Christ which strengtheneth me" (Philippians 4:13). "I will fear no evil for Thou art with me Lord, Your Word and Your Spirit they comfort me" (Psalms 23:4).

PAM'S PRIVATE PROGRAM

THE TRUTH, THE WHOLE TRUTH, AND NOTHING BUT THE TRUTH, SO HELP ME GOD!!
(Everything you wanted to know and were brave enough to ask!)

I would like to take this opportunity to answer some of your questions about my own personal exercise program and eating habits, as well as other questions about my life you have asked. Some of the following questions are from your letters, and some from the many radio and T.V. interviews conducted while I was on tour promoting *BUTTER BUSTERS THE COOKBOOK.*

YOU: By looking at you, I can see that you are not overweight, Pam. Have you ever had a weight problem, and if so, is that why you wrote the book?
— F.M. Baton Rouge, Louisiana

Pam Age 9   Xmas 1958

ME: I was a fat baby, a fat toddler, and a fat child. I was also very short until I turned 14. I grew from 4'11" to 5'4" in one year. Finally I was of normal weight for my height. Afraid to be fat again, I over-exercised and underate for 25 years. Even though I didn't APPEAR to have a weight problem, I really did. In my opinion, that IS a weight problem. If I over-ate one day, then I would go to the gym the following day and work out for 2-3 hours to punish myself for lack of control. I over-ate a lot, because I didn't eat any food (on most days) until about 4.00 in the afternoon, when I became so hungry that once I started eating I couldn't stop. It was a vicious cycle. Starving (because I didn't eat all day), over-eating (because I felt like I deserved it), guilt (because I consumed so many calories in a few hours and felt stuffed), and over-exercising

**Pam and Dad
Age 11   May 1960**

(to cancel out my lack of control). This was a typical day for me! It would all start over the next day by not eating until late afternoon. I felt I would become obese if I ate three meals a day like a normal person. I WAS MISERABLE! I tried every diet that came along, which in most cases consisted of some kind of deprivation. The real reason I wrote the book was to teach others what I had learned. After a high cholesterol scare in 1990, and lowering it by cutting the fat in my diet, I realized I was on my way. I also realized that I could eat like a normal person (at least three to five low-fat meals a day), exercise moderately, and not gain weight. As a matter of fact, I lost about 15 pounds when I started cutting the fat in my diet to lower my cholesterol. I felt, at this time, there was a need for a book to teach others this new-found liberation that had taken me twenty-five years to figure out. By your letters, I found there were a lot of people (like me) who lived the same way and could identify with my story!

YOU: You have three kids. Do they eat low-fat, and will most children adapt to low-fat changes?
—W.P Seattle, Washington

ME: My children eat low-fat MOST of the time. They are all three aware of the fat content in most foods. They found, through experience, they feel better when they limit their fat intake. I don't push my eating habits on anyone (even family), and never say anything when they order what I might consider a poor choice when eating out. They have told me, on more than one occasion, they don't feel as good when they consume a lot of fat in their diet. Children need about 30% fat (of their total calories per day) in order to grow and develop properly. If a child eats about 2,500 calories a day, that would amount to about 84 fat grams. This should allow plenty of foods your children enjoy and still fall within "healthy guidelines." On the other hand, if you have a child who eats bacon and

Tyler tasting low-fat goodies.

eggs for breakfast, hamburger and fries for lunch, pizza with pepperoni for dinner, and a Hot Fudge Sundae for a late night snack, it might require a little creativity on your part. Don't give up, my youngest son Tyler fits in this category. All you have to do is serve their favorite foods MODIFIED to low-fat (without them being able to tell the difference). This is where the creativity comes in. By substituting Egg Beaters for eggs, low-fat Canadian Bacon for regular bacon, ground venison, Vermillion Valley, or Maverick Lite low-fat beef for regular hamburger, this feat can easily be accomplished. Try baking your fries, using fat-free cheese and Healthy Choice sliced sausage on the pizza. Serve their Hot Fudge Sundae made with fat-free ice cream or frozen yogurt topped with fat-free fudge topping. Your children will BE HAPPY AND HEALTHY!! With all the great substitutions available today our children, in most cases, will not even realize they are eating anything different and therefore adapt quite nicely. What they don't know won't hurt them! In fact it will probably help them later in life. With YOUR help they will develop a taste for healthy low-fat food. As a result of their low-fat diet, they might not be forced to contend with the obesity and weight-related problems many of us adults face today.

YOU: What do you do for exercise? Do you exercise every day?
—*S.C. Arlington, Texas*

ME: I try to do something aerobic most every day because it serves as a stress release, gives me more energy, and is the only time that truly belongs to me. I consider it a gift to myself. This is my time to read, meditate, pray, let my mind wander and totally relax. I turn on the answering machine and don't allow interruptions. You might think this sounds kind of selfish, but I feel I can be a better wife, Mom, and friend if I take care of myself first. If you don't believe this, just ask my family! I enjoy the Stairmaster and stationary bike because I can read while doing these activities. If I am in the mood to watch T.V. I use the treadmill and walk. I also enjoy bench step aerobics. I have several exercise video tapes, which allow me to work out at home. I include a light weight routine 2-3 times a week to build lean muscle mass, help prevent osteoporosis, and increase strength. I usually take one day off (either Saturday or Sunday) during the week, depending on my schedule and the kid's activities. This is what I DO, but I'm not saying this routine is for everyone. If you exercise aerobically 3-5 times a week and incorporate some kind of weight or resistance training into your program, you will benefit greatly. Remember aerobic exercise burns body fat, and resistance or weight training builds lean muscle mass (which enables you to eat a whole lot more calories and not gain weight). I would rather eat a lot of low-fat food and not much fat. If you eat A REALLY HIGH-FAT DIET, and try to control your weight, YOU WON'T BE ABLE TO EAT A LARGE QUANTITY OF FOOD, TRUST ME!! In other words, if you have a double hamburger, french fries, and a vanilla milk shake for lunch, you will probably consume your fat budget for the day in that one meal. I would rather eat three to five filling low-fat meals a day, and never feel hungry or deprived.

YOU: Do you count calories, and if so how many do you eat in a day? What percentage of your calories come from fat?   —*K.S. San Antonio, Texas*

ME: I really don't count calories! In order to answer your question concerning percentage of fat, it was necessary for me to know how many calories I eat in a day. When I kept track, I was amazed how many calories I really did eat. Let me first explain that for my height, frame size, and activity level, I should be able to consume about 1800 calories (providing I eat 30% fat) a day and maintain my weight of 120 pounds. I do, however, eat very low-fat. I consume 10% fat which amounts to about 20 fat grams a day. However, I eat about 3,000 calories a day and maintain my ideal weight. I would rather eat a lot of food, and not much fat. Because I know how to modify and make substitutions in my recipes, I am able to eat anything I want and a lot of it! I do, of course, exercise aerobically. I've said it before and I'll say it again: Regular aerobic exercise in conjunction with a low-fat diet is a system destined to succeed! I believe this to be true, because I've eaten low-fat and exercised aerobically for five years and I know it works!

YOU: How long do you exercise aerobically?   —*R.L. Dayton, Ohio*

ME: In order to burn body fat most efficiently, you need to exercise aerobically for a minimum of 35 minutes in your target heart rate zone (not counting warm-up and cool-down). Your target heart rate zone is approximately 220 minus your age, taking that number times 70% and 85%. The two numbers you end up with are your "personal" heart rate zone. By taking your pulse on the radial artery (located on the thumb side of the wrist), or carotid artery (located on the side of your neck under your ear), for 10 seconds and multiplying that number by six you can determine if your number falls within your personal zone while exercising aerobically. Refer to page 146 for more information regarding exercise and heart rate.The first 15 minutes of your work-out, after warm-up, your body primarily burns carbohydrates for fuel by depleting your glycogen stores (how your body stores carbohydrate for future energy use). The twenty minutes, following the initial 15 minutes of your aerobic work out is when the fat-burning mechanism really "kicks in" and your body burns fat most efficiently. I exercise 45-60 minutes at a time. I begin by warming up about five minutes. I then stop to stretch the muscles I will be using during my workout. I begin increasing my intensity gradually. After 45-60 minutes I start decreasing my intensity until I feel cooled-down. I add about

15 minutes of abdominal work at this point three times a week. I end my work-out with a slow static (constant never bouncing) stretching of my major muscles groups. If it happens to be a day that I am also doing weights I move into that segment as soon as I complete my aerobic activity. It is better to engage in your weight training after aerobics because your muscles are warm and sufficiently stretched. If you exercise in the order I suggested, your risk of injury or muscle damage will be reduced. If you do not exercise aerobically before your weight training session, please be sure and warm-up (5-10 minutes) and adequately stretch, before you begin.

YOU: Do you go out to eat very much? What kind of restaurants do you prefer to eat in? How do you order, get what you want, and not appear demanding or picky?
—S.I. Hurst, Texas

ME: I go out to eat a lot. When I was on my book tour I ate every meal away from home for 4 1/2 weeks. My favorite kind of restaurants are those serving Mexican, Italian, and Chinese foods. Eating out is no excuse to disregard healthy low-fat eating. I ALWAYS ASK how a dish is prepared. If the preparation includes oil or butter, I ASK the waitperson if they could please use broth or another low-fat substitution in it's place. I ASK for all dressings and sauces on the side. This puts me in control of how much or how little I eat. You can still enjoy the taste of a salad dressing without destroying your fat budget for the day. By dipping your fork in the dressing, then spearing the lettuce, you will enjoy the taste without all the extra fat.

This method also works with sauces. As long as you are polite and make your requests in a nice friendly way, you should be able to get what you want to eat and not offend anyone. Most restaurants will be very accommodating because they want your business. If you aren't pleased with your food, chances are you won't be back and they realize this. It IS POSSIBLE to be assertive without being offensive. While traveling on tour I ate many of my meals in my hotel room. It was easy to bring along my own salad dressing, fat-free margarine, and other low-fat condiments. I always take healthy snacks along while traveling on planes. You never know when or what you will get to eat. If you find yourself on a long flight, or the meal is high-fat or delayed, by bringing your own food you always have a healthy option. A few of my regular take-a-long airplane staples are bagels, fruit, fat-free granola bars, pretzels, fat-free string cheese, and my own bottled water. Sometimes it takes forever to get your complementary beverage due to delays. I also carry my favorite candy in my purse or briefcase- Twizzlers! I don't leave home without it! My kids give me a hard time about my food on trips, but are usually the first ones to ask, "Hey Mom, what do you have in your bag to eat, I'm starving!" The Twizzlers are usually the first to go. It might take a little preparation, but I find the effort well worth the time and planning.

YOU: You have over 350 recipes in your book. How did you come up with all of those recipes?
—J.K. Atlanta, Georgia

ME: When I got married in May 1970, my Mom had a recipe shower. Everyone that received an invitation to the wedding was requested to send their two favorite recipes for Mike and me to enjoy. All were placed in a yellow wooden box (hand-painted by one of Mom's friends) and became my family's favorite recipes. Here is a copy of the recipe shower poem my Mom sent to the wedding guests:

PAM'S RECIPE SHOWER

The big day has come;
The news you have heard
My daughter, Pam, to wed Mike is the word!

I pondered the problem—
I thought and I thought
And one day it came, the solution I sought!

Eureka, I've found it—
Hooray I cried!
An idea for a shower
Just made for a bride!

I'll write all my friends,
Good cooks everywhere,
And ask for a secret—
A recipe they'll share.

So look in your files, your cookbooks high and low,
A recipe "from Grandma"
Or a favorite you know.

Then write it on this card—
With a note to Pam from you;
I know she'd really like it
If you should send her two.

Her home is very new—
Her pots are all quite bare,
I know each dish you send her
She will prepare with care.

So now I have reached
The end of my tale,
Thank you for being part
Of my recipe shower by mail!

—Mother Doehler May 1970

Many of the great recipes found in *BUTTER BUSTERS THE COOKBOOK* and this book (modified to low-fat, of course) came from that little yellow wooden box.

In March 1990 when I learned of my high cholesterol, I began to cut the fat in my diet by modifying those same recipes (we had enjoyed the past twenty years) to low-fat. By using simple substitutions and modifications my family never felt deprived because they were still eating all their favorite foods. A lot of the recipes in the book came from that "Little Yellow Wooden Box." I also modified several recipes I found in various newspapers and magazines. I made up a bunch of the recipes by experimenting through trial and error. If I ordered something really good in a restaurant, I asked the chef what was in the dish. Although most chefs won't give out their recipes, they will usually tell you the basic ingredients. I would then go home and start putting ingredients together until I duplicated the dish, or at least came close enough that I, as well as my family, was satisfied. A good example of this is the "Fancy Bar-B-Q Chicken with Pasta" on page 256 (in *BUTTER BUSTERS*). I had a similar dish in a restaurant while vacationing in Palm Springs, California. I went home and developed this recipe. On page 338 in *BUTTER BUSTERS* you will find "Spicy Marinara," another recipe I developed after tasting a dish in Port Charlotte, Florida. Some recipes were more difficult than others. Some of the recipes were just plain good luck. One day I was modifying a creamy chicken recipe to low-fat. After tasting the dish, I decided I didn't really care for it, but hated to throw it away. I had spent a lot of time, money, and energy preparing the dish. I started adding ingredients until I came up with "Spicy Beans and Chicken Supreme" found on page 260. If you read that recipe in the book you will find a long list of ingredients. I just kept adding to it until I was happy with the taste. I love that recipe and am so glad I didn't "dump it" when it didn't turn out well, initially. I hope you have enjoyed the recipes as much as I did developing them. My kids often joke to their friends, "Our crazy mom is back in the lab working on her experiments." I'm expecting a white lab coat with my name on it any day now! Actually, they are pretty good sports about trying my new creations......... MOST OF THE TIME!

YOU: I love baked potatoes. I know most toppings are loaded with fat. What do you put on your baked potato?   —*B.L. Shreveport, Louisiana*

ME: I use the Kraft Peppercorn Ranch Fat-Free Salad Dressing (also good on steamed vegetables) on my baked potato if I am at home or have the dressing with me. I sometimes use fat-free sour cream and fat-free cheese. If I am in a restaurant, I ask for salsa, fat-free plain yogurt, or Bar-B-Q sauce to put on my baked potato. I usually carry Weight Watchers' fat-free individual packets of salad dressing in my purse. Sometimes I use these on my baked potato as well as on my salad.

YOU: What kind of oil do you use in your own home?   —*B.N. Aspen, Colorado*

ME: You probably won't believe this, but I don't use any oil. I have found there are so many substitutions that oil is not really necessary. For baking I use Liquid Butter Buds (made from the mix), Fleischmann's Fat-Free Squeeze Margarine, and Promise Ultra Fat-Free Margarine. Other low-fat substitutions used in baking, and new on the market, are Wonderslim and Just Like Shortenin'.

They are both derived from plums and work great in most baked goods. Check the NEW PRODUCTS chapter to find more information regarding these products on page 525. If I need a fat substitute for cooking, stir frying, or sautéing I use clear chicken broth, cooking wine, vermouth, vinegar, or water. I also use a low-fat cooking spray (such as PAM) to coat my pans and skillets. Remember these sprays do contain fat. You might try spraying a little on a paper towel, then spreading it on the pan. Using this method reduces the amount of oil you use dramatically. Another option is to fill a (never been used) perfume anatomizer with olive oil. It might be cheaper since you could continue to refill as needed. I strongly suggest investing in a good set of non-stick skillets. You might not even need a cooking spray if you purchase really good-quality cookware. If you feel oil is necessary in your home, I would recommend Olive oil or Canola oil. They are more heart-healthy than the saturated fats and most poly-unsaturated fats. Even though they are mono-unsaturated (liquid at room temperature and contain no trans-fatty acids), they are still 100% fat and contain about 12-14 fat grams a tablespoon! PLEASE USE ALL OILS IN MODERATION!! Refer to page 305 in "A Change for the Better" chapter regarding oils.

YOU: OK Pam, fess up!! No one eats a perfect diet every day of their life. Do you ever just blow it and eat what you want? I know you must, so tell me what you eat when YOU cheat?
—J.L. Houston, Texas

ME: To tell you the honest truth, I don't deviate from low-fat food too often. I can make just about any food I desire by using modifications and substitutions in cooking. However, when I eat out and "cheat" my favorite is pizza (still topped with vegetables and light on the cheese). I really consider this a pretty healthy "cheat." I order Caesar Salad if I know it is good at that particular restaurant. If there is something on the menu I really want, I order it. That is the point I am really trying to make. If you eat low-fat most of the time, IT'S OK TO SPLURGE ON OCCASION! The problem begins when you do so on a regular basis. It is no longer a splurge at that point, but a way of life. This can mean trouble for your heart as well as your waistline!! I would like to cite an example: There is a restaurant on Captiva Island, near Sanibel, Florida called *The Bubble Room*. They have a dessert called BUTTER CRUNCH ICE CREAM PIE. It is made with chocolate cookie crumbs, Butterfinger candy bars, ice cream, some kind of hardened chocolate shell, and caramel with whipped cream on top. There, now you know!! That is my major "CHEAT." I order it every time I visit that restaurant and eat every bite. It is a HUGE SERVING by the way, and I enjoy every morsel without guilt!! I THEN JOG THE SEVEN MILES BACK TO THE HOTEL. *(JUST KIDDING)!!!*

YOU: I love desserts. They are my weakness. Do I have to give them up to be skinny? I've made about twenty of your main course recipes and have not had a dud yet!! I've actually lost about seven pounds so far since I started cooking out of your book. All the recipes have been easy, quick and tasty! I think I really could live the low-fat way the rest of my life. I do have one little problem, however. To tell you the truth, I am afraid to try making any of your breads, muffins, or desserts. O.K. I hadn't planned on this, but here it goes. I have been a "Compulsive Overeater" most of my adult life. I don't have the problem with other food, just desserts. If I get started on sweets, I just can't stop. I really hadn't planned on telling you that part, but you seemed so honest

in your book, I didn't think it would be fair if I wasn't honest with you, too! Do you have any secret weapons to help people like me? Do you think it is possible to learn to control my sweet tooth? I don't feel like a normal person, but at this point, I am too scared to even give it a try. Do you know of any ideas to keep my overeating under control with sweets? I've tried not buying them, hiding them, exercising when I got the urge to cheat, eating them until they made me sick, and just about everything else I can think of. Nothing works. I'm afraid that I am doomed and don't know where else to turn for help. I hope my letter doesn't gross you out. This is the first time I have ever written a letter to anyone about my problem. I can't even sign my name or give you my real address. I am too embarrassed, so you can send your reply to this post office box. Thank you for your time!
—*Unhappy in Utah*

ME: It might take a little work, but I do think you can learn to control your sweet tooth. The reason I say this is because I have been where you are, and know I can easily return on any any given day. My name is Pam. I am a "Compulsive Overeater." I have been since the age of 14, when my brother died. I'm not sure if there is a relation to his death or not, but feel there probably is. In 1987, I finally came to a place in my life that I couldn't stand the way I was living. I had hit rock bottom. I was miserable and felt my life was unmanageable.

I looked in the phone book and found an organization called "Overeaters Anonymous." I attended "Overeaters Anonymous" meetings once a week for well over a year before I began writing *BUTTER BUSTERS* in August 1990. If you read my interview with Jennifer in the first part of the book (actually the first question) you will realize "what" I was talking about when I said I deprived myself of food and over-exercising to stay slim. I was a compulsive overeater for many years. The only way I could control my weight was starving myself all day (out of guilt) because I pigged out the night before, and exercising way too much (to make up for my lack of control). To tell you the truth, Unhappy in Utah, I wasn't planning on including that little tidbit of information in this book either, but because you were honest with me, I felt the need to share my story with you and others who might need to hear it!

I'm not exactly proud, nor can I really explain why, but do know it can happen to "anyone" and there ARE WAYS to deal with the problem. I believe most people must reach "rock bottom" before they will admit they have a problem. That is what happened to me, anyway. When your life seems out of control and is unmanageable, you will start looking for some kind of solution, I promise! When I went to *SHAPE* Camp in August 1990 it was the first time in my life that I felt "safe" or "desperate" (probably a better word) enough to even begin to think about giving some other way of eating a try. Even though I had been attending the "Overeaters Anonymous" meetings, I was still "in charge" of my eating habits. It was one of the few things in my life I felt like I could control. On the outside I looked happy, healthy, and slim, but on the inside I was insecure, miserable, and angry! After attending "Overeaters Anonymous" I learned, by talking to others and opening up, that my problem wasn't really the food, but I medicated my insecurities by eating because it made me feel better temporarily. I always felt worse after I overate, and that is why I punished myself with obsessive exercise the next day. I don't know about you, but I did all my overeating late at night. I knew what I was doing, but I just couldn't stop. An upsetting situation (or sometimes my kid's fighting) would set me off. I would start with a handful of Fritos or chips, thinking it was no big deal. From there I would move into the candy or cookies. I can remember eating a pound of Twizzlers Red Licorice and not even being aware what I had done until I realized the bag was empty. I would usually go from sweet to salty, and back to sweet again. I think I was borderline anorexic (around November 1981 when our home burned and we had to move to an apartment for five months while they rebuilt it), because I actually skipped a period. I was under a great deal of stress and honestly felt my life "was out of control" at that point.

I think I felt my eating was the ONLY thing I COULD CONTROL (at that time). In Jennifer's interview when I said that I came home from *SHAPE* Camp with "a new lease on life" and "an improved self

image," that is what I was talking about. At *SHAPE* Camp I was finally able to "give up the control" of my terrible eating habits by turning them over to someone else. I learned how to love and trust myself (for the first time in my life). I learned how to spend time alone and not be afraid (another big step). I made some "big changes" at *SHAPE* Camp in August 1990. It was definitely a turning point in my life!!

I was so excited when I didn't gain weight after eating like a "normal person" for a whole week at camp. I know the main reason I overate all those years. By the time I finally did give myself permission to eat (around 4:00 in the afternoon), I was starving!! Even after six months of cutting the fat in my diet and lowering my cholesterol almost 100 points (from March 1990 to August 1990), I still over-ate, just low-fat!! Most compulsive overeaters are hiding some kind of feelings they don't want to deal with. To tell you the

I was too thin! 1981

I "appeared" to have it all

truth, I really don't know "the" exact reason. I had several to choose from!! I don't want to go into that (in this book anyway). It really doesn't matter what the reason was, only that I realized and admitted I DID HAVE A PROBLEM! One thing that has helped "me" and might help "you" with your compulsive overeating of sweets might sound kind of crazy, but it works for me. Instead of depriving myself of those trigger foods I try to eat them occasionally in moderation (and around other people). Most compulsive overeaters do not overeat in front of, or with, other people. You might try having a sweet treat or dessert "with" your family or a trusted friend that understands your problem. Take your time and enjoy it. Another thing I found when I ate compulsively was that I ate so fast I didn't even taste or enjoy the food.

My worst culprit is Twizzlers Red Licorice! I love it, I love it, I love it!!! You might find this interesting, but as a small child it was my very favorite candy. I can remember getting 100 sticks of red licorice in my Christmas stocking every year during my childhood. I can remember going to the T G & Y in Shawnee Mission, Kansas and buying 100 sticks of red licorice with my

A Twizzler's Moment   February 1994

$1.00 allowance. One dollar went a lot further back then, didn't it? Maybe there is some connection to my childhood and my obsession with red licorice. I do find when I am really down, that I REALLY want red licorice. Maybe I equate the red licorice with making me feel better because I relate to eating it at a happy time in my life (early childhood). Who knows? I do know that I always carry a package of Twizzlers in my purse or briefcase every day just to remind myself that it is there if I want it so I never "feel" deprived. I have been carrying the same package in my purse about two months now, so that tells me that things are going pretty well (right now) and it works for me.

I realize now (with God's help), I do live one day at a time, but also understand that I can still slip back into that behavior on any given day. I know it is something I will deal with the rest of my life. Like alcoholism, the disease never really goes away, you just learn to deal with it (one day at a time) and always with God's help!!

My suggestion to you, Unhappy in Utah (and anyone else reading this part of the book), is to PLEASE GET HELP!! Check in your phone book for the "Overeaters Anonymous Organization" in your community. You might be embarrassed to go (afraid someone will know you), but believe me, it is worth the risk! You will find you are not alone, and it is much easier to face our problems when we find someone we can trust to share them with. I hope, by reading my story, you realize you are not the only person with this problem. I know one thing for sure, it made ME feel better to share my story with you. I wish you the best of luck and if you ever feel the need to write or call me, please do. I'm here waiting, and I'm Listening if you want to talk! God Bless! (Refer to page 257 in the "Disease Section" for more information regarding eating disorders).

YOU: Upon listening to your KLIF interview on Larry North's talk show, I immediately purchased your book. You offer so many ideas, and the best part is that your book is so "real life" - nachos, pizza, Mexican. It is the most reality based cookbook I've ever read.

What intrigued me the most is that in your "How I Got Started" section, your background seems much like mine. I am 30 years old with a great husband and child. I have worked out continually for the past six years. I have been on the roller coaster of exercise, overeating, and starvation for 15 years. I am currently, and have been for many years, a size four. I can greatly identify with your text referring to the fear of gaining weight by eating breakfast and even lunch, holding out to eat dinner with your husband, etc. I always receive much more satisfaction by reading someone's personal experience, especially when I can relate to it. Because of the similarities, I would appreciate your addressing two concerns. I am addicted to diet drinks- Diet Rite Cola more specifically (no sodium, calories, or caffeine, but feel I overdose on all that nutrasweet). I drink lots of water during my meals. I want to cut out my in-between snacks of 3-6 cans of Diet Rite a day. Do you have any suggestions on how to make water more interesting? I want to keep it fat/calorie free, along with a desirable taste. Next, I still struggle with 3 meals a day, etc. I am curious to see what your daily pattern of eating might be. What if I am not truly hungry until about 9:00/9:30 A.M.? Should I allow myself a snack late in the day if I'm hungry? I tend to be a "black & white" person when it comes to food, afraid to deviate from the plan. I would appreciate your advice on how to obtain the ability to find some "grey" area and not be so regimented.

Also do you have a recipe for low-fat biscuits? My husband especially likes to cook "breakfast for dinner" sometimes. This can end up a very high-fat meal. Any suggestions would be appreciated. Finally, I was delighted to read your verse in Leviticus. I have searched the scriptures many times for God's Word regarding my eating and food patterns. The fact that you were courageous enough to place a Bible scripture in your book is a witness to others. It gave me even more reason to like your book and believe in your message about health. I know you are inundated by letters and calls, but please write me back when you can.

I am enjoying your book and would highly recommend it to anyone.
—*J.H. (a small town in Texas)*

NOTE: I didn't think I should list the city in this case, because the person who wrote the letter might not want others to know who she is. For this reason I must protect her privacy.

ME: I would like to thank you for your sweet letter and I will attempt to give you some answers to your questions. I can identify with your Diet Rite dilemma. I, myself, used to be addicted to Diet Coke. I drank about 4-5 a day. I drank the kind with caffeine. I think it helped me keep going because my eating habits were so messed up. Since I didn't eat anything before 4:00 P.M. most days, I needed something to fill me up and give me some energy. Even though your Diet Rite doesn't contain a large amount of sodium and is caffeine free, it does contain Nutrasweet. I happened to be doing a T.V. show in Arlington, Texas about the time my "Diet Coke habit" was in full swing. It just so happened the guest right before me was a woman named Mary Stoddard. I was in "The Green Room" (a place you wait when you are doing a T.V. show- I don't care what show you are doing they always call it that) waiting for my turn. The more I listened to Mary, the more intrigued I became. I learned later this woman is "on a mission" to inform people of the dangers associated with Aspartame. As "I LISTENED" (remember we all learn by listening) I learned there are some people (in particular) who MUST STAY AWAY FROM ASPARTAME. These people are born with a rare metabolic disorder called phenylketonuria, or PKU. They are unable to metabolize an essential amino acid in the aspartame called phenylalanine. Once a child consumes the product, it builds up in their body and can ultimately cause severe problems such as mental retardation. Remember when your baby was born and you had to take him back to the hospital (three days after you took him home) to have a blood test performed? Well, I do. That was the test they were performing. Because of this problem, labels on cans of diet soda and other foods containing aspartame must carry the warning: "Phenylketonurics: Contains Phenylanine." Aspartame affects people in different ways. It is believed to cause seizures in some, headaches, hyper-activity, and a host of other problems. In my case, I believe it was the culprit behind the headaches I was experiencing on a regular basis. I had attributed the headaches to not eating until late in the day, UNTIL I DISCONTINUED AND GAVE UP DIET COKES. My headaches stopped within two days! When you mentioned you were "addicted" to Diet Rite, I could identify with this behavior. Maybe aspartame is addictive. If you would like to contact Mary Stoddard and receive additional information concerning Aspartame, please send $1.00 and a self-addressed stamped envelope to:

Ms. Mary Stoddard
Aspartame Consumer Safety Network
P.O. Box 780634
Dallas, Texas 75378 (214)352-4268
(800) 969-1650 (Book Order Dept.)

There are several bottled flavored waters on the market. However, most of them contain aspartame. I think drinking water is a habit you can learn. I would invest in a bottled water service such as Ozarka. That is what I did. Place the water cooler in your home where you see it all the time. This will remind you to drink it. It took me about three weeks to develop the habit of drinking water, and now I actually crave it. Some folks like to squirt some lemon or orange juice in their water for added taste. The neat thing that happened at our house (with the kids) was when we bought the water machine, they quit drinking so many canned drinks. I don't remember ever seeing them go to the faucet to just get a drink of water before. They were always drinking juice, milk, or soda pop. Once the water cooler was installed, I found they used it as much as I did. If it's there, they WILL use it!

As far as eating three meals a day, that is also a habit that takes getting used to. Once you realize your body can accommodate much more food (if you spread it out over the day) and not gain weight (providing it is low-fat), you are on your way. If you are not hungry at 9:00 A.M., you can wait a little while to eat breakfast. Many (myself included) prefer to workout before breakfast. I feel your body moves right into burning fat a little quicker (due to the depletion of glycogen stores from the fast you experienced while sleeping) if you work out before you eat. The jury is still out on that one, but I've read a lot about this process and understand why many believe it to be true. It does make sense. If I'm NOT working out first thing, then I do go ahead and eat breakfast shortly after I get up. If you try to eat something every three hours (it doesn't have to be a huge meal) you will find you have more energy and will be able to consume more food. The secret is to keep your body moving and metabolizing calories on an even keel throughout the day. If you are hungry, by all means have a snack (no matter what time it is).

As far as the recipe for low-fat biscuits, check out the Pioneer Low-Fat Biscuit Mix. It is a great product that can be used to make waffles, pancakes, muffins, cookies, and fat-free biscuits. If you can't find it in your area call: (210) 227-140l. (I actually sent this person the recipe, but lack the room here to include it.)

In response to your last comment about the Bible Scripture, I too found it interesting, and wanted to share the information with my readers. My reference can be found on page 103 in the 7th edition of *BUTTER BUSTERS*. If you have one of my earlier editions, it can be found on page 83. Good luck!

YOU: Congratulations on the success of your cookbook, *BUTTER BUSTERS*. As a physician practicing bariatric medicine (weight management), I was delighted to discover a truly low-fat cookbook to recommend to my patients. At our clinic we teach behavioral modification and nutrition. We encourage our patients to make a commitment to a more active, healthy lifestyle. Your cookbook provides an excellent source for health conscious individuals desiring tasty low-fat recipes to incorporate into their new lifestyle. Is it possible to order books for my patients directly from you?
—*R.P. Ft. Worth, Texas*

ME: Thank you, doctor, for your nice comments. I'm so glad your patients have enjoyed the book. There are several low-fat cookbooks on the market, but I have found many of them aren't really THAT low-fat. I also think my shopping guide really helps folks just getting started with low-fat cooking. There are so many new products on the market. Some of them are great, but some of them aren't so great. Even though we have the new labeling in effect, there are still a lot of label deceptions that people need to be aware of. Label deceptions are my pet peeve! Nothing makes me madder than an uninformed consumer purchasing a product they feel is a wise choice due to what the information states on the front of the package. I always tell folks to turn the package over and READ the nutritional information. So many times the 80% fat free (on the front) is according to weight, not the percentage of fat in the food. All products contain water. If you take an 8-oz. glass of water and put 2 teaspoons of butter in it, it can legally be touted as 90% fat free. What a joke that is! Do you catch my drift. The new labels are better.....but far from perfect!! Since *BUTTER BUSTERS* is now published by Warner Books, you must contact them regarding ordering the books in bulk. I'm sure they can give you the name of a distributor in your area. I first published the book myself in March 1992, but sold publishing rights to Warner Books in January 1994.

Note: Check the acknowledgments page for information regarding Warner Books, Inc.

YOU: I saw you on T.V. last weekend. I was interested in the information you were sharing. I am a diabetic with high blood pressure (190/160). My cholesterol is 368 with triglycerides around 300.

I did not get the whole address before the program went off the air and I was so upset. Would you believe the next day there was an article about you in the *Ft. Worth Star Telegram* with the address I needed. I thanked the Lord for your address. Since I purchased your book I have learned so much about cholesterol. I wasn't aware of all the hidden fats in food. I started walking again and hope to lower my cholesterol like you did. My questions are: Do you have a newsletter? I try to keep up on all the current information regarding diabetes, high blood pressure, and cholesterol. Do you think the exercise will help to lower my cholesterol?
—*N.C. Cleburne, Texas*

ME: I'm so glad you are enjoying the book. I do have a bi-monthly newsletter, and there is ordering information in the back of this book. I am anxious to share current health information with my readers as well as inform them of all the new products appearing in the grocery stores every day. I offer a very practical (easy to read and understand) newsletter with all the latest information on health and fitness (in layman's terms). I include New Recipes and New Product News. I do recipe makeovers on the recipes my readers send in.

As for exercise; aerobic exercise (such as walking) can contribute to lowering your total cholesterol because it raises the good cholesterol (HDL) which serves as our cholesterol transport, by taking the bad cholesterol (LDL) to the liver where it can be excreted. We want our HDL around 45 (for a man) and 55 (for a premenopausal woman).

After menopause it is even more important to be involved in some form of aerobic exercise (and weight bearing exercise to help prevent osteoporosis) because the estrogen level goes down at this point and you lose some of the protection regarding your heart health. We are shooting for a high HDL (good cholesterol) and a low LDL (bad cholesterol). Please refer to page 194 in the "Disease Section" for more information concerning the new cholesterol guidelines. Keep up the aerobic exercise. It can do nothing but help with your cholesterol, as well as heart health, blood pressure and weight control. Good luck!

YOU: I've just come home from a family reunion get-together. "The Basic Vanilla Non-Fat Frozen Yogurt" (from your book) was a big hit! Your cookbook was often the topic of conversation. I've talked about your book so much that now my mom, sister-in-law, three aunts, a good friend, and a co-worker now have and use your *BUTTER BUSTERS* cookbook.

The main thing that makes your cookbook unique is that it contains "everyday people food" and not recipes that call for ingredients that need to be bought in a specialty shop. I personally liked the special hints for modification and substituting, so I can make my own favorite recipes low-fat.

Within three months my cholesterol was lowered 26 points. My husband's was lowered 13 points, but his triglycerides were down to 170. Three months ago they were 512! His family asks how our "diet" is going. I always correct them and say we are not dieting. We have made a lifestyle change.

I do have one suggestion. How about a newsletter with all the new product updates?

Well, I better get busy. I'm making your "Layered Bean Dip" for supper. My husband also wants some "Orange Slice Candy Oatmeal Cookies!" Thanks for your help!
—*T.W. Leeds, Alabama*

ME: I'm so glad you are enjoying the book. Thank you for spreading the word about low-fat living! I really appreciate your comments. As far as a newsletter is concerned, I am in the process of putting one together. I'll put you on my mailing list. I hope you will continue to enjoy the book. It's people like you (who take the time to write), that keep me inspired and excited about my work. Thank you for your kind words, and don't ever lose your wonderful attitude!

Note: Refer to the back of this book for newsletter ordering information.

YOU: I am 33 years old, the mother of three, and a stay-at-home mom. My youngest is 4 months and my other two are 7 and 8. My hubby and I have have been married 12 years. (Just wanted to tell you a tid-bit about myself!)

My first and most important "New Years Resolution" is to get rid of the fat! I've tried diets but the awful problem I have is, I love to eat! I need to lose 50 pounds (combination "baby" weight and weight from quitting smoking that I've had for two years).

I absolutely love your book. I am really determined to change my family's eating for life! I don't want my kids to grow up with the wrong kind of eating habits. I've really enjoyed reading your book and cooking your great recipes. I have a couple of personal questions:

1. If a recipe is 0 fat grams, can you eat as much as you want?
2. Rumor has it that unused calories, turn to fat. Is this true?
3. I've been stair climbing since January 1st, 30 minutes a day with one pound hand weights and taking Sundays off. Will it hurt to do a 30 minute routine in the morning and a 30 minute in the evening? Does it just get rid of the fat twice as fast?
4. Does chewing gum have any fat grams?
5. How long did it take you to start seeing results?
6. Do you take any vitamin supplements?
7. Are the fat grams in Egg Beaters any different than using egg whites? Also, is the correct ratio 2 egg whites for every 1 Egg Beater? We are having trouble finding Egg Beaters.

Thank you for sharing your secrets to healthy, happy bodies! I've been able to use your secrets with my own recipes, too. Please respond to my questions whenever you can. Thanks a million!
Sincerely, —K.H. Richmond, Texas

ME: I am so glad you are enjoying the book. I think it is wonderful that you are anxious to take control of your life and eating habits, and especially excited you want to help teach your children how to eat healthy, too. The best way to teach your kids is to set a good positive example through what YOU DO to stay healthy and fit. (Please refer to "KIDS ARE PEOPLE TOO!" for ideas concerning children.)

If a label states 0 fat grams, this means that it can legally contain as much as 0.49 fat grams. (If a product contains 0.5 fat grams per serving, the label **MUST** read "Low-Fat.") In other words, if a salad dressing says it is fat-free and one serving is 2 tablespoons, it will depend on how much you use. If one serving can contain 0.49 fat grams and you use 1/2 cup, you will be consuming 1.96 fat grams (4 x 0.49). There are 16 tablespoons in one cup. Since 2 tablespoons are one serving that would be 4 servings in 1/2 cup. I know this doesn't seem like much (and it isn't), but my point is that just because it says fat-free it doesn't always mean that is ENTIRELY true.

As far as unused calories "turning into fat," this is the deal. First it depends what kind of calories they are and how many extra calories you are eating on a regular basis. If your extra calories come from fat then, yes, they will turn into fat (easily). If your extra calories are from carbohydrate sources, chances are they will be burned off for energy to make room for the next day's intake (or stored in your body in the form of glycogen within your muscles to be used for energy when you exercise). Your body has a limited capacity to store carbohydrates. Even if you occasionally consume an excess of carbohydrate calories, chances are the increase of weight on the scale is due to water retention. Carbohydrates are stored in your body in the form of glycogen. It takes four grams of water to store 1 gram of carbohydrate. When you deplete your glycogen stores (through aerobic exercise) you will quickly lose the extra pounds you see on your scale. I'm not saying you can eat 3,000 extra calories of carbohydrates every day and not gain weight and get fat! If you overeat anything on a regular basis, you will get fat! Exercise is the real key to permanent weight (fat) loss. Another contributing factor (to lose fat quicker) would be eating small meals throughout the day. Both of these habits will increase your metabolic rate (rate at which your body burns fat and calories) and help with weight reduction and management.

It is fine to do your aerobic activity twice a day. You need to exercise 35 minutes (not counting warm-up and cool-down five minutes each) to burn body fat. The first 15 minutes of your aerobic activity you will be burning those glycogen stores (I spoke of earlier) for quick energy fuel. The twenty minutes (following that segment) is when the fat burning mechanism "kicks in" and you start burning body fat. This also depends on whether you are within your own "personal heart rate zone." I assume you know what that is: 220 minus your age and then take that number times 70 and 85 percent. Since you are 33 years old, that would be 220-33 = 187 (187 X .70 =131 and 187 X .85 =159). Your target heart rate zone would be between 131 and 159 beats per minute. Take your pulse for ten seconds and multiply times 6 to see if you are within your zone to burn body fat efficiently. Refer to page 145 in the "Exercise and Fitness" section for an explanation concerning exercise and your heart rate.

As a matter of fact I had a good friend who was anxious to lose body fat quickly for a high school reunion. I advised her to do aerobics twice a day (like I described) and she lost fat very quickly. It makes sense if you put your body into an intense "fat burning mode" twice a day, you will lose fat quicker. However, one long (say 45 - 90 minute) session of aerobic exercise will work just as well. What it really boils down to is this: Incorporate some kind of aerobic activity as often as possible (4-5 days a week is sufficient) into your life and you will speed up your metabolic rate (which is the KEY to fat loss)!!

Gum does not contain fat, however, it does contain calories. I don't think you could actually chew enough gum to make a real difference in your weight. I would recommend sugar-free gum, however, to prevent and guard against cavities (providing you don't have a problem with Nutrasweet).

It took me about 6 weeks to see a major improvement when I first started exercising on a regular basis and eating low-fat. If you have eaten a very high-fat diet in the past (and switch to 10% fat), and have never exercised on a regular basis (and start to do so), it is possible to see results within a week or two (especially in your energy level and mood).

I do take vitamins (especially the antioxidants). I will list the vitamins I take myself, but understand that this is not what I recommend for everyone. Because I work out on a regular basis, I feel it necessary to supplement my healthy diet. I also feel antioxidants play an important role in disease prevention. Since I am 45 years old (and premenopausal) I know how important calcium is to help prevent osteoporosis so I take a supplement that contains 1,000 mg daily. I take 400 IU of vitamin E. I take 500 mg of vitamin C, and I take 50 mg of Beta-Carotene daily (the major antioxidants). I also take 100 mcg of Selenium (another anti-oxidant). I take 100 mg of Zinc (to aid in muscle repair and healing). I take 500 mg of Potassium/Magnesium Aspartate (because I sweat a lot when I work out). I take 200 mcg of Chromium Picolinate daily (because most diets are deficient in this nutrient). ALONG WITH MY CALCIUM SUPPLEMENT I try to add dietary sources such as skim milk, broccoli, fat-free frozen yogurt, fat-free cheese and I also sprinkle non-fat powdered milk over foods I eat as well. Most women need a lot more calcium than they realize. Osteoporosis is a major concern for all women (especially after menopause when their estrogen levels have declined). The estrogen hormone helps protect women from developing osteoporosis. There is a book called *BONE BUILDERS* by Edita Kaye. I would highly recommend this book to everyone that would like to learn more about osteoporosis. If you can't find it in your local bookstore write to Edita at: P.O. Box 2661 Ponte Vedra Beach, Florida 32004. (800-77-COOK-1) Refer to page 240 in the "Disease Prevention" chapter of this book to learn more about calcium and *BONE BUILDERS*.

I do not suggest you (or anyone else) follow my personal supplemental vitamin program. I HIGHLY RECOMMEND EVERYONE CONSULTING THEIR "OWN PHYSICIAN" CONCERNING VITAMINS OR SUPPLEMENTS! Whatever you do, please don't self-prescribe thinking "more" is better. We all have different needs, so the best thing to do is ask your physician for his nutritional advice (and by doing so) come up with a plan that is right for YOU!! Refer to page 227 in the "Preventive Medicine" chapter, concerning vitamins and supplements.

There aren't any fat grams in Egg Beaters. They are fat-free. However, one Egg Beater equals 1/4 cup of the egg substitute or the equivalent of one whole egg. Two egg whites (whites contain no fat, but they are a rich source of protein) can be substituted for one whole egg. There are six fat grams in the yolk of one egg and 200-300 milligrams of cholesterol (depending on the size of the egg). It is best to avoid an abundance of egg yolks (especially if you are concerned with lowering your cholesterol)!

I hope this answers your questions and I wish you the best of luck in "changing your life for the better" regarding your new diet and exercise program (and the health and welfare of your family as well)!!

YOU: I know you are in the business to make money! How-ever I am disabled n- handicapped; n- can only work as a volunteer, so, I can only hope -n- pray you'll send me the cook book "Butter Busters The CookBook" as a donation, free of charge!!
—*D.P. Benicia, California*

ME: I received your letter yesterday. You might think people like me are in this for the money, but I want you to know that I NEVER wrote this book with that intention. You see, I had a cholesterol problem. Once I started cutting the fat in my diet, my cholesterol came down almost 100 points in six months. My brother died of heart disease at the age of nineteen. THOSE were the two reasons I wrote *BUTTER BUSTERS*. I hoped by doing so (and teaching others what I had learned) it might help people obtain a healthy life-style. I would be happy to send you a book. I appreciate the fact that you want one so much. I hope my book helps you learn how to incorporate healthy habits into your own life. The Low-Fat Lifestyle (I enjoy living myself) can be your answer, too!
Good Luck! Pam Mycoskie

(I sent this woman a complimentary book and NEVER DID hear from her again!)

NOTE: I included this letter to let others know the motivation behind my book, *BUTTER BUSTERS*, and really the motivation behind all of my books, and my work in the health and fitness field. I know it may be hard for some people to realize this, but I honestly believe in my heart that this is God's plan for my life. I can't think of one other reason why He has put the tremendous drive and dedication behind what I do. Nothing in my life has ever felt better than thinking I have helped (through God's blessings) someone change their life for the better.

October 23, 1994
As I sit here in Dallas, in a hotel room (where I have been living the past five days working on this

My hotel room.............

book), I have wondered why it is so important to me. (In case you are wondering what in the heck I am doing in a hotel in Dallas, when I only live 20 minutes away in Arlington, I will try to explain.) It is very difficult to write a book such as this one when you only have bits and pieces of un-interrupted time during the day. I have three children that I love very much, but the life of a Mom (as many of you know) consists of a lot of running around, driving, cooking, cleaning, etc., etc. This is the life I have chosen and I love it (don't get me wrong), but I also want to finish this book before the holidays (which are quickly approaching), so I CAN ENJOY THAT SPECIAL TIME WITH MY FAMILY!!

.............work, work, work

In order to accomplish this feat, I have found a week here and there (spent alone in a hotel room) gives me the quality un-disturbed time that writing this kind of book requires. It might sound kind of selfish to some, but I think in the long run, by doing this, I will be able to offer my family the FULL TIME ATTENTION they deserve when I go back home.

I am very, very lucky to have a wonderful husband who supports me and even recommended the idea of going to a hotel to work the first time (I've made three 5 to 6-day trips all together). It has

given Mike a chance to spend even more time with the kids (and everyone knows how important that is in this day and age). I must admit that I do feel a little guilty missing a volleyball game, hockey

game or tennis match, but my kids have been quite understanding regarding my work. (I would NEVER schedule one of these weeks away during a REALLY IMPORTANT game or match.) I check their schedules thoroughly before making reservations to leave town.

I have really enjoyed writing this book because it has given me the opportunity to go back through my letters, audio and video tapes (from my book tour), reminding me of the thousands of wonderful people I met and talked to (as a result of writing *BUTTER BUSTERS*).

| Mike, Blake, and Pam | Pam and Paige | Tyler and Pam |

My readers are VERY IMPORTANT to me and, for that reason, I have to go with my "gut feelings" on this. I believe if your heart is in the right place and you do things for the right reasons, then you can "feel secure" with your ultimate decision. I know now that my work has a purpose and that it has not been accomplished by me alone. It has all come through God's grace, and because of that, I feel there is a reason WHY I am writing this book. I feel there are a lot of folks who need this information, and might just be afraid to ask. This book is for all of you who need the answers, but might not be quite ready (or willing) to sit down and write me a letter. I hope, through this book, you find the inspiration you are seeking, and the answers to your questions. I want you to know, I'M LISTENING! and I REALLY DO CARE!!!

As far as this book is concerned, I must say, my publisher wasn't real excited about me even writing it (at first). They were quite anxious for my next cookbook. They were convinced that another cookbook (more recipes) was what the people really wanted. They may have been correct in their thinking, but I personally felt this book would be helpful to people with all kinds of questions, and an inspiration to folks who might be looking for encouraging words as well. I don't think my publisher realized (in the beginning) that people really would have a genuine interest in this type of book. I am the kind of person that looks in their heart and asks God's help and direction when making decisions. Because I have had an OVERWHELMING DESIRE to write this book, I knew there was a reason behind it. I had even considered self-publishing this book, because I felt so strongly about my commitment. I wasn't sure I could turn over something so dear to my heart, as *I'M LISTENING!* when I didn't think my publisher shared my passion and feelings concerning the importance of a book such as this.

I'm so glad (after much discussion) they came to believe in me and trusted my feelings regarding this book. Sometimes you have to ALMOST lose something before you can realize just HOW MUCH it means to you. Warner Books and I ALMOST lost each other. I'M SO GLAD WE BOTH REALIZED EACH OTHERS IMPORTANCE (BEFORE IT WAS TOO LATE)! The good faith we shared initially has grown into a unique trusting relationship. But, as I said earlier in the book, I liked the folks at Warner Books the first time I met them back in April, 1993. I truly believe good first impressions are the best way to begin strong long-term relationships. Besides, when it came

**Warner Books and Butter Busters
A Good Combination**

right down to the real nitty-gritty, they have always done the right thing in the end! Sometimes it took some convincing, but when push came to shove, they have trusted my feelings and believed in me. I can only hope that I won't let them down. This book was written for YOU, my readers, and partly BY YOU! Together, we have ALL made it happen! You, my readers, will be the true test. I can only hope through your interested positive response, we will be able to convince Warner Books that they made the right decision!

YOU: I am writing in regard to your cookbook.

I have nothing against the book itself. It was given to me as a present from my cousin, and I have really enjoyed using the book. However, I saw a paragraph in the *"Shopping Tips"* section under **"A Final Thought"** and wanted to comment on it.

When someone is quoting the Bible, I feel that all of God's points should be brought out and not just the ones that we want to tell about. You quote Leviticus, chapter 7: 22-24. I wonder if you have read chapter 11: 1-47? We not only shouldn't eat the fat of an animal, but there are certain meats that we shouldn't eat at all! I only eat chicken, fish (only those with fins and scales), and turkey. I have been long before you wrote the cookbook. I eat no red meat at all, any fish that has a shell, or pork of any kind.

I know you aren't trying to preach to your readers and neither am I. I just wanted to bring this to your attention before you quote the Bible again. By the way, you might find this chapter in the Bible VERY interesting. Thank you for giving me the opportunity to comment on this manner. Respectfully Submitted,   —*G.K. Wallburg, North Carolina*

ME: I wanted to thank you for taking the time to send your letter. When I included the quote from the Bible I didn't mean to offend anyone. I just found the passage quite interesting. I read Leviticus, Chapter 11: 1-47, and I understand what you mean concerning eating all kinds of animal products.

You said you felt that I should bring out all God's points when quoting from the Bible. I'm afraid that would be impossible. I feel all God's words are important too, but there is no way I can relay every message He intended through my work. People quote the Bible every day and I honestly don't think they include every point God intended to make. It would take volumes to do so. I only included that segment because I found it interesting. I'm really sorry if it offended you in any way.

I am a Christian woman and live my life for God every day. I feel blessed that He has chosen me to deliver this message through my work. I have written this book to simply teach others what I have learned. I feel this is my way to minister to the people who need hope in their battle concerning this subject manner.

I can only hope you will continue to use and enjoy the book.

YOU: Last March I saw you on the Joan Rivers' "Can We Shop?" show and ordered your book. I can't tell you how much it has helped me. After watching Joan eat that "Hot Fudge Pudding Cake" on the show, I just had to find out for myself if it REALLY tasted as good as she said it did. Well, it did!!! It was one of the first recipes I tried. A couple of months later (I think it was in May) I saw you on the show again with your workbook and video series. Well, I ordered that, too. After I saw you in that leotard on her show, I figured your system must work! I've been cooking and eating out of your book for about six months now and following your advice about exercise, too. I am really enjoying the step or bench aerobics. My husband even made me my own bench following your instructions in the workbook. I am proud to say that I have lost 27 pounds, and lowered my cholesterol, too! I have lost inches all over and am fairly happy with my body. My problem, however, is my outer thighs (saddlebags) and my big behind. Is there anyway to get rid of fat in this area? I know you say the only way to burn body fat is with aerobic exercise. I walk and do the bench 3-4 times a week. What do you do? Are there any great exercises that work on those areas?

Do you have any more books planned? After watching you on T.V., my husband and I both think you should have your own show. Have you ever thought about it? I watch *Home Shopping* all the time (as I exercise) and wondered if you have ever been on "QVC?" I haven't seen you, but thought you would be perfect. As a matter of fact, you should do an infomercial. You know those 30 minute shows that are on late at night? I don't mean to tell you what to do, but you might be missing out on ways to market your products. Just a suggestion. The main thing I would like to know is if you are going to write another book and when?

Was Joan Rivers nice? Have you been on any other neat shows? If you had your pick, who would you like to meet? I know that seems like a silly question, but I was just wondering. You have proba-

bly met all kinds of stars. Who did you like best? I know you are busy, but I would love some suggestions about my bottom and thigh problem. Thanks for your time. I'll watch for you on T.V.
—*P.L. New York, N.Y.*

ME: Thank you so much for your kind letter. I am so happy you have enjoyed "The *BUTTER*

BUSTERS Low-Fat System." It sounds like you are doing great with your eating and exercise. I will address your main concern first. Your problem (saddlebags) plagues most women in America. For some reason it is the first place we gain weight (if you are a pear shape like me), and the last place to lose. The good news is, if you are pear shaped (bottom heavy) your risk of heart disease is lower than a person who is apple shaped (carrying most of their weight around the middle and in the tummy). Doesn't that make you feel better? I didn't think so. It's true that aerobic exercise is the most efficient way to lose body fat all over the body. I have never

Bowler's Lunge - Position #1

been much of a believer in spot reduction exercises, because in my experience I have found they just don't work. That goes for leg lifts and sit-ups. However, sit-ups are still effective because once you lose the body fat through your aerobic exercise, you can tone your stomach muscles. However, don't think you will lose your tummy fat by sit-ups alone. It just doesn't happen! Squats seem to be the most effective exercise for the hips and thighs. Even those didn't give me the results I expected. **The good news is: I do have a couple of secret exercise weapons that have really helped me more than anything else that I have ever tried. I call them Morris' Kick-Butt**

Bottom Busters. A very good friend of mine and a personal trainer, Morris Kiker, showed me two exercises that have given me the results I wanted. You can even do them in a hotel room (and I have using the bathtub). I will try to explain how you do them. The first one Morris calls his "Bowler's Lunge" because it resembles the position you are in after you roll a bowling ball. You squat down on your right leg placing your left leg behind you extended straight out to the right side with your toe resting on the floor. The exercise involves dropping your left knee to the floor and then straightening it again. I do 20 repeti-

Bowler's Lunge - Position #2

tions, change legs (squatting on left leg with the right leg straight behind me and out to the left side) and do 20 on that side. I rest a couple of minutes and do 20 more on each side. This is the best exercise I know of to firm up your fanny.

The other one I named the "Bathtub Squat" because I did it while on book tour with *BUTTER BUSTERS THE COOKBOOK* as I was traveling all over the country staying in a different hotel every night for 4½ weeks. Sometimes it was so late when I got to my hotel that the health club was already closed. However, I must say the people working at every Ritz Carlton Hotel I stayed in were VERY accommodating. They would let me use the club (after hours) and even lock me in so I would be safe. I would then call for assistance when I was finished and they would make sure I got back to my room safely. For that reason, The Ritz Carlton Hotels (along with their great room service food) were my favorite hotels. Anyway, back to the exercises. Sorry, I get sidetracked sometimes. The second exercise "The Bathtub Squat" can also be done on a bench and something to hold onto for support (it can be the wall). You stand with both feet on the

Bathtub Squat - Position #1

bench. While holding onto something for support and balance, you bend the right knee and squat extending your left toe to touch the ground behind you. This works

Bathtub Squat - Position #2

the bent supporting leg that is still on the bench. Just tap it on the floor gently, and straighten that leg coming back to a standing position. Do 20 on each leg. Rest a couple of minutes and then do 20 more on each leg. These are very isolated exercises and I promise you will feel the burn! It only takes a few minutes (two or three times a week), but the results are amazing. After four weeks of doing these exercises all my pants and jeans were loose in the bottom and leg area. I went down a size in all my pants. Believe me at the age of 45 it isn't easy to firm up your bottom. I have tried everything, and **these are the only exercises that have ever given me positive results.**

"Can We Shop?" March 1994

As far as other books go, I am in the process of writing a book called, ***I'M LISTENING!*** due out in September 1995. It is a question/answer format book with over 100 quick and easy low-fat recipes. As far as Home Shopping, I did do two Q-2 (a division of QVC) shows in New York last August. I was on the "Ricki Lake Show" and "The 700 Club" while on tour. I really enjoyed the Joan River's "Can We Shop?" show the most. Joan is a real sweetheart and couldn't have been nicer. As far as who I would like to meet goes... That is easy. I would love to meet Oprah and Dave Letterman (at the same time). I know that will probably never happen because (after watching Dave EVERY night) it sounds like he hasn't met Oprah, either. He always jokes about her not wanting to be on his show. That might not be true at all, but regardless, those are the two people I would most like to meet someday!

As far as the infomercial goes... I have done an infomercial (it was filmed in L.A.) that will air all over the country in the near future. It is called, "BUTTER BUSTERS THE LOW-FAT SYSTEM." As far as the T.V. show goes, that is also in the works and will be called, ***I'M LISTENING! with Pam Mycoskie***.

I really appreciate your letter and am so glad you have enjoyed the recipes. Let me know what you think about "MORRIS' KICK-BUTT BOTTOM BUSTERS!" Good Luck!

This picture was taken after I taped Joan's show in May, 1994. I'm only sitting by Dave's picture at the CBS studio.

FOOD AND NUTRITION

YOU: How can you really make the food taste good when you remove the fat?
—*J.S. Seattle, Washington*

ME: SMART SUBSTITUTIONS, THAT'S HOW! There are several ways. In baked products you simply substitute the fat-free products for the high-fat items. Use Egg Beaters in place of eggs, Promise Ultra Fat-Free margarine, Fleischmann's Fat Free Spread, or the mix to make Liquid Butter Buds in place of oil, butter, or margarine. Use chicken broth to sauté or stir fry instead of oil. There are so many great fat-free products on the market that it really is easy. We have fat-free cheese, sour cream, and cream cheese to use in place of the high-fat products. We have fat-free mayonnaise and fat-free salad dressings. Most people can't taste the difference in recipes modified to low-fat if you don't tell them. The selection of GOOD LOW-FAT PRODUCTS increases daily. We have great tasting low-fat hot dogs, beef, and even sausage. With all the fat-free desserts, snacks, chips, crackers, and cookies, I can't imagine ANYONE not switching to this healthy way of eating. After all if the food tastes good, why not?

THE FOLLOWING QUESTIONS WERE TAKEN FROM A TALK RADIO SHOW
(USA TODAY SKY RADIO/BETWEEN THE LINES)
Arlington, Virginia

YOU: I'm looking in your book and see recipes for Country Chicken with Creamy Gravy, I lot Fudge Pudding Cake, Chicken Fettuccine Alfredo, and Banana Cream Pie. OK, now all the skeptics are saying, "Come on you can't make any of that stuff and actually cut the fat by any significant amount, now can you?"
—*B.T. Arlington, Virginia*

ME: Actually you really can. As a matter of fact most of the recipes in my book are under 5 fat grams and many of the desserts are under one fat gram. Thanks to all the great low-fat products on the market you can have all the foods you have ever enjoyed modified to low-fat if you know a few simple tricks.

Bill Thompson and Pam
Arlington, Virginia
January 1994

YOU: Do we have a natural taste for oily, greasy, buttery things?
—*B.T. Arlington, Virginia*

ME: I think we do. A lot of time people think they are craving sugar, when in all reality, they really are craving fat. I think that's the problem a lot of people have with over-eating. They just think they want sugar, but when you really think about it, what do they reach for? It's usually a piece of cake, a cookie, or a candy bar. Most of these items contain a great deal of fat.

YOU: If it was just the sugar we wanted, we would reach for the old sugar bowl and grab us a couple of sugar cubes, right?
—*B.T. Arlington, Virginia*

ME: Right, but you don't see people do that too often, do you?

YOU: Do you think we just like the way fat feels in our mouth?   —B.T. Arlington, Virginia

ME: I definitely do. Think about it, creamy sauces, fried chicken, potato chips...But that is where good low-fat substitutions come in handy. We need to learn how to trick our palates into thinking they are eating high-fat foods, then you won't feel deprived or feel like you are missing out on the good taste. Most people find as they cut the fat out of their diet gradually, they will acquire new taste preferences. An example involves Caesar Salad. I started ordering it with the dressing on the side in restaurants so I could control how much dressing I used. I stick my fork in the dressing and then spear the lettuce. You still have the great taste with a fraction of the fat. Well, I got so used to eating less dressing on my salad that even at home when I'm using a fat-free salad dressing, I still eat it on the side. After eating low-fat for a period of time, most people find they really lose the enjoyment of eating high-fat, heavy, and greasy foods.

YOU: Many people are dissatisfied with the low-fat foods, because they just don't taste as good. They know they should cut the fat because of health-related problems or need to lose weight, but won't give up the good taste in exchange for good health. What do you tell those folks?
— V.C. Jackson, Mississippi

ME: There are some low-fat products I don't care for myself. That is why I recommend different name brands in the shopping guide of the book. I've found most people have a problem finding fat-free cheese that melts and tastes good. Some people may try a fat-free salad dressing and think it tastes awful. Well, the problem is, next time they go to the store, they say to themselves, "I've had it with that fat-free stuff, I'll just buy the 'Light' this time. It has to be lower in fat and maybe it will taste better, too." The problem with "Light" on the label doesn't necessarily mean low-fat. A leading "Light" brand of mayonnaise contains 90% fat. I would hardly consider this product a wise choice if you are trying to cut the fat in your diet, would you? Be sure and read the nutritional information on all low-fat foods, ESPECIALLY the products with "Light" on the label. Watch for new low-fat products every time you visit your local grocery store. The low and fat-free products have improved greatly since 1990 when I wrote *BUTTER BUSTERS!*

YOU: I love cheese, but haven't found a fat-free one I like yet. Can you obtain the same result by sticking to just plain old regular cheese and just eat a whole lot less of it?
—L.K. Birmingham, Alabama

ME: Well, you can if that will satisfy your palate. In my opinion, you are still depriving yourself if you do this. I love cheese on my pizza. I like A LOT OF CHEESE on my pizza. If I only had a couple of tablespoons sprinkled over my pizza, I wouldn't be satisfied. I would feel deprived. I know the great fat-free and low-fat cheeses that melt and taste good, so I would rather load it on and feel like I was eating pizza just the way I always have.

YOU: Is there one food that there is just no substitute for that you're just going to have to live without because it's terrible for you and you can't substitute any thing for it?
— *R.E. New York, New York*

ME: Nuts are very high in fat. Chestnuts are the only nut I know of that is actually low-fat. Four ounces are only 1.4 fat grams. Some believe walnuts help lower cholesterol. There have been several articles concerning this recently. Walnuts are 16 fat grams an ounce, so if you are counting fat grams they still wouldn't be a terrific choice to consume on a regular basis. It's hard to find a substitute for nuts. What I do is use Grape Nuts Cereal in place of nuts. It provides that crunchy nutty texture, and most people don't realize it isn't nuts unless you tell them. You can also use extracts in place of high-fat items such as coconut and walnuts. By using a nut flavored extract, along with Grape-Nuts Cereal, most people will THINK they are eating nuts. Another food that contains a lot of fat and hard to substitute or replace is the avocado. This can be a problem if you happen to like guacamole dip. However, I have a new recipe for MOCK GUACAMOLE DIP that is made with split peas. It may sound gross, but wait until you taste it. I've served it at parties and no one could tell the difference. Check the recipe section of this book (page 353) to find my new "MOCK GUA-CAMOLE DIP." I think you will be pleasantly surprised!

YOU: I heard about *BUTTER BUSTERS* at a garage sale I had at my home on August 28. A lady came looking for size 12-14 clothes just to hold her over until she reached her goal of size 10-12. Everything I had was 18-20 and too small for me! She told me about this cookbook and the success story of a whole family-the loss of 150 pounds-4 people. I'm sorry I didn't get her name.

On August 30, two days later, I purchased two copies-one for a friend and one for me. I showed mine to a daughter-in-law and gave up my copy, so off to purchase my THIRD copy. Now I hide it when anyone comes! This weight loss is just costing me too much in books!

Since August 30 to September 13, I have gone from 188 to 172 and my husband from 204 to 186. We are thrilled and not hungry. We neither had any other health problems, just ate wrong. We're active, take care of a big yard-one acre, square dance, walk 3-4 times a week, and love to eat! I was the typical "don't eat till 4:00 P.M. and then don't stop till bedtime!"

I do have one problem and hope you can help me. I'm referring to recipes for fruit breads and cakes such as Pumpkin Bread, Mock Banana Nut Bread, and Carrot Cake. All of these are very good soon after baking, but I store them covered (either foil or bake box sealed) and they get sticky or gummy. What am I doing wrong? I mix the Butter Buds mix with water until it dissolves and proceed as the recipe says, but can't seem to keep them from getting sticky, like I said. Please help. I've had great results with all the salad and meat dishes and love the part of the book with shopping tips (names and items). Some I can't get in my area, but have called the numbers you listed and had some items sent to me.

I do keep a food diary and right now limit myself to 20-25 grams of fat a day. Anyway, I want to tell you how much help this book is to someone that has ALWAYS had a problem with weight!
—*D.W. Duncan, Oklahoma*

ME: I want to thank you for your sweet letter, and am so glad you are enjoying using the book. Since you have one of my earlier editions of the book, I have made some changes you might not know about. When I signed with Warner Books, I revised and updated the book and made several changes. One change I made was to give the reader a choice in most of the recipes that call for the mix to make Liquid Butter Buds in muffins, cakes, and breads. I give them the choice of using the Promise Fat-Free Margarine or Fleischmann's Fat-Free Spread (squeeze bottle) instead. I too, had a problem with some of the baked goods getting sticky after a few days. They were fine if you served them immediately, but did get gummy after sitting. I still recommend the liquid Butter Buds in all my sauces, soups, puddings, gravies, etc., but have found the Promise Ultra Fat-Free margarine and the NEW Fleischmann's Spread Fat-Free Margarine BOTH WORK BETTER in baked goods. Even though the containers say not to bake or microwave with with the margarines, that never stops me! The reason behind that statement is the large amount of water contained in the products. I have had great luck using both of these fat-free margarines in all my cakes, muffins, and breads, and the gummy problem is gone. The Promise Ultra Fat-Free Margarine comes two tubs to a package. It is a yellow package and you use it just like you would margarine or oil. If the recipe calls for 1/2 cup margarine, you would use 1/2 cup of the Promise Ultra Fat-Free Margarine.The fat-free Fleischmann's margarine comes in a squeeze bottle. Measure it as you would the Promise Ultra fat-free margarine. Another wonderful product I've also had great luck with is Wonderslim (also fat-free). It is an egg and fat substitute that comes in a jar (found in health food stores), and is derived from plums. This product is used a little differently. If a recipe calls for 1/2 cup oil or margarine, you would use 1/4 cup of the Wonderslim. If you can't find Wonderslim in your area, ask your health food store to order it for you or call: (800)497-6595. There is another similar product called Just Like Shortenin' (also derived from plums) and can be ordered by calling: (203)245-7893. I wish you continued success!!

YOU: I recently had the opportunity to glance at your book. Although it was borrowed and I only got a glimpse, I was really impressed. *BUTTER BUSTERS* is the most logical approach to a healthy life-style I have ever come upon. After convincing my husband that changing our lifestyle might prolong our lives and ensure good health for our two year old daughter, he agreed to buy the book. Before buying the book, however, I soon realized I may not be able to use the book and I decided not to buy it after all. You see, we spend only $50.00 a week on food. Most all our meals come in boxes and packages that are ready to mix. Therefore, I don't have many of the spices and ingredients needed for a lot of the recipes in your book. We don't have the extra money to go out and buy all of the low-fat foods. They are more expensive than the high-fat items. I also noticed you have a video series and workbook to teach low-fat cooking, eating, and shopping. I think I will save my money for that instead. Maybe it would help teach me what to do. I do have a VCR.

I have heard it is healthier to cook from scratch. My family would benefit from a change in diet to healthier foods, less fat, and more exercise. Could you respond with advice on how to get started on the right track towards a healthier lifestyle? Please keep in mind our income and food money are very limited.
Sincerely, —H.C.

ME: I can understand where you are coming from and would love to share these items (*BUTTER BUSTERS THE COOKBOOK* and my *BUTTER BUSTERS* GuideBook and Video Series) with you and your family. You are right that a lot of the low-fat products are more expensive than the high-fat foods. You can make wise inexpensive choices, however. You mentioned that many of your meals are prepared from box mixes. You can even reduce the fat in those products by substituting egg whites in place of eggs and powdered non-fat milk in place of whole milk. There is another product you might consider purchasing that will save you a lot of money. It is called ENER-G Egg Replacers. It is a powdered egg substitute you mix with water. It only costs about $4.69, but is equivalent to 162 eggs. It doesn't require refrigeration and works great in all baked products. It can be found or ordered through any health food store. Most of the more expensive low-fat items are convenience foods. For instance the fat-free cream cheese. It doesn't cost any more than the regular cream cheese, but still might be out of your budget. In that case, you can make your own fat-free cream cheese substitute with yogurt (the recipe is in the guidebook) or fat-free cottage cheese which is a great protein source and it might be a little cheaper. The recipe is in the cookbook.

Since meat, chicken, and turkey can add expense to casseroles, try using more beans (a great protein source), rice, pasta and vegetables. Think of using meat in small amounts for taste as a condiment, rather than the main course, and you will cut the fat content as well as the expense. Try buying your fruits and vegetables in bulk at farmer's markets or roadside produce stands. Share the cost with a neighbor or friend and you will get more for your money. Invest in a card at Sam's Club or some other price club. Your investment will save you a lot of money in the long run. When you can buy in bulk, and split the cost with a friend, you can save a tremendous amount of money. If you have another family that lives close by (that is also interested in cooking healthy low-fat food), you might make a deal with them. When you prepare casseroles, make two and trade one with the other family. This provides variety and is another way to be more cost efficient. I can identify with your problem. When my husband was in medical school in New Orleans, our budget was VERY LIMITED!! I worked as a waitress at the Roosevelt Hotel and later at Steak'N Ale Restaurant when they opened in Louisiana. This was in the 70's and food was a lot cheaper, but our income depended on my tips waiting tables. (Mike waited tables with me on weekend nights.) We were able to sell our blood at the Oschner Clinic in New Orleans every three weeks for extra money (which you can no longer do, but could back then). We were lucky because my husband has a very rare blood type, so he got paid twice as much as I did. Mike also participated in drug studies which enabled him to earn a little more (much needed) money. The drug studies consisted of him taking medication (such as a type of aspirin), and having blood drawn every 2 hours over a forty-eight hour weekend. The purpose was to find out how fast the medicine was absorbed into the bloodstream, etc. I honestly don't think we could have made it without the added income the drug studies provided. Our experience also made us appreciate our lives even more when things got easier. Back then hamburger was 49 cents a pound. We lived on Hamburger Helper and macaroni and cheese. I was also on a diet most of those four years in medical school trying to lose weight. As a result of our high-fat diet, and lack of exercise I remained heavy during those years. I hate to think how much my high-fat diet and lack of exercise contributed to my cholesterol problem (that I didn't even know I had). I wish I would have known about low-fat substitutions and aerobic exercise during those years.

I'm telling you all of this, because I have been where you are, and I truly understand how hard it can be to make ends meet. I found, because of our limited income, that I could cook in bulk and freeze in small servings, which saved me a lot of time and money. That is also when I got involved in food co-ops (sharing with other families that I spoke of earlier). This method also works well with child care. Take turns with a friend keeping each other's kids so you can exercise or have some time for yourself. This way you aren't out any money, but still have some quality alone time (which we all need when our children are small).

Other inexpensive ideas you might try are baking your own bread (using whole wheat flour), making your own low-fat chips (oven baked corn tortillas- recipe in cookbook, or potato chips- recipe in guidebook), making your own frozen fruit juice bars (these can be frozen in ice cube trays and are a lot cheaper than store bought popsicles). Canned beans and other vegetables are cheap, but loaded with sodium. Always rinse thoroughly before using. Learn to make your own jams, jellies, and preserves. Most children love pasta. Make your own spaghetti sauce adding fresh vegetables such as onions, green and red peppers, garlic, tomatoes, and mushrooms and you will be adding the antioxidant vitamins so important in disease prevention. It is a lot cheaper to "stay healthy" than to "get sick." Make your own granola and cereal bars from scratch. Use Grape-Nuts Cereal in place of nuts to save fat grams and money. Use nut and coconut extracts for the taste without the fat, in your baked items. Use clear chicken broth to stir fry and sauté vegetables instead of oil. I have a recipe for chicken broth in the book, or you can purchase sodium reduced chicken broth in cans. They come in huge cans at Sam's Club. When you open a can, pour what you don't use in plastic ice cubes trays and freeze for later when you just need a small amount. Take advantage of buying fresh vegetables in bulk during their prime season and freeze for later. If you feel the low-fat and fat-free cheeses are too expensive, reduce the amount of regular cheese you use by grating it finely and using moderately. This allows the taste, but will help you reduce the fat content. You can make many of the desserts, sauces, and puddings from scratch using powdered skim milk (cheaper) or evaporated skim milk in place of whole milk. The Promise Ultra Fat-Free Margarine and Fleischmann's Fat-Free Spread are no more expensive than regular margarine and work great in most baked products. You can save money making your own baby food by puréeing fruits and vegetables. This helps you control the sugar and sodium content as well. You can freeze portions in ice cube trays as you do the chicken broth and fruit juice frozen snacks. There are many low-fat snacks you can make from scratch that don't require special ingredients. As I said before, many of the expensive low-fat snacks are for convenience only. If you have the time, and don't mind the extra work, you CAN eat, shop, and cook low-fat for the rest of your life (even on a limited budget)! I'm sending you my video series and guidebook to help with your shopping and cooking since you did mention that you have a VCR. I'm also sending along a couple of boxes of the mix to make liquid Butter Buds so you can give them a try. Please accept these items and see if they don't help. Please keep me posted on your progress!!

The following is a letter from the same person:

Dear Pam Mycoskie:

Thank you so much for your kindness. Now that I have your cookbook, some Butter Buds, your video series and guidebook, and all of your helpful suggestions, I can get started. They are all so informative towards a healthier lifestyle. I would also like to thank you for opening my eyes to what I put into my body and what I am feeding my family. All it took was to begin reading labels and I realized that eating healthy wasn't so hard (or expensive). As a matter of fact, it's better AND cheaper (in some cases). I've only just begun, but it feels great to know that I am helping my daughter grow up healthy and with less risk of heart disease and obesity. I don't go through one day without learning something new about my healthy lifestyle and I have you to thank for that!

P.S. It is people like you who make it easier to live in this world for people like me. All my best to you and your family! Gratefully,   —H.C.

NOTE: I've included these letters (not to make me look good, I promise), but to let you know just how much my readers mean to me, and how strongly I feel that this is my true purpose in life! Nothing is more rewarding than knowing you have helped change someone's life for the better!!

YOU: My husband has high blood pressure. So many of the low-fat foods (especially salad dressings) contain high levels of sodium. Is there any way to tell how much sodium is in the food in restaurants? They don't list nutritional information on menus and we eat out a lot. I used your suggestion in the book and purchased the Papa Dash Lite Salt and we just love it. It is the first and only lite salt we have ever liked. I rinse all my canned vegetables (like you suggested). My kids even love your recipes! Thanks for real food (not diet food) and all the great shopping tips too! —L.K. Chicago, Illinois

ME: As a matter of fact there is a neat gadget that measures the sodium content in food. It is called the "Lumiscope Salt Detector." It retails for about $15.00 in drug stores. It has a probe you place in hot or cold food or liquid to determine the sodium content. If you can't find it in your area you can call: (908)225-5533. I'm so glad you and your family are enjoying the recipes. If we teach our children low-fat healthy cooking, shopping, and eating early on, they might not have to contend with the fat-related problems we, as adults, have been forced to deal with today. Good Luck!

YOU: Having had the opportunity to work with your cookbook and one of our cardiac patients, I would like to purchase your workbook and video series for low-fat cooking, shopping, and eating. These materials would be used in the education of new heart patients who have had a heart attack or have had surgery. Your information seems easier for the patient and family to understand as compared to some of our texts. I continue to look for a book that approaches Diabetes and Heart Disease with diet. Often the reduced calorie need is overlooked when a book is prepared. If you have further resources concerning sugar reduction, please let me know.

As we are considering using your book as a source for our patients to purchase, would you please quote a price if more than one is purchased? Thank you for your assistance.

ME: I appreciate your comments regarding my book. Many hospitals, doctor's offices, and clinics have purchased my materials to distribute to their patients. I realize (more than most) that physicians simply do not have the time to discuss diet and exercise in great detail with their patients. My husband is an orthopedic surgeon, and I realize their workload and lack of time. He is quite lucky to have a very qualified staff that takes up the slack concerning patient education regarding treatment and instructions. Not all physicians are so fortunate. Since you have one of my earlier editions of the book, you are not aware of the updated revisions concerning sugar substitutes. In the 7th edition of the book I've included the choice (mostly for the diabetics) of using one half Sweet'N Low for one half of the sugar in all the recipes that contain sugar. This has helped all of those folks who need to be concerned with sugar consumption.

Note: The following is new information about diabetes. It was not included in the letter to the physician, however, I feel it will be of value to you.

Because of the recent dietary guideline changes established by the American Diabetes Association, sugar is no longer the taboo it once was, and has been placed with all carbohydrates (sugars and starches) as a single category of foods among which trade-offs are possible. Starches are made of long chains of glucose that digestive enzymes quickly break down into individual glucose molecules. Sucrose, or table sugar, on the other hand, is made of one molecule of glucose and one molecule of fructose. The glycemic index of fruits is very low, 20 as against 100 for glucose, and this may be why a potato, which is all starch, and therefore breaks down into pure glucose, has a higher glycemic index than table sugar, which is a 50-50 combination of glucose and fructose.

Instead of setting rigid ratios of proteins, fats, and carbohydrates, the new guidelines recommend that protein make up 10% to 20% of the calories consumed each day and the remaining 80% to 90% of calories be divided between carbohydrates and fats,depending on the individual's weight concerns and other health risks (like blood levels of cholesterol and triglycerides). For patients of reasonably normal weight with normal cholesterol, a diet of 30% and less than 300 mg of cholesterol is satisfactory. Only 10% of those fat calories should come from saturated fats, however. The majority should come from the heart-healthy monounsaturated sources, such as olive or canola oil. If they are overweight or suffer from high cholesterol, they should reduce their TOTAL FAT to 10% of their daily caloric allotment.

As you can see, all diabetics need to be concerned with the fat in their diet. For this reason, my book will appeal to diabetics as well as heart patients (especially with the new Sweet'N Low additions). Thank you for your kind words!

YOU: I recently purchased your book, *BUTTER BUSTERS*, and I think it is the best low-fat cookbook I have ever seen. I have shared this with many of my friends and co-workers and have encouraged them to buy the book. The shopping information is wonderful!

I have made several of the recipes and have been pleased, but did have a problem with one recipe and I was hoping you could help me figure out what I did wrong. The Chocolate Meringue Pie was great, EXCEPT for the pie crust. The crust was quite hard and tough around the edges. I used the Promise Ultra Fat-Free Margarine like you suggested. What did I do wrong? Thank you for your assistance and for publishing a realistic low-fat cookbook.
— M.S. Tallahassee, Florida

ME: If it makes you feel any better, you are not the first to have trouble with the pie crust recipe. In my earlier editions of the book, I used corn syrup in place of fat, but that was even more difficult to not overwork, due to the sticky dough. I have had good luck with the Promise Ultra Fat-Free Margarine, providing I don't overwork the dough. I also suggest placing foil around the edge as it bakes. I have found that once the filling sits in the crust for a few hours in the frig, the crust softens up considerably. I know it is not perfect, but I do have some other suggestions you might want to try. Since the pie crust proved difficult for many people, I experimented with some new options. If you don't mind a little higher fat crust, you can try this:

BASIC PIE CRUST

1 1/4 cups all-purpose flour
2 Tbs. sugar
1/4 tsp. Papa Dash Lite Salt
3 Tbs. cold Fleischmann's Lower Fat Margarine (4.5 fat grams a Tbs.)
4-5 Tbs. ice water
Prepare as you would any other pie crust.

Total Fat for the whole pie: 14.4 fat grams
Serves 8: Per serving: 1.8 fat grams
I hope you will continue to enjoy the book.

> *Note:* For more pie crust options, refer to page 431 in the Recipe section of this book.

YOU: I am writing to tell you how thrilled I am with your cookbook. I have been overweight my whole life, and never found a way to keep the weight off once I lost it (which I have done many times, lose it that is). I've lost 22 pounds in the last three months and have eaten more delicious food from your book than I ever thought possible. My friends at work kid me because I take your book with me everywhere I go. I'm not worried about gaining the weight back this time because I don't ever WANT to go back to my old way of eating!! If I can have all my favorite recipes modified to low-fat, why would I ever want to? I have a few questions. Do you have a recipe for Honey Mustard Dressing? Do you think store brands are just as good as name brands? How do you eat at

parties, cookouts, and vacations away from home? I haven't ventured out much, because I can control my food at home, but you can't always trust others to cook low-fat and healthy. What are good snacks to carry in your car? Can I still use box prepared mixes and substitute the liquid Butter Buds (made from the mix) in place of oil? Anyway, I could go on for hours about how your book has changed my life, but I need to get back to cooking. Your delicious "Rum Cake" I made for bridge club tonight is ready to come out of the oven! Please don't ever stop writing low-fat cook books! There are a lot of us out here who need your recipes!
—B.B. Midland, Texas

ME: It sounds like you are "on a roll" with your weight loss. That is wonderful and I am so happy

Pam, Dorcas Pohl, and Ann Gilcrease
Dallas, Texas   1993

my recipes have made it easier for you. You might have one of my older editions of the book, because since then I've added a new Honey Mustard Dressing called "Dorcas Pohl's Honey Mustard Dressing." It was sent to me by a reader, Dorcas Pohl, and I asked her permission to use it to replace the honey mustard recipe I had in my original book. It is one of my favorites. I make it in big batches (it stays fresh several days in the frig), so I always have plenty on hand for sandwiches as well as salads. It is on page 146 in the 7th edition of the book. I know you will love it too.

Note: The photo was taken in 1993 when Dorcas came to Dallas to visit her daughter Ann.

I think store brands are GREAT in most cases and always cheaper. Some examples are the Kroger brand (Lite Classics) low-fat cheese products, Kroger brand salad dressings, ice cream, and ice cream toppings. They also have their own brand of fat-free egg substitute. If you have Kroger stores in your area, check out their brands. They have their own brand called Deluxe Fat-Free Frozen Dessert (their answer to fat-free ice cream) that is just delicious and much cheaper than the name brands. Food Lion has their own brand of egg substitutes called Egg Mates which is great and much cheaper than most name brands. Most stores have their own brand of fat-free sour cream, fat-free cream cheese, and fat-free salad dressings. Winn Dixie has their own brand of several low and fat-free products that are inexpensive and delicious. I have tried many of the store brand items and can't tell much difference other than getting more change back when I pay for them.

Eating out is never a problem. I don't care what kind of restaurant (even fast food) you find yourself in, YOU CAN MAKE A WISE CHOICE! You might need to be a little assertive and ask some questions and make requests, but it can be done. Trust me! As far as parties are concerned, I usually eat a healthy filling low-fat snack BEFORE I go to the party if I think the low-fat options will be scarce or non-existent. Since most folks are interested in healthy eating, even party foods have changed dramatically due to all the great new products on the market (fat-free cream cheese, fat-free sour cream, etc.) over the past few years. Most thoughtful hosts and hostesses will include low-fat options. The only thing they might not offer is a low-fat dessert. I don't know why, but most people think it is impossible to make a really good and tasty low-fat dessert. Most folks won't even attempt to make one! I've never had that problem at my parties. I've had guests make me swear my desserts are low-fat. Some people even insist on seeing what I used to make them (especially my Famous No Guilt Mud Pie on page 438, my Carrot Cake with Vanilla Sauce on page 372, Chocolate Caramel Bars on page 410, Cherry Cheesecake Delight on page 413, Hot Fudge Pudding Cake on page 358, and my Cream Cheese Cake Bars on page 391). No one believes they are REALLY LOW-FAT because they taste so rich, but every one of those recipes are UNDER 1 FAT GRAM PER SERVING!!

I always carry low-fat snacks in my purse and car. I drive a suburban so I have plenty of room for a small ice chest (for my fat-free salad dressing, fat-free margarine, and bottled water). Some of my favorite car snacks are pretzels, bagels, low-fat microwave popcorn, the cinnamon or caramel corn flavored rice cakes, Frito brand baked Tostitos and hot sauce, fat-free string cheese, boxes of Snackwells crackers or cookies. You can also keep fresh fruit and fat-free Dannon Light yogurt in your car if you have an ice chest like I do. I also bring plenty of low-fat food in my carry-on bag when I travel by plane. You never know when or what they will serve you!

In answer to your last question about using the liquid Butter Buds (made from the mix) in place of oil in your cake or muffin mixes. Yes, you can. I actually prefer the Promise Ultra Fat-Free Margarine in most baked goods, but you can use the liquid Butter Buds in place of margarine in many of the mixes such as macaroni and cheese and powdered sauce and gravy mixes. Keep up the great job and thanks for your letter!

YOU: Do you have any recipes for venison? I prefer it to beef.   — B.B. Millsap, Texas

P.S. I ordered your *BUTTER BUSTERS COOKBOOK* and started marking my favorite recipes with sticky notes. I was marking every other page!!

ME: I love venison too! I had never really eaten it before I got into low-fat cooking (and wanted another low-fat option besides turkey) a few years ago. There is one brand called Broken Arrow Ranch Brand Venison I use all the time. It is from Ingram, Texas and comes in the regular ground, chile ground, and chunk varieties. If you can't find it in your area call: (800)962-4263. It is only 11 fat grams a pound. If you have a friend or husband that enjoys deer hunting, you also have that option. Most children will not be able to tell the difference between ground venison and ground beef. They CAN tell the difference between ground beef and ground turkey (because it is white). If it is only the taste you prefer, then the venison is your answer. However, if you gave up red meat because of the cholesterol and fat content, you now have a wonderful new option. It is an extremely low-fat beef called Vermillion Valley Beef (formally Covington Ranch). It is sold by mail order and comes in a variety of options from ground beef to ribeye steaks. A six ounce Vermillion tenderloin is only 3 fat grams. It actually has less cholesterol than flounder and 50% less fat than a skinless chicken breast. I've included more information about this great product in the "New Products" chapter on page 273 and also in the "Resource Guide" on page 539.

YOU: In the past year my husband has managed to lose 40 pounds and I have lost 25 just by cooking out of your great book. We were already walkers, so we did exercise too, but had never eaten low-fat until we bought your book. We couldn't believe how quickly the weight came off with little effort. I do have a question. With everything in the news about trans-fatty acids, would we be better off to switch back to butter? I know butter contains cholesterol, but which one is worse? Please let me know if you can. My husband and I are your biggest fans. He never used to talk about cookbooks or cooking, but I can't shut him up now. Everywhere we go, he spreads the word. Of course, everyone wants to know how he managed to lose so much weight, and your book always comes up in the conversation. We both appreciate you and what you have done for so many people who need to make the switch, but just don't know how to get started. You make it so easy!! — *J.H. Tallahasse, Florida*

ME: I'm so glad the book has helped both of you. As far as going back to butter, I would not recommend that at all. Stick for stick, both butter (rich in saturated fat and cholesterol) and margarine (packed with chemicals called trans-fatty acids) raise the levels of "bad" LDL cholesterol. Trans-fatty acids have also been found to lower the levels of "good" HDL cholesterol. Should you go back to butter? I say NO! The American Heart Association says margarine is still better than butter, but to choose tub or squeezable margarines over the sticks (which contain more trans-fatty acids). BUTTER ALSO CONTAINS MORE OF THE SATURATED FATS THAN MARGARINE (A TABLESPOON OF MARGARINE HAS 2 GM. OF SATURATED FAT, VERSUS 7.5 GM. OF SATURATED FAT IN BUTTER). Instead I would recommend switching to one of the great fat-free margarines that contain NO TRANS-FATTY ACIDS! Your total daily fat calories should not exceed 30% of your overall intake. So, if you consume 2,000 calories a day, only 600 calories should come from fat. This comes out to a total of about 66 grams of fat a day (600 divided by 9 = 66). One tablespoon of either butter or margarine has around 11.5 grams of total fat.

Note: *The American Heart Association recommends 30% or less as a healthy total fat allowance. However, if you are trying to lower your cholesterol or lose weight I would recommend between 10-20% total fat of your total caloric intake for the day. Check the section on "Butter versus Margarine" on page 301 of this book for some great suggestions!*

YOU: I love your wonderful book and have been cooking out of it for several months. I've purchased many as gifts. I just found out that I am pregnant and wanted to know if low-fat eating was OK if you are pregnant? Also, do you know of any guidelines as far as gaining weight? I've heard everything and am a little confused. Thanks for a great book. You outdid yourself!
—*F.T. Rochester, New York*

ME: As long as you are eating a healthy diet and consuming enough calories for you and your growing child, a low-fat diet is just as healthy when you are pregnant as when you are not. You want to gain healthy weight during your pregnancy, not unhealthy fat, right? There is nothing healthy about eating too much fat. It is important to choose more healthy kinds of fats, however, when you are eating fat. Olive Oil and Canola are the most heart-healthy oils (but still 14 fat grams a tablespoon). The fats you really need to be concerned with are foods containing the trans-fatty acids. These are the fats that start out as innocent polyunsaturated or monounsaturated fats, but because of a process called hydrogenation, are transformed into saturated fats (which have been shown to be detrimental to our health for many reasons). For one thing they raise the levels of the "bad" LDL cholesterol and reduce the "good" HDL cholesterol. If you want to keep them off your plate, be on the look-out for the following foods. I know it is extra hard when you are pregnant because some of us have some very strange cravings when we are "with child."

Food	Trans-Fatty Acids (In Grams)	Total Fat (In Grams)
French Fries (4 oz. order)	5.5	16
Glazed Donut (1.6 oz.)	3.2	12
Danish Pastry (2.5 oz.)	3.0	11
White Cake (1 slice)	1.0	14
Cherry Snack Pie	2.0	20
Sugar Cookie (.6 oz.)	1.0	6
Margarine, Stick (1 Tbs.)	1.8	12
Margarine, Tub (1 Tbs.)	0.9	7-10

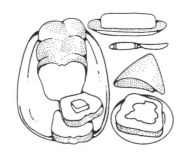

After a woman gives birth, many are likely to retain about 10 pounds or more for years. Although you should NEVER DIET DURING PREGNANCY, you can help limit excessive weight gain through a two-step method: Follow good nutritional habits and stay active through regular exercise (if your physician permits). Here are the standard recommendations for what you should be able to safely gain, depending on your height and weight before pregnancy:

Body Mass Index* before pregnancy	Recommended weight gain (in pounds)
Underweight (less than 19.8)	28-40
Normal weight (19.8 to 26.0)	25-35
Overweight (26.1 to 29.0)	15-25
Obese (more than 29.0)	15
If carrying twins	35-45

*Your body mass index (BMI) compares your weight in relation to your height.

To calculate your BMI:
1. Multiply your weight (in pounds) times 700.
2. Divide the result by your height (in inches).
3. Divide that result by your height again to determine your BODY MASS INDEX.
I hope this information helps but keep in mind this is only an example. Each person is an individual and has different nutritional needs.

NOTE: ALWAYS CHECK WITH YOUR PHYSICIAN CONCERNING DIET AND EXER-CISE DURING PREGNANCY!!!!

YOU: I love your book and have been using it about six months. My family loves the recipes and the kids are even into watching fat grams. They really read the labels and have quit eating so much junk as a result of your book. I do have a couple of concerns. Since I use many of the non-fat products in place of the old high fat versions, I have noticed a lot of strange sounding ingredients on the label. Are these non-fat products highly chemicalized concoctions that might not be as healthy as we think? Thanks for any information you might offer.
—*J.H. Jackson, Mississippi*

ME: I'm so glad the book has been helpful. I know what you mean about the kids reading the labels. I made an infomercial a few weeks ago, and we had two children help us out in one of the cooking segments (Gabrial and Dominique). While I was talking to the kids between shootings, they asked me about the fat content of Liquid Butter Buds (we happened to be using this product to make Hot Fudge Pudding Cake). They asked me what it was made of and how much fat it contained. I was impressed. They were only eight years old! The children of our country definitely understand the importance of a low-fat diet. Many of the strange sounding ingredients listed on low-fat products (locust bean gum, carrageenin, guar gum, cellulose gum) may sound threatening, but they are the names of soluble fibers and other substances extracted from plants. They provide the same creamy "mouthfeel" of butterfat without the fat and calories. You are smart to be concerned and if you ever question an ingredient look it up or ask at your local health food store. They have several books concerning ingredients you might want to check out.

YOU: I bought your great book about three months ago and have really enjoyed cooking the great recipes. I was really getting into the habit of cooking and eating low-fat. My weight started dropping within the first week, so I knew this was something I could do the rest of my life. I was eating all the food I wanted and was still losing weight (even with desserts)!

Two weeks ago, my life changed dramatically. My husband informed me that he wanted a divorce because he was in love with someone else. No one was surprised more than me. I had NO IDEA! We have two small children (pre-school age) and I haven't worked since we got married (7 years ago). I'm not going to cry on your shoulder about all of my problems, but would like your help (if you have the time to write) with some food related questions. My problem is my schedule. I just recently went back to work full time (an adjustment in itself) and I am always on the run. I eat lunch in my car many days. I usually stop by the house to pick something up to eat, but don't even have time to sit down and eat it there. Any suggestions for quick portable lunches? My mornings are really wild (trying to get myself ready and the kids dressed, fed, and to day care). I know breakfast is important for my energy level, but don't have time to cook a big meal. Any suggestions for quick (less than 10 minutes) and healthy low-fat breakfast ideas? Some days I never leave the office all day. We do have a small kitchen and microwave at work. Are there any good munchies I can stock at my office in my desk, when I don't have time to get away? I refuse to eat out of those vending machines! Please help if you can. I was doing so well with my weight loss before HE "gave me the good news!" Ha Ha!! I can see a big picture of me pigging out with my eating (because I am depressed) and gaining it all back again. There are other fish in the sea, and I plan on catching one if possible. Please help me. I don't want to be single the rest of my life! I'm only 37 years old. I'm not bad looking (most people find me attractive). If I ever get married again, I'll get back to cooking your great recipes. By the time I get home from work, I really don't feel like cooking. Besides there are just so many things children under the age of five will eat. I do use low-fat substitutions when I can in preparing the kid's meals. Thank goodness they like noodles, beans, fruits and vegetables (and those foods are pretty cheap, too). Have you considered a newsletter? I would love to have a regular source of new information about low-fat living! I'm sure there are a lot of people like me that could use some advice!   —K.L.

ME: I must commend you for retaining your sense of humor. You have experienced a major jolt to your life, and I respect you greatly for the continued interest and concern you show for the health and welfare of your children and yourself. One suggestion I might make (if you can fit it in) would be to take a couple of hours (on Sunday afternoon perhaps when the kids are napping) and cook several meals to freeze for your busy days during the week. It's just an idea, but it might help. It will save you time and money in the long run.

When you drop by the house to grab a bite to eat for a portable lunch try these suggestions:

1. Pile a couple of slices of fat-free turkey and fat-free sliced cheese on a fat-free flour tortilla and roll it up. Grab some carrot sticks and a carton of Dannon "Light" fat-free yogurt with a plastic spoon. You can always eat a banana or apple while driving for dessert. Don't forget a carton of juice or a plastic bottle of water.

2. Split a bagel in half and spread with fat-free cream cheese and raisins. Eat it like a sandwich. If that filling doesn't appeal to you try another low-fat filling. Make my Basic Low-fat Tuna Salad on Sunday (when you do your cooking), and you will have sandwich filling for several days. Grab some pretzels or baked tortilla chips. Polly-O and Healthy Choice make fat-free string cheese. These are quite portable and easy to eat while driving (also great for the kid's lunch boxes). Keep rice cakes, pretzels, fat-free cookies and crackers in your car at all times. You can always stick in a frozen carton of juice for later in the day. It will defrost by lunchtime and you don't have to worry about refrigeration.

Mornings can be really hectic in any household with children! Try some of these quick fixes:

1. Add applesauce and raisins to microwave oatmeal.

2. Sprinkle fat-free granola in a carton of Dannon "Light" flavored fat-free yogurt. Add toast or an English muffin.

3. Microwave a frozen fat-free pancake. Spread fat-free cream cheese, sprinkle cinnamon and fat-free granola on top and roll it up. Stick a toothpick in it to hold it together. Pour some fat-free maple syrup in a small dish for dipping. Head for the bathroom to put on your make-up. You can use all kinds of fillings (sliced bananas, raisins, strawberries, etc.). You can put on your make-up or dry your hair while you eat these rolled-up pancake treats.

4. Grab a SnackWells fat-free breakfast bar and a piece of fruit. Head for the kid's bedroom to wake them up. You will finish your breakfast before you get back to the kitchen. (This one works if you ARE REALLY pressed for time!)

5. Place a sliced tomato on a bagel half or English muffin. Top with a slice of fat-free cheese and run under the broiler for 1-2 minutes. Add some grapes and you are ready to roll!

6. You can always drink your breakfast. In a blender, combine 2 ounces of frozen orange juice concentrate, 1/2 cup vanilla flavored Dannon "Light" fat-free yogurt, 3/4 cup skim milk, a dash of vanilla, and 1 or 2 ice cubes. Munch on a whole wheat bagel or piece of toast while you are making your smoothie. There are all kinds of variations for healthy low-fat smoothies. Use your imagination! The kids might even enjoy this breakfast drink once in a while. Check page 352 for a yummie orange smoothie.

7. When you are REALLY in a hurry, do what I do. Grab a bag of Back to Nature No-Fat Added Granola and a spoon (not totally necessary, but helpful) and head for the door! Maybe you will be lucky and find a defrosted carton of juice or a banana (that slipped between the seats in your car) and munch away as you drive the kids to day care!

8. You can always drive through McDonald's. They offer fat-free muffins and they really are delicious!

If your office has a refrigerator, you can dine on leftovers from dinner the night before. You might consider storing yogurt and skim milk in the office refrigerator. Stash a box of cereal, fat-free crackers, fruit, and other healthy low-fat munchies in your desk. Try to eat something every 3-4 hours to prevent low-blood sugar and uncontrolled hunger!

I hope you meet a wonderful man who will appreciate what you have to offer. By reading your letter, I feel like YOU are the Angel Fish in the sea that will be someone's GREAT CATCH! Don't fall for the first worm (no pun intended) that happens to come along. Watch out for the sharks! Be choosy! You're worth it!!! Good luck!

YOU: Love your book! Have you heard of a fat substitute called Appetize? I was listening to a talk radio show and caught the tail end of some guy talking about fat substitutes you could fry with. He also mentioned low-fat pork. Is there such a thing? Please let me know if you have any information regarding these matters. —*K.P. Billings, Montana*

ME: I don't know if this is what you are talking about, but I read an article in a health magazine that mentioned a new product called (you guessed it) Appetize. The product was created by researchers at Brandeis University. Appetize contains no trans-elaidic (or fatty) acids, which are found in the hydrogenated vegetable oils and linked to heart disease. Three types of Appetize will be manufactured. They are derived from natural fat blends that can be used in deep fat frying, shortening for baking, margarine or butter substitutes, and in dairy products for cheese and ice cream. The products will first appear in universities, school systems, and large food service businesses in 1995 the article stated. Look for products made with Appetize in the near future. The article did not mention the fat content, however. Even though Appetize doesn't contain cholesterol or trans-fatty acids, it must contain some kind of fat. The article stated that it was derived from "natural fat blends." I'll watch for more information and pass it on when I have more answers.

Pork tenderloin is a very low-fat pork product. A three ounce serving of roasted pork tenderloin is only 4.1 fat grams. Even though pork (in general) is considered a high-fat food, Americans are eating two more pounds of pork yearly than they consumed in 1990. I've heard of a manufacturer in Missouri who claims they are raising low-fat pork. I'm sure it is possible because Vermillion Valley Beef (in South Dakota) has accomplished the feat of raising low-fat beef. Who knows what the future holds? I'll keep you posted if I uncover any new info. Good luck!

YOU: Your book is a miracle. I would have never thought I could eat desserts and not gain weight. I always thought sugar was the culprit in my weight problem, not the fat. With all the fat substitutions you list in the shopping guide, low-fat cooking is a breeze. I've lost about eight pounds and haven't even had to cut out my nightly sweet treats. I feel that I still eat too much sugar. Are there any foods that satisfy your sweet tooth without sugar? I know sugar is void of nutrients, but it sure tastes good. I imagine if I cut my sugar intake (along with cutting the fat), I could REALLY speed up my weight loss. Thanks for all the work. I can't imagine writing a book. It must have taken you forever!   —S.S. Fayetteville, Arkansas

ME: I always thought it was the sugar that made me fat, too. Unfortunately, I love sugar myself (especially the kind found in Twizzlers Red Licorice)! The American Diabetic Association has changed their guidelines (for patients) due to new information concerning simple sugars and complex carbohydrates. They feel all forms of carbohydrates affect the insulin reaction in your body in much the same way. For this reason diabetics are now allowed to consume some simple carbohydrates along with the complex carbohydrates (they have always been able to eat in the past). Since sugar has no nutritional value, however, we are wise to substitute foods that contain natural sugar and taste sweet, but still offer an abundance of nutrients and vitamins. The following is a list of foods that might help control your sweet tooth because they contain a "naturally" sweet taste!

Breads, Corn, and Rice	Breakfast Cereals	Fruits	Vegetables	Peas and Beans
whole wheat bread corn on the cob brown rice	oatmeal all-Bran Shredded Wheat Cornflakes	apples oranges bananas raisins	sweet potatoes yams beets white potatoes carrots	chick peas baked beans green peas

You can always substitute one half Sweet 'N Low or Necta-Sweet Saccharin tablets for one half of the sugar in your recipes to help cut down on simple sugar consumption!
•Note: Some folks do not like to use sugar substitutes. The choice is up to you.

As a matter of fact it did take me a long time to write *BUTTER BUSTERS*. From start to publication about 2 years! I'm so glad you are enjoying the book. I have been paid back for my hard work many, many times by the wonderful letters from my readers! It's your inspirational letters that keep me motivated!

YOU: I've heard it is better to eat several small meals rather than two large meals to lose weight. Is that true? I read that you only ate one meal a day for several years to stay slim (but were miserable). Now, you say you eat every 3 or 4 hours. Don't you eat a lot more food that way? Do you have to exercise more to keep the weight off? I've only eaten one meal a day for several years myself. I'm afraid to eat more often (for fear I couldn't stop if I got started). Do you have any ideas to help me change my eating patterns? I know this is unhealthy, but change is hard for me. Please help if you can.   —E.M. Raleigh, North Carolina

ME: I know how difficult it is to "give yourself permission" to eat more often when you are trying to lose weight. It sounds crazy. Eat more food and you will lose weight. Well, I didn't believe it myself until I gave it a try. I was a "one-meal-a-day person" for many years (as you know). I was slim all right, but I felt very deprived and honestly thought if I ate like a normal person I would be obese. When I did overeat, I worked out a couple of hours the next day to make up for my lack of control. When I finally changed my eating habits (back in August 1990), I became a free and happy person. By free, I mean that I finally broke away from the ridiculous mind-set of deprivation and compulsive exercise I practiced to remain slim. I put so much pressure on myself to "look good" no matter how much I suffered in the process I was one of those "people pleaser types" that thought I had to "look good" to be accepted. It took me REALLY accepting and liking myself (for the first time in my life) to make the big change. So, you see, that is what I mean by free!

Today I eat about every three hours. I'm not saying I eat huge amounts of food, but I do eat often. I've found by keeping my body fueled on a constant basis, I am able to consume a much greater amount of food over the course of a day and not gain weight. I eat a lot of carbohydrates. With my hectic schedule, I need the energy provided by carbohydrate-rich foods. I predict over the next year or so many Americans will adopt my style of eating. It makes sense if you really think about it.

It's kind of like my computer. As long as I leave it on it is easy to sit down and write or add to what I have already written. After all, the file is open and ready to go. When I turn it off and shut it down (like I do when I know I am finished working for a while), it takes a few minutes to turn it on and get back to what I was working on. I have to kind of start all over again (if you know what I mean). Our metabolic rate (rate at which our bodies burn calories) works in a similar way. When you turn it off, by not eating for several hours, it takes a while to turn it back on so it can efficiently use your food for fuel. If you keep your body fed on a constant basis, you don't have to worry about it shutting down to conserve energy (or store fat). It will constantly be working and burning fuel (or calories) to make room for more.

Another added bonus of eating five meals a day instead of the traditional three, you will find that it doesn't take as much food to fill you up. You simply won't be as hungry. I know this is true. When I only ate one meal a day, it began about 6:00 and wasn't over until about 8:00 P.M. I was so happy to finally be eating, I just couldn't stop once I got started (the fear you spoke of). Oh, I didn't eat for two straight hours, but those were the hours I gave myself permission to eat, and I guarantee I was consuming a huge amount of calories at once (because I had deprived myself all day). Since my poor body thought it was starving and wasn't quite sure when it was going to see the next meal, it became an expert at hoarding all those calories and sending them straight to my fat stores to wait out the next famine (not knowing when the food would come again). It's amazing how efficient our bodies are at storing fat, but on the other hand, so stingy at giving it up, isn't it? I find when I feed it constantly (on a regular basis), it's much more generous giving up the fat (and calories) as I exercise aerobically. It knows from experience (because I eat often now) that the next meal is only a couple of hours away! When I ate one meal a day, even exercise didn't work to budge that fat from my thighs!

When I was in New York a few months ago there was a show on T.V. discussing this very subject. It caught my attention because someone had even made up names for the new added meals. I'm not sure who said it, but I wrote down the names, because I thought it was funny. Don't be surprised if these terms become real meal names some day. After all it works, so why not?

DAYSTART ....**(Breakfast 7:00-7:30 a.m.)**
PULSEBREAK ....**(10:00-10:30 a.m.)**
HUMPMUNCH ....**(Lunch 12:30-1:00 p.m.)**
HOLDMEAL ....**(4:00-4:30 p.m.)**
EVESNACK ....**(Dinner 6:30-7:00 p.m.)**

Those were the five, but I need to add one more, because I must have my nightly snack of Guilt Free (sugar and fat-free) ice cream mixed with fat-free granola that I enjoy around 9:00 p.m. I think I'll call it: SWEETTREAT (9:00-9:30 p.m.) This is my treat before I go to bed and have "Sweet Dreams." What do you think? I hope this convinces you to at least give it a try. Who knows, you might free yourself of deprivation and dieting, too! After all "diet" is just DIE with a T. Since most people feel dead (from the lack of energy) when they are on a diet, I say enjoy yourself! Eat to live, don't live to eat!! Good luck!

YOU: I love your book because I love to bake. Your book is the only low-fat cook book that I have come across that actually has real desserts. Not only do you have a bunch, but they are just delicious! Many of your recipes call for low-fat buttermilk. I've never understood how something called buttermilk could be low-fat. What is the scoop on that stuff? How is it made? Does it keep in the refrigerator as long as regular milk? Since I don't use it too often, it's a shame that it doesn't come in a dry mix like dry non-fat powdered milk. Thank you for your time and most of all for your wonderful recipes! I never would have dreamed that low-fat could taste "so fattening!" My family loves your "Cream Cheese Cake Bars." My kids can even make them because they are so easy! I hope you plan to write another book. It must have taken forever to figure out how to make those recipes taste so good without the fat.   —*F.S. Montpelier, Vermont*

ME: Thank you for your letter. The "Cream Cheese Cake Bars" are my husband's favorite dessert, too! I got the original recipe from a good friend named **Mary Sue Hayes**. She used to make them and include a few with her annual tray of Christmas goodies she graced us with each year. I had to ration them out among the family members because they were EVERYONE'S FAVORITE (especially Mike). When I started modifying recipes for *BUTTER BUSTERS*, that was one of the first ones I tried. Once the low-fat cake mixes hit the market it was no problem. I saved 120 fat grams by using a low-fat cake mix. When I wrote the book (back in 1990) they didn't have fat-free cream cheese. I devised my own recipe for cream cheese and called it "Mock Cream Cheese." That substitution (made from fat-free cottage cheese) cut 80 fat grams from the original recipe. I originally used Liquid Butter Buds (made from the dry mix) in place of the 2 sticks of butter (in the original recipe). That

Mary Sue Hayes

was a huge savings of 184 fat grams. Later, when the Promise Ultra Fat-Free Margarine hit the market (in 1993), I had another choice to use in place of butter. The Promise Ultra Fat-Free Margarine as well as the New Fleischmann's Fat-Free Margarine actually work a little better in baking than the Liquid Butter Buds. The texture seems to be a little more tender. The Liquid Butter Buds is still a great product, and I use it in many of my recipes (especially my gravies, soups, sauces, puddings, and pie fillings, etc., etc.). By using Egg Beaters in place of eggs, I was able to cut 18 more fat grams. Mary Sue's original "Cream Cheese Cake Bars" were just delicious, but unfortunately they contained 426 fat grams (for the whole recipe) and 10.6 fat grams per bar. After making a few changes, I was able to turn our favorite dessert into a low-fat treat. The whole recipe (the low-fat way) only contains 24 fat grams. That amounts to 0.6 (less than one) fat grams a bar. Now we are able to enjoy this wonderful dessert on a regular basis (instead of just splurging by eating it at Christmas time). That is a classic example of how I changed many of the dessert recipes to low-fat with a few modifications.

About the buttermilk questions. I agree the name buttermilk is a poor choice of terms for such a low-fat product. Buttermilk actually has very little fat. The low-fat variety has about the same as skim milk. Buttermilk is low in calories too (at 85 calories for one 8-oz. cup). Buttermilk earned it's name in the early days before refrigeration. The dairy farmers used to mix safe bacterial cultures into whole milk to give butter longer shelf life. They skimmed off the cream to make butter. The thickened, remaining liquid had a slightly sour-cream flavor, and for that reason, was dubbed "buttermilk." Today buttermilk is made by adding formulated bacterial cultures to milk (very much like yogurt and cottage cheese are manufactured). The fermentation process of buttermilk allows slightly easier digestion for people who happen to be lactose intolerant (those who experience gastric distress or diarrhea after drinking milk). Buttermilk is quite popular for baking. I use it in biscuits, pancakes, cookies, breads, salad dressings, gravies, sauces, and other desserts and baked products. The rich taste adds a wonderful texture and richness to many of my recipes (without adding much fat). Buttermilk will keep in the refrigerator as long as regular milk. The good news is IT DOES COME IN A DRY POWDERED MIX. You simply combine three or four tablespoons of the powdered mix with hot water to get reconstituted buttermilk. One 8-oz. serving is less than one fat gram. Once the can is opened the remaining contents should be refrigerated. It will keep in the frig. for months. I hope you will continue to enjoy the book.

YOU: I know the new labels are supposed to be easier to read, but I am still quite confused. I'm so glad you taught me how to figure out the percentage of fat in different foods. Your way is much easier for me to understand. Are the new labels required on all foods now? Could you explain some of the terms such as "Low," "Light," "Good Source," etc.? Can I really trust the new labels? Why don't they list the poly and monounsaturated fats on the label too? At least they HAVE TO LIST the saturated fat content. Since that is the main culprit in heart disease and cholesterol problems, I guess we don't really need to worry about the poly or monounsaturated fats do we? You have a way of explaining things that is much easier for me to understand (than what I read in the newspapers and magazines). Thank you for putting medical and technical terms in every-day language so everyone can understand! I appreciate your gift of teaching. I'm sure there are a lot of folks out there that feel the same way I do. Bless you! —*J.D. Norfolk, Virginia*

ME: I really appreciate your sweet comments. I am basically a very simple person. Sometimes I have to read something several times myself before I REALLY understand what they are trying to say. I guess it sounds more important and official when it is written in such a way, but I agree with you. It sure is difficult to figure out what some of the information means when I can't even pronounce some of the words and have to use a dictionary to grasp the true meaning.

Unfortunately the new labels are not required on all foods. If the package is too small or oddly shaped to fit the standard-sized label, the products are exempt from the law. These companies must list an address or telephone number on the package, however, and provide nutrition information upon request.

Products such as coffee, tea, and most spices and herbs do not have to comply because they lack nutritional value. Foods containing less than 5 calories, 2 milligrams of cholesterol, 0.5 grams of fat, 5 milligrams of sodium, and 2% of the RDI of vitamins or minerals fit in this category.

Even though labeling became effective May, 1994, in order to accommodate food manufacturers who had huge inventories of old product labels, The Food and Drug Administration extended the label deadline to August 1994. That was the last date they could ship products without the new label, but it could take several months for grocery stores to sell out of products with the old packaging.

Small businesses were eligible to file for exemptions. With regulations based on food sales, total company sales, number of food units sold, and even the number of full-time employees, many food manufacturers (who make no health or nutrition claims) do not have to provide nutritional information on their products.

Products sold for immediate consumption, such as fast foods, are also exempt. Most established food chains will provide nutritional information upon request, however.

Fresh produce, meat, and seafood aren't required to carry individual labels, but grocery stores must display posters or have brochures available with nutrition information for the most commonly purchased items.

Up until the new food labels were adopted, manufacturers could use terms like "lite" and "cholesterol free" as they saw fit. Because of the lack of mandatory industry standards (in the past) the manufacturers could get away with just about anything. For example, a microwave popcorn could be labeled as "lite" based on the snack's color, and potato chips were labeled "cholesterol free" (despite the fact that all plant products contain no cholesterol anyway). Cholesterol products come from animal sources, period. If it walked, swam, or had a mother, it contains cholesterol. I know it's silly, but I bet you will always remember that little tidbit. I consider that example a "word picture." Word pictures (usually an extreme or oversized ridiculous picture in your mind) are a great way to remember things. I use word pictures all the time to help me remember information I find important and don't want to forget. I even use them to remember people's names. As part of the new labeling standards, all terms must fit strict government definitions before they can be used. Many of the definitions of claims on the new labels have been changed and made more accurate.

The following list should prove helpful when deciphering the new label terms:

LABEL CLAIM	DEFINITION *
Calorie free	Less than 5 calories
Low Calorie	40 calories or less**
Light or Lite	1/3 fewer calories or 50% less fat than the original
Light in Sodium	50% less sodium
Low Fat	3 grams or less of fat **
Fat Free	less than 1/2 gram of fat
Cholesterol Free	less than 2 milligrams of cholesterol and 2 grams or less saturated fat **
Low Cholesterol	20 milligrams or less cholesterol and 2 grams or less saturated fat **
Low Sodium	140 milligrams or less sodium **
Very Low Sodium	35 milligrams or less sodium **
Sodium Free	Less than 5 milligrams sodium **
High Fiber	5 grams or more fiber

*Per Reference Amount (standard serving size). Some claims have higher nutrient levels for main dish products and meal products, such as frozen entrees and dinners.

** Also per 50 gm. for products with small serving sizes (Reference Amount is 30 gm. or less, or 2 Tbs. or less).

Some food packages make claims about specific vitamins and minerals. Claims like "good source of vitamin C," "high calcium," or "added iron" describe the amount of certain vitamins and minerals in a food. These claims can only be used if a food meets strict government definitions. The following chart lists some of the basic vitamin and mineral definitions:

LABEL CLAIM	DEFINITION
Good Source, Contains,Provides	10-19% of the Daily Value
High, Rich In, Excellent, Source Of	20% or more of the Daily Value
More, Fortified, Enriched, ...	Contains at least 10% more of the Added Daily Value, compared to the reference food

Some new label terms concern sugars. The following chart explains the definitions of those claims:

LABEL CLAIM	DEFINITION
Sugar Free..	Less than 0.5 gram sugars
Reduced Sugar	Example: "These cornflakes contain 25% less sugar than our regular sugar coated cornflakes."
Less Sugar	Sugar content has been lowered from 12 to 9 grams per serving.

In regard to your question asking if we can trust the new labels, well "yes and no." Did I confuse you? It is a little confusing, but I will attempt to explain it in a way even I can understand. You asked why the labels don't include poly and monounsaturated fats on the labels, but they do include the saturated fats. Well, as a matter of fact, listing poly and monounsaturated fats on labels is optional. It is true that saturated fats are the culprits responsible for raising our LDL (bad cholesterol) levels in our total blood cholesterol. The saturated fats and cholesterol containing products are detrimental to our health. Have you heard the term "trans -fatty acids?" Trans-fatty acids actually start out as innocent unsaturated fats and are certainly quite harmless. Unsaturated fats tend to go rancid (or spoil) quickly, and lack some of the sensual pleasures of their saturated cousins. Attributes such as spreadability in margarine and creaminess in cupcake fillings (found in the saturated fat products) are chiefly accomplished by a process called hydrogenation. This simply means turning unsaturated fats into saturated fats to accomplish the taste associated with the highly saturated fat products. The hydrogenation process produces the dreaded "trans-fatty acids" (which may promote cancer as well as heart disease). You would think the food manufacturers would have to be more specific concerning the amount present in the different food products. No such luck! The good news is trans-fatty acids CANNOT be listed as an unsaturated fat. My advice to you is if you see a label where the amounts of unsaturated and saturated fats don't add up to the listed total, you can be quite sure the "phantom fat" is of the trans-fatty nature. The other bad news is if the manufacturer chooses NOT TO LIST unsaturated fat (because it is not required), you won't have a clue. In this case, you would be wise to check the list of ingredients. If you find partially hydrogenated oils or fats, you can be assured the product contains trans-fatty acids. Like I said, the new labels are better, but far from perfect! I hope this helps.

YOU: I know the new labels are better, but there are some new terms (such as % Daily Value) that are so confusing to me. It seems like the labels were designed for people who eat 2,000 or 2,500 calories a day. Why did they do that? What if I eat 1800 calories a day and my husband eats 3,000 calories a day? I read the American Heart Association changed their guidelines, but the new labels don't reflect their advice. That seems a little strange to me. What about all the health claims many of the new labels are including. Are they accurate? What are the most important things to look for on the labels? I am more than a little confused. Please clear this up if you can. I have really enjoyed your book. It was a Mother's Day gift from my daughter. My husband and I have really enjoyed the recipes. We love the "Shopping Guide." Thank goodness you have done the leg work and tested the low-fat products for us. Otherwise we would be spending hours in the store trying to figure out what the new labels really mean. Your recommendations have proved to us that low-fat eating can be a pleasant experience. Thank you for your time.   —*P.J. Memphis, Tennessee*

ME: I appreciate your thoughts and concerns with the new labels. They are a challenge for all of us, believe me! The "% Daily Value" addition that replaced the term "recommended dietary allowance" was really hard for me to understand at first, too. The % Daily Value (found on the right side of the label and corresponding to the amount of each nutrient supplied by a single serving) shows how a food fits into your daily diet. For example, if you are contemplating buying a package of bagels, and the nutrition information states it's fiber content in grams per serving, you can look to the right of that number and find the % Daily Value information. This new information informs you how much that particular individual serving will contribute towards your total daily intake of fiber (% Daily Value). I'll try to make it easy. Let's say you drink a glass of juice for breakfast that accounted for 60% of your vitamin C requirement for the day. If you happen to eat an apple later that afternoon, you will most likely reach your vitamin C quota (for the day).

Unfortunately the % Daily Value figures are based on a 2,000 or 2,500 calorie a day allotment of the "normal person." I wonder how many people actually fit into that category? Since the % Daily Value uses a 30% fat allotment, many feel this is too high if you are trying to lose weight, or control your cholesterol. I know it makes it even more confusing, but you should try to limit your fat intake to less than 30% of your total caloric intake if you fall within those situations (losing weight or lowering cholesterol). On the other hand, to simplify matters, the % Daily Values for sodium and cholesterol are the same for everyone, regardless of calories consumed. However, if you happen to suffer from high blood pressure or high cholesterol, you will probably want to adhere to lower guidelines. The National Academy of Sciences recommends that all healthy adults consume no more than

2,400 milligrams of sodium daily (even though the new American Heart Association guidelines recommend 1100 milligrams or less of sodium). No matter what your height or weight, The National Cholesterol Education Program recommends no more than 300 milligrams of cholesterol (even though the new American Heart Association guidelines recommend 150 milligrams or less of cholesterol). I don't understand the discrepancy of the dietary recommendations, either. Quite possibly the American Heart Association guidelines are recommended for those with heart disease risks. It appears to me that we all have different dietary requirements, so it is really hard to accept a standardized food label that covers the "blanket population." The Daily Values for vitamins and minerals are based on the U.S. Recommended Daily Allowances for each specific nutrient. These allowances are uniform for everyone and not based on any particular calorie count (thank goodness)! Just remember when it comes to sodium, cholesterol, and nutrients, daily allowances are standard. What this really means is you can take the % Daily Value column at face value (in that particular area). In other words, if the packaged macaroni and cheese dish you are preparing for dinner supplies 30% of your sodium intake for the day, it provides approximately the same percentage for your husband or your friend that lives next door. One healthy tip would be to aim for the lower end of the first four % Daily Values (which include total fat, saturated fat, cholesterol, and sodium). On the other hand, you should try to aim towards the higher range of the % Daily Value recommendations listed near the bottom of the label. These would include the total carbohydrates, fiber, and the four vitamins and minerals listed (vitamin A , vitamin C, calcium, and iron).

The following chart shows personalized nutrition amounts for eight different calorie levels according to the % Daily Value recommendations. I hope you fit into one of these categories:

CALORIES	1,200	1,400	1,600	2,000	2,200	2,500	2,800	3,200
Total fat (gm.) (30%)	40	46	53	65	73	80	93	107
Saturated Fat (gm.)(10%)	12	15	18	20	24	25	31	36
Total Carbohydrate (gm.)	180	210	240	300	330	375	420	480
Dietary Fiber (gm.)	20*	20*	20*	25	25	30	32	37
Protein (gm.)	46**	46**	46**	50	55	65	70	80

* 20 gm. is the minimum amount of fiber recommended for all calorie levels below 2,000.
** 46 gm. is the minimum amount of protein recommended for all calorie levels below 1,800.

Note: To lose weight most experts recommend cutting your total fat to 10%-20% of your caloric intake for the day. For example, if you eat 2,000 calories a day you should consume 20 (10%)-40 (20%) fat grams and you will lose weight providing you stay within your personal caloric allotment, height, frame size, and activity level.

One of the most dramatic differences between the new labels and the old is that the new format may include a health claim (if it is relevant). In seven very specific situations, a manufacturer may call attention to the connection between a particular food or nutrient and a reduced risk of a certain disease, an action that was forbidden by law before.

NUTRIENTS AND HEALTH CLAIMS ON FOOD LABELS

*Calcium	Osteoporosis
*Fat	Cancer
*Saturated Fat and Cholesterol	Coronary heart disease
*Fiber-containing grain products, fruits and vegetables	Cancer
*Fruits, vegetables and fiber-rich grain products	Coronary heart disease
*Sodium	High Blood Pressure
*Fruits and vegetables	Cancer

My straight-forward easy-to-understand advice for all of us who wish to lose or control our weight and increase our longevity is to eat less fat and exercise aerobically (on a regular basis).

P.S. It probably wouldn't hurt to increase your fiber intake by eating more fruits and vegetables (which also provide the antioxidant vitamins and minerals) that could prove helpful in the fight against diseases we may all face in our lifetime. Good luck!

YOU: I, for one, thought the old labels were easier to use and understand. I was so excited when I heard they were requiring mandatory nutrition labels on all foods. I was really disappointed when they turned out to be so confusing. More information doesn't necessarily mean better. At least the serving sizes are a little more realistic than they used to be. Who on earth ate 4 tablespoons of cereal for breakfast? The 1/2 cup serving is a lot more practical. So many of the new foods state the term "healthy." What do they have to contain in order to print that on the package? Why don't fresh meat, fish, and poultry have to abide by the new label regulations? I'm really glad you explained how to figure out fat grams and the percentage of fat in foods in your book. Otherwise, I wouldn't have a clue what any of this means. Since I don't have any health problems, and just want to lose weight, I am primarily concerned with fat and it's percentage of the calories anyway. I guess I am one of the lucky ones! Thanks for the great shopping tips and ideas to modify recipes. You have made this low-fat lifestyle change really easy to follow. The food is great and since I added exercise to my routine, I have managed to lose about 26 pounds with little effort. Keep up the good work! —G.C. Toledo, Ohio

ME: I know what you mean about the new labels. I agree with you about the serving sizes. That was the best change they made. In all reality the food manufacturers could make any food look low-fat or low-calorie by reducing serving sizes. Since most people never checked serving sizes (in the past) they really thought they were making wise choices. The new labels have certainly forced the food manufacturers to finally get busy with reducing the fat and calories in their products to keep up with the competition instead of resting on their laurels as they did in the past.

Serving size information is very important. It tells the amount of the food that will give the calories and nutrient levels listed. It is stated in both common household and metric measures (the latter to further confuse people like me). Under the new regulations, serving sizes better approximate the ACTUAL AMOUNTS most people eat, although they are not necessarily the amounts recommended by various health groups. The best part is the new serving sizes must be about the same for like products. For example, different brands of potato chips, pretzels, and corn chips are within the same category of snack foods. This makes it easy to to compare the nutritional qualities of related foods.

Even foods that are naturally low in fat can cause weight gain if you overeat with huge servings (on a regular basis). The examples listed below will give you an idea of the amounts of food that constitute one serving:

MILK, CHEESE, AND YOGURT	One Serving ➡	1 cup milk 8-oz. yogurt 1- 1 1/2 oz. natural cheese 2-oz. processed cheese
BREADS AND CEREALS	One Serving ➡	1 slice bread 1/2 hamburger bun 1 English muffin 1 roll or muffin 4 small or two large crackers 1/2 cup cooked cereal, rice, or pasta 1-oz. ready to eat cereal *(The actual measure would depend on the density of the cereal.)*
VEGETABLES	One Serving ➡	1/2 cup cooked or chopped raw vegetables 1 cup leafy vegetables (such as lettuce or spinach)
FRUITS	One Serving ➡	a medium-sized piece of whole fruit (such as a banana, apple, orange, a grapefruit half, or a melon wedge) 1 cup of berries 1/2 cup cooked or canned fruit 1/4 cup dried fruit 1/4 cup juice

MEAT, POULTRY, FISH, AND ALTERNATES:

Serving sizes will differ. Consider a serving of meat to be about the size of a deck of playing cards (3-oz.). You can usually consider 1 egg, 1/2 cup dried beans, or two Tbs. of peanut butter to amount to the same nutritional protein value as 1-oz. of meat. Remember the egg and peanut butter contain a much greater amount of fat than the bean source for the same amount of protein.

CAN WE BELIEVE WHAT WE READ?

At long last, "healthy" is a word that has to be lived up to. That is because the Food and Drug Administration (FDA) and the U.S. Department of Agriculture (USDA) have agreed on a strict definition of the term. Under the new definition, one serving of a food labeled "healthy" must contain the following:

- •At least 10 percent of the Daily Value of vitamin A, vitamin C, protein, calcium, iron or fiber
- •Sixty milligrams of cholesterol or less
- •No more than 480 milligrams of sodium (some foods have higher limits)
- •Three grams of fat or less, including no more than one gram of saturated fat

Meat, poultry, and seafood must meet the USDA's definition of "extra lean" by containing no more than five grams of fat per serving, including a maximum of two grams of saturated fat.

Nutritional labeling for fresh meat, poultry, and fish is voluntary, but they do require two other labels. All fresh meat and poultry products must have labels detailing procedures for safe handling and cooking. The information on those outlines common-sense principles to avoid bacterial illness, such as: keeping uncooked meat refrigerated or frozen until use; washing utensils and work surfaces after touching raw meat or poultry; cooking thoroughly; and, after cooking, keeping hot foods hot, and refrigerating leftovers.

A new label in the produce department tells which items have been waxed, and with what. This includes produce "coated with food grade animal, vegetable, petroleum, beeswax" and/or "shellac-based wax or resin to retain freshness." Many fruit suppliers wax items such as cucumbers and bell peppers to make them look better or keep longer.

LOOPHOLES IN THE LABELS!

There are a few loopholes in the new labels you should be aware of. Somehow products like milk were conveniently exempted from the new labeling law. A prime example is "low-fat 2% milk." By reading the labels most people will assume it only contains three grams of fat per glass, right? I mean after all that is the new guideline for a low-fat label (under 3 fat grams per serving). Well, it actually contains 5 grams of fat. Three of those five grams are saturated fat. So what if "low-fat 2% milk" is as popular as whole milk, because people think it's really low in fat and that is why they buy it? It looks like to me what's good for the dairy industry is good for—well, the dairy industry.

Another problem I have run across concerns packaged cookies. For example, at first glance the new low-fat version of the original appears to have less fat than the original. The new cookie's serving size amounts to one cookie that weighs in at 17 grams. The original version of the same cookies list 3 cookies per serving that weigh in at 32 grams (about one ounce). Ounce for ounce, they are equally fatty. I thought the new labels were supposed to end serving-size trickery, didn't you? The answer is yes they were, and yes they do. The FDA set "reference" serving sizes for all foods, based on what people typically eat. Almost all cookies, for example, have to use one ounce for a serving size. And claims like "low-fat" are only allowed if they're valid for the reference serving. The new low-fat version are an exception because they are so big. Here is the rule: Any food that comes in a "unit" (like a slice of bread, a roll, or a muffin) can use a single unit as a serving if that unit weighs at least one-half of the reference serving. That makes sense, because people don't eat fractions of cookies, slices of bread, etc. My advice and the bottom line is: Check the serving size. If it is not the same on two foods you are comparing, adjust accordingly!

I'm sure you have run across the many products that state "Made with fruit" on the label. They are all over the cereal and snack food aisle. The main reason is because the food companies are striving to cash in on the advice of the National Cancer Institute to eat "5 a day" (fruits and vegetables that is). The problem is that many foods don't really contain much fruit. The new labeling rules don't address most claims about an ingredient like fruit, bran, or whole wheat. My advice: Consumers, Be Aware!

WHAT IF THE FAT DOESN'T ADD UP?

One of the worst offenders in my opinion are the labels that boast "no cholesterol." Swell you say, this product won't raise my blood cholesterol one iota. Wrong!! There is a cookie (and I won't mention any names) that is made with "partially hydrogenated oil." In case you don't know that means they contain the dreaded "trans-fatty acids" (which by the way is responsible for raising our blood cholesterol levels as much as any saturated fat does). The FDA doesn't count trans fat as saturated (although it has been asked to). The FDA has wisely limited the saturated fat in foods that make "no cholesterol" claims to no more than two grams per serving. But, if you add the previously mentioned cookie's trans fat to it's saturated fat, it REALLY contains three grams of artery-clogging fat! Until the FDA starts treating trans fat as saturated (and it will probably be forced to eventually), you must assume that the "saturated fat" number is an underestimate in foods that are made with partially hydrogenated oils. Here are some tips that might help uncover the real scoop, Sherlock! After all, we must be well informed in the field of "detective investigation" in order to even walk in the door of a grocery store these days (if you know what I mean).

1. If the food is labeled "low-fat," the amount of trans is too small to worry about.

2. If a label lists "Monounsaturated Fat" or "Polyunsaturated Fat" as well as "Saturated Fat," you can add the three and subtract them from the "Total Fat" to get a rough estimate of how much trans the food actually contains. (It's rough because the numbers have probably been rounded.) In this case the three cookies (I spoke of earlier) have about two grams of trans fat. Surprise!!!

I have one more tid-bit of information and then I will be quiet about it, I promise. What food adds the most saturated fat to the average American's diet? Red meat (aside from the Vermillion Valley Low-Fat Beef and a few others). What food doesn't require "Nutrition Fact" panel on it's package? You guessed it. (Neither does fresh poultry, fish, fruits, or vegetables.) Congress decided that if 60% of supermarkets voluntarily provide "Nutrition Facts" for these foods, it won't require labels. But, aside from the fact that your supermarket could be one of the 40% that don't, there are three catches.

First, the information could be stuck on a sign or looseleaf binder. **Second,** it can (and you bet it will) omit crucial % Daily Values. And **third,** the serving size is a skimpy 3 ounces. And the bad news, we can't do a darn thing about it!

I'll get off my soap box and let you enjoy the rest of your day. I'm sorry I got so carried away, but label deceptions are my "pet peeve" and they make me VERY ANGRY!!!!! I'm glad you are enjoying the book. Thank you for taking the time to ask. I hope my answers didn't offend you.

YOU: I love fat. Sorry, but I do. I love chocolate, too. The reason I am writing is because your book has fooled my brain into thinking that I am still eating both. The good news is I am dropping weight like crazy and I'm still eating foods that taste "fried" (like your "Country Chicken with Creamy Gravy"). Your desserts taste so sinful, I feel guilty eating some of them (like your "Hot Fudge Pudding Cake"). I don't know how you did it, but you are a genius when it comes to making healthy food taste great! I just wanted to know if you have any more great new tips. You don't have a recipe for onion rings in the book. Am I asking for the impossible? Please let me know if there is a way to make low-fat onion rings. I love them, but haven't even considered eating them since I started eating low-fat. When can we expect another book with more "fattening tasting recipes?" Please put me on the top of your mailing list. I don't want to miss anything!
—K.O. Clearwater, Florida

ME: It's people like you that keep me inspired. Thanks for taking the time to write. You said that you loved chocolate. I do have a few tips you might want to try. In your brownies substitute half of the granulated sugar with brown sugar. It will give them a delicious caramel chocolate taste. Coffee really intensifies chocolate flavor. Try adding 1/2 tsp. of instant espresso coffee powder (available in specialty food stores) to cake and brownie batter. I use brewed coffee for part of the liquid in some of my chocolate cakes. Check out the new chocolate cake recipe in this book on page 429. I call it "Cup of Coffee Chocolate Cake." When making chocolate dessert sauces, substitute brewed coffee for half the water. If a recipe calls for cocoa to be dissolved using water, use boiling water to heighten the chocolate taste.

For a meaty tasting stew, try substituting cubed eggplant instead of beef. In lasagna substitute mushrooms and white beans to replace meat. When you want a rich spread, top your bread with fat-free cream cheese and apple or pumpkin butter (both have a fattening tasting rich luscious texture). For a rich tasting quick healthy dessert, brush a peeled, cored apple with orange juice concentrate and cinnamon. Bake at 350 F. 20-30 minutes. Top with fat-free frozen yogurt and fat-free granola for crunch. You can also use bananas.

As far as onion rings, I do have a new recipe you might enjoy: Preheat your oven to 450° F. Coat onion rings with seasoned flour (use your imagination), then dip in egg whites, then dip in crushed Pepperidge Farm Stuffing cubes (or other seasoned crushed bread crumbs). Arrange onion rings on a cookie sheet that has been lightly sprayed with a low-fat cooking spray. Bake 5 to 6 minutes. There is a great new product called Shake 'N Bake Perfect Potatoes. The "Herb and Garlic" flavor is my favorite. It can be used to make oven baked french fries. You could probably use it for onion rings as well. On the box it says to use 1/4 cup oil on the pan, but IT ISN'T NECESSARY! Just spray a little Pam Spray on the cookie sheet. I also have a recipe, in the cookbook section on page 388 called "All Shook Up, Not Fried Onion Rings." Good luck!

YOU: I recently purchased a copy of your book and love it! I've made several of the recipes and my family hasn't even realized they are low-fat. My kids even like the food. I've learned so much about modifying my recipes with your great suggestions. I've actually lost nine pounds in about two weeks by just cooking out of your book. I've started walking three times a week at the mall for exercise. I have a long ways to go, but with your help, I might just make it.

I bought another book first, and didn't agree with some of the information. I won't mention any names, but in the other book it said to forget calories and just count fat grams. The book said if you eat high volume food and exercise, anyone can lose weight. I did what the book said, but actually gained five pounds the first week. I knew it sounded too good to be true. I love to eat, so that kind of diet appealed to me. The other book said I had to exercise, so I walked three times the first week. There is something I don't understand. I wrote to the author, but she never wrote back. You probably won't write back either, but I thought I'd give it a shot anyway. I am 34 years old and weigh about 190. I never had a weight problem before I had kids. I've had three children in the last seven years and my body looks worse than my grandmother's (she is 74). My first question is: How can you eat 20 cups of brown rice and not gain weight? The other book said I could eat one chocolate chip cookie or 20 cups of brown rice for the same amount of fat. They both contain 6 fat grams. I looked them up in my fat gram counter. The book said not to worry about the calories and just eat all you want, providing it is low in fat. I looked up the calories in the same book and found the cookie to be 78 calories and the rice to be 3,242 calories. I'm sorry, but I don't see how you can eat 3,242 calories at one meal and not gain weight. I think you have to count calories too. What is your opinion on this? Also, is there a really simple way to figure how many fat grams you can eat a day? How much fat a day can I eat and still lose weight? Is it possible to eat too little fat? How much fat does your body need to to be healthy? Does alcohol contain fat? When a label says "light," is that REALLY true? What is your opinion on spot reducing? Will leg lifts help to firm up my thighs, or is it just a waste of time? I know you are busy, but I really need help. I hope you find it in your heart to answer my letter.   —M.D. Grand Forks, North Dakota

ME: I'm so glad you are enjoying the book. I know what you are talking about when you question the idea of eating so many calories. I try to be more concerned with fat grams, too, but you have to be realistic. I believe in comparing foods with the same amount of calories. For example, you can eat 6 ounces of potato chips or 8 medium baked potatoes. They are both 900 calories, but the potato chips contain 60 fat grams and the 8 baked potatoes contain 1.6 fat grams. I understand the other person's idea with her example. I think the point she is TRYING to make is that most people couldn't even eat 20 cups of brown rice, so it doesn't really matter. I don't agree with that idea, because some people will take that as permission to eat as many calories as they want, and THINK they won't gain weight. I LIKE TO LET PEOPLE KNOW THEY CAN EAT A LOT MORE FOOD IF THEY EAT LOW-FAT, BUT YOU HAVE TO USE COMMON SENSE! For example, you can eat ONE McDonald's Quarter Pounder with cheese (512 calories) or TWO AND ONE HALF "Maverick Natural Lite" low-fat beef quarter pounders with fat-free cheese and low-fat buns (510 calories). The one McDonald's burger is 28 fat grams. The two and one half low-fat beef burgers are 12 fat grams. In my opinion, that is a fair comparison. Obviously you can eat more food, if you make wise low-fat choices for THE SAME AMOUNT OF CALORIES! THAT is the key to weight loss. I'll list some more examples:

For the same amount or less calories, you can eat a lot more food, if you make wise low-fat choices!

1 Oscar Mayer frank on a regular bun	306 calories	(19.3 fat grams)
3 Oscar Mayer FREE fat-free franks on low-fat buns	300 calories	(1.5 fat grams for buns)
8-oz. Fritos Scoops Chips	1,200 calories	(72 fat grams)
52 cups of Pop Weaver's Gourmet "Light" low-fat microwave popcorn	1,196 calories	(15.6 fat grams)
4 Tbs. Kraft Ranch salad dressing	280 calories	(28 fat grams)
15 1/2 Tbs. Kraft Ranch Free (fat-free) salad dressing	280 calories	(0 fat grams)
1 slice Borden American cheese	110 calories	(9 fat grams)
3 1/2 slices Borden Fat-Free cheese	110 calories	(0 fat grams)

I hope this helps. Figuring how many fat grams you can eat in a day really depends on many factors. To be really accurate, you would need to know your frame size, your height in feet and inches, your desired weight, and your activity level. I explain how to figure all of this in my Butter Busters Low-Fat System Guide Book and video series (only available through mail order (800)476-2253), but I am going to give you a simple method. This will not be quite as accurate, but will give you a good idea. You said you weigh 190 pounds. I assume you would like to lose weight. I will show you how to figure 30% fat, 20% fat, and 10% fat. Although The American Heart Association says you can eat 30% fat and fall within the healthy guidelines, I have found in order to lose body fat, you must reduce your fat consumption to between 10-20% fat of your total caloric intake.

- For a **30%** fat diet, divide your ideal body weight (in pounds) by 2.

- For a **20%** fat diet, divide your ideal body weight (in pounds) by 3.

- For a **10%** fat diet, divide your ideal body weight (in pounds) by 6.

Example: If your ideal body weight is 140 pounds, the 30% limit is 140 divided by 2 = 70 fat grams. If you choose 20% fat, you would divide 140 by 3 =46 fat grams a day. If you cut your fat consumption to 10% fat, you would divide 140 by six = 23 fat grams a day.

You asked me if it was possible to eat too little fat. Your body only needs between 5-7% calories from fat to prevent fatty acid deficiency, to carry fat-soluble vitamins, and for normal cell metabolism. There are exceptions, however. Most pregnant women, adolescents, and children need an intake of 25-30% fat (although there is some dissension on this matter). Everything I have read says children grow a bit slower when their fat intake is reduced to less than 10% before the age of 12. Since most pregnant women are not trying to lose weight, but still wish to remain healthy, I would recommend between 25-30% fat of their total caloric intake. For the average ACTIVE adolescent, between 25-30% fat should be adequate. This would depend on their activity level. If your teenager happens to be a "couch potato" they may want to limit their fat consumption to between 15-20% of their total caloric intake. Rather than limit their fat intake, I would suggest getting them interested in some form of aerobic exercise. Not only will this allow them to eat a lot more food (and more fat grams), aerobic exercise will strengthen the heart muscle as well as increase their bone density. This is especially important for teenage girls (due to their increased risk of osteoporosis later in life).

Alcohol does not contain fat grams. Refer to page129 for a complete explanation. However, I AM NOT SAYING that alcohol is not fattening. Alcohol is a form of sugar. As I said before, you must use common sense when it comes to calories (regardless of where they come from), because calories do add up. Whether they come from fat or not, a tremendous excess of calories ON A REGULAR BASIS (that your body doesn't use for energy, growth, or repair), may be stored as fat. You are probably saying to yourself right now, "OK Pam, why do I need to avoid fat if my body is going to make fat out of everything I eat anyway?" My answer is because fat calories are more fattening. One gram of fat equals nine calories, while one gram of protein and carbohhydrate only contains four calories each. Unfortunately, most of the fat we eat ends up in storage because our bodies rely on fat for survival if the food supply decreases. It's our natural built-in survival kit against starvation. Carbohydrates, on the other hand, are converted to glucose and used immediately for energy, or stored in the muscle (in the form of glycogen), and used later. Whatever can't fit into the "glycogen storage tank" (which

FOOD AND NUTRITION

holds about 800 calories a day), and you don't use for energy (exercise, growth, or repair), can be stored as fat. If you over-eat carbohydrates once in a while, this is not a problem. When you eat an over-abundance of carbohydrates (say an extra 2,500 calories occasionally), your body works twice as hard to get rid of them (to make room for the next day's intake). It's like a shock to the system and your body will turn up it's fat-burning engine to accommodate the increased amount of calories. However, if you consume an over-abundance of carbohydrate calories on a regular basis, your body will get used to the increase of fuel and slow down it's engine (if you are not exercising) which could eventually put on a few pounds. Carbohydrates have a tougher time being converted to fat because in order for your body to transform carbohydrate into glucose (or fuel) to be used for energy, it uses about 96% of the calories in the process. This only leaves 4% of the carbohydrates you consumed to be stored as fat. Fat, on the other hand, is a different story! It doesn't take as much energy to convert fat into fuel for our bodies. Only 3% of the calories are used to process the fat we eat. Ninety-seven percent of the calories in fat are stored for later use in your body in the adipose tissue. The adipose tissue can contain as many as 145,000 calories of fat. Your body uses two to three times more energy metabolizing carbohydrates compared to fat. As long as you continue to eat more and more fat, you will keep getting fatter and fatter until you reach the point where the expanded energy needs of your fatter, heavier body match your high fat intake. To explain this, let me use an example:

YOU CAN WIN THE FIGHT AGAINST FAT, IF YOU KNOW WHERE IT'S AT!

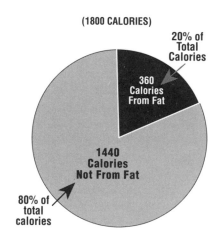

(1800 CALORIES)

20% of Total Calories

360 Calories From Fat

1440 Calories Not From Fat

80% of total calories

(1800 CALORIES)

40% of Total Calories

720 Calories From Fat

1080 Calories Not From Fat

60% of total calories

1800 calories
40 fat grams
20% fat

Calories From Fat: 360
Since there are 9 calories in one gram of fat, this means that only 360 of your 1800 total calories come from fat.

1800 calories
80 fat grams
40% fat

Calories From Fat: 720
Since there are 9 calories in one gram of fat, this means that 720 of your 1800 total calories come from fat.

WHICH DIET WOULD YOUR BODY UTILIZE IT'S FUEL MOST EFFICIENTLY?

If you guessed the LOW-FAT DIET, then you are correct! By eating a low-fat diet YOU can become a winner!

As for the "Light" label question, let me explain.

1 serving of Kraft "Light" mayonnaise—90% fat
1 serving of Kraft Free (fat-free) mayonnaise—0 % fat
1 serving of Land O Lakes "Light" sour cream—45% fat
1 serving of Land O Lakes Fat-Free sour cream—0% fat
1 serving of Philadelphia brand "Light" Cream Cheese—78% fat
1 serving of Philadelphia brand Free (fat-free) Cream Cheese—0% fat

How can this be you say! It's really quite simple. You look how many calories are in one serving. In the "Light" mayonnaise, one serving is 50 calories. One serving is 5 fat grams. You take 5 times 9 (because there are nine calories in one gram of fat) = 45 FAT CALORIES. Now, you find that 45 of the 50 calories contain fat. Divide the big number into the little number and you find the percentage of fat in the food. 45 divided by 50 = 90% fat. "Light" doesn't necessarily mean low-fat. In some cases it does. For example the "Pet" evaporated "Light" skimmed milk is fat-free. You need to look at the nutritional information label. It doesn't take long to determine if the "Light" label really is accurate. Even with the new labeling (effective May 1994), label deceptions are still out there. Watch out, they can still fool you!

There is no such thing as spot reducing. Aerobic exercise is the only way to reduce body fat. You can tone your abdominal muscles by doing sit ups, but in order to lose the fat under the toned muscle, you must reduce your total body fat through aerobic exercise. For example: Just because a person talks a lot, doesn't mean they will have skinny cheeks. All the leg lifts in the world aren't going to reduce the body fat on your legs. Walking 45 minutes three to five times a week (in your target heart-rate zone according to your age and fitness level) will reduce the size of your thighs. I can promise you that!! I hope this helps! Good Luck!

YOU: I love your cookbook. Your research has saved me a lot of time. I value your book as a wonderful resource. I have some basic cooking questions. I hope you can help. If I am baking a pie crust without the filling, how do I keep it from shrinking? How can I make a meringue pie "not weep?" How long can I freeze baked goods? Can I freeze dairy products? Why do beans fill you up so much more than potatoes? Since they are both carbohydrates, I was just wondering. Whenever I eat beans, I seem to stay full longer. Thanks for your time!
— *S.A. Conroe, Texas*

ME: When I bake a pie crust to be filled later (such as a chocolate cream pie), I line the crust with foil and fill it with dry beans or rice before baking. The weight of the beans or rice help the crust retain it's shape. Simply discard the foil, (and beans or rice) after baking and fill as directed by your recipe. Most meringue toppings will start to give off a clear liquid after a day or so. This is because the beaten egg white starts to break down. Liquid egg whites take on air as they are beaten. The air is held in little bubble pockets of the beaten egg white (the liquid is mostly water with small amounts of protein) that are strengthened as the white is beaten. When the egg whites are baked, some of the protein that forms the pockets coagulates so the air inside them remains forever trapped. Soft meringues (such as those that contain sugar or possibly a small amount of acid) are only partly cooked, so the protein does not set completely. Over time, the little pockets will begin to break down and the water from the egg whites will begin to "weep out" of the structure. Under-cooking the meringue is usually the main culprit in this problem. If your oven temperature is too high the protein in the egg whites will coagulate too quickly, also causing "weeping." I recommend a 350° F. oven for baking soft meringues. Humid weather will also cause a meringue to "weep." I found if I beat my egg whites in a copper bowl, this seems to help. I guess a small amount of copper leaches itself to the egg whites, which seems to stabilize them. Another hint is to add cream of tartar to the egg whites as you beat them. This seems to help a great deal too.

Baked bread freezes better than raw bread dough. Baked quick and yeast breads can be frozen 2-3 months. You can freeze fruit pies, baked cookies and cookie dough. I don't recommend freezing custard or meringue pies. I usually freeze cake layers (individually wrapped) without the filling or icing. Cooked frosting does not freeze well. You can freeze cookies up to six months and the dough about 4 months. Cakes and pies can be frozen 6 months.

Milk and cream can be frozen, but will separate when thawed. Heavy whipping cream should not be frozen (or probably eaten anyway due to it's high fat content). It will not whip well when thawed. Milk and cream can be frozen up to two months. I freeze cheese and cream cheese up to five months. Freezing cottage cheese, cooked eggs, yogurt, and mayonnaise affects their texture. I do, however, freeze fat-free ricotta with no problem. Cheese products can be frozen about six months. Uncooked egg whites can be frozen up to one year. Do not freeze the fat-free margarines. When they thaw, the texture will be distorted. On the package it says not to bake with the fat-free margarines. However, I do not agree with that information. I've use the Promise Ultra Fat-Free margarine and the Fleischmann's Fat-Free margarine for baking with wonderful results. They mean what they say about not freezing them, however. Trust me on this one!

Beans do seem to suppress our appetites. I know, because I eat beans on a regular basis and they really fill me up. Potatoes fill me up, too, but I tend to get hungry a lot quicker after eating them. I feel the reason is because beans are digested slowly, causing a gradual increase in blood sugar (which three hours later is still higher than pre-meal levels). Potatoes, on the other hand, are digested quickly, causing the blood levels to decrease after two or three hours. Low blood sugar is the main cause of hunger. I hope you will continue to enjoy the book.

YOU: I am delighted with your book. The information is excellent. I've never seen a book like yours. It is so organized and easy to read. I especially like the large print. I'm blind in one eye and don't see real well with the other, so I really appreciate the large print you used in your book. I do have a couple of questions. If a recipe calls for cake flour and I don't have any on hand, can I sub-

stitute all-purpose flour? The other question concerns me and my energy level. Do you think the foods we eat have anything to do with how we feel? Since I started cutting the fat out, I do seem to have more energy than I used to, but still feel tired a lot of the time. You mentioned eating a lot of carbohydrates in your book. It's so hard to make myself eat that way. I've always cut carbohydrates to lose weight in the past, and it is so hard to change my way of thinking. Do you have any suggestions? Oh yes, one other thing. Do you know anything about those hormones they are injecting cows with? I don't like the idea of hormones being added to my milk. Please let me know if you have any information concerning this matter. Any plans for future cookbooks? I hope so!
—*H.K. Grand Rapids, Michigan*

ME: Thanks for your comments about my book. When I wrote *BUTTER BUSTERS*, I wrote a book that I would enjoy using myself. Since I am a cook, I knew what was important to me and hoped it would appeal to others as well. I am a very simple person, and have always had a terrible time with detailed instructions. As a matter of fact, I think I must have some kind of learning disability, because I have always had trouble reading and following instructions. I do much better if someone just shows me something. All three of my kids can put things together so easily by reading and following directions. Thank goodness they must have taken after Mike, not me!! Anyway, I am really glad you are enjoying the book. I wear contacts, so without my glasses or contacts, I am probably legally blind myself. I chose the large print for my own selfish reasons. It's easier for me to read, too! I've found when you are following a recipe and cooking at the same time, it is much easier to follow a recipe when the ingredients are written in bold type. I tried to make it as easy as possible to follow. Thank you for noticing, and being so kind to write and tell me so.

I used to drag around myself when I ate a high-fat diet. I've found the more carbohydrates I eat, the more energy I tend to have. Complex carbohydrates provide the time-released, long-term energy needed to carry out all my day-to-day activities, as well as my exercise program. Since I have a very active life-style, at least two-thirds of my calories come from carbohydrates. We should each consume from six to eleven servings of carbohydrate-rich grain foods a day. In all reality only 5% of Americans actually consume the amount recommended. Unfortunately, when folks decide to cut back on calories or start some kind of diet (DIE with a T), carbohydrate rich foods are the first to go. After all, when you think about it, that is the only thing we heard growing up. I remember thinking If you wanted to lose weight, you had to cut calories. Since none of us had a clue about fat (or what it did to our bodies), we all cut out the starchy foods to lose weight. No wonder we couldn't keep the weight off! You can only take that kind of deprivation for so long. I can remember my typical diet meal if I was trying to lose a few pounds. I would eat a hamburger patty with melted cheese on top, cottage cheese with pineapple chunks and more grated cheese on top of that, and a green salad with Italian dressing. I would not have dreamed of eating any kind of bread and there is no way I would have considered a baked potato. What was I thinking? Somehow I don't think I was alone. Everyone I knew ate this way if they were on a diet. As a matter of fact, I can remember meals such as this were usually listed on most menus as the "Diet Plate." It's just so funny, because I eat the exact opposite of that now, a ton more food, and I don't have to worry about gaining weight. I always wondered why those diet meals didn't work for me. I just thought it was my metabolism, or something. Little did I know I was eating a high-fat meal and every bit of the fat was going straight to my hips and thighs. Well, it was a happy day for me when I discovered eating carbohydrates was the REAL WAY to lose body fat. A typical meal for me today would be a huge baked potato with fat-free sour cream and fat-free cheese, two or three slices of homemade bread with fat-free margarine, a big green salad with fat-free salad dressing, a big plate of beans or vegetables, and a venison or low-fat ground beef hamburger with fat-free condiments. I would probably have a "Guilt-Free Brand" (my favorite) fat-free and sugar-free ice cream sundae with fat-free hot fudge or caramel and fat-free granola on top. It's really hard to believe that you can eat all that food, feel full, and not gain weight. I'm just sorry it took me so many years to figure it all out.

Unfortunately, carbohydrate-rich foods such as bread, pasta, cereal, and other grain foods are the first to be eliminated by many people when making weight loss resolutions. This is such a mistake, but some folks just don't believe they can lose weight eating carbohydrates. One gram of carbohydrate equals 4 calories and one gram of fat equals 9 calories. Most people know that, but still refuse to change the way they eat. Besides that, the body burns carbohydrates faster and is less likely to store them as fat. My point is you don't have to starve yourself to lose weight. As a matter of fact the exact opposite is true. The more carbohydrate-rich foods you eat, the faster your body works to burn them off to make room for more! Instead of focusing on what you shouldn't eat, start enjoying all the wonderful filling, energy providing foods you should and can eat!

Eat at least two grain foods with every meal. Have toast or a bagel with your cereal in the morning. Order pasta or a baked potato with your sandwich at lunch. Remember carbohydrates get your metabolism working and provide so much energy for your busy days!

Eat breakfast. It's the easiest meal to plan. You have so many great options that are filling and provide the much needed energy for your day ahead. With foods such as cereal, toast, English muffins, bagels, fat-free waffles or pancakes, fat-free biscuits, fruit, fat-free granola or granola bars, and all kinds of fat-free muffins, there is no excuse to skip this important meal. (Check pages 321-330 for meal plan suggestions.)

Carbohydrates are so portable and easy to take along in your car, purse, or briefcase. I always stash bagels, fat-free crackers or chips, rice cakes, pretzels, or fat-free muffins in my car. If you bring along healthy low-fat snacks with you to work, chances are you won't be raiding the vending machine around 3:00 when the mid-afternoon "snack attack" strikes.

In restaurants try dipping your bread in marinara sauce and forgo the butter. Always keep pasta on hand and plenty of fat-free and low-fat sauces. You can always throw in some vegetables, ground turkey or venison, or some boiled shrimp or crab.

When you eat sandwiches out try using more bread and fewer fillings. When you are cooking chicken or fish and want the fried taste without the fat, try dipping the meat in Egg Beaters and crushed fat-free crackers and baking it in the oven. You can lightly spray the chicken or fish with a low-fat olive oil cooking spray to add the flavor without much fat. After exercising always refuel within 30 minutes with a carbohydrate-rich snack such as bagels, graham crackers, fat-free granola or granola bars, or raisins. You need to replenish those glycogen stores used during exercise. I honestly feel your energy level will improve if you start incorporating carbohydrate-rich foods into your diet.

As for the bovine growth hormone issue, this is what I learned after much research. Dairy cows are routinely injected with a lab-produced bovine growth hormone, causing them to produce additional proteins and 20% more milk. The hormone is actually a substance that is naturally present in all cows. The big question and concern is whether the hormone will raise the risk of cancer and other health problems in humans. Many have shown concern of the protein stimulating cancerous cells in the stomachs and intestines of humans. According to the U.S. Food and Drug Administration (and most scientists), there isn't enough of the protein to cause concern. Besides they (the FDA) studied the milk of cows treated with the hormones for twelve years before they decided it was safe. They say the amount is within the normal range among untreated cows. The human stomach is capable of breaking down the protein into harmless amino acids before any negative effects can take place. Some are worried about the other drugs given to cows. Some consumers feel they may be ingesting drug residues in the milk and meat from the animals. My suggestion would be to write to your U.S. senators and representatives urging stronger laws to prohibit illegal use of animal drugs.

When a recipe calls for cake flour and you don't have any on hand, you can easily make your own using a blend of all-purpose flour and cornstarch. Use a mixture of three parts all-purpose flour to one part of cornstarch. Substitute this for an equal amount of cake flour. Check page 336 for emergency substitutions. When using store-bought pre-sifted flour you do not need to make any changes to the recipe. If the package says the flour is "pre-sifted," there is no need to sift it again. I wish you the best and hope you will try adding some carbohydrate-rich foods to your diet. Let me know if it affects your energy level. Happy cooking!

YOU: First I want to say how much I love the *BUTTER BUSTERS COOKBOOK*. It was bought for me as a gift and it's nice to know I don't have to live on bland food. Do you have any tips on making fat-free mayonnaise taste better? Are there any packaged seasonings that are OK to use (such as Stroganoff, ranch dressings, or packaged gravies) where you just add water?

Last question. If I put myself on say 15 grams of fat a day, and a label says 3 grams of fat per serving, do I have 12 grams of fat left for the day? I know that seems simple, but I was told I was not figuring correctly.

Thanks again for the book. Please send me information to order your videos and workbook. Do you have a newsletter or something similar to help us keep up with new ideas and recipes? I would like more ideas on easy to prepare ordinary everyday meals. I make tacos using taco shells and fat-free re-fried beans and I load them with veggies and salsa. Do you have any other quick good ideas? —*M.K. Roswell, New Mexico*

ME: Thank you for your letter. I'm so glad you are enjoying the book. Have you tried the Kraft Free Miracle Whip? When I ate regular mayonnaise the only kind I used was Hellmann's. I hated Miracle Whip. It's a different story with the fat-free variety. I do not care for any of the brands of fat-free mayonnaise, but like the Kraft Free Miracle Whip. Have you tried the recipe on page 342 in *BUTTER BUSTERS* for "Substitute Mayonnaise Spread?" Another great substitution on sandwiches is "Dorcas Pohl's Honey Mustard Dressing" on page 146. I know it isn't mayonnaise, but it is delicious on sandwiches as well as salads.

The packaged seasonings are fine (in some cases). Check the ingredients. Some contain a large amount of sodium and in some cases, oil. As long as you substitute skim milk, liquid Butter Buds (made from the mix), and Egg Beaters in place of what the seasoning packet calls for, you will be cutting a tremendous amount of fat. The ranch dressing seasonings come in the diet low-fat variety. I don't think they contain any oil. The Stroganoff mixes probably contain some fat, but if you prepare them with liquid Butter Buds and skim milk in place of oil and whole milk, you will reduce the fat content a great deal. Pioneer (the folks who make the low-fat biscuit mix) now offer fat-free gravy mixes. It comes in brown and white varieties and is delicious. All you do is add water and heat briefly.

As far as your fat question is concerned, yes, if you are trying to eat 15 fat grams a day and one serving of a food contains 3 fat grams, then you would have 12 left. I must say that 15 fat grams a day is really low. I eat very low-fat myself. I eat about 20 fat grams a day, but I eat 3,000 calories. I should be able to eat about 1800 calories a day to maintain my 120 pounds if I were to eat 30% fat (which would be 60 fat grams). I would rather eat more food and less fat. How much do you weigh? Are you at your ideal weight? Do you exercise? If you decide to order my workbook and video series, this is all explained in video #1 (along with information how to figure your own personal fat gram budget). **Note:** For ordering information on my 160 page workbook and video series, call: (800)476-2253.

I am in the process of putting together a newsletter. (There is ordering information in the back of this book.) You mentioned that you would like some "regular food" recipes. Have you checked out some of mine? I have Meat Loaf, Country Chicken with Creamy Gravy, Chile, Lasagna, Macaroni and Cheese, Nachos, etc. Check out "Pam's Personal Favorites" on pages XV-XVIII. I think you will find plenty of regular food recipes (nothing fancy). Also check out the "Modifying Recipes" section pages 21-28 in *BUTTER BUSTERS* and "A Change for the Better" chapter in this book. I have 7 days of meal plans on pages 321-330 in this book, as well. I give you all kinds of tips to change your own recipes to low-fat. Good Luck!

YOU: My husband and I have really enjoyed your wonderful book. I've had to learn to cook all over again due to my husband's triple bypass last Spring. I don't know what I would have done without your book. When we were told we would have to change our eating habits, needless to say we were extremely upset. I love to cook and we both love to eat. I just knew we were destined for baked fish the rest of our lives. While my husband was in the hospital recovering from surgery I began my search for low-fat cookbooks. I happened to be in a bookstore in Portland, and saw your book with a huge display in the cookbook section. I learned later you had just visited the city on your national book tour. As a matter of fact you had been on T.V. the day before. I'm sorry we missed it. Anyway, the girl at the bookstore recommended your book because she herself had lost 24 pounds using it. It seems she had the original book you had published yourself before you went with Warner Books. I took it back to the hospital that evening to show my husband. As I was sitting with him as he slept, I began reading the front section. Two hours later I was still reading. I couldn't put it down. I felt like I knew you personally. As I was thumbing through the recipes my husband woke up from his nap. I couldn't wait to show him "our" new book. He couldn't believe you actually had real food and many of the dishes I had prepared for years were included. He was a bit skeptical at first. He said, "Just because they sound good, doesn't mean they will taste good!"

I went home that night and made a shopping list. I couldn't wait to go to the store and buy the low-fat products so I could start cooking. The rest is history. The food was wonderful, I've lost 17 pounds, my husband looks and feels great and we are eating all the foods we have enjoyed for years (just made the healthy way). We don't miss anything, because we aren't deprived in the least! Thank you for making our lives healthy and happy.

I have a few questions you might be able to answer. I've heard you can rinse ground beef to remove most of the fat. Is that true? What are your recommendations to replace ground beef besides ground turkey? We aren't too wild about the ground turkey. Do you know much about Buffalo. I heard it was low-fat. Is that true? What about other low-fat meats? Are there any out there? My energy level has been kind of low lately. My doctor suggested I increase my fiber intake. I know eating fiber is important. Do you have any new ideas concerning fiber in the diet? What is the difference between soluble and insoluble fiber? I always get confused on that. Thanks so much for you wonderful book. Because of you we can enjoy great food and not miss out on anything! Write another book. PLEASE!!   —S.B. Portland, Oregon

ME: Your letter made my day! You have no idea what letters from people like you mean to me. It seems they always arrive on days when I really need a lift, too! I was having a difficult day before I went to the post office and picked up my mail. I was going to wait and read my mail when I got home, but decided to open your letter because of the cute envelope and sticker on the back. I'm so glad I did. The rest of the day went great. I guess I just needed an attitude adjustment!

In answer to your question about rinsing ground beef, here is the deal. What you are referring to is a method I've used before and it really works quite well. Brown the ground beef as you would normally. Place it in a strainer and rinse well with hot water. Put it in a bowl and pour more hot water with a bit of lemon juice over the meat. Swish it around. Place the meat back in the strainer and drain off the liquid. Most of the fat will go right down the drain. Once you season the meat, no one will be able to tell you washed it. I wouldn't try it in the dishwasher, however. The drying cycle really toughens up the meat! Just kidding!

There are several other choices to use in place of ground beef. Have you tried ground venison. It is only 11 fat grams a pound. In my opinion it tastes and looks like ground beef. My kids really like it. There is a company is South Dakota called Vermillion Valley Beef. It is extremely low-fat and tastes great. It is available by mail order. (Check the Resource Guide of this book for ordering information.) A six ounce tenderloin is only 3 fat grams. They carry all varieties and cuts of beef.

As far as buffalo is concerned, I used to think it was a very good choice. I had read quite a bit about the product (even though it was not available in Texas). I thought it was very low in fat. However, when the new labeling came out in May 1994, the nutritional information changed quite a bit. The FDA states in order for a product to be called "low-fat" it must contain three fat grams or less per serving. Furthermore, for a product to be considered low cholesterol it must contain 20 milligrams or less of cholesterol and 2 grams or less of saturated fat per 100 grams. After checking out the nutritional information with a particular meat company concerning their buffalo I found that it listed their buffalo as 1.4 grams of fat per serving and 40 milligrams of cholesterol. Another thing I found interesting was they compared the buffalo (round) to beef (bottom round) and not the eye of round or top round. I wonder why? Maybe it was because those two cuts of meat are lower in fat than the bottom round. I guess what I am saying is it all depends on what part of the animal you choose to compare. On that particular beef company nutritional information, it showed the buffalo ground round to contain a mere 7% fat. I did some checking and found after the buffalo meat had been analyzed (in an approved FDA lab) that 100 grams of that same buffalo ground round meat contained 210 calories and 11.55 (almost 12) grams of fat!! That amounts to 49% fat (not 7% as stated on the nutritional information label). I wanted to give them the benefit of the doubt, so I considered the explanation that the two cuts of buffalo came from different parts of the animal. Maybe the meat analyzed by the FDA approved lab was really regular ground buffalo along with everything except the round. According to the USDA's Handbook Number 8, the fat content of regular ground beef is 66% fat calories, while "lean" ground beef is 58% fat calories. When you compare buffalo to those numbers, it appears slightly lower in fat, but not low enough to warrant switching from poultry to buffalo. Buffalo is higher in cholesterol, too. Ground extra lean top-round steak is about 30% fat. **My advice is to be aware of companies selling the public a product when they are allowed to print their own nutritional information that has not been approved by the USDA.** It's not always the butcher's fault. The vendors who sell their products to the butchers are responsible for supplying the nutritional information to the butchers. If a vender decides to trim as much fat as possible from his meat before sending it to the lab, he has a better profile on the meat to use in advertising and a better sales pitch to the butcher as well. When the actual meat is sold to the butcher shops, a dishonest vendor could add more fat into the meat before shipping it. Since meat is sold by weight, greater profits could be made by the vendor. Even though the nutritional analysis may use round steak as it's profile, that may not be what the ground buffalo really contains when it makes it to the vendor. It could actually contain scraps from other parts of the animal. As long as it contains "some" round steak within the ground meat, the company could state that, it is in fact, ground round.

We know top round and eye of round are about the leanest parts of a cow. Tenderloin, ribs, T-bone, and regular ground beef are all very high in fat. Unless you are able to have your buffalo meat analyzed through a chemical analysis every time you buy it (or has been USDA approved), how will you really know what part of the animal has been used? My advice would be to only purchase buffalo meat that has been nutritionally analyzed and labeled by USDA standards. This is just another time you really need to be aware of label deceptions. I would love to believe we could trust every label on the market, but unfortunately that isn't always possible. Hopefully the FDA will continue to crack down on the offenders and maybe some day we REALLY WILL be able to trust what we read!

I spoke of the Vermillion Valley low-fat beef earlier. The reason I recommend their products is because THEY ARE USDA APPROVED.

The chart on page 106 compares different kinds of meats. As you can see the Vermillion Valley Beef Products are a wise low-fat choice if you are interested in red meat without the fat!!

NOTE: Ordering information can be found in the "Resource Guide" on page 539 of this book.

FOOD AND NUTRITION

Nutritional Comparisons of Other Meats
With
Vermillion Valley Low-Fat Beef

Vermillion Valley Beef 6 oz serving	Fat (gms)	%of Recommended Daily Fat*	Cholesterol (mgs)	Calories
Tenderloin	3.0	3.8	94	168
Sirloin	3.0	3.8	94	168
Ribeye	3.0	3.8	92	168
Dakota Striploin	3.0	3.8	94	168
Roast	3.0	3.8	96	168
Stir Fry/ Fajita	3.0	3.8	92	168
Kabobs	3.0	3.8	92	168
Ground Beef (our 4 oz serving)**	4.7	5.9	67	132

Source: Vermillion Valley Quality Assurance Data, USDA
Approved Green Meadows Laboratory, Ft. Collins, CO.

Some Typical Meats 6 oz. serving	Fat (gms)	% of Recommended Daily Fat*	Cholesterol (mgs)	Calories
Flounder	2.6	3.3	116	198
Skinless Chicken Breast	6.0	7.5	144	280
Skinless Turkey (light meat)	5.4	6.8	118	266
Buffalo	3.3	4.1	106	237
Elk	1.6	2.0	114	235
Venison	2.4	3.0	198	255
Ordinary Beef Tenderloin	17.0	21.3	142	356

Source: USDA Handbooks (8-5, 8-13, 8-17)   *Based on 30% of a 2400 calorie diet
North Dakota State University   **Different portion size

As far as fiber is concerned, I will attempt to provide you with the most current information available. Fiber is important in our diets for a number of reasons. Fiber (which is actually the structural part of plant food) has been shown to aid in the fight against various diseases such as digestive problems, irritable bowel syndrome, colon cancer, hemorrhoids, breast cancer, obesity, blood sugar control for diabetics, and high cholesterol to name a few. A low-fat high-fiber diet may be the answer in controlling many diseases we face.

There is no doubt that people who consume the two types of fiber (soluble and insoluble) on a regular basis can improve their health. Soluble fiber blocks fat absorption, which in turn lowers cholesterol and reduces the risk of heart disease and high blood pressure. Some examples of soluble fiber are: oat bran, barley, beans and legumes, barley, lentils, and many fruits and vegetables. Insoluble fiber is the indigestible part of fruits, vegetables, and whole grains. These are the sources responsible for moving food through the intestines. Some examples of insoluble fiber are: wheat bran, corn bran, peas, and seeds.

High fiber foods supply a tremendous amount of vitamins and minerals to our diet as well. Another added bonus concerning fiber is the more we eat the less room we have for the fatty foods we should try to avoid. High fiber foods are very filling. I would recommend eating between 20-35 grams of fiber daily. At least 10 grams should come from the soluble sources. Soluble fiber is the key to reducing cholesterol levels (in some cases). Insoluble fiber may be responsible for cutting the risks of various cancers (especially colon cancer). If you consume more than 50-60 grams a day, you may lower the amount of vitamins and minerals the body absorbs, so don't go too fiber crazy.

The following is a list of ways to increase your fiber intake GENTLY:

1. Add dietary fiber slowly so your body can adjust.

2. Try to drink A MINIMUM of half your body weight in water a day. For example if you weigh 120 pounds, you should try to consume A MINIMUM of 60 ounces of water daily.

3. Try to eat beans, peas, legumes, or lentils every day to boost your fiber intake. A serving would be 1/2 cup. Aside from the fiber benefits, these foods are also rich protein sources.

4. Try to eat 5 servings of fruits and vegetables a day. It isn't as much as it sounds. A typical serving is only one half of a banana.

5. Use 100% whole grains rather than white breads, pasta, and rice. Whole wheat pasta and brown rice also contain a much greater amount of vitamins (as well as fiber) than their plain white cousins.

HIGH-FIBER FOOD GUIDE

CEREALS
Eat a variety.
samples: (1/2 cup serving)

Kellogg's All-Bran with Extra Fiber (15 gm.)
General Mills Fiber One (13gm.)
Kellogg's All-Bran (10gm.)
Back to Nature (No-Fat added) Granola (4gm.)
Post Raisin Bran (4gm.)
Quaker Oat Bran (3gm.)

BREADS
Try to eat whole-grain breads and
baked goods.
samples: (2 slices per serving)
*Some slices are larger than others.

Arnold/Brownberry Bran'ola Original
or Hearty Wheat (6 gm.)
Orowheat "Light" 100% Whole Wheat (6 gm.)
Wonder "Light" Wheat or 9-Grain (6 gm.)
Whole Wheat Pita (1 whole) (5 gm.)
Roman Meal "Light" White or Wheat (5 gm.)
Arnold Oatmeal (4 gm.)

GRAINS AND PASTAS
samples: (1 cup serving, cooked)

Barley (6gm.)
Bulgur (5 gm.)
brown rice (4 gm.)
Couscous (2 gm.)
regular macaroni or spaghetti (2 gm.)

FRUITS
Those with edible skin and seeds
contain the most fiber.
samples: (1 medium-sized piece
unless otherwise stated)

kiwi fruit (5 gm.)
pear (4.5 gm.)
apple (4 gm.)
Apricots, dried (1/3 cup) (4 gm.)
two figs (4 gm.)
1/2 cup blackberries (3.5 gm.)
banana (3 gm.)
orange (3 gm.)
1/2 cup raspberries (3 gm.)

VEGETABLES

Choose vegetables with edible
skin and seeds.
samples (1/2 cup serving, cooked)

Green peas (4 gm.)
1 medium sized Baked potato
   (or Sweet variety) with skin (4 gm.)
Brussels sprouts (3.5 gm.)
carrots (2 gm.)
corn (2 gm.)
broccoli (2 gm.)
asparagus (2 gm.)
spinach (2 gm.)

BEANS AND LEGUMES

These are a rich source of protein, too.
samples (1/2 cup serving)

Navy beans (6 gm.)
kidney beans (5 gm.)
Black beans (5 gm.)
lentils (4 gm.)
Lima beans (4 gm.)

BEAN SOUPS

samples (1 cup serving)

Health Valley Real Italian Minestrone Soup (11gm.)
Pritikin Split Pea Soup (10 gm.)
Progresso Healthy Classics Lentil Soup
   (6 gm.)
Campbell's Black Bean Soup (5 gm.)
Progresso Split Pea Soup (5 gm.)

CRACKERS AND SNACK FOODS

samples (1 ounce serving)

Wasa Fiber Plus Crispbread (3 pieces) (9gm.)
Wasa Hearty Rye Crispbread
   (3 pieces) (7 gm.)
Wasa Multigrain Crispbread
   (3 pieces) (6 gm.)
Health Valley Fruit Bars (1 bar) (4 gm.)
Nabisco Wheat'n Bran Triscuits
   (7 pieces) (4 gm.)
No-Oil baked Tortilla chips
   (15-20 chips) (2-4 gm.)
Whole Wheat Matzos (1 piece) (4 gm.)
Health Valley fat-free Granola Bar
   (1 bar) (3 gm.)
Nabisco low-fat Wheat Thins
   (16 crackers) (2 gm.)
Archway Oatmeal Cookies (1 cookie) (1 gm.)
Nature Valley Low-fat Chewy Granola
   Bars (1 bar) (1 gm.)

I recommend eating food to obtain your fiber quota. Most Americans simply don't monitor their food choices like they should. If you just can't seem to get enough fiber through the foods you eat you might be interested in a new product called LiFiber. It contains (ounce for ounce) 8 times the soluble fiber of oat bran. For information concerning this product call: (800)748-8288.

Most people find when they increase their fiber intake, their energy level is enhanced as well. This just might be the answer to your low energy level since all high-fiber foods are also carbohydrate-rich. Good Luck!

YOU: I love your book and have really enjoyed learning about all of the great new products on the market. I just don't have the time to find them all myself in the grocery store. In fact I hate shopping, so you have saved me a lot of time and frustration. Even though I don't like to shop, I do like to cook. Can you recommend any good low-fat cooking gadgets that might help me when cooking low-fat?

I am a bit confused when it comes to Olive Oil. What does "Extra Virgin" mean? I travel by car during the day with my business. Can you give me some take along low-fat snacks and low-fat choices available in most convenience stores? Thanks for all the time you have saved me! I really appreciate your hard work and dedication.
—J.K. Lafayette, Louisiana

ME: Thank you for your sweet comments. It's funny, but I honestly love going to the grocery store. I guess I enjoy finding all the great new products. I think I find at least one new product every time I visit the grocery store. I admit it takes a lot of time, but since I enjoy looking, I don't consider it work.

There are several gadgets you might consider to help with low-fat cooking.

A **STEAMER** is a great investment. It can be as fancy as an electric appliance or as simple as a bamboo basket, a metal colander, or a fold-up wire basket that fits into the pots you already own. A steamer cooks quickly, uses no fat, and minimizes nutrient losses. Steamers are easy to use and require little clean-up.

A **WOK** (preferably non-stick) is a great low-fat cooking aid. You can purchase electric woks or a very inexpensive version. If you choose a wok with a non-stick coating, oil is not even necessary. I use clear fat-free low-sodium chicken broth in place of oil when I stir fry. You can actually use any non-stick skillet in place of a wok. Since you cook quickly when using a wok, the nutrients are greatly retained in your vegetables.

The **GRAVY PITCHER** looks like a spouted cup. You pour your pan juices into it and the fat rises to the top. You pour off the fat-free broth from underneath. In this same category you might might wish to purchase a ladle for skimming fat from a soup or sauce. Placing poultry on a rack in the pan as you cook it will allow the fat to run off the meat into the bottom of the pan. You can always refrigerate your soup or sauce. The fat will rise to the top for easy removal. If you notice fat floating on the surface of your soup or sauce, quickly dip an ice cube into the hot liquid. Excess fat will congeal on the surface for easy removal.

A **CHEESE GRATER** allows you to add a lot of cheese flavor with a minimum of cheese. This is helpful when using a low or moderate fat cheese. If you are using fat-free cheese, you don't have to worry about the amount so much. You will find some of the fat-free cheeses don't melt too well. If you grate them finely they tend to melt a little better. Another good idea is to use the fat-free cheese in the casserole or dish and sprinkle grated low-fat cheese on top. For some reason the fat-free cheeses melt fine when mixed into a dish. There are several fat-free cheeses that do melt well. Polly-O fat-free mozzarella is a good example of a fat-free cheese that melts well. (Check the "Name Brand Shopping Guide" in this book for other good fat-free cheese options that melt well.)

A **YOGURT FUNNEL** is a great gadget. You can buy one, or make your own with a coffee cone and filter paper or a strainer and cheesecloth. Simply spoon the yogurt into the funnel and let the liquid (whey) drain out. This leaves a thick "yogurt cheese" that can be used in place of sour cream or cream cheese in your dips, spreads, salad dressings and other sauces. You can always use the fat-free sour creams and cream cheeses, but making your own fat-free variety with yogurt and a yogurt strainer will probably be cheaper.

You might already own a **PRESSURE COOKER**. They were very popular in the '70s. They have gained back their popularity with low-fat cooking because they are similar to a streamer. They cook very fast (even pre-soaked dried beans and other legumes), and therefore help retain the vitamins and nutrients in the foods you are cooking.

Most people own a **BLENDER** or **FOOD PROCESSOR**. If not, you can purchase a small, inexpensive, easy-to-wash model that does a good job. These appliances will come in handy when you want to pureé fruits to use as fat substitutions. Pureéd vegetables are great fat-free thickeners for soups and sauces, too. Fat-free smoothies (made with skim milk, fruit, and yogurt) are a great refreshing snack after a workout. You can chop herbs, garlic, onions and even grate cheese in food processors. I use my food processor to grind turkey breasts (without the skin) into ground turkey. I purchase Family Packs of turkey breasts, take them home and grind in my food processor and freeze them in one pound plastic baggies. One pound of ground white meat turkey (without the skin) is a mere 4.8 fat grams. A **FOOD GRINDER** will do the trick, too.

I would strongly suggest investing in **non-stick baking sheets, muffin tins, and cake pans.** They require little, if any, low-fat cooking spray and are a snap to clean up. I especially like the Cushion Air brand of baking products.

A **FISH POACHER** allows you to add herbs, a little cooking wine, lemon juice, clam juice, or fish stock, and get a delicious result without frying. Fish filets can bake nicely in almost any shallow pan with a little liquid covered with foil.

MICROWAVE OVENS have become one of the most popular kitchen appliances in the American home. You can use it to quickly defrost frozen foods as well as cook them in half the time. Because the foods cook so quickly, they retain a greater amount of vitamins and nutrients compared to foods baked in conventional ovens. There is a product called Micro-Crisp (similar to waxed paper and found in many grocery and discount stores) that allows your food to brown as it cooks in the microwave. It works great with baked potatoes (the one food that doesn't generally do well in a microwave). For ordering information, call: (800)998-8750.

A **GARLIC PRESS** is a neat gadget that saves a lot of time. Just place the unpeeled clove into the press and squeeze. Garlic is one of the "wonder foods" associated with disease prevention.

GRILL RACKS are a must when broiling meat, vegetables, or fish. Many will fit over a regular burner or a gas, electric, or charcoal grill. Some models come with non-stick surfaces making clean-up fast and easy.

KITCHEN SCALES take the guesswork out of portion control.

ELECTRIC FOOD DEHYDRATORS are used to create delicious dried fruit snacks, healthy long-storing dried vegetables and low-fat turkey jerky. You can even make fresh yogurt with this neat kitchen appliance.

ELECTRIC BREAD MACHINES are a great addition to any low-fat kitchen. There are all kinds of machines and the prices vary greatly.

I know what you mean about the Olive Oil terms, they are confusing. Let me try to explain.

EXTRA VIRGIN OLIVE OIL has a deep aroma and the lowest acidity (less than 1%). The colors range from dark yellow to green. The prices range from $8.00-$30.00 a quart. The flavor evaporates quickly under heat, so this oil is best on salads or used as a marinade.

VIRGIN OLIVE OIL are first-pressed oils with a higher acidity (usually 1 1/2-3%).

FINO OLIVE OIL means Italian for "fine." These oils are blends of extra-virgin and virgin olive oils.

PURE OLIVE OIL is often processed lower-grade oil that is bolstered with 5-30% virgin or extra-virgin to replace lost color and flavor. It makes a good all-purpose cooking oil and a great deal cheaper. In January 1991 the term "pure" was dropped from most labels. They now simply read "Olive Oil."

LIGHT OLIVE OIL is pure olive oil with less than 5% extra virgin content. Many consumers buy it because of the "light" label, but the only difference between the "light" and "pure" is the milder (almost bland) flavor. It has the same amount of calories and fat grams as other oils (about 14 fat grams a tablespoon).

OLIVE OIL is a monounsaturated fat and is more heart healthy than most other oils. It helps raise the HDL (good cholesterol) in your total blood cholesterol and helps lower the LDL (bad cholesterol). Another monounsaturated heart-healthy oil (and probably cheaper) is Canola oil which is actually lower in saturated fat than Olive oil. If you are counting fat grams to control your weight, please realize all oils are 100% fat. For that reason, I would suggest limiting your consumption of all oils when possible.

There are several good low-fat snacks to take along in your car. Pretzels, rice cakes, low-fat chips, fat-free crackers and cookies, fruit, and bagels are all quite portable and require no refrigeration. If you have room for an ice chest in your car the possibilities are endless.

When you find yourself in a convenience store and want a low-fat snack try to make wise choices. Soft giant pretzels, fruit, yogurt, pretzels, or baked chips can be found in most convenience markets. Bagels, mozzarella string cheese, graham crackers, juice, and even fat-free frozen yogurt are stocked in most gas station stores as well. Some small convenience stores even carry a variety of fat-free muffins delivered fresh daily. I hope this information will be helpful when you are on the road. I WISH YOU CONTINUED SUCCESS!

YOU: Hi Pam: Help! I purchased Joyce Vedral's *BOTTOMS UP* book a month ago. I wrote to her complaining about the lack of recipes and food ideas. She recommended your *BUTTER BUSTERS COOKBOOK* which I went out and immediately purchased. I have been unable to use it much because I have been unable to find the Butter Buds Liquid. I know it comes in a powdered form and you have to add it to water, but where in the world can I find it? I tried Shop-Rite, Shop and Stop, and Waldbalums. We don't have Food Lion, Albertsons, Krogers, or Tom Thumb. Any ideas would be helpful! I love your book. Very helpful! I've lost 15 pounds in 2 months. Only 40 more to go! (But I love fat— Boo Hoo!) Thank you!
—*S.P. Burlington, Connecticut*

ME: I was glad to hear that Joyce answered your letter. I haven't actually met Joyce, but have talked to her on the phone and she seems like a very fine woman! I have all her books MYSELF, including the new one she authored with her daughter, *THE COLLEGE DORM WORKOUT*. I use and follow her book called *THE FAT-BURNING WORKOUT*. It caught my eye in the bookstore because even though it is a weight work-out, you also burn fat because you stay aerobic (you don't stop between sets). As far as the liquid Butter Buds, I must clear up one thing. This product comes in a box that looks like a box of stick margarine (same size). It contains eight packets. You mix one packet with 1/2 cup of hot water. It DOES NOT come in liquid form, you have to make it. I realize that you know that because you mentioned mixing it, but I felt I must include the information for others reading this book. The folks at Cumberland Packing Corporation (the people who manufacture Butter Buds) have told me some people call or write them asking for "Liquid Butter Buds."

Butter Buds also comes in a jar that you can sprinkle on food but CAN NOT BE MIXED WITH WATER! It doesn't work! I get letters every day about this product. I've tried to let the people at Cumberland know that many folks CAN'T FIND THEIR GREAT PRODUCT! They assure me it is out there, but people are looking in the wrong place in the store. There are three locations that I have found the mix to make Liquid Butter Buds. It can be found in the "diet food" section, the "spice" section, and, in some cases, the "refrigerator butter and margarine" section. If you can't find it in your area, call (800)231-1123. That number is listed in your *BUTTER BUSTERS COOKBOOK* on page 69 in the 7th edition. On page 63 (of the 7th edition) you will find information about the product and how to mix and use it. I have also included information about Butter Buds on page 119 of this book as well.

I first met the folks at Cumberland in August 1992 when I visited them in New York. I met Abe Bakal, the chemist who developed so many of their great products. He and his wife Fi Fi took me to dinner and gave me a tour of the lab. At that time they were experimenting with a new product (Butter Buds Solid). They were working on a tub form and a stick form (the sticks never made it). I tasted the product and just couldn't believe how great it was. It tasted so buttery, and MELTED just like butter. It was only 2.6 fat grams per tablespoon. Even though it wasn't fat-free, it melted and tasted so great! I couldn't wait for it to hit the market. They sent me samples and I cooked and tested the product in many of my recipes. It made a great pie crust!! Butter Buds (solid) went into the test market later that year in Grand Rapids, Michigan and St. Louis, Missouri. I just knew it would be in the stores everywhere soon. How could a product this great not test out as a success? I guess it's harder to break into the market than most people think. Here we are three years later, and it still isn't on the shelves. I understand there were packaging problems. The latest report is that it's being tested in Detroit, Michigan and Indianapolis, Indiana currently so we will all be watching for the BUTTER BUDS SOLID (IN TUB FORM) TO HIT THE SHELVES ANY DAY NOW! I can't wait!!

Good luck and keep up the good work. By calling the number I listed, you can have the mix to make Liquid Butter Buds sent to you by the case!!

YOU: Please rush me your video series and 160 page guidebook. I love your book and want to learn even more! I was wondering if you have heard about Medium Chain Triglycerides (MCT's) vs. LCT's? From my reading, I have learned that MCT's bypass the stomach and go to the liver and provide extra energy and burn fat more effectively. So what's your opinion on the new studies of MCT's vs. LCT's?

By the way, I weigh 236 and am 34% body fat. I am 27 years old. Can you help me GET A LIFE? Thanks for reading my letter. P.S. Have you heard of Wonderslim? It is a fat substitute used for baking and cooking derived from fruits and vegetables (I think).   —D.P.

ME: MCT stands for Medium Chain Tryglycerides and moves through the portal vein system to the liver and is absorbed into the bloodstream for energy. It is made up of carbon chains. Whatever is left over (and not used for energy) is excreted in the urine in the form of ketones. Many people in the fitness industry take MCT Oil as a supplement. MCT have been used in treating some people who, because of some metabolic abnormality, have trouble absorbing fats. The only problem is how it might affect healthy people. After testing, some healthy people did gain weight using MCT oil. In one small study involving humans, patients who drank large amounts of MCTs did burn more calories than men who ate large amounts of conventional fat. You must remember that gram for gram, they contain the same amount of calories as regular fat-nine. Another thing most folks don't realize is MCTs are derived from coconut oil, which, as we know, can have the nasty side effect of raising your cholesterol, not to mention causing cramps, bloating, and possibly a serious acid imbalance in the blood of diabetics.

Now for the good news. Twin Labs is one of the many manufacturers that make this essential fat supplement. It can be found in most health food stores. The good thing about this oil is it gives your body the energy it needs, but does not easily convert to body fat like all other kinds of oils. MCT oil contains 114 calories per tablespoon. Many folks use it on their salad mixed with vinegar as a salad dressing. It can also be used to cook with. It will smoke if the temperature is too high, however, so be careful if using this product for cooking. LCT(Long chain Triglycerides), on the other hand, travel through the body (via the lymphatic system) as do all traditional fats. It is easily converted to body fat. I felt I should give you the pros and cons of MCTs so you will have all the information available. I hope this explanation gives you the general idea and will aid in your decision as to using or not using this supplement.

My suggestion to you (in order to lose body fat) would be to decrease your fat intake to 10% to 20% of your total calories. You didn't mention your height or body frame, but I will attempt to explain how many calories you should eat a day (on the average). I'm glad you ordered the guidebook and video series, because this information is outlined in detail in that material. First take your ideal weight times 15. I will use myself as an example, since I don't know your ideal weight. My ideal weight is 120. 120 X 15=1800 calories per day. This would really depend on your fitness level and exercise, too, but we will use 15 to make things simple. Since I recommend (in order to lose body fat) you cut your fat intake to 10% of your total calories. This would be 1800 X 10%=180 fat calories. Next you would divide by 9, because there are 9 calories in one gram of fat. 180 divided by 9=20 fat grams. This would be how many fat grams a day you should be eating to lose body fat. If you add aerobic exercise (using your large muscle groups in a rhythmic motion for 35 minutes not counting warm-up and cool-down) and exercise within your target heart rate zone your fat loss should be accelerated. To find your target heart rate zone subtract your age from 220. Then take that number times 70% and 85%. Example: 220-27 (your age) =193. Take 193 X 70%=135 and then take 193 X 85%=164. You will find your target heart rate zone to be between 135-164 to burn body fat most efficiently. Most experts agree working out in the lower to middle part of your range burns body fat just as well as working out in the top of your target heart range. If you are just beginning to exercise (for the first time), I would strongly suggest working out in the lower portion of your range and increasing to a higher level gradually. You find your heartrate by counting the beats on your radial artery (on your wrist just up from your thumb) or carotid artery (on the side of your neck down about 3-4 inches from your ear) for ten seconds and multiply times 6. If you work out within your zone (135-164) aerobically, 3-5 times a week for a minimum of 35 minutes (not counting warm-up and cool-down), and eat 10% fat of your total calories (determined by your ideal weight), you will lose body fat!!

If you have never cut the fat in your diet, you might start with 20% or even 30% of your total calories. Most people can maintain their weight at 30% fat, but, in order to lose fat, most folks find they need to cut their fat intake percentage down to 20%, or even 10%, fat (in some cases). I hope this helps. Like I said, I'm glad you ordered the videos and guidebook. I'm sure it will be much easier to understand because I go through each step very slowly.

Wonderslim is a new fat and egg substitute derived from plums. It can be found in most health food stores and is fat-free. I use it for baking, and love the results. If you can't find it in your area call: (800)497-6595. There is another product called Just Like Shortenin' (also derived from plums) found in some super markets and health food stores. If you can't find it in your area call: (203) 245-7893. Good luck!

YOU: Are there any low-fat choices for prepared mixes? I love the convenience of the taco, soups, and sauces that come in the little packets.
— B.A. Baton Rouge, Louisiana

ME: McCormick makes a "light" Taco mix. Hidden Valley makes a fat-free dressing mix. Those are only two, and there are many on the market now (too many for me to list them all). You can make most mixes low-fat by using low-fat ingredients when you make them. For instance, for an Alfredo Sauce mix use liquid Butter Buds in place of oil and skim milk in place of whole milk. Even though most of the mixes contain some added fat, you will be cutting quite a bit if you make them using low-fat products. Be careful, because most of the prepared mixes contain a high amount of sodium.

YOU: My kids love taco or nacho flavored Doritos. They are so high in fat (9-12 fat grams an ounce). Do you know of any low-fat taco flavored chips? The whole family has enjoyed your recipes (especially the Chicken Enchiladas and Tortilla Soup). My husband and I started exercising along with our low-fat diet and we have each dropped about twenty pounds (he lost it quicker than I did) since we started using your book. Thanks for making healthy food taste so good!!
—J.K. Jefferson City, Missouri

ME: There is one new low-fat taco flavored chip on the market by Guiltless Gourmet. Tyler, my youngest, didn't care for them (but he doesn't like many of the low-fat chips in general). I thought they were OK, and my Mom loved them! However, you might give them a try because chips are a personal matter. What tastes great to one person is gross to another. I can tell you how to make your own: buy a bag of Smart Temptations Chips, Amaizing Taste Chips (not a typo—that is how they spell amazing), or Frito Lay Baked Tostitos low-fat chips. Use 1 tablespoon McCormick "Light" Taco Seasoning Mix and 1 tablespoon "Best of Butter" brand Cheddar Flavor Butter Substitute. Mix the two seasonings together (you can mix up a large amount and store in a salt shaker). Spread the chips on a large cookie sheet that has been sprayed with a little Pam Spray, and sprinkle the seasoning mixture on both sides of the chips. Bake at 300° F. for 5 minutes. My son Tyler loves these. I bet your kids will, too!

YOU: There are three products that I can't find anywhere that you recommended in your shopping guide. I have the fourth edition of *BUTTER BUSTERS THE COOKBOOK*. Is there a chance they have been taken off the market? I've looked everywhere! They are Alpine Lace Fat-Free Fresh Parmesan cheese, Alpine Lace Italian Style Mozzarella Cheese, and Weight Watchers' Fat-Free Croutons. I just want to tell you that I have never used and enjoyed a cook book the way I have yours. You make everything so simple. Your recipes are good and easy to fix. I can buy most of the ingredients in the local grocery stores (except the ENER-G Egg Replacers, but worth a trip to the health food store). Thank you for your many hours of cooking and writing to give us this wonderful book. I will treasure and use it the rest of my life!!
—M.S.Huntington Beach, California

ME: I'm so glad you like the book. You are correct about those products. They were removed from the market in 1993. The croutons have not returned, but you can purchase the Pepperidge Farm Herb Seasoned Stuffing Mix. It is very low in fat (1.5 fat grams per 3/4 cup).The cubed style stuffing works great as croutons. The stuffing can be used in salads as well as coatings or crust for various meats. Other fat-free ideas for coating are Corn Flakes Cereal (you can crush it yourself with a rolling pin or it also comes crushed and ready to use in a box), or Premium Fat-Free Saltine Crackers by Nabisco (also comes crushed in a box for convenience). As far as the cheese products are concerned, the Alpine Lace brand Fat-Free Parmesan Cheese is back on the market. It comes in a plastic cup found in the Deli section, rather than the plastic bag that hung on the cheese rack before. It is improved (longer shelf life), melts well, and tastes great!! The Alpine Lace "Italian Style" mozzarella cheese has not returned. There was a problem with the shelf life, due to the ingredients used to make the cheese. After several months of testing, they have introduced a NEW mozzarella cheese that melts well and taste good, too. Don't look for "Free & Lean" on the label anymore, however. When the new labels came out in May 1994, all of their labels were changed to accommodate the new label guideline regulations. All of their cheeses are now called "Alpine Lace Fat-Free Cheese" or "Alpine Lace Reduced Fat Cheese." I am also happy to report that Alpine Lace has introduced a whole new line of cheese spreads and a wide variety of flavored cream cheese products. They have one in particular (an herb flavored cream cheese) that is delicious heated and mixed with fettuccini noodles. All you do is cook and drain a 16-oz. bag of fettuccini noodles. Stir 1 tablespoon of Liquid Butter Buds or clear chicken broth into the noodles (to coat them). In a saucepan, heat 1 (6-oz.) package of Alpine Lace Fat-Free Cream Cheese (the Garlic & Herbs flavor), and 1/2 cup skim milk. Blend with a wire whisk until it is thoroughly blended and smooth. Add 1/4-1/2 tsp. Papa Dash Lite Salt and fresh ground black pepper (to taste). Toss with pasta and you have a fat-free Fettuccini Alfredo that is quick and easy. This recipe serves eight and is about 130 calories per serving and less than one fat gram. Be sure and check out all their new products!! They are fantastic!!

YOU: I noticed you use Sweet 'N Low in your recipes. I prefer Nutrasweet. Will it work just as well? I was really glad you added the sugar substitution choices in your new 7th edition. I am not diabetic, but try to watch my sugar consumption. I have seven grand kids that visit quite often and I like to make their sweet treats with less sugar. I think sugar makes them hyper. One of them has ADD (Attention Deficit Disorder) and his Mom told me he shouldn't eat too much sugar. They all love your cakes (especially "Best Pound Cake"), your cookies (especially the "Snickerdoodles"), and your pies (especially "Chocolate Cream") so much. I want to still treat them once in a while with my homemade goodies, but try to limit the sugar in my recipes. They have loved everything I have made so far, but I personally like the taste of Nutrasweet better in my iced tea. I haven't tried using it yet for baking, because I try to always follow recipes the way they are written.

My husband, by the way, has been eating out of your book since he had by-pass surgery 17 months ago. His doctor recommended it to us! He loved to eat steak, eggs, bacon, peanuts, lunch meat, and just about everything else that was bad for him. His doctor told him he was lucky that he didn't have a heart attack years ago (especially when he smoked three packs of cigarettes a day). He loves all the recipes in your book, quit smoking, walks every evening, and has never felt better. I thank you for helping my husband be able to eat food that tastes good and enjoy living again. God Bless You!   —*M.K. Miami, Florida*

ME: I'm so glad you have both enjoyed the book. It sounds like your husband REALLY changed his life-style. Not only has he added years to his life, he has added life to his years!! That is wonderful. I use Sweet 'N Low in my recipes for a reason. Nutrasweet contains Aspartame and Aspartame breaks down at 85 degrees and loses it's sweetness. That is why you can't bake or cook with the product. If you don't care for Sweet 'N Low, you might try using NECTA SWEET. It is a saccharin based product that comes in tablet form. It easily dissolves when you mix it into your batter. You don't have to crush it or anything. I've used it in baking and it works well and tastes great! It can be found in most grocery stores, but if you can't find it in your area call: (800)952-5130. I hope your grandchildren will continue to enjoy the recipes. Next time they come for a visit, let them HELP YOU make the "Hot Fudge Pudding Cake" on page 358. You can make it with the Sweet 'N Low Brown Sugar Substitute (to cut down on sugar) for one half of the sugar. It's one of my favorites, and a fun recipe for children to make. It's like a science experiment. All the ingredients go into the dish, then you pour hot water on top. It looks like a mess, but as it bakes the water goes to the bottom and forms a delicious hot fudge sauce, and the cake rises to the top. If they like chocolate, they will love eating AND making this recipe!! Have Fun! It is best served warm with fat-free ice cream or frozen yogurt on top!!

Pam serving "Hot Fudge Pudding Cake"

YOU: I purchased your book about two months ago at a B.J. Warehouse Store in my area. I really love this book. I have read it from cover to cover more than once, and each time I find something new I want to try.

I was born with a heart condition and a cholesterol level that was once more than 351, so you were just what the doctor ordered. I found your recipes a great change from the usual "diet" recipes.

The reason I am writing to you is to ask for help. I have searched eight large chain supermarkets in a 20 mile radius of my home and no one sells Butter Buds in the mix (packets) to make liquid. All they have is the sprinkle form. Can the sprinkle kind be used to make liquid?

I also can't find the Sweet 'N Low Brown. I have asked each store to order these products for me but they say they can't get them. In some of your recipes you use Promise Ultra Fat-Free Margarine, but others list Butter Buds Liquid. Are the two interchangeable? If they are, could you please let me know the amount of margarine that is equal to the Butter Buds?

If you have any other suggestions on how I could get Butter Buds or any other substitutions such as Sweet 'N Low Brown I would greatly appreciate it. *R. G.* (I misplaced her envelope with the return address, so I don't know where she is from) I wrote her back when I received her letter back in June 1994.

ME: I'm so glad my book has been helpful and you have enjoyed the recipes. Another liquid Butter Buds question. I honestly get 3-5 letters a week from people looking for this product. I just don't understand why they have such a hard time getting it distributed in the various grocery stores. It is one of the best fat-free products on the market. It should be in every grocery store in the country. Maybe if you keep requesting it, SOMEONE WILL GET THE MESSAGE!!

The Promise Ultra Fat-Free Margarine and the Fleischmann's Fat-Free Spread (in a squeeze bottle) work great in most baked items. I use them in place of oil or margarine in all cakes, muffins, and breads. I do prefer the Liquid Butter Buds in sauces, soups, gravies, puddings, and pie fillings. You can use clear chicken broth for pan frying or sautéing vegetables in your soups, casseroles, and stews instead of liquid Butter Buds. As far as the Sweet 'N Low Brown, guess what? It is also made by Cumberland Packing Corporation (as is Butter Buds). It is a wonderful product but hard to find. It really bothers me that I recommend and talk about these great products all over the country (on T.V., radio, workshops, book signings, etc., etc.) and no one can find them in the grocery stores! I just can't understand it. Every time I contact the people at Cumberland Packing Corporation (and I know them all personally), they insist their products are in the stores. Maybe  they are being sabotaged by the grocery store stock clerks who are hiding their products from us folks trying to cook low-fat. I don't know what is going on, but I do believe my readers when they say they can't find the products!! I get too many letters every week not to believe what they are saying! If you can't find the Sweet 'N Low Brown or Butter Buds Products please call: (800) 231-1123, and in New York call: (800)336-0363 and tell them I told you to call! I really love those people. I have been to their plant. They are a family owned business and they couldn't be nicer. As a matter of fact Abe Bakal, the chemist responsible for many of their great products (and a personal friend), shared this story with me and I would like to share it with you. I hope I get all the facts right.

Abe Bakal

From what I understand, during World War II a gentleman named Benjamin Eisenstadt owned a cafeteria across the street from the Navy Yard in Brooklyn, New York (this is where the company is currently located). It was called Ben's Brooklyn Navy Yard Cafeteria. After the war, the cafeteria closed down (the Navy guys went home) and Benjamin and Betty, his wife, were left with an empty building and a large family (four children and newly immigrated in-laws) to support. As a child Ben had worked at a tea factory and vaguely remembered a machine used to package tea bags. After selling everything in the cafeteria, he had enough money left to purchase one tea-bag machine. Even though the machine was designed to make tea bags, it was used to package individual packets of sugar, instead. When the cafeteria was in business, the sugar in the sugar bowls had always been a problem. Because the cafeteria was located near the water, the humidity caused the sugar to clump together. Not to mention the problem of flies hovering over the bowls of sugar, and the obvious lack of sanitation. This had always bothered the Eisenstadts, but at the time no one had a solution. Thus Cumberland Packing Corporation was born. Ben went into the packaging business. In 1956, his son Marvin joined the family business. Along with sugar, they began packaging everything from ketchup to glue. They were the first company to package soy sauce for Chinese take-out restaurants. Business was going well, but Ben was anxious to come up with a product of his own to package. Other packaging plants began cropping up and the competition

Brooklyn Navy Yard

was tough. Together, in 1957, Ben and Marvin developed a sugar substitute. Betty, who had stopped using sugar in her tea because she was trying to drop a few pounds, complained because the only sugar substitute on the market was a bitter tasting tablet called saccharin. Ben and Marvin began to experiment with different blends of sweeteners until they came up with a product Betty liked. There was a song popular in the 1940's that Ben and his family loved called, (you guessed it) "Sweet 'N Low." The title of the song actually came from a poem written by Lord Tennyson. Ben thought it was a marvelous name for his new product. It was sweet, yet low in calories! Barbara Eisenstadt, Marvin's wife, came up with the musical G-clef idea (the familiar logo we have all come to know and love) and they decided on pink because they thought it would stand out and be noticed in sugar bowls. They were right, and it does. The rest is history.

I personally think it is a wonderful story, and I have told it many times. Benjamin is still living in New York. His son Marvin, and grandson Jeff, run the family business. I have had the opportunity to talk to Marvin several times over the last four years, and the thing that impresses me most about this successful businessman is actually not his wonderful products. I have a lot of respect for his work and for the contribution he and Benjamin made back in 1957, when they developed a product that has made the life of diabetics more enjoyable by replacing sugar with a great -tasting alternative. But to let you know the kind of person he is, let me share this with you. In November 1994 I had called Marvin to inquire about the distribution of the mix to make Liquid Butter Buds. It seemed a lot of my readers were having trouble locating the product in their grocery stores. Marvin suggested the problem could be that they were looking for a product ALREADY IN LIQUID FORM instead of in a box containing packets to be mixed with hot water to "make" Liquid Butter Buds. Before I could even finish asking him about distributors, he couldn't wait to jump in and ask me, "Pam, have I told you what Debra is up to now?" I said, "No, what?" He proceeded to tell me that his

Pam visits Cumberland Packing Corporation

darling daughter was in L.A. (where I was headed to film my Butter Busters Infomercial) and was in the play "Sisters Rosensweig," and, on top of that, had recently landed a part in a movie, too. In a previous phone call he had told me about the two books his other daughter, Jill, had written. The conversation shifted to our children and to how proud we were of them for what they had managed to accomplish on their own (without our help). I guess that is why I admire and respect Marvin Eisenstadt so much. He has his priorities in order. His business is important, and he has a lot to be proud of concerning his accomplishments (without a doubt), but what his daughters have managed to accomplish is what he wants to talk about. He is, and will continue to be, an inspiration for all of us in the business world who struggle to divide our time between family and work, hoping to make the right decisions regarding both.

I wonder if Debra and Jill have any idea just how proud their Dad is of what THEY have accomplished all by themselves! Knowing Marvin, he probably tells them each and every day! So, next time you open a package of Sweet 'N Low to pour in your coffee, remember this story that made it all possible! I don't know about you, but I think it is pretty neat!

YOU: This is my second letter of praise. Thank you for writing me back last time. As I said before your *BUTTER BUSTERS* is the very best of all of them! When oh when are you going to write another cookbook (not just an updated edition)? I have tried writing and sending a self-addressed stamped envelope to Flavor House, Inc. to inquire about their Caramel Corn with no response. Can you help me? I've written four times! Also do you know of a way to make low-fat yogurt dipped pretzels or raisins (a good idea for your next new cookbook, huh?) Where can I find fat-free Buttermilk? Is there a fat-free Cheddar Cheese sprinkle powder for popcorn? My stores are not very friendly when I ask them for fat-free items, but I keep asking anyway! I could go on and on, but I better get this in the mail so you can read it and then get back to WRITING ANOTHER COOKBOOK!!! Keep up the great work, and send me any information you can. I'll watch for you on T.V.
—*J.S. Cedar Lake, Indiana*

ME: I have good news. The Flavor House Caramel Corn is now sold under the label "Nature's Classic" and can be found in every K-Mart Store in the country. If you still can't find it in your area call: Flavor House Products, Inc. (205)983-5634. I spoke to the customer service representative for the company (her name is Karen) and she assured me they answer all correspondence regarding their products. I don't know what happened to your requests, but now you know where to buy the great product! There are several fat-free Cheddar Cheese sprinkle powder products available. I've used one called "Best of Butter" brand Cheddar flavor by McCormick and Molly McButter makes a Cheddar as well as sour cream flavor fat-free sprinkle powder. You should be able to find both of these products in the spice section of your grocery store. I wish I had an answer to your yogurt dipped pretzels and raisins. Unfortunately, the reason that yogurt mixture hardens and does so well to coat pretzels and raisins (you have seen sold in the grocery store) is because they are made with hydrogenated vegetable oil (one of the five saturated fats we all need to be concerned with when tracking our cholesterol). It is impossible to get a hardened product without adding the fat. I know, because I tried to make low-fat chocolate chips. It follows the same premise. I even tried adding edible wax. It still didn't work. I don't give up easily. My kid's love "Magic Shell" on frozen yogurt. You know the stuff, like the chocolate they make dip cones with at Dairy Queen!! Unfortunately, it's loaded with saturated fat. I would love to figure out a way to do it. If I do, you will be the first to know!

In answer to your final question: Surprise, I have two more books "in the works." Look for them in late 1995 or early 1996.

YOU: I love your cookbook. I wish you would include more soup recipes in your next one, though. I live in Michigan and we eat a lot of soup in this part of the country. Do you have any tips to help me de-fat some of my own soup recipes? Also, have you ever heard of taking pectin, or sprinkling it on your food, to fill you up? Can you really use prune pureé in place of fat in baking? I saw you on the "Joan Rivers Show" twice. I saw you the first time in March and I just happened to be clicking through the channels one day in May, and there you were again. I don't think it was a re-run because you had on a leotard the second time and I think you had on a T-Shirt the first time I saw you. What is Joan Rivers like, anyway? I'm a very health conscious woman with grown up children married to a man who loves high-fat food. I would be happy eating fruits, vegetables, bread, and beans. He, however, is a meat and potatoes man. The good news is, my husband has been very pleased with everything I have made from your book. Your book is fantastic! You pleased both of us! I think you are the greatest and would love to meet you in person if you ever visit Michigan on one of your book tours! Please don't ever stop writing cookbooks. The whole Country thanks YOU for making healthy eating so delicious and easy!!
—R.D. Lansing, Michigan

ME: Thank you for the sweet comments. I also love soups and plan to include a bunch in my future books. I do have some tips that might help de-fat your own soup recipes. You can skip the heavy cream or half and half so many recipes call for and substitute evaporated skimmed milk OR you can pureé cooked rice, potatoes, or vegetables with thinned skim milk or broth. This makes a great base for "cream" soups and a thickener for hearty stews. When your recipe calls for oil to sauté the vegetables for your soup or stew, use clear chicken broth instead. When you open a can of chicken broth, pour what you don't use in a plastic ice cube tray and freeze. That way when you need a little broth to sauté some vegetables, you can just pop out a cube and there you are. Cheese soups are always fat-laden (unless made with skim milk and fat-free cheese). There are several fat-free cheeses that melt. Some good ones to use are Alpine Lace Fat-Free Parmesan, Kraft Fat-Free sliced American cheese, Borden sliced fat-free Sharp Cheddar cheese, Lifetime by Lifeline fat-free cheeses (many varieties), Weight Watchers' fat-free cheese slices, SmartBeat fat-free cheese slices, Polly-O Free (fat-free mozzarella cheese or Ricotta cheese), and Healthy Choice "Velveeta Style" Cheese (also great for Rotel Dip). Look in the "New Products" chapter of this book to find telephone numbers if you can't locate these products. To de-fat chili or other meaty soups or stews, chill, and skim off congealed surface fat, and then reheat. Another good trick is when you notice fat floating on the surface of your sauce or soup, quickly dip an ice cube into the hot liquid. Excess fat will congeal on the surface for easy removal. If your recipe calls for canned broth, please use the sodium reduced variety, such as Campbell's Healthy Request or Health Valley sodium reduced chicken or beef broth. You might try cooking your soup or stew in a cast-iron Dutch oven. You will give your soup a healthy dose of iron when doing so! I have heard of sprinkling pectin on your food, to add soluble fiber. Pectin (found naturally in apples) can be purchased in the grocery store in the section where the spices are located. It comes in little packages that look like JELL-O. It also comes in liquid form. It is the ingredient cooks use to make homemade jams and jelly. It's the stuff that makes the fruit mixture gel and thicken so it can be used for spreading on your bread. Pectin is found on many food labels. Small amounts are used to stabilize and improve the texture in some soft cheese products and even yogurt. It is actually a carbohydrate that's added to thicken a product and still allow it to maintain it's structure. Pectin is not some weird additive, but only a natural food. Actually it's a soluble fiber (the kind that helps lower your cholesterol). Pectin can actually be found in many fruits besides the apple I mentioned. It's in apricots, peaches, prunes, pears, plums, raspberries, raisins, carrots, onions, sweet potatoes, beans, grapefruit, oranges, grapefruits, and even lemons.

I did some research on what you heard about pectin filling you up as well. Interestingly enough, there have been some studies on this matter. In Southern California many people found (in controlled research testing) when they added pectin to their food, they felt full longer. It makes sense if you think about it. Since the pectin gels when combined with ingested food, it probably stays in the stomach longer and that is why you "feel" full longer. When your stomach stays full longer, you don't get hungry as soon. In some respects, it can be compared with fat. High fat foods stay in your stomach longer and leave you with a full feeling longer. The difference is fat is fattening, while pectin is a form of fiber. When fat is eaten and digested it is absorbed as calories, and too many of those fat calories will make us fat. Pectin, on the other hand, moves out of the stomach and is not digested or absorbed, but moves out of the body in our stool because it is fiber. I don't see a problem adding pectin to your food. If it makes you feel full, satisfied, and increases your fiber intake, I certainly don't see anything wrong with it. **However, I would still ask your personal physician before you add anything new or unusual to your diet!**

You heard me right on the Joan Rivers' Show "Can We Shop?" You can use pureéd prunes or prune baby food in place of fat for baking. The recipe for making prune pureé is: Take 2 cups of pitted prunes, 4 Tbs. vanilla, 3/4 cup water and process in blender until pureéd. This will give you about 1 cup of pureéd prunes. If a recipe calls for 1/2 cup oil, use 1/4 -1/2 cup prune pureé in it's place. The amount depends on how many other liquids are in the recipe. If it contains milk or water, cut the prune pureé to 1/4 cup. If there is no other liquid, use 1/2 cup.

As far as Joan is concerned, she is an absolute doll!! She was funny, kind, smart, and VERY personable!! It was a real honor to meet and work with her! She is so talented. When I appeared on her show in May, my husband and I also had the privilege of attending her performance of "Sally Marr and Her Escorts" on Broadway. She wrote the play herself. It is the story of Lenny Bruce's mother Sally Marr. It is basically a "one woman play." Joan was on stage throughout the whole performance. She was wonderful and was nominated for a Tony as a result of her fantastic performance. Unfortunately, she didn't win, but she is still a "winner" to me. I also watched her in the T.V. movie she made with her daughter Melissa called, "Tears and Laughter, The Joan and Melissa Rivers' Story." It was also excellent! Joan has had a very difficult life, with the suicide of her dear husband Edgar followed by the estrangement with Melissa following his death. After that came the "much publicized" disagreement with Johnny Carson concerning hosting his show. Maybe the trials and tribulations Joan has bravely encountered during her lifetime helped contribute to the genuine compassion she radiates when you meet her. I have nothing but admiration

New York May 1994

and respect for the woman. She may appear hard and brash to some, but I'm here to say she is a very kind, sweet lady, and I feel very lucky that I even got to meet her, not once, but twice. I have a

New York   March 1994

signed photograph from Joan hanging in my pool house right above my computer where I write my books. She is a real inspiration to me!

YOU: I recently purchased your cookbook and just love it. I am from the South and love good ole home cooking. I grew up with a can of bacon grease sitting on the stove. In the winter nothing beats black bean soup, gumbo, chili, and thick soups or stews. Most of my favorites contain sausage, ham hocks, or bacon for that great rich flavor. Do you know of any good substitutions I can use in place of the high-fat items? The desserts in your book are wonderful. I feel like I am eating rich "fattening-tasting" desserts without the consequences. I've never ENJOYED losing weight so much! It's usually an unpleasant chore I contend with January 1st each year that lasts until Super Bowl time. That is usually about how long I can stand it. This year will be different, however. Why go back to high-fat eating when I can have anything I want eating this low-fat way? Thank you for making healthy food taste good. I will never diet again!!   —R.B. Baton Rouge, Louisiana

ME: I am thrilled you feel the way you do about low-fat eating. I couldn't have said it better myself. As a matter of fact, folks do ask me all the time, "What would you eat if you could have anything you want to eat?" My answer is always the same. "I CAN EAT WHATEVER I WANT!" When you know the tricks of substitution, you can make just about anything (you have ever eaten and enjoyed) low-fat and healthy. I use several different substitutions in place of high-fat meat items. Healthy Choice has a great low-fat sausage. It is only one fat gram an ounce. Hormel and Healthy Choice make low-fat (1 fat gram a frank) hot dogs that do quite nicely in some soups and stews. Oscar Mayer has introduced a fat-free frank that is fantastic! Another idea is using baked chicken that has been cooked in liquid smoke and Bar-B-Q sauce. Canadian bacon is much lower in fat than regular bacon. Two tablespoons of Imitation Bacon Bits (a soy product) only contain about 1 fat gram. It doesn't take a lot to give you that great bacon "flavor." These substitutions will give your soups that spicy rich fattening taste with much less fat.

YOU: I love cream soups, rich desserts, high-fat sauces, and red meat! I guess that is exactly what got me in trouble too! I've always prided myself by cooking. I've been a gourmet cook for several years and never considered substituting anything less than the richest and the best for the "real thing." Six months ago my eating and cooking habits finally caught up with me. It was fun while it lasted, but thanks to a triple by-pass, I've been forced to change my ways, or I'm not going to see my next birthday. (That is what my doctor says anyway.) As a matter of fact, he was the one who recommended your book. I must admit, I was surprised to find so many rich sounding desserts and cream dishes. I really couldn't believe you had "Grand Marnier Soufflé" in the book. I wondered how in the world you could ever make a dessert like that without all the butter, cream, and eggs and still resemble one of my favorite dishes. Well, I am here to say you did manage to convince me. "The Grand Marnier Soufflé" was delicious and that sauce was pure Heaven! What are some of your best thickening agents for cream soups? I thought I was doomed to tasteless food for the rest of my life, until I discovered your book. Thank you from one great cook to another. Bon Appetit!!

ME: I consider your letter a real compliment. Thank you for your very kind words. It is funny that you mentioned my "Grand Marnier Soufflé." That was always my very favorite "fancy restaurant splurge" dessert I reserved for very special occasions. One reason being, you usually have to order it ahead of time. Besides, it is so delicious and rich that you just couldn't eat it all the time. I worked hard getting that one just right. By the way using Sweet 'N Low DOES NOT WORK IN THAT RECIPE! You can use it in the sauce, but not the soufflé. Don't even try it, unless you want a real mess in your oven. It took three real messes in my oven to make me realize it just didn't work with Sweet 'N Low. They blew up (exploded or whatever)!

I use arrowroot, flour, or cornstarch for thickening along with Pet evaporated skimmed milk. I add Liquid Butter Buds (made from the mix) for a rich buttery taste. Cooking sherry adds a rich taste without adding any fat. It is especially good in gravies and sauces. Another great way to thicken soups is simply pureéing vegetables and adding them to your soup stock. In the case of the potato or corn soup, simply pureé 1/2 cup cooked corn or potatoes with a little fat-free chicken broth or skim milk and add them to your soup. When making cheese soup, be sure and use one of the great new fat-free cheeses that melt well. There are quite a few on the market. (Check the "Resource Guide" pages 527-528 for some great suggestions!) When sautéing vegetables for soups or sauces, always use clear chicken broth, wine, vinegar, vermouth, or water in place of oil. If you have a good set of non-stick cookware, cooking spray might not even be necessary. You do not need oil, butter, or margarine to sauté or stir fry! You might consider increasing your herbs and spices for added flavor. Always add these the last 15-20 minutes of cooking time for best results. Fresh herbs contain more flavor. There is an herb seasoning mix called "Spike" found in the spice section of most grocery stores that tastes great in most soups and stews. I hope you will continue to enjoy eating good low-fat healthy food as well as COOKING IT!

YOU: I can't tell you how much my whole family has enjoyed your recipes. We honestly feel like we are cheating, but the weight is falling off like crazy. I have to admit that we WERE "die-hard junk food junkies" until my husband gave us all a wake-up call with a heart attack last Christmas. Since I had to start cooking differently for him, I decided that I just didn't have the time to cook different meals for everyone. At first the kids resisted, but after a few great meals, they soon adapted to low-fat foods over greasy hamburgers. That's not to say we don't all enjoy a good pizza once in a while, but our days at Dunkin' Donuts are definitely over! About a month ago, I caught the tail end of Good Morning America, and I swear they had a guy on who said potatoes are about 30% higher in fat-forming ability than table sugar. Did I hear him right? I thought potatoes were fat-free. Please clear this up for me if you have any idea at all what I am talking about. We're ready for another cookbook. Do you have one in the works? If so, when?
—*J.B. Madison, Wisconsin*

ME: I'm so glad the book has been a hit with your family. I too was a junk food junkie (for many years). The crazy thing is a lot of those foods don't even sound or smell good to me anymore. I guess miracles never cease!

I watch Good Morning America every day (if I am home). I did see that show and this is what I understood him to say. I'm not saying I agree with him, but everyone is entitled to their own opinion. I won't mention any names, but this person claims to have a "revolutionary new diet program." He claims that carrots, potatoes, bread, rice cakes, and a long list of other foods are all made up of what he called "bad calories." As a matter of fact he proceeded to tell Joan Lunden that "baked potatoes are about 30% higher in fat-forming ability than sugar." You did hear him correctly. He went on to say, "You're better off eating the same number of calories of sugar." His angle is that in some people foods such as potatoes create a lot of blood sugar which he says produces excess fat in people with a "metabolic condition" he called the "starvation response." He sited symptoms such as eating rapidly, overeating regularly, late night snacking, and gaining a lot of weight after a pregnancy.

It may be true that eating potatoes by themselves (without any other foods or topping) are likely to cause a rapid rise in the blood sugar level as they are digested by the body. However, blood sugar isn't automatically turned into fat. Blood sugar enters the cells of the body where it can be used as fuel for energy. It's true you can't over consume any kind of fuel (on a regular basis) and not gain weight (or body fat). I don't care if it comes from potatoes or any other food, an overabundance of anything is not healthy. However, I do not agree with his view. In my opinion (and the opinion of most real experts) the only type of foods that appear more likely than others to turn into fat are not the high carbohydrate items like potatoes, but the fatty foods such as sour cream, butter, cheese, and bacon bits folks put on their spuds! Most agree that compared to calories from carbohydrates, calories from fat are more easily converted into body fat. Like I said, we are all entitled to our own opinion, but I have to wonder **just how many** innocent folks he happened to convince (of the six million estimated viewers tuning in that day!) Thanks for your comments. I hope this cleared up your questions!

YOU: Thank you for writing *BUTTER BUSTERS*. It is like my second bible. My husband and I have been living the Butter Busters Life-Style for close to seven months now. He is so funny. I have NEVER in the twenty three years of our marriage seen him so excited about anything! Maybe it's because he can wear pants he hasn't worn in years, maybe it's because everyone keeps telling him how much younger he looks, maybe it's because he feels better, or maybe it's because he feels so much better about himself (for all the above reasons). After all, he has lost 23 pounds, started exercising and quit smoking. I have lost close to 20 pounds myself, but I have always exercised (or so I thought). Thanks to your book, I learned about the benefits of aerobic exercise and boy has it made a difference! All those legs lifts and sit-ups never did a thing for me. I've found my sit-ups seem more effective since I added the aerobics four times a week. The best part of all is we don't feel deprived. We just can't get over how delicious all your recipes are. From appetizers to desserts, they are all just great! I do have a couple of questions and I would love to know the answers if you have the time. Please send me your video and workbook too. I am anxious to see the tape of all the new products. #1. What are the leanest cuts of red meats? I've heard that buffalo is is really low-fat. I can't find it in the stores here in Mississippi. Do you know anything about buffalo? #2. I love caramel corn. Are there any new low-fat caramel corns on the market? #3 Do you know of any way to make low or non-fat whipped topping? Dream Whip and Cool Whip Light both contain saturated fats (even though Dream Whip lists 0 on it's label). Is there anything else on the market? #4. Does alcohol contain fat grams? I love your segment on label deceptions! That really opened my eyes for shopping! Thanks for answering my questions in advance! I hope another book is in the works. We can't wait!

ME: I'm so glad my book has helped you and your husband. That is wonderful that he has developed such a great positive attitude about his life-style and the changes he has made. Letters like yours really make my day. I will try to answer your questions. As far as the leanest meats are concerned, you heard right about buffalo. However, the numbers can be deceiving. See page 104 for an explanation. I will list the different types of meat along with their percentage of calories from fat. This is not how many fat grams they contain, but the percentage of calories from fat. Remember these cuts are uncooked and trimmed of all visible fat. I must tell you about a great product, however. If you like red meat, you will be happy to hear about a low-fat beef called Vermillion Valley Beef. A six ounce tenderloin is only 3 fat grams. The beef was developed through selective breeding and feeding programs. It is produced without fillers or preservatives. It displays the healthy heart sticker from The American Heart Association, so you can trust the nutritional information. My family cannot tell one bit of difference. My husband had given up red meat when he switched to a low-fat diet, but can now enjoy beef without the guilt. They offer all different cuts and it is sold by mail order. If you are interested call: (800)365-2333. (There are several new low-fat beef products on the market as well. Refer to page 539 for other options.) We don't have buffalo in the grocery stores in Texas (that I am aware of), but I use venison in place of red meat quite often, too. My family cannot tell the difference. I've heard of another low-fat red meat called emu. It is actually a large bird that looks like a giant ostrich. They are imported from Austrilia. Many ranches in the United States have started raising them. Their fat content is similiar to buffalo. Watch for more information about this new product in your area. For more information regarding emu, call: (800) 374-6362 or (800) 791-2669.

WHERE'S THE FAT?

TYPE OF MEAT	PERCENT OF CALORIES FROM FAT
buffalo top sirloin	15%
Vermillion Valley Low-Fat Beef	16%
venison	18%
veal cutlets	24%
pork tenderloin	27%
beef top round	29%
beef eye of round	32%
leg of lamb	34%
beef round tip	35%
rabbit	7%
beef sirloin	38%

I love caramel corn, too. As a matter of fact, I don't like regular popcorn that much, but I do love caramel corn. Have you tried my recipe for "Pam's Sweet Trash" on page 455 in *BUTTER BUSTERS*? There are some fat-free caramel corn products on the market that are delicious. Louise's Fat-Free Caramel Corn, and Houston Foods Co. low-fat caramel corn (only 1 fat gram per cup) are two my family really likes (check the "New Products" section on pages 537-538 of this book for ordering information).

I know what you mean about whipped toppings. That is a tough one. I've tried making it all kinds of ways with evaporated skimmed milk, and most of them have tasted awful. I've tried mixing it with powdered sugar, regular sugar, honey, etc. Most of the toppings made with evaporated skimmed milk turn to liquid after about 30 minutes in the refrigerator. Of all the methods I've tried this is one of my favorites. It's not exactly like Cool Whip, but it makes a nice dessert topping. You will need: 3-oz. fat-free cream cheese, 2 Tbs. powdered sugar, 3 Tbs. fat-free sour cream and 1 tsp. vanilla. Beat cream cheese and sugar. Add vanilla and sour cream. Serve as a dessert topping. This is pretty good, but it will be different than your regular cool whip topping. Another idea, and one I use all the time, is the Betty Crocker Fat-Free Fluffy Frosting Mix that comes in a box. All you do is add 1/2 cup hot water and blend well. It is like a marshmallow topping and I have used it many of the places I would normally use Cool Whip Light. It keeps well in the refrigerator for several days and is fat-free. It may be a little higher in calories than Cool Whip Light, but I would rather have the calories than the fat. Six tablespoons of Cool Whip Light is 60 calories and 3 fat grams. Six tablespoons of Betty Crocker Fluffy Frosting is 100 calories, but fat-free!

Alcohol does not contain fat grams, however, the beer we once thought of as liquid bread (as well as wine and hard liquor) react in our bodies more like oil than sugar. Just because alcohol is a "form" of sugar many of us think we are free to consume liquor much the same way we do other carbohydrates. Alcohol reduces the body's metabolism of fat. In other words, it promotes fat storage. Therefore, if you are are keeping track of fats and carbohydrates you consume, then alcohol calories should be counted as fat. I have had friends who switched to a low-fat diet and just couldn't understand why they didn't lose weight. More often than not, the culprit was the two or three glasses of wine (margaritas, beer, etc.) they consumed four or five times a week. Alcohol can slow down your weight and /or fat loss by slowing down your fat-burning metabolism! If you can't give up your happy hour, at least hit the gym that morning to speed up your metabolic rate through exercise. It might make you think twice about overdoing the cocktails when you see the toll it takes on how you look and feel the next day! I'm not telling you to never drink again. I just wanted to let you know how alcohol can be detrimental to your weight and/or fat loss even if you eat a low-fat diet (especially if you don't exercise)! I didn't mean to give you a lecture about this. I just wanted you to know all the facts.

I wish you continued success and I hope you will continue to enjoy the book. Thanks for asking!

YOU: I am really enjoying the recipes in your book. My family has liked everything I have made for them. I also take items to work to share with my co-workers. Five of my friends at work have bought your book as a result of tasting the food I brought for them to taste. You have helped make cooking enjoyable for me again and also low-fat. I have a few questions you might be able to answer. Many of the fat-free cereals and granola bars are made with fruit juice instead of sugar for sweetening. Is the fruit juice more healthy than sugar? What causes cookies to spread when you bake them? I've had that problem with a few of my own recipes that I modified to low-fat. Do I need to be concerned with everything I've read in the press about poultry, eggs, and beef being unsafe to eat?

Do you have plans for more cookbooks? Your recipes are so good and easy to make. My kids can cook a lot of them. Please write another book soon. Thanks for making healthy eating so delicious!

ME: I'm so glad your friends and family have enjoyed the recipes in my book. Don't be fooled into thinking foods sweetened with fruit juices are nutritionally better than foods sweetened with sugar, corn syrup, or other sweeteners. When fruit juice is added to a food, it is usually void of all the vitamins and other nutrients. All that is left is the sugar (in most cases). Fruit juice causes the same rise in blood sugar (in the body) as refined sugar. It might sound more healthy, but in most cases it isn't. There are several reasons for cookies spreading as they bake. There could be too much liquid in the recipe. This happens sometimes when you use fat-free margarines in baking. The reason is they contain more water than regular margarine. You can always add an extra tablespoon of flour to the dough. I wouldn't add much more than that or your cookies might turn out tough. Spreading can also occur when you leave your dough sitting out before you bake the cookies or if the cookie sheets are too hot when you place the dough on them to bake. Always chill your dough 20-30 minutes when baking low-fat cookies (especially my Snickerdoodles and cut-out sugar cookies). Any time you handle food of animal origin, there is a chance of bacteria. That bacteria could make you sick if the food isn't refrigerated properly or not cooked thoroughly. Try not to thaw your meat at room temperature. Don't recontaminate cooked meat with juices from raw products found on your cutting board, hands, or your counter. Refrigerate cooked meat (leftovers) within two hours (or sooner). For other safety concerns regarding meat and poultry call: (800)535-4555. It is the USDA's Meat and Poultry Hotline. I hope this helps. I wish you continued success with your low-fat lifestyle.

YOU: I am in love with your cookbook. I have had so much fun making all the great recipes! I went through it page by page, read it thoroughly, and found it all very interesting. I love microwave popcorn and am so confused when I go to the store to buy it. All of the labels are different. Some of them are according to weight before the corn is popped, and some of it is analyzed after the corn is popped. I spent 45 minutes looking at the popcorn labels the other day, and finally left without buying any. Can you please tell me the best and lowest-fat microwave popcorn on the market? It sure would save me a lot of frustration.

By the way, your cookbook is the best one on the market. When I decided to go low-fat, I went to Barnes & Noble and they told me to buy your book. It seems the lady who worked there had lost close to 60 pounds following your recipes. That was good enough for me! I've lost 7 so far and I've only been at this two weeks now. I'm just about ready to join a health club. I'm sure the exercise will really help me take it off quicker.

Well, thanks for your time and research. I hope you have figured out the popcorn labels, so the rest of us won't have to. Keep up the good work. You really are providing a service to mankind! God Bless You!   —*J.L. Shreveport, Louisiana*

ME: I know what you mean about the microwave popcorn. Just when I thought I had it all figured out, a bunch of the companies changed their labels to reflect weight in grams (before it was popped). I was just as confused as you are. I contacted quite a few of the manufacturers and found out the real scoop. Here is what I found:

The lowest fat microwave popcorn on the market (and it really is good, too) is the Orville Redenbacher's Smart-Pop (with 80% less fat). It only has 2 fat grams for 5 cups popped. The following chart might make it easier. Just zerox this page and keep it in your purse when you go to the store.

POPCORN (3 cups popped)	CALORIES	FAT	% of FAT	SODIUM	MY RATING
Orville Redenbacher's Smart-Pop	45 calories	less than 1 gm	20 %	165 mg sodium	EXCELLENT
Original Weaver Movie Popcorn (Butter) Light (formally Pop Weaver's Gourmet Extra Light)	70 calories	1 gm	12 %	85 mg sodium	THE BEST
ACT II.	60 calories	less than 1 gm	15%	90 mg sodium	EXCELLENT
Weight Watcher's	90 calories	1 gm	10 %	0 mg sodium	FAIR
Pop Secret by Request	60 calories	1 gm	15 %	160 mg sodium	REALLY GOOD
Orville Redenbacher's Butter Light	60 calories	2 gms	30%	95 mg sodium	EXCELLENT
Orville Redenbacher's Natural Light	60 calories	2 gms	30 %	125 mg sodium	VERY GOOD

You can see by the chart that the percentage of fat is affected by how many calories the popcorn contains. I try to count fat grams myself, rather than figure out the percentage of fat in everything I eat. That is too much trouble. I hope this chart helps. I would recommend trying to choose a popcorn 20% fat or less and, to accomplish that, you would probably need to pick a popcorn with 2 fat grams or less per serving. In this case, the nutritional information has been calculated with a serving size of three cups popped. If you try to go by Tbs. and the amount of grams per weight, you will never figure it out. I promise. Some kernels are larger than others, and some weigh more, and some pop up bigger than others. I hope this chart comes in handy! Thank you for your nice comments about the book. I wish you continued success.

P.S. Have you seen the Louise's Low-Fat Popcorn? It is 2.5 fat grams for 3 1/2 cups and is already popped. It contains 130 calories. Because it is a little higher in calories, it's only 17 % fat. The sodium is a little higher at 180 mg. Louise's now offer a fat-free caramel corn that is really fantastic. I'm not that big on popcorn, but my first choice is the Original Weaver Movie Popcorn. It's the same company who used to sell Pop Weaver's Extra Light Gourmet popcorn. I haven't seen Pop Weavers in the stores, so I assume the Original Weaver Movie Popcorn took it's place. I happen to like caramel popcorn better than regular popcorn, so I am probably not the best judge. However, Mike, my husband, loves popcorn. His favorites are Orville Redenbacher's Smart-Pop and Weaver's Original Movie Light Popcorn. Good Luck!

NOTES

EXERCISE AND FITNESS

ATTENTION READERS:

Let me begin this chapter by telling you that I do not have a degree in Exercise Physiology, nor do I have the initials R.D. after my name. I, in no way, consider myself an expert regarding nutrition or exercise. However, I have done a tremendous amount of research and have consulted experts regarding both fields. The information regarding health, nutrition, and fitness is ever-changing. One day we read that aerobic exercise is the "only way" to lose body fat. The next week we learn if you build lean muscle mass through anaerobic exercise (such as weight training) you will burn calories at a faster rate. Therefore, anaerobic exercise is the best way to lose body fat.

Some experts claim that "only fat" is burned for fuel when you are within your heart rate zone during aerobic exercise, while others insist "it's a blend of carbohydrate and fat" burned during any physical exertion. Many experts feel fat loss is determined by the total amount of calories burned rather than fat calories, specifically. Most experts recommend aerobic exercise at a low intensity to burn body fat most efficiently because most people will give exercise a try if they don't think they have "to kill themselves" to achieve results. It's a known fact that the higher the intensity of your workout, the more calories you will burn. However, the ratio of fat to carbohydrate calories burned is determined by the intensity **and** duration of your workout. If you were told that you had to exercise every day aerobically at the high end of your target heart rate zone for one hour to lose body fat, how many of you you would say, "Forget it!" On the other hand, if you were told to exercise aerobically 3-5 times a week at a moderate pace (within your heart zone) for a minimum of 35 minutes to achieve results, would you consider giving it a try? I can't argue with the fact that the longer and faster you exercise the more total calories you will burn, but I also think it is important to recommend choices that are more realistic and have proven effective for myself as well as many of you that have written and insisted that my method worked for you, too!

We hear from one source that you must work out within your aerobic target heart rate zone for "X" amount of minutes in order to burn body fat efficiently. Within weeks there is an article in a major newpaper stating that "It doesn't matter if you are within your zone for an extended period of time at all." Instead, it has been recommended by some experts that all you need to do is use the stairs instead of the elevator and you will improve your fitness level, control your weight, and strengthen your heart. To me, this is rather misleading. Some people will read a statement such as this and think they are fit and will burn body fat if they use the stairs more often. This is exactly what I am trying to say. You must consider everything you read, but still form your own opinion as to what will work for you. Because we are all individuals and our metabolic rates differ (the rate at which your body burns calories), many factors must be considered. **THERE IS NO SINGLE EXERCISE PRESCRIPTION FOR EVERYONE!** Basic guidelines that are realistic and liveable to the majority of the people is the most important factor to consider when discussing exercise (in my opinion).

The same holds true in the field of preventive medicine. One day we read that hot dogs cause cancer and the next day it's the growth hormone in cow's milk that we need to be concerned with. My point is that ideas, theories, and recommendations change every day. You just have to read everything and make your own personal choice as to what you will believe and follow and what you won't. Ultimately, the choice is up to you. My intention is ONLY TO PROVIDE INFORMATION. I speak from experience. When I recommend the way I exercise to a reader who has written and asked, I try to give them all the information available along with my personal experience and what has worked for me. I have found through your letters that many of you have followed my program and it has obviously worked for you, too. (Please refer to the chapter, "MY READERS INSPIRE ME.") If you don't agree with my ideas, that is fine. Believe me, I AM NOT TRYING TO TELL YOU WHAT TO DO. I am only trying to present you with all of the information available. In some cases, experts differ on their opinions. However, I have found one common thread. Everyone agrees that regular exercise and a low-fat diet are two of the major components necessary to achieve a healthy lifestyle. Regarding exercise, the experts may disagree about how long, how strong, or how often, but the bottom line is **they all agree** that we should all "Do something!"

You have written and asked for my opinion, and after much research (along with my personal experience), I only wish to offer options. My book is not intended to prescribe, but only to inform. I hope you will read this section with that thought in mind and hopefully my suggestions and ideas will continue to help each of you change your life for the better, for that is my intention...to simply help YOU! Concerning this chapter, or for that matter the whole book: Take what you want and leave the rest. The "one idea" that doesn't interest YOU, may be the "very thing" someone else is searching to find. We are all individuals. Our desires and needs differ (as do our personalities). I hope YOU will find what YOU are looking for regarding exercise and fitness. But remember, the ultimate choice is YOURS!

NOTE: The American Heart Association offers a report on Exercise Standards. To obtain your copy of this report write to: Office of Scientific Affairs, 7272 Greenville Ave., Dallas, Texas 75231.

"JUST DO IT!"

YOU: I can't afford a health club membership. I have three small children and must do something at home. Do you have any exercise suggestions that are easy, quick, and cheap? I live in an apartment, so I don't have much room to move around.
—*W.S. Baltimore, Maryland*

ME: I understand where you are coming from. When my kids were small my neighbor and I took turns watching each other's kids so we could work out. We each had an hour (without distractions) to ourselves. If you can't get outside to walk, I would suggest making your own bench. You could also purchase a cheap one at your local discount store. However, I would not suggest the bench if you have knee problems. The bench is nice because you don't need a large area to get a great workout. If you like to watch T.V. as you work out, set the bench in front of the television. You could follow an exercise step video (many benches come with a free video). What I do (if I want to watch T.V.) is use my cassette player with an aerobic music tape on low (so I will stay with the beat) but still able to hear and watch T.V. All you have to do is step up and down in a rhythmatic motion for 35 minutes and you have a great workout. A pattern I use (even on the porch steps outside if I don't have a bench) is to step up, knee up, step down, step down, step up, knee up, step down, step down. If you do this as you read the words it will make sense to you. This is very simple and you don't have to think about it. Changing your arm motions as you step increases the intensity of your workout. Remember to decrease your intensity gradually, cool down, and stretch your muscles to increase flexibility and help prevent soreness. For weight training fill milk gallon jugs with water or sand. These work great because they have handles and are easy to use. A gallon jug (filled with water) weighs about ten pounds. A half-filled jug equals about five pounds. Canned goods can also serve as light weights. You can purchase large rubber bands (in an office supply store) and place around your ankles to aid in resistance for leg lifts. Your child's rubber ball (a volleyball works great) can be placed between your knees as you do sit-ups squeezing your legs together as you lift. This gives you a great inner-thigh workout. Most kids have a jump rope. This can be a wonderful aerobic exercise you can do with the kids. Don't forget to play. Get the kids involved (if they are old enough) and make fitness fun for the whole family. Mall walking is cheap, fun, and entertaining. All you need is a good pair of shoes and a cassette player to keep you moving. Sunglasses and a wig add a nice touch if you have a problem with interruptions (such as friends stopping you to visit). The mall walking option works when you are out of town and don't know anyone living in the area. Good luck!

Madearis Studio ©

Pam "Just Listening" between workouts
February 1995

YOU: My girlfriend bought your book and after tasting the food, found I actually liked some of the recipes (especially the Mexican food). You mentioned aerobic exercise and said it was necessary to lose body fat. I am forty-six years old, 6'2", and 245 pounds. I am an ex-football player (who loves to eat), but doesn't like to work out. I had my fill of that when I played football! I don't have time to work-out anyway because I travel 3-5 days a week, so a health club would be a waste of money. Can I lose weight by eating low-fat without exercising?
—*C.L. Nashville, Tennessee*

ME: You CAN LOSE WEIGHT by a low-fat diet alone, but YOU MIGHT NOT BE LOSING FAT. You will initially shed water weight, followed by a loss of lean muscle if you don't exercise. Our body's preferred fuel is protein (found in the muscle) rather than fat. By exercising aerobically, we force our body to protect the muscle by burning fat stored in the adipose tissue. When my husband first decided to start eating low-fat back in January 1991, he did not include exercise with his low-fat diet. He lost about twenty pounds in a little over two months, but was not pleased with his new body. He lost most of his upper body muscle mass, because his body consumed the preferred fuel (muscle) for energy. Once he added aerobic exercise along with weight training into his work-out, he continued to lose weight, but this time in the form of fat. Through aerobic exercise, he forced his body to burn fat for fuel. He developed lean muscle mass as a result of the weight training. Lean muscle mass is metabolically active, which enables you to eat a lot more food and not gain weight. It also speeds up your metabolic rate (how quickly and efficiently your body burns calories), which in turn increases the fat burning process. Your body will continue to burn fat after your work-out is completed for several hours. Regular aerobic exercise in conjunction with a low-fat diet is a system destined to succeed. It's YOUR choice!

YOU: Pam, I work out every day. I do six miles on the Stairmaster as well as lift weights four days a week. Do I need more than 1200 calories a day? I eat about 10-15 fat grams a day. Am I working out too much? I feel tired and sore all the time. My mom is really overweight and I don't want to end up like her! I am a college student, 18 years old, 5'7" and weigh 125 pounds.
—*S.C. Brooklyn, New York*

ME: Is 125 your ideal weight? If so, you should be consuming around 1900 calories (minimum). Take 15 times your ideal weight and this is approximately your calorie allotment for the day. Since you are SO ACTIVE you could probably consume 2,000-2,500 calories and maintain your weight (even with 30% fat which would amount to about 60 fat grams a day). Have your body fat measured to determine if you are over-fat. I doubt you are, but could be burning muscle (the body's preferred fuel choice) instead of fat if your caloric consumption is too restricted. You might not be eating ENOUGH calories to force your body to burn fat rather than muscle and protein. If you want to lose weight, decrease your fat to 10% which would be 20 fat grams a day. I WOULD NOT DECREASE YOUR CALORIES due to YOUR active life-style and intensive exercise program. You are probably tired because you aren't eating enough calories for your work load. Carbohydrates (fruits, vegetables, beans, rice, pasta, and bread) all serve as great energy sources. When you cut the fat in your diet and add more carbohydrates, you will have more energy. I only do light weights twice a week for 30 minutes. You really don't need more than that unless you are involved in body building. I think you need to take at least one day off a week, to rest your muscles. They need a chance to rebuild, so give your body a break, and space the weight training out over the week. In order to burn body fat, you must be within your personal heart-rate zone. This would be approximately 220 minus your age times 70% and 85%. In your case it would be: 220-18=202. Next take 202 x 70% and 85%. YOUR target heart range would be between 141-171 beats per minute. You determine your pulse by counting beats of the radial artery (about two inches down from your thumb on the side of your wrist) or carotid artery (on the side of your neck down from your ear) for 10 seconds and multiplying that number by six. Any health club or fitness facility could explain this to you if you don't understand. Another option would be to purchase a heart-rate monitor. I own the Polar Pacer (retails around $125.00). I received mine from my Mom three years ago and it is still running on the same batteries (even using it about one hour 5-6 days a week). If you work-out higher than your target zone, you will be burning carbohydrates and glu-cose for fuel. You don't have to kill yourself! Longer moderate aerobic exercise is the most effec-tive method for burning body fat. You sound a bit compulsive about your exercise program. I say this, because I used to be the same way. You can overtrain and, by doing so, increase your risk of injury and burn-out! Check the Up-Front and Personal chapter to find out what I do to stay fit.

Note: This girl reminded me of myself so I sent her a long letter explaining my program. I felt she might benefit from my words of experience.

YOU: Are personal trainers really worth the money? How much do they cost anyway? I AM VERY MOTIVATED to workout, but my husband isn't. I'm worried about his health because he is about fifty pounds overweight, smokes, and his only workout involves changing the channels on the remote control and an occasional walk to the refrigerator to get a beer!!
   Signed: Depressed and Desperate in Delaware

ME: I think in your husband's case a personal trainer just might be the answer. The cost ranges between $20-$50 (maybe less) per session. Check your local YMCA or fitness clubs for names and prices. Sometimes an active, fit, wife can pose a threat to her out-of-shape couch potato hus-band and vice versa. With a personal trainer, your spouse won't have to compete with YOU! The personal time and attention might be just what they need to get started. A personal trainer will determine his body fat, suggest a healthy diet, and monitor and motivate your spouse to obtain his goals. If your husband needs a cheerleader to get started and keep him motivated, a personal trainer IS WORTH THE MONEY! You cannot put a price on a healthy life-style, but in the long run it will save you money. Poor health habits usually wind up costing you a bundle. It costs more to fix the problem, than to prevent it! Be patient, not pushy. Let him THINK it's HIS idea! (This letter could also apply to a man with an out-of-shape wife.) I don't want this book to only appear written for women readers. Everyone SHOULD BE CONCERNED with their own health! YOUR LIFE COULD DEPEND ON IT!!

YOU: My husband left me because I am so fat. I weighed 120 when we got married and have gained about twenty pounds with each baby. I have three kids. I weigh about 170 and can't get the weight off. My husband bought me a health club membership for my birthday. I am a klutz and feel very uncomfortable in a leotard next to all those "aerobic queens" at the club. My husband is dating my EX-Sister-in-law (one of the aerobic queens), but says he doesn't love her. He said we can get back together if I lose 50 pounds. He is about 20 pounds overweight himself, but says it's OK for a man to be a little heavier. Can I lose the weight without exercise? I hate to sweat!! (Besides I can't stand to face HER at the club.) All her friends know the story and work-out there, too. It is very humiliating!   —A.M.

ME: Do you really want him back under those circumstances? You need to be happy with yourself. Are you comfortable at 170 pounds? It doesn't sound like it. I hate to judge your husband without knowing the whole situation, but it sounds like he is on a "power trip" going no-where! I can understand your feelings regarding working out at the health club. You could try to go different times of the day when you know THEY won't be there. Does your health club offer water aerobics classes? Water aerobics is virtually no-impact, so it's safe for most anyone. Just because it's gentle on your body doesn't mean that it's not a super fat burning work out. Besides, you don't have to sweat! Adding a light weight program will build lean muscle mass which enables your body to burn fat at an accelerated speed. Determine your ideal weight and take that number times 15. If it's 120, that would be 1800 calories a day. Try to eat only 10% total fat and exercise 3-5 times a week, and he will be begging you to take him back before you know it. The only decision you will have to make at that point is if you really want him! It's always nice to have an option. Let it be your choice, not his. Your happiness is the main concern, not what makes HIM happy. Get my drift?

YOU: I am 64 years old, have a bad knee, and don't know what to do for exercise. I can't walk at the mall with all my lady friends, because it hurts my knee. I need someone to exercise with, because I'm not self-motivated. I am a widow and live alone. I love to watch T.V. (my soaps) and reading for entertainment.   —B.B. Galveston, Texas

ME: I understand your problem. My Mom is 75 years old and also had a knee problem. She found a stationary exercise bike her only "pain free" mode of exercise. You should, of course, check with your physician before starting anything new, but it worked for her. It would, of course, depend on your specific problem. Another option is water aerobics. If you have access to a pool (check at your local Y.M.C.A.) this might be a possibility. The water aerobics class would provide the fellowship of working out with other people (it sounds like you miss your "lady friends"). You can always read or watch T.V. as you pedal away on a stationary bicycle. I hope these suggestions help!

YOU: I recently had cosmetic surgery and can't use my arms, bounce, or do aerobics for six weeks. I'm afraid I'll gain a lot of weight just sitting around even if I do eat low-fat. Do you have any ideas? —S.K. New Orleans, Louisiana

ME: Do you have access to a stationary bike? As long as you work a large muscle group (in this case your legs by pedaling) you can burn body fat. You don't need to use your arms or bounce. Try to "ride" at least 35 minutes, not counting a five minute warm-up and cool-down. You should monitor your heart-rate and try to stay within your target heart-rate zone in order to burn fat. You are usually "in your zone" if you break a sweat after 10-15 minutes and can talk and carry on a conversation, but not sing.(This would be an indication you are working too hard, thus defeating your goal of burning fat.) The nice thing about the stationary bike is you can read or watch T.V. as you exercise! You should continue sit-ups, squats and lunges to keep you lower body toned as well. You don't have to use your arms or bounce to get a great aerobic workout. The same holds true for a person that can't use their lower body to exercise. You can get an excellent aerobic workout in a wheel chair by using your arms in a rhythmatic motion for 35 minutes. Don't forget to warm-up and stretch before you begin. Intense arm movements WILL elevate your heart-rate. You can burn body fat (even sitting down), if you work out long and hard enough within your personal target heart-rate zone! Good Luck!

YOU: Today is my daughter's 17th Birthday. My gift is helping her develop a low-fat lifestyle. She is 5'8" tall and weighs 150 pounds. She is very busy performing in the drill team and studying very hard to keep her "B" average. She was a lifeguard this summer and probably ate all the wrong foods at the pool. I feel she is slightly overweight and wonder how she can weigh this amount when she is so physically active in practicing every night after school for drill team. She has gained 15 pounds in the last year. I would like your recommendation for a camp that could help her learn about eating correct foods, along with aerobic activities. The *SHAPE* Magazine Camp in Malibu sounded really great. Could you give me some information on that camp? I would be interested too.

Your book, *BUTTER BUSTERS*, is very informative and I appreciate all your thoughts and recipes. We are convinced that a low-fat lifestyle is the best way to live. I also appreciate your thoughts on how in the Bible it says we are to not eat fat. I feel God wants us to be the best temples we can. My body is a temple and it needs to be nourished the right way so I can live my life to the fullest and give God and my family the best I can.
—S.B. Blue Springs, Missouri

ME: What a wonderful birthday gift for your daughter! You are obviously a very caring, concerned and loving mother who wants the best for her family. She might not appreciate it now, but I know she will later. I speak from experience. I never really appreciated my parents until I had children of my own. It's true, she is active, but my question to you is, "is she AEROBICALLY ACTIVE?" In order to lose body fat, we must exercise aerobically a minimum of 35 minutes (not counting warm-up and cool-down) three to five times a week. Even though she is up at the school practicing drill team every night, chances are there is a lot of standing around listening to instruction, as well as constant starting and stopping of activity. In order to be aerobic (and lose body fat efficiently) we need to be using our large muscle groups in a rhythmatic motion. You should be within your personal target heart rate zone (approximately 220 minus your age times 70% and 85%) and you should exercise continuously (for at least 35 minutes). It's true that all physical activity burns calories. Any form of exercise is better than nothing. The neat thing about aerobic exercise is the "after effect" it gives us. After you have completed your aerobic activity, your body continues to burn fat and calories at an accelerated speed. Aerobic activity puts our bodies (like a car engine) in the idle mode. In other words, it continues to burn the fuel after we stop.

It doesn't matter what aerobic activity you pick (and there are many to choose from), just be sure you are working hard enough to break a sweat and your breathing becomes somewhat labored. If you have a heart rate monitor you will be able to tell if you are working hard enough. If not, you should be able to carry on a conversation, but have trouble singing. I call it the talk/sing test. If you can sing, you are probably not working hard enough to be beneficial. Hard breathing is proof that you are forcing oxygen through the body. By doing this, you deplete the glycogen stores (how we store carbohydrates in our body) and force the body to burn fat as fuel. This is the key to FAT LOSS and why aerobic exercise is so important.

I have an example. I have a good friend who lives out in the country. Granted she works very hard every day. She paints, cleans, scrubs, hangs wallpaper, repairs, mows, etc. However, she does not exercise aerobically. Even though she is exhausted at the end of the day, and feels she is working hard, she cannot seem to lose body fat. She does sit-ups to trim her tummy, but doesn't understand why she can't seem to lose weight (more specifically the mid-section). My answer to her is all the sit-ups in the world will not flatten your stomach until you first get rid of the body fat. This CAN ONLY BE ACCOMPLISHED through aerobic exercise. Aerobic exercise burns fat all over the body (including the stomach). Once you lose the body fat, abdominal exercises (such as sit-ups) will help tone and strengthen those muscles. The biggest misconception regarding exercise (in my opinion) is people always want to equate how hard they work with how much they think they should be losing. The key is moderate aerobic activity for an extended period of time (at least 35 minutes) on a regular basis (three to five times a week). Their answer to me is always the same. But Pam, I don't have time to exercise that way and besides it's boring. My answer is this: Is your heart and health worth it? NOT ONLY IS THE AEROBIC EXERCISE BENEFICIAL TO BODY FAT LOSS, IT STRENGTHENS THE HEART MUSCLE! I don't know about you, but I think it is worth the time to ensure a healthy heart. Most folks CAN find the time. If you have a tread mill, walk on it as you watch the news at night. If you have a stationary bicycle, pedal as you read the paper or a good book.

I didn't mean to get off on a tangent about aerobic exercise, but so many people do not understand the importance of aerobic exercise regarding body fat and how to lose it. I will try to explain the importance of your personal heart rate zone in relationship to aerobic exercise.

AEROBIC EXERCISE AND YOUR PERSONAL HEART RATE ZONE

After warming up approximately five minutes (followed by a three to five minute stretch) you are ready to get moving and elevate your heart rate so it is within your personal zone. You should remain within this zone (after you reach it) for approximately 35 minutes. After 35 minutes, cool down gradually (about 3-5 minutes) and finish your aerobic workout with static stretching of all your major muscle groups. Try to incorporate this routine into your day three to six days a week for maximum results. By adding thirty minutes (twice a week) of light weights (or some other type of weight bearing exercise), you will build lean muscle mass, improve your strength, and increase your bone density (so important in the prevention of osteoporosis). Lean muscle mass is metabolically active (meaning it forces your body to burn calories and fat at an accelerated speed). This will allow you to consume a much greater amount of calories without adding fat to your body.

DO YOU WANT TO BECOME FIT?
(Aerobic exercise could be your answer!)

IN ORDER TO RECEIVE MAXIMUM BENEFIT REGARDING AEROBIC EXERCISE YOU MUST BE F.I.T. TO BE CONSIDERED FIT, YOU MUST EXERCISE AEROBICALLY! Does this seem confusing? I'm telling you to exercise aerobically to get fit, but that you must be fit before you exercise aerobically. This is like one of those crazy questions such as, "Which came first, the chicken or the egg?" If you are a bit confused, please don't be discouraged. It's really not as bad as it sounds! Let me attempt to explain myself.

If you want your aerobic exercise to be effective, you must go about it in the right way. There are three basic ideas you need to keep in mind. The guidelines actually spell the word F.I.T. so it will be easy to remember. When I say you must be fit to exercise aerobically, I mean you must incorporate these guidelines into your work-out. The goal you will achieve through exercising aerobically, is that you will become a "FIT" person.

HOW TO GET FIT!
(Frequency, Intensity, and Time)

F. (Frequency) **You must exercise on a regular basis**. Sometimes it's hard to work it into your day, but the best thing to do is schedule exercise as if it were an appointment. I know you would not intentionally skip an important appointment. Try to think of your exercise session with the same importance. Put it high on your list of priorities and follow through by keeping it. Three to six times a week will achieve maximum results. Three days are better than none, and five days are better than four. Find a schedule you can live with and stick to it.

I. (Intensity) If your goals are to burn body fat (as it is for most of us) and to strengthen your heart (which it should be for all of us) then you must be within your personal heartrate zone for a minimum of thirty-five minutes (for best results) during your exercise session. I REALIZE THIS IS NOT POSSIBLE FOR EVERYONE! If you are exercising for the first time in your life, the most important thing to remember is to just start moving. In the beginning, it doesn't really matter how long or how hard you exercise. Just "do something" on a regular basis. Listen to your body. How are you feeling as you exercise? If you ever feel faint or dizzy slow down gradually and stop. Remember to work out within YOUR OWN PERSONAL FITNESS LEVEL! This is very important. Don't compete with anyone. Don't think you have to kill yourself to reach your target heart rate zone (or it won't do you any good). That simply is not true. Any exercise is better than no exercise. **Your aerobic heart rate zone should be approached gradually.** It might take several sessions to reach the intensity (according to your age) where you need to be for maximum results. Progress takes time! The duration is also based on your age and fitness level. If, in the beginning, you can only walk to the mailbox and back, that is just fine. These guidelines are WHAT YOU SHOULD TRY TO WORK TOWARDS to achieve the ultimate goal of BECOMING FIT! **Gradual is the key concerning intensity and duration.** As for frequency, this concerns all of us (no matter what level of fitness) and how you should start your exercise program from the beginning. I don't care if you can only walk to the garage (and have to rest a couple of minutes before you go back inside the house). If that is the case, you need to take that walk as often as possible. Eventually you will be able to walk further (longer) and faster (within your target heart rate zone).

T. *(Time)* As I said earlier, time should NOT BE an issue when you first begin incorporating exercise into your life. For those who have never exercised, any type of movement will be an improvement towards obtaining the goal we are striving towards: To Be FIT!!! On the other hand, if you have already achieved fitness in your life, for maximum results, try to reach your target heart rate zone by increasing your intensity gradually and work out within that zone for a minimum of thirty-five minutes (not counting warm-up and cool-down)during each exercise session.

No matter what your level (beginner, intermediate, or expert), fitness is the ultimate goal to improve the quality (how good we feel) as well as quantity (how long we live to enjoy it) of our lives!

HOW TO FIND YOUR HEART RATE

TAKING YOUR HEART RATE (PULSE)
(The neck and wrist are the best places to take your pulse.)

1. **NECK:** First locate your carotid (pronounced ca-rot-id) artery on either side of your neck. Place the first two fingers of your hand just below the line of your jaw. (Do not use your thumb, because it contains a pulse.)

2. **WRIST:** Turn your hand palm side up. With the first two fingers of the opposite hand, locate the pulse on the thumb side of your wrist.

Count the beats for ten seconds and multiply this number by six to determine your heart rate per minute.

DETERMINE YOUR PERSONAL TARGET HEART RATE RANGE
(According to age and fitness level)

The best guide for determining the intensity of a cardiovascular (aerobic) workout is your target heart rate. For best results, a training range between 70%-85% of your maximum heart rate is desired. Your maximum heart rate is 220 minus your age. DO NOT WORK OUT AT THIS LEVEL!!!!!

By taking your maximum heart rate times 70% and 85% you will find the heart rate range appropriate for your age. The other factor you should keep in mind is your personal fitness level. This would determine the intensity (or how hard) you should work to achieve maximum results. Your personal fitness level determines if you should work out in the lower or higher portion of your range (lower-beginner/higher-expert). This range allows you to improve your fitness level without working harder than your heart can handle.

The chart on page 148 will simplify things. All you need to do is locate your age and look under the appropriate percentage (according to your personal fitness level.) However, if you don't happen to have this chart with you (as you exercise), you need to multiply the beats you count in a ten second period times 6. If the number falls under the percentage of your fitness level, then you are within your fat-burning zone. For example:

I am 45 years old. 220-45= 175 (my maximum heart rate)

I would take 175 X 70%=123 and 175 X 85% =149. This would determine my heart rate zone to burn body fat. I have been exercising aerobically for ten years and consider myself quite fit. For that reason I try to keep my heart rate around 140-145 to burn body fat efficiently. If I go over 149 (highest number in my range), I will most likely become anaerobic and start burning glucose (or sugar) for fuel. This is not my goal. If I work out under 123, I am not working hard enough to be considered aerobic (or burn body fat). In other words, my range is between 123 and 149 beats per minute. The higher (within your range) you exercise aerobically, the stronger your heart will become. Check your pulse periodically throughout your workout and immediately after you complete the aerobic segment. Be sure your pulse is within your range. If it is too high, slow down. If it is too low, speed up a bit.

It is important that you figure out your personal range and memorize it. This way, you will know if you are working within your heart rate zone (and burning body fat).

EXERCISE AND FITNESS

TARGET HEART RATE RANGE
(The key to fat loss)

•**Take your pulse for 10 seconds and multiply times 6 to find the beats per minute.** Compare your number with the chart below to determine if you are working out within your heart rate zone.

YOUR AGE	BEGINNER 70%	INTERMEDIATE 75%-80%	EXPERT 85%
25	136	146-156	165
30	133	142-152	162
35	130	138-148	157
40	126	135-144	153
45	123	131-140	149
50	119	128-136	145
55	116	124-132	140
60	112	120-128	136
65	105	113-124	132
75	102	109-116	123

•If you are under the age of 25 or over the age of 75, simply subtract your age from 220 and multiply that number times 70% and 85%. The two numbers represent your personal target heart rate range (or zone) to burn body fat. If you are just starting to exercise aerobically for the first time, I would suggest staying near the low number. Otherwise you may work at the higher end of your range. Pay attention to signs of overexertion. If you feel dizzy, faint, or start to sweat profusely slow down gradually, but don't stop abruptly. Walk around slowly for 5-10 minutes. If symptoms persist, consult your physician immediately!

I hope this information helps your daughter understand the importance of aerobic exercise and how to determine her personal target heart rate range to burn body fat efficiently.

As for *SHAPE* Magazine Camp, I am sorry to report that it no longer exists. I spoke to Barb Harris, the Editor in Chief of the magazine, and she told me they were trying to get it started again. I have heard of other fitness camps around the country. As a matter of fact there is one called "Fit Camp." For information regarding this camp (or their video) call (800)727-2888. It's for women of all ages!

I appreciate your comments regarding the Bible. I believe we honor God by taking care of the wonderful temple (our body) He has provided. The better the fuel, the better the performance. As long as we "start our engines" every day (by exercise) we won't have to worry about a dead battery (which will happen to any machine if it isn't used for an extended period of time)! I hope your daughter has a wonderful birthday, and by incorporating aerobic activity into her life, she will be able to lose body fat and increase the strength of her heart as well.

YOU: I love your book, and especially like the fact you included an exercise section. I understand all about aerobic and anaerobic exercise and their benefits. I would like your thoughts concerning what time of day is best for losing the most body fat? In your book, you said some people think mornings are best, but it should be up to each individual and when THEY HAVE THE TIME to work out. Do you have any new information regarding this matter?
—K.A. Cincinnati, Ohio

ME: I have done a great deal of research regarding this matter. I have heard all kinds of theories, but the most popular answer "does seem" to make sense. The majority of sources state: For optimal fat loss, working out before breakfast is the most beneficial. Early morning aerobic exercise kicks the body's metabolic rate up immediately. Since the body's glycogen levels are depleted (due to fasting during the night) early morning sessions (on an empty stomach) tend to burn lipids (or fat in the blood). The body prefers to burn carbohydrate for fuel, but if your body is carbohydrate-depleted, it will burn whatever fuel is available. Aerobics before breakfast quickly depletes the fuel of choice (carbohydrates) and forces your body into the fat-burning mode. This is only a theory (as I said), but it does seem to make sense, doesn't it?

YOU: I attended one of your workshops and learned so much. Thanks for sharing all the great shopping tips and new product information. You said one thing that I would like to know more about. You mentioned eating more than three meals a day. You also said that exercise increases your metabolic rate. Could you explain metabolic rate in greater detail? You mentioned weight training helps you lose body fat, too. I thought aerobic exercise was the only way to lose body fat. Can you clear up these questions for me? I had to leave early and didn't get to hear all of your talk regarding exercise. Thanks so much for your time and effort.*—C.P. Arlington, Texas*

ME: I'm so glad you enjoyed the workshop. I've always enjoyed speaking and giving workshops, but don't have as much time to do them as often as I did in the past. That is one reason I wrote a workbook and produced three videos (*Butter Busters The Low-Fat System*). There are so many folks that just don't have the time to attend a workshop, but still need and want to learn the information. As for eating often to increase your metabolic rate, let me explain. First of all your BMR (basil metabolic rate) is the rate at which your body burns calories at rest. If you are able to increase your metabolic rate, you will lose fat quicker. The very act of eating actually increases your body's metabolic rate. Eating small amounts of food frequently actually helps stimulate the body's calorie-burning abilities. The body increases it's metabolism in order to burn away newly consumed foods. After eating, your metabolic rate is increased for 2-3 hours while digesting the food. Therefore, if you eat often (every two or three hours) you ensure a continually stimulated basal metabolic rate. This also explains why we can eat more food if we break it down into smaller amounts and eat more often.

The other way to increase your metabolic rate is through aerobic exercise. Aerobic exercise stimulates muscle growth. Aerobic means "with oxygen." By forcing oxygen through the body, aerobic exercise increases the size and number of blood vessels. Your blood vessels carry oxygen and nutrients to the body tissues and remove waste products as well. Muscle size and development is limited to the size and quantity of the supply routes (or blood vessels). Muscle is metabolically active (meaning it burns fat and calories at an accelerated speed). You will develop lean muscle mass through aerobic exercise. If you incorporate weight training into your workout (say two times a week), you will develop even more lean muscle mass (which will enable you to burn fat and calories at an accelerated speed), and also help prevent osteoporosis (by increasing your bone density). The key to weight (or fat) loss is to increase your basal metabolic rate through frequent small low-fat meals and aerobic (using large muscles in a rhythmic motion for at least 35 minutes) and anaerobic (weight training) exercise on a regular basis! Good Luck!

YOU: I work out all the time and have really enjoyed your cookbook, because it's real food. I have had some trouble with my deltoid muscles. When I do certain shoulder routines, my right shoulder "feels like" it is tearing inside. Is it possible that I might have a rotator cuff injury or do you think I am doing the exercise wrong? I've worked out for years and am in really good shape. I am 42 years old and played football all through high school. I've lifted weights on a regular basis for the past two years. I haven't been to the doctor about it yet, but thought I might just ask your opinion since I was writing to you anyway. Thanks for all the great recipes. I'm single and don't cook much, but you have made it easy for me with your shopping tips and restaurant guide.
—D.R. Lansing, Michigan

ME: Although I am not an authority on the subject, it sounds like you might have simply overstressed your shoulder joint. The shoulder is an extremely versatile joint, but because of it's flexibility, can be highly susceptible to trauma. The rotator cuff consists of four muscles that cover the anterior and posterior portion of the shoulder blade and are found beneath the deltoid (shoulder) muscle. Weight training can cause injury if you are pressing or lifting extremely heavy weights. As a matter of fact, swimming, playing golf, tennis, or even walking with hand weights can result in tearing those muscles. In other words, it doesn't take much to injure the rotator cuff muscles. I would suggest a decrease in activity (in this area), ice application, and possibly some kind of anti-inflammatory medication. ALL OF THIS WOULD DEPEND ON THE OPINION OF YOUR PHYSICIAN. I would have it checked out immediately. If you do have a tear or injury, continuing to exercise will only increase the possibility of permanent damage. It's not worth the risk! You mentioned that you played football for many years. Were you the quarterback by any chance? Maybe you have an old injury that has been irritated by increased use. If your physician gives you the OK to continue with weight training, there are a couple of exercises that might help to strengthen the rotator cuff muscles. The first is called the External Rotation Strengthener: lie on your side with one arm tucked under your head and the other arm at a 90 degree angle with the elbow resting on your hip bone. While holding a one or two pound weight, slowly move your hand upward as high as you can go without moving your elbow away from your side. Do this 15 times with each arm. The other exercise is called the Supine Hand Stretch: lie face up on a bed or bench and let one arm simply hang down holding a light weight (one or two pounds). Be sure the surface you are lying on is tall enough that your extended arm doesn't touch the ground. While keeping your arm somewhat straight stretch the arm forward and hold it for about 20 seconds. Next stretch it back and hold that position about 20 seconds. Repeat the stretch about five times in each position and then switch arms. I'm sure your physician can give you other ideas and suggestions regarding strengthening those muscles. Good luck!

YOU: My wife has bought your book and changed my opinion of low-fat food. I can't believe how good it tastes! She didn't tell me for about a month. She just started cooking out of your book every night and didn't say a word. I asked her why she was cooking all new recipes, but she just said she wanted to try some new things. She didn't mention they were low-fat and I sure couldn't tell. All I know is it tasted great and I started losing weight. After I lost about seven pounds, I became a little curious. I mentioned the weight loss and she started laughing. I wanted to know what was so funny. After much coaxing she told me the "big secret." I think she was afraid to tell me because she thought that I wouldn't like the food anymore once I knew it was low-fat. Instead I was so excited to find out the great food she had been serving was actually helping me to lose weight and I wasn't even on a diet!

Now, about my question. Since I have started losing weight, I feel it is time to start some kind of exercise. I know about aerobic exercise and how it burns body fat. I read the section on exercise in your book. I am an attorney and my job involves long working hours. I try to go to the gym during lunch to work out. By the time I get home it is usually quite late, and I want to spend time with my wife. I can only go to the gym three times a week. What do you recommend as far as weight training is concerned? If I do aerobics about 45 minutes, that leaves me with 45 minutes in the weight room. I don't want to get "huge," but would like to have a nice physique. Can you give me a simple routine that might help and be easy to follow. The guys working at the gym are pretty intimidating. I'd rather figure it out on my own. Thanks for any help you might offer!
—J.K. Woodland Hills, California

ME: I'm so glad you are enjoying the recipes. I've found most people love low-fat food if they don't know the difference. There are so many great low-fat products on the market now, that it really is easy to prepare most anything low-fat and still taste good. As far as weight training goes this is what I would suggest: I recommend that you split it up so you train your upper body on Monday and Friday, and lower body on Wednesday the first week. The next week, train your lower body on Monday and Friday and upper body on Wednesday. This will help keep a good balance of all body parts. If your goal is to gain nice shape (without getting huge), I would suggest 10 to 12 reps of each exercise. Choose two exercises per body part and do three sets of each for a total of six sets a body part. For legs, try squats, leg presses and leg extensions. You might go to the bookstore and check out the many books and manuals on weight training. I know what you mean about the people at the gym being intimidating. A friend of mine, Larry North, has a great book out called *GET FIT*. It can be found in most bookstores, but if you can't find it write to Larry at: North Bodies Gym, #30 Highland Park Village, Suite 110, Dallas, Texas 75205. His book is very easy to understand and a great way to learn the mechanics of weight training on your own.

YOU: I just love your cookbook. I had my first child last year and have not been able to get those last ten pounds off. I am hoping to be successful by using your book. The food part is easy. I have had a hard time trying to find an hour to exercise. My husband works 14 hours a day and I don't have anyone to watch my son while I exercise. How did you do it with three small children? I don't have a lot of money to join a health club or buy expensive equipment. I live in an apartment so I don't have much room to follow an exercise video tape in front of the T.V. The only time I have for exercise is when my son naps in the afternoon, but I can't leave the apartment. Do you have any ideas that don't cost much, but will give me results? I am a pear-shaped person. In other words, I am bottom heavy. I've read that it is more healthy to carry your extra weight in your hips and thighs (rather than your stomach), but it doesn't look too great in stretch pants! Please help me get started with some kind of exercise program. Any suggestions would be great!
—G.M. Jackson, Mississippi

ME: I'm so glad you are enjoying the book. I know what you mean about finding the time. When my kids were really small I traded out with a friend. I watched her kids while she exercised and she watched mine while I exercised. It worked pretty well unless one of us was sick, one of our kids was sick, or we had other plans. Unfortunately, this was the case more times than not. That routine didn't work as well as we thought it would when we began. For that reason I did eventually join a health club that had a nursery. It was a birthday gift from my husband one year and it was the best thing he could have ever given me. It got me out of the house and around other moms with small children. I found the adult conversation quite stimulating. The health club became my emotional as well as physical outlet for stress. Anyone with small children understands the word STRESS!!

However, I do have another suggestion. I recommend you invest in a step aerobics bench. You can purchase them in discount stores (such as Target or K-Mart) as well as fitness or sports stores. Some benches come with a video tape. The reason I am suggesting a bench or step is because it doesn't take much room to get an excellent workout. The bench lets you move in a vertical space in your living room in front of the T.V., so you need less space than you would following a traditional aerobic exercise video. It is an excellent muscle firming workout for the buttocks, thighs, and calves. As you step on and off the bench, you work at an intensity similar to running or high-impact aerobics, but with little or no impact. It should be easier on your joints. YOU SHOULD ALWAYS CHECK WITH YOUR PHYSICIAN BEFORE STARTING THIS OR ANY OTHER FORM OF EXERCISE! Providing you don't have any knee problems, the bench might be a great investment for you. If you do decide to invest in a bench, I would like to offer some suggestions:

1. Keep your eyes on the bench. It is fairly easy to catch your foot on the bench by misjudging where you place your feet (especially towards the end of your workout when you are getting tired).

2. Know your training heart rate range. Take your pulse two or three times during the workout, or wear a pulse monitor. Slow down if your heart rate gets too high. Continue the steps, by doing them on the floor to the side of your bench until your heart rate is where it should be for your age and fitness level.

3. Wear aerobic dance shoes, cross trainers, or tennis shoes. DO NOT WEAR RUNNING SHOES! THEY HAVE A TREAD DESIGN ON THE BOTTOM THAT MIGHT CATCH ON THE BENCH.

4. Be sure and place your whole foot on the bench, not just your toes or the ball of your foot. Otherwise your calves will be extremely sore the next day.

5. Choose music that is 122 beats per minute or less. If your music is too fast, your chances of stumbling or tripping on your bench increases. To determine the average beats per minute of a song, count the main beat for 15 seconds and multiply by four.

6. If you choose to use hand weights during your bench workout BE SURE AND USE HALF SPEED WITH YOUR WEIGHTS. Do not try to keep the exact beat of the music with your hand weights. Never use over 5 pound weights, and I would recommend 1-3 pounds when you are first getting started. I don't use hand weights myself, but some people insist on doing so. My only advice is to PLEASE be careful, work through a full range of motion, and go SLOWLY!!

I hope this helps. Bench stepping can be quite effective in reducing and toning the lower body (especially the upper legs and bottom).

Bench aerobics are fun, challenging, easy to do at home (in a limited space), inexpensive, and most definitely a "STEP" in the right direction!!

Madearis Studio ©

YOU: I've read the best time to exercise is first thing in the morning before breakfast to ensure maximum fat loss (regarding aerobic exercise). Is this also true of weight training? That is wonderful for those who have the time in the morning, but I don't. My work day begins at 6:00 A.M. I am a male nurse and I have a very stressful job. There USED to be all kinds of high-fat snacks at the nurse's station to tempt me and I had a hard time not eating all the junk (especially during a stressful day). That is, until a good friend bought me your book. I can't tell you what an impact it has made on all of us at work. My shift now eats and breathes the words of *BUTTER BUSTERS!* We

take turns bringing your recipes to share with each other at work. As a result of your book, we are all looking leaner and feeling better. Back to the exercise dilemma. I can't exercise until 3:30 or 4:00 P.M. when I get home from work. Will this really affect my fat loss? Thanks for your dedication with the book and teaching all of us how easy it can be to eat low-fat!
—G.S. Houston, Texas

ME: I'm so happy to hear you are enjoying the book and have shared it with your friends at work. My husband is a physician and I have heard stories about the abundance of food sitting around the nurse's stations in most hospitals. Mike doesn't have a lot of will-power when it comes to sweets, so he generally avoids the doctor's lounge and nurse's stations (if at all possible). You are smart to bring low-fat snacks to enjoy at work. We all tend to eat when under stress, and I KNOW the kind of stress you face in your job. Some experts feel aerobic exercise first thing in the morning when your glycogen stores are depleted (due to your overnight fast) is the best time for maximum fat loss. Please realize this is only a theory. Weight training is a different story. The most important thing to consider in weight training is regularity. The time or hour of day makes no difference. Since the body adjusts itself naturally to the day's changes, constant repetition of the same training time will provide your body with a mechanical and physiological expectancy that will give you the physical gains you are seeking in your weight program. In other words, your answer would be the same hour of the day is best (no matter what time that might be). Our bodies are amazing. They really will adjust to our schedules if we give them a chance. As far as aerobic exercise is concerned, it will help to do your aerobic exercise on a relatively empty stomach. I do not recommend doing aerobic exercise right after you have eaten a large meal. Your body is working hard enough digesting what you just fed it. Besides, if you exercise aerobically right after a meal, you aren't going to feel very good afterwards. I know because I have tried it. If you do your aerobics around 4:00 in the afternoon, chances are your glycogen stores will be depleted (especially if you ate lunch around 11:00). If your work day starts at six, there is a good chance you eat an early lunch. My advice is to exercise the SAME TIME OF DAY and don't be too concerned what time that might be.

YOU: I have been eating low-fat since my Mom bought me your book last Christmas. It was the best gift she could have ever given me. It kind of pissed me off when I opened it, because I thought she was hinting that I needed to lose a few pounds. Even though she never said anything, I knew it bothered her that I was about twenty pounds overweight. I took the book home and put it on the shelf in my kitchen. I continued eating the same high-fat way trying to cut calories to lose some weight instead. I knew I could lose weight if I didn't eat much. I had done it before and it always worked. The only problem was I could only stand it about one week before I pigged out and ate everything in sight (after depriving myself of food). Towards the end of January (still twenty pounds overweight) I pulled down your book to look over one night when I was depressed about my weight. I stayed up until 4:00 A.M. reading. Your story was so interesting and I found out this book was a whole lot more than some kind of diet cookbook! After looking at the recipes, I found you had included all my favorites. I noticed how you changed regular food to low-fat with all kinds of substitutions. It all looked great, but I couldn't help but wonder if there was any way they could really taste good, too. The next day I went to the store and bought some of the basic low-fat products you suggested in the shopping guide. You had even done the foot work and checked out all the good stuff for me. I went home and started cooking. I don't even like to cook, but this was a new challenge and I wanted to give it a try. I made the "Mexican Layered Dip" and tried it with some of those low-fat tortilla chips you recommended. I couldn't believe my taste buds. It was delicious!! I even took the leftovers to work the next day to share with my friends. They couldn't believe it was low-fat. Everyone in my building now owns your book! Anyway, to make a long story short, your book changed my life. Not only have I lost twenty pounds without dieting, I'm now even considering starting to exercise. That is why I am writing you. I've never been able to stick with exercise. Do you have any tricks of the trade that might get me motivated? By the way, It took me a while to admit to my Mom that your book was the key to my weight loss. Somehow when you leave home and try to "MAKE IT" on your own, it's really hard to admit that your Mom might know more than you do about anything! Do you know what I mean?   —L.N.

ME: I know what you mean about admitting you don't know as much as you thought you did. It happens to me all the time. It takes a lot to admit you have made a mistake, and I applaud you for your honesty! As far as exercise is concerned, I will try to help you with some suggestions that keep me motivated. It takes about six weeks for exercise to really become a habit. I know, six weeks sounds like a long time! If you have been a couch potato for quite a while, six weeks might sound like an eternity. Trust me, it will become a habit, and once it does, you will have a hard time going back to your old sedentary ways. Why, you ask? Because you are going to feel so much better, have a ton more energy, and be giving yourself the gift of improved health. I think you will find it well worth the effort.

The hard part is getting started. Make a list of potential reasons why you might skip exercise. For example, how can you fit exercise into your lunch hour? You could bring your lunch, go for a walk and eat at the park. You could always stop by the deli (on the way back from your walk) and grab a turkey breast sandwich to eat at your desk when you return to work. Another good motivator is to find a role model. Do you have a friend or someone you know who always seems to fit exercise into their day? Ask them how they have managed to succeed with their exercise program. Wear headphones when you walk or work out. This really helps me. I can do the treadmill or stair climber for 45 minutes if I am listening to music. Without my music, I can't stay on those machines five minutes! If you don't like music, try listening to a novel on tape. It will hold your interest and motivate you to keep going. Set your exercise bag by the front door the night before you want to exercise. This way you won't forget to take it to work. Most folks find they have better luck sticking with an exercise program if they go straight from work, rather than going home first to change clothes. They can always find something else to do around the house and usually have a hard time making themselves go out to exercise, once they have come home and "gotten comfortable." Make appointments to exercise with a friend. This will usually encourage you to show up because you don't want to disappoint your friend (or let them down). Try different forms of exercise (better known as cross training). This simply means participating in a different kind of activity every time you work out. Not only will it cut down on boredom, it will help prevent the overuse of various muscles (which could lead to possible injury). Some aerobic exercise ideas would be walking, running, swimming, stairclimbing, bicycling (outside or inside on a stationary bike), hiking, aerobic dancing, or bench stepping. These are just a few aerobic suggestions. I also encourage you to incorporate some kind of light weight routine into your program once or twice a week. This will help build lean muscles mass which, in turn, enables you to eat a lot more food. The possibilities of exercise are endless. Don't push yourself too hard. Exercise should be challenging, but if it is too hard, chances are you won't continue. Choose activities you enjoy. If you like to read as you exercise, choose the stairclimber or stationary bicycle and you will have better luck sticking with your program. Make up a reward system to work towards. Promise yourself a treat if you stick with your program for so many days. "Treat suggestions" would be things such as a new outfit, a book, a C.D., a weekend trip, a movie, or anything YOU truly enjoy and consider "a treat." If you are the kind of person that needs to write down your accomplishments, then by all means do so. Keep a log of hours that you exercise. The visual reminder of your accomplishments will make you feel good about yourself for exercising so many times, and help keep you motivated to continue (especially when you start seeing results)! Read everything you can get your hands on regarding exercise and fitness. The more knowledgeable you become, the more you realize (by incorporating exercise into your life), you are taking an active interest towards improving your health.

Most of all, have a positive attitude. Use self-talk to motivate yourself. Repeat things like, "I'm living a healthy lifestyle because I eat low-fat and walk three times a week at lunchtime." You might feel silly repeating this over and over to yourself (especially if you haven't reached your goal). You might even feel like you are lying to yourself, but that is OK. As long as your statement is a believable and attainable goal, you might start "doing" what you "keep saying" to yourself! I wish you luck and continued success!!

YOU: I am so excited about *BUTTER BUSTERS*! Several of us at church have purchased your wonderful book, and are having a blast making the recipes. We have a ladies group that meets every Wednesday to learn how to take care of our bodies (through exercise) and how to cook and prepare healthy foods. There are a number of us that have struggled with the same up and down yo-yo system of weight loss over a period of years. There is one lady in particular who really doesn't need to lose weight, so she told us she wasn't interested in low-fat eating or cooking. She says she has no need to exercise because she isn't overweight and exercise is only for people trying to lose weight. I don't know a lot about diet, but I have read that many diseases are diet related. I really care about my friend, and feel she could benefit from low-fat eating for the sake of her health. Her Mom died of heart disease at the age of 53, and she has no idea what her cholesterol is. For this reason, I would think some kind of aerobic exercise would be beneficial for her own heart health. Do you agree? She thinks just because she is thin, she is healthy. Do you have any information I might share to get her interested in healthy cooking, eating, and exercise? I'd like to order your workbook and video series for our ladies Wednesday group. Can we purchase one set of videos and several copies of the workbook so we can each have our own copy? I hope to hear from you soon because we are most anxious to get started! We have all purchased your cookbook and love everything we have tried so far! Thanks for your research and dedication in helping Americans learn the importance of eating to live, rather than living to eat!
—*S.W. Springfield, Illinois*

ME: I am so glad your ladies group is using the book and enjoying the recipes. I spoke at my church a few weeks ago to a group of women, and was surprised to find so many tend to be compulsive overeaters (myself included). I've found most Christian women will not succumb to drug or alcohol addiction for religious reasons, but will medicate their problems and emotions through the mis-use of food. We should realize that our bodies (and the way we take care of them) is a wonderful way to honor and thank God for what He has blessed each one of us with. The human body is a miraculous thing, and it will take care of us for many years (in most cases), providing we nourish and treat it in a healthy way. I do have some information regarding diet and exercise (and how it affects our health) you might want to share with your friend. Every day more and more diseases are being linked to "poor diet" and "lack of exercise." In 1992, the American Heart Association added "physical inactivity" to their list of risk factors for heart disease. They found that exercise not only helps keep heart disease at bay, but can also improve the long-term survival rate of people who have already had a heart attack. Even modest exercise can have a beneficial and cumulative protective effect on our health. The other heart disease risks are smoking, high blood pressure, and high cholesterol. Does your friend suffer from any of these disorders or unhealthy habits (such as smoking)?

Research has shown that exercise helps boost blood levels of high density lipoproteins (the good cholesterol) in our blood. In a three year study which included 500 women (women's HDL levels usually drop after menopause due to lack of estrogen) it was noted that women who quit exercising with age boosted their risk of heart disease by 9%. The risks for the women who remained active (exercising the equivalent of three one -mile walks per week) rose only 3% (and that could have been a result of genetic factors). It has been proven that moderate to vigorous exercise is great for lowering blood pressure (IN MOST CASES). Many individuals with mild hypertension may not require medication if they exercise on a regular basis. HOWEVER, YOU SHOULD ALWAYS CHECK WITH YOUR PHYSICIAN FIRST, BEFORE STARTING ANY KIND OF EXERCISE PROGRAM!

The risk factor for adult-onset diabetes is usually reduced with exercise. A recent study showed that women who exercised at least once a week had one-third less risk of adult-onset diabetes than sedentary women or those who exercised less than once a week. Men who burned at least 2,000 calories a week exercising had 24% less risk than inactive men. Although exercise alone is not the answer for such a complex disease, you might have a better chance at good health by avoiding a sedentary lifestyle as you grow older. The risk of colon cancer doubles for inactive people. A Harvard study of more than 17,000 men between the ages of 30-79 showed exercise helped prevent colon cancer by speeding food through their digestive systems, giving carcinogens (cancer causing substances that may increase the formation of free radicals) less of a chance to contact colon linings. Weight loss (resulting from regular exercise) may lessen the risk of arthritis. Exercise increases the range of motion and reduces the pain of arthritic joints.

I honestly feel exercise is a wonderful way to ensure better health for everyone. Most people can handle the low-fat eating, but many have a really hard time working exercise into their day. I say the benefit is well worth the effort!! I wish you continued success with your group, and especially your friend. She doesn't realize how lucky she is to have a "real" concerned friend like you! I'll have my business manager, Mike McWithey, contact you regarding the video series and workbooks. Please stay in touch and let me know how your friend takes the suggestions!

YOU: After becoming a "gum addict"a little over a year ago I was thrilled to receive your *BUTTER BUSTERS COOKBOOK* as a Christmas gift. I've been interested in counting fat grams and cooking low-fat for sometime. I feel your cookbook can be a great help to people just beginning to cook low-fat, as well as veterans (like myself). I really am thrilled about my introduction of the mix to make Liquid Butter Buds. It is great!

I think that you offer valuable information concerning diet and exercise. However, I do have a concern about a comment you made in the exercise section. After my daily workouts I am, more often than not, very tired and sore. Soreness is good.....it shows hard work and accomplishment. Your muscles should be tired and soreness takes time to appear, sometimes days! I'm afraid that saying you should not be exhausted or really sore is just the excuse the average person is looking for to curtail their exercise program. Pain is another thing-one needs to know the difference! Thanks for listening and a reply would be appreciated.   —*B.C. Chesapeake, Virginia*

ME: I'm glad you are enjoying the book. As far as your questions concerning exercise and soreness, I will try to explain myself. In the book I stated, "You should not be exhausted, or you are over-doing it. If you are sore from your activity TWO DAYS later, you have overdone it. Aches and pains from exercise that don't go away are warning signals that you shouldn't ignore. If you continue exercising when you have pain in a particular area, you are more apt to really injure yourself further." As you can see, I did not say that you shouldn't be sore. I said if you are sore two days later, you might have overdone it. As far as being exhausted, there are different degrees of exhaustion. I agree that many people find all kinds of reasons "not" to exercise, and obviously I feel exercise is very important. I only felt the need to warn people about overdoing it, because this can be a problem, too! I know, because I have done it myself. If you continue to exercise when you have a stress fracture or a torn muscle, you are looking for trouble. That was the point I was trying to make. Many bodybuilders welcome a slight soreness as a sign they have worked their muscles hard (like you say has happened to you). However, a very deep and severe soreness probably means that you did too much and you should take it easy and give your body a chance to heal. I would like to site an example: Before 1985, my aerobic exercise consisted of swimming. When my son Tyler was eight months old, my husband gave me a membership to a women's health club called Cosmopolitan Lady. I started taking aerobics classes for the first time in my life. I found the dancing and music really appealed to me. In November 1985 high impact aerobics was in full swing. The classes consisted of about 35 minutes of aerobics and 20 minutes of toning or what they called "contour." After 3-4 weeks of classes my back started bothering me. I just attributed it to doing something new and kept going to class every day. In the contour part of the class we did a lot of sit-ups. The instructors were very good and always explained the safety measures as we performed the exercises. Sit-ups actually help to strengthen the back, so, even though my back was sore, I continued doing the sit-ups thinking it would get better. Because I was new to this kind of exercise, I must have strained a muscle in my back doing sit-ups (even though I was doing them correctly).

The first week of December 1985 is one I will never forget. I woke up one day, and could not get out of bed. My husband is an orthopedic surgeon and, after examining me, said I must have strained my back and should take it easy. About two days later, it felt better so I went back to class. It just hurt a little during sit-ups so I didn't do the full amount. To make a long story short, my back went into spasms a day later, I spent two weeks flat on my back with ice, I had physical therapy, and before all this happened, I had to be carried out of The Tandy Center in Ft. Worth on a stretcher, because my back went into spasms during my kid's ice skating lesson. I'll never forget the pain or humiliation. Blake was nine and Paige was four and they still talk about Mom being carried out of the Tandy Center on a stretcher. My point is that I had overdone it, ignored the fact, and ended up really injuring myself. That is why I feel it necessary to warn people of over-use and over-training. Later that year I suffered from a stress fracture in the ball of my foot (from high-impact aerobics). I continued with the classes ignoring the pain until I could no longer walk. My husband x-rayed me and found the stress fracture. Did that stop me? No! I continued with the classes wearing a pad in my shoe against my husband's advice. It finally got so bad I was forced to give up high impact aerobics forever. Thank goodness low-impact aerobics became popular about that same time. If you have pain in an area, please get it checked out. A little soreness is normal, but severe pain is not!! I hope you can understand WHY I feel this way.

YOU: I started using your book about two months ago and love everything that I have made so far. I exercise by walking on a treadmill for 30-45 minutes a day. Is this enough exercise a day, or should I do more? Can you explain what the Body Mass Index is? I don't really understand what it means. I love to listen to music when I exercise. Where do you get your aerobic tapes? I read in your book that you like to exercise to music, too. Can you tell me a good moderate priced walking shoe? Mine are worn out and I need to buy a new pair. How often should you buy new walking shoes, anyway? I've thought about buying another kind of exercise machine. Would you recommend a stair climber or stationary bicycle? I've lost about 15 pounds in the last two months (by using your book and walking), but can't seem to lose any more no matter what I do or what I eat. Do you know why? I'm usually in a rush and don't take the time to warm-up or cool-down. Is it really all that important? I never stretch. Is that bad? I know I have asked a lot of questions, but I need some answers. Since most of this is new to me, I just want to do the right thing. My kids love your "Orange Slice Candy Cookies" and "Cream Cheese Cake Bars." My husband loves your "Quick Spicy Chile." He even made it for a chile cook-off and won first prize in the "healthy division." No one believed it was low-fat. I hope you plan to write more books. I'll be first in line when you do! Thanks for your time in answering my questions. I know you are busy!
—C.H. Akron, Ohio

ME: I am so glad you are enjoying the book and it looks like it is working since you have lost 15 pounds in two months. That is wonderful! Walking on the treadmill is a great form of aerobic exercise. I would recommend a five minute warm-up and stretch, and a five minute cool-down and stretch. People often skip the warm-up due to lack of time. This mistake could lead to an injury that might keep you out of commission for several days. Take a few minutes to warm-up and stretch to avoid soreness and increase flexibility. Rent or purchase an exercise tape that demonstrates effective warm-ups, stretches, and cool downs. Learn a few and use them. If you fail to cool down gradually, your blood pressure may drop significantly (due to the abrupt change from vigorous aerobic exercise). This could lead to irregular heart beats or even fainting. Slow down gradually (never abruptly) by walking around for three to five minutes or until your heart rate decreases dramatically. Stretching is best performed after your muscles are warm. Although stretching helps with flexibility, most of your flexibility is genetically related. All of your bones are held together by ligaments. This helps determine your flexibility. If your ligaments stretch easily, you probably have flexible joints. Another factor involves how well your connective tissue (or fascia) binds the bone to the muscle, ligaments, and tendons, and surrounds each muscle (like a whole-body web) that is held together by collagens. Collagens are the body's tough insoluble proteins. As our connective tissue ages and is subject to wear and tear, the collagens lose some of their stabilizing qualities. If calcium deposits and adhesions develop, the supply of water decreases. All these changes can result in decreased flexibility. Stretching delays this loss (by stimulating the production of lubricants between the connective tissue fibers), thus preventing the formation of adhesions. Active isolated stretching increases the blood and oxygen flow that generates and provides muscles and facia (connective tissue) with the essential nutrients, keeping them fresh and supple. While stretching, hold the stretch at least 15 seconds. Stretch all the major muscle groups used during your exercise session. Be sure and stretch through a full range of motion. Un-stretched muscles tend to cramp up easily and might appear more bulky. Stretching may help prevent soreness. As you can see, stretching is important.

You mentioned you can't seem to lose more than 15 pounds. Are you sure you are still overweight? There are many ways to determine this without ever stepping on a scale. Since you asked about Body Mass Index (BMI) I will explain this and it may help answer your other question. The BMI is the most effective way to determine your ideal weight. This is how to figure yours: take a calculator and multiply your desired weight (or the weight you wish to maintain) in pounds times 700; divide the result by your height in inches; finally divide by your height again. I'll use myself as an example to make it easier to understand. I weigh 120 pounds. 120 X 700= 84000. 84000 divided by 67 inches (I am 5'7") = 1253.73. 1253.73 divided by 67 inches again =18.71. I am forty-five years old. This number would fall within the acceptable range. The acceptable BMI ranges are 18-24 for women younger than 35 years and 21-26 thereafter. For men the desirable body mass ranges from 20 to 25. Above 29 is considered obese and above 40 is extremely obese. Once the BMI gets up to 28, experts say, there is an increased risk of obesity-related health problems like diabetes and high blood pressure. If your BMI is higher than the norm, you should consider losing a few pounds. Refer to page 74 in the "Food and Nutrition" chapter for more information concerning the Body Mass Index in pregnancy.

Another way to determine if you are overweight (and probably at risk regarding heart disease), is to measure your waist-to-hip ratio. The waist-to-hip ratio determines if you are an apple (less healthy) or pear shaped (more healthy) body type. Apple shaped persons (who carry excess weight around their abdomen, have a higher waist-to-hip ratio (which is associated with high blood pressure and increased risk for developing adult-onset diabetes and heart disease). Take a tape measure and measure your waist. Next, measure your hips at their widest point. Divide your waist measurement by your hip measurement. The healthiest ratios are below .80 -.85 for a woman and under .95 for a man. I will use myself as an example. My waist is 24 inches. My hips are 35 inches. Divide 24 by 35=.68. I am in the healthy range. My daughter, Paige, drew this picture as an example and I used it in my *BUTTER BUSTERS GUIDEBOOK*. I've included it here to explain the waist to hip ratio.

WHAT KIND OF SHAPE IS YOUR BODY REALLY IN?

You might not like the way your pear shaped body looks in a bathing suit, but scientific evidence has shown that **YOUR RISK OF HEART DISEASE DECREASES IF YOU HAPPEN TO CARRY YOUR WEIGHT IN YOUR HIPS AND THIGHS.** The people that resemble the apple, unfortunately, have a lot more to be concerned with. It has been shown if you carry the majority of your weight in your abdomen, your risk of heart disease is greatly increased. We can't change the way our bodies are built, because that has to do with heredity and genes, but we can engage in aerobic activity on a regular basis, helping to reduce our total body fat percentage, and therefore reduce our risk of heart disease tremendously!!!

**Paige with her drawing
July 1993**

"ORANGE" you glad to hear this? No pun intended!! Women with a ratio above 1.0 and men with a ratio above 1.1 are extremely apple shaped and should take steps to trim their waistlines.

Another way to determine if you are overweight is by having your body fat tested. There are several methods. The most accurate is the hydrostatic, or underwater weighing, method. Unfortunately, it is also the most expensive. Other methods include skin-fold calipers (used by pinching excess skin at different sites on the body), electrical currents or infrared rays, sonograms, etc., etc. The list goes on and on. For more information regarding body fat testing check with your health club, the Y.M.C.A., local gym, doctor's office, clinic, or hospital. Your body fat will most likely help determine if you are REALLY overweight or just over-fat. Do you see yourself as others see you? I ask you this, because even though I am of normal weight, I used to see myself as a size 11-13 even after I lost weight and was a size 5-7. Many people feel fat when in fact they really aren't. If you feel fat, but others say you look great, then you probably aren't overweight. You can always tone and tighten your body with continued aerobic exercise and weight training. You will continue to lose body fat if you stick with your program. Refer to page 180 in this section regarding body fat testing methods.

You might try switching aerobic activities. You mentioned buying another piece of equipment. That is why cross-training is so popular. Not only does it help relieve boredom, it also taxes different muscles. If you feel that you are at a plateau (in your weight loss), a change of aerobic activity might just be your answer. The stationary bicycle is great if you enjoy reading or watching T.V. while exercising. It is also a good choice if you have a knee problem (in some cases). Before my Mom had knee replacement surgery, the exercise bike was the only form of aerobic exercise she could handle. I personally own a recumbent Lifecycle 5500R stationary bicycle. It has a back rest and you sit on the same level as your legs (rather than higher as on most stationary bicycles). It is very comfortable (because you don't lean over) and easy on the back (great for those with back problems). It is also a good alternative if you happen to suffer from Morton's Neuroma (pinched nerves in the feet) because it doesn't cause additional stress to your feet (like a treadmill or stairmaster). I also own a Stairmaster. It is my favorite piece of equipment. I can read while working out and I reach my target heart rate zone in about five minutes after I begin exercising. I can only do the Stairmaster while listening to music. Many people find the Stairmaster quite difficult and I would agree if I didn't have my music. Without my headphones, I can't do the Stairmaster five minutes. With music, I can exercise on the Stairmaster forty-five minutes to one hour. The only problem is I do happen to have Morton's Neuromas (pinched nerves in my feet), so the Stairmaster is quite uncomfortable after twenty minutes. I am getting ready to have foot surgery in the near future. This should take care of my problem. Prices range for both pieces of equipment. When you asked me what kind of machines I recommend, that is kind of hard to answer. My advice would be to go to a gym or local YMCA and try both pieces of equipment to decide which one you enjoy most. Since you already have a treadmill, you might consider the stationary bicycle to give you a sitting down way to exercise. REMEMBER TO ALWAYS CHECK WITH YOUR PHYSICIAN BEFORE STARTING ANY NEW EXERCISE PROGRAM!

I mentioned listening to music and you had asked me about it. I order my aerobic tapes through the mail. I order from two companies. I like Power Productions (800)777-BEAT and Aerobics Music Inc. (800)748-6372.

Before you choose a walking shoe there are a few factors to keep in mind. Your foot shape and walking gait are the most important. Next time you step out of the shower, note the shape left by your wet foot on the bath mat. If your whole foot shows, you have a low arch. If only the outer trace remains, you have a higher arch. Also check your old walking shoes for signs of overpronating (when feet roll inward) or oversupinating (when feet roll outward). If you are an overpronator, your shoes will be worn down on the inner edges, and you will be more susceptible to shin splints and knee pain. To avoid both problems, select walking shoes with a cradled midsole and a firm heel fit. If you are an oversupinator, your feet lean outward when they hit the ground, resulting in less shock absorption and shoes worn down on the outer edge. To avoid stress fractures, choose shoes with solid cushioning, rear foot stability, and firm midsoles. I will give you a few suggestions in three different categories.

For low-mileage walkers (three times a week under two miles) some choices would be Asics Aero Gait ($55.00), Rockport W7450 ($60.00), and LA Gear Eureka Tech ($64.99). For high-mileage walkers (walking 45 minutes to one hour every day at 3.0-4.5 mph) I would recommend the Avia 384 ($70.00), Reebok Inspiration ($74.99), K-Swiss Bria ($69.99), Ariel Walker by Avia ($70.00), or the NaturalSport Eclipse ($70.00). For run-walkers (for someone that walks a mile, runs a mile or two, and then walks another mile) you might check out the Ryka 560 ($59.95), Brooks Destiny ($49.95), New Balance WW590 ($70.00), Nike Air Speed RW ($70.00), and Saucony G.R.I.D. Jazz Step ($59.95). Your shoe life depends on many factors. Your weight, walking style, and walking surface all need to be considered. One walker's shoes might last three months, while another's may last six months. Wear is not always visible. The first thing to go is the cushioning ability of the midsole. If you feel unusual pain or discomfort in your feet, legs, knees, back (or your feet start to develop blisters or callouses) you should probably consider buying new shoes. When your shoes feel flat, no longer provide cushioning, or the edge of the outsole wears through the heel it's probably time to head for the shoe store. I hope this answered your questions.

YOU: I must tell you that I have never written to an author before, but felt the need to let you know what an impact your book has had on my wife. She has been very overweight since the birth of our third child. I hated to nag her about the weight, because she really did try. She has always watched what she ate and exercised when she had the chance (which isn't often with three small children) but still continued to fight her weight problem. It's not like she sits around eating Bon Bons! She was always concerned with calories, and after reading your book, we both feel that was probably her main problem. She cut way back on calories to lose weight, always felt deprived, and had a terrible self-image (especially after the last baby). Then everything changed. Her mother gave her *BUTTER BUSTERS* for her 40th Birthday. Not only are we all eating great food (even the kids like the recipes), my wife and I are both losing weight. She has lost 16 pounds and I have lost 12. This has happened in less than seven weeks. Not only has my wife lost weight, but her whole attitude about life has changed. She has more energy than she has had in years. I used to run for exercise, but switched to speed walking about six months ago. At first I thought it looked whimpy, but now I really don't care what people think, because I really enjoy walking and I can walk a lot further than I used to run. I'm hoping to get my wife started, too. Our only problem is having someone to watch the kids if we were to walk together. I would like to order your video series and workbook, because I understand you have an exercise and fitness video in the set. I have some questions you might be able to help me with. I developed tendonitis in both my knees about a year ago. That was the main reason I quit running. My question is will walking help my tendonitis or make it worse? It hasn't seemed to get much worse, but I just wanted your thoughts on the matter. Sometimes when I walk a really long distance my feet get really hot. I'm not just talking about a little hot, I'm talking burning! I use Vaseline to help prevent blisters but it seems to add to the problem making my feet feel like they are cooking in my shoes. Have you ever heard of anything like this before? Do you have any sugges-

tions? I might be over-doing it, but I also suffer from shin splints occasionally. Can you address these problems? Thank you so much for your time and again I owe you a giant THANK YOU!!
—M.W. Chicago, Illinois

ME: I appreciate your kind letter and really appreciate YOU for taking the time to write me. You obviously love your wife very much and are concerned with her health and welfare. That is a wonderful and refreshing thing to see, and I wish you both continued success with your weight loss and many, many more happy years together! As for your hot feet, I know what you are talking about. It only happens to me when I run in Central Park in New York. I know that sounds crazy, but that is the ONLY time I ever run. I don't like to run, but when my husband and I go to New York (which is quite often due to my book business) we enjoy running/walking in Central Park together. We have so much to look at and watch that we tend to run a lot further and longer than we would anywhere else. For that reason, my feet get really hot. I have some suggestions. Are your shoes too large by any chance? If so, the movement of your feet in your shoes could be causing the heat to build up. Always wear acrylic socks which will help draw heat and moisture away from your feet. Cotton socks tend to trap heat and moisture. Try placing disposable odor-eating charcoal insoles in your tennis shoes. Be sure and replace them daily if you are wearing the shoes every day. There is a prescription cream called Zostrix which will sooth and cool your feet. It can be used 3-4 times a day. There is also a product called Tannic acid 10% which is also known as "tough skin." It can be applied to the bottom of your feet. It toughens the skin and might reduce some of your symptoms. I found out about that product because my son, Blake, had trouble with blisters playing tennis (especially when he was in tournaments and playing several matches a day). As far as the tendonitis, walking can actually help people with tendonitis providing you walk on even ground. Since tendonitis is an inflammation of the knee, it can usually be attributed to overuse of the tendons. Walkers can lessen the stress on their tendons by avoiding hills. Walking up and down hills puts extra strain and stress on those tendons. Since there are several kinds of knee tendonitis, I would highly recommend you seek the advice of your physician. An orthopedic doctor or physical therapist can also give you suggestions on your exercise program. The doctor might prescribe an anti-inflammatory medication and a patella (knee cap) wrap to be worn during physical activity. For quick relief, you might try ice massage or a general friction massage. A physical therapist will probably suggest specific stretching and strengthening exercises to help your condition. It is treatable, but might involve a little time off or switching to another form of aerobic exercise for a short time. As far as shin splints go I have had those more times than I care to remember. It happens every time I run in New York. I think part of my problem is I don't warm up or stretch enough first. Shin splints involve pain along the front of the lower leg. Running long distances (which is what I do in New York), or walking on uneven terrain, can aggravate the problem. Your best prevention is well-fitted tennis shoes with good arch supports. Always make sure you warm-up, stretch, and cool-down properly. There is an exercise you might try to help strengthen your lower leg muscles. Secure a band or rubber tubing in a door frame or around an immovable object. Place the rubber tubing around the toes of one foot so the band is taut. Pull the toes toward your nose. Return to starting position. Repeat this exercise 10-15 times with each foot. There is one other thing you might try if you don't mind people REALLY looking at you. It's called reverse walking. Walking or running backwards has proven beneficial in assisting athletes recovering from knee injuries. It is also a good cardiovascular workout if you can keep it up long enough without running into anything. Running backwards strengthens the entire leg, especially the quadriceps which act as a stabilizer for the knee joint. It also places less stress on the knee. The only problem is you can't see where you are going! Good luck!

YOU: Your book is the greatest! Wow! I get to eat "real food" again. I was getting really sick of those diet frozen dinners! It was quick and easy, granted, but not my idea of fun. I bought myself your book one Saturday at Sam's Club when I was feeling down and out. I took it home and started reading immediately (since I didn't have a date) and didn't go to sleep until I reached the cookbook part. What an inspirational story! I could really identify with your eating patterns. It's always nice to see someone else admit they have problems, too! Well, I'm here to tell you, after losing 38 pounds, I have a new lease on life. I know the exercise was the biggest change for me and probably the main reason I've been able to lose so much weight and still eat a ton of great food. I have a couple of questions. Sometimes when I am exercising I get a terrible headache. I swear it feels like someone is hammering nails into my eye sockets. Sometimes it feels like my head is in a vice. Sometimes I even feel sick at my stomach. The other question concerns the calorie meters on exercise machines in health clubs. I work out at a health club and usually walk on the treadmill or use the stairclimber. If all of those machines are occupied I ride the stationary bicycle. My question is can you trust the calorie meters on the machines? Sometimes it says that I have burned as much as 600 calories in one hour. I just don't know if they can be trusted. What do you think? Thanks for your book. I've never been so excited about anything in a very long time. Thanks for making life worth living. I even have dates now. As a matter of fact I meet lots of guys at the health club. You have opened up a whole new world for me. You're cool!!   —J.D. Houston, Texas

ME: I loved your letter. You are a breath of fresh air. I love hearing from young people. I think it is so great that young folks are beginning to show interest in their health. Believe me, I didn't have a clue about health and fitness until I was forced to take stock of my diet and eating habits right before I turned forty and was diagnosed with a high cholesterol. I salute your interest and dedication. I think it is just wonderful and I hope you continue to enjoy your life for many, many, many more years!! As far as the headaches go that is amazing that you asked me that question. The reason it is amazing is because that has been happening to my husband, Mike, recently when he exercises. There is actually a pain known as (you guessed it) "exertion headache!!" It is brought on by physical activity. Lifting weights (which is when it hits Mike), aerobics and walking have all been known to trigger the exertional headaches. It doesn't even have to be really vigorous. There doesn't seem to be any rhyme or reason to their onset. Extreme coughing and sneezing can even cause them to crop up. I don't know if this is the kind of headache you are experiencing or not, but in case it isn't, you should probably have it checked out by your physician (especially if it happens often). Headaches, in some cases, can be warning signs of a medical condition that might require immediate attention. I don't want to scare or alarm you, but severe headaches can mean serious problems such as hidden hypertension or even an aneurysm (this is serious). If your physician is concerned he might even order a diagnostic test such as a CAT scan or an MRI to rule out anything serious. The cause of "exertional headaches" is really unknown. They were first described in medical journals and given their name in 1968. So, you can see, they have been around quite a while. My husband has had exertional headaches for a long time. I can remember him complaining of this kind of headache on really hot days when he was playing golf and usually wearing a hat. I always thought it was due to the heat or his tight fitting hat. It wasn't until recently that he experienced the headaches while working out and lifting weights. This is when I did some research on the matter and discovered there really is a name for his headaches. Some over-the-counter medications you might try taking an hour before you work out are aspirin or ibuprofen. **Please, get checked out by your physician before you take any king of medication. Do not self-prescribe. It could be dangerous to your health!!** Chances are, your physician might wish to prescribe some kind of medication to relieve the pain, but this would be up to him.

I've often wondered about the calorie meters on the exercise machines, too. Thanks for asking about that. It forced me to research the information available. This is what I found. The best thing about the calorie meters on cardio equipment is that it gives you something to watch and helps to pass the time. I've found they vary greatly depending on the manufacturer and the price tag on the equipment. For example, I usually do the Stairmaster 45 minutes. I've used three different brands and received three different calorie counts working out on the exact same level. I've even had different calorie numbers on the exact same brand of equipment used on the same level for the same amount of time. Manufacturers insist the counters are only an average of calories burned. Most commercial equipment found in health clubs is relatively accurate. However, you should be aware that some home models might be severely mis-metered. Calorie meters average caloric, or energy consumption. Don't take your calories, multiply times nine, and assume you can walk or bicycle away an equivalent amount of fat. How many calories you actually burn is related to weight, fitness level and the speed and intensity of your workout. Calorie meters simply can't factor in all of that information. For example, the calorie counter or meter on a stair-stepper reads the same whether the user leans on the hand rails or swings their arms by their side as they step. It is a proven fact that folks who lean on the rails as they step use much fewer calories. The machines that allow you to enter your weight are more accurate than those that don't factor in weight. The first 15 minutes of your aerobic workout you will be burning primarily carbohydrates for fuel. It isn't until the twenty minutes following the initial 15 minutes that your body starts burning a larger percentage of fat in comparison to carbohydrate for fuel, if you are within your target heart rate zone (according to your age and fitness level). Men tend to burn fat sooner than women (probably because they have more lean muscle mass) in most cases, and a conditioned athlete begins burning fat quicker, too (within five minutes in some cases). If you are really concerned with how many calories you burn during exercise, or anytime for that matter, you might want to check out a neat gadget called CAL-TRAC. It's a small instrument that simply clips onto your belt or waist band and worn throughout the day. It accurately (within 2%) measures the amount of calories you are burning all day long. It's not quite as easy as it sounds. I bought one myself. You have to enter in the calories you consume as well. It comes with a calorie counter, but you have to figure (by using the guide) the amount of calories of everything you put in your mouth. However, it comes with a video and can really be a helpful tool for those concerned with caloric consumption as well as calories used through exercise and basic movement. For information on CALTRAC call: (800)467-6319. Have fun and hold onto your wonderful attitude and personality. You have what it takes to succeed in whatever you choose to do with your life!

YOU: I love your wonderful cookbook and am constantly striving to teach my large family about healthy eating and exercise. With five children, ages 6 to 17 years, it's really hard to get the whole group to sit down and eat our meals at the same time. Your casseroles have been a life saver. I love making your soups and chili. I just leave them on the stove and everyone can help themselves. I love to cook myself, but unfortunately I just don't have the time to do so right now. I have a very demanding job which requires some travel and long hours. I do most of the cooking on weekends when I am home. I am lucky enough to have a full-time nanny and cook. I bought your book for our cook about eight months ago. I just go through the book every Sunday and pick out all the recipes I want her to prepare that week. It has worked out just great. We live out of your book. I don't even use anything else.

As I said, I have five children, and that is why I am writing. I am very concerned about my 14 year old daughter. I, myself, am in pretty good shape (because I have to be due to my job), but my daughter has become obsessed with working out. I have friends who tell me that I should be happy she is interested in her health instead of boys (like most of her friends). She is 5'8" and is a beautiful girl. She is slim, but not too skinny. I've noticed that she doesn't see her friends much anymore, and seems to spend every waking moment at the health club. If her brothers or sisters eat something fattening, she asks them if they know what they are putting in their body and acts like they have committed a deadly sin. I am happy she is concerned with her health, but to tell you the truth, I feel like I have created a monster. Maybe it is my fault. I have always been very concerned with my weight and appearance. I have to be for my job. I am in the entertainment business. My appearance is very important. I've always made a point of playing looks down, because we have one child with Downs Syndrome and the last thing I want is for "that child" to ever feel less than perfect. I know you are reading this letter thinking what kind of mother is this? You probably want to know why I work outside the home (with five kids) and don't stay home to be with my children. My career is very important to our income. My husband is a lawyer, but we really need my salary. OK, enough about me. Like I said, I think my daughter is obsessed with exercise. Last month she injured her knee and wouldn't stop exercising. I know she was in pain, but nothing stopped her from going to the gym. One of the personal trainers even called me and said he was concerned with her compulsive behavior. Do you have any suggestions? She is also compulsive about her food. She is hooked on sweet potatoes. She has one every night for dinner. She won't eat any meat (including chicken, turkey, or fish). Like I said, she is slim, but not too skinny. I fear she might be developing some kind of eating disorder because she only eats about six different foods. Although what she eats is healthy, I feel she needs more variety in her diet. She doesn't like dairy products, and I fear she could have problems with osteoporosis down the road. She also suffered from a stress fracture on the ball of her foot about six months ago. Could this be related to her diet? Please help me. I love my daughter very much and it is very hard to watch what is happening to her.   —(no name given, only a P.O. Box)

ME: I appreciate your frankness. It sounds like you have a very demanding job, but have a genuine love and concern for your family. Your daughter doesn't realize how lucky she is to have a Mom who REALLY CARES! I have a fifteen year old daughter myself, so I know how you are feeling. We want the best for our children, but don't want to infringe on their privacy and risk driving them away from us. I've found it difficult sometimes to "bite my tongue" and not say anything even when I felt she was making an unwise choice. I've been very fortunate because my daughter, Paige, and I get along great. We have done so since I stopped trying to tell her what to do and how to run her life. I try to set a good example myself, and hope she learns through "osmosis."

There are some symptoms of exercise addiction you might look for in your daughter's behavior. You mentioned the stress fracture. This is quite common because they won't stop working out even though they suffer from injury. You mentioned a sore knee. Tendonitis (inflammation of the elbows, knees, hips, wrists, shoulder, or ankle) is quite common with this disorder due to overuse. Has she ever skipped a period? Since she is only fourteen, she might not be that regular yet anyway, so that one might be hard to spot. Is she tired all the time? Extreme fatigue is common with exercise addicts. Does she suffer from colds, sore throat, the flu, etc., etc.? Depressed immune response is another common symptom. Has she been to the doctor for a physical lately? Anemia (low red blood cell count) is also common with this disorder (especially with her limited diet). Does she ever complain of sore joints? Premature arthritis can strike at any age. Have her arms or legs appeared swollen at any time? There is a syndrome called "compartment syndrome" which is associated with the swelling of arms or legs causing potential nerve or vascular damage. Excessive breakdown of lean muscle (due to diet and over-exercising) can cause Myoglobinuria (which could ultimately lead to kidney damage). I don't want to scare you, but there are some serious repercussions related to exercise addiction. There are four signs you might watch for as well: 1. Is exercise the number one priority in her life? (It sounds like it is to me.) 2. Does she appear to enjoy exercise, or does she just seem "driven" to continue? 3. Does she exercise despite pain, injury, bad weather, and other's advice? 4. Is exercising and food always on her mind?

Unless you are an athlete in training, there is no real benefit in exercising more than five times a week. Most exercise addicts think if they miss one workout, they have failed and sometimes work out twice as long the next day to make up for their lack of control. Excessive exercise can be dangerous to your health. Overuse injuries (caused by over-exercising the same muscle group of muscles with minimal rest), like stress fractures and sprains, are very common with exercise addicts. Women are at additional risk of developing gynecological problems like amenorrhea (discontinuing their periods) and eating disorders. Until the exercise addict admits there is a problem, there is little we can do as parents except stand by and watch. The more you pressure her to stop, the more driven she will be to continue. Maybe you could talk to one of the trainers at the health club she likes and respects. Let them be "the bad guy" and try to get through to her. Ask them to provide information about exercise addiction. Maybe if she reads some of the statistics and symptoms, she will realize (on her own) what she is doing to her body. Has anything traumatic happened to her that would cause this compulsive behavior? Is there a possibility that she has been sexually abused and you aren't aware of it? Sometimes young women with compulsive exercise addictions are running away from other problems. They choose exercise or eating as something in their life THEY CAN CONTROL. This is especially true if they have been violated in some way.

Does she seem easily agitated, depressed, restless, or withdrawn? I wish you luck and pray (with God's help) you can help her recognize she does have a problem and guide her in the right direction to overcome whatever is causing her exercise addiction. Please stay in touch. I am very concerned for your daughter, and hurt for her, knowing she must be going through some sort of inner turmoil and has found excessive exercise the only way she can deal with it at this time. I would like to recommend a book called **Raising Strong Daughters** by Jeanette Gadeberg. I met Jeanette while I was on book tour. She lives in Minneapolis, Minnesota and was in the

Pam and Jeanette Gadeberg
Minneapolis, Minnesota   January 1994

process of writing her book when I met her. It was published in April and is full of wonderful information any parent would find beneficial. You can contact her through Fairview Press, 2450 Riverside Ave. South, Minneapolis, MN 55454 (800) 544-8207. **Note: Refer to page 257 in the "Preventive Medicine" chapter concerning eating disorders.**

YOU: I have recently lost sixteen pounds cooking out of your book, and am ready to begin some kind of exercise program. I feel walking is my best choice, but need some advice how to get started. How often and long do I need to walk? How does walking compare to running? I used to jog when I was younger. Is there a difference between walking on a treadmill and outside or the mall? I've heard of power walking, race walking, and aerobic walking. What do those terms mean? How long does it take to see results? Will walking firm up my legs and bottom? Should I walk with ankle or hand weights? I am interested in reducing my body fat (especially in my legs and bottom). Is this a good way to do that? Thanks for your time. I have several friends that walk at the mall. I'm not ready to join them yet, because I am still extremely overweight, and know I couldn't keep up. I would like to try and get started doing something, however. Do you have any other suggestions? I love to sit in the sauna because I lose a lot of water weight and it makes my skin so soft. Is it dangerous to sit in the sauna every day? What are the best exercises to flatten your stomach? I've read about a pill that helps burn fat. It's called "Chromium Picolinate." Have you ever heard of it?
—S.A. Augusta, Georgia

ME: I'm so glad my book has helped you with your weight loss. You are very smart to be interested in an exercise program. Walking is a fantastic way to begin. You need to start slowly and BE SURE AND GET CHECKED OUT BY YOUR PHYSICIAN BEFORE YOU BEGIN ANY KIND OF EXERCISE PROGRAM! Your goal should be three miles at least three to five times a week for the greatest benefit. Start with one mile and add a quarter mile each week. Even moderate walking will help to raise your HDL (good cholesterol) associated with decreasing your heart disease risk. As far as comparing walking with running, walking has an injury rate of virtually zero which is not true with running. As you increase your speed with walking you will also increase your cardio-respiratory fitness. Once you increase your speed to say a 12 minute mile, the benefits of walking are equivalent to other forms of aerobic exercise such as running or aerobic dance. Most people begin by walking a 15-20 minute mile. As you increase your speed to a 12 minute mile you will need to shorten your arm frequency and increase your stride frequency. Don't try to lengthen your stride, but work on a quicker stride, keeping your hips forward, shoulders back, and chin up. As you increase your speed, you might experience some fatigue in the front of your lower legs (the dreaded shin splints). Be sure and warm-up and stretch before you get moving too fast. Good posture is important no matter what kind of walker you are. Strive to keep your head erect (ears over shoulders), chin lifted, shoulders back, and keep your elbows bent at a 90 degree angle with your hands cupped loosely (do not clench your fists). If you are obese or suffering from any kind of medical problem ALWAYS CHECK WITH YOUR PHYSICIAN before you even take that first trip out to walk. The most important thing is to get out there and walk on a regular basis. You might have to start with a trip to the mailbox. As you feel more comfortable, increase your length of walks 5 or 10 minutes each day. Always start slowly building up your time, speed, and exertion.

Race walking is a sport that involves special hip movements and a very fast stride. It is completely different from aerobic walking and requires practice to learn the technique. Race walking is a sport in itself. Aerobic walking (or power walking) refers to walking at a pace of a 12 minute mile in order to reach your target heart rate zone. Aerobic walkers move at a brisk pace and bend their arms at a 90 degree angle (allowing them to swing their arms faster and increase their stride frequency). Some people find walking on a treadmill easier than walking outside. The treadmill will definitely keep you moving at a constant pace. You have the advantage of making your course difficult or easy at the tip of your fingers. You can incorporate hills into your workout or remove them with the push of a button. Weather is not a problem and you can watch T.V. as you work out. On the other hand, walking outside gets you out of the house and the change of scenery is a nice distraction for many people. As far as results, that will vary on your duration, frequency, and exertion. I would give yourself about three months to see a major change in the shape of your body and about one week to see a difference in your state of mind! Aerobic exercise is definitely a mood enhancer and you will benefit from a better attitude almost immediately. The most important advice I can give you is to be consistent with your walking. Schedule it into your day as you would any other appointment. You will most definitely lose body fat when walking for exercise. As a matter of fact two years ago my husband gave me a treadmill for Christmas. I had always exercised on a stair climber and loved it because I could read as I exercised. I started using the treadmill three times a week the first of January and by March all of my pants and slacks were loose in the bottom and legs. I hadn't changed another thing. Walking is a great exercise to firm and tone the lower body. Sometimes it just takes changing your routine to see a difference in the shape of your body. I began using different muscles when I switched from the Stairmaster to the treadmill. That is the reason cross training is so beneficial. By working different muscles every day, your body constantly changes to accommodate your various routines. This will definitely work to your benefit in achieving over-all fitness and strength. I do not recommend ankle or hand weights while walking. Ankle weights will disrupt your gait and and throw off your stride which could lead to injury. I see folks walking with hand weights all the time, but I do not recommend them. They just aren't necessary. Instead I recommend walking at a faster pace which will automatically increase your arm movement. As you walk faster, increasing your arm speed, you involve the large muscle groups in the upper body. By incorporating extreme movement of your upper body you will increase your heart rate and the intensity of your workout. If you are holding weights, you tend to weigh yourself down, and by working against the weight and trying to maintain the arm movement speed, you risk tearing or injuring muscles. Save your weights for the weight room. When you engage your upper arms fully (without weights), you will be working the same muscles as when you are cross-country skiing. Everyone knows what a great aerobic workout cross country skiing can be.

If you want to burn maximum calories, walk as quickly as you can for as long as you can. **F**requency, **I**ntensity, and **T**ime (or duration) are the keys to success regarding walking. Did you notice what the first initials in those three words spell? ...F.I.T. Add the speed slowly. Alternate 4-mph walks with 3-mph walks. Gradually increase the number of days you walk fast. Interval walking will add endurance. Combine short bursts of fast walking with periods of slower walking, gradually lengthening faster intervals as you gain strength and endurance. After you have been walking a while begin walking up hills. You will burn more calories, build muscle, and increase your endurance. If you feel the need to add something to your walk, add walking poles (not weights) for added intensity and variation. Good walking shoes are important. Refer to page 162 in this section for walking shoe recommendations.

As far as the sauna is concerned, please use safety guidelines. A sauna is a nice way to relax after your workout, but don't overdo it. You shouldn't stay in for more than five minutes when first using a sauna (until your body gets used to it and then no more than 15 minutes). Only use the sauna once a day. If you have heart or other health problems be sure and check with your physician first. DO NOT USE THE SAUNA, STEAMROOM, OR HOT TUB IF YOU ARE PREGNANT OR SUSPECT YOU MIGHT BE PREGNANT!! This sounds really gross, but think of how your baby would feel taking a bath in very hot water. By increasing the heat of your body, you turn up the heat inside your body, too (specifically the amniotic sac where your baby is living and growing). Don't stay in a sauna that is warmer than 103 degrees. Re-hydrate your body by drinking plenty of water after using the sauna. Don't jump into extremely cold water, take an ice cold shower, or roll in the snow (I know, I have done it too), because this puts a lot of stress on your heart. Don't rub your skin with baby oil before using the sauna (even if you think it will help soften your skin), because the oil will inhibit sweating and might cause you to become overheated.

The best way to flatten your tummy is through aerobic exercise. You need to get to the root of the problem before you think about toning and this can only be accomplished through aerobic exercise which removes body fat from all over the body. Sit-ups are the best way to gain abdominal strength (which will make your tummy APPEAR FLATTER). Even toned muscles won't help the looks of a stomach if they are covering layers of abdominal body fat. Ten minutes of sit-ups three times a week should be sufficient to keep your abdominals taut. It's better to do 10 correctly than 50 sloppily. I'm sorry to report sit-ups will not get rid of "love handles." To do that you must reduce dietary fat and burn calories with regular cardiovascular aerobic exercise. Always exhale as you sit-up. Inhale as you return to a starting position. Contract your stomach muscles as you lift yourself off the ground. Do not use your neck muscles to lift or pulling with your hands behind your head. This is working your neck muscles, not your stomach muscles. To avoid back injury, keep your lower back pressed against the floor. Never lift yourself more than half-way up. If you have any kind of back problem or experience ANY PAIN while doing sit-ups, please GET CHECKED OUT BY YOUR PHYSICIAN IMMEDIATELY! There are several variations of sit-ups, but I would like to give you the basic form to use. Lie flat on your back. Put both calves on a bench so your knees are bent at a 90 degree angle. Tilt your pelvis to flatten your lower back against the floor or mat. Place your hands next to your ears and pull your elbows in. Don't place your hands behind your head and pull on your neck. Tuck your chin into your chest and slowly curl your shoulders up about 6-8 inches off the floor. Slowly lower (but not all the way to the floor), don't relax and lay back to rest, and then repeat the process. Start with 5-10 reps, building to 30-50. Abdominals are the one weight bearing exercise that you can safely perform every day and not risk injury. Three to five times a week are adequate, however.

Chromium Picolinate, like you have read, has been touted the fat-burning pill of the '90s. Chromium is actually a nutrient that occurs naturally in the body. The problem is the average American eats about 30 mcg of chromium a day. Most of us get very little of this nutrient in our American diets. Many sources believe there is a profound effect on overall health when we increase our dosage to 200 mcg. Chromium (or Chromium Picolinate which is the form best utilized by humans) plays a major role in supporting the insulin sensitivity of body tissues. Insulin is imperative in the metabolism of protein, carbohydrate, and fat. Dosages of 100-200 mcg have been shown to improve glucose control in diabetics, reduce elevated cholesterol, and some believe it may reduce body fat and increase lean muscle mass. I read about thirteen articles from all different sources concerning this nutrient and this was the consensus of the material available. Again, PLEASE CHECK WITH YOUR PHYSICIAN before adding any kind of supplement or exercise to you program. I hope this information helped. Good luck!

YOU: I have eaten healthy most of my life. I grew up on a farm and ate lots of fruits and vegetables when the kids in the city snacked on junk food, candy, and gum. I have always been pretty active working in my garden and walking everywhere I go. I am now 66 years old and and have never had a weight problem, but my cholesterol is a little high (around 190). My granddaughter came to visit a few weeks ago and was appalled that I had recently enrolled in a dance aerobics class (for senior citizens) at church. I've never done any kind of weight training, but have considered giving that a try, too. I've read so much about osteoporosis (in older women) that it must be important. Am I really too old to exercise? Am I pushing my luck or is an active lifestyle OK for someone my age? I love the recipes in your book. Everyone in my church has your book. As a matter of fact, your book is what got our senior citizen's exercise class started. We all decided we needed to get moving to keep up with our grandchildren. Any information you give me I will pass on to my lady friends. —*L.M. Richmond, Virginia*

ME: I admire your spunk and determination! As a matter of fact, exercise can make all the difference between becoming sick (and household bound) and staying active. When folks retire, they finally HAVE THE TIME to exercise. Unless you have an underlying medical condition which makes working out risky, your doctor should be delighted that you WANT to exercise. If you have been active all your life (and it sounds like you have), there is no reason to slow down now. Aqua-aerobics classes are a great choice for older folks (in case some of your lady friends find the traditional aerobics class too taxing on their bones and joints).

Weight training is not just for the young, but also for the young at heart! A study was performed on 50 frail nursing home residents (ages 72-98) to find out how adding a vigorous exercise regimen and weight machines three days a week, for 45 minutes at a time, would affect their strength and endurance. The study lasted ten weeks. Compared to 50 residents (who did not participate in the program) they increased their walking speed by 12% and their ability to climb stairs by 28%. Four of the participants started the program using a walker, and at the end of the study were walking with a cane.

Physical activity is critical in combating frailty and maintaining a good quality of life in the elderly population. The key is to start slowly and allow the body to adjust to the activity. Research has consistently shown the fitness and health benefits of exercise later in life. As people grow older, bone mass lessens and they are susceptible to broken bones that can incapacitate them. With the proper amount of exercise, we can maintain bone mineral density and possibly remain injury-free regardless of our age. Increasing bone mass will help prevent osteoporosis (a major risk of older people, especially post-menopausal women). Exercise slows down and helps to control many of the disease risks and problems associated with aging. Risks of heart disease, blood pressure, diabetes, arthritis, cancer, and osteoporosis can often be controlled (to some extent) by simply adding exercise to your life as you age. Please refer to page 205 in the "Disease" section of this book concerning cholesterol levels in older people.

I say, go for it! Don't let anyone get you down! Do your own thing! More power to you! I wish more older people had your attitude. If they did give it a try, like you and your friends, they might just find out they enjoy it! Keep up the good work and I wish you many, many more healthy, active, fun-filled years (all of you)!

YOU: I am a lean, mean, low-fat eating machine! That is, since I found *BUTTER BUSTERS* and started using it. I've lost 22 pounds and have NEVER had so much energy and vitality! How did you ever find the time to write a book with three children and such an active lifestyle? I have a few questions. I've read about BMR and I understand that it means your Basal Metabolic Rate. I know that means the calories your body burns at rest. My question is how in the heck do you figure out what your BMR is? One more thing. Is it safe to continue working out if you have a cold or flu symptoms? *—M.F. Orlando, Florida*

ME: The book took me over a year to write. (I explained the whole story to the lady in a letter, but since I have already explained it in the first part of the book, I'm not going to repeat it again here.)

Figuring your BMR varies from one individual to another and is kind of "iffy" at that. This is really confusing to me, but since you asked for it......

Male resting metabolic rate=900 + [7 X (weight in kilograms)]

Female resting metabolic rate=700 + [7 X (weight in kilograms)]

NOTE: One pound = 0.454 kilograms

The result is a fair estimate of a resting metabolic rate. However, to further tailor the results to your particular energy needs, you need to adjust for your level of activity. Multiply the figure by 1.2 if you are very sedentary, 1.4 for moderately active, and 1.8 for very active.

Again, the figure is imprecise, but it is a good starting point to calculate your personal weight-loss regime. Adjusting your daily caloric intake so that it is consistently less than your calculated BMR should lead to a gradual but steady weight loss (ESPECIALLY IF YOU ARE EATING A LOW-FAT DIET!)

I know this is confusing, so I will walk you through it using myself as an example:

My weight in kilograms is 120 X 0.454= 54.48
700 (female resting metabolic rate) + [7 X 54.48] = 1081.36

I am very active so 1081.36 X 1.8= 1946.45

In other words, I burn about 1,946 calories a day at rest. By adding my aerobic activity, I burn even more calories, which explains why I can eat so much more food (without gaining weight) provided I exercise aerobically and eat low fat!

There are quite a few factors to consider if you are trying to lose body fat:

1. Your body size and composition strongly determines how you utilize energy (or calories) even while you are sleeping. If you have more muscle tissue and less fat you will burn calories at a much faster rate.

2. Exercise intensity and duration will give you a temporary boost in your metabolic rate (rate at which your body burns calories).

3. Genetic factors may play a role in your body type and frame size, but have a small effect on your resting metabolism (BMR).

4. Thyroid disorders may affect your metabolic rate. Some people must take thyroid medication to help regulate these problems. Any type of medication should be determined by your own personal physician.

5. Your resting metabolic rate (BMR) tends to slow down with age.

6. Diet has a temporary effect on the metabolic rate (rate at which your body burns calories while active), but little affect on your resting metabolic rate (BMR).

The good news is.....you can boost your metabolic rate! If you exercise aerobically on a regular basis, build lean muscle mass through weight training, eat small meals frequently, and stay active, you should be able to boost your metabolic rate and control your weight for the rest of your life!

If you are interested in losing weight this information may be beneficial. Adjusting your daily caloric intake so that it is consistently less than your calculated BMR, should lead to a gradual but steady fat loss. Since 1 gram of carbohydrate or protein contains 4 calories and 1 gram of fat contains 9 calories, it is easy to see how you can eat a lot more food if you eat low-fat. Add aerobic exercise and some form of weight training and you have a winning combination!!

Many people wonder if it is safe to continue their exercise program if they happen to have a cold or flu symptoms. If you have a cold, most physicians say to cut back on your training by 50% (and listen to your body). If you feel light-headed or faint, or can't breathe through your nose, it probably isn't a great idea to exercise and get over-heated. Most doctors would probably advise people with flu symptoms to stop exercising and begin again when symptoms (fever, loss of appetite, and muscle aches) disappear completely. Even at that point, you should start again slowly. Even though it is rare, a flu virus can travel to the heart (which could happen from over- exertion). I don't want to frighten you, but I would not recommend strenuous exercise if you are running a fever or experiencing other flu related symptoms. Keep up the good work and don't ever lose your great attitude and interest in fitness!!

YOU: I'm writing to you because I am pregnant with my second child, and I don't want to go through again what I went through the first time to lose weight. I am four months pregnant, feel good, and have a lot of energy. I really wasn't too sick this time like I was during my first pregnancy. My two year old keeps me busy, so I'm not exactly sitting around the house twiddling my thumbs, but I would like to get more involved in some kind of exercise program this time around. I have a membership to an all women's health club (it was a birthday gift from my sister before she knew I was pregnant), so I have exercise equipment available. I've only gained 5 pounds so far because I have been eating low-fat thanks to your great cookbook. I gained 64 pounds with my first pregnancy and I never even got back to my pre-pregnancy weight before I got pregnant this time. I am determined NOT to let that happen again!! What do you suggest concerning exercising? I can't believe you have three kids and look like you do. Did you exercise when you were pregnant? I read that you swam, but was that all you did? Thanks for answering my questions.
—G.F. Las Vegas, Nevada

ME: You are smart to be concerned with your weight during pregnancy. While it is true most physicians recommend a weight gain of 25-35 pounds (if you are of normal weight when you become pregnant), many women still consider pregnancy an unlimited meal that never stops. Your weight gain in pregnancy should be determined (to some extent) by how much you weigh when you become pregnant (especially if you are overweight). Refer to page 74 in the "Food and Nutrition" section to learn more about weight gain during pregnancy. As long as you are eating an adequate amount of calories for you and your growing child (not under 1800), and making wise nutritional choices (not a lot of high-fat junk food), you shouldn't have any problem staying within a reasonable weight gain range (that you and your physician both approve). As far as exercise, yes I did swim during all three of my pregnancies. I found it to be a nice aerobic work-out that I enjoyed, and it was the only kind of exercise that I had ever participated in before I got pregnant. Back in 1975 most pregnant women didn't exercise at all. Most women can participate in some form of aerobic exercise throughout their pregnancy providing they have experienced no unusual problems. THIS SHOULD BE DISCUSSED WITH YOUR O.B. PHYSICIAN AT YOUR VERY FIRST APPOINTMENT!

Heavy weight-bearing and high-impact aerobics should be avoided (in most cases) in favor of walking, stationary bicycling, and aqua or less intense low-impact aerobics. Step aerobics are fine in the beginning, but, as your tummy grows, you might have trouble keeping one eye on the bench (due to the obstruction of view). This could cause you to trip or stumble and possibly fall. Moderate seems to be the key word in judging and picking your routine. I like to use the "talk-sing" test to determine if you are working out within a safe heart rate zone. If you can carry on (even a broken) conversation while exercising, you are probably within your heart rate zone. If you can easily sing, you probably aren't working out quite hard enough. I would recommend your work-out intensity be determined by how you feel that particular day (not by the way you usually work out).

MOST DOCTORS RECOMMEND NOT WORKING OUT AT ALL if you have experienced premature labor, cardiac disease, or more than two miscarriages (at least not without their OK). The main thing to remember is your fitness program should be especially tailored for YOU and fit YOUR NEEDS and ALWAYS SUPERVISED BY YOUR PHYSICIAN!

One of the most controversial issues is abdominal work during pregnancy. Many doctors warn of the dangers of performing crunches while pregnant (especially after the first four months). The main reason is because physicians are concerned that while a woman is on her back, the weight of the fetus can depress major blood vessels, resulting in dizziness and reduction of oxygen to the baby. Another concern is that the exercise could lead to a condition called "diastasis recti" (a separation in the abdominal muscles). You need the abdominal muscles to push your baby out during the birth process. If you have access to machines, chances are you could use the crunch and torso twist machines (after four months) which allow the abdominals to be exercised while upright.

My last bit of advice is to work with your doctor to develop a routine that keeps you in shape, but most importantly, one that is safe. Make sure your trainer or instructor is certified in prenatal exercise by a major sports medicine association. (The Aerobic & Fitness Association of America

[AFAA], the International Association of Fitness Professionals [IDEA], and the American College of Exercise [ACE] all offer specialized certification in this area.) For more information regarding exercising during pregnancy, call:

1. Aerobic & Fitness Association of America: (818)905-0040
2. American College of Exercise: (619)535-8227
3. IDEA: (619)535-8979
4. Moms in Motion (a division of Sara's City Workout): (800)545-CITY
5. Pregnagym: (813)221-8050

I wish you a happy healthy pregnancy and a short and easy delivery!!
P.S. Please send me a picture of the baby!

YOU: I have a couple of questions I hope you can answer. What do you think about those thigh creams? They are in every newspaper and magazine article in the country. They sell the stuff everywhere. I am quite young, never had children, normal weight, but I have cellulite on my thighs and buttocks. Is it possible to get rid of it with exercise? I will do whatever it takes to make the cellulite go away. Do you know what causes cellulite? My mom and three sisters have it, too. They are all a lot heavier than me, however. I didn't have it when I was younger. What causes it to appear? Does diet have anything to do with it? Does your body type have anything to do with it? I've read about the three kinds of body types. Do you know what I am talking about? Any suggestions would be deeply appreciated! I will wait anxiously for your answer.
—D.S. Jackson, Mississippi

ME: I don't know a woman alive who isn't familiar with cellulite. It is one of those problems we can all "identify with" at sometime in our lives. Cellulite is not a "special" kind of fat like we would all like to think. Unfortunately it is nothing more than a "buzz word" to describe the dimpled fat on the buttocks and thighs of at least 80% of American women (and a few men). If you were to look at the thigh fat under a microscope, it looks no different than fat on other parts of the body. What creates the dimpling effect is the connective tissue beneath the skin. When we gain weight, fat fills the little pockets around the connective tissue and creates a dimpled appearance. Unfortunately the only way to smooth out the appearance is by losing body fat through aerobic exercise. Leg lifts don't work, trust me on this! As far as diet, a low-fat diet (rich in fruit and vegetables) is your best defense against fat in general. I also recommend drinking water constantly throughout the day. Soda pop, because of it's high sodium content, causes the body to retain fluid.

NOTE: This letter was written before I discovered Morris' Kick-Butt Bottom Busters. Refer to pages 56 and 57 for a couple of specific exercises I have found effective (along with my aerobics).

As far as exercise goes, I've found the best ways to firm buttocks and thighs are walking, the Stairmaster, squats, and lunges. If you have exercise equipment available, leg curls and leg presses are also good choices. We inherit a tendency to store fat in a certain order, say the stomach first, then the legs, then the face. Unfortunately we tend to lose the fat in reverse order. Doesn't it seem like most people notice when you have lost weight in your face first? Fat cells are laid down early in life. Your body won't produce more after puberty unless you chronically overeat or binge severely. When you gain weight, your existing fat cells simply plump up. New fat cells might form (in extreme cases) if you gain a lot of weight. Once new cells develop, they are there for the duration, unless you have them sucked out through liposuction. Losing body fat CAN shrink fat cells. Where we store body fat is determined by genetic factors (in most cases). If your Mom is bottom heavy, chances are, you and your sisters will be, too. This brings us to the subject of body types you asked about. Body types are also hereditary to some extent. The three basic body types are as follows:

Endomorph: (rounded, curvy form, possibly large hips) People with this type body tend to be shorter in stature, have a little more body fat, and are probably pear-shaped. Your best choice of exercise is aerobics. Strive to burn more calories and minimize your curves with regular low intensity aerobics. Endurance is the key for you. The treadmill (45-60 minutes) would be a great choice. You tend to bulk up easily, so use lots of reps and light weights in your resistance exercise program. [Marilyn Monroe] ***Your challenge is to slim your hips which will make you appear taller and leaner.**

Ectomorph: (usually tall and thin) This is the one most women would pick if they had a choice and is the body type of most models. This body type has less body fat, a lean torso, and probably small breasts. Concentrate on building lean muscle mass. Be more concerned with building muscle rather than calorie and fat burning. Low impact aerobics for 35 minutes is all you need. Try to enhance your slim figure with curves and contours. You might enjoy Nautilus type machines, free weights, exercise bands, and other forms of resistance exercise. If you use less reps and heavier weights you will be able to build and define your figure easily. [Heather Locklear] ***Your challenge is adding curves and shape to your body.**

Mesomorph: (muscular, solid, athletic, and block-like form) If you are a mesomorph body type you are probably large boned, have broad shoulders and are strong. You probably have well-developed limbs and may be stocky in stature. Unless you are a professional body builder you would choose lighter weights and higher repetitions in the weight room. You should concentrate on endurance aerobic activities to burn body fat most efficiently. Light body sculpting classes would be perfect for you. Jogging, power walking, jumping rope, and aerobic dance might be good choices for your aerobic activities. You will probably need to concentrate on your mid-section with plenty of abdominal work (you tend to gain weight in this area easily). [Martina Navratilova] *** Your challenge is looking lean and long, not chunky.**

The easiest way to figure out your body shape is to put on a leotard and stand in front of a full length mirror. If you carry your excess weight all over, you are probably an endomorph. If most of your weight is around your lower body (and you have a strong and stocky build), you are probably a mesomorph. If you are tall and lean (lucky you) you are an ectomorph.

Now, for the news you have been waiting for. Do you like the way I saved this question for last? I know what you mean about the thigh cream (aminophylline) popularity. It's everywhere! I did a little research on the subject myself. I haven't had the nerve to buy any myself, because I am afraid someone I know might see me and I would be really embarrassed. I guess I could always say it was for "research purposes!" Ha Ha! Most women probably feel the same way I do about that. I am curious, and I, like you, read every article that comes out. Wouldn't it be nice if you REALLY COULD smear a little cream on your thighs and get rid of the fat forever? Unfortunately, I don't think that is the case. There is a cream that has been around for years in the bodybuilder world called "Thiomucase." I thought it might be similar, but after reading a ton of information found this not to be the case. Although Thiomucase can be rubbed on the skin the same as Aminphylline, it works in an entirely different way. It causes fat cells to discard water (as much as 20% of their volume) and gives the "appearance" of being smaller. Many competitive bodybuilders use Thiomucase for a period of a week or two before a show to look tighter and a little more ripped.

Aminophylline (originally designed as an asthma medication), on the other hand, supposedly works by targeting the beta receptors which produce a chemical that temporarily initiates fat loss. Aminophylline advocates claim that the drug raises levels of this fat-releasing chemical. They say the more you rub on, the more fat is released. Where exactly these fatty acids go after obtaining their new-found freedom is unknown. Is it possible they get used as energy or is there a chance they could be stored somewhere else in your body (like maybe in your heart)? I have read numerous reports stating women have lost up to 1/2 inch in each thigh after six weeks of applying the product twice a day. When treating asthma, aminophylline dilates the bronchi by working on certain receptors called alpha-2 receptors. These receptors are known to be found in other locations in the body including blood vessels and fat cells. Women happen to have more alpha-2 receptors on thigh fat cells compared to abdominal fat cells. This makes thigh fat more difficult to mobilize during weight loss. As thigh fat accumulates in women, the distended fat cells can put tension on connective tissue under the skin forming a dimpling effect we call cellulite. Even though the girth of those women's thighs was reduced by 1/2 inch, their actual body fat was not tested. Most of the reports insisted there was no toxicity in the cream and no aminophylline detected in the blood stream when tested. They also stated a strength of at least 2% was necessary to achieve results.

Other reports gave entirely different information. Aminophylline has been reported to produce an array of side effects including nausea, vomiting, diarrhea, dizziness, headaches, insomnia, heart palpitations, circulatory failure and even a coma (when absorbed through the skin). Some subjects reported a metallic taste and pressure in their lungs within minutes after applying a cream containing 2% of the drug. Two percent of the 700 women testing the product reported a mild to severe reaction after using the 2% aminophylline product. One of the sources stated not to use the thigh cream if it feels gritty. This happens as a result of the compound breaking down into ammonia and crystals, which can be irritating to the skin. Most manufacturers are aware of the watchful eyes of the FDA, so their only claim is the promise of smoother skin. It's safety, not the claims that bother the FDA. The FDA still remains unconvinced that aminophylline is safe at any level no matter what the manufacturers say about it not entering the blood stream. The official statement from the FDA is that it is still investigating the use of aminophylline in cosmetics. All the reports do agree on one thing. The results ARE TEMPORARY and only work as long as you use the cream......twice a day!

I hope this answers your questions. I don't know about you, but I'd rather eat a whole lot of low-fat food and exercise aerobically to maintain my weight rather than worry about rubbing cream on my thighs for the rest of my life. Besides, aerobic exercise is a great stress release, and I don't think I need the extra stress of worrying about what those thigh creams might be doing to my body on the inside. How about you?

YOU: Thank you for writing your book. It has been the "pot of gold" at the end of the rainbow for me. I've searched for a healthy way of eating that tastes good for most of my adult life. I've been on every diet known to man. I've been obsessed with the scales since I can remember. My parents are both fat and so are the rest of my relatives. I've decided to make a change in our family tree. I refuse to turn out like the rest of my family. I know genes play an important part in the body type of a person, but believe me, I intend to change that. I've lost about 17 pounds and started walking four evenings a week. Everything I've read (also included in your book) states that your percentage of body fat is much more important than how much you weigh on the scale. Would you please explain how you have your body fat tested and exactly what it all means. My other question is what should I eat before I exercise (if anything) and after I exercise (even if I'm not hungry). I'm really trying to do this whole thing the healthy way, so please humor me even though my questions probably sound kind of dumb. You don't know how much I appreciate you and what you have done for people like me. Thank you from the bottom of my heart!!   —J.T. San Diego, California

ME: Your letter meant a great deal to me. Thank you so much for taking the time to tell me how you feel. You sound like a very determined, strong young woman, and all of us could learn from your positive attitude. There are several ways to have your body fat measured. I will attempt to explain the most common methods:

Hydrostatic (underwater) weighing is considered the most accurate method of measuring body composition. You are completely submerged in a water-filled tank and body density is measured according to weight under water. You blow all of the air out and hold your breath during the test. It is considered the most valid method available, but it is expensive, time-consuming, and a little uncomfortable (since you have to hold your breath even though you have blown all of the air out of your lungs first). There is a small possibility of error if guidelines (such as water temperature, posture, and scale accuracy) are not followed exactly.

Circumferential Measurements use tape measures to determine limb and body girths without taking subcutaneous (under skin) fat density into consideration. The results (measured in centimeters) are plugged into formulas that don't differentiate muscle mass from fat. I feel this is the least accurate.

Ultrasound testing is another method. Ultrasound waves penetrate the skin and pass through the fat layers to measure underlying muscle tissue. This method is used in many hospitals and clinics.

Near-Infrared Acterance is another method based on light absorption theories using fiber optics. The Futrex 1000 Body Fat Home Tester uses this concept. I purchased this device and found it quite accurate. For ordering information: 1-800-255-4206. It retails for about $100.00

Bioelectrical Impedance, another method, is performed by attaching electrodes to the body to measure a weak electrical current as it passes through the body. The faster the current, the less fat in the body. This method is used in many gyms, clinics, and hospitals. Your water consumption before the test can influence it's accuracy. You should have this test performed prior to working out or physical exertion.

Skinfold Calibration involves pinching inches of fat at various sites on the body. Several formulas are then applied to determine the body fat percentage as it relates to age, sex, and weight. This method can be quite accurate if you are able to have the same person perform the test every time. By using the same person, this should guarantee that the sites would be taken and measured in the exact same places on the body. Otherwise, this method can have a large margin of error (due to different people using different sites on the body). This is the most inexpensive test. Most gyms, health clubs, and Y.M.C.A.'s provide this service.

The National body fat averages are as follows:

College age males	12-15%
College age females	22-25%
Optimal health/fitness range for all males	12-18%
Optimal health/fitness range for all females	16-25%
Male obesity standard	over 25% body fat
Female obesity standard	over 30% body fat

About two hours before you work out you should consume food that is easy to digest and high in carbohydrates, such as fruit, fruit juice, dried fruit, fat-free crackers, pretzels, low or fat-free cereal with skim milk, or bagels. This will help regulate your blood sugar. If your work-out is very intense and lasts more than an hour, along with water, you might want to choose a sports drink, dried fruit, low-fat energy or granola bars, or fat-free fig newtons. Sports drinks containing 50-60 calories per 8 ounces are best. Try to steer clear of drinks containing fructose, since it can cause gastrointestinal problems. Alternative sources of energy are sucrose or glucose.

Once your work-out is completed you have a window of 15-30 minutes when it is very important to consume about 100 grams of carbohydrates (which amounts to about 400 calories). If you are a casual exerciser who walks or jogs two or three miles a couple of times a week, this isn't as important. However, stocking up on carbohydrate-rich foods is heart-healthy and would certainly be a better post-exercise snack than a greasy hamburger and fries! Some great post-exercise snacks would be orange juice, apricot nectar, apple juice, grape juice, watermelon, cantaloupe, fat-free frozen yogurt (my personal favorite with fat-free granola on top), sherbet, raisins, brown rice, pasta, pizza with fat-free toppings, bagels with fruit spread or fat-free cream cheese, a banana, grapes, or dried fruit.

Potassium is vital in muscle glycogen replacement after exercise to help maintain fluid balance, blood pressure, and body temperature. While some sports drinks and energy bars supplement this mineral loss, they are actually much lower in potassium than many foods. Although there is no RDI for potassium, 1,600-2,000 milligrams of potassium should be ingested daily. A regular sports drink contains only 45 mg.

SOURCE	SERVING	POTASSIUM (MG)
watermelon	one slice	600
banana	one medium	569
cantaloupe	half	502
orange juice	one cup (8-oz)	496
raisins	1/4 cup	271

NOTE: REMEMBER TO ALWAYS DRINK WATER BEFORE, DURING, AND AFTER EXERCISE!!

If you are going hiking for three hours or more, be sure and pack plenty of carbohydrate-rich foods to replenish your energy (or glycogen) stores. A piece of fruit, a sandwich and some cut-up vegetables are ideal. Bagels, rice cakes, fat-free granola, and dried fruit are also easy-to-pack carbohydrate rich snacks that don't add much weight to your backpack. DON'T FORGET THE SUN SCREEN!!

I HOPE THIS HELPS AND MAY YOU CONTINUE TO LIVE LIFE TO IT'S FULLEST, AND ENJOY EVERY MINUTE OF EVERY DAY NO MATTER WHAT OBSTACLES COME YOUR WAY!!

YOU: Now that I have mastered low-fat cooking (thanks to your book) my husband and I have decided we would like to invest in some fitness equipment for our home. We really enjoy working out together. Since my husband retired six months ago, we have changed our eating habits. Since I have so much more time to spend in the kitchen, I have taken up cooking again. Since we are getting older, we thought it might be smart to learn healthy cooking and eating so we could share more years together. After all, we finally have the time to spend together, so we thought it might be more enjoyable if we felt good too! So many of our senior citizen friends are sickly, overweight, and miserable. We have both trimmed down a bit, our cholesterol is in the safe range, but we are both out-of-shape. Our past exercise has consisted of riding in a golf cart and pushing the remote con-

trol buttons on the T.V. (Oh yes, and an occasional stroll around the mall on Sunday afternoon.) As you can see, we need your help and advice. We are in our 60s and we don't have any serious medical problems (that we know of). We were both checked out recently at our annual physical exams and everything looked pretty good. Any ideas would be greatly appreciated. Please write another book.....Soon!
—P.L. Boca Raton, Florida

ME: What a darling couple you must be. I can just see you now tooling around the golf course in your golf cart laughing and holding hands like two teenagers. It's obvious you love each other very much. It shows in your letter. There are all kinds of possibilities available. Since aerobic exercise helps burn fat, prevents heart disease, boosts your energy level, helps prevent osteoporosis, and improves your mental health and attitude, I would highly recommend you invest in some kind of cardiovascular equipment you will use and enjoy. All the experts say we need vertical, linear, and lateral movement to keep up with the challenges we face every day. Your choices include stair-climbers or bench steppers (for vertical), stationary bicycles and treadmills (for linear) and slide boards, tennis, or rollerblading (for lateral). Now is the time to narrow down the choices. Let me help. I bet your choices consist of a treadmill, stationary bicycle, or possibly a stair climber. Am I close? My mom is 75 and her choice of exercise equipment is a stationary bicycle. If you are thinking of two pieces of equipment I would recommend a treadmill and a stationary bicycle.

Stationary bicycles are pretty compact, easy to use (you can read or watch T.V.) and are great for burning fat (remember to pedal at least 35 minutes, not counting a five minute warm-up and five minute cool-down). I would recommend an electronic model which relies on electromagnets to create resistance. I personally own a recumbent style Lifecycle 5500R model. It is really nice because it has a back rest and is very comfortable to use. Make sure the bicycle you choose has toe clips or straps to secure your feet to the pedals, adjustable seat and handlebars, and, most of all, a comfortable saddle. The more expensive the machine, the more gadgets it contains. It might be worth the money to invest in a model with an electronic screen that computes calories burned per minute and distance traveled. They help keep you motivated and give you something to watch while you ride. They range in price from $300.00 to $2,000.00. Shop around and compare prices and features until you find the right model for you.

Safety features are important with stationary bicycles especially if you have grandchildren, other small children, or pets around the house. All moving parts should be covered even if there is a visible wheel. Watch for a sturdy metal seat post and a sturdy leather seat. A plastic seat may collapse or break. Watch for high-quality chains, straps, or cables in the construction of the machine. Treadmills are the most frequently used piece of home exercise equipment. Most top brands rely on motors with at least 1.5 - 3.0 horsepower to drive the belt you walk on. A programmable control board is mounted on the front. All you need to do to increase or decrease your speed is push some buttons. Pushing a button raises or lowers the bed (or platform) you walk on. There are some check-points you should be aware of. Be sure the treadmill you choose has a two-ply belt and a bed long enough for the stride of the tallest person using the equipment. For safety purposes your treadmill should include a stop button or safety strap you clip to your clothes (or strap around your waist) that attaches to the machine with a magnet. If the magnet breaks away, the machine automatically stops, immediately. Automatic slow-starting speed is another nice safety feature. Your treadmill should start slowly at a speed less than 2.0 mph. Watch for enclosed wiring and motor, along with front or side handrails.

A fancy home gym isn't really necessary for weight or resistance training. Dumbbells, weighted bars, free weights, or even rubber tubing will do the trick. However, if you are interested in a home gym, there are several brands available. Multi-station gyms that combine many different exercises into one piece of equipment are safer and easier to use than dumbbells. You don't need a spotter, and to change the weight all you have to do is move the pin. The main thing to remember when choosing a home gym is to make sure it allows you to work all of the major muscle groups. It should also allow you to move directly from one exercise to another. Watch for a durable heavy gauge steel frame with strong welds. As far as safety is concerned, watch for properly placed weight stacks that won't catch on clothing or body parts. Look for stacks covered in plastic or metal. A sturdy frame, quality materials, and good construction are imperative.

Exercise equipment buying tips:

1. Don't buy anything you won't use. It's a waste of money and space.

2. Shop around and compare prices. Watch for sales, rebates and get ready to bargain. Prices are not set in stone, believe me on this one!

3. Measure your space before you buy. Be sure it will fit through the door after you get it home. Make sure you have plenty of room to walk around your equipment without running into the wall or each other.

4. Don't take anyone's word for anything. Try it out for yourself. Make sure it is comfortable and fits your body size and type.

5. Check out the warranty and service agreements. If you have a choice between two machines, choose the one with the better warranty. It will save you money in the long run. Ask the dealer who is responsible for fixing it. Find out if they charge for service calls, handle them in their store, or make house calls. Some dealers hire independent service companies to service their equipment. This can be a problem at times if the service company is located in another town or city. I personally recommend Busy Body, Inc. for purchasing fitness equipment. They have stores all over the country. To find out if there is a store in your area call (800) 536-2639.

6. Buy the best equipment you can afford. This doesn't always mean the most expensive (but it usually does). Look for sturdy construction and quality workmanship.

7. Buy for total fitness. Keep all three fitness components in mind when making your purchases. Endurance, strength, and flexibility are all necessary to accomplish your fitness goal. Supplement a stationary bicycle with free weights and a mat for sit-ups and stretching, and you will have all the bases covered!

Have fun and continue to enjoy each other every single day that you share together for the rest of your lives (which should be a mighty long time at the rate you are going)! God Bless You Both!!

YOU: Thank you so much for the *BUTTER BUSTERS* cookbooks! My husband and I have been using your cookbook and information since February 1994. Al lost about 60 pounds and is in much better health! (He does not even snore anymore.) I have lost 43 pounds and feel better getting back into the sizes I used to wear. We came to your book signing at Books A Million in Birmingham last February. I was delighted to find that you are what you preach. Your enthusiasm and energy inspired us. We took both editions of your cookbook on a 29th anniversary weekend to the beach. We read and walked and enjoyed working on the new eating ideas together. Our children (ages 23 and 17) like the home cooking and don't even miss all the hamburger.

I am having trouble losing the last 15 pounds. I keep bouncing between -45 and -40 pounds lost. Please send the information on your video and workbook. I really need your help to finish getting this last bit off. Thank goodness this is not a "diet" but a way of life to keep us healthy! Keep up the good work!   —B.C. Odenville, Alabama

ME: Thank you so much for your sweet note. It was so great to hear from you. I remember you and your husband perfectly! It sounds like you are both doing great! I'm sending you the order form for the video series and workbook that you requested. I hope this helps with some new ideas. You might try switching to another form of aerobic exercise for a while (to shock your fat-burning system). When I hit a point that I couldn't lose, I switched from walking to the stair climber and the stationary bike. You might also incorporate some kind of light weights twice a week (to build even more lean muscle mass). This will help you burn fat at a faster rate, too! I wish you and your family the best and please stay in touch! I hope to see you again when I'm out on book tour.

Note: This letter was written by Betty Corley. As it turned out, she and her husband gave their testimonies in my "Butter Busters Low-Fat System" Infomercial. Read about Betty and Al in "My Readers Inspire Me" chapter pages 500-501.

NOTES

PREVENTIVE
MEDICINE
AND DISEASE

RISK FACTORS YOU CAN CONTROL
(Change your behavior)

YOU: I am a 17 year old Black female and I would like any information you can give me regarding diseases. I have several hereditary risks for various diseases in my family, and would like to take any and all preventive measures possible. My mom received your book from her best friend for her 40th birthday. My whole family appreciates all your southern recipes such as New Orleans Seafood Filé Gumbo, Jambalaya, Creole Red Snapper, Shrimp Etoufeé (New Orleans Style), New Orleans Barbecue Shrimp, etc., etc. I am a little curious why you included all the "New Orleans" recipes? Since we live in New Orleans, we found it quite interesting. Thanks for making OUR FOOD tasty and healthy!!   —*S.B. New Orleans, Louisiana*

ME: I am so happy to hear from you. I am really impressed that a 17 year old young woman is concerned with her health and welfare. I think that is wonderful and I applaud you!!!

As far as the New Orleans dishes... My husband attended Tulane Medical School in New Orleans, so we lived in the city almost five years. Many of my recipes were taken from various restaurant's dishes that Mike and I enjoyed (the high-fat way) during our years in New Orleans.

Your disease risks are determined by many factors such as family history (hereditary factors), lifestyle (diet and exercise), habits (alcohol consumption, smoking, or drugs), age (different diseases affect us at different times in our lives), and sex (male or female). These risks are all important factors to consider.

You mentioned a concern regarding all the disease risk factors in your family. This, alone, puts you at a hereditary risk, so you are smart to be concerned. For instance, if one of your first-degree relatives had bypass surgery or if you smoke, your chances of developing heart disease would be higher than average. You can reduce your risks by changing your behavior. Even if this particular problem is not one you are concerned with, eating right and plenty of exercise can lower your odds regarding many different diseases. Do remember that if you have a one in 1,000 chance of developing heart disease, there is still a 999 out of 1,000 chance that you won't!! Disease risks generally go up with age. Five of the top ten causes of death in this country are related to lifestyle. It has been proven that diet can influence your chance of developing heart disease, cancer, stroke, diabetes, or osteoporosis.

I will address the different diseases, how risks go up with age, and preventive measures. I hope this answers your questions and helps in your preventive fight against disease. Good luck!

ARE YOU AT RISK?
(Prevention is the key to protection)

Disease and Preventive Measures	Age	The Odds
Lung Cancer: Do not smoke (if you do, get medical help to stop). Eat a low-fat diet. It has been proven that those who ate less than 30% fat were five times LESS LIKELY to develop lung cancer than those who ate between 40-45% fat. Eat lots of fruits and vegetables.	age 20-29 age 30-39 age 40-49 age 50-59 age 60-69 age70+	1 in 50,000 1 in 33,300 1 in 4,300 1 in 1,000 1 in 559 1 in 485
Breast Cancer: Eat less than 20% fat in your diet. Eat about 35 grams of fiber per day. Try to eat 5-9 fruit and vegetable servings a day. Use self-breast exam after age 20 (monthly). Start mammograms every 1-2 years at age 40 (depending on your family history).	age 20-29 age 30-39 age 40-49 age 50-59 age 60-69 age 70+	1 in 25,000 1 In 2,200 1 in 625 1 in 403 1 in 226 1 in 220
Ovarian Cancer: Check out your family history. Heredity is a risk factor. Women whose mother and/or sisters have had ovarian cancer may be at significant risk. Special testing (such as the CA-125 blood test and vaginal sonography) may be helpful.	age 20-29 age 30-39 age 40-49 age 50-59 age 60-69 age 70+	1 in 33,300 1 in 14,300 1 in 5,900 1 in 3,100 1 in 2,000 1 in 1,700
Diabetes (Type II-Adult Onset): Keep your weight under control (more than 85% of people with Type II diabetes are obese). Consider the new dietary findings that the amount of total carbohydrates are more important than the type. Some sugars may actually be less harmful than certain starches!	age 20-29 age 30-39 age 40-49 age 50-59 age 60-69 age 70+	1 in 478 1 in 175 1 in 84 1 in 45 1 in 20 1 in 13
Osteoporosis: Consume at least 1,200 mg. of calcium a day until the age of 24 (especially during the teenage years). After that consume a MINIMUM of 1,000 mg daily. Limit alcohol, caffeine, and sodium in your diet. Try to consume adequate magnesium (your ratio of calcium to magnesium should be 2 to 1).	age 20-29 age 30-39 age 40-49 age 50-59 age 60-69 age 70+	Rare Rare 1 in 25 1 in 4 1 in 3 2 in 3
Heart Disease: Cut your SATURATED FAT intake to 10% or less of your total calories. Cut your TOTAL FAT consumption to 30% or less of your total calories. Limit your total cholesterol. Try to stay under 300 mg. of cholesterol per day (less if your cholesterol is at a dangerous level). Reduce these numbers further if your total cholesterol is over 200 and your HDL is under 35.	age 20-29 age 30-44 age 45-54 age 55-64 age 65-74 age 75+	Rare 1 in 1,000 1 in 250 1 in 100 1 in 71 1 in 16

YOU: I read in your book that you lowered your cholesterol almost 100 points in six months by cutting the fat in your diet. I don't know much about cholesterol. Could you send me some basic information. If there are any new ideas, please let me know about those, too. I haven't had it checked yet, but high cholesterol runs in my family. I think your book is great. I cook out of it every day. In fact, it is the only cookbook I really use. I sold all the rest in a garage sale. When you have *BUTTER BUSTERS*, that is all you need!   —*M. C. Colorado Springs, Colorado*

ME: I appreciate your note. I am really glad you feel that way about the book. When I wrote it, I had no idea if people would really like and use it. I just wrote a book that I would like to have myself and that is how it turned out. I guess there are other people, like me, who like an easy to follow- basic food recipes- with a grocery store name brand shopping list- cookbook all in one.

You mentioned that you hadn't had your cholesterol checked yet. For the most accurate cholesterol measurement, make sure you are on a stable diet and at a stable weight for at least two weeks before your test. Make sure you are feeling well. If you have just gone through major surgery, a heart attack, stroke, viral infection, bacterial infection or have been under unusual stress or trauma to your body, put it off for a while (at least six weeks). If you have just had a baby, wait 3-4 months before you have your cholesterol tested.

AS I WAS ANSWERING THIS PERSON'S LETTER, I DECIDED THIS WOULD BE A GOOD TIME TO INCLUDE ALL THE NEW INFORMATION REGARDING CHOLESTEROL. I HAVE SEVERAL LETTERS WITH ALL KINDS OF QUESTIONS, SO I FELT THIS WAS THE BEST WAY TO GIVE ALL MY READERS THE NEW INFORMATION IN AN EASY-TO-READ AND UNDERSTAND WAY!

ALL THE NEWS THAT'S FIT TO CHEW
(Revised Cholesterol Guidelines for Healthy Hearts)

Just when I figured out what all those cholesterol numbers meant, the rules changed. With the new evidence we now know the high density lipoproteins (HDL) cholesterol is a strong predictor of heart disease. The National Cholesterol Education Program recommends advising doctors to measure HDL levels as well as total cholesterol during routine screenings. Even if your total cholesterol is within the "desirable" level (under 200 mg/dL), you may still be at increased risk for heart disease if your HDL levels are low (under 35 mg/dL). On the other hand, a high HDL (over 60 mg/dL) may help protect against **heart disease, which is the number one killer of the American people.**

Thanks to estrogen (a female sex hormone), premenopausal women generally have higher levels of HDL than men. HDL is the "good cholesterol" that carries harmful cholesterol out of the bloodstream. However, when a woman reaches menopause, levels of estrogen drop and it's protective benefits diminish as well. This is one reason why women tend to develop heart disease about ten years later (on the average) than men. The new guidelines recommend a cholesterol check at least once every five years.

Low-density lipoproteins (LDL), the "bad" cholesterol that tends to build up in the artery walls, continues to be the main target of cholesterol-lowering treatment, according to the new guidelines. The experts now advise that only those who have a low HDL (under 35 mg/dL), high cholesterol (more than 239 mg/dL), or borderline cholesterol (200-239 mg/dL) with two other risks factors undergo a more detailed lipoprotein analysis to determine LDL levels.

The new guidelines suggest delaying cholesterol-lowering drug therapy for premenopausal women unless they have very high LDL levels (220 mg/dL or above) or a high risk of developing heart disease due to a combination of factors such as diabetes plus a family history of heart problems.

You would be smart to begin tracking, and possibly raising, HDL levels when you are young. Don't wait until you are 40 like I did to find out the bad news! You can do so by exercising regularly, stopping smoking (if you smoke), losing excess weight and moderating your alcohol consumption. To lower your LDL levels, try to maintain a low-fat (especially saturated fat), low-cholesterol diet, keeping your fat intake below 30% of your total daily calories. Preventive medicine is well worth the effort. Maybe our future generations (if they follow these guidelines) won't be faced with the cholesterol related problems so many of us have had to deal with in our lifetime (myself included)!

CHOLESTEROL LOWERING OATRIM–A FAT SUBSTITUTE
There is a fat substitute on the market called Oatrim. It is made from the cholesterol-lowering soluble fiber in oat bran, and was developed by the U.S. Department of Agriculture for use in commercial baked goods and processed foods. In a government study, Oatrim lowered harmful low-density lipoproteins (LDL) cholesterol 6-16% without lowering the beneficial high-density lipoprotein (HDL) cholesterol. The volunteers in the study, without restricting calories, also managed to lose an average of 4 1/2 pounds during the 10-week study. The "fake fat" only has 1 calorie per gram, while real fat has 9. Unlike other fat substitutes, Oatrim absorbs water, causing it to swell, so you feel full with fewer calories. Oatrim can be found in such products as Healthy Choice Hot Dogs and some of the Healthy Choice cheese products. It can also be found in Quaker Oats' GatorBar. It's sold in some grocery stores on the West Coast and Midwest in powder form for baking. Oatrim powder is available by mail. For more information regarding this product write to: Bob's Red Mill Natural Foods, 5209 Southwest International Way, Milwaukee, Oregon 97222.

FIBER AND CHOLESTEROL
Another cholesterol-lowering product you might not be aware of is Psyllium seed, found in Kellogg's Bran Buds cereal and some over-the-counter fiber supplements such as Metamucil. Total cholesterol was reduced approximately 5% (and LDL, 7%) by the participants who were involved in a 8-week study. Half of the participants were given 5.1 grams of psyllium supplement

twice a day and half of the participants were given a placebo. Before you bulk up on any kind of fiber supplements, BE SURE AND CONSULT WITH YOUR PHYSICIAN!

COULD YOU HAVE A GENE DISORDER?
(Familial Hypercholesterolemia)

There is a small group of people with a big problem. Because there has been so much attention in the news about lowering our cholesterol, little concern has been given to a small group of people who suffer from a very serious genetic disorder (and more at risk than any of us). I learned about this disorder while I was on my book tour in January 1994. I was actually in Detroit, doing a remote talk radio show from my hotel room (that was being broadcast in Florida at the time). A lady called in about her mother who happened to have this severe cholesterol disorder. By the grace of God, I had just read an article (about the disorder) the day before in *U.S.A. Today*. Something had made me tear out the article and stick it in my briefcase as I flew from Chicago to Detroit. I had found the information interesting and wanted to research it further. It was as if God had planned the whole thing. When the lady called in, I was able to give her the new information and a number to call for help.

There are 1 in 500 people missing a gene that causes a severe cholesterol disorder called FH (familial hypercholesterolemia). The disease affects the liver. In most normal situations the liver produces a gene that builds proteins to remove cholesterol from the blood. If you suffer from this disorder, your liver fails to produce the much-needed substance. Most victims have high cholesterol levels by the age of 2 and can suffer from heart attacks in their 20s. People suffering from this disorder usually produce total cholesterol levels in the high 300-600 mg/dL range. Some of their cholesterol levels can be controlled with the proper medication (if they know they have the problem), but their response to drugs is less dramatic. That is why it is so important for all of us to not only know our family history, but also have our blood cholesterol levels tested. As a matter of fact, a 30 year-old woman in Pennsylvania has undergone gene therapy, possibly prolonging her life by months or even years. Since the technique proved beneficial to the woman, it has been administered to four other victims with the disorder. While not eliminating the risk of heart disease, the promising therapy may provide a longer life to those afflicted. Let's hope so.

To find out if you are a FH gene carrier, you begin by having your cholesterol checked. If you happen to be affected, you can write to: MED PED FH Coordinating Center, 410 Chipets Way, Room 161, Salt Lake City, Utah 84108 or call (801)581-3888 for more information. Since the disorder is a hereditary problem there is a chance your children could be affected as well. A blood test would determine if that is the case.

HOME CHOLESTEROL TESTING
(Is it really worth the time, effort and money?)
Several companies have introduced home cholesterol testing kits. They have been approved by the Food and Drug Administration, and are available in drug stores across the country.

Here is how it works:
- You prick your finger and squeeze a few drops of blood into a container that contains a test strip.

- Once the strip changes color (about 15 minutes), you compare the height of the color with the kit's conversion chart to find your cholesterol level.

The main drawback is it only measures the total cholesterol (cost is $19.95 for a single-use disposable kit), not the HDL or LDL levels which are critical when assessing your heart disease risk. You really have to be careful not to squeeze your finger too hard. By squeezing your finger to get more blood out, you could cause the tissue fluid to dilute the blood and possibly lower the cholesterol readout. It's probably as accurate as the cholesterol screening you might have had at a health fair, or the mall, where they offer the finger-stick tests to screen the general public. If you do choose to purchase one of these tests and the result is over 200 milligrams per deciliter, please make an appointment with your physician for a total blood cholesterol profile immediately. Unless you are taking cholesterol-lowering drugs (and need more frequent testing), I would skip the home test and get checked out by your personal physician for a full cholesterol screening (ranging from $25.00-$50.00 depending on where you live).

If you have other risk factors, I would strongly consider being tested by a physician initially. Don't get me wrong, the home cholesterol test is better than not having your cholesterol checked at all. If you choose to use one of the home tests to save a little money, just remember that it is a lot cheaper (in the long run) to STAY WELL than it is to go through the long (and sometimes very expensive) process of TRYING TO GET WELL! I'd rather be safe than sorry! You really can't put a price tag on your health!

YOUR CHOLESTEROL GUIDELINES
(Up with the "good" and down with the "bad")
Even though cholesterol levels have dropped in the past twelve years, about half of all Americans have cholesterol levels that are too high. Bringing down the bad cholesterol (LDL) is still the main concern. However, the new cholesterol guidelines emphasize the importance of the good cholesterol (HDL). Since heart disease becomes much more likely as we age (over 45 in men and 55 in women), our age has in fact become a risk factor. Lifestyle changes remain the first choice for lowering cholesterol, but cholesterol-lowering medication should be strongly considered if the lifestyle adjustments don't make a difference after three months, especially those who already have coronary artery disease (CAD), or who have at least two other risk factors.

HEART DISEASE RISK FACTORS
(Do any of these apply to you?)

Age	Men 45 or older, and women 55 or older (also women in premature menopause who aren't taking estrogen).
History of Coronary Artery Disease	Even though you have recovered, you will always be at risk and should be monitored carefully.
Family History	A heart attack or sudden death in a father or brother before the age of 55 (this one hits close to home since my brother died of heart disease at the age of 19), or a mother or sister before the age of 65.
Lack of Physical Activity	Regular physical activity helps reduce your risk of heart disease by raising the HDL cholesterol (in most cases).
Currently Smoking	Quit!! What more can I say!!
Hypertension	If your blood pressure is 140/90 or greater, or you are taking antihypertensive medication.
Low HDL Cholesterol	If your HDL (good cholesterol) is less than 35 mg/dL (35 milligrams per deciliter).
Diabetes	This in itself, puts you at increased risk. If you are diabetic AND overweight your heart disease risk increases. **Try to maintain your ideal weight.**

WHAT IS CHOLESTEROL?
(A Basic Review in Case You Have Forgotten)

Cholesterol is actually a waxy substance that is essential in all animal tissues. It provides the structural support for cell membranes and is used to manufacture hormones. It is converted by the liver into bile acids that digest fats. Cholesterol is produced, for the most part, by the liver, and your body can easily make all it needs. We add to our cholesterol account by eating animal food products, such as meat and eggs. **Remember, if it walked, swam, or had a mother, it definitely contains cholesterol!** I bet every one of you reading this book, is getting really tired of me saying that, aren't you? I do it for a reason, you see. I DON'T WANT YOU TO FORGET IT!

All cholesterol, no matter what it's source, circulates through the blood in water-soluble, protein-wrapped packages called lipoproteins. Lipoproteins transport cholesterol to the body's tissues (LDL), or sweep up the excess and return it to the liver for repackaging or excretion (HDL). The LDL is a problem when it deposits itself in the arterial walls which could lead to **coronary artery disease** (CAD). It could also lead to carotid artery disease (a stroke) or peripheral vascular disease in the legs. You remember the carotid artery? It is the one on the side of your neck where we count our heart rate during aerobic exercise. If it gets blocked, a stroke may result. Very low density lipoprotein or (VLDL), is manufactured by the liver and transports mainly triglycerides. Triglycerides, a type of fat produced by the liver, are used by the body for energy, the muscles for energy and the excess is stored as fat.

THE NEW CHOLESTEROL UP-DATES
(What do the numbers mean?)

A total cholesterol reading doesn't necessarily give you all the information you need. Oh, it's a good place to start, but there is so much more to it. Between 60-70% of the total cholesterol comes from the LDL, so an elevated total cholesterol almost always indicates a high LDL, as well. High levels of the good protective cholesterol (HDL) may contribute to a somewhat elevated total cholesterol that is not dangerous. This is especially true in premenopausal women and post menopausal women taking estrogen.

On the other hand, you may be at greater risk if you happen to have a low HDL. The National Cholesterol Education Program (NCEP) recommends specific values concerning HDL and LDL cholesterol. They also take into consideration other risk factors for heart disease.

Total Cholesterol: Under 200 mg/dL is the most desirable. If you happen to have coronary artery disease (CAD) your total cholesterol should be under 160.

HDL: Low levels (under 35) of the protective (HDL) cholesterol is considered a risk factor. If you happen to be a lucky soul with your HDL over 60, this would be considered a negative risk factor (meaning it would help protect your heart). The female sex hormone estrogen helps elevate the HDL, which may be why women don't usually develop CAD until after menopause. Estrogen-replacement therapy (after menopause) reduces CAD risk as well. In women it was found, with every 10 point increase in HDL, there is a decrease in the risk of heart disease by 40-50% according to two studies (the Framingham Heart Study and a study funded by the National Heart, Lung, and Blood Institute (NHLBI).

LDL: Your desirable level of what we usually refer to as the bad cholesterol (LDL) is under 130 mg/dL. You are considered borderline high if you are within the 130-159 range. If your LDL is over 160, it would be considered high. If you happen to have **coronary artery disease** (CAD), your LDL should be kept below 100.

BLOOD LIPID AND LIPOPROTEIN GUIDELINES

Type of Cholesterol	Desirable	Borderline High Risk	High Risk	Very High Risk
TOTAL CHOLESTEROL	less than 200	200-239	240+	
HDL CHOLESTEROL	35+	less than 35		
LDL CHOLESTEROL	less than 130	130-159	160+	
TRIGLYCERIDES	less than 200	200-400	400-1,000	1,000+

HDL (Good Cholesterol)

The healthy average HDL for a man is 45 (the higher the better)
The healthy average HDL for a premenopausal woman is 55 (the higher the better)
Anything less than 35 is considered a heart disease risk factor!

CHOLESTEROL TESTING
(The New Standards)

1. All adults over the age of 20 should have their total and HDL cholesterol checked every five years if their values are in the desirable range. Additional CAD risk factors may require more frequent testing.

2. The initial test measures your total and HDL cholesterol blood levels. This simple test requires no fasting. If your total cholesterol is under 200 and your HDL is over 35 mg/ dL, you need not be tested again for five years (unless you have two or more risk factors).

3. If your total cholesterol is high (240 mg/ dL or more), or if you have CAD, or if your total cholesterol is borderline high and you have two or more risk factors for CAD, you should have a complete lipid profile (even if your HDL is above 35). This comprehensive evaluation requires an overnight fast. It measures triglyceride levels as well as total and HDL cholesterol. LDL cholesterol levels are calculated from these other values.

4. If your cholesterol is borderline, and you have fewer than two CAD risk factors, you should have your total cholesterol rechecked in one year.

5. If your HDL is below 35, even if your total cholesterol level is desirable, you should have a complete lipid profile if you are a man over 45, or a woman over 55 (since this combination constitutes two risk factors).

6. If the complete profile shows your LDL in the desirable range, you can wait five years to be retested. If your LDL is above 130, you will need to lower it, as well as have annual testing.

CHOLESTEROL TEST RESULTS
(Go with the Flow Chart)

You will need a basic cholesterol screening to complete this chart. You do not need "to fast" in order to have this test performed.

Total Cholesterol = _____
(Insert YOUR value)

The Good News & the Bad News	Now What?
Over 240 mg/dL	Complete Lipid Profile
Over 200 mg/dL with HDL under 35 or other risk factors	Complete Lipid Profile

HDL = _____
(Insert YOUR value)

The Good News & the Bad News	Now What?
HDL under 35 and you are a male 45 years (or older)	Complete Lipid Profile
HDL under 35 and you are a female 55 years (or older)	Complete Lipid Profile
HDL over 35	Recheck in 5 years

Note: This "flow chart" is only provided to give you basic guidelines regarding your cholesterol screening. Your personal "risk factors" will determine the frequency in which you should be re-tested and the type of testing needed. **ALWAYS CONSULT YOUR PHYSICIAN!**

TRIGLYCERIDES
(Are you at risk?)

1. Triglycerides are the main types of fat transported in the blood, and are derived directly from the food you eat.

2. Elevated triglyceride levels appear to be a risk factor for coronary artery disease.

They are frequently associated with low levels of HDL and / or elevated levels of total and LDL cholesterol. Individuals who are obese, diabetic, or consume excess alcohol are at risk for elevated triglyceride levels.

3. Most physicians don't usually consider mildly elevated triglycerides to be a risk factor for coronary artery disease (CAD) in older men. If your LDLs are high, many doctors ignore triglyceride levels because they don't add any useful information about your risk of a heart attack. However, if a man is under the age of 70, has normal or low LDLs, and turns up with elevated triglycerides, further investigation would be in order. Mildly elevated triglycerides seem to be less troublesome for older adults. The majority of physicians agree that elevated triglycerides in men are (more often than not) a result of high blood sugar levels, or being overweight.

4. The National Cholesterol Education Program guidelines state that the desirable level for triglycerides is less than 200 mg/dL for men and women.

5. The key to lowering elevated triglycerides is the same for everyone: Lose weight (if you are overweight), exercise (on a regular basis), avoid alcohol (or limit your consumption), and EAT A LOW-FAT DIET!! With this plan, you will not only lower your triglycerides, but will also lower your coronary artery disease risk as well.

TIPS TO HELP YOU LOWER YOUR CHOLESTEROL
(Your mission if you choose to accept it!)
In most cases, the first step to lowering your cholesterol involves lifestyle changes, and a blood cholesterol re-check in three months. YOUR primary concern is to lower your total cholesterol (if it is over 200), lower your LDL cholesterol (if it is over 130), and raise your HDL cholesterol (if it is under 35).

1. **Eat less saturated fat!** Meat, butter, whole milk, cheese, palm oil, palm kernel oil, coconut oil, cocoa butter, and hydrogenated vegetable oil (trans-fatty acids) all contribute to a high cholesterol. **Limiting, or omitting, these products from your diet is probably the single most important change you can make to lower your cholesterol levels.** Cut down your total fat percentage to 10-20% of your daily caloric intake if you haven't already done so. Modify your recipes using low and fat-free products.

2. **Lower your cholesterol intake!** Cholesterol containing products (those of animal origin) should be limited to no more than 300 mg. a day. **The American Heart Association has cut their recommendation to 150 mg. or less.**

3. **Eat foods rich in antioxidants!** LDL cholesterol causes trouble when it is oxidized (it reacts with certain oxygen molecules). The antioxidant vitamins E, C, and beta carotene (commonly found in fruits and vegetables) may help block this process. Vitamin E has shown particular promise at being protective. The opinions of physicians differ concerning

antioxidant vitamin supplementation. The majority of the sources I consulted recommend (especially those at risk for CAD) supplementing 200 - 400 mg. of vitamin E to their diet daily. (The standard recommended dosage has yet to be established.) **HOWEVER, ALWAYS CHECK WITH YOUR PHYSICIAN BEFORE TAKING ANY MEDICATION OR SUPPLEMENTS!**

4. **STOP SMOKING!** Not only is this a good reason to quit, it will even help raise your protective HDL cholesterol.

5. **Lose weight!** For every two pounds of excess weight, you increase your total cholesterol 1 mg/dL.

6. **Exercise!** In addition to helping you lose weight, aerobic exercise is one of the best ways to raise your good cholesterol (HDL) level. Brisk walking 35-45 minutes three or four days a week may do the trick.

*NOTE: Some experts feel moderate alcohol may raise the HDL level of your good cholesterol and even lower heart disease risks. However, the dangers of excessive alcohol intake far outweigh the benefits, so I personally do not recommend this method. I wanted to mention it, however, because I know many of you have read about the "French Paradox," and I didn't want you to think I was withholding information. I feel there are other ways to raise your HDL cholesterol. Aerobic exercise, in my opinion, is a much healthier way to go about it!

7. **Medication is the last resort!** Diet and exercise should be the initial lifestyle changes in management of your cholesterol problem. Medication should be the last resort if lifestyle changes fail to do the job. Medication **should be considered** under the following circumstances:

   •In men younger than 45 or women younger than 55 with fewer than two risk factors, if the LDL is greater than 220 after three months of lifestyle modifications.

   •In men older than 45, or women older than 55 (or women with premature menopause who aren't taking estrogen), regardless of the number of risk factors, if the LDL cholesterol level is greater than 190 mg/dL after three months of lifestyle modifications.

   •In those with two or more risk factors, if the LDL cholesterol level is greater than 160 mg/dL after three months of lifestyle modifications.

   •In those with known coronary artery disease (CAD), if LDL is greater than 100 mg/dL after three months of lifestyle modifications.

A heart-healthy diet is a must, even for those taking medication. A number of cholesterol drugs are available. Your doctor is the best judge of which drug, or combination of drugs, is best for you.

NO MORE RATIO CONFUSION
(Let's figure out what the numbers really mean)

In the past we were all concerned with our ratio. This meant comparing your total cholesterol level to your HDL cholesterol or comparing HDL cholesterol to the LDL cholesterol. Ratios became popular because people were trying to simplify cholesterol. Most experts never really endorsed it. The "ratio" was not effective because it just wasn't specific enough for physicians to use as a guide for treatment. When the physicians were focusing on the ratio they felt they lost sight of the specific LDL level. They became so concerned with how the two numbers related to each other, instead of getting it down to where it needed to be. The latest thinking, is to assess HDL and LDL levels as separate risk factors concerning heart disease. This means both numbers should be considered **separately** when trying to improve your cholesterol levels.

CHOLESTEROL TALK—BE AN INFORMED PATIENT!
(The questions you should ask your doctor)

All healthy adults should have their cholesterol levels tested at least once every five years after the age of 20. Some people should be tested more frequently depending on their total cholesterol, HDL cholesterol level and other risk factors. Talking with your doctor about your test results can be a little confusing, and somewhat intimidating, if you don't know the questions to ask. I know because I am married to a doctor, and I know how confusing medical terms can be. Many people don't want to appear uninformed, so instead of asking, they leave the doctor's office with unanswered questions, simply because they were embarrassed to ask. I want to give you some vital questions to ask your physician in order to understand what your cholesterol levels really mean:

1. **IS MY CHOLESTEROL READING IN THE SAFE RANGE?**

   Your doctor says that your cholesterol is 220. This only tells you your total cholesterol level. Since YOU know the general guidelines for total cholesterol levels are: under 200 is desirable; 200-239 is borderline high; and over 240 is considered high, you already know the answer, but ask anyway. He didn't mention your HDL or LDL did he? Well, you need to ask for those numbers as well.

2. **WHAT ARE MY HDL AND LDL LEVELS?**

   If your doctor says "Well your ratio is....." Stop her, or him, and say, "I would like to know my specific HDL and LDL levels." Once you get those numbers, ask: "Are these results safe for me based on my risk factors?" "What would be the best levels for me?" Because you are informed, you know your HDL should be over 35. Forty-five is average for a man and 55 is average for a premenopausal woman or a postmenopausal woman taking estrogen. Your LDL should be under 160. It's such a nice secure feeling knowing the answers before you ask the questions. It's like a little test, if you know what I mean. I hope my husband doesn't read this part, because then he will know what I am doing when I start quizzing him about some medical question. Ha! Ha!

3. ARE THERE WAYS TO IMPROVE MY CHOLESTEROL WITHOUT TAKING MEDICATION?

If your doctor wants to prescribe medication right off the bat, you might ask about other treatments that could be tried before medication. Don't ever agree to this idea, without asking questions. A lifestyle change (including a low-fat diet and some kind of exercise program) should be your first plan of action. Six weeks to six months (depending on YOUR risk of heart disease) of changing your lifestyle should show results. Ask your physician for recommendations that might be helpful. You already know what to do, but ask him, or her, for fun. If, after changing your lifestyle, your cholesterol levels remain unchanged, it might be time to start discussing the various medications. If you do need to consider medication here are some questions you might ask:

1. **How long will I need to take medication?**
2. **How often should I recheck my cholesterol levels?**
3. **Are there drug side effects and if so, how can I prevent them?**
4. **What is my target level after treatment?**

CHOLESTEROL-LOWERING DRUGS

There are several cholesterol-lowering drugs on the market. We have all heard the names. They range from Nicotinic acids (such as Niacin) to Bile-acid-binding resins (such as Questran and Colestid). Then we have the HMG CoA reductase inhibitors (Mevacor, Pravachol, Lescol, and ZOCOR), the Fibrates (Lopid and Atromid-S), and the Estrogens (specifically for women).

After a five year Scandinavian study of 4,444 people with heart disease who took ZOCOR or a placebo, the results are in. This drug, made by Merck & Co., was shown to reverse or stop progression of coronary blockages over time. The findings, presented in November 1994, at The American Heart Association's 67th Scientific Sessions in Dallas, Texas, is expected to dramatically change treatment and may help thousands delay or avoid bypasses and angioplasty to open blocked arteries. They felt the 5-year Scandinavian study had the definitive answer. Results of the study showed many important breakthroughs that the drug had produced: reduction of heart disease related deaths by 42%, reduced over-all deaths by 30%, the need for bypass surgery or angioplasty had been cut by 37%, the LDL (bad) cholesterol had been lowered 38%, by raising HDL (good) levels by 8%. Total cholesterol had been reduced 28%. The study was done on people with mild to moderately high cholesterol levels (ON THE AVERAGE OF 260), with either chest pain or an earlier heart attack. Researchers said the results of the study indicated most people with severe heart disease should be put on a cholesterol-lowering drug (similar to ZOCOR) and a LOW-FAT DIET! (We knew that part, didn't we?) The drug has actually been on the market since 1992, and has accounted for 16% of cholesterol-lowering drug sales. **Most doctors feel other medications (of the same class) may have similar effects.**

HMG CoA reductase inhibitors: lovastatin (Mevacor), pravastatin (Pravachol), simvastatin (ZOCOR), and fluvastatin (Lescol) are the cholesterol-lowering drugs that seem to be the most potent. Their attributes include lowering the LDL, raising the HDL, and lowering triglycerides. Since the drugs are relatively new (1989) long-term safety has not been conclusively established. The unusual complications associated with these drugs include a rise in liver enzymes and muscle inflammation (which could be quite serious and life threatening). For this reason, people using these drugs should have a blood test to check their liver enzymes periodically.

CAN YOUR CHOLESTEROL BE TOO LOW?

If you read the scary studies reporting a link between low cholesterol levels (below 160) and an increased risk of death, you may have thought twice about lowering your cholesterol. According to those studies, men who decreased their cholesterol through drugs or diet were less likely to die from heart disease, but more likely to die from such diseases as lung cancer, alcoholism, accidental death, or suicide. The findings were questioned by researchers at The University of California. They found an adverse effect of low cholesterol occuring only in those who had certain medical conditions, or in those who smoked or drank heavily. Healthy men who lowered their levels had no increased risk.

If your doctor warns you to reduce your cholesterol, I would take his advice. Keep in mind that **the number one killer of both men and women is heart disease!**

NEW CHOLESTEROL TECHNIQUES AND TREATMENTS
(A LOOK INTO THE FUTURE)

CHOLESTEROL VACCINES
(A shot in the artery?)

When it comes to lowering cholesterol levels a low-fat diet doesn't always do the trick (even when it is combined with proper exercise). A lifetime of medication is nothing to look forward to as an alternative measure and, for some, it might not even be an option. In Washington, D.C., a physician from the Walter Reed Army Institute named Carl Alving, M.D. stumbled upon the possibility of an anti-cholesterol vaccine. While testing the safety of new drug-delivery methods, he had injected mice with drugs enclosed in liposomes (which are mostly cholesterol). He found the mice developed antibodies to cholesterol when injected. Subsequently, liposome injections kept the cholesterol levels of rabbits fed a cholesterol-raising diet, 30 percent lower than those of untreated rabbits that were fed the same diet. The possibility that antibodies can actually clear clogged blood vessels (since arterial plaque also resembles liposomes) is being explored further. The next step will be to find out if people with naturally high levels of antibodies do, in fact, have lower cholesterol levels. Even if the vaccine does become a reality, it will probably be used in conjunction (as a supplement) with diet modifications and medication to treat and/or control cholesterol disorders.

NO-STICK CHOLESTEROL TEST: PHOTON CORRELATION SPECTROSCOPY
(On the lighter side)

I don't know anyone who actually looks forward to an injection (shot). It's pretty hard to avoid the needle, however, if you want to have your cholesterol checked, right? Fortunately (for those of us who hate the sight of blood), sometime in the near future there may be a way to measure your "good" protective (HDL) cholesterol and your "bad" artery-clogging (LDL) cholesterol. This feat is accomplished by simply shining a low-power red beam light into your eyes. The results are immediate. You see, the low-power red beam bounces off the HDL and LDL particles present in the fluid within your eyes. Next, the particles are "counted" by a process called photon correlation spectroscopy. Don't run to the phone to call your doctor (for an appointment) just yet. The test won't be available until 1996. Be sure and "keep your eyes open" for any new "light" shattering developments! (No pun intended!)

X-RAY CHOLESTEROL SCREENING
(Computerized Tomography)

Until a few years ago, the only way to determine the extent of coronary artery disease (CAD) was through angiography, a sometimes uncomfortable, often scary procedure that involved injecting an opaque dye into a narrow tube that was threaded through the blood vessels leading to the heart. There is a new test known as Ultrafast CT (computerized tomography) or, by its trade name, Imatron, that can scan the coronary arteries by means of an electron beam in less than 15 minutes, using an X-ray. The test measures the amount of calcium in the heart's vessels (which is believed to cause the "hardness" or hardening of the arteries we are all familiar with). Unlike the angiogram, the test does not show the extent to which blood flow through a given artery is reduced.

Ultrafast CT is new, and not yet ready to be used as a measure of coronary disease. More study is needed before the device can be used as a screening tool. At this time, the best application for the test is for "ruling out" heart disease (particularly in people under the age of 60 who are having chest pains that aren't typical of heart disease). If no calcium shows up on the Ultrafast CT scan, some physicians feel the possibility of heart disease is very low. Other physicians disagree, feeling there is not a clear correlation between the amount of calcium in the arteries and coronary disease. Some feel Ultrafast CT can be used to screen people for coronary artery disease whether they have symptoms or not. Some feel the test would be especially useful to people in their thirties and forties who have high cholesterol levels or a strong family history of heart disease and, therefore, are at an increased risk of a heart attack 10 or 15 years down the road.

APOPROTEINS AND APOLIPOPROTEINS
(Cholesterol screening of the future?)

We haven't always known about cholesterol's contribution to heart-disease. Cholesterol screening gained popularity in the 1980s and was a major leap forward in preventive medicine. Recently we have gone from "ratio concern" to measuring the good (HDL) and the bad (LDL) cholesterol levels individually as a more accurate method. Who knows what the future holds? We will probably look back some day and think of even these refinements as relatively crude.

Many researchers have switched to more sophisticated measurements of HDL and LDL, using antibodies to detect proteins that surround cholesterol and carry it through the blood. Apoproteins or apolipoproteins (the cholesterol-carriers) may provide the clearest picture yet of who is at risk for heart disease. There are some people at risk for heart disease who do not test high for cholesterol. Those people, on the other hand, usually have elevations of apoprotein B (which carries LDL). Some feel it might be more accurate to count the carriers, rather than the cholesterol.

Until recently, it has been hard to test for apoproteins because they constantly change shape, often hiding from the antibodies sent to find them. (Think of it as hide and seek in your body.) A pathologist from the University of Rochester Medical Center, Charles Sparks, M.D., has devised a technique that creates a rigid core in the cholesterol center, which stabilizes the protein coating. Using this method doctors could test for apo B (which carries LDL) and apo A (which carries HDL), as well as others. More research needs to be done to find the exact role each apoprotein plays. Who knows? Maybe the answers will be found in our lifetime, or in that of our children!

IS HIGH CHOLESTEROL AFTER AGE 70 A RISK?
(Don't believe EVERYTHING you read!)

As of November 1994, according to a report that was published in the *Journal of the American Medical Association,* it is now believed by many experts that a cholesterol reading over 200 is not as important for our senior citizens as once thought. The study found that, unlike younger people, those who are 70 years old (or older) do not appear to be of increased risk of heart attack, angina, or death from any cause by having either a high total cholesterol or a low HDL (good cholesterol).

In 1988 testing began at Yale University using blood samples for cholesterol analysis from 610 women and 387 men between the ages of 70-104. The average age was 79. They took health histories on all the participants. In 1992 they checked the death records for each participant who died during that period. They then compared the information in each person's records with his or her cholesterol readings. They found only 32% of the women and 16% of the men had cholesterol levels greater than 240 mg/dL, and only 9% of the women and 26% of the men had low HDL levels. There did not appear to be any significant association between either total cholesterol or HDL levels and the occurrence of heart attacks or deaths in either group.

Although the results of larger studies are needed before any major policies on managing cholesterol are written, some experts are advising physicians to stop performing cholesterol tests or treating high cholesterol of people in their late 70s. They feel that cholesterol-lowering drugs are more likely to have a toxic effect or to possibly interact with other medications older people may be taking. However, the study's findings should not be extended to people who are younger than 70 or interpreted as an excuse to overindulge in high-fat foods or discontinue exercise!

Restricting your fat to 30% or less is important at any age. There are many diseases linked to a high-fat diet (besides an elevated cholesterol). Any testing over the age of 70 would definitely be up to YOUR personal physician. I just wanted to mention this, because it has been all over the news and I don't want senior citizens to think their diet or exercise program is any less important than it ever was. Please follow the advice of your personal physician, and take everything you read in the newspaper "with a grain of salt" until proven beyond a questionable doubt. In other words, don't self prescribe based on what you read somewhere (including this book). I only offer information from a vast amount of sources to let you be aware of the tremendous amount of research going on every day. Please discuss anything and everything you read with your physician before taking action!

YOU: I read somewhere that you are more at risk for heart disease if you carry your weight in the tummy. Is that true? I love your book, and have lost about thirty pounds, but am having a hard time getting rid of my gut (please excuse my frankness). Are there any good exercises that might help me? My husband also carries the majority of his weight in his stomach. Is it a problem for men too? —*P.S.Little Rock, Arkansas*

ME: As a matter of fact you read correctly. If you carry the majority of your weight in the stomach area (and resemble the shape of an apple), this would mean you have a large waist in comparison to your hips which could increase your risk of heart disease. I don't want to scare you, but I feel you need to be aware that the larger the waist in comparison to the hips, the greater the risk of diabetes, some forms of cancer, and most definitely heart disease. Women who are "pear shaped," however, and carry the majority of their fat in the hips and thighs might not like the way their jeans fit, but in all reality their disease risk factor is greatly reduced. (Somehow that never made me feel a whole lot better when my inner thighs rubbed together when I walked!) I guess no one is ever totally happy with their body shape, are they?

I speak of women specifically (when I discuss the "pear" shape) because most men carry their extra fat in the stomach area. This brings up your husband and his stomach. Yes, men are just as much at risk when they carry the highest percentage of fat in their mid-section. You hardly ever see a bottom heavy man unless he is extremely obese. That may explain why men generally die younger than women, and the majority of their deaths are "heart related."

It is important for all of us to determine if we have an "apple" or "pear" shaped body type, regardless of your sex. All you need to determine your waist-to-hip ratio is a simple tape measure. While standing, measure your waist just above where you feel the top of your hipbone (or where it should be if you can't feel it). Next measure your hips at their widest point. Divide the waist's measurement by the hip measurement. I will give you an example. Say your hips are 36 inches and your waist is 24 inches. Divide 24 by 36 and you get .66 which would mean you are a "pear" shaped person. On the other hand, if your hips are 38 inches and your waist is 34 inches your ratio would be .94 (not so good for a woman, but satisfactory for a man). For a woman, a ratio under .85 means you are a "pear" shape (lucky you) and under .95 for a man. Your ratio contributes to your disease risk, but please realize your lifestyle choices can be just as important. Smoking, a high-fat diet, and lack of exercise can be just as detrimental to your health as your body shape! And just think, WE ALL HAVE COMPLETE CONTROL over "lifestyle" disease risk factors! (Refer to page 161 in the "Exercise and Fitness" chapter for more information regarding "body shape.")

For women (since their hips are naturally wider) the waist should be "quite a bit" smaller than their hips. For men the waist only needs to be slightly smaller. Somehow that doesn't seem fair, since men tend to lose weight (and body fat) faster than women, too! Please don't freak out if your test determines you are an "apple" shape. Even though the "shape" of your body is somewhat genetic, a low-fat diet in conjunction with regular aerobic exercise will reduce fat all over your body (quicker for men because they usually have more lean muscle mass than women), thus lowering your disease risk. "ORANGE" you glad to hear that tidbit of news? (No pun intended!)

You will notice I mentioned aerobic exercise to reduce body fat all over. There really is no such thing as spot reduction. We would all like to believe those sit-ups will flatten our stomachs, but unfortunately this is not the case. A low-fat diet and regular aerobic exercise is the only way (besides liposuction), to accomplish that feat. However, once you've sweated off a few pounds, the crunches and abdominal exercises will strengthen, firm, and tone up your abs giving them that "washboard look" most of us can only dream about!

I hope this answers your questions, and I wish you the best of luck and continued success with your weight (more importantly fat) loss in the future.

YOU: I love your cookbook. At last, I feel I really got my money's worth! I bought another "Hot" low-fat cookbook expecting great recipes, but was very disappointed when the food turned out to be gourmet and there were only 50 recipes in the book. Just because a famous person happens to lose weight using someone's recipes, does not make for a great cookbook. I won't mention any names, but you probably know what book I am talking about. As a matter of fact I took it back to the bookstore and asked for a refund. I asked the girl in the bookstore if she knew of any good low-fat cookbooks, that had regular food recipes and a lot of them. Guess what? She suggested *BUTTER BUSTERS*! I couldn't be happier. I've already purchased several more as gifts. Your book is so complete with the shopping guide, modifying recipe section, restaurant guide, cholesterol info., and even exercise tips. I don't think you left anything out. The best part is the recipes. How did you know all my favorites?

I have lost 13 pounds in seven weeks and I have never felt better. As I was reading the first part of the book, I noticed the book was in memory of your brother, Tom. How on earth did he die of heart disease at the age of nineteen? If you don't want to tell me I understand. I'm sure it is very painful for you to talk about it, but I was just curious.

I'm spreading the word all over San Diego about your book. Most of us people in California are quite concerned with healthy eating and exercise. That is nice you got inspired to write the book at *SHAPE* CAMP right here in California. My daughter attended that camp several years ago. Maybe she was even there when you were. Keep up the good work and let me know if you write another book! —*S.A. San Diego, California*

ME: I appreciate your kind words regarding my book. I feel the book has helped a great many people because the recipes are (like you put it) real food. When I turned up with a high cholesterol in March 1990 and started cutting the fat in my diet, it was a real challenge! There weren't many low-fat products on the market back then. As a matter of fact, I had the Liquid Butter Buds (made from the dry mix), Egg Beaters, and Alpine Lace came out with a line of fat-free cheese in August of that year. Gradually (at first) more and more low-fat products began to appear on the grocery store shelves. I can remember the day I tasted my first low-fat baked tortilla chip. Even those chips have improved greatly over the past four years. The assortment of wonderful low and fat-free products is unbelievable (considering there were very few five years ago). Like the commercial says, "We've come a long way baby!" I, for one, am thrilled. I get so excited every time I find a new product that is really good. I can hardly wait to share the "good ones" with my readers.

As for my brother's death, I don't mind talking about it at all. As a matter of fact, that is one thing that really bothers me. It seems when you lose a close family member many people choose to ignore or avoid the subject. I guess it makes most people uncomfortable to talk about death. Speaking from experience, since I've lost my brother and my father, I want to talk about them. By talking about the memories of your loved ones, you are able to keep their spirit alive within your heart. I'm sure most people don't want to bring up the death of someone, because they don't want to upset you by reminding you of them. On the other hand, when they don't ask or avoid the subject entirely, it forces us to deal with the loss by stuffing our feelings inside because we have no one to talk to about them. Eventually, we must all face the death of our friends and family. By choosing to avoid the idea they ever lived (because it is an uncomfortable subject) is the worst thing you can do to those of us who are left behind to grieve alone. I didn't mean to give you a lecture. I'm really sorry I got so carried away. I guess I'm just kind of sensitive about this matter, because I recently went through an experience regarding my father's death that was very upsetting.

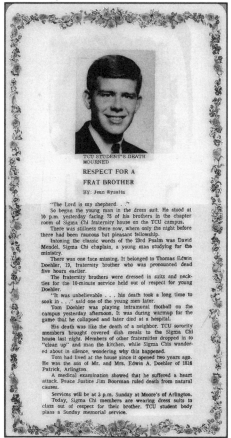

Tom Doehler
November 13, 1945 - October 7, 1965

In answer to your question about Tom, the autopsy didn't give us an answer. As a matter of fact the report read, "cause of death: unknown cardiac arrest." Tom's unexplained death was very hard for my parents and me to accept. He was the epitome of health. The only risk factor I can think of is he did smoke. He was only nineteen years old, however, so he hadn't smoked that long. I read everything I can get my hands on regarding "sudden death" and have recently come across some new information I found very interesting.

"Sudden death" is a general phrase dealing with any case in which a person goes into cardiac arrest and dies quickly. People who die suddenly almost always have some underlying heart condition. About 250,000 people die suddenly each year.

The challenge to doctors is that death is often the first symptom. Obviously people known to be at risk are usually given drugs to lessen their chances of cardiac arrest, or automatic defibrillators to restart the heart if it stops. The risks of suffering a heart attack can be reduced by avoiding smoking, lowering blood cholesterol and treating or preventing other contributors to heart disease. Hypertrophic Cardiomyopathy (or an enlarged heart) is one of the most common causes of sudden death in young people. The thicker heart muscle narrows the opening of the chambers and makes the heart more prone to lapsing into an irregular beat.

Long Q-T Syndrome (an electrical flaw) also strikes the young. Many of the deaths are children between the ages of 8 and 14 years old. The heart looks normal, but it has an electrical flaw that can disrupt its normal beating pattern. The name refers to the peaks and valleys which are named P,Q,R,S, and T that represent a heartbeat on an electrocardiogram. Long Q-T means that the interval between the Q and the T points is unusually long. Most scientists theorize that perhaps the heart takes longer to recover after each beat, so that there is some inherent disorganization in the cardiac electrical system. The victims usually die during stress or exercise. The condition is often overlooked because it is impossible to find after a child dies, even with an autopsy. The heart and every other organ look normal. That sounds like what could have happened with my brother, Tom. What typically happens is the autopsy report says, "Probably cardiac arrhythmia" (meaning irregular heartbeat), but doesn't specify what caused the disorder. Researchers are constantly searching for clues in the electrocardiograms and other tests performed on their patients. In the case of my brother, he had never had an electrocardiogram test, so there was no way of knowing if he had an enlarged heart or an electrical flaw. An electrocardiogram is not a common test performed by pediatricians on most children during a routine visit. The other most common warning sign is so subtle, it is often dismissed. A frequent loss of consciousness can be a warning signal. The electrical disturbance caused by long Q-T is often activated during extreme exertion or emotional excitement. Sometimes, when the heart starts beating irregularly, it kicks back into its normal rhythm seconds later. From outward appearances, it looks like an ordinary fainting. If it happens a lot, or during exercise, there is definitely reason for concern. Most doctors don't want to upset parents, or get them overexcited about the loss of consciousness in children, but I feel they should be made aware of the possibility of an electrical disorder. The sudden deaths (from cardiac arrest) are nothing new. In July 1993 Reggie Lewis (the Boston Celtics basketball star) collapsed and went into cardiac arrest. Hank Gathers (another basketball star) died suddenly with heart failure as well. Both of those young men happened to have some symptoms before they died, but thousands of cardiac arrest deaths occur with no warning (as in the case of my brother). Some people are known to be at risk because they have already had a heart attack. Heart attack survivors only account for about 20% of sudden death victims. The other 80% never saw it coming.

Victims of sudden cardiac death almost always have some underlying condition (whether it's recognized or not). The arteries are usually narrowed from plaque buildup. Sometimes people have a silent electrical flaw that disrupts the heart's rhythm (as in the Long Q-T Syndrome). The challenge to medical science is that in these patients, death is often the first symptom. Warning signs aren't always there. There is no chest pain or even labored breathing present. Then, without warning, something interrupts the rhythmic beating of their hearts. Scientists are looking at the problem from two different angles. There seems to be a distinction between the disease that makes the victims susceptible to it, and an event that triggers it. Many of the victims experience an adrenaline rush just before the cardiac arrest occurs (as in exercise or exertion).

All of us can reduce our risk of heart disease by avoiding known contributors such as smoking and inactivity. The secret to combating sudden death in young people (who don't usually have clogged arteries) may lie in their genes. Hypertrophic cardiomyopathy (or enlarged heart) is the most common cause of sudden death in young people. This disease causes the heart to develop excessively thick walls. People don't know about the condition because they feel fine. The bigger hearts can provide a more powerful beat, often drawing teenagers into athletics and other physical activities. Many of these athletes are a little "supernormal." The enlarged heart is more rigid and prone to lapsing into an irregular heartbeat. The chambers are often narrowed because the walls are so thick. Almost all of these victims die under exertion. Exercise produces a deadly combination by making the heart pump harder while the body is dehydrated. The heart can contract so forcefully in a person with hypertrophic cardiomypathy that it actually squeezes all the blood out of one chamber. This sends the heart into a series of rapid convulsions called fibrillation. When a heart fibrillates, it isn't pumping blood. In 1990 scientists located the gene believed responsible for hypertrophic cardiomyopathy. The gene normally makes a protein called myosin (also known as the "motor molecule" of muscle). It actually prompts the heart to contract. In people with hypertrophic cardiomyopathy, the gene is mutated, so they don't make the right form of myosin. The defective myosin leads to an enlarged heart. Some evidence suggests the molecule does not work properly, so the heart (early in life) goes into an accelerated growth pattern. People at risk can be tested to determine if they have the gene disorder. There are ways to decrease their chance of sudden death. If a person is found at risk, they are encouraged to purchase an automatic defibrillator. Unfortunately defibrillators are very expensive. Drugs called beta blockers can also slow down the heart and are much cheaper. Discuss all options with your physician.

The search for the defective gene responsible for the Long Q-T is underway. They have already narrowed the search to the point that they are in the neighborhood of the gene on chromosome 11, although scientists feel there is more than one gene involved. Once the gene is pinpointed, researchers will have a better idea what causes long Q-T and will be able to custom design a treatment.

Other causes of sudden cardiac arrest have been traced to viral infections, heatstroke, or, in some cases, the extreme loss of potassium as a result of ingesting diuretic medication prescribed for (ironically) patients with congestive heart failure. Diuretics lower blood pressure, which should reduce the incidence of sudden cardiac deaths. It is unknown whether the diuretics had any connection with the sudden deaths occurring when victims happened to be taking the medication, but it would probably be a good idea to be closely monitored by your physician if you are taking any kind of medication that could possibly affect your heart in any way.

Each school year, a small number of students collapse and die during or after athletic participation, most frequently as a result of heart problems. Between 1982 and 1992, 133 U.S. high schoolers died suddenly after sports exertion. More than 90% of the deaths were male. Parents, in my opinion, should ensure their teenagers are in good health before they try out for any sport. In most states, high school students participating in interscholastic sports must first be examined by a doctor. About half of all states require high school athletes to have subsequent annual exams.

Even though routine physicals may fail to detect potentially fatal heart problems, more thorough screening, including an echocardiogram could save the life of a child. I encourage all parents to get their kids checked out and never brush off suspicious symptoms (such as unexplained fainting). It's always better to be safe than sorry. As in the case of my brother, there was no way of knowing back then If he had a heart disorder. Even though the autopsy showed Tom's heart to be normal, after reading the information about Long Q-T Syndrome and how in the autopsy of a victim with this disorder the heart does appear normal, I feel there is a good possibility my brother suffered from this electrical flaw disorder. I will continue to search for an answer. Even though we will never know for sure what caused Tom's death, it does make me feel better to learn more about heart disease. If there is anything we can do as parents to protect our children against heart disease, I want to know about it.

Thank you for allowing me to learn even more about heart disease by asking me about my brother. It always makes me feel better to talk about it! THANK YOU FOR LISTENING TO ME!!

YOU: I received your book for Mother's Day and haven't put it down since. I KNOW WHERE BUTTER BUDS IS LOCATED in every major grocery store in the greater Nashville area. I even found it in some spots you didn't mention. I actually found it in the cereal section (it might have been misplaced because the cereals are across the aisle from the health food section). I took your advice and tried the Promise Fat-Free margarine in your pound cake recipe and loved the taste and texture. Your book changed the way I shop, cook, and eat. As a result of my new-found knowledge, I have managed to drop the extra 22 pounds of baby fat I had been carrying around way past the time I should have lost it. Thanks for the yummy recipes (especially the "Mexican Spaghetti" and "Cherry Cheesecake Delight"). Now for my question. I am thirty years old, the mother of an eighteen-month-old daughter and have been plagued with bladder infections for the past two years. My grandmother swears by cranberry juice to ward off various urinary tract infections. I beg to differ with her, but it sounds like an "old wives tale" to me. Do you have any information that might substantiate her recommendation? I can't wait to show her your reply. She thinks she knows the answer to every problem of mankind. Please answer my letter as soon as possible, because we are going to Topeka to visit her over Thanksgiving. Thanks a bunch!!
—*A. K. Nashville, Tennessee*

ME: I am so glad you are enjoying the book, and if YOU know where to find the mix to make Liquid Butter Buds, then you are definitely a die-hard low-fat shopper!! Did you know that is the #2 most asked question I receive a week? The #1 most asked question is, "When are you going to write another book?" The Butter Buds question is a close second. I list a telephone number in the book to order the mix to make Liquid Butter Buds, but I think a lot of people are mistakenly looking for Butter Buds (already in liquid form).

BUTTER BUDS DOES NOT COME IN LIQUID FORM. YOU MIX THE POWDER, FOUND IN A BOX CONTAINING EIGHT PACKETS, WITH HOT WATER TO MAKE LIQUID BUTTER BUDS! I list where to call for information concerning Butter Buds in _BUTTER BUSTERS_ on page 69 of the 7th edition. The number is: (800)231-1123 and in New York: (800)336-0363. I've also included instructions how to mix it on page 63 of the 7th edition in the "Shopping Tips" section. As YOU know the product is generally found in the diet food section, the spice section, and in some cases the butter or margarine section. If you can't find it in your area, you can always order by mail.

About your bladder infections...... I hate to tell you, but your Grandma might just win this one. In 1993 Harvard Medical School completed a six month study at Brigham and Women's Hospital regarding cranberry juice and it's impact on urinary tract infections. They ran the test on 153 women. They gave half of them 10 ounces of cranberry juice every day. They gave the other half a placebo look and taste alike drink. The juice drinkers, after six months, had 58% less infection-causing bacteria in their urine than those who drank the placebo. They first thought cranberry juice worked because it made urine more acidic. The final conclusion, however, is that cranberry juice contains a compound that inhibits bacteria from adhering to the bladder lining. A daily cranberry juice cocktail might just be a great preventive measure for you to consider trying. You don't have to tell your Grandma, but I'm afraid her advice is a good idea!

YOU: I've followed your book throughout my pregnancy and am happy to report I only gained 22 pounds and felt great the whole time. I exercised (by riding my stationary bike) the entire nine months. My baby son is precious and even sleeping through the night at three weeks. I plan to teach him healthy eating from the beginning, once I quit nursing. There is one thing that concerns me and I wanted to ask if you know anything regarding this information. At the end of my pregnancy there were several articles in the paper regarding hot dogs and cancer. The first article I read associated hot dogs with brain tumors in children. Since the damage was already done, there wasn't anything I could do about it at that point. I haven't eaten one since. The reason I am so concerned is because I got on a hot dog kick when I was pregnant. I ate the Healthy Choice low-fat hot dogs, but I did eat hot dogs.

I averaged 3-4 a week, I'm afraid, and now I am wondering if my hot dog consumption could have a detrimental affect on the health and welfare of my son, Michael? Please let me know if this information is true. —_A.L. Las Vegas, Nevada_

ME: Your letter really hit home for me!! I, like you, while pregnant with my daughter Paige who is now 15, ate hot dogs like they were going out of style. I ate them back in 1979-1980 and they were not the low-fat variety. I even went a step further, and ate them in a cheese omelet about 4-5 days a week for lunch. I hate to think how many fat grams that lunch contained!! I ate pretty healthy most of my pregnancy, until the last three months, when I developed the "bizarre craving" for hot dog cheese omelets. When the "hot dog scare" appeared in the newspapers, I also sat up and took notice. I was, and still am, a little concerned if my crazy eating habits could have or will affect Paige's health. I have read everything I can get my hands on regarding this matter. This is what I found:

There have been three studies thus far. The first study of 440 children in the Denver, Colorado area "suggested" a higher incidence of childhood cancers (brain tumors and leukemia) among children who ate hot dogs at least once a week or whose mothers had eaten hot dogs during pregnancy. THE KEY WORD IS *"SUGGESTED."*

The second study of 310 children "suggested" a link between the consumption of hot dogs and other cured meats by pregnant women with a higher risk of brain tumors in the children they bore. THE KEY WORD IS *"SUGGESTED."*

The third study, which received the most attention, examined the diet of 232 children in the Los Angeles area who were diagnosed with leukemia. The researchers found that the "only persistent significant associations" were that the children or their FATHERS had eaten 12 or more hot dogs a month. All of the research came with disclaimers that the findings were preliminary, and that NO cause-and-effect link had been established and much more research was needed before any conclusions could be drawn.

There have been several flaws pointed out concerning the studies. The main question that arose was the selection of control groups of healthy children they compared to the cancer victims and what researchers refer to as "recall bias." This means when people are asked what they did or ate years ago, they may focus on something that they already suspect might not be healthful (such as eating hot dogs). Most experts do not consider this a very credible study. If you think about it, there is a new danger or cancer-causing food in the news almost every week. I guess we can all drive ourselves crazy if we believe everything we read (myself included).

The culprit in the hot dogs that warrants question are the nitrites used to process meats. (There is a new brand of healthy fat-free franks on the market called, "Smart Dogs." They can be found in some grocery stores and many health food stores. They are meatless and DO NOT contain nitrites.) Nitrites are converted (in the body) to highly carcinogenic nitrosamines. However, it might be noted that vitamin C and other substances found in plant foods have been shown to help block nitrosamine formation. This information, in my case, is good news!! You're not going to believe this, but with my hot dog cheese omelet, I always ate an orange. Don't ask me why? It just tasted good together. Maybe God was watching over me, back in 1979-1980, when I was pregnant with Paige, and I didn't even realize it until now!!

Despite the possible increased incidence of disease reflected in the hot dog studies, it is still a very low rate! This does not compare with the warnings on tobacco causing cancer and the proven relationship of cancer to high-fat diets. Most feel there is no case concerning hot dogs, but we must recognize the fact that animal studies have established that nitrites can cause cancer. Other factors were not taken into consideration. We don't know if the participants were undernourished, had adequate exercise, or other disease risk factors (possibly hereditary problems) that could have led to their medical condition.

I hope this information didn't make you feel worse. I will be watching for any updated information and promise I will keep you posted, too!!

YOU: I have really enjoyed using your cookbook. The food is great and the whole family is losing weight. I've been walking for exercise for six months and have really enjoyed getting outside. About two weeks ago my legs started cramping up every time I went out for a walk. I took off for a few days, but when I tried walking again they came back. Have you ever heard of this before? I am 37 years old and in pretty good shape. I've lost about 12 pounds so far by just cutting the fat, but would like to continue with my exercise program. Any suggestions would be greatly appreciated. —P.L. Jackson, Mississippi

ME: I'm glad you are enjoying the book. I can't be sure, but there is a possibility you might have a disorder referred to as "intermittent claudication." The only reason I even know about it is because a friend of mine was recently diagnosed with the problem by my husband. My husband, Mike, is an orthopedic surgeon. The cramps you are experiencing could be a symptom of peripheral vascular disease, which is basically a narrowing of the arteries in the legs due to a buildup of plaque (deposits composed of fat and other material) along the artery wall. The only way to get relief is to stop walking and rest until the symptoms subside. Fortunately, intermittent claudication is not life-threatening, and treatment usually helps. Most patients can be helped by conservative measurers such as exercising, not smoking, eating a low-fat diet (to help control your weight, blood pressure, and cholesterol).

If you do happen to have this disorder immediate treatment by your physician might be your answer. I would recommend making an appointment and finding out. In some cases, the conservative treatment doesn't work. There is another method that has been used to treat this disorder. It is angioplasty. I'm sure you have heard of this in relation to heart problems. It is a technique that pushes aside the blockages by inflating a tiny balloon inserted into the artery through a catheter. Many patients have benefitted from this procedure.

The problem occurs when the arteries narrow due to plaque build-up, less blood, and the oxygen it carries can't reach it's destination. When you start walking, this increases the amount of oxygen the legs require, and the pain occurs because the arteries cannot keep up with the increased demand. Symptoms are always the same. The cramping usually begins in the same part of the leg, and almost always during or after exertion. For some walkers it begins after a few steps, while others may walk a mile or more before the cramping starts. Sometimes the pain only occurs when walking uphill or climbing steps.

A conservative approach is nearly always preferred as the initial treatment. About 75% of most patients improve enough to avoid any dramatic procedures or treatments. Please get it checked out as soon as possible! I wish you the best.

YOU: Let me introduce myself. I am about 27 years old and am not married. I have dealt with a weight problem all my life until (about six months ago) when I discovered your book at The Tattered Cover Book Store in Denver, Colorado. It was the best day of my life. I was the classic yo-yo dieter. I'd lose 10 pounds and gain back 15. I'd lose it again and gain back a little more. It's amazing to me that so many people live this way that they even gave it a name. I want to thank you for making me a happy person. I have changed my life around and I owe it to you. Maybe I will get to meet you some day if you ever come back to Denver on a book tour. I saw you on the news several months ago (but that was before I knew who you were) and before I was ready to listen to anyone about low-fat eating anyway. I have a rather odd question, but you might be able to help. I work out with my boyfriend 4 evenings a week after work. I really like him a lot, in fact I think I love him. He is sweet, kind, good looking, funny, and most of all he thinks I am wonderful. I think he is wonderful, too, but there is one thing that kind of bothers me. I know you are going to think I'm nuts, but here it goes. My boyfriend is a body builder and loves to work out. In fact, the gym was where we met. When we work out together he smells like ammonia. I know you think I am crazy, but it really has me wondering. He doesn't smell like that any other time. At first I thought it was the detergent his clothes were washed in, but I have even done his wash with MY detergent and he still smells like that when he wears clothes that I have washed myself. Have you ever heard of anything so wild? We are really close, but not enough for me to ask him why he smells like Mr. Clean or Lysol. Is there a possibility that something could be wrong with his health? I know what he eats and drinks, and it's not much different from what I eat and drink. Please if you have EVER heard of anything like this, write me and tell me. I've even asked my doctor, and he couldn't give me an answer. Granted, he is a dermatologist, but don't all doctor's have basically the same training? I'll pray for an answer.   *—E.R. Denver, Colorado*

ME: I'm really glad you found the book and it has helped you change your life. I love the book store where you bought the book. Do they still have the statue of the old man reading the newspaper upstairs on the second floor? My escort while on book tour in Denver, Lisa Maxson, pulled a fast one on me when we visited that bookstore. She asked me what I thought about the guy reading the paper? He looked so real that I started to talk to him. Anyway, enough about me.

The Tattered Cover Bookstore

I think I might have an answer for you. After pouring over medical journals, and consulting several sources, this is what I found. The reason body sweat MAY smell like ammonia is because your boyfriend MIGHT BE CONSUMING TOO MUCH PROTEIN IN HIS DIET. The foods we eat are made up of fats, carbohydrates, and protein. Of the three, only protein contains nitrogen. Many athletes or people who work out a lot mis-

Lisa Maxson
Denver February 1994

takenly load up on an overabundance of protein (thinking it's going to make their muscles bigger and stronger). The only problem is the body has no way of storing all the extra protein. If your boyfriend is taking in more protein than his body needs, the liver removes the nitrogen from the protein and the nitrogen is actually converted to AMMONIA as it passes through the SWEAT GLANDS (sound familiar) and kidneys. I am hoping this is the case with your boyfriend. You might check out his diet a little closer. Is there a chance he is overdosing on protein?

There is another explanation, but this one is quite rare. Some people smell like ammonia even when they don't eat a lot of protein if they happen to be infected with helicobacter, which is a bacterium that removes nitrogen from protein. People that suffer from duodenal ulcers are infected with the bacteria. If your boyfriend belches and burps a lot, and complains of a sour taste in his mouth, he could be infected. Has he ever complained of a burning or pain in his stomach when he is hungry? A simple blood test can detect this infection. The good news is it CAN BE CURED with about a week of medication. Either way, it isn't too serious and it can be fixed. Good luck! I wonder if he can smell himself?

YOU: We have really enjoyed using your book. You have made healthy eating so easy to follow. For the past two years I have really watched what I eat. I take all the antioxidant vitamins and exercise every day. Since my Mom died of breast cancer three years ago, I have made a real effort to eat healthy. I've read so much about preventive medicine and how we can affect our destiny through our diet. I'm always interested in new information concerning cancer (specifically breast cancer). I have my annual mammogram and have limited my fat consumption down to about 10%. So many cancers seem hereditary, so I am doing everything in my power to protect myself. Any information you have concerning cancer would be greatly appreciated.
—*M.T. Bismarck North, Dakota*

ME: I'm glad you have found my book helpful. You are on the right track towards cancer prevention. A low-fat diet along with regular aerobic exercise is very important. The antioxidant vitamins and plenty of fiber in your diet are also great preventive measures. Some cancers, as you probably know, are genetic diseases, in which inherited or acquired mutations damage the genes that control cell division. Most of the cancer research involves trying to find the specific genes where the damage occurs, and ultimately trying to repair or fix them. It is strongly believed that our diet and lifestyle may have a direct influence on some types of cancer. I don't have the answers (by any means) but only wish to provide you with information regarding diet and lifestyle changes concerning cancer risks. Please realize this information should be discussed with YOUR personal physician and never self-prescribe. **It could prove detrimental to your health!**

IS THERE A CONNECTION BETWEEN A HIGH-FAT DIET AND BREAST CANCER?

Research has shown that women who gain an extra 10 pounds between the ages of 25 and 30 may increase their risk of breast cancer by 23%. Women who gain 15 pounds increase their risk by 37%, and those with a 20 pound gain increase the danger by 52%. We may not be able to control hereditary risk factors, **but we can control our diet and exercise lifestyles!**

As early as the 1960s, researchers discovered a correlation between animal-fat intake and breast cancer-mortality. These tests were made all over the world. They found the higher a country's fat intake, the higher it's breast-cancer-death-rate. The lower it's fat intake, the lower the rate. It sounds logical, but there could be more determining factors responsible. Some countries with fatty diets could also be among the most industrialized. The pollutants associated with industrialization could be the carcinogens (cancer-causing substances). High-fat diets have been associated with breast cancer because they lead to earlier menstruation, and an early onset of menstruation has been identified as a risk for breast cancer. We do know that dietary fat can raise estrogens, and high levels of estrogen have long been suspected as a breast-disease culprit. Experts know estrogen causes breast cells to divide. This repeated cell division may lead to genetic mutations in breast cells. The hormone (estrogen) can also make existing tumors more aggressive. Most of the studies on premenopausal women have been inconclusive. However, a high-fat diet may be particularly risky after a woman reaches menopause because of the hormonal changes that take place at that time.

CAN ALCOHOL INCREASE MY RISK OF BREAST CANCER?

Many studies have indicated that the greater the alcohol intake, the greater the risk of breast cancer. Researchers have found that moderate alcohol use (two drinks a day) increases a woman's breast-cancer risk by 30-60%, while one drink a day can raise it by 10-40%. A National Cancer Institute study of 34 premenopausal women found that when women were given the equivalent of two drinks per day, their estrogen levels rose 32%. Some studies have indicated that moderate alcohol consumption may reduce the risk of heart disease, however. Since heart disease accounts for 40% of deaths in women, and breast cancer is associated with 4% of women's deaths, it does give us something to think about, doesn't it? However, there are a great many  other diseases associated with alcohol consumption. I would never recommend that anyone increase their alcohol consumption under any circumstance (even if a few studies linked alcohol consumption to decreased heart disease risks). There are other healthy ways you can reduce your risk of heart disease (such as a low-fat diet and regular exercise) besides drinking alcohol. Any woman at risk for breast cancer should do all she can to lower her chances. Modifying alcohol consumption is one of the factors within her control.

PREVENTIVE MEDICINE THE CURE OF THE FUTURE
(Fight cancer through your diet!)

DIET IS ONE OF THE TWO LEADING CAUSES OF CANCER IN THE UNITED STATES!
The good news is that we all have control over what we put in our mouths!!

The National Academy of Sciences, National Cancer Institute, and American Cancer Society have all urged people to eat foods low in fat and high in fiber, vitamin A, and vitamin C. Fortunately, foods that fight cancer also protect against other diet-related diseases. Eating foods low in fat, cholesterol, sodium, sugar, and high in fiber and calcium reduces the risk of heart disease, stroke, diabetes, obesity, and a vast array of other diseases. Even though no diet will GUARANTEE PROTECTION against cancer, the cost of preventive measures far outweigh corrective surgery. Besides, it gives you a sense that you are doing everything in your power to ensure good health!

CANCER FIGHTING GUIDELINES

FAT: The evidence linking fat to cancer is stronger than any other dietary component. **Colon, breast, and prostate cancers are clearly less common in populations that eat a low-fat diet.** About 40% of the calories in the typical American diet come from fat. We should be eating about half that much. Both saturated and unsaturated fats seem to contribute to cancer.

Healthy Tip: Try to cut your fat consumption to 20% of your total caloric intake to guard against cancer (10% If you have strong hereditary risk factors and/or obesity).

FIBER: Dietary fiber, or "roughage," is the indigestible material in plant foods. Fiber-rich diets may help prevent colon cancer by increasing stool bulk, which dilutes the concentration of cancer-causing substances that contact the colon. The typical American only eats about 15 grams of fiber daily. We would all be better off eating between 30-45 grams. Since too much fiber can prohibit the body's ability to absorb certain minerals and vitamins from the food, don't go overboard with your daily consumption.

Healthy Tip: Increase your fiber intake GRADUALLY by eating an abundance of fruits and vegetables. Eat 30-45 grams a day to DECREASE your risk of cancer.

SELENIUM: Studies involving rats have shown a reduction in cancer rates when the animals were given generous (not excessive) doses of selenium prior to exposure to cancer-causing chemicals. Too much selenium is highly toxic, but a moderate amount (50-200 micrograms per day), is considered safe and adequate. The amount of selenium in food varies, depending on the selenium content of the soil where it was grown. Since we have no way of knowing that information (in most cases) selenium supplements may be recommended for some people. If your diet doesn't include seafood, beef, pork, eggs, and chicken, you might consider a supplement of 100 micrograms. ALWAYS CHECK WITH YOUR PHYSICIAN FIRST! If you are following a low-fat diet, some of the selenium-rich foods may be missing from your diet.

Healthy Tip: Consume 200 micrograms a day, from FOOD or a (ALWAYS CHECK WITH YOUR PHYSICIAN FIRST!) natural supplement. Some breads and cereals are rich in selenium.

ALCOHOL: Heavy drinking may cause liver disease. Alcohol also contributes to cancers of the mouth, throat, larynx (voice box), and esophagus, particularly in smokers.

Healthy Tip: Drink in moderation (or not at all)!

CONTAMINANTS: Pesticides and other agriculture and industrial chemicals contaminate many of our foods. Some are suspected of causing cancer. The following are some suggestions to help cut your cancer risks.

1. Buy organically grown food.

2. Avoid high-fat meat and dairy products. (The contaminants accumulate in an animal's fat cells.)

3. Avoid certain high-fat fish such as bluefish, striped bass, lake trout, mackerel, as well as the bottom feeding fish, such as carp. The fish in your supermarket may come from clean water, but the above species are more likely than others to contain high levels of contaminants. HOWEVER, THERE IS NO NEED TO LIMIT YOUR CONSUMPTION OF OTHER TYPES OF FISH! To be safe, limit eating fish (only the ones I mentioned) to no more than once a month.

Healthy Tip: Limit your intake of high-fat animal foods (cholesterol containing products)!

VITAMIN C: Stomach cancer is more common in countries where people consume very little vitamin C, than in the United States. It has been found that most people who suffer from cancer of the esophagus or larynx usually ingest little vitamin C. Vitamin C may prevent cancer by blocking formation of cancer-causing nitrosamines. Even though there is little evidence that mega doses of vitamin C will prevent cancer, we do know that fresh fruits and vegetables (rich sources of vitamin C) are fat-free and provide plenty of fiber which do decrease your risk of cancer.

Healthy Tip: Try to eat at least 25 milligrams in every meal. Eat fruits and vegetables raw or slightly cooked to get the most vitamin C benefit. One orange contains 70 milligrams.

VEGETABLES: All vegetables may help prevent cancer. A few scattered studies have found that people with cancers of the stomach, lung, colon, breasts, esophagus, or larynx eat fewer vegetables than people without cancer, when their diets were compared. However, it is not clear whether it is the fiber, vitamin A, vitamin C, lack of fat, or some other attribute of vegetable-rich foods that ward off these cancers. Two anti-cancer constituents might be the indoles and isothiocyanates in cruciferous vegetables. These substances have shown a reduction in the the number of tumors in mice treated with carcinogens.

Healthy Tip: Try to eat three or more (½ cup) servings of vegetables a day. Include cruciferous vegetables as often as possible. Some examples of cruciferous sources include: broccoli, Brussels sprouts, kale, cauliflower, bok choy, collards, mustard greens, rutabaga, and turnip greens.

VITAMIN A: Chemical relatives of vitamin A clearly inhibit cancers of the breast, skin, and urinary bladder in laboratory animals and may help in the fight against several other types of cancer as well. Studies of people who smoke show that a diet rich in vitamin A is associated with a reduced risk of lung cancer (though non-smokers have even lower risks). **Retinol, the form of vitamin A in dairy products, liver, and most supplements, may be toxic at doses of 50,000 International Units (IU) per day or more. Doses in excess of 20,000 (IU) per day taken in pregnancy may cause birth defects.** Beta-carotene (not retinol), has been shown to protect against lung cancers in smokers.

Healthy Tip: Aim for 10,000 IU per day, with at least 7,500 IU coming from fruits and vegetables. There is no evidence that amounts over 10,000 IU per day are beneficial, therefore a beta-carotene supplement (available in 25,000 IU doses) is a reasonable insurance policy. **Your body only takes and uses the vitamin A found in beta-carotene it needs.** It is impossible to overdose on vitamin A by taking beta-carotene supplements as long as you stay within the guidelines (25,000 IU per day or less).

COFFEE: The high temperature of roasting coffee may create cancer-causing substances in coffee beans. Test results are mixed, but some studies have suggested that coffee (regular or decaffeinated) may be responsible for urinary, bladder, and pancreatic cancers. The key word is "may." Many other studies disagree with this theory. A small cancer concern is a substance called methylene chloride, a chemical used to decaffeinate various coffees. Brands that DO NOT use methylene chloride include: High Point, Nescafé, and Taster's Choice.

Healthy Tip: Keep your coffee consumption to a minimum. Two cups a day (or less) would be considered safe by most sources.

COOKING TIPS: Certain cooking methods, such as charcoal broiling or smoking cause carcinogens (cancer causing substances) to form in meat, chicken, and fish. To insure safety when charcoal broiling, use low-fat cuts and shield food from the flame with aluminum foil. **Avoid frequent consumption of smoked foods.** Choose "smoked" products made with liquid smoke flavor (available in the spice section of the grocery store). Try to avoid high temperatures and long cooking times when broiling, frying (you shouldn't use this method any way), or baking meats, chicken, and fish and you will reduce your risk of cancer. Another idea is to cook your meats partially in the microwave or oven first, and simply place on the charcoal grill for a couple of minutes for flavor.

SOMETHING TO THINK ABOUT:
• **Tobacco is the greatest source of cancer.** Cigarettes, pipes, cigars, and chewing tobacco account for 1/3 of all cancers!

• Natural foods are composed of all kinds of different chemicals. Scientists are discovering every day that some of these chemicals may promote cancer, while others actually help to inhibit it. Make wise choices and you will be taking charge of your cancer-causing risks!

• Air and water pollution, asbestos fibers, and work place carcinogens are also serious problems. Many of these factors are difficult to avoid, however. IT TAKES GOVERNMENT ACTION TO REDUCE THESE RISKS. WRITE TO YOUR CONGRESS PERSON URGING THEM TO SUPPORT STRONGER PROGRAMS FOR A CANCER-FREE SOCIETY! YOUR LIFE COULD DEPEND ON IT!!!

GETTING HELP:
The Cancer Information Center: (800)-4-CANCER (referrals to local cancer care programs)
American Cancer Society: (800)-ACS-2345
Cancervive: (310)-203-9232
The National Coalition for Cancer Survivorship: (310)-650-8868

YOU: You can't pick up a magazine or newspaper and not read something about free radicals and those antioxidant vitamins. Well that is all fine and good, because I eat a lot of fruits and vegetables anyway. My question is this. If the antioxidant vitamins are so hot, then why did I read about some research done in Finland that found the antioxidants to be detrimental to smokers? I would think the antioxidants would help everyone no matter what your lifestyle? Have you heard anything about this study? I must say, that your book has changed my life. I used to "suffer" with low-fat eating, but now I "celebrate" healthy eating, because you managed to bring back the great taste I had been missing before your wonderful book came along! I would appreciate any information you might have regarding the antioxidant vitamins. I don't want to do the wrong thing and take a supplement that might do more harm than good. One more question. What does the term phytochemical mean? I have also heard a lot about them in the news too. Thanks for your time.—*J.P. Colorado Springs, Colorado*

ME: As a matter of fact, I did read about the Finland study research results. After reading several articles regarding the information, I am pleased to announce the news is not as bad as you thought. We have heard about the benefit of the antioxidants (vitamins C, E, and beta-carotene) for some time now. They are touted as the cancer and heart disease preventers of the '90s. As a result of this, more and more people are eating foods rich in antioxidants as well as taking antioxidant vitamin supplements. In April 1994, the newspaper headlines stated it was all a "big hoax."

The results involved a 6-year study in Finland on the effect of beta-carotene and vitamin E on long time smokers. They stated the antioxidant vitamins gave the smokers no protection against lung cancer. In fact, they stated the smokers who received beta-carotene supplements had an increase of lung cancer by 18% more than the smokers who did not take the beta-carotene. It seemed like this single test had disputed everything research and scientists were recommending. I decided to do a little research on my own. It proved quite interesting: The people involved in the study were all older men who smoked an average of one pack of cigarettes a day for more than 35 years. The doses of beta-carotene given (20 mg.) and vitamin E (50 mg.) were MUCH LOWER than those, that had proven protective, in all other studies. Even researchers acknowledged that the increase in lung cancer "might have been" a coincidence. It is quite possible the dosage of antioxidants was not high enough to prove beneficial. It is obvious that supplements alone cannot reverse the damage of many years of heavy smoking.

Other factors, such as proper diet, exercising regularly, quitting smoking (if you smoke), limiting alcohol consumption, and even reducing stress are all important in obtaining good health. You can't expect a couple of vitamins to reverse all the damage accumulated over the years due to bad health habits.

I take the three major antioxidant vitamins (vitamin C, Vitamin E, and Beta Carotene, as well as some antioxidant nutrients) myself, and plan to continue doing so. I tend to believe "everything else I've read concerning their benefits" rather than one isolated study that took place in Finland with "less than ideal" conditions. Be sure and check with your physician before taking ANY medication or supplements. Please do not self-prescribe medication OR supplements even if it is YOUR constitutional right. YOU MUST UNDERSTAND, IT COULD BE DETRIMENTAL TO YOUR HEALTH, AND MORE IMPORTANT, TO YOUR LIFE!!

Note: Antioxidant supplements have not been established according to dosage, combinations, or even benefits. Although many experts in the medical field suggest antioxidants beneficial in preventive medicine, it is only their opinion. For this reason, please understand I am not recommending anything. My only intention is to provide information. Dosages of any type of supplement or medication are determined by many variables (sex, age, weight, and other health factors). For this reason PLEASE DO NOT SELF PRESCRIBE! If you acquire the antioxidants through diet, rather than supplements, you will not only include vitamins and minerals, but fiber as well. Fiber has been proven beneficial in reducing risks of many various diseases.

In response to your question about phytochemicals, coincidentally American's released results of a study about the same time as the Finnish study results. It confirmed a chemical, sulforaphane, found in broccoli to contain cancer fighting potential. The chemical is not a vitamin at all, but, you guessed it, a phytochemical. Phytochemicals are simply chemicals that exist naturally in all plant foods. The word "Phyto" actually means plant in Greek. They can be found in all fruits, vegetables, and grains. Like antioxidants, some phytochemicals appear to contain disease fighting benefits. The difference being they don't come in pill form (so far) as do the antioxidants.

PHOTOCHEMICALS
(Where do they come from?)

Phytochemicals	Food Sources
Capsaicin	Hot peppers
Flavonoids	Citrus fruits, tomatoes, peppers, carrots, and berries
Indoles	Broccoli and cabbage
Isothiocyanates (also known as sulforaphane)	Broccoli, cabbage, mustard, and horseradish
Lignans	Flaxseed, wheat, and barley
Lycopene	tomatoes and grapefruit
Genistein	Various beans, peas, and lentils
S-allycysteine	Garlic, onions, and chives
Triterpenoids	Licorice root and citrus fruits

The proposed benefits of phytochemicals are varied. Some believe they aid in prevention of cancer-promoting hormones, stimulate anticancer enzymes (by preventing blood clotting), and help prevent cancer-promoting hormones from attaching themselves to normal cells (thus inhibiting estrogen related cancers). Many feel they help protect DNA from carcinogens by acting like an antioxidant and blocking the formation of nitrites in the stomach which stimulates anticancer enzymes. They are also believed to inhibit hormone dependent steps in the formation of tumors thus protecting against breast, prostate, and cervical cancers. **Again these are proposed attributes.**

I didn't mean to go off on a tangent about all of this, but once I started researching the material, I found it all quite interesting and wanted to share the information with you, too.

I guess the gist of all this scientific data is: **If you eat a variety of fruits, vegetables, and grains on a regular basis, you will reap the benefits of various protective substances that have already been proven and identified.** Who knows what the scientists and research experts will uncover in the future? Some of those designer fruits and vegetables (with all kinds of added nutrients) might not be such a bad idea! This will probably become commonplace in our lifetime. I'm sure we are all anxious to find what the future holds. Chances are scientists, even with their newfound discoveries, will still recommend "getting back to basics" (regarding food in it's natural state), and this will continue to be a wise choice concerning our good health. I hope so!!

YOU: Pam, I love your workbook and video series. I found your section on antioxidants quite interesting. My husband is a physician and treats patients with cancer. He read over your material and was very impressed! Most physicians simply don't have the time to go over diet and supplements with patients in a detailed manner. Your book has made the work of MANY DOCTORS a lot easier. As a matter of fact, several doctor's offices in our area actually write prescriptions for your book to give to their patients. What antioxidants do you personally take and how much? It seems the information changes daily. Thanks for making this important information SO EASY TO UNDERSTAND!
—B.K. Tyler, Texas

ME: I really appreciate your kind words. Several physicians have written to let me know they recommend my book to their patients. Since my husband happens to be a physician (orthopedic surgeon) himself, he has been pleased that "his peers" consider my book a valuable source of information. Since the antioxidants, a unique group of vitamins and minerals, have been linked to a reduction in the risk of cardiovascular disease and certain cancers, I personally feel everyone should incorporate foods containing antioxidants (or in some cases supplements) into their diet. Of the major antioxidant vitamin supplements, I personally take 10,000 IU of Beta Carotene (split up in two doses), 500 mg. of vitamin C in a time-released tablet, and two 400 IU of vitamin E daily (one in the morning and one at night). I also take a few of the lesser known antioxidants such as manganese, selenium, zinc, and chromium. EVERYONE SHOULD CHECK WITH THEIR OWN PERSONAL PHYSICIAN BEFORE ADDING ANY KIND OF SUPPLEMENT TO THEIR DIET!! PLEASE DO NOT SELF-PRESCRIBE!! Nutritional supplement needs differ according to your individual life-style and eating habits (as well as your weight and age)!

YOU: I have never written anyone like this before, but I had to write and tell you how your book has changed my life. Not only has your book taught me to learn to cook low-fat, it has given me the push I needed to improve my health in general. I quit smoking, started exercising, and feel and look about ten years younger than my 51 years. I have lost about 22 pounds and have kept it off this time (a first)! Since I am really into taking care of myself now, I've decided that I need to learn more about vitamin supplements and especially the antioxidants I've read and heard so much about lately. You can't pick up a magazine or newspaper that doesn't mention the benefits of the antioxidants and their fight against the free radicals. I'm not so sure I really understand all I read, so I thought you might be able to help me out. What do you think about vitamins? Do you take them? What do you think about the antioxidants and should everyone be taking them? If so, how much and how often? I hate to put you on the spot, but any information at all would be deeply appreciated. I want to thank you Pam Mycoskie for giving me a new lease on life, but best of all a new and improved self image. Thanks for your time. —H. S. Lincoln, Nebraska

ME: I can't tell you how much I appreciated your letter. Letters from folks like you really keep me motivated to learn all I can about health and nutrition. It's funny, but I never was interested in health until I discovered something as easy as changing my diet to low-fat could have such a tremendous impact on lowering my cholesterol. I guess that is when I realized we do have some control over our bodies and the way we feed and exercise them can have such positive results on our health and welfare.

As far as vitamins are concerned, yes I do take a few. After much research, I feel the antioxidant vitamins may help reduce the risks of a vast array of diseases. I sure don't see any harm in taking the antioxidants (as long as they are approved by YOUR physician). If you are taking vitamins to supplement your diet that is one thing. If you are "living on" vitamins and supplements, you might re-examine your motives!

ATTENTION READERS:

I decided to include an extensive segment on antioxidants in this section. Everyone is interested in the antioxidant vitamins and minerals. I receive questions about supplements every day. For this reason, I decided to put all the new information in one place, so it would be easier to understand. Please realize the benefits of antioxidants are still controversial. If you obtain the antioxidant vitamins and minerals through food sources, however, you will benefit your health regardless of the antioxidant issue. No one can argue with the idea of eating plenty of fiber-rich fruits and vegetables in your diet. If they happen to provide antioxidant protection, then that is great, too. I recommend food sources over supplements, but felt this information may be of interest to some and provide the latest information regarding the antioxidant vitamins and minerals.

> **WARNING:** Always check with your personal physician before you ingest any kind of supplement or medication. **I CAN'T STRESS THIS ENOUGH!**

There is a group of vitamins, minerals, and enzymes (protein product in living cells) called antioxidants that help protect our body from the formation of free radicals. If you have picked up a magazine or newspaper lately, you will know what I am talking about. It's the "News of the '90s!" Free radicals are simply atoms or groups of atoms that cause damage to our cells. They are responsible for disrupting our immune systems which lead to infections causing all kinds of various diseases. **There are three known free radicals.** They are **superoxide**, **hydroxyl,** and **peroxide.** The most common reasons for their formation are overexposure to the sun's rays, exposure to radiation and toxic chemicals, or as a result of various metabolic processes (such as stored fat molecules). Free radicals are usually kept in check as long as the body's army of free radical scavengers (enzymes that occur naturally in the body) are "on the job" so to speak. The scavengers (or enzymes) attack and neutralize the free radicals. Enzymes are proteins found in all living plant and animal matter. They are essential for maintaining proper bodily functions such as digesting food and aiding in muscle repair. While it's true enzymes are manufactured in the body, you can also obtain them indirectly through protein food sources. (They are broken down into amino acids in the body.) Low degrees of heat will destroy enzymes in the food, however. For this reason, you must eat the enzyme-rich foods raw in most cases. Avocados, mangos, and bananas are all rich in enzymes, but sprouts are the richest source. Because enzymes are the only substances that can supply the body with energy needed for it's activities, overuse can disrupt the functioning capacity of the body, increasing the risk of cancer, obesity, cardiovascular disease, and all kinds of other problems. The body makes the enzymes naturally, but they can be supplemented by a diet rich in antioxidant vitamins and minerals. These antioxidants are scavengers, too (kind of like the back-up or reserve forces), that also gobble up the free radical particles as they are formed.

If your diet is inadequate, lacks appropriate antioxidants, or if your system is overwhelmed by free radicals, you might need the assistance of antioxidant supplements. HOWEVER, PLEASE CONSULT YOUR PHYSICIAN BEFORE TAKING ANY KIND OF SUPPLEMENT OR MEDICATION! The following chart includes the recommended levels of vitamins and minerals for healthy adults through **FOOD** and/or supplements.

Antioxidants bind to free radicals rendering them inactive and unable to create damage.

WARNING!!
DAILY DOSAGES MAY BE SUGGESTED, HOWEVER, BEFORE USING ANY SUPPLEMENTS OR MEDICATION, ALWAYS CONSULT WITH YOUR PHYSICIAN FIRST!! DOSAGES WILL VARY ACCORDING TO WEIGHT AND AGE!!

Proposed Vitamins and Minerals for Healthy Adults

Nutrient	Women	Men
Vitamin A	4,000 IU	5,000 IU
*Beta-carotene	6-15 mg	6-15 mg
*Vitamin C	500 mg	500 mg
Vitamin D	300-400 IU	400 IU
*Vitamin E	100-400 IU	100-400 IU
Vitamin K	65 mcg	80 mcg
Thiamin (B1)	1.1-2 mg	1.5-2.5 mg
Riboflavin (B2)	1.3-2.3 mg	1.7-2.7 mg
Niacin (aka niacinamide)	15 mg	19 mg
Vitamin B6 (aka pyridoxine)	1.6-2.6 mg	2-3 mg
Folic Acid	400 mcg	200-400 mcg
Vitamin B12	2 mcg	2 mcg
Biotin	30-100 mcg	30-100 mcg
Pantothenic acid	4-7 mg	4-7 mg
Calcium	1,000 mg	1,000 mg
Phosphorus	800 mg	800 mg
Magnesium	300-350 mg	350 mg
Iron	15 mg	10 mg
*Zinc	12 mg	15 mg
Iodine	150 mcg	150 mcg
*Copper	1.5-3 mg	1.5-3 mg
*Manganese	2-5 mg	2-5 mg
*Selenium	55 mcg	70 mcg
*Chromium	50-200 mcg	50-200 mcg

*Antioxidant rich vitamins and minerals

Many of these nutrients can be obtained through the FOOD you eat. These are not RDA's (or as they are now called RDI's), but simply a list of important dietary nutrients recommended for healthy female and male adults. The antioxidant vitamins and minerals are starred. *

The following terms found on vitamins and other supplements:

IU: This stands for International Unit and is the standard unit of measurement for fat-soluble vitamins (A, D, and E).

DV: This stands for Percent Daily Value, the reference term for the percentage of the recommended daily intake (RDI) for each nutrient for adults and children over the age of four.

mg: This stands for milligram.

mcg: This stands for microgram.

They are both units of measurement for water-soluble vitamins (C and B-complex) and minerals. A milligram is equal to 1/1,000 of a gram. A microgram is equal to 1/1,000 of a milligram.

Vitamins and minerals are of vital importance to our good health. Notice, I didn't say supplements! Many of the essential nutrients can be found in a healthy low-fat diet. Supplements are intended for that purpose, TO SUPPLEMENT A HEALTHY DIET!! By now, you have probably noticed the new nutrition labels on food packages. As of May 1994, most food packages were required to include a "Nutrition Facts" label with key nutrient information to help consumers make better decisions regarding food products. They are better, but far from perfect. A similar label was required on dietary supplements by July 1995. The term "U.S. RDA" was replaced by "Percent Daily Value," which shows the percentage of the Recommended Daily Intake (RDI) for nutrients in dietary supplements. In January 1994, the FDA proposed establishing RDI's for seven additional nutrients not before included. They were vitamin K, selenium, chloride, manganese, fluoride, chromium, and molybdenum. Once RDI's have been established these nutrients will be allowed to be listed on the nutrition label and provide a basis for nutrient claims.

YOUR GUIDE TO UNDERSTANDING THE DIETARY SUPPLEMENT LABEL

1. **BRAND NAME:** This is the brand name of the product.

2. **DIRECTIONS:** This is the recommended dosage by the manufacturer and directions.

3. **SERVING SIZE:** Serving size indicates the manufacturer's serving expressed in the appropriate unit (such as tablet, softgel, capsule, teaspoon, etc.).

4. **AMOUNT PER TABLET:** The Amount Per Tablet heads the list of nutrients contained in the dietary supplement. This is followed by the quantity present in each tablet or capsule (if the serving is one tablet).

5. **PERCENT DAILY VALUE:** Percent Daily Value (DV) is the reference term for the percentage of the recommended daily intake (RDI) for each nutrient for adults and children over the age of four.

6. **INTERNATIONAL UNIT:** International (IU) is a standard unit of measurement for fat-soluble vitamins (A, D, and E).

7. **MILLIGRAM AND MICROGRAM:** Milligram (mg) and microgram (mcg) are units of measurement for water-soluble vitamins (C and B-Complex) and minerals. A milligram is equal to 1/1,000 of a gram. A microgram is equal to 1/1,000 of a milligram.

8. **(*):** An asterisk under the Percent Daily Value heading indicates that a Daily Value is not established for that nutrient.

9. **INGREDIENTS:** A complete list of all the ingredients will appear outside the Nutrition Facts box. This list includes nutrients and other ingredients used to formulate the dietary supplement, in decreasing order according to weight.

10. **STORAGE:** Under the storage instructions you will find all supplements should be stored in a cool, dry place in their original container.

11. **"KEEP OUT OF THE REACH OF CHILDREN"** will appear on all dietary supplements.

12. **EXPIRATION DATE:** The product should be used before this date to ensure full potency.

13. **MANUFACTURER'S OR DISTRIBUTOR'S NAME, ADDRESS, AND ZIPCODE** are required to appear on the label.

BRAND NAME ❶
MULTIVITAMIN AND MINERAL SUPPLEMENT

Directions: One (1) tablet daily as a dietary supplement ❷
Servings Per Container 100

NUTRITION FACTS
Serving Size 1 tablet ❸

Amount Per Tablet ❹	% Daily Value ❺
Vitamin A 5000 I.U. ❻ 50% as Beta Carotene	100%
Vitamin C 250 mg ❼	417%
Vitamin D 400 I.U.	100%
Vitamin E 200 I.U.	667%
Thiamin 5 mg	333%
Riboflavin 5 mg	294%
Niacin 20 mg	100%
Vitamin B₆ 5 mg	250%
Folate 0.4 mg	100%
Vitamin B₁₂ 6 mcg ❼	100%
Biotin 150 mcg	50%
Pantothenic Acid 10 mg	100%
Calcium 200 mg	20%
Iron 18 mg	100%
Phosphorus 200 mg	20%
Iodine 150 mcg	100%
Magnesium 200 mcg	50%
Zinc 15 mcg	100%
Selenium 25 mcg	*❽
Copper 2 mg	100%

❾ **Ingredients:** vitamin A acetate, beta carotene, vitamin D, di-alpha tocopherol acetate, ascorbic acid, folic acid, thiamin mononitrate, riboflavin, niacinamide, pyridoxine hydrochloride, vitamin B-12, biotin, d-calcium pantothenate, potassium chloride, dicalcium phosphate, potassium iodine, ferrous fumarate, magnesium oxide, copper sulfate, zinc oxide, manganese sulfate, sodium selenate, chromium chloride, sodium molybdate, microcrystalline cellulose, calcium carbonate, sodium carboxymethylcellulose

❿ **Storage:** Keep tightly closed in dry place, do not expose to excessive heat.

⓫ **KEEP OUT OF THE REACH OF CHILDREN**

⓬ **Expiration Date:** Nov. 1996

⓭ Manufacturer's or distributor's name, address and zip code

Some nutrients and vitamins affect the absorption of others, so it is important to know which supplements help and which supplements hinder each other. The following chart may help you determine if your vitamins and minerals are helping or hindering each other:

UNDERSTANDING THE ANTIOXIDANT VITAMINS

BETA-CAROTENE	
(RDI)	NONE ESTABLISHED
Proposed amount for antioxidant protection: (through food and/or supplements). Note: Beta-Carotene is a relative of Vitamin A found only in plant foods and unlike Vitamin A) is non -toxic.	6-15 mg a day (or 10,000-25,000 IU a day)
LOW-FAT FOOD SOURCES: (Recommended over supplements)	carrots, melons, peaches, squashes, sweet potatoes, broccoli, and spinach, pink grapefruit, apricots, pumpkin, cantaloupe, and most dark leafy vegetables
PROPOSED BENEFITS:	The body converts this antioxidant to vitamin A which is necessary for good eye (has been shown to lower the risk of cataracts) and skin health. It helps to fight infection and assists the immune system in general. The body regulates the conversion of beta-carotene to vitamin A at the rate in which the body requires it. It will only take as much as it needs. It IS NOT a good idea to take Vitamin A because large amounts could be toxic. Beta-carotene, unlike vitamin A, is safe. The worst thing an over-abundance (like a pound or two of carrots a day) of beta-carotene could do is possibly turn your skin a little yellow or orange.
IF YOU CHOOSE TO TAKE THIS SUPPLEMENT:	Supplement Beta-Carotene with vitamin E because beta-carotene can depress E in the blood. Always take beta-carotene with meals (that contain a SMALL amount of fat) to increase absorption. It doesn't take much, so don't even think about that burger and fries at the closest fast food chain. That is not what I had in mind. This supplement may cause side effects if taken with alcohol. Pregnant women should not take this supplement without their doctor's approval. Smokers should also seek the advice of their physician concerning Beta-Carotene supplements.

VITAMIN E

(RDI)	(RDI) 8-10 mg.
Proposed recommended amount for antioxidant protection:(through food and/or supplements).	100-400 IU a day
LOW-FAT FOOD SOURCES: **(Recommended over supplements)**	sweet potatoes, oatmeal, asparagus, green leafy vegetables, wheat germ, peaches, whole grain breads and pasta, soybeans, and corn
PROPOSED BENEFITS:	Vitamin E is believed to support cellular functions and give anti-aging protection (by attacking free radicals associated with aging and disease). Many feel it is beneficial in the treatment of arthritis, and may provide protection against arteriosclerosis and the fight against some types of cancer. Vitamin E has also been shown to reduce the risks of cataracts and boost the immune system in general. Vitamin E is associated with benefits to the skin as well. The vitamin actually has a small sunscreen effect comparable to an SPF of about 3. Many people claim vitamin E aids in healing wounds, preventing stretch marks (as in pregnancy) and even slow down the effects of aging (facial lines). There really is no scientific evidence to support these theories, but if it makes you feel better, it certainly won't hurt you to spread a little vitamin oil on an old scar.

VITAMIN E (cont.)

PROPOSED BENEFITS (continued):

Vitamin E is the ONLY vitamin whose natural form is significantly different than the synthetic forms. Don't worry though because it is easy to tell the difference. Natural vitamin E will have the letter "d" before it's chemical name on the label (as in d-alpha tocopheryl or d-alpha tocopheryl acetate). Synthetic forms have the letters "dl" instead of "d." The "d' and "dl" refer to the molecular structure. When shopping for vitamins, you will find the natural E vitamins are more expensive than the synthetics. The benefits and potency are worth the extra cost. Try to include Beta-Carotene with vitamin E. Fish oils use up vitamin E because they are so easily oxidized. If you happen to take fish oil supplements (AND I DO NOT SUGGEST THIS), you might need to take vitamin E supplements. Ask your physician about this. Vitamin E may increase blood lipids (or fat). An overdose of this supplement could result in decreased thyroid hormone levels, increased blood pressure, extreme fatigue and even blurred vision. Vitamin E should not be taken with blood thinners (such as aspirin) in most cases. Vitamin E CAN CAUSE BLEEDING in people on anticoagulant drugs or patients who have recently undergone surgery. Intakes of over 400 IU a day over a long period of time (according to some reports) could prove detrimental to your eye health. "Retinitis Pigmentosa" a condition that could possibly lead to blindness (in individuals at risk) have shown their condition to accelerate when taking high doses (over 400 IU) of vitamin E over an extended period of time. Always consult with your physician before taking any kind of supplement or medication. PLEASE, DO NOT SELF-PRESCRIBE!! There have also been reports suggesting a connection of large consumptions of vitamin E with a decreased ability of the white blood cells to fight bacteria and therefore an increased need of vitamin K. Vitamins (in excess) could be detrimental to your health! Please check with your personal physician regarding all supplements!!

VITAMIN C

(RDI)	60 mg.
Proposed amount for antioxidant protection (through food and/or supplements)	500 mg. a day.
LOW-FAT FOOD SOURCES: (Recommended over supplements)	citrus fruits, dark-green leafy vegetables, strawberries, tomatoes, potatoes, green peppers, red peppers, most fruit juices, Brussels sprouts, melons, sweet potatoes, and broccoli (Even fish and skim milk have small amounts.)
PROPOSED BENEFITS:	For many years we have known vitamin C increases the high density lipoproteins (HDL) or good cholesterol in the bloodstream. HDLs can be equated to the busboy in a restaurant. They take the dirty dishes back to the kitchen to give them to the dishwasher. In much the same way, HDLs remove the fat from the artery walls and take it to the liver, where it can be broken into bile acids and excreted. Vitamin C aids in healing wounds, increases resistance to infection, helps support the immune system, and aids in collagen reconstruction. Vitamin C is believed to protect against esophageal, oral, and stomach cancers, and it has been strongly suggested that it may help lower other cancer risks as well. Vitamin C helps to promote healthy gums and teeth, it aids in iron absorption, and helps to maintain normal connective tissue.

VITAMIN C (CONT.)

IF YOU CHOOSE TO TAKE THIS SUPPLEMENT:

*WARNING! If you take vitamin C supplements, wash them down with water instead of crunching on the chewable type. Chewing large doses (500 mg or more) of vitamin C on a regular basis can raise the acidity level in your mouth. This could dissolve the enamel and lead to tooth damage!! I recommend the vitamin C tablets that can be swallowed! Many feel there is a distinct protection against cataracts if an adequate intake of vitamin C is included in the diet. A chronic low intake of vitamin C has been associated with cancers of the stomach and esophagus. However, huge doses of vitamin C will not cure any of these conditions nor prevent them from occurring. There is no need to ingest large amounts, because any excess (not needed by your body) will simply be excreted in the urine. Levels over 4,000 mg per day could cause diarrhea, liver problems, or even kidney stones. Megadoses of ANY supplements can cause diarrhea and even distort the results of some medical tests so PLEASE DON'T SELF-PRESCRIBE!

UNDERSTANDING THE ANTIOXIDANT MINERALS

Along with the antioxidant vitamins, many minerals have been associated with antioxidant protection as well. Like vitamins, minerals are needed for proper composition of body fluids, the formation of blood and bones, and responsible for the maintenance of a healthy nervous system. Minerals are naturally occurring elements found in the earth. Rock formations are made up of mineral salts. Now for your your science lesson: As rock and stone are broken into small fragments over millions of years of erosion, dust and sand accumulate, forming soil. These minerals are passed from the soil to the plants which are eaten by herbivorous (plant-eating) animals that don't eat meat. Humans, in turn, obtain these minerals (for use in the body) by eating these plants and herbivorous animals. Minerals belong to two different groups: They are known as macro (or bulk minerals) and micro (or trace minerals).

BULK MINERALS	**TRACE MINERALS**
calcium	zinc
magnesium	iron
sodium	copper
potassium	manganese
phosphorus	chromium
	selenium
	iodine

Bulk minerals are needed in larger amounts than trace minerals. However, trace minerals are important for good health. Because minerals are stored in the body's bone and muscle tissue, it is possible to overdose on minerals if extremely large doses are taken. However, toxic or dangerous amounts will only accumulate if massive amounts are taken over a prolonged period of time. Bulk and trace minerals are found in vitamin supplements and multivitamin formulas. Check your vitamin bottle to see if the desired mineral supplements are listed.

Mineral supplements seem to be more effective when taken with a meal. After a mineral enters the body, however, the battle is on. They all have to compete with each other for absorption. For this reason minerals should be taken in balanced amounts. For example, too much zinc can deplete the body of copper and excessive calcium can affect magnesium absorption. Always use a balanced mineral supplement. Fiber decreases the body's absorption of minerals, too. For this reason, it is a good idea to take supplemental fiber and minerals at different times.

The minerals believed to be associated with antioxidant benefit are: copper, manganese, selenium, zinc, and chromium. You will notice they are all considered trace minerals. In other words, it doesn't take a lot, but they are very important to your good health.

NOTE: My intention is to simply offer information. **I DO NOT RECOMMEND THAT YOU SELF PRESCRIBE!** In regard to supplements and medication, I urge you to consult with your personal physician and follow the advice he or she prescribes.

COPPER

Proposed safe intake through food and/or supplements:	1.5- 3 mg a day
LOW-FAT FOOD SOURCES: (Recommended over supplements)	beans, barley, beet roots, blackstrap molasses, broccoli, garlic, lentils, mushrooms, oats, oranges, radishes, raisins, salmon, seafood, soybeans, and green leafy vegetables
PROPOSED BENEFITS:	Copper aids in the formation of bone, hemoglobin in red blood cells, and works in balance with vitamin C and zinc to help repair tissue and aid in the healing process. It is involved with energy production and is necessary for proper nerve function. ONE OF THE EARLY SIGNS OF COPPER DEFICIENCY IS OSTEOPOROSIS. Copper is essential for the formation of collagen, which makes up the connective tissue within the bones.
IF YOU CHOOSE TO TAKE THIS SUPPLEMENT:	Copper levels in the body are reduced if high amounts of zinc or vitamin C are taken. If copper intake is too high, the levels of vitamin C and zinc will drop.

MANGANESE

Proposed safe intake through food and/or supplements:	2-5 mg a day
LOW-FAT FOOD SOURCES: (Recommended over supplements)	dried peas and beans, blueberries, pineapple, spinach, and green leafy vegetables
PROPOSED BENEFITS:	Small quantities of manganese are needed for protein and fat metabolism, healthy nerves, aids with the immune system, and regulates blood sugar. It is required for normal bone growth and aids in energy production. It is necessary for iron-deficient anemia and also needed for the utilization of thiamine (B-1) and vitamin E. Manganese, along with the B-Complex vitamins give an over-all feeling of well-being.

MANGANESE (cont.)

PROPOSED BENEFITS:	It aids in the production of mother's milk and is one of the key elements in the production of enzymes needed to oxidize fats and metabolize carbohydrates.
IF YOU CHOOSE TO TAKE THIS SUPPLEMENT:	An excess of this trace mineral may interfere with iron absorption. Manganese is essential in re-production and energy production. Problems in those areas could signal a manganese deficiency.

SELENIUM

Proposed safe intake through food and/or supplements:	55-70 mcg a day
LOW-FAT FOOD SOURCES: (Recommended over supplements)	Whole grains, seafood, onions, beans, fish, shell-fish, chicken, garlic. (The amount in vegetables depends on the soil they were grown in.)
PROPOSED BENEFITS:	This trace mineral is a vital antioxidant (especial-ly when it is combined with vitamin E). Selenium protects the immune system from free radicals, which can damage the cells and lead to infec-tions and other various diseases. It is also impor-tant in the proper function of the heart muscle.
IF YOU CHOOSE TO TAKE THIS SUPPLEMENT:	Large doses can be toxic, so make sure you have the approval of your physician before taking this supplement and PLEASE don't self-prescribe-EVER!! Some effects of overdoses of selenium have been hair loss, garlic odor breath and sweat, diarrhea, and nausea.

ZINC

Proposd safe intake through food and/or supplements:	12-15 mg a day
LOW-FAT FOOD SOURCES: (Recommended over supplements)	seafood (especially oysters), whole grains, legumes, mushrooms, milk, whole wheat bread, brewer's yeast, rice, wheat germ, sardines, soybeans, and lima beans
PROPOSED BENEFITS:	Next to iron, zinc is the most abundant trace mineral in the body. It aids in cell division, growth, and repair (as in wound healing). It keeps our immune system in check and running properly. Zinc is important for the growth and development of bones, muscles, and sex organs. It plays an important role in our taste and smell senses and is involved in the metabolism of carbohydrates. It displaces loosely bound iron, preventing oxidation, which can cause cell damage. Zinc is a natural insect repellent and sunscreen. Products like zinc oxide, for example are used to relieve minor skin irritations as well as protecting those noses on our kids in the summer at the pool. Some even feel the proper amount of zinc in the diet may increase memory.
IF YOU CHOOSE TO TAKE THIS SUPPLEMENT:	Sufficient intake of zinc is necessary to maintain the proper concentrations of vitamin E in the blood. Zinc can block copper absorption, affecting the function of the body's immune system. For that reason you would be wise to take zinc and copper at least two hours apart. Zinc deficiency is quite rare, but there are some groups of people at risk. Heavy drinkers (alcohol speeds zinc excretion), endurance athletes (sweating causes zinc depletion), and strict vegetarians (fruits and vegetables contain little zinc) should all be especially aware of their diet and zinc consumption. Zinc is relatively non-toxic but extremely high doses may cause an increased LDL (bad) cholesterol.

CHROMIUM

Proposed safe intake through food and/or supplements:	50- 200 mcg a day
LOW-FAT FOOD SOURCES: (Recommended over supplements)	orange juice, legumes, brewer's yeast, wheat germ, brown rice, whole grains, fortified cereals, dried beans, chicken, corn, mushrooms, and potatoes
PROPOSED BENEFITS:	This trace mineral is very important in the metabolism of carbohydrates and fats. It helps the body's cells absorb insulin, a hormone that burns sugar and fat and helps to build muscle tissue. Strong evidence suggests it might be responsible for lowering the LDL (bad) cholesterol and raising the HDL (good) cholesterol. This essential mineral helps to maintain stable blood sugar levels through proper insulin and regulation of glucose in the blood. Chromium deficiency has been associated with blood-sugar malfunctions such as those suffering from diabetes and hypoglycemia. A deficiency in this trace mineral could increase your risk of developing heart disease. If you exercise frequently, are under a lot of stress, or eat a high-sugar diet, you may need to increase your chromium consumption. Check with your physician to find out!

NOTE: There is still a lot to learn concerning trace minerals and how they interact with each other and with other nutrients to help maintain health and prevent disease. It is not enough to concentrate on the intake of any one in particular since proper functioning depends on maintaining the delicate balance among them.

YOU: I have really enjoyed your book and my family loves your recipes. I have three daughters and I am doing everything in my power to teach them healthy eating habits so they don't have the weight problem I have had most of my adult life. I think there is a good chance I could develop osteoporosis as well, so I was wondering if you have any suggestions concerning my diet and should I be concerned with this problem regarding my girls. I've heard osteoporosis can be hereditary. My mom had the disease so I feel I might be at risk. Do you have any diet or exercise recommendations for me and my girls?
—*L.K. Lansing, Michigan*

ME: Osteoporosis is a disease in which your bones gradually thin, leading to a high risk of fractures. The best way to determine if you're at risk for osteoporosis is to have a bone density analysis performed by your physician. As far as the girls are concerned, you didn't mention their ages. The younger you are when you find out you may be at risk, the earlier you can take preventive steps. There are several factors you should be aware of regarding yourself, and your daughters. If you are Caucasian (white) or Asian and have a small frame you might be at risk. Postmenopausal women are at greater risk because of the decline in estrogen due to the absence of menses (monthly periods). The average woman experiences menopause around the age of fifty. If you are around this age, and have other hereditary risks, you should be especially concerned with ways to increase your calcium intake as well as incorporating some form of weight bearing exercise into your life. If you have gone through menopause early, as a result of having your ovaries removed by surgery, you are also at risk unless you take estrogen supplementation. If you suffer from other diseases such as asthma, cancer, arthritis, or even a thyroid disorder and take some form of medication to relieve the symptoms, you may have already experienced bone loss and thus increased your risk of osteoporosis (and not even know it).

Your lifestyle and dietary habits can be a major contributing factor concerning osteoporosis and the destruction it can cause. If you are "lactose intolerant," meaning you have trouble digesting milk products because of a lack of the enzyme lactase, you might consider trying lactase tablets or drops to aid in their digestion. You can also purchase milk that has been especially treated for folks suffering from lactose intolerance.

Smoking can contribute to a decrease in bone mass. Excessive alcohol consumption may result in the inability of your body to absorb calcium. As far as your girls are concerned, do they drink a lot of soda pop? Phosphorous, found in regular and diet sodas diminish calcium absorption, thus robbing the body of that much needed nutrient. Crash dieting (decreasing your calories dramatically) can also contribute to the lack of calcium needed to build strong bones. Most people restrict dairy products when cutting calories. If you happen to suffer from diabetes, your bone mass is probably 10% less than someone without the disease. As you can see, there are a lot of contributing factors we need to be aware of concerning the risks and treatment of osteoporosis.

The teenage years are when women develop a great percentage of their total body and spinal bone density, as well as their skeletal bone mass. Unfortunately, because of the typical teenage lifestyle (crash dieting, smoking, lack of exercise, consumption of soft drinks and too much high-fat junk food), many young girls deprive their bodies of the much needed calcium necessary in the bone building process. There are several ways we can teach and influence our daughters (and sons, too) regarding the importance of consuming an adequate amount of calcium, as well as the importance of weight bearing exercises. We can educate them with reading material. We can set a good example ourselves, by our diet and exercise program, and we can offer supplements (such as consuming 5 calcium-rich Tums tablets a day, thus meeting the U.S. RDI calcium requirement of 1,000 mg). Another great way to increase your calcium intake is to sprinkle non-fat dry milk on most anything before you eat it. This adds no fat and very few calories. This is an easy, inexpensive way to add calcium to our diet (and you can't even taste the difference)! By providing our children with a vast array of the many preventive measures regarding diet and exercise available, they might not be forced to deal with all the diet-related problems we (as adults) have had to face.

If you suffer from osteoporosis, or know someone at risk, I would like to suggest a wonderful book every household, doctor's office, clinic, school, hospital, etc. etc., should include in their library. It is a relatively new book called *BONE BUILDERS* by Edita Kaye. It contains more information on calcium and osteoporosis (prevention and treatment of) than any book I have ever read. Not only does her book offer a tremendous amount of pertinent information (in an easy to understand manner), Edita has also included over 150 wonderful low-fat, calcium enriched delicious recipes as well. The recipes have all been nutritionally analyzed, so you know the benefits of the foods you consume and how they will contribute to your good health and welfare. Edita also offers a video that compliments her book. The video is full of important information and produced in a way that is interesting, fun to watch, and loaded with practical applications. This information will be quite beneficial to those "at risk," as well as ANYONE interested in the prevention of osteoporosis for themself or someone they care about! I highly recommend this book to EVERYONE!! If you can't find *BONE BUILDERS* in your local bookstore, call: (800) 77-COOK-1 or write to:

BONE BUILDERS™
830-13 AIA North
Suite 313
Ponte Vedra Beach, FL 32082

Edita Kaye

Note: I met Edita in May, 1994 when she interviewed me in New York for an article she was writing for *Woman's World* magazine. As a result of our meeting, we have become very good friends. You will find Edita listed in my "Earth Angels" segment on page XXI. Aside from our friendship, I respect her tremendous knowledge of osteoporosis and preventive measures concerning the disease.

YOU: I've really enjoyed the recipes in your book and have lived the low-fat lifestyle for several years due to a cholesterol problem that runs in my family. I was really excited when I started using your book, because I found I REALLY COULD EAT all the foods I had ever enjoyed modified to low-fat with your recipes and ideas. Thank you for your time, research, and dedication to make low-fat living easy, fun, and delicious. When I was younger I exercised all the time. I used to play tennis, golf, water ski, and snow ski on a regular basis. Since I was diagnosed with arthritis about six months ago, I have basically given up on all forms of exercise due to stiffness and soreness in my bones and joints (especially in the morning). I am very unhappy. I didn't realize what a "mood enhancer" exercise was in my life, not to mention the major source of social interaction with my friends. To put it bluntly, I miss my exercise and it's benefits. Am I doomed at the age of 42 to sit back and watch the world pass me by? I admit that I'm probably not a lot of fun to be around these days (as a result of my constant pain). Any ideas? I would appreciate any suggestions you might have. Thanks in advance for your reply!   —G.F. Scottsdale, Arizona

ME: Does it make you feel any better knowing that you are one of over 37 million Americans who suffer from arthritis? Probably not, but I just thought I would mention it so you would know that you are not alone. You might need to take it a little slower, and some days you won't be able to do much without experiencing pain, but please don't stop exercising entirely. Try walking on a firm surface three to five times a week. Begin by strolling around the mall. Just get out there and start moving, slowly at first. Exercise strengthens the ligaments and cartilage that support your joints. It will also help to increase bone strength and will naturally aid in weight reduction (which could be taxing on your joints if you happen to be overweight). If you can't handle walking, why not try water aerobics or a stationary bicycle?

You have heard the saying, "If you don't use it, you'll lose it." This applies to our muscles. You might check with your physician regarding some type of anti-inflammatory medication to help ease the soreness and pain. PLEASE don't do ANYTHING that causes extreme discomfort or pain! However, WITH YOUR DOCTOR'S PERMISSION, a little exercise might prove to be quite beneficial. It will definitely help your mood. I can promise you that!!

YOU: Dear Pam: I just purchased your new 7th edition of *BUTTER BUSTERS* and was so excited to find the Sweet'N Low option in all the recipes that contain sugar. My husband was just diagnosed with Type II diabetes. I really don't understand the difference between Type I and Type II. Anyway, my question is if I can make the recipes with just Sweet'N Low? I guess we need to cut out all sugar. This is going to be really hard on my husband, because he loves sweets. Do you have any new information on diabetes? Thanks for your time.
—M.C. Montgomery, Alabama

ME: Let me explain what diabetes is and the difference in Type I and Type II. For someone WITHOUT DIABETES, the body breaks down food into a type of sugar called glucose and delivers it to the bloodstream. As the sugar enters the blood, it triggers the pancreas to produce a hormone called insulin. This helps to move the sugar out of the blood and into the cells of the body tissues where it fuels their activities. When a person HAS DIABETES the blood sugar can't get into the cells of the various body tissues, because the pancreas doesn't put out enough insulin. The cells in a diabetic resist the insulin's attempt to deliver the sugar. This results in chronic high blood sugar. This problem, in turn, throws all the bodily functions out of whack. It damages the nerves, blood vessels, eyes, heart, kidneys, and other organs as well. Type I means it usually appears quickly (as in children and young adults) and requires insulin injections for treatment. In this case, the body destroys it's own insulin-producing cells, and the pancreas stops making insulin entirely. It can lead to such a severe blood sugar overload that physical symptoms set in early. The body tries to get rid of the excess blood sugar by flushing it out in the urine. **Most people with Type I complain of frequent urination and constant thirst. Fatigue and weight loss are two other symptoms that show up because the body simply can't utilize the sugar for fuel.**

Type II Diabeties, on the other hand, is harder to detect and many don't even realize they are afflicted. This type of diabetes usually develops over the course of several years in older individuals who are most frequently overweight. This is too bad because if left undetected can damage blood vessels, cause strokes, affect eyesight, harm the kidneys, and contribute to heart disease. A way to avoid this is to have your blood sugar checked in routine yearly exams. This is especially important for those at high risk. **If you are over 40, have a close relative with diabetes, and more than 20% over your ideal weight, you should be checked periodically. If you suffer from high blood pressure, high cholesterol or high blood sugar during pregnancy, you could be at risk as well.** For some reason diabetes is more prevalent in American Indians, Hispanics, and African Americans. Many physicians run routine blood sugar tests on all their patients, but if you don't visit your physician at least once a year, you could have Type II Diabetes and not even know it. Type II diabetics usually make "some" insulin, so they DO ABSORB SOME SUGAR into their cells. This is why the disease might not show up for years, until the pancreas literally wears out due to pumping extra insulin. Many of these patients can be treated with oral medication rather than insulin shots.

The recipes can be prepared with Sweet'N Low alone, but it takes getting used to the flavor. Some find the taste quite bitter. There is some new information regarding sugar and it's consumption for diabetics. It's now believed that complex carbohydrates such as bread, potatoes, rice, and pasta break down into glucose just as rapidly as the simple carbohydrates found in foods like candy, cookies, and other sugar laden desserts. DIABETICS NEED TO BE CONCERNED WITH TOTAL CARBOHYDRATE CONSUMPTION, rather than a separate sugar limit or prohibition. The *American Diabetic Association* has updated their guidelines. There is no specific "Diabetic Diet" as before. The old advice specified the exact percentage of calories that were supposed to come from protein, carbohydrate, and fat in diets of all people with the condition. Except recommending 10-20% of the calories coming from protein, the new guidelines reject the idea of promoting the same proportion of major nutrients for everyone. As a matter of fact the new recommendations give diabetics more flexibility in food choices and no longer single out sugar as being any more damaging to blood sugar control than other carbohydrates.

The total amount of carbohydrate in the diet is the key to controlling blood sugar. The experts now say, moderate amounts of sugar may be eaten as part of an individualized and balanced nutrition plan. The new guidelines were published in the Diabetic Association's journal *"DIABETES CARE."*

Diabetes, especially Type II, often appears with other health problems that are just as important to consider when planning your diet. Heart disease is the major concern. **In fact, heart disease is the number one killer of people with diabetes.** For this reason diabetics need to plan a diet that will not only control their blood sugar, but also lower their blood cholesterol (especially blood triglycerides which is a type of fat in the blood), which can be linked to heart disease. For more information regarding diet, exercise, and other concerns related to diabetes, contact The American Diabetes Association at: (800)232-3472. Good luck!

YOU: Diabetes runs in my family. I heard something on the radio about a new test for early detection that involved some kind of light. Have you ever heard about this? If so, please send me any information you have. Thanks for adding the Sweet'N Low choices in your new 7th edition. I had your original book you published yourself, and have used it for two years. My family loves all the recipes, especially the desserts. "Pam's Famous Guilt Free Mud Pie" is our favorite! I bought the new one because I think we all need to monitor our sugar consumption (even if we aren't diabetic). My husband has lost 53 pounds and I have lost 35 since we started using your book. Thanks for making healthy eating taste so good!   —N.B. Atlanta, Georgia

ME: I'm so glad you have enjoyed my book and hope you will enjoy the new edition with all the updates and revisions. I had all the recipes re-analyzed because so many of the products have changed since 1992 when I first self-published the book. As a matter of fact, I have heard about the early diabetes detection test. From what I understand, it involves a light being shined into the patient's eyes. The device shines a blue light in the eye and measures changes in the eye's lens which are related to the levels of glucose (a simple sugar) found in the body. A high glucose can indicate diabetes. The early indication of diabetes (especially Type II because it usually goes undetected) with the new device could lead to treatment. Blindness is a major concern associated with diabetes. From what I've heard, the test doesn't require needles and provides results immediately. Blood test results can take up to 2 days. A portable hand-held version of the device could enable screening tests at public places, such as shopping malls. Approval of the new device by the U.S. Food and Drug Administration is expected in 1995. If we can detect diabetes in the early stages, the problem of blindness (associated with the disease) might eventually be eliminated. I hope this information helps. Be on the look-out for more information regarding this early detection device. I will watch for it, too!!

YOU: I have really enjoyed your cookbook and want you to know that the recipes have been a hit with my whole family. I am concerned with sodium since I suffer from high blood pressure. I followed your directions about rinsing all canned vegetables and using Papa Dash Lite Salt. It really is the first lite salt that tastes decent! This may sound kind of funny, but my husband has VERY low blood pressure. As a matter of fact I think it really is too low. He used to have a problem with high blood pressure so he started taking medication to lower it. In my opinion it is too low now. It is 90/60. Is it possible to have a blood pressure that is too low? Thanks for all your tips for modifying recipes. You have made it so easy to eat healthy. Some of your recipes do contain a high amount of sodium, but with your suggestions I have been able to modify them. Do you have any new informa-

tion concerning high blood pressure or low blood pressure? I know there are all kinds of medications available to treat high blood pressure, but is it still important to eat a low-salt diet? I'm afraid mine must be hereditary. My Mom and Dad both have high blood pressure, too. I was also wondering about my kid's blood pressure. Can I prevent my children from developing high blood pressure if it does happen to run in my family? I hope you have a new book in the works. I need some more great recipes! Keep up the good work and let me know if you discover any new secrets!
—*K.L. Seattle, Washington*

ME: Thank you for your comments regarding my book. Although I am very lucky and have very low blood pressure myself, my mother-in-law, my Dad, and my Mom have all suffered from high blood pressure over the years. Since high blood pressure can lead to heart attacks and strokes, you are wise to be concerned. Most physicians seem to be most concerned with the second or "bottom" number when it comes to your blood pressure reading. In other words, the "80" in "120 over 80" seems to indicate whether the pressure is high enough to cause concern as a risk towards heart disease. This makes sense because the first (or top) number represents the pressure exerted as the heart contracts to pump blood to all the arteries throughout the body and is relatively high in most cases. The second (or lower) number represents the pressure exerted by the blood in the walls of the arteries between beats. If that number happens to be elevated, it means the arteries, or blood vessels, are under a great deal of pressure even when the heart is relaxed between beats. It is at this time (between beats) when the heart is filling with blood getting ready for the next beat. If the second (or bottom number) known as the diastolic pressure is above 90 (which would be considered high) your physician might recommend trying a blood-pressure lowering change in life-style or perhaps even medication.

Until recently the top number wasn't considered to be as much a risk regarding heart disease as the bottom number. Many experts feel there is cause for concern if the first (or top number), known as the systolic pressure, is elevated as well. This also holds true if only the top number is elevated and the bottom number remains in the normal or safe range. As a matter of fact, there is even a name for it. Borderline Isolated Systolic Hypertension (which generally affects people over the age of 65) has been ranked as the most common type of high blood pressure that usually goes untreated. Unfortunately, besides being one of the most under diagnosed and least treated types of blood pressure, Borderline Isolated Systolic Hypertension has most physicians puzzled. Because certain medications affect both numbers, the most effective method of treatment, at this time, seems to be life-style (as in exercise) and dietary changes.

SOME IMPORTANT LIFE-STYLE CHANGES YOU MIGHT TRY:

1. **Limit your daily sodium intake to less than 2,300 milligrams.** This is the amount found in one teaspoon of regular table salt. Switch to Papa Dash "Lite" salt if you must use salt. One-fourth teaspoon of Papa Dash "Lite" salt contains 90 mg. of sodium compared to 595 mg. per ¼ tsp. of regular salt. Because the new labeling that was effective in May 1994, sodium content MUST be listed on all packaged foods. You might consider investing in a Lumiscope (an

electronic sodium detector). It is battery operated and detects the sodium content in hot, warm, or cold foods and liquids.   It retails for about $17.99 in most drug stores.   If you can't find it in your area call: (908)225-5533.   It would come in especially handy when eating out since you have no idea how the food might have been prepared.

2. **Limit your daily alcohol consumption to no more than one ounce** (the amount found in 24 ounces of beer, 8 ounces of wine, or 2 ounces of 100- proof whiskey). I do not advocate drinking at all, but wanted you to be aware of the guidelines recommended by most physicians. If you don't drink now, PLEASE don't start!

3. **Try to lose excess weight if you are currently overweight.** With a loss of as little as ten pounds you will significantly lower your blood pressure (in most cases).

4. **Incorporate exercise into your life if you haven't already done so.** If you have been sedentary in the past and start walking 30-45 minutes three to five times a week (at a brisk pace) chances are you may be able to lower, as well as control, your systolic pressure in the future.

Although most folks work to keep their blood pressure down (less than 140/90 is normal), some people actually have blood pressure that is too low. Readings of 90/60, or even 80/50 are not that uncommon. A sign your blood pressure may be too low would be a woozy feeling when you stand up after eating a large meal or when first getting out of bed in the morning. If your vision seems to be dimming, or you suffer from a pain in the back of your neck or head, you would be wise to have yourself checked out by your physician. Some other causes of low blood pressure could be a result of: Dosage higher than needed (over medicated), other medications such as diuretics, or even diet pills that contain phenypropanolamine. You may suffer from a very low blood pressure if you happen to be diabetic, have a heart valve defect, or an imbalance of body chemicals that regulate the widening and narrowing of blood vessels (when vessels widen, your blood pressure falls). If you have always had low blood pressure, and have no symptoms, you probably have nothing to worry about. You can always get out of bed a little slower (try dangling your legs over the side of the bed for a few minutes before you get up). If you feel light-headed when you get up quickly after a meal, try drinking a cup of coffee after you eat (caffeine tightens blood vessels, which raises your blood pressure temporarily). There is probably no need to change your habits unless you are taking hypertension drugs (which could be the culprit). When diastolic pressure (the smaller and bottom number) is lower than 85 in people who have reduced their blood pressure with drugs, it could actually raise their risk of a heart attack, because there is not enough blood going to the heart (which could damage the heart muscle). The blood flows to the heart mainly during diastolic pressure. Please have your husband talk to his physician about this if he is taking hypertension medicine that may be lowering his blood pressure too much. Home monitoring of blood pressure can be helpful to those taking medication to lower their blood pressure.

Low-sodium diets are one of the safest and most effective ways to treat high blood pressure. Many blood pressure medications are a form of a diuretic (or water pill). They force the kidneys to leak out salt by increasing the flow of urine. Some common side effects could be high glucose levels, low potassium levels, and gout. A low-sodium diet can help you correct the problem without losing important vitamins and minerals from your body. Since a high-sodium intake can lead to blood pressure problems, there are some foods you should try to cut down on if possible. You will notice that many of the foods on the following chart are VERY HIGH IN FAT as well as sodium:

HIGH SODIUM FOODS

Food	(mg/100 gm)
bacon	1,021
butter	987
ketchup	1,300
bouillon cubes	24,000
some salad dressings	1,094
canned soups	300-800
caviar	2,200
cheddar cheese	700
olives	2,400
canned sardines	760
sausage	1,300
soy sauce	7,325
self-rising flour	1,079

Many of these products come in a low or sodium-reduced version. Check your labels before you buy or eat a product. Many of the soups and canned goods have reduced their sodium content over the past year. Watch for the words "low-sodium" or "reduced-salt" on the products you purchase. Your heart will thank you for it!

As far as your children are concerned, you can certainly help them develop habits that might lower their risk of developing high blood pressure. We all know that a high blood pressure can lead to all kinds of health problems, so the earlier we develop good habits, the better our chances of cutting the risks involved. Encourage your children to maintain a normal weight. Overweight children often grow into overweight adults. Set a good example by exercising yourself. Maybe they will catch the drift. Don't force exercise on your children. IT DOESN'T WORK!! You can reduce their sodium intake by cooking with low-sodium products and using Papa Dash "Lite" salt in your home. Try to include sources of calcium in their diet, such as skim milk, fat-free yogurt, and low or fat-free cheese. (I do not recommend low or non-fat dairy products for children UNDER the age of two.)

It has been shown that children who get plenty of calcium have lower blood pressure. I don't know if this will help prevent high blood pressure as they reach adulthood, but the healthy habits learned as children usually carry over into later years. That is why it is so important to start by teaching your children, from the very beginning, about healthy habits. The best way to do this is through YOUR personal example.

Some suggestions would be to use more spices in place of salt, substitute salt-free additives and condiments, try cutting down on alcohol (which raises blood pressure), avoid fast food restaurants (unless they have healthy choices), read labels before you purchase many pre-packaged snacks, cookies, and crackers, and PLEASE give some kind of aerobic exercise a try. Regular aerobic exercise has been shown to lower blood pressure in many people that haven't changed another thing in their life.

Potassium prevents sodium from raising your blood pressure and therefore decreases your risk of a stroke. Try adding at least one serving of a potassium-rich fruit or vegetable to your daily diet and

Tyler, Paige, Mom, and Blake Christmas 1992

cut your risk of a stroke by as much as 40%. Do you like bananas? My Mom has increased her potassium-rich foods (bananas, oranges, dried fruits, yogurt, poultry, and potatoes with the skin on), started riding a stationary bicycle for thirty-five minutes four days a week, and cut down on her alcohol consumption. She was able (because of her life-style changes) to discontinue taking blood pressure medication at the ripe young age of 75 this past year. It's NEVER too late to adopt life-style changes and take control of your health. She also dropped over 50 pounds and lowered her cholesterol to a safe level by adhering to a low-fat diet and incorporating aerobic exercise into her life on a regular basis. I am so proud of her and what she has accomplished! My Mom truly is a "walking example" of what I teach. She is an inspiration to many people, myself included!!!

If you are currently taking blood pressure medication, NEVER discontinue without approval from your personal physician!

There are quite a few blood pressure monitors on the market. You can find a good selection at most drug stores. If you have trouble finding one in your area, try calling A & D Medical, a leading manufacturer and distributor of blood pressure monitoring equipment and health care products for home and professional use at: (800)726-3364. I wish you luck with your new lifestyle changes and thank you for taking the time to write and ask about blood pressure. Because of folks like you, I continue with my research to find the answers that just might help someone reading this book. Good Luck!!

YOU: I love your book and have enjoyed learning how to cut the fat, but save the taste! Not only have I dropped about 25 pounds, I even started exercising for the first time in my life! I have a couple of medical questions that I hope you can help me with. First of all, what is considered high blood pressure? Could you explain what blood pressure really means? I am confused by the numbers and terms. Second, could you explain what the liver does in conjunction with cholesterol? I know it has something to do with the HDL, but don't quite understand what. I just had my yearly physical and was a little overwhelmed by all the new information. I was pleasantly surprised to find I had lost more weight than I realized and my cholesterol, for the first time ever, dropped below 200. It was my physician who suggested your book in the first place six months ago when I complained of the extra weight I had picked up over the past year. Thank you for taking the time to answer my questions. I know how busy you must be cooking all the time so you can write more cookbooks! I hope that is what you are doing anyway!

—F. S. Trenton, New Jersey

ME: It sounds like you are on the right track and I am so glad my book has helped you. I agree with you that blood pressure readings are confusing. I will try to explain what the numbers mean. Your blood pressure varies with the beat of your heart. When the main chamber of the heart squeezes or beats (as we know it), blood spurts into the large arteries stretching the arterial walls. When our heart relaxes (between beats), the arterial walls spring back keeping the blood flowing between heartbeats. The high pressure (or top number) in your blood pressure reading is called the "systolic pressure." The lower (or bottom number) in your blood pressure reading, that is generated as your heart relaxes, is called the "diastolic pressure." In most adults, the blood pressure is considered normal when the top number (systolic) is less than 140 and the bottom number (diastolic) is less than 90. (This is assuming the test is taken while you are sitting down and are relaxed.) Your blood pressure can vary greatly throughout the day. There are quite a few factors that may affect your reading. The top number (systolic) will increase during exercise and may fall while you are sleeping. Your blood pressure will increase under stressful situations. Your blood pressure is usually highest in the morning and is typically lower in the evening (especially while you sleep). Most physicians like to have more than one reading to determine the accuracy of the test. If the bottom number (on more than two or three occasions) is over 90, there is a good possibility you could have high blood pressure (also known as hypertension). There is also room for concern if the top number (systolic) is elevated (even if the bottom number remains normal). This is more common in older folks (usually over 65) and in people with diabetes. It's a wise idea to become familiar with your blood pressure reading because it will allow you to keep track of your progress if you are on a special diet or taking blood pressure medication. The goal for most healthy adults is the bottom number (diastolic) to be below 90 mm Hg and the top number (systolic) to be below 140 mm Hg. The units of blood pressure measurement are millimeters (mm) of mercury (Hg.).

Now, for your chemistry lesson: A systolic blood pressure of 140 mm Hg. means the pressure in the artery is enough to raise a narrow column of liquid mercury 140 millimeters, or about 5.5 inches. Mercury is used instead of water because it is about 13 times heavier, and much shorter tubes can be used for the measurement. A systolic blood pressure of 140 mm Hg. would raise a similar column of water almost six feet (providing you had a container that tall). I hope this wasn't too confusing, but I find it all rather fascinating myself!

As for the liver, it really is an amazing organ. Found behind the ribs in the upper right section of the abdomen, the liver is actually in two parts or lobes. It has over 200 functions and is the largest internal organ in our body. It manufacturers essential blood proteins that aid in clotting, oxygen transport, and even immune functions. It produces MOST of the body's cholesterol (converted from saturated fats) and regulates blood levels of amino and fatty acids. This is the problem with people who have hereditary high cholesterol. Have you ever known someone that lived on bacon, eggs, steak, and greasy, highly-saturated fatty food and still have a low cholesterol? Well, this is because they have a very efficient liver that can handle getting rid of the bad cholesterol. Cholesterol is manufactured and excreted by the liver. Some of us are more fortunate than others. Many people, myself included, are lucky because they can control their cholesterol by eating a low-fat diet. Others must take medication (no matter what kind of diet they eat). This all has to do with your liver and how efficient it is at getting rid of the bad cholesterol (LDL).

The liver removes damaged blood cells and foreign organisms from the blood. It joins forces with the kidney and filters toxins out of the blood. The liver stores excess nutrients and corrects problems by returning some of the reserves to the bloodstream. The fat-soluble vitamins (A, D, E, and K), for example, are stored in the liver, as is glucose. Glucose, derived from carbohydrates eaten, is stored in the form of glycogen and provides body's fuel for cell metabolism and energy for exercise. It takes four grams of water to store one gram of carbohydrate for energy. This is why we sometimes weigh more the morning after we eat a carbohydrate-rich meal. Our body is retaining fluid to store the extra carbohydrates. I have found the extra "water weight" usually disappears after my aerobic exercise session (even if I drink a couple of quarts of water while I work out). This is because your muscles primarily raid the glycogen stores for energy the first 15-20 minutes of your aerobic activity before it starts burning body fat. If your glycogen stores are depleted (due to fasting during the night while sleeping), your body will automatically head for stored body fat to be used as energy (if you work out before you eat breakfast). Some feel aerobic exercise is more beneficial (regarding fat loss) if you work out before you eat a meal, when your glycogen stores are depleted. **This is only a theory and not substantiated by concrete evidence, but it does seem to make sense.** This is the reason aerobic exercise (preferably long in duration and low in intensity) is so important if you are trying to lose body fat no matter what time of day you choose to exercise.

The liver is the body's primary detoxifying center as well. It manufactures and regulates many of the body's chemicals, removes poisons from the blood (including alcohol and drugs), and plays a major role in the digestion process. The liver is so important that we would die in a couple of days if it completely shut down. It's amazing, however, that this three-pound organ has a surplus of active tissue and can actually function when up to 75% of it has been removed or is diseased. You might compare it to the EverReady Battery (It just keeps going!). I wish you luck and continued success with your new healthy lifestyle! Thank you for taking the time to write. People like you encourage me to learn so much more than I would if you hadn't asked a question! Thanks for the push I needed to learn all about blood pressure and the many functions of our miraculous liver!

YOU: Thank you so much for changing my life. I never knew low-fat food could taste so great. I've made several of the recipes in the main course section and a ton of the great desserts. What I really liked is the way you taught me to change my own favorite recipes to low-fat. You took all the guess work out. THE WHOLE FAMILY HAS LOST WEIGHT AND FEEL GREAT! I do have a question you might be able to answer. If you are too busy, I understand, but I just thought I would ask anyway. I have terrible migraine headaches. I know it must be hereditary because my mom had them and now my 15 year old daughter has them too. She just gets them during her period. Do you have any new information about treatment of migraines? I've read a few articles in different magazines about them, but wanted to know if you knew of anything official. How can I be sure if my daughter's headaches are migraines? I think they are because she feels sick at her stomach like I do. Please help if you can. Our favorite recipe is "Fancy Barbecue Chicken with Pasta." I make it once a week. We also love the "Chicken Enchiladas" and the "Quick Spicy Chile." Everyone loves the "Cream Cheese Cake Bars" and "No Guilt Mud Pie" (just to mention a few). By the way your "Pam's Best Beer Bread" is to die for. It makes wonderful cinnamon toast for breakfast. Thanks for making healthy food taste wonderful!   —P.H. Harrisburg, Pennsylvania

P.S. I have lost 27 pounds and my husband has lost 16 (and he didn't even realize he was eating low-fat until I finally told him).

ME: Thank you for taking the time to write. Some of your favorite recipes are my favorites, too! I'm so happy you have lost weight without feeling deprived. I really think that is why the book has helped so many people. The food really does taste good. Believe me, I sure wouldn't stick to something that didn't!

ARE YOUR MIGRAINES GIVING YOU A HEADACHE?
Headaches are something we all deal with on occasion. However, if you suffer from migraines you are in a whole different league. We get headaches from all kinds of things such as:

1. **EYESTRAIN** (Long periods of focusing on close work- like me at my computer.)

2. **HUNGER** (Fasting for more than 5 hours while awake, or 13 hours while asleep causes blood vessels to dilate as blood sugar levels drop.)

3. **SINUS** (Infected swollen sinuses push against nerve endings.)

4. **ALCOHOL** (It lowers blood sugar dilating blood vessels in the brain.)

5. **HOT DOGS** (Nitrite compounds found in hot dogs and many other processed meats dilate blood vessels.)

6. **MSG** (A flavor enhancer found in foods some people can't metabolize.)

7. TMJ (A misaligned temporomandibular joint in the jaw can lead to muscle spasms.)

8. ICE CREAM (Very cold food can stimulate nerve endings in the mouth.)

9. REBOUND (Withdrawal from caffeine causes blood vessels to constrict. When you take it away, if your body is used to it, the blood vessels dilate causing pain.)

10. WEEKEND HEADACHES (You may get these from sleeping too much or too little.)

11. STRESS (Tension headaches occur regularly in the late afternoon.)

I have (over the past 45 years) had MOST of these types of headaches, but I have never (knock on wood) experienced the dreaded "migraine headache." I guess I have my parents to thank for that, because from what I understand migraine headaches (in most cases) are thought to be hereditary. I'm sorry to hear you suffer from migraine headaches. I have a very good friend who has migraines and from what she tells me they must be terrible. Her two daughters (ages 18 and 14) started getting migraines around the time they started menstruating. I feel sure it must be related to hormones. Since there is a drop in estrogen before or during your menstrual flow (and that is when most women have problems) there is a good chance the hormonal changes trigger the headaches. If your problems occur around or during your period, you might check with your physician who may be able to prescribe supplemental medication to balance your hormone fluctuations. (This would depend on many factors, SO PLEASE CONSULT YOUR PHYSICIAN regarding any kind of supplements.) As far as your daughter is concerned, this would depend on her age. You mentioned that you weren't sure if your daughter is having migraines or just (what most of us to refer to as) tension headaches. You mentioned they only occurred during her period. For that reason, there is a strong possibility she may be having hormonally related headaches. The best way to find out is to make an appointment with her physician and let him investigate the problem further. About 70% of those suffering from migraine headaches are women. Oral contraceptives, because they involve hormonal changes, have been associated with migraines, as well. Many experts feel specific foods could be the culprit. If you have suffered from migraines for sometime, you are probably aware of the foods to avoid: chocolate, alcohol (especially red wine), aged cheese, smoked meats, and caffeine have all been associated with the trigger responsible for the onset of migraines.

Besides the foods I mentioned, monosodium glutamate (MSG), a food additive, can trigger migraines in some people. You must realize that MSG can be labeled as hydrolyzed vegetable protein or sodium nitrites in processed foods, such as hot dogs. Migraine headaches have a typical set of symptoms that occur in characteristic order. Most migraine sufferers receive warnings before the actual headache occurs such as blurred vision, zigzag lights, yawning, weakness or tingling (on one side of the head or body), chills, nausea or vomiting. Migraine headaches can last several days. Migraines, from what I understand, are a throbbing or steady ache usually on one side of the head, forehead, or temple. When my friend feels a migraine "coming on" (remember there are usually warning signs) she heads for bed and a dark room.

Smoke, loud noises, and strong perfume have been known to set them off too. Migraine headaches are usually hereditary, but they can be triggered by physical causes, as well. Diet, stress, menstruation, and environmental changes have all been associated with migraines. There is a good chance your daughter has inherited migraine headaches from you and your mother. I find it interesting that childhood migraines are more common in boys than girls before the age of 12. By the time girls reach the age of 20 the numbers change and twice as many women as men suffer from migraines.

Years ago, migraine pain was blamed on the constriction and swelling of blood vessels in the brain. Some feel all headaches are linked to an imbalance of chemicals in the brain. Here is an example of how some people feel they get started: Say, something in your day really upsets you and you have already been dealing with a lot of stress in your life. This emotion activates a decrease in your level of serotonin (a nerve chemical that regulates pain and sends messages to your brain). This chemical drop causes the blood vessels in the brain to swell. The swelling causes pain. **My point is that the stress did not cause your headache, but the stress interacted with your brain's serotonin level and THAT is the cause.** We can't control our serotonin levels, but there are many other contributing factors we can control such as diet and environment.

Some feel migraines could be an inherited neurological disorder. A few experts think they could be associated with the trigeminal nerve system which carries impulses from the head and face to the brain. Some experts feel during a migraine headache the nerve system becomes inflamed causing extreme pain. No one really knows how many people are affected by migraines. (It has been estimated at sixteen million for women alone.) It is believed that many people possess the disposition to get migraines, but for some unknown reason never suffer a single symptom because the migraine must be "set off" by some form of trigger. It's kind of like cancer. Many people carry genes that increase their risk of developing cancer, but not everyone of those people will develop the disease. If we knew all the answers, there would BE NO disease. If only one parent has migraines, there is a 50% chance the child will inherit migraines, but if both parents have migraines the child's risk increases to 75%.

CLUSTER HEADACHES
There is another type of headache called the "cluster headache" which falls under the heading of migraines, and generally affects men. The cause of cluster headaches is relatively unknown, but they can be worse than a severe migraine. They usually occur on one side of the head or behind the eye area and can last from 15 minutes to three hours. My father-in-law has had this type of headache. I'll never forget Thanksgiving day back in 1974 when he had (what must have been) a cluster headache. He was in severe pain. I think they might be hereditary, too, because my husband Mike gets this type of headache every once in a while. His are usually triggered by intense heat. Most cluster headaches begin while sleeping. When you wake up you may notice nasal congestion or discharge, or tearing from the eye on the side of the pain. However, this could also be the symptom of a sinus headache.

BIOLOGICAL OR PSYCHOLOGICAL?
(Oh come on, give me a break!)

Over the years some people actually had the nerve to blame migraines in women on the fact we just couldn't handle stress or were too emotional! I DO NOT AGREE WITH THAT THEORY! I feel quite sure migraine headaches are biological rather than psychological.... and I'm not just saying that because I am a woman! There is too much evidence pointing to hormonal fluctuation that substantiates that theory. Another reason I believe this to be true is because **the only time my friend DOESN'T suffer from migraines** is when she is pregnant. Tell me that has nothing to do with hormones! I'm just sure!

HEADACHES CAN BE A REAL PAIN!

The following information addresses the three major types of headaches. If you recognize the symptoms of the cluster or migraine headaches in yourself, please get checked out by your physician as soon as possible. There are other kinds of headaches with all kinds of causes, but I wanted to address the ones that are most common.

TYPE OF HEADACHE: Tension

CAUSE: Tension headaches are usually a result of sustained contractions of the head and neck muscles which cause the blood vessels in our heads to become restricted. An example would be looking down to read or holding the same position for an extended period of time. In my case, tension headaches have occurred a lot the past few weeks, because I have been sitting at my computer trying to finish this book. As a matter of fact, let me tell you about the tension headache I had yesterday.....never mind, I know you don't want to hear about it.

LOCATION, SYMPTOMS, AND SEVERITY OF PAIN:
- mild to moderate (or intense in the eye area which is what mine was)
- dull ache frequently described as a vice-like squeezing of the head
- usually in neck, eye area, temples, or shoulders
- last from 30 minutes to one day
- frequently start later in the day (about the same time each day)

TREATMENT:
- rest
- hot shower
- neck or back massage (This works best for me!)
- over-the-counter analgesics such as: aspirin (Bufferin or Bayer), acetaminophen (such as Tylenol, Anacin III, or Panadol), ibuprofen (such as Advil, Motrin IB, or Nuprin), or one of the combinations (such as Excedrin or Anacin) *ALWAYS CHECK WITH YOUR PHYSICIAN BEFORE TAKING ANY MEDICATION!! Migraine drugs are sometimes prescribed if your headaches are chronic.

TYPE OF HEADACHE: Cluster

CAUSE: Cluster headaches may be a result of neurotransmitter levels being affected by disturbances in a part of the brain called the hypothalamus. Most cluster headaches occur in the spring or fall. For that reason it is thought that they might be brought on by seasonal changes. Daily biological reasons such as smoking, alcohol, cold wind, consuming foods that contain nitrites, or any other substance that causes the blood vessels to dilate may be the culprit. Ninety percent of those suffering from cluster headaches are male. (Maybe they can't handle the stress or are too emotional!) Just kidding. I couldn't resist that one.

LOCATION, SYMPTOMS, AND SEVERITY OF PAIN:
- knifelike pain in or near one eye
- lasting 15 minutes to three hours
- eyes become bloodshot and teary
- nasal congestion, sweating, or flushing
- Attacks can occur several times daily for months (usually at the same time) then disappear for years.

TREATMENT:
Stay away from alcohol and tobacco smoke. Appropriate medications can help. Check with your personal physician for recommendations.

TYPE OF HEADACHE: Migraine

CAUSE:
- may be caused by fluctuation in neutrotransmitters (especially serotonin) that regulate the perception of pain
- may be caused by spasm and swelling of blood vessels in the head which irritate nearby nerve endings

Triggers:
- drop in estrogen
- oral contraceptives
- eating aged cheese, smoked meats, chocolate, or alcohol
- bright or flashing lights
- changes in altitude
- lack or sleep
- stress

Note: There could be a genetic predisposition (hereditary).

LOCATION, SYMPTOMS, AND SEVERITY OF PAIN:
- mild to severe pain
- often one-sided and throbbing
- can last three days
- nausea
- sensitivity to bright lights
- vomiting
- perceiving flashing lights, or strange smells (usually before pain strikes)
- numbness in an arm or leg

TREATMENT:
- rest or sleep in a quiet room
- ice pack to back of neck and scalp areas
- avoid chocolate and aged cheese
- Prescriptions may be helpful. *CHECK WITH YOUR PERSONAL PHYSICIAN FOR RECOMMENDATIONS!

HOW TO TREAT A MIGRAINE
(All the new methods and how they work)
Some people find over-the-counter medication quite effective. Some do well with relaxation exercises and biofeedback. Some take beta-blockers to relax blood vessels. There are serotonin inhibitors and calcium channel blockers to prevent blood vessel constriction. Estrogen supplements taken premenstrually work well for some women. There are more powerful prescription drugs like ergot compounds, which also constrict blood vessels. There are some new medications on the market that have proven quite effective for many people. Sumatriptan is a prescription that works by shrinking swollen blood vessels back to their normal size. The medication lasts about five hours and can halt a full-blown migraine. Another drug, Ergotamine, has been around longer and your physician may suggest this initially. The newest medication on the market is Migranal. It is a therapeutic nasal spray. Out of 100 people tested (79 women and 21 men) all reported quick relief from migraine pain and nausea within minutes. IT IS ALWAYS BEST TO CHECK WITH YOUR PHYSICIAN FIRST!

WARNING: How do you know if your headaches are severe enough to consult a physician? If you have persistent and severe headaches or migraines, and what you are taking for them does not alleviate the pain, you should see your doctor and get a formal diagnosis. There are other serious causes of headaches that should be considered (such as a brain tumor or aneurysm) **which could be life threatening**. If you experience numbness in one or both legs, difficulty with balance, or loss of vision (or blurred vsion), consult your physician immediately. Sudden occurence of symptons in someone who has never experienced headaches warrants immediate attention, as well. You might try keeping a journal concerning your headaches. Try jotting down when they occur, how often, time of month, foods eaten near their onset, etc.

These are all factors that could help your physician determine the best plan of attack. Make a note of the duration and severity, too.

Good luck! I hope I answered your questions. For more information contact: The American Council for Headache Education at: (800)255-ACHE (2243) or contact: The National Headache Foundation, 5252 North Western Ave., Chicago, IL 60625 (800)843-2256.

EATING DISORDERS

YOU: I would like to start my letter on a happy note, because that is how I feel when I read your book. You seem to have it all together. Have you always been so slim? Do you exercise a lot? Do you ever lose control and eat everything in sight? You must love to cook or you wouldn't have written a book, but do you eat a lot of sweets? I noticed you have a lot of desserts in your book. I can only dream about those. You see, if I ever start eating a cookie, or a piece of pie, or something like that, I can't stop. You guessed it. I am a compulsive overeater, I guess. However, I also throw up a lot, too. I just can't stand the thought of being fat again (I used to weigh over 200 pounds) so, instead of gaining weight, I just get rid of all the terrible things I eat (when I lose control and can't stop) by throwing up. You probably think I'm crazy, but I really don't know who else to tell about this. I figure you don't know me and I don't really know you (except I kind of feel like I do after reading the first part of your book). You see, I'm not sure if I am a compulsive overeater (because I honestly can't stop eating once I get started), or bulimic (because I throw up to control my weight), or maybe I am anorexic (because I'm scared to eat and risk getting fat again).

Can you possibly help me? Do you have any suggestions or some kind of meal plan for people like me? Maybe if you could tell me what to eat every day for a week or two, I could get used to eating normally. To tell you the truth, I am scared to death of food. It is controlling my life. I'm scared to eat because sometimes I can't stop once I start. However, I know if I starve myself, I will die. I know the vomiting isn't good for me either, so as you can see, I really need some help! Oh yes, I also exercise constantly (especially after a major pig-out).

Please don't judge me because everyone else does (including my mother), and I just couldn't stand one more person yelling at me. It seems that I just can't please her. When I was fat all she ever did was tell me how fat and disgusting I was. Now that I am thin, she tells me I look like "a prisoner of war" and need to gain some weight. I don't think I could ever please her, but want to change because I really am miserable. I know I should ask for help, but I am really embarrassed about my problems. Besides, I finally found a man who really loves me. (Of course, he doesn't know about all of my weird hang-ups.) I guess I will have to tell him some day, but I was hoping that maybe you could help me get myself straightened out first.

I've made several of the recipes in the main course section and they really are great. I don't seem to have a problem overeating those kinds of foods. Do you think some foods set off binges? I've read a book that says some people are kind of allergic to carbohydrates, and when they start eating them, they can't stop. That sounds like me. I'm so confused. I read everything I can and have really tried to help myself, but I don't know how much longer I can live this way. I'm not using my real name on this letter and please, if you do write back, just send your letter to the post office box on the envelope. I know you are probably really busy (with your three kids). I saw their picture in the book. You have a lovely family. I really appreciate all your hard work in writing the cookbook and hope you will write more books. I especially liked the first part of your book about yourself. You made me feel like I could talk to you and that is why I wrote this letter. If you can find it in your heart to write back, please do and soon if possible! Thank you for reading this letter.

ME: I am so glad you took the time to write. Please don't feel alone. There are hundreds of thousands of others "just like you" all over the country (or should I say world). As a matter of fact one out of every 100 women suffer from anorexia or bulimia in the U.S. alone. I'm sure the percentage is much higher than that, because so many cases go unreported. You didn't mention your age or how long you have lived under these conditions. You said your Mom yelled at you. How was it growing up? You mentioned that she made fun of you when you were heavy and now complains because you are too thin. Is there any special reason why you feel the need to please (or displease) her? Did you get along with the rest of your family as a child, and how about now? Where is your father and what kind of relationship do you have with him? Do you have brothers or sisters? You didn't really mention your family (except your Mom). Did you experience any kind of trauma as a young child? Were you ever sexually abused? I know you wrote to ask me for help, but I need some more information in order to understand the circumstances that could be contributing factors to what is going on with your eating disorder. You see, the problem is usually not the food (in most cases). With most eating disorders, there is usually an underlying problem and the excessive eating pattern, or bulimic behavior, is most likely a way of dealing with your hurt feelings, disappointment, or other problem you have been forced to face. To get through it many people use food as a source of medication (so to speak). They do feel better temporarily (as they stuff in the food to forget the pain), but the end result is NEVER A HAPPY ONE. That is because most of those people are actually stuffing their feelings even deeper down inside as they consume a tremendous amount of food, in record time. Believe me, they aren't eating for the enjoyment or savoring every bite. They just want to get rid of it as fast as possible hoping their misery and unhappiness will disappear just as fast as the food does. Unfortunately, that isn't the way it works. Oh, the food is gone alright, but the resentment, pain, and unhappiness are still there and now they have been joined by tremendous guilt for what they have just done. I've known compulsive overeaters who have told me in the middle of a full blown-out binge they actually feel numb, literally. Others have told me they actually go into some sort of trance (like an out-of-body experience). They can see what they are doing, know that it is wrong, want to stop, and yet they keep right on eating! It's almost like, a "Well, I'll just show them!" attitude. Of course, the only one "they show" is their own self, and most don't exactly like what they see. The guilt they experience is usually worse than the event that drove them to binge in the first place. Many people eat compulsively because they just can't face what is bothering them "on the inside."

Eating disorders, to some extent, resemble drug and alcohol addictions. Food just happens to be your medication, or way of coping. I'm not trying to make you feel bad, because I know exactly how you do feel. You see, I am a compulsive overeater myself. I have been since I was 14 years old and my brother died. I found by eating when I felt bad, I didn't have to think about the things that were really "eating me" so to speak. I'm not trying to make a joke about this, but sometimes a little humor works wonders when we are feeling "really down." I have never been bulimic (probably because I hate to throw up), but I found other ways to deal with my excessive eating after a major binge. I would simply exercise for 2-3 hours the next day. Believe me, that is just as "sick" as throwing up! I guess I felt like I had this image to live up to. **I thought I had to look good for others to like me. I found out**

August 1984
137 lbs.

later (after I worked so hard to look good) that was why people didn't like me. I was very confused. I felt like I had to be the perfect child, the perfect wife, the perfect mother, and the perfect friend. When you think about it, that is a lot to live up to. On the days when I couldn't accomplish that feat, I turned to my best friend who never judged me, food. It was a love/hate relationship. I'm telling you all of this, because I want you to know that I really do understand and I'm really glad you decided to write me this letter.

February 1985
112 lbs.
I still saw myself as heavy.

As far as a particular food setting you off on a binge, I understand your feelings. Before I got into low-fat eating, Frito Corn Chips did it for me. I couldn't eat just one, literally. I couldn't believe it (a couple of years ago) when I read some study about sniffing Frito Corn Chips to help you lose weight. Did you see that? Somehow, I don't think that would have worked out too well for me. Although compulsive overeating is a lifelong illness (much like alcoholism) I have gotten a lot better and don't really lose control very often, but when I do it is usually with Twizzlers Red Licorice. That is my "binge friend." There is probably a psychological reason behind that, too. You see, when I was a child it was also my favorite candy. I remember getting 100 pieces of red licorice in my stocking on Christmas and I associate that particular food with the good times of my childhood. So, doesn't it make sense, when I feel down or unable to cope with my feelings, to reach for something that reminds me of the happy times in my life? I have found the best plan for me, however, is not to prohibit myself from eating it or keeping it in the house. As a matter of fact, I ALWAYS carry a package in my purse and briefcase and keep it in the house as well. My kids love Twizzlers and so does my husband! Lucky for me it is very low-fat! Ha! Ha! I carry it with me to remind myself that I do not control my life. It is only when I try to do just that, that my problems begin. I have to remind myself every single day that God is the one in the driver's seat, and I'm just along for the ride. The licorice is just a little token I carry with me to remember to turn over the control (on a daily basis) to God. He always shows me the way as long as I follow His lead and don't try to be the one running the show. It is only then, that I do feel in control (so to speak) of my life. I'm not saying that I can't eat red licorice like a normal person and enjoy it. I can go to the movies and share a bag with Mike or the kids. I can even have 4-5 pieces and feel fine, but it is only when I feel good about things and happy that I can eat Twizzlers safely like a normal person. When I am down, upset, hurt, mad, etc., etc., is when licorice is my enemy. I can easily go through a (1-lb.) package in a matter of minutes without stopping (and I have many times)! Now, you're probably wondering if I am some kind of nut, right? Well, I think we are all a little nuts (if you know what I mean). Most people just don't like to admit it. I haven't always been so honest myself, but after reading thousands of letters that came my way as a result of writing *BUTTER BUSTERS,* I found there were a lot of other people who shared many of the problems and concerns I had experienced. They were all honest enough to share their secrets with me, and not fear rejection. So, I guess you could say I learned by "listening" to all of you that it was OK not to be perfect. Your letters enabled me to be honest and share my faults, knowing and trusting that you will understand. I thank each of you for writing and the gift you gave me with YOUR trust. As a result of my honesty, I can only hope that someone reading this book will realize that they are not alone, no matter what their problem may be, and there are many of us in the world that just need someone to talk to.....someone that will "REALLY LISTEN." Take the risk and trust someone. They might need you just as much as you need them!

I'd like to share with you a little information concerning the different eating disorders and their characteristics. Hopefully by reading some of the symptoms, you may be able to pinpoint the reason behind your feelings, and why you are using food to get through them. Most eating disorders start quite young. I told you mine started at the age of 14. How about you? Not everyone suffers from abuse or a traumatic experience, but it is quite common in people with eating disorders. Some disorders begin in young girls (it is more common in girls and women) with someone telling them they are heavy or need to lose a few pounds. Some young girls have obsessive mothers who count every calorie they put in their mouth, are thin as a rail, and still complain constantly that they "feel fat." This is a crime, in my opinion. I hope that I have never relayed this kind of message to Paige. I can't stress enough how important it is for the mothers of this country NOT to push your obsessive behavior on your children. Instead, set a positive example by eating a healthy diet and exercising a reasonable amount. And most important, please don't tell your child, "If you eat those cookies, you're going to get fat!" That is one of the the worst things you can do to a child. Try to equate low-fat eating with feeling good, having more energy, and a healthy heart, rather than being fat or getting skinny!

Anorexia is most common in young girls between the ages of 14 and 18 (but has been reported in children as young as eight or nine) when there are increased stresses associated with puberty and sexuality. So many young girls want to grow up, but when they start showing the physical signs of maturity, they get scared and want to go back to being children again. This is a very confusing time, and the beginning of eating disorders in MANY young girls. This is also a time when peer pressure is at it's height. It is SO IMPORTANT to "fit in" and be liked. When I think about it, not only did my brother die when I was 14, but it was also about the same time I moved to Texas from Kansas. Let me tell you that moving to a different state at the age of 14 IS NOT A PLEASANT EXPERIENCE! It is even more difficult when you look different, talk different, and dress different. Talk about not fitting in.....that's putting it lightly! I think I dealt with my lack of confidence and poor self-esteem by eating (to cover up my feelings and not "fitting in"). Let me tell you, it takes a long, long time for those feelings to go away. It has only been since I wrote *BUTTER BUSTERS* that I realized I really did have something to offer others. I found through your letters that I really could do something to help people and that my work, had in fact, affected other people's lives in a positive way. I found this out from each of you that took the time to write and tell me what the book had done for you, or how it had changed your life for the better. I realize that all of this has come as a result of me giving up the control (I held on to for so many years) by letting God guide and direct me. It was only then I experienced a freedom that I had never known.

July 1974

August 1976

Most young girls have a distorted body image as well. I can remember when I was 26 right after Blake was born. I had always been a "little" overweight. That is, until I had my son. For some reason, my metabolism changed for the better. Maybe it was lack of sleep, or never having time to eat (Blake was very active and didn't sleep much), or maybe a combination of things, but for the first time in my life I was really thin (AND I LOVED IT). Three weeks after Blake's birth I had lost the weight I had gained in my pregnancy, plus 15 more. I had only gained 14 with the pregancy (I was a little overweight when I got pregnant) so I didn't have a lot to lose, but when the next 15 pounds came off, I just couldn't believe it. However, in my eyes I was still fat. Even though my friends and family told me I was getting too skinny, I didn't believe them. I just thought they were jealous. When I look back at pictures from that time, I can see they were telling me the truth. So many people that have been overweight can NEVER see themselves as thin, no matter HOW THIN they do become. Many people who do lose weight have the overwhelming fear of gaining it back, and this, in itself, can lead to eating disorders. You said in your letter that you used to weigh over 200 pounds and didn't EVER want to be fat again! Could this apply to you?

Although I haven't suffered from bulimia, I do have a good friend that has lived with the disease for many years. It may be hard to believe, but some bulimics can consume as many as 20,000 calories in one eating binge. Bulimia is a disease of secrecy, while anorexia is more a disease of control. I also have a close friend who

November 1976

has battled anorexia for over twenty years. Anorexics usually have an outward self-confidence, but suffer from a terrible self-image on the inside. They put on a good show! Your typical people pleaser (so to speak)! While on the other hand, most bulimics live in shame, hating how they live, but too embarrassed to let anyone find out. They eat until they are physically ill, and then feel so guilty because they lost control that they punish themselves by vomiting, using laxatives, or, in my case excessive exercise. Excessive exercise really is (in my opinion) a form of bulimia.

Eating disorders can lead to all kinds of physical and medical consequences, as well. Anorexics and bulimics often faint or pass out, weakened from lack of food. Many suffer from gastrointestinal problems. Bulimics often destroy their throat muscles and gag reflex due to vomiting so often. A tell-tale sign is when their tooth enamel is eroded from continued vomiting. Many times a young girl's dentist is the first to suspect bulimic behavior. Many anorexics stop menstruating and some even become infertile temporarily, or in some cases indefinitely.

Most people with eating disorders tend to have a low self-esteem. They tend to be perfectionists and many times come from families where achievement is a big deal and are often criticized by their parents for not living up to the family tradition of being smart, pretty, artistic, athletic, etc., etc., ...and the list goes on and on. Why do parents love to relish in their child's accomplishments (as a reflection of them), but when the coin is turned (and the child messes up), the parents often act embarrassed and might even say, "I wonder where in the world he got that problem." I say give your children trust and understanding and let your children be.....anything they choose, NOT what will make YOU LOOK GOOD!!

Many feel there is a definite link between eating disorders and child or sexual abuse. It is believed that 50-60% of women with eating disorders have had some sexual trauma in their childhood. Others feel there might be some sort of chemical imbalance in the brain. It has been found that some people with eating disorders have lower levels of certain neurotransmitters such as serotonin (in bulimics) and norepinephrine (in anorexics) that influence mood. So please realize, there may be a chemical imbalance responsible for your behavior. Maybe you just can't help it. Did you ever consider that possibility? Stop blaming yourself. It might not be your fault, after all!

Unfortunately the American society puts as much pressure on us as we do ourselves. Whoever thought up the saying, "You can never be too rich or too thin" had a problem themselves (in my opinion). Of course, it doesn't help matters when our young teenagrs have girls who look like toothpicks (in the fashion magazines) as role models. (As if they don't have enough pressure on them already!) I'd like to know what happened to the healthy, athletic, and fit look that was "in" a few years ago? I just can't understand WHY anyone would WANT to look sick?

I wish I had the perfect answer for you, but, unfortunately, I don't. I would begin by checking into one of the many organizations for people with eating disorders. I know you said that you were embarrassed, but how do you think everyone else feels who does go for help? It's a cinch they aren't proud to be there. I'm not telling you that you will be cured by going to a meeting, but you might find out that you are not alone, nor the only person who has a problem with food. I attended

Overeaters Anonymous' meetings for over a year, and it was one of the best things I ever did. I cared enough about myself to try and change my behavior. I found out that I was not alone, and that was enough to keep me going back again and again. Why is it when we are hurt or feel miserable, that the first thing we all do is run away and retreat to be alone with our unhappiness?

I would recommend finding someone to share your feelings with on a regular basis. Think of it as "purging your thoughts of destruction" by telling someone else. Don't you always feel better when you get things off your chest? You said you had a man who loves you. Have you considered sharing your feelings with him? He may be more receptive than you think, especially if he really loves you. Trust and honesty can give us all a sense of freedom, if we only give it a chance. No one is perfect and everyone has something they might not be proud of or want to admit about themselves, but if you can be brave and take the first step and risk it, you might just open up the line of communication that is so important in a loving relationship between two people.

I "appeared" to have it all together in 1989 - NOT!

I hope my letter shows you that there are a lot of people in the world who may appear to have it all together (on the outside), but really need a friend just like you to share their feelings with, too! I hope you will stay in touch and know that I am here and would be happy to talk or help any other way I can. Please let me get to know you better. It sounds like we have a lot in common!

I'm including some phone numbers of various organizations that may be of interest to you. Good luck and God Bless!

1. National Association of Anorexia Nervosa and Associated Disorders (ANAD), P.O. Box 7, Highland Park, Illinois 60035
    (708)831-3438

2. American Anorexia/Bulimia Association (AABA), 418 East 76th Street, New York, NY 10021; (212)734-1114

3. Anorexia Nervosa and Related Eating Disorders, Inc. (ANRED), P.O. Box 5102, Eugene, OR 97405; (503)344-1144

4. National Anorexic Aid Society (NAAS), Harding Hospital, 445 East Granville Road, Worthington, OH 43085; (614)436-1112

5. Overeaters Anonymous, 6075 Zenith Court N.E., Rio Rancho, New Mexico 87124
    (505) 891-2664

"Peer pressure"

NEW PRODUCTS

HOW TO CHOOSE THEM AND USE THEM

YOU: I live in a small town near Shreveport, Louisiana. I love your book and especially the NEW PRODUCTS SECTION. The only low-fat baked tortilla chips we have are made by Guiltless Gourmet. Do you know of any other baked tortilla chips on the market?
—*C.C. Shreveport, LA*

ME: There are several new baked tortilla chips on the market. Four of my favorites are SMART TEMPTATIONS by Charlotte Charles in Niles, Illinois (708) 647-0787, BAKED TOSTITOS by Frito Lay in Dallas, Texas (800)352-4477, INDULGE SNACKS manufactured by El Paco (which also offers fat-free flour tortillas) in Dallas, Texas (800)225-6915, and AMAIZING TASTE of Gates Interprises in Dallas, Texas (800)858-2783. Other baked tortillas you might find in your area are EL GALINDO (512)478-5756, and a few new varieties of GUILTLESS GOURMET CHIPS such as "White Corn" and "Nacho" flavors (512)443-4373. Watch for new products every time you visit your local grocery store. I find at least one new product every time I go. Check the "Resource Guide" on pages 525-541 for a complete list of new low-fat products.

YOU: Since I have lost 45 pounds, people have asked how I did it. Actually, I tell them it wasn't a diet, but a new way of eating. Then comes the part about your *BUTTER BUSTERS COOKBOOK*. When I tell them about all the great low-fat and no-fat things to make and eat, they can hardly believe it until I give them a sample. The girls at the beauty shop last week sampled the Snickerdoodles. Immediately, they called the local bookstore. The store happened to have three copies left, which was exactly how many they needed. The girls went directly up and purchased them. My two good friends also purchased one. I feel like I'm a walking advertisement for your book. It's great! The item that I am looking for and can't find is the Pioneer No-Fat Biscuit Mix that you mentioned in the book. Well, I just wanted you to know that your book is very much appreciated in Elmore, Ohio. I intend to keep up the good work. —*P.D. Elmore, Ohio*

ME: You should be proud of yourself, but I really can't take all the credit. It took a tremendous dedication and desire on your part to make your weight-loss possible. I'm just glad that I could be a small part of it. I can understand why you want to find Pioneer No-Fat Biscuit Mix. You might be having trouble finding it because the label now reads "Pioneer Low-Fat Biscuit and Baking Mix." They had to change the label in May, 1994 when the nutritional information guidelines became mandatory by law. If a product contains 0.5 fat grams per serving, it can no longer be considered fat-free. The product is still VERY LOW FAT, so I still recommend it. It is a wonderful product. I use it to make waffles, pancakes, biscuits, cookies, muffins, and some quick breads. They also offer two NEW fat-free gravy mixes. They have a "Country White" and "Brown Gravy" that are both delicious. All you do is add water to the mix. If you can't find them in your area, call (210)227-1401. They are manufactured by Pioneer Flour Mills in San Antonio, Texas.

YOU: I heard Guiltless Gourmet makes dips, too. Is that true? I heard you on a talk radio show talking about some fat-free cheese dip. Please advise me if I heard you correctly.
—*S.D. Chicago, Illinois*

ME: You did hear me correctly!! Guiltless Gourmet has a whole variety of fat-free dips. They have both mild and spicy Black Bean Dips, Pinto Bean Dips (mild or spicy) and even Cheddar Queso (mild or spicy). Another company, Frito-Lay, has their own brand (Tostitos) of Fat-Free dips as well. Their Black Bean flavor is great. If you can't find these products in your area call:
Guiltless Gourmet: (512)443-4373   Frito-Lay: (800)352-4477.

YOU: Can you tell me if there are any new fat-free cheeses on the market that really do melt? I have your very first edition of *BUTTER BUSTERS* and don't care for the cheese you used in most of the recipes. I love all of the desserts, especially the "Cream Cheese Cake Bars." They are a regular treat in our home. The teenagers especially love them and they are easy enough for them to bake, too. I appreciate this fact because it saves me time!
—D. K. Orlando, Florida

ME: Did you say you have my very first edition? I self-published that edition in March 1992. There were only 5,000 copies of the first edition printed, so hold onto it. It might be a collectors item someday. Just kidding!! It's just that I went through a lot to publish my book. I actually tell that whole story in *BUTTER BUSTERS TOO! THE ULTIMATE COOKBOOK*. It's a great (sad but funny) story! In August 1990 when I first started writing the book, Alpine Lace Brand low and fat-free cheeses were the only ones available. At that time they offered mozzarella, Swiss, American, and Cheddar. It's true they didn't melt too well. They later introduced two products that did melt well and tasted great, too.

I highly recommended their fat-free Parmesan and Italian mozzarella cheeses when they hit the market. The only problem was their limited shelf-life. For this reason, they were temporarily removed in June 1993. I must say, I was very sorry to see them go. The people at Alpine Lace told me they had some problems with those two products because they lacked preservatives necessary for extended shelf-life. I am happy to say Alpine Lace has introduced a whole new line of fat-free cheeses that DO MELT AND TASTE GREAT! If you have been disappointed by their products in the past because they lacked meltability, it might be worth another try. I especially love their NEW FAT-FREE FRESH PARMESAN CHEESE (it comes in a plastic sealed cup now). They offer a large variety of fat-free and low-fat cheese as well as fat-free flavored cream cheese spreads. For information regarding all of the GREAT "NEW" ALPINE LACE PRODUCTS call: (201)378-8600.

There are several other good brands of fat-free cheese available as well. My favorite fat-free mozzarella cheese is POLLY-O FREE out of Mineola, New York. They also offer fat-free ricotta I use in my Italian dishes that tastes great. POLLY-O recently introduced a "Lite" mozzarella cheese that is 2.5 fat grams an ounce as well as "Lite" String Cheese (my kids love these). If you can't find the Polly-O Products in your area call: (800)845-3733. Another favorite manufacturer is LIFELINE FOOD COMPANY that makes LIFETIME CHEESE PRODUCTS. They offer several varieties of low and fat-free cheese. Their Mild-Mexican fat-free is delicious. Some of their other choices include Cheddar, Swiss, Monterrey Jack, Vegetable Garden, Mozzarella, and many more. If you can't find these products in your area call: (408)899-5040. The company is located in Sand City, California. There are some other fat-free and low-fat cheese products that melt and taste good, too. Borden and Kraft offer fat-free sliced cheese my kids love on sandwiches. SmartBeat, Frigo, Weight Watchers, Healthy Choice, and Healthy Favorites by Kraft offer low and fat-free cheeses, too. As a matter of fact Healthy Choice makes a fat-free "velveeta style" cheese that tastes and melts great in Rotel Dip. I did want you to be aware of the many great choices available now. The low and fat-free cheese products continue to get better every day! Refer to the "Resource Guide" on page 527 for a complete list of cheese manufacturers and ordering information.

YOU: Thank you for the BEST down-to-earth cookbook I have ever used! Discovering a book devoted to fat-free cooking is such a relief. There are a million low-fat cookbooks out there. I know because I own half of them. The only problem is they just say LOW-FAT on the cover. The difference with yours is THAT IT REALLY IS LOW-FAT!! Preparing healthy meals for my friends and family is really important to me. I do have one question you might be able to help me with. I like REAL CREAM in my coffee. I've tried evaporated skim milk, but it just didn't taste rich enough for me. I use the evaporated skim milk in my sauces like you suggest and they taste great, but my coffee needs help. Any suggestions!
—J.H. Baton Rouge, LA

ME: I'm glad you are enjoying the book. Thanks! I have found a product you might enjoy. The product is a liquid non-dairy flavored fat-free creamer. It is called COFFEE-MATE and made by Carnation. Be sure and watch for the blue fat-free label. Carnation also makes a regular creamer that is not fat-free. They offer a variety of flavors such as Irish Cream, Hazelnut, and even Kahula.

MOCHA MIX brand also offers a fat-free non-diary creamer. Again, please read the label because MOCHA also sells "Lite" and "Original" that both contain fat. Another idea I have tried that tastes great to me is to use fat-free ice cream or fat-free frozen yogurt in place of cream. While on my book tour in Dayton, Ohio a young girl at my booksigning shared her family's secret with me. The problem was they couldn't stand skim milk on their cereal. She told me they use fat-free Carnation Creamer on their cereal for the rich taste they love. I didn't even realize she was really listening to my speech. I had noticed her on the front row sitting next to her mother while I was talking. After I was finished

Books & Company Book Store
Dayton, Ohio January 1994

speaking, I asked for questions from the audience. A gentleman had the same problem with skim milk on his cereal. The young girl (about 10 or 11) raised her hand and offered her great suggestion. I continue to be amazed by our children and how much we can learn from them, if we just take the time TO LISTEN!! It was at a BOOKS & COMPANY Bookstore. I only wish I could remember her name, but everyone at the signing (who might be reading this) knows who I am talking about!

YOU: Hi Pam. I just bought your book after seeing you on T.V. with Tom Bergeron in Boston, Mass. I haven't been able to put it down! I've tried several recipes and they are delicious! I just have one problem ... I'm having trouble finding Smart Temptations' low-fat tortilla chips. I also love cheese, but can't find fat-free Parmesan. HELP! Are there any fat-free potato chips out yet?
—D.S. Worcester, MA.

ME: I'm glad you saw the show. Tom was a character and a lot of fun. Did you also see him spraying PAM Cooking Spray all over the set? His show was one of my first (and favorites) while on tour.

Pam and Tom Bergeron "Eyewitness News at Noon"
W.B.Z. - TV   Boston   January 1994

Smart Temptations are in most parts of the U.S. now, but in case you haven't found them yet their number is: (800)242-7568. Alpine Lace has introduced a brand new fat-free Parmesan cheese that melts well and taste great! It is one of their BEST products. If you can't find the Alpine Lace fat-free Parmesan call: (201)378- 8600. Weight Watchers' makes a fat-free Parmesan as does Kraft and Frigo brands. Weight Watchers' products can be found most everywhere. For information regarding Weight Watchers' products call: (800)333- 3000. The Frigo products come from Greenbay, Wisconsin and are manufactured by Steller Foods. They offer fat-free ricotta cheese, too. If you are interested in more information concerning their products call: (800)558-7315. I'm glad you asked about fat-free potato chips. We now have several to choose from along with some great low-fat chips as well. LOUISE'S brand out of Louisville, KY offer several flavors of fat-free and low-fat potato chips. They also offer low-fat tortilla chips. Their number is: (800)284-8280. CHILDERS fat-free potato chips manufactured by Childers Food Products in Charlotte, N.C. can be located by calling: (704) 377-0800. POP CHIPS from POP SECRET manufactured by Betty Crocker are a new low-fat chip that is baked instead of fried. It runs 130 calories and 3.5 fat grams for a 1 1/2 cup serving. They may not be fat-free, but are certainly a better choice than regular potato chips. My kids love them (especially the Butter flavor). They offer a variety of flavors. Pacific Grain Products offers NO FRIES, a low-fat potato snack shaped like french fries. They are manufactured in Woodland, California. A 1-oz. serving is 120 calories and 1-2 fat grams depending on the flavor. Information can be obtained by calling: (800)333-0110.

YOU: The world was ready for a sensible low-fat cookbook and am I ever glad my Mom gave me yours! What intrigued me the most was your "How I Got Started" section because your background is much like my own. Now for my question. I was in the grocery store last week and came across the new Louis Rich FAT-FREE OVEN ROASTED TURKEY BREAST! My question is how do they do that? How can turkey be fat-free? I thought the new labels were supposed to clear those deceptions and misleading information up for us consumers!
—J.H. Waco, Texas

ME: I know what you mean. I saw the turkey breast, too, and checked it out. You must realize a food can be considered fat-free if it contains 0.49 fat grams, or less, per serving. The Louis Rich Turkey breast lists one slice as one serving. This means one slice PROBABLY contains 0.49 fat grams. Do you use one slice on your sandwich? I didn't think so. Four or five slices is a little more realistic. If you take 0.49 X 5 your turkey would contain 2.45 fat grams provided you didn't add anything else to the sandwich that contained fat. My point is when a product states it is fat-free on the label, please assume that it probably isn't (in most cases). A good example of this is Dream Whip Topping. It states that is fat-free on the label. One serving is 0.49 fat grams (I know because I checked it out myself). One serving amounts to one tablespoon. One package of Dream Whip prepared with skim milk equals 11 fat grams. Be careful! You STILL can't always trust what you read. The new labels are BETTER, but far from perfect!

YOU: I just finished listening to you on Larry North's "Weekend Workout" radio show on KLIF in Dallas. I immediately purchased your book. You offer so many ideas, and the best part is that your book is the most realistic low-fat cookbook I've read. It contains recipes that my family have always eaten, just made healthy. I do have a question you might be able to help me with. I love to cook, but don't always have the time (I work two jobs and have three children). My kids love pizza, but I know the store-bought kind is loaded with fat. When I make it myself there is no problem. I've seen the "diet brands" but my kids didn't care for the one I bought. Do you know of any Fat-Free PIZZA? Please help if you can.
—*H.J. Duncanville, Texas*

Larry North and Pam
KLIF Talk Radio   Dallas   May 1993

ME: Larry has a great show and I always enjoy being his guest. As a matter of fact, I do know of a Fat-Free Pizza. It is called FIT'N FREE. Each microwaveable pizza is 9-inches in diameter and serves two. They come in packages of six. Each serving contains 253 calories and 0 fat. For more information if you can't find them in your area call: (800)779-5588. The manufacturer is PIZZA FREE INC. in Akron, Ohio. They are also available by mail order.

YOU: I don't know if you will receive this note. However, in my heart I feel the need to write. Thank you for the best cookbook on the market. It was a lucky day when I found your super book! As a matter of fact I later purchased a copy for my new daughter-in-law. My question is this. Have you ever heard of a new product called Wonderslim? I heard some ladies talking about it in the Health Food Store where I buy my vitamins. I thought I heard one of them say she had baked with it instead of oil. Can you help? Again, thanks for helping me enjoy eating again and for all your personal tips. I hope you are writing another book. Let me know, because I will be first in line to buy it. Keep me on your mailing list, PLEASE!!
—G.P. Bentonville, Arkansas

ME: I receive all letters addressed to me personally. I try to answer them all, too! I had not heard of Wonderslim myself until I received your note, so thank you for writing. Because of you and your question, I found a new product that was worth looking for. It is, as you thought, a substitute for oil. As a matter of fact it is an egg and fat substitute used in baking. It comes in a jar and consists of plums, water, citric acid, and lecithin. You can use it to replace butter, margarine, or oil in your baked goods. If a recipe calls for 1/2 cup of oil, you would use 1/4 cup Wonderslim in it's place. I made Snickerdoodle cookies with it and they turned out great! It is manufactured by Natural Food Technologies, Inc. It can only be found in Health Food Stores as far as I know. If you are interested in finding out about this amazing product call: (800)497-6595. There is another similar product called Just Like Shortenin'. It is derived from plums as well, and used the same way. This product is manufactured by The PlumLife Company. Just Like Shortenin' can be found in some grocery stores. If you can't find it in your area call: (203)245-7893. I'm glad you were "LISTENING" to those ladies in the store that day. Because of you, we both learned something. Thanks!

Note: I recently found another great low-fat substitute that can be used in place of butter, margarine, or oil in baking and cooking. Refer to page 282 in this chapter for more information.

YOU: I'm very excited about your book. My husband and I love all kinds of food. You name it, we love to eat it, which is why we both used to be overweight. This is one reason we're enjoying your book so much. We are both losing weight so fast and haven't given up our large portions. With your help, we learned how to de-fat our own family favorites too! Your recipes are "real food," and that is what made it so easy to change over to the low-fat life. Our favorite recipe is your "Country Chicken with Creamy Gravy." When I first saw it in your book my first thought was: There is no way she can make THAT DISH low-fat and please MY husband. Well, I'm writing to tell you that he LOVED IT and we have it every Sunday for supper. The only thing missing from your great book is meat. You have a couple of recipes and they are good, but we sure miss our roasts and other red meat. I guess you just have to give up some things, don't you? If you ever hear of a place that sells meat that isn't so fattening, will you please let me know? I'm dreaming, but wouldn't it be nice if there was? Thanks again for your "Down Home" cookbook!
—M.T. Topeka, Kansas

ME: I've thought of you and your request for low-fat beef. I, like you, thought it would never happen, but I was wrong. SURPRISE!! I have found the answer and I think you are really going to be excited. There is a company in Yankton, South Dakota called VERMILLION VALLEY (formally Covington Ranch) that raises and sells (drum roll please!) LOW-FAT BEEF!!! The good news IT TASTES GREAT, TOO! I promise you, no one will be able to tell the difference. We're not talking reduced fat beef here. No ma'am! Would you believe 3 fat grams for a 6 ounce tenderloin? I know, I couldn't believe it either. That is why I called them up and ordered some to be sent to my home. It can only be purchased through mail order at this time. Along with those tenderloins I mentioned, they offer Beef Chuck Roast, Beef Round Roast, Beef Brisket, Beef Eye of Round, very low- fat and lean ground beef, Ribeye steaks, Top Sirloin, Round steak, Eye of Round, Filet of Sirloin, Sirloin tip Steak, Beef Kabobs, Stir Fry or Fajita Beef, etc. Do you get the drift? These folks have it all and it is absolutely WONDERFUL! I sent a case to my Mom and my husband's Mom for Mother's Day. They both love steak, and had almost given it up for health reasons. Boy, were they excited! You are probably wondering, as I did, how in the world can they raise low-fat beef. The beef, developed through selective breeding and feeding programs, is produced WITHOUT fillers or preservatives. The American Heart Association also gave the company it's "seal of approval" as a healthy meat. This means the company can put the association's "Heart Smart" sticker on it's products and they have been graded and tested by the USDA, too! The beef is 50% lower in fat than a skinless chicken breast, and has less cholesterol than flounder. I know it "sounds too good to be true," but it is!! It really is wonderful news for those who love and have missed eating red meat! Oh yeah, I forgot to tell you where to get it didn't I? I'll never tell! Just kidding! For more information about ordering call: (800)365-BEEF. I'm so glad we "Found the Beef!!" The Beef section in my first cookbook was called "Where's the Beef?" I think I'll call the chapter "I Found the Beef!" in *BUTTER BUSTERS TOO!* What do you think? For this reason, *BUTTER BUSTERS TOO!* and *KIDS IN THE KITCHEN* will both contain an extensive beef section! Refer to the "Resource Guide" on page 539 for other options regarding low fat beef.

YOU: I am writing to thank you for your new edition of *BUTTER BUSTERS* that includes the choice of sugar substitutions. My husband was recently diagnosed with diabetes. Needless to say, I am in the process of changing the way I cook. I've noticed you only recommend Sweet'N Low. Can I use Nutrasweet? We like the taste better. The reason I'm asking is because I tried it in a cake and it didn't taste sweet enough. I used the same amount of Nutrasweet in place of the Sweet'N Low. Do you use different amounts, and if so can you send me substitution information?
—*J.S. Charlestown, Mass.*

ME: There is a reason I use Sweet'N Low in the book. You cannot use Nutrasweet for baking. Nutrasweet contains aspartame. When aspartame is heated to 85 degrees the sweetness breaks down. Until recently Sweet'N Low was the only suitable substitution. I have found another saccharin based product called NECTA SWEET. It comes in tablet form and is available in three different sweetness strengths. The tablets dissolve easily and taste great in baked products. The product can be found in most grocery stores all over the country. If you have trouble locating it call: (800)952-5130. The only brown sugar substitution available is Sweet'N Low Brown. Sweet' N Low products can be found in most stores in the country. For information regarding the Sweet'N Low products call: (800)231-1123. I hope this helps. I tried the NECTA SWEET sugar substitute tablets in the "Best Pound Cake" from *BUTTER BUSTERS* (page 357) yesterday and the whole family loved it!

YOU: I can't tell you how pleased I am with your wonderful cookbook. I have been following your book since September and I've lost thirty pounds so far. I've been a yo-yo dieter all my life. I love all the cakes and desserts you have in your book. I firmly believe when you can still have desserts and not deprive yourself, you can stick with this kind of eating forever. I have a couple of questions. I love turkey and because it is low fat we eat it a lot. Are there any new turkey products on the market? I read about the Vermillion Valley Low-Fat Beef that you recommended in the column you write for *Fitness Magazine.* I didn't even know you wrote a column for the magazine, but just happened to come across it one day when I was looking at the magazine at my health club. I loved all the new product suggestions with ordering information and telephone numbers. I wish the column listed new products every month. Any chance of that? Since I live in a small town, we don't have a lot of the products you recommended, but since you gave the telephone numbers I ordered several of the new products. I also ordered the Lifetime Cheese from California. The Mexican flavor was delicious (just like you said it was). Your recommendations are wonderful. I wish you lived in my town so I could pick your brain all the time. You must go to the grocery store every day to find all that stuff. Thank you for taking the time to read my letter. I know you must be very busy, but if you have time, I would love to hear from you.
—A.D. Athens, Georgia

ME: I'm so glad you are enjoying the book and the *FITNESS MAGAZINE* columns, too. I actually wrote three columns for *FITNESS MAGAZINE.* I enjoyed doing it, but it took a lot more time than I thought it would. When you work for a magazine, you are basically working for someone else, and must write to their specifications. That is kind of hard for someone like me, who is used to writing what I want to write about and how I want to write it as well. It was a learning experience and the folks at the magazine were very nice, but I felt the many hours I spent working on those columns could be better spent working on this book. I, too, feel that new product information is one of the most valuable pieces of information I can offer my readers. For that reason, I decided to start a Newsletter so I will be able to keep my readers informed of all the new tips, tricks, and products hitting the market every day. Check the back of this book for *THE BUTTER BUSTERS NEWSLETTER* ordering information. There is a new turkey product I found here in Texas. I don't know if you have **The Turkey Store** brand in Georgia. The product is a real time saver called "Seasoned Cuts." They are fresh boneless steaks, chops, and filets and they come in three flavors (Italian, Hickory, and Teriyaki). They are 99% fat-free. You can heat them up in the microwave for a quick meal in about ten minutes.They also offer extra lean ground turkey breast at 6 fat grams a pound. **ButterBall** brand also offers a variety of marinated, skinless and boneless chicken breasts that are only one fat gram each, as well as other low-fat chicken and turkey products. See the "Resource Guide" page 539 for ordering information on both products. Speaking of new products, I came across another meat substitute called "MEAT *of* WHEAT." It is actually a meat substitute made from (you guessed it) wheat. Would you believe a ball of dough can be kneaded, stretched, rinsed, and cooked in seasoned broth to produce a truly convincing meat substitute? This is actually a process the Chinese and Japanese have been doing for centuries. It sounds pretty good to be able to enjoy the taste of meat, poultry, and sausage, without the fat, cholesterol, and excess calories, doesn't it? "MEAT *of* WHEAT" can be found in some grocery and most health food stores. It is manufactured by White Wave, Inc. If you can't find the all-natural, preservative-free meat substitutes in your local store, call: (800) 488-9283. The following chart shows the difference between "MEAT *of* WHEAT" and traditional meat and poultry products:

Item	Calories	Cholesterol	Fat
MEAT *of* WHEAT Burger/3.5 oz.	237	0 mg.	1 gm.
Hamburger/3.5 oz.	319	99 mg.	23 gm.
MEAT *of* WHEAT Chicken/100 gm.	214	0 mg.	0.4 gm.
Chicken White Meat/100 gm.	175	86 mg.	4.5 gm
MEAT *of* WHEAT Sausage/100 gm.	185	0 mg.	1.1 gm.
Pork Sausage/100 gm.	343	78.6 mg.	29.3 gm.

I ordered all the products and have really enjoyed them. My family thinks they taste great, too. I use this product in "MEAT *of* WHEAT CHILI BURGERS" on page 413 in this book. I hope you will continue to enjoy the book. Please let ME know if you find any great new products in Georgia. Good luck! Check the "Resource Guide" pages 525-541 for other great new products.

YOU: I want you to know that your book has saved my husband's life. He was overweight, smoked, didn't exercise, and was headed for a heart attack. Since I bought your book and started cooking out of it over the past nine months, he has lost 47 pounds, quit smoking, and goes to the gym four to five days a week. He thinks he is Jack La Lane. I just want to thank you for all your hard work and research. It must have taken you years to accumulate all that information and test those recipes. I love to cook, but didn't have time to learn how to cook low-fat. I didn't have a clue what products were good and what products were bad. That is, until I bought your book. I love letting "Pam Mycoskie do the walking" for me. You have saved me time, money, and frustration! I have a question about Pam Cooking Spray. I know you say it is so many fat grams per spray. How do you know exactly how long to spray? Is that the only brand you use? I love your "Mandarin Orange Sweet Potato Casserole." I made it for Christmas dinner and everyone loved it (even the kids). It tasted like dessert. Thanks for giving me more years to enjoy my husband. The way he was headed (before I found your book) is something I don't even like to think about. Thanks to you, I don't have to! Keep up the great job!   —*G.B. Baton Rouge, Louisiana*

ME: I want to thank you for taking the time to share your good news. I am so glad the book has helped your husband. That is the reason I stay so motivated. Letters like yours serve as a constant inspiration to me and my work. It shows me that I am making a difference in people's lives (for the better). Concerning Pam Cooking Spray, it is 1 fat gram per two seconds. I have found a new great product that just came out on the market. It's called, "I Can't Believe It's Not Butter!" It is a pump spray that can be used to spray on any food you might use butter or margarine on such as toast, corn on the cob, a baked potato, etc. You can also use it to coat your non-stick skillet when frying. Four (1-second) squirts equal 1 fat gram, so you can see that it is VERY low-fat (depending how much you use). It has a delicious "butter" taste. My son Tyler loves it! You can find it in the refrigerated section of the grocery store with the margarine products. It is made by Vadenburg Foods. If you can't find it in your area call: (800) 735-3610. I hope you will continue to enjoy the book. Good Luck and continued success to you and your "healthy" husband!

YOU: I met you while visiting in Houston at a Target store when you were on your book tour. I've used the book since that day, and pushed all the others back on the top shelf. I don't need any other cookbook, now that I have *BUTTER BUSTERS*. I love all of the great recipes in your book, and most of all I love your "Shopping Guide." I always take my cookbook with me to the grocery store so I can add new products when I find them in the various stores. Thanks for that suggestion. It was a great one. I have a couple of questions regarding some products you recommend in the shopping guide. The first one is the Pioneer No-Fat Biscuit and Baking mix. I can't find the No-Fat anymore in the grocery stores. Did they take it off the market? I hope not because I love that stuff. The other question concerns the Pop Weavers Gourmet Light Microwave Popcorn they sell at Target stores. I've bought that popcorn since I met you in Houston at a Target signing and you were passing out samples. At 1 fat gram per serving, it was a great low-fat snack! I've noticed they changed their package and the nutritional information changed, too. What happened? In fact, I've noticed the fat and calories changed on a few other products when they changed over to the new labels in May 1994. Can we trust the labels now? My husband and I have both lost close to thirty pounds each and we attribute every pound to what we learned in your book. Thanks for making us healthy, not wealthy, but wise! Ha Ha! That was a joke, get it? I guess in a sense you did make us more wealthy, too, because we both quit smoking (thanks to your suggestions) and I guarantee that has saved us a lot of money (not to mention medical bills as well). We were both heavy smokers. We smoked 1 ½ -2 packs a day (a piece). Do you know that I can't stand it now when people smoke around me. It's not that I want one or anything, I just can't stand the way it smells anymore. I was really worried when I quit smoking. I thought that I would gain a lot of weight. I have quit before over the years, but always gained weight before. This time I'm losing weight. Now, that is a switch! I guess it's because I can still snack and eat more often. As long as my snacks are low-fat, I seem to be able to get away with it. I guess you could say that my low-fat lifestyle even helped me to quit smoking. It's hard to believe I smoked for over twenty years and I never noticed the smell back then! Any new information would be great! I hope another book is in the works! I want some more great recipes!
—*U.M. Santa Fe, New Mexico*

ME: I'm so glad you both stopped smoking. Smoking contributes to so many different diseases. I smoked myself when I was in college and the first couple years of my marriage. Once I had kids though, I never really wanted to smoke again. I've noticed most people my age (45) have quit. I still see a lot of older people smoking and some young people, but not near as many as you used to see. As a matter of fact, in Arlington (where I live), smoking is not allowed in many of the restaurants. You are right about the Pioneer No-Fat Biscuit Mix. The label now reads Low-Fat. The new labeling is responsible for the change. If a product contains 0.5 fat grams (half a gram rounded) or more, it must say low-fat (not fat-free) on the label. However, when you look at the nutritional information on the back, they are allowed to round the information. If the product contains 0.49 fat grams per serving, the fat listed per serving will read 0. The Pioneer folks have also come out with new fat-free gravy mixes. All you do is add hot water and you have a delicious cream or brown gravy. Both are delicious and real time savers. Check the "Resource Guide" for ordering information.

The Pop Weavers Light Microwave Popcorn has changed their packaging. The new labeling laws affected their label, too, because of the serving size guidelines. One serving is 6 cups now instead of 3 cups (as it was before) and the fat grams per serving is 3.0. The serving size is twice as large and the fat gram count is a little higher, but still a great tasting low-fat snack. The label you were looking at on the new package was for unpopped corn. If you will notice on the other end of the box, there is another blue nutritional label. I didn't see it the first time, either. Many of the products were forced to change their nutritional information due to the regulation guidelines concerning serving sizes. Even though most have gone up, I would still rather have the realistic serving sizes. I'm sure most people ate more than one serving and never could understand why they weren't losing weight. It makes it easier to track fat grams and calories when you really do eat one serving instead of two or three and count it as one. I know, because I did it, too! My next book, *KIDS IN THE KITCHEN*, will be out in early 1996. *BUTTER BUSTERS TOO! THE ULTIMATE COOKBOOK* will follow. I hope you will continue to enjoy the recipes.

YOU: Since I bought your book, I'm eating three meals a day (I used to skip breakfast), and losing weight like crazy. I think you know what you are talking about when you say eating more food makes you lose weight, if you eat low-fat! Thanks so much for teaching me so much about healthy eating and exercise. I've lost 6 pounds in the last two weeks, and I'm eating more food than ever. This is a great way to live!! I have one question. We love caramel corn and have loved your "Pam's Sweet Trash" recipe. Since it does take a little time to fix, I tried to order the caramel corn you mentioned in your shopping guide under "New Products." I sent my request, but never heard from the company. Are they still in business? Please let me know if you have any information on the Flavor House Caramel Crunch product. Eating low-fat and loving it!!
—*P.L. Springfield, Illinois*

ME: It is always great to hear from people like you. It's hard to convince folks they REALLY CAN eat more food, if they eat low-fat. I know from first hand experience. It took me twenty-five years to give up the control of "not eating to stay slim" to find out.

I have had several letters regarding that product in the past few weeks, so I called and checked it out myself. Here is the deal. The Flavor House Caramel Crunch is now packaged under a new label. It is "Nature's Classic." The good news is they sell it in every K-Mart store in the country. If you still have trouble finding the product you can call: (205)883-5643. It contains 0.5 fat grams per 2/3 cup. It isn't fat-free, but quite low-fat for a generous serving. My kids love it! I have recently found four other caramel corn products on the market that are great and much easier to find as well. The first one is my favorite, but when I contacted the company they did not want to be mentioned in my book. I can't understand WHY ANY COMPANY would not want free advertising (I don't get paid by these companies, but only try to inform the consumers of all the great products available) and to be listed in a positive way, but who knows? I'll give you a hint. It comes in a white box and the name will be familiar when you see it! Good luck! My other favorite is Houston Foods Co. Caramel Corn. It is delicious and 1 fat gram per cup. A company called Pacific Snax makes a Caramel Flavored rice snack that tastes just like caramel corn and I love it. If you can't find the Pacific Snax products in your area call: (800)494-4100. I have another favorite that is just as good and fat-free. It is Louise's Fat-Free Caramel Corn (my husband's favorite). It is 100 calories per serving. If you can't find this product in your area call: (502)495-0494. We take it with us to the movie theater. I would like to share a little interesting information concerning movie theater popcorn. My kids used to get popcorn, but with all the new information about movie popcorn, even they don't want to eat it anymore!! One medium bag of unbuttered popcorn prepared with coconut oil contains an average of 900 calories and 60 grams of fat! Add butter to that medium-sized bag of popcorn and you bring the calories up to 1,225 calories and over 100 grams of fat! That is just a medium-sized bag! How many of us eat a large bag every time WE visit the movie theater? Did you realize that one medium-sized bag of buttered popcorn equals as much fat as a bacon and eggs breakfast, PLUS a Big Mac and fries for lunch, PLUS a steak dinner with all the trimmings for dinner? Think about this. How many of us actually go out to dinner after the movie? Refer to the "Resource Guide" on pages 536-537 for additional carmel corn products.

You probably consumed more fat in that medium-sized bag of popcorn (especially if you put butter on it) than you should consume in two days!! Now where did you say we were going out to dinner after the show? As a result of all the press, some movie theaters plan to start passing out brochures with the nutritional information of all the snack items they sell on the premises. You can always bring along your own snacks like I do (if you have a big purse!). If you must have the movie popcorn, you might consider a small bag, leave off the butter, and share it with a friend. I'd rather have A LOT of something that is low-fat and tasty (such as low-fat caramel corn) than 1 cup of high-fat movie popcorn, and feel guilty about it the rest of the evening. How about you?

YOU: Your book has changed our lives!! I've never written a letter to anyone like this before, but felt I must let you know what an impact you have had on seven people who live in Salt Lake City, Utah. My husband and I have had a weight problem during our 27 years of marriage. We have seven children who inherited our terrible eating and exercise (lack of) habits. We ate a lot of junk food and our physical activity consisted of shopping at the mall for larger clothes. My sister-in-law sent me your book for Christmas last year. Things haven't been the same around here since. Not

only have we all lost weight, but we joined a health club and bought a family membership. The whole family started exercising and the good news is WE LOVE IT! We play racquet ball, tennis, swim, and even take aerobics' classes together. I love everything about your book, especially the "Shopping Guide." I really don't think I would have ever "even tried" to eat low-fat if it hadn't been for you, telling me what to buy and how to use the products for cooking. Your exercise tips helped us all change our lifestyle, and I thank you for that too! You are a saint, and I honestly feel it was fate when I got your book for Christmas. I guess God knew we couldn't go on much longer the way we were, or we just weren't going to last long. I guess he wanted us around a little longer (maybe to help spread the word). That is JUST WHAT I DO, SPREAD THE WORD! It was obvious when our whole family started losing weight, our friends started noticing, and wanted to know what we were doing. Well, I told them. I think half of Salt Lake City must own your book now. I have a big mouth! I could go on and on, but I need to get to the health club for the 10:00 aerobics class. Oh, I almost forgot, I do have a quick question. I'm not wild about the fat-free potato chips and neither are my kids. Do you know of any new products that resemble potato chips? I really do miss those.
—P.T. Salt Lake City, Utah

ME: What can I say? You made my day! Wow, what a great letter and believe me, nothing makes me happier than hearing from folks like you. I wish you and your family continued success. I always say, **"a family that plays together, stays together."** As far as the potato chip question. I know what you mean about some of the fat-free

Beaver Creek, Colorado
December 1993

Calloway Gardens, Georgia
July 1989

potato chips. There is a product made by Betty Crocker called "Pop Chips." They aren't fat-free, but low-fat. They come in three flavors: Original, Butter flavor (these taste like buttered popcorn), and Sour Cream and Onion. They are baked and not fried. If you can't find them in your area call: (800)328-6787. As I said they aren't fat-free, but MUCH LOWER IN FAT than "regular" potato chips. However, my family really likes Louise's Fat Free Potato Chips.

Cayman Islands
March 1994

YOU: We love homemade bread, but honestly don't have time to make it. Do you know of any low or fat-free bread mixes that are quick and easy? We love your book. I do try to cook in bulk one day a week (and freeze casseroles), for my busy days like you suggested. I love hot homemade bread with dinner, and don't have time to bake it every day. Any suggestions?
—*L.K. Memphis, Tennessee*

ME: I have the answer for you. I found these wonderful bread mixes about a year ago at the Albertsons' stores in Texas. I don't know if you have that grocery store in Tennessee, but you might be able to ask your grocer to order the product. It is called "Quick Loaf" by Daily Bread Company. It is fat-free and so easy! All you do is add one beer (regular, non-alcoholic, or lite) or 12 ounces of club soda to the mix. Stir, pour into a loaf pan, let it set 15 minutes, and bake at 350 F. for 40 minutes. It comes in Garlic & Herb (my personal favorite- it tastes like Focaccia bread), Cinnamon-Raisin, Hearty Cracked Wheat, Honey Oatmeal, Nine Grain, and Onion-Dill. If you can't find these bread mixes in your area call: (800)635-5668, or write to them at the following address:
Daily Bread Co., Inc., P.O. Box 1091, Portsmouth, N.H. 03802-1091.

YOU: I own one of your very first editions of *BUTTER BUSTERS*. I just purchased the updated 7th edition, and wondered why you changed the binding? I liked the other style much better. I do appreciate all the updated shopping information and the new recipes you added are wonderful (especially the Tortilla Soup and Chocolate Caramel Bars). I think it's really nice that you continue to add new information as you reprint. Most people would just publish a book and not care about keeping the information current. I know it takes time on your part, but wanted you to know your efforts have not gone un-noticed. Since you added the Promise Ultra fat-free margarine as a choice when baking, I decided to give it a try. I used it instead of the liquid Butter Buds in your pound cake recipe (like you suggested) and really liked the texture better, too. Is that the only fat-free margarine on the market? My husband and I started low-fat eating in April 1992 when we bought your first book. We are now healthy, happy, and slim thanks to you! Do you have plans for more cookbooks? Your recipes in *BUTTER BUSTERS* are so much better than other low-fat cookbooks. Thank you for making low-fat eating taste so good!   —*G.N. Fort Walton Beach, Florida*

ME: I understand your feelings concerning the binding on the 7th edition. When I signed with Warner Books, they said the spiral binding (like I had used) was just too expensive to produce. They wanted to keep the price down on the book, so I went along with their wishes. Many of my readers felt the same way you do. I finally convinced Warner to change back to my original binding. Look for the return of the spiral binding on *BUTTER BUSTERS* in the near future.

I love the Promise Ultra Fat-Free margarine for baking, too. Even though the package instructions do not recommend their product for baking, I decided to give it a try anyway. I had used SmartBeat (a very low-fat margarine) for baking with satisfactory results. The reason fat-free margarines are not recommended is because of the high water content in the products. There is another fat-free margarine on the market. It is Fleischmann's Fat-Free Spread. It comes in a squeeze bottle. I've used it for baking cakes, breads, and muffins with wonderful results. I even used it in Oatmeal Cookies and the texture was great. It has a very buttery flavor. As a matter of fact, when I first tasted it on bread, I didn't really care for the flavor. I wasn't sure why at first, but soon realized it was because of the rich buttery taste. I guess I had gotten so used to margarine that didn't taste like butter, that I had lost my taste for that flavor. The true test came with my son Tyler. Even after the rest of the family switched to low or fat-free margarine, Tyler continued to use his Fleischmann's squirt margarine (at ten fat grams a Tbs.). It was the only margarine he liked. Since he didn't use margarine on that many foods, I continued to buy it for him. I was so excited when the new Fleischmann's Fat-Free came out, because I thought maybe I could convince Tyler to give it a try. The main reason he liked that particular brand was because it came in the squeeze bottle. I was a little nervous when I gave Tyler a taste test because, after all, the regular Fleischmann's squeeze margarine was 10 fat grams a Tbs. I was sure he would hate the fat-free variety. SURPRISE!!! He loved it! That was the true test. Tyler loved it because it has a very distinct butter taste (just like his favorite high-fat version). That was a happy day in the Mycoskie household when Tyler switched to fat-free margarine. I personally prefer Promise Ultra Fat-Free margarine on my bread, but I really like the buttery taste of the Fleischmann's fat-free margarine for baking. My husband prefers the SmartBeat Trans Fat-Free margarine on his bread, so I guess it is all a matter of individual taste. It's really great that we have so many low and fat-free margarines to choose from. If you can't find the new Fleischmann's Fat-Free Spread in your area call: **1-800-NABISCO.** I'm so glad you have enjoyed the recipes!

Butter Busters Publishing, Inc.   ## Warner Books, Inc.

March 1992	**May 1992**	**July 1992**
August 1992	**December 1992**	**February 1993**

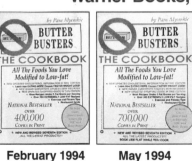

February 1994	**May 1994**	**August 1994**

July 1995

ATTENTION READERS:

There is a WONDERFUL new butter flavored fat substitute on the market called MRS. BATEMAN'S BAKING BUTTER. The product actually contains a very small amount of butter which explains it's rich buttery taste. The BAKING BUTTER DOES NOT CONTAIN trans fatty acids or hydrogenated oils. The key ingredient is maltodextrin, a naturally occurring carbohydrate found in rice, corn, and potatoes. The BAKING BUTTER can be used as a fat replacement for baking and cooking. Mrs. Bateman DOES NOT RECOMMEND using the product as a spread or in frying because there is very little fat in the formula. The Baking Butter contains a mere 13 fat grams per cup (and 35 mg. of cholesterol) compared to 184 fat grams in one cup of regular butter (not to mention 496 mg. of cholesterol). The product will keep on the shelf without refrigeration until it is opened. It will keep in the refrigerator for up to six months and can even be frozen. The product is available in one, three, and five pound tubs. MRS. BATEMAN'S BAKING BUTTER can be found in several Sam's Club and Price/Cosco stores across the country. It is sold in some Albertson's stores (in various locations) and the King Sooper's grocery stores in Colorado. The product has been adjusted so you can substitute the EXACT SAME AMOUNT of BAKING BUTTER for the fat (butter, margarine, or oil) in any recipe, which eliminates additional measuring. In other words, you would use 1 cup of BAKING BUTTER if your recipe calls for 1 cup of butter, margarine, or oil (so you don't have to adjust your regular recipe) making it easy to use! I've personally had great results using the product in cookies, cakes, breads, sauces, soups, biscuits, rolls, brownies, pie crusts, frostings, and candies. If you can't find this wonderful product in your area and would like to order by mail call: (800) 574-6822. The mail order size is 5 pounds for $8.99 (plus shipping and handling). Helpful hints for using MRS. BATEMAN'S BAKING BUTTER are included with the product. If you haven't tried it yet, YOU SHOULD!!

Note: Mrs. Bateman has even developed a low-fat chocolate chip to be used for baking and has applied for a patent. One ounce of her low-fat chips is only 1.5 fat grams compared to 6 fat grams found in one ounce of standard chocolate chips. Let's keep our fingers crossed that the low-fat chocolate chips will be on the market in the near future!

NOTES

A CHANGE
FOR THE BETTER

HOW TO CUT THE FAT GRADUALLY
(Try a little tenderness!)

What is the meaning of change? Have you ever really thought about it? We all experience some kind of change in our lives every day. Some days more than others. Well, I looked up change in the dictionary and this is what I found: to make or become different, to put something in place of another, a passing from one form to another, something to be used in place of another of the same kind, and money returned to you when you have given a larger amount than the price of what you were buying (an unexpected pleasure in my opinion). There are sudden changes and gradual changes. Most people prefer gradual changes that evolve slowly changing their behavior or habit, over a period of time, which allows them to get used to the change. On the other hand, there are others who simply take a running start and jump right in with both feet (never giving the consequences a second thought until it's too late to do anything about it). Oh, yes, there are some compulsive people in the world (myself included), who don't take the time to think things through, but react on emotion without considering the consequences.

Everyone has their own "comfort zone" which basically means a place they feel secure and comfortable. When you leave your comfort zone (or make a change in your life), you may feel a little apprehensive and not quite sure of yourself. We all experience these feelings when we do something new or different. This can apply to anything in life from a new school or church, changing hairdressers, buying a type of clothing different from your usual style, or even changing the way you drive to work. The point I am trying to make is that change is never easy once we GET USED to something a certain way. Change involves taking a risk and, to some, that can be kind of scary.

Changing the type of food you eat can be very difficult if you have eaten the same way most of your life, especially if the new foods look different or strange. If a food LOOKS different (than you are used to) chances are you might not want to even give it a try. It may end up tasting great, but most folks would rather NOT "risk it" by finding out (especially kids). I guess that is why I worked SO HARD to make the recipes in *BUTTER BUSTERS* (and now this book) as familiar as possible. I knew if I changed the food to low-fat and it didn't look and taste like the original recipe, no one was going to eat it (myself included). So, it is of utmost importance and why I try VERY HARD to give my readers the foods they are used to eating that taste just as good as the original version. It's really easy with some recipes, and quite a bit harder with others. That's what makes it so fun and challenging, but most of all rewarding when it turns out well!

I've found most people like to change gradually (when it comes to their lifestyle and eating habits) instead of "all at once" (or cold turkey), unless they are forced to do so because of health reasons. As a matter of fact, most people refuse to change their eating habits unless they have a deep desire to lose weight, or have received a bad cholesterol reading at their yearly physical.

I could be Pollyanna and pretend everyone wanted to start eating low-fat and exercising on a regular basis just to be healthy, and feel good, but I would be fooling myself. I'm not that naive. No, I realize many of you are reading this book because it was prescribed by your doctor, or you really want to lose a few pounds and you are at the end of your rope. That's OK. Don't worry, I'm human, too! You didn't see me making a great change from my junk food habits until I turned up with a cholesterol reading of 242. No, changing my diet to low-fat was definitely not my idea of fun (in the beginning)! That is, until I discovered how easy it was to change my favorites to low-fat and still taste great!

However, I was one of the lucky ones. In a very short time (after only 6 months) I saw a tremendous positive CHANGE in my cholesterol as a result of a few VERY MINOR CHANGES in my diet. The best part of all was I could still eat all the foods I had always enjoyed. I only CHANGED the way I prepared them. Since all my favorites still tasted great, I didn't feel like I was missing out on anything, especially the great taste! I discovered that I could live and enjoy the low-fat lifestyle for the rest of my life! After all, why on earth would I want to go back to something that was detrimental to my health that I didn't even miss! That is really the key to the whole *BUTTER BUSTERS* Low-Fat System and the difference between a "diet" and a new healthy way of living. I was going to say lifestyle, but I am getting kind of tired of everyone calling it that. I do agree with the concept, but it's just that it seems to have become a catch-all phrase for every single plan to control your weight and improve your health. I will work on figuring another name to call it, and let you know when I do!

I think most people would agree to give it a try **if they knew for a fact** the change would be a positive experience. If that were the case, I'm sure most people would be more willing. After all, that would not be a risk at all, if you were GUARANTEED that it would work for you. I'm sorry to say there are no guarantees in life, but my *BUTTERS BUSTERS* Low-Fat System comes pretty close to a guarantee. After all, it has helped thousands of people lose weight, control their cholesterol, and learn to live a healthy lifestyle (that is what I have been told by my readers). Since we all resist change (because it involves a risk), I've decided to make it easier for everyone. I'M GOING TO HELP YOU CHANGE VERY GRADUALLY. In fact, it's going to be so gradual you probably won't even notice the difference. That is my intention. What do you say we take a risk together and try something new (for a change). You will never know "what it could have been like" if you don't give it a try. Who knows....YOU MIGHT EVEN SURPRISE YOURSELF AND ACTUALLY LIKE IT!

If you are willing, I would like to lead each of you on a journey through the process of gently and gradually cutting the fat in your diet. You may travel at your own speed. Some of you will get there quickly and some may take a little longer. That part doesn't really make any difference. All that matters (in the long run) is that each of us will eventually reach our destination, that which a low-fat journey can provide, GOOD HEALTH! So, fasten your seat belts! I know that I'm ready if you are! Of course, I've already been there and liked it so much I came back to get you. Trust me, I wouldn't take you anywhere that I wouldn't want to go myself! All of this talk about change made even more sense after I talked to a good friend of mine about modifying one of her favorite recipes to low-fat. This is how it happened:

I have a very dear friend named Nina Burgett. You might have read about her in my "Earth Angels" Tribute on page XXI. She is one very special lady!! Nina has provided me with tremendous love and support over the past year as I was writing this book. She always had time to "listen" to me when I needed encouragement and someone to "unload on." She always stood by me and never turned her back no matter how busy she was. Nina is a wonderful person. She is kind, giving, sincere, compassionate, and trustworthy. Not only that, I think she has a direct prayer line to God, because whenever she prays for me God seems to be listening! I can't think of many people who can fill that bill.

My daughter Paige and Nina's daughter Haley are very good friends and, over the past year, Paige has spent a lot of time in their home. As I was driving Paige and her friend, Julie, to the mall one evening we started talking about *I'M LISTENING!* and how it was almost finished. I had been cooking day and night for about four weeks so the subject of food was the topic of our conversation. Out of the blue, Paige said, "Mom, you need to get Mrs. Burgett's recipe

Haley Burgett and Paige
June   1994

for Cinnamon Pull-Apart Bread." Well, that was the first time I had ever heard a thing about it. Paige went on to say that Mrs.

Haley Burgett and Paige
July   1994

Burgett made the bread with a garlic and butter seasoning version, too, and they were the best two breads she had EVER eaten. She said, "Mom, if you could make her recipes low-fat I would just love it!" Paige then said that Mrs. Burgett had told her she loved the bread, too, but that it was VERY FATTENING, so she didn't make it much anymore (for that reason).

I had been working on my "Modifying Recipes" section of the book and the more I thought about it, I realized that Nina's Bread (if I could make it taste good) would be a perfect example of how you can gradually cut the fat in your recipes by changing a few little things. I was looking for an example in which you didn't have to go from high-fat to fat-free in one step. I wanted a recipe that could give my readers a choice and let THEM decide how low-fat THEY wanted to go. Well, it sparked my interest, so as soon as I got home, I gave Nina a call. I asked her about the bread, and she said it was really quick and easy, but unfortunately VERY FATTENING, too! Since Nina had started eating low-fat, she had pretty much given up making the bread that everyone loved so much. I asked if she would consider letting me try to modify it to low-fat and she said she would be thrilled if I could do it.

Jon Ellis, Luke Brentlinger, Tyler, and
Kyle Derrick
Official Testers   January 1995

So the next morning I went to work on the recipe (trying 8 different ways to make it low-fat), and I came up with four versions that I was pleased with. Next I had twenty-seven different people: men, women, children and one dog (Roxie, our Lab puppy who enjoyed crumbs from all four versions that ended up on the floor) taste them. The true test came when we delivered the favorites to the Burgett home to let Nina, Randy (Nina's husband), Haley, Cari, and Lindsey (Nina's daughters) try the various breads. They were torn (no pun intended...pull apart bread. Get it!) between the Breadstick and French Bread Methods. For that reason, they are the ones I've included, along with Method #1 (a simple change in the original recipe), and Method #4 (a made from scratch method).The

Cari, Lindsey, and Haley
Nina and Randy
January 1995

four recipe versions I've included were the over-all favorites tested by more than 27 different people. You can see by the various methods how easy it is to change a couple of little things and make a big difference.

I'll show you how to gradually cut the fat in Nina's recipe one step at a time. I tried several methods, but wanted to stick with something very quick and easy (as hers was). By changing a couple of products, I was able to come up with a recipe that Paige loved as much as Nina's "Original" version. As a matter of fact, she couldn't really tell the difference between the "Original" and the "Light" (the breadstick method). I invite each of you to try one of my low-fat versions and find out for YOURSELF just **how easy it is to cut the fat, but not the flavor!**

Remember, everyone has to start somewhere. How low you go is entirely up to you! Isn't it nice to have a choice? I hope you enjoy Nina's wonderful bread as much as I did while modifying it to low-fat for all of us to enjoy! When Nina gave me the recipe, it sounded very similar to the Monkey Bread I had made for years. It was always Blake's favorite, but I had never added the cinnamon and sugar or the garlic and butter seasonings. I had just made it plain, but it gave me some ideas how I might be able to change her recipe (with some of my low-fat tricks) and still keep the great taste and texture of the original bread. I couldn't wait to get started when she gave me her recipe, and I hope you will feel the same way! Have Fun!

ORIGINAL METHOD:
NINA'S FAVORITE CINNAMON PULL-APART BREAD
(15 fat grams per servintg)

3 cans (10-count) Pillsbury Buttermilk Biscuits
1 ½ sticks of butter, melted
1 ¼ cups sugar
2 heaping Tbs. cinnamon

Nina Burgett

Turn the oven on and set the temperature at 325 degrees. Combine the cinnamon and sugar in a small bowl. Melt the butter in a glass measure in the microwave (about 1 minute). Spray a bundt pan with cooking spray. Layer one package of biscuits in the bottom of the pan. Sprinkle ⅓ of the cinnamon/sugar mixture over the biscuits and ⅓ of the melted butter. Layer the second can of biscuits over the cinnamon/sugar/butter mixture and repeat with the next ⅓ cinnamon/sugar and butter. Layer the last can of biscuits and top with melted butter and the rest of the cinamon/sugar mixture. Place in the oven and bake at 325° F. for 40-45 minutes. Serve warm.

Method #1: You can reduce the fat content of the original recipe by substituting Fleischmann's Fat-Free Squeeze Margarine in place of the butter (still using the regular biscuits) and **cut the fat to 6.5 fat grams per serving.**

Variation: Prepare the recipe just the same, but instead of the cinnamon/sugar mixture, combine 1 tsp. garlic powder and 1 tsp. onion powder (or any seasonings you prefer). Layer the biscuits in the pan sprinkling a little onion and garlic powder and melted butter in between each biscuit layer.

Option: I tried adding some basil, oregano and ½ cup Alpine Lace Fat-Free Parmesan cheese along with the other seasonings and thought it was good that way, too.

Yields: Serves 16

Per Serving:

Fat:	15 g	Calories:	298	Protein:	3 g
Cholesterol:	23 mg	46 % Calories from Fat		Carbohydrate:	38 g
Fiber:	<1 g			Sodium:	651 mg

NINA'S "LIGHT" CINNAMON PULL-APART BREAD
(This was the favorite by the majority of the twenty-seven people who tested all four versions.)
(3.8 fat grams per serving)

Method #2:
3 (11-oz.) cans Pillsbury Soft Breadsticks (2.5 fat grams per breadstick)
¾ cup Fleischmann's Fat-Free Squeeze Margarine
1 ¼ cups sugar (or 1 cup sugar and 3 packets Sweet 'N Low)
2 heaping Tbs. cinnamon

Turn the oven on and set the temperature at 325 degrees. Combine the sugar and cinnamon in a small bowl. Unwrap three cans of Pillsbury Soft Breadsticks. There will be eight segments in each can. Pour the Fleischmann's Fat-Free Squeeze Margarine in a small bowl. Form each of the 24 segments into balls. (Paige liked it better when I cut each segment in half making 48 segments total.) Dip each ball into the margarine and then coat with the cinnamon/sugar mixture. Place all the coated balls in a bundt or angel food cake pan that has been sprayed with I Can't Believe It's Not Butter! Spray (or other cooking spray). Bake at 325° F. 40-45 minutes. Serve warm.

Note: I found by coating each ball individually with the margarine and cinnamon/sugar mixture, the flavor is more evenly distributed when using the fat-free margarine (because it is not as thin as melted butter).

Variation: Prepare the recipe the same, but instead of the cinnamon/sugar mixture, combine 1 tsp. garlic powder and 1 tsp. onion powder (or your choice of seasonings) and sprinkle between layers along with the ¾ cup Fleischmann's Fat-Free Squeeze Margarine. You can coat the balls with margarine, and sprinkle the seasonings over the balls as you layer them.You can also add ½ cup Alpine Lace Fat-Free Parmesan Cheese (or another fat-free cheese) between the layers if you desire. Use your imagination. I tried basil and oregano along with the garlic and onion powder and it tasted great!

Yields: Serves 16

Per Serving: (All sugar)

Fat:	3.8 g	Calories:	231	Protein:	5 g
Cholesterol:	0 mg	15 % Calories from Fat		Carbohydrate:	44 g
Fiber:	<1 g			Sodium:	529 mg

Per Serving: (1/2 Sweet 'N Low)

Fat:	3.8g	Calories:	220	Protein:	5 g
Cholesterol:	0 mg	15 % Calories from Fat		Carbohydrate:	41 g
Fiber:	<1 g			Sodium:	529 mg

NINA'S "LIGHTER" CINNAMON PULL-APART BREAD
(This was my favorite and a close second to the breadstick version)
(1 fat gram per serving)

Method #3:
3 (11-oz.) cans Pillsbury Crusty French Loaf (5 fat grams per can)
¾ cup Fleischmann's Fat-Free Squeeze Margarine
1 ¼ cups sugar (or 1 cup sugar and 3 packets Sweet 'N Low)
2 heaping Tbs. cinnamon

Turn the oven on and set the temperature at 325 degrees. Combine the sugar and cinnamon in a small bowl. Unwrap three cans of Pillsbury Crusty French Loaf bread. Cut each can into 10-12 segments. Pour the Fleischmann's Fat-Free Squeeze Margarine in a small bowl. Form each of the segments into balls. Dip each ball into the margarine and then coat with the cinnamon/sugar mixture. Place all the coated balls in a bundt or angel food cake pan that has been sprayed with I Can't Believe It's Not Butter! Spray (or other cooking spray). Bake at 325° F. 40-45 minutes. Serve warm.

Note: I found by coating each ball individually with the margarine and cinnamon/sugar mixture, the flavor is more evenly distributed when using the fat-free margarine (because it is not as thin as melted butter).

Variation: Prepare the recipe the same, but instead of the cinnamon/sugar mixture, combine 1 tsp. garlic powder and 1 tsp. onion powder (or your choice of seasonings) and sprinkle between layers along with the ¾ cup Fleischmann's Fat-Free Squeeze Margarine. You can coat the balls with margarine, and sprinkle the seasonings over the balls as you layer them. You can also add ½ cup Alpine Lace Fat-Free Parmesan Cheese (or another fat-free cheese) between the layers if you desire. Use your imagination. I tried basil and oregano along with the garlic and onion powder and it tasted great!

Yields: Serves 16

Per Serving: (All sugar)

Fat:	1 g	Calories: 208		Protein:	6 g
Cholesterol:	0 mg	4 % Calories from Fat		Carbohydrate:	43 g
Fiber:	<1 g			Sodium:	443 mg

Per Serving: (1/2 Sweet 'N Low)

Fat:	1 g	Calories: 197		Protein:	6 g
Cholesterol:	0 mg	4 % Calories from Fat		Carbohydrate:	41 g
Fiber:	<1 g			Sodium:	443 mg

NINA'S "LIGHTEST" CINNAMON PULL-APART BREAD
(Pam's made-from-scratch recipe) (This one is almost as quick as the other methods and a lot cheaper)
(0.4 fat grams per serving)

Method #4:
Bread:
2 cups lukewarm water
2 pkg. dry yeast
¼ cup Egg Beaters
¼ cup sugar (or 2 Tbs. sugar and 1½ packets Sweet 'N Low)
¾ cup Fleischmann's Fat-Free Squeeze Margarine
4 cups self-rising flour
¼ tsp. Papa Dash "Lite" Salt

Filling:
¾ cup Fleischmann's Fat-Free Squeeze Margarine
1 ¼ cups sugar (or 1 cup sugar and 3 packets Sweet 'N Low)
2 heaping Tbs. cinnamon

Bread: Turn the oven on and set the temperature at 325 degrees. In a large bowl, mix water and yeast. Add sugar, Egg Beaters, and ¾ cup margarine. Gradually add flour. Mix well. Chill dough about 15 minutes. Coat your hands with flour and form dough into 30 balls.

Filling: Pour the remaining ¾ cup margarine in a small bowl. In another bowl combine the sugar and cinnamon. Dip each ball in the margarine and then coat with the cinnamon/sugar mixture. Layer the balls in a bundt or angel food cake pan that has been sprayed with I Can't Believe It's Not Butter! Spray. Bake at 325° F. 40-45 minutes. Serve warm.

Yields: Serves 16

Per Serving: (All sugar)

Fat:	0.4 g	Calories:	197	Protein:	4 g
Cholesterol:	0 mg	4 % Calories from Fat		Carbohydrate:	45 g
Fiber:	1 g			Sodium:	596 mg

Per Serving: (1/2 Sweet 'N Low)

Fat:	0.4 g	Calories:	181	Protein:	4 g
Cholesterol:	0 mg	4 % Calories from Fat		Carbohydrate:	40 g
Fiber:	1 g			Sodium:	596 mg

I've shown you how to gradually cut the fat in Nina's Pull-Apart Bread by changing one or two ingredients. With all of the great new products on the market, I'll show you how to change a high-fat recipe to low-fat if you just know which substitutions to use. Check the "Name Brand Shopping Guide" starting on page 513 to see if there are any new products you haven't yet found. I've already told you about all the new products in the "New Products" chapter, but wanted to show you a "before and after" on a recipe my sister-in-law Sally gave me. Sally has been making these enchiladas for years, but as you can see the original recipe contained quite a bit of fat. I want to show you how easy it is to change your family's favorites to low-fat. You can see what a tremendous difference a few fat-free substitutions can make. Sally lives in Arlington with her husband Cliff (Mike's brother) and their two children Katy and Jordan.

AUNT SALLY'S CHICKEN ENCHILADAS

1 package extra large flour tortillas (6)
1 can enchilada sauce (10-oz.)
1 can re-fried beans (16-oz.)
1 can Campbells' Cream of Mushroom Soup
1 (16 oz.) sour cream
12-oz. grated longhorn Cheddar cheese
1 boiled and deboned hen

Serves 6 (1 large enchilada per serving)

Per Serving:

Fat: 58 g   Calories: 965

Cliff, Katy, Sally, and Jordan Mycoskie
September   1994

AUNT SALLY'S (SLIMMED DOWN) CHICKEN ENCHILADAS

12 "El Torito" fat-free flour tortillas or Mission "Light"
   (1 fat gram a tortilla) Flour Tortillas (Neither of these brands
   come in the extra large size so use two tortillas per serving.)
1 can enchilada sauce (10-oz.)
1 (16-oz.) carton Land-O-Lakes No-Fat sour cream
1 can Campbells' 99% fat-free Cream of Mushroom Soup (or Weight Watchers')
1 can fat-free refried beans (Old El Paso or Rosarita brand)
12-oz. fat-free grated Cheddar or Mozzarella Cheese (your brand choice)
1 package ButterBall brand "Mesquite Seasoned"
   fresh skinless chicken breast filets (16-oz.)

Per Serving:

Serves 6 (2 enchiladas per serving)

Fat:1.5 g   Calories:473

A CHANGE FOR THE BETTER

AUNT SALLY'S CHICKEN ENCHILADAS

REGULAR METHOD	FAT GRAMS	LOW-FAT METHOD	FAT GRAMS
6 extra large flour tortillas	23.3	12 "El Torito" fat-free flour tortillas	0
1 can enchilada sauce	0.5	1 can enchilada sauce	0
1 (16-oz.) sour cream	95.0	1 (16-oz.) carton Land O Lakes No-Fat sour cream	0
1 can Campbells' Cream of Mushroom Soup	23.0	1 can Campbells' 99% fat-free Cream of Mushroom soup	5.5
1 can refried beans	37.2	1 can Old El Paso or Rosarita brand fat-free refried beans	0
12-oz. grated Cheddar Cheese	112.7	12-oz. grated Alpine Lace or Lifetime by Lifeline fat-free Cheddar Cheese or 12-oz. Polly-O fat-free mozzarella cheese (grated)	0
1 boiled hen	54.3	1 16-oz. package Butter Ball brand "Mesquite Seasoned' fresh skinless chicken breasts (These are only 1 fat gram each.)	4

Serves 6: (1 LARGE enchilada per serving)		Serves 6: (2 regular-sized enchiladas per serving)	
CALORIES PER SERVING:	965	CALORIES PER SERVING:	473
TOTAL FAT GRAMS IN RECIPE:	348	TOTAL FAT GRAMS IN RECIPE:	9.5
FAT GRAMS PER SERVING:	**58**	**FAT GRAMS PER SERVING:**	**1.5**

As you can see, with a few changes, this recipe can easily be de-fatted and most people won't even know the difference. I always say, "If you can eat the foods you have always eaten and they still taste good (modified to low-fat), this is something most people CAN and WILL live with for the rest of their LONG, HEALTHY lives."

AUNT SALLY'S (SLIMMED DOWN) CHICKEN ENCHILADAS

12 "El Torito" fat-free flour tortillas or Mission "Light" (1 fat gram a tortilla) Flour
    Tortillas (Neither of these brands come in the extra large size so use two tortillas
    per serving.) If you use the "Mission Light" tortillas, add 2 fat grams per serving.
1 can enchilada sauce (10-oz.)
1 (16-oz.) carton Land-O-Lakes No-Fat sour cream
1 can Campbells' 99% fat-free Cream of Mushroom Soup
1 can fat-free refried beans (Old El Paso or Rosarita brand)
12-oz. grated fat-free Alpine Lace or Lifetime by Lifeline Cheddar Cheese,
    or 12-oz. Polly-O-Free Mozzarella cheese (grated)
1 package Butter Ball brand "Mesquite Seasoned" fresh skinless
    chicken breast filets (16-oz.) (cooked and cut in bite-sized pieces)

Spread tortillas with refried beans. Combine enchilada sauce and mushroom soup in a saucepan
and bring to a boil. Simmer until ready to use. Place a few pieces of the cooked chicken in the
tortillas and sprinkle with cheese. Roll up and place in a large (9 X 13-inch) glass casserole dish
(that has been sprayed with a low-fat cooking spray) seam side down. Pour the enchilada sauce
mixture over the tortillas. Cover dish with foil and bake 20-30 minutes at 350 F. Remove from oven
and spread fat-free sour cream and remaining cheese on top. Bake uncovered 5-7 minutes.

Note: You can also add my "Mock Guacamole Dip" (page 353) on top if desired. You can make
this ahead and freeze. Add the sour cream, however, when you bake the enchiladas.

Yields: Serves 6 (two enchiladas per serving)

Per Serving:

Fat: 1.5 g	Calories: 473	Protein: 53 g
Cholesterol: 69 mg	2% Calories from Fat	Carbohydrate: 67 g
Fiber: 6 g		Sodium: 1420 mg

**Blake, Sally, and Cliff
Christmas 1994**

**The original recipe from my
recipe shower.**

Thank you, Sally, for sharing your great recipe with all of us!

SUBSTITUTIONS—THE KEY TO SUCCESS!

With the vast array of low and fat-free frozen yogurts, ice creams, cakes, cookies, chips, and snacks we have available (check the "Name Brand Shopping Guide" on page 513 for suggestions), no one has to worry about giving up their treats. You can easily cut the fat in cooking and baking, as well, by making low-fat substitutions. Choose fat-free salad dressings and you will fight the "number one fat culprit" in most people's diets. Switch to fat-free sour cream, fat-free cream cheese, fat-free ricotta and fat-free Parmesan and you will save hundreds of fat grams you won't even miss. The options are unlimited. No one is asking you to give up anything. Instead, I want to take your hand and lead you down "the road of low-fat living." Don't worry, I'm not going to dessert you (no pun intended)! I'm going to teach you how to substitute and I'm even going to give you name brand products that I have personally tested, and highly recommend.

If you want to take the trip slowly travelling by ship, train, or car (what I recommend if you are trying this for the first time) or "blast off" in a jet plane (full speed ahead), that is up to you. I promise this is a journey you won't regret. It is your personal trip to health, fitness, and even weight loss (if you so desire). If you remember, the tortoise and hare both finished the race. One just made it there a little quicker (and it wasn't the rabbit). It really depends on you and your personality. Positive results are the goal we are seeking. I'll give you the tools (low-fat substitutions) and you decide just how quickly you would like to reach your destination.

Good Luck !
Pam

The following chart lists ideas for substitutions and modifications. Try cutting the fat gradually. You don't have to cut all the fat in every recipe at once. By making a few modifications, you will ease into the low-fat lifestyle and not even notice the difference (except you will look and feel great)!

HIGH-FAT OR LOW-FAT?

(It's your choice!)

DAIRY PRODUCTS

High Fat:
whole milk, 2% milk, cream, half & half, condensed sweet milk, evaporated canned milk, whipped cream, ice cream, non-dairy type creamers, sour cream, cream cheese, most cheeses, Parmesan cheese, ricotta cheese, and creamed cottage cheese

Low-Fat Substitutions:
Nonfat dry milk, skim milk, 1% milk, low-fat buttermilk, nonfat yogurt, non-fat frozen yogurt, fat-free ice cream, non-fat ice milk, sherbet, fat-free cottage cheese, fat-free cream cheese, fat-free ricotta, fat-free sour cream, non-fat evaporated skimmed can milk, low-fat sweetened condensed milk, non-fat non-dairy creamers, fat-free cheeses, low-fat cheeses (less than 4 fat grams an ounce), fat-free Parmesan Cheese

PROTEIN SOURCES

High Fat:
Salmon, shark, mackerel, trout, swordfish, anchovies, sardines, dark poultry meat, white poultry meat with skin, bacon, duck, sausage, hot dogs, cold cuts, organ meats, nuts, seeds, peanut butter, tofu, egg yolks, most beef, most pork, most lamb

Low-Fat Substitutions:
Flounder, haddock, red snapper, sole, tuna steak, cod, halibut, butterfish, squid, shrimp, clams, mussels, scallops, crab, white poultry meat without skin, fat-free and low-fat luncheon meats (several brands available), Canadian bacon, low-fat sausage (Healthy Choice), pork tenderloin, flank steak, venison, buffalo, eggwhites, beans & legumes, rabbit, Vermillon Valley brand low-fat beef (information in Resource Guide pg. 539)

FRUITS & VEGETABLES

High-Fat:
olives, avocados, coconut, creamed vegetables

Low- Fat Substitutions:
Aside from the few high-fat items I listed, fruits and vegetables are great low-fat sources of fiber, nutrients, and vitamins that fill you up, but not out! Fruits and vegetables are also rich in the antioxidant vitamins and minerals. The antioxidants have been proven effective in reducing and eliminating many of the free radicals and carcinogens (associated with many diseases).

STARCHY FOODS

High-Fat:
biscuits, cornbread, waffles, pancakes, granola, muffins, croissants, pastries, butter-soaked garlic bread, doughnuts, french fries, hash browns, chips, some bagels (only if they contain chocolate chips or other high-fat ingredients), crackers, microwave or oil-popped popcorn

Low-Fat Substitutions:
most breads, cereals, bagels, English muffins, pasta, rice, corn, barley, bulgur, oats, bran, potatoes, corn tortillas, low-fat or fat-free flour tortillas, baked low-fat or fat-free chips and crackers, pretzels, rice cakes, air-popped popcorn (or low-fat microwave brands such as Pop Weaver's Gourmet "Light"), matzo, couscous, and soft giant pretzels

SAUCES, SOUPS, AND CONDIMENTS

High-Fat:
Creamed soups, most salad dressings, mayonnaise, most margarines, all oils (even Olive Oil although it is more heart-healthy), lard, butter, tartar sauce, cream sauces, pesto sauces, REAL bacon bits, peanut butter, puddings and creamy or nutty pie fillings

Low-Fat Substitutions:
bouillon, broth, tomato-based soups, 99% fat-free cream soups, fat-free soups, spices, herbs, salsa, ketchup, mustard, fat-free mayonnaise, fat-free puddings, fat-free salad dressings, fat-free tartar sauce, horseradish, fat-free sour cream, fat-free margarine, Butter Buds (in liquid form made from the mix), Sprinkle on Butter Buds (or other butter flavored substitutes), low-sodium soy sauce, wine, vinegar, steak sauce, Worcestershire sauce, teriyaki sauce, most Bar-B-Q sauces, imitation bacon bits, pickles, and sauerkraut, most red and marinara sauces, reduced fat peanut butter

SWEETS AND DESSERTS

High-Fat:
chocolate, candy bars, most cookies, sweet rolls, coffee cake, donuts, sopaipillas, cakes, pies, fudge, granola bars, ice cream, ice cream bars and sandwiches, puddings, fudge toppings, caramel and butterscotch ice cream toppings, coconut and nuts for baking, whipped cream toppings, and whole fat yogurt (frozen, too)

Low-Fat Substitutions:
jam, jelly, apple butter, jelly beans, gummi bears, red licorice, hard candies, candy corn, lollipops, frozen fruit bars, fruit roll-ups, sorbet, fat-free fig bars or cookies, low-fat or fat-free granola bars, animal cookies, gingersnaps, low and fat-free cupcakes and snackcakes, low and fat-free cookies, fat-free muffins, fat-free pastries, angel food cake, marshmallows, gelatin, fat-free ice cream toppings, cocoa, chocolate syrup, fruit toppings, coconut and almond extracts, Grape-Nuts Cereal or Fat-Free Granola (in place of nuts), low and fat-free whipped cream toppings (Reddi Wip "Lite" contains soybean oil which is more heart-healthy than palm or palm kernel oil found in many of the whipped toppings), fat-free puddings and pie fillings

BUTTER VERSUS MARGARINE—THE TRANS-FATTY ACID DISPUTE

Your first thought is margarine must be better for my heart than butter, right? Let's examine both possibilities and I will let you decide for yourself. It's true that butter contains cholesterol. Remember, if it walked, swam, or had a mother it contains cholesterol! If a product comes from animal origin, it does contain cholesterol and is therefore a form of saturated fat. We all know how important it is to limit cholesterol and saturated fats from our diets. For this reason, we should LIMIT OR OMIT BUTTER FROM OUR DIETS! OK, you say, then what is the deal with margarine and those trans-fatty acids I've been hearing and reading about? The "DEAL IS" even though most margarines are made from vegetable oil containing "heart smart" polyunsaturated fats, many have been transformed to solid form by a process called hydrogenation. Trans-fatty acids are formed in vegetable oils when they are processed to make margarine, crackers, chips, cookies, and a lot of other foods we consume on a regular basis. Trans-fatty acids have been linked to heart disease, high cholesterol, and even growth disorders in newborn babies. Since trans-fatty acids do not appear on food labels (in those exact words), we may not be aware of the fact that they are found in many foods. If a label lists **partially hydrogenated oil**, this means **it contains trans-fatty acids.** Don't expect the food manufacturers to slap a sticker on the front of a package advertising it contains trans-fatty acids. That is the **last thing** they want you to know. Instead they camouflage it in a way that we have to be an "educated consumer" to detect these cholesterol-raising culprits in the foods we buy and eat.

Fats are made of three different kinds of fatty acids. They are saturated, monounsaturated, and polyunsaturated fats. The food's fatty acid make-up determines whether it will be liquid or solid at room temperature. This process is what affects our health. I will try to simplify this process for you. Saturated fatty acids stack on top of each other to form a solid mass because of their linear structure (it is straight). Butter and coconut oil are very high in saturated fat content which explains why they have a solid appearance. Saturated fatty acids alter how fats and cholesterol are moved through the body in our blood. They are the culprits that clog the arteries to our hearts, raise our cholesterol levels, and sometimes cause heart disease followed, possibly, by the dreaded heart attack!! Saturated fats are BAD NEWS! Mono and polyunsaturated fatty acids look and react in our bodies differently. They actually have a bend or curve in their chemical structure, so they can't stack up in a uniform fashion. Because of their shape, they remain in liquid form. Olive oil and canola oil are rich in monounsaturated fatty acids. For this reason they tend to lower the bad low density lipoproteins cholesterol (LDL), and raise the good high density lipoproteins cholesterol (HDL) in our bodies. Polyunsaturated fatty acids such as corn, sunflower, and safflower oils DO NOT increase our cholesterol levels (unless they are put through the hydrogenation process). For this reason we must realize if a label states a polyunsaturated fat in the nutrition label and list partially hydrogenated oils in the ingredients, you can be quite sure they "nuked the good oil" and turned it into a trans-fatty acid.

Most food manufacturers have switched from saturated to unsaturated fats over the years to please the consumers. Unfortunately, it has affected food textures in many cases. Liquid oil didn't work well in many foods. What was their solution? HYDROGENATION or partial hydrogenation! OK, you say, so what does that mean to me? Well, I will tell you: T R O U B L E ! ! ! **Hydrogenation converts unsaturated healthy fatty acids into unhealthy trans-fatty acids by straightening out their chemical structure**. Once the trans-fatty acids are straightened they stack better and take on THE DREADED SOLID FORM! This might be nice for food texture, but it is bad news for our arteries. Trans-fatty acids are just as detrimental to our health as saturated fats and cholesterol containing products! Great, you say, now what? You probably couldn't avoid them completely (even if you wanted to), but I will give you some helpful tips that might help you monitor your intake:

1. **ALWAYS READ FOOD LABELS** on everything you buy or eat (especially cookies, crackers, chips, and snack foods) for hydrogenated oils. You won't be able to avoid them completely, but you can limit yourself.

2. In recipes when cooking, always use liquid Butter Buds (made from the mix), Promise Ultra Fat-Free Margarine, or Fleischmann's Fat-Free Spread (squeeze bottle) in place of oil, butter or margarine. The substitutions I recommend **do not contain trans-fatty acids.**

4. If you must use oil, please choose **Olive oil or Canola oil.**

5. Use Promise Ultra Fat-Free Margarine, Fleischmann's Fat-Free Spread (squeeze bottle), or SmartBeat Trans-Fat Free Margarine to spread on your bread. None of those products contain trans-fatty acids. You could also dip or drizzle olive oil on your bread, but be aware that one tablespoon of olive oil contains 14 fat grams. This would be 125 fat calories (14 X 9=125). Remember, there are 9 calories in one gram of fat.

6. **When eating in restaurants avoid fried foods.** They may be cooked in vegetable oil shortening which contains trans-fatty acids.

7. If a label lists "monounsaturated fat" and "polyunsaturated fat" as well as "saturated fat," you can add the three and subtract them from the **"total fat"** to get a rough estimate of how much trans fat the food contains. (I said rough because the numbers have probably been rounded.)

8. **TRY TO REDUCE THE TOTAL FAT IN YOUR DIET** and **Increase your intake of complex carbohydrates** and you will be making a **wise heart-healthy choice!!**

WHAT ABOUT THOSE FAT-FREE MARGARINES?

You will find that the fat-free margarines don't generally melt too well. Don't let that discourage you from using these products. It's true if you put a little fat-free margarine in a frying pan, most of it will evaporate (not so much with the Promise Ultra Fat-Free Margarine) because they contain so much water. If, instead, you spread the fat-free margarine on the bread (as if you were making a grilled cheese sandwich) and cook it in a non-stick skillet, it will brown beautifully and make a great fat-free cheese sandwich (considering you used fat-free cheese). Even though the fat-free margarines state on the package not to bake with or use in the microwave, that never stops me from trying. I have tested and used Promise Ultra Fat-Free Margarine and Fleischmann's Fat-Free Margarine in baking breads, cakes, muffins, crusts, brownies, and some cookies (it doesn't work as well in sugar or chocolate chip cookies) with GREAT RESULTS!! I guess the food manufacturers thought because the fat-free margarines contain a large amount of water, the baked product would not be satisfactory. That simply was not the case. The baked products using the fat-free margarines were as moist and tender as any baked goods using regular high-fat margarine.

I also use Liquid Butter Buds (made from the mix) in baking and cooking with wonderful results. I tend to use that product in my soups, sauces, and gravies rather than my baked goods, since the newer solid fat-free margarines have hit the market. They seem to give me a more tender texture in baked items. Remember Promise Ultra Fat-Free, Fleischmann's Fat-Free Squeeze Margarine, SmartBeat Trans Fat-Free, and Butter Buds Liquid (made from the mix), contain NO TRANS-FATTY ACIDS!

THE LOW-FAT MARGARINES AND HOW THEY "STACK UP"
(How their linear structures differ)

MARGARINE	TOTAL FAT (PER TBS.)	CONTAINS TRANS-FATTY ACIDS
Fleischmann's Fat-Free	0	NO
Promise Ultra Fat-Free	0	NO
SmartBeat Fat-Free	0	NO
Butter Buds Liquid	0	NO
SmartBeat Trans-Fat-Free	2	NO
Land O Lakes Light Whipped Butter	3.5	YES
Promise Ultra Lite	4	YES
Weight Watchers' Extra Light	4	YES
Fleischmann's Lower Fat	4.5	YES
Blue Bonnet Lower Fat	4.5	YES
Imperial Whipped	5	YES
Fleischmann's Diet	6	YES
Promise Extra Light	6	YES
Land O Lakes Country Morning Blend Light	6	YES
Mazola Diet Imitation	6	YES

NOTE: If a margarine contains more than 6 fat grams a tablespoon, I would not recommend using the product. Why ruin a great low-fat food with a high-fat margarine when you don't have to (thanks to all the great low and fat-free margarines available)?

I personally use Promise Ultra Fat-Free Margarine to spread on my bread, my husband uses the SmartBeat Trans Fat Free, Paige likes the Fleischmann's Lower Fat Margarine, Blake prefers Blue Bonnet Lower Fat, and Tyler just switched from the regular Fleischmann's squeeze margarine (at 10 fat grams a tablespoon) to the New Fleischmann's Fat-Free Spread (squeeze bottle) margarine (0 fat grams) and WE ARE ALL SO GLAD HE DID!!

I'm sure you have a big picture of what our dinner table looks like with five different margarine containers. With all the great low-fat choices available, there is definitely something FOR EVERYONE!!

People are always asking me what kind of oil to use (if they want to use one), so I decided this would be a good place to list the different oils and how they are broken down according to saturated, monounsaturated, and polyunsaturated fatty acids. You will notice the percentages don't always add up to 100%. It is because those oils (that don't add up to 100%) contain "other" fat-like substances. These **could be** trans-free acids. **However, this does not mean they contain trans-fatty acids!!** Trans-fats (for the most part) do not occur in natural oils. Trans-fats are a result of hydrogenation, a process performed by man. It involves turning a polyunsaturated fat into a saturated fat by changing it from a liquid to a solid form. Look for the oils with the highest ratio of unsaturated fat to saturated fat. These would be more healthful. Remember ALL OILS ARE 100% FAT and if you are trying to lose weight by counting fat grams, you NEED TO BE AWARE OF ALL KINDS OF FAT! It's true, that some oils are better than others. The monounsaturated fats are the best choice regarding your heart-health. Monounsaturated fats help lower the LDL (bad cholesterol) and raise the HDL (good cholesterol). For this reason, **Olive oil and Canola oil would be your best choices!** Palm Kernel oil and Coconut oil would be poor choices. Try to avoid those two, along with cocoa butter, palm oil and hydrogenated vegetable oil (such as Crisco), when possible. They are all highly saturated and may be detrimental to your health!

VEGETABLE OILS VARY

The chart below lists the breakdown of fatty acids in various oils. As you can see, they really do vary. The higher the ratio of unsaturated fat to saturated fatty acids, the more healthful the oil. However, this doesn't mean you should add unsaturated fats to your diet. **The idea is to cut down on all fats!** If you do choose to use an oil, please make it as unsaturated as possible and the more monounsaturated, the better!

FATTY ACID CONTENT

Oils, least to most saturated	Poly-unsaturated(%)	Mono-unsaturated(%)	Saturated (%)	Unsaturated/ Saturated Fat Ratio
♥ Canola	32	62	6	15.7/1
Safflower	75	12	9	9.6/1
Sunflower	66	20	10	8.6/1
Corn	59	24	13	6.4/1
Soybean	59	23	14	5.9/1
♥ Olive	9	72	14	5.8/1
Peanut	32	46	17	4.6/1
Sesame Seed	40	40	18	4.4/1
Cottonseed	52	18	26	2.7/1
☠Palm kernel	2	10	80	0.2/1
☠Coconut	2	6	87	0.1/1

YOU: I don't know if this letter will get to YOU or not, but I felt in my heart that I just had to write and tell you how much I love your book. It was a lucky day when I found it. As a matter of fact, I have purchased several copies for my friends and family.

I have changed the way I cook and have even joined a health club. My only problem is eating out. I have read your restaurant guide in the book, but wondered if you could give me suggestions for other types of restaurants as well. What are some good low-fat choices in Greek or Indian restaurants? Since I am an international fight attendant, I eat out a lot (all over the world). Any ideas or suggestions would be greatly appreciated.   —*H.M. Los Angeles, California*

ME: What a fun job you have. Since you do eat out on a regular basis I've decided to include this section in the book for you and anyone else that eats out on a regular basis.

RESTAURANT GUIDELINES

CHINESE

AVOID OR EAT ONLY OCCASIONALLY:
Fried Dumplings
Szechuan Beef or other beef dishes
Kung Pao Anything (unless you ask them to remove the peanuts)
Fried Rice (contains oil and eggs)
Sesame Noodles
Peking Duck (or any other dish with Duck)
Anything Fried
Egg Rolls
Sweet and Sour Pork (or anything dish that contains pork)

FILL UP ON THIS INSTEAD:
Anything steamed
Stir-fried vegetables, chicken, or fish (ask them to use chicken broth instead of oil)
Steamed Vegetable Dumplings
Bean Curd
Velvet Chicken
Steamed rice
Hot and Sour Soup
Vegetable Lo Mein (or chicken or fish)
Wonton Soup
Fried rice (if you can convince them to use broth and egg whites only)

JAPANESE

AVOID OR ONLY EAT OCCASIONALLY:
Tempura anything (This is a deep fried food loaded with fat.)
Chicken Sukiyaki
Beef Negimaki (or beef anything)
Pork Katsu (or pork anything)
Any Duck dish
Anything fried

FILL UP ON THIS INSTEAD:
Sushi
Sashimi
Seafood Yosenabe
Chicken or Fish Teriyaki
Miso Soup
Hijiki Salad
Steamed rice
Steamed vegetables

MEXICAN

AVOID OR ONLY EAT OCCASIONALLY:
Refried beans
Enchiladas
Beef Flauta (or any beef dish)
Carne Asada
Cheese Quesadilla
Guacamole
Sour Cream
Nachos
Taco Salad (especially with ground beef and a fried shell)
anything fried
chips (eat tortillas instead or limit yourself to ten)
Beef Burrito
Tostadas (unless you leave off the shell, guacamole, sour cream, and cheese)
any egg dish
any pork dish
any cheese or cream sauce
chile (unless vegetarian)
Chile con queso
Beef Fajitas

FILL UP ON THIS INSTEAD:
Black Bean Soup (try to avoid the bacon or sausage that might be floating in this)
Mexican rice (ask if they fry it- some restaurants do)
Chicken Enchilada (ask them to leave off the sour cream and go light on the cheese)
Chicken Fajitas (ask for them dry- no oil)
Chicken Fajita Salad (leave off the guacamole, sour cream, and cheese) Don't eat the shell it comes in!
Gazpacho
Tortilla Soup (leave off cheese & sour cream)
Charro Beans
Bean Soup
Salsa
Soft corn tortillas
Flour tortillas (ask if they are made with lard, and if so, limit yourself)

GREEK OR EASTERN

AVOID OR ONLY EAT OCCASIONALLY:
Falafel
Gyro
Moussaka
Baba ghanoush
Spinach Cheese Pie
Pastitsio
anything fried
any pork dish
any beef dish
any duck dish
Bourekakia

FILL UP ON THIS INSTEAD:
Couscous
Tabouli
Yogurt Tzatziki
Fish or Chicken Shish Kebab
Pita Bread
Hummus
Torato
Souvlaki

ITALIAN

AVOID OR ONLY EAT OCCASIONALLY:
Any dish that includes the word "Alfredo"
Pasta Bolognese
Cheese Ravioli
Lasagna
Veal Chops
Zucchini Fritti
Fried Mozzarella Cheese Sticks
Eggplant or Veal Parmigiana
beef, sausage, or pepperoni pizza
garlic bread
cheese bread
anything fried
anything in a garlic/butter sauce
anything in a cream sauce
Cheesecake or any other rich dessert
Antipasto (you can eat the vegetables, but try to avoid the cheese and meats)
Caesar Salad (ask them to leave out the egg yolk and go light on the oil and cheese)

FILL UP ON THIS INSTEAD:
Caesar Salad (have your dressing on the side so you can control how much you use)
Vegetable Antipasto
Pasta Primavera (provided it isn't in a cream sauce)
Pasta in a Marinara or Red Clam Sauce
Chicken Cacciatore
Minestrone or Bean Soup
Pasta e Fagioli
Ribollito
Pizza (topped with vegetables, except olives, and light on the cheese)
Plain French or Sourdough Bread
Sorbet
Sherbet

INDIAN

AVOID OR ONLY EAT OCCASIONALLY:
Chicken Kandhari
Lamb Curry (or any other Lamb dish)
Beef Vindaloo
Samosas
Pakoras
Paratha
Poori
Kandhari
Malai
Korma

FILL UP ON THIS INSTEAD:
Chicken or FishTandoori
Fish Vindaloo
Chapati
Fish Tikka
Vegetable Biryani
Chicken Dal
Basmati Rice
Yogurt Curry

Indian
Restaurant

FRENCH

AVOID OR ONLY EAT OCCASIONALLY:
Steak Tartáre
Caesar Salad (unless you ask them to leave out the egg yolks, and go light on the oil and cheese)
any liver or pork dish
Rack of Lamb (or any other Lamb dish)
Pâté
Croissants
Stuffed Mushrooms
Beef Burgundy (or any other beef dish)
Duck à la Orange
Cassoulet
Gratins of any kind
Vegetables with Hollandaise (unless you order the sauce on the side)
Veal Cordon Bleu
anything fried or in a puffed pastry
Escargot (usually dripping with butter)
pastries and desserts

FILL UP ON THIS INSTEAD:
French Onion Soup (ask them to hold the cheese)
Chicken Calvados
Consommé
Green Salad or Caesar Salad (ask for the dressing on the side)
Salad Nicoise
Poached Salmon
Dover Sole
Pasta in a red sauce
Shrimp Cocktail
Oysters on the half shell
Crab Cocktail
French Bread (without butter)
Sorbet/Sherbet
Fresh Fruit

> *Note: The key to success in this restaurant is to ask for all sauces and dressings on the side! You can still enjoy the taste, **without** all the fat!*

FAST FOOD

AVOID OR ONLY EAT OCCASIONALLY:
Double or Triple anything
Fried fish sandwich
Roast Beef sandwiches
Hamburgers
French Fries
Chicken Nuggets
any egg or sausage sandwiches
Hash Browns
anything fried
Tuna salad
Egg Salad
Cole Slaw
Potato Salad
Whole milk cottage cheese
Puddings
ice cream
Hushpuppies
Fried Fish
Corn Bread
Pasta Salad
Pizza (unless you top it with vegetables
    and cut the cheese)
Garlic or Cheese Toast
Cobblers
Chips
Croissants
Fried Fish of any kind
Fried Chicken of any kind
Chili
Cinnamon Rolls
Pastries or Donuts
any sandwich with salami, sausage, beef,
    or ham
mayonnaise
oil dressings
tartar sauce

FILL UP ON THIS INSTEAD:
Grilled Chicken sandwich (with low-fat condi-
    ments
Baked Potato (with low-fat condiments)
Corn on the Cob (no butter)
Beans
Salad (with dressing on the side or fat-free
    dressing)
Mashed Potatoes (no butter or gravy)
Frozen Yogurt
Pasta with Red Sauce
Vegetarian Chili
Bar-B-Q Chicken (white meat with skin removed)
Baked Chicken (white meat with skin removed)
Baked Fish
Turkey Breast Sandwich
    (no cheese or mayonnaise)
Soups (as long as they aren't cream based)

Most of us eat out on a regular basis. I hope this guide helps you make wise choices no matter what kind of restaurant you choose. It is possible to find low-fat options. Just ask, and you shall receive!!

Besides the traditional restaurants, many of us find ourselves in all kinds of places at mealtime when we need to make a low-fat healthy choice, but sometimes it's not so easy! This guide is for you!

HOW TO MAKE WISE CHOICES IN THE REAL WORLD

HOW TO SURVIVE THE MOVIE MUNCHIES:

TRY TO AVOID

SNACK	AMOUNT	FAT GRAMS	CALORIES	% Fat
King size Chocolate-Nut Bar	5-oz.	45 fat grams	750 calories	54% Fat
Kit Kat Bar	4-oz.	33 fat grams	588 calories	51% Fat
Butterfinger	4-oz.	21 fat grams	492 calories	38% Fat
Reese's Peanut Butter Cups	4 cups	22 fat grams	380 calories	52% Fat
Goobers	2.2-oz.	21 fat grams	320 calories	59% Fat
M & M's, peanut	2.6-oz.	20 fat grams	363 calories	50% Fat
M & M's, plain	2.6-oz.	16 fat grams	350 calories	41% Fat

BETTER CHOICES

SNACK	AMOUNT	FAT GRAMS	CALORIES	% Fat
Raisinets	2.3-oz.	10 fat grams	270 calories	33% Fat
Junior Mints	3-oz.	9 fat grams	360 calories	23% Fat
Skittles	2.6-oz.	2 fat grams	286 calories	7% Fat
Twizzlers	4-oz.	1.5 fat grams	385 calories	3% Fat

Be aware of movie popcorn. A small popcorn (without extra butter or salt) still has 350 calories and 32 grams of fat! Check out the nutritional information if it is available. Many theaters now offer air-popped popcorn. Some movie theaters offer bagels, giant soft pretzels, and frozen yogurt. You CAN make a wise choice at the movies!

UP, UP, AND AWAY! AND......... IN CASE YOU GET GROUNDED!

Most regular in-flight meals weigh in at about 600-800 calories and over 45% fat. Remember, **anyone can request a special meal.** It just takes a little advance planning. Some airlines are really making an effort. American Airlines, for instance, now serves all of their sauces on the side. They also offer 14 different options.

If you get stuck on a lay-over or become stranded at an airport, there are plenty of great low-fat snacks available. Bagels, non-fat frozen yogurt, giant soft pretzels, a turkey sandwich with mustard, vegetarian pizza, cold cereal with skim milk and fruit are a few ideas. Skip the burgers, hot dogs, and fries. Make healthy low-fat choices, and chances are you won't come back from your trip with any extra baggage!

TRY TO AVOID:	**HAVE THIS INSTEAD:**
THE REGULAR AIRPLANE MEAL	FRUIT PLATE SPECIAL MEAL
Cheese Lasagna, salad, and cookies	(or one of the other great Special Meals) fruit platter, yogurt, skim milk, and roll
778 calories	345 calories
53 fat grams	3 fat grams

A DASH TO THE DELI!

This is a snap. Your best choice would be a turkey breast sandwich. Skip the mayonnaise and you will save 200 calories and 20 fat grams! If they have vegetable soup that is usually a safe bet. Don't even look at anything made with mayonnaise (such as tuna or egg salad) it's a cinch they didn't use fat-free mayonnaise. There are a few exceptions. A restaurant chain (here in Texas) called Jason's Deli offers fat-free salad dressings and other low and fat-free condiments. Make low-fat requests at your favorite restaurants. There is no harm in asking, and maybe, just maybe they will jump on the low-fat band wagon and join the rest of the world!

TRY TO AVOID:
4-oz. of salami and Swiss Cheese
with mayonnaise on a roll
1,026 calories
76 fat grams

HAVE THIS INSTEAD:
2.5 -oz. turkey with lettuce, tomato, pickle, and
mustard on a 6-inch whole-wheat bun
351 calories
9-10 fat grams

Paige and Julie Blank
(between volleyball matches)
October 1994

A CHANGE FOR THE BETTER

TAKE ME OUT TO THE BALL GAME!

Although nachos, hot dogs, peanuts, and burgers are definite strike-outs, you can still find some home runs at the concession stand. Just remember to let the bad ones go by and you will WALK away with a big win!

TRY TO AVOID:
1 cheese hot dog, fries,
and a beer
680 calories
31 fat grams

HAVE THIS INSTEAD:
1 hot dog with mustard, a giant pretzel,
and a "lite" beer
530 calories
16 fat grams

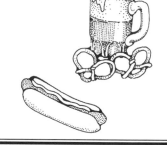

TRY TO AVOID:
1 ounce of roasted peanuts
164 calories
14 fat grams

HAVE THIS INSTEAD:
1 box of Cracker Jacks
120 calories
3 fat grams

YOUR LOW-FAT SCORECARD

STRIKE OUTS:
Three of these and you're not only out,
but you might lose the game, too!

☒ Cheese nachos
24 fat grams (320 calories)

☒ Hamburger on bun with mayonnaise and cheese
48 fat grams (670 calories)

☒ large order fries
19 fat grams (396 calories)

☒ 1 cup shelled or dry roasted peanuts
70 fat grams (850 calories)

☒ 1 Personal Pepperoni Pan Pizza (made by Pizza Hut)
29 fat grams (675 calories)

HOME RUNS:
Why not go home a winner!!

HR Grilled Chicken Sandwich with barbecue sauce
6 fat grams (310 calories)

HR 1 box Cracker Jacks
3 fat grams (120 calories)

HR 3 cups popped popcorn
6 fat grams (150 calories)

HR 1 large soft pretzel with mustard
0 fat grams (170 calories)

HR 1 large non-fat frozen yogurt
0 fat grams (180 calories)

Mike and Rich Ashton
Nolan's 5000th Strike Out
August 22, 1989

I'm sure Nolan would agree with me!

LET'S PARTY!

We all love parties, but as you know they can "lead us into temptation" and "deliver us to evil." Sometimes it really is hard to "Just Say No!" It's fine to splurge sometimes as long as you don't make it a habit. Don't starve all day waiting for the big event. Instead, eat small low-fat meals throughout the day. This way you won't arrive starved and eat everything in sight. Only eat what YOU REALLY WANT!

TRY TO AVOID:		HAVE THIS INSTEAD:
1-oz. potato chips (a handful) 150 calories 10 fat grams		1-oz. pretzels (a handful) 110 calories 1 fat gram
1 ½ inch slice chocolate cake with frosting 300 calories 17 fat grams		¾-inch slice of chocolate cake with frosting 150 calories 8 fat grams
2-oz. Cheddar cheese and 5 crackers 220 calories 20 fat grams		6 large boiled shrimp with red sauce 120 calories 1 fat gram

You can usually find healthy snacks at most parties. Don't go for the onion dip when they have salsa. Choose pretzels over the chips. Some other healthy snacks you might watch for are vegetables, fruit, shrimp, mini-pizzas, bagels, and popcorn. Hard candy, gummy bears, jelly beans, red licorice, and candy corn are all fat-free sweet treats. You might pass on the chocolates or after dinner mints. Leave the crust and eat the pie filling. The crust usually contains most of the fat. Have a good time. Pay more attention to the guests and less attention to the food. Conversation is fat-free!

Reception for President and Mrs. Bush - Arlington, Texas - April 1990

NOTES

MEAL PLANS
AND
RECIPE SUGGESTIONS

YOU: I heard you on the radio last week, got *BUTTER BUSTERS THE COOKBOOK* at Sam's Club, and am motivated to try all the recipes. They look great! However, I really need help with meal planning. I really wish you had serving suggestions with the main dishes that cross-referenced the side dishes, salads, bread, and desserts. I have lost my creativity over the years and I don't have the time to pull it all together just before mealtime. Any suggestions?
—*M.G. Dallas, Texas*

ME: I sent this lady some suggestions. The following segment is the answer to her question. I hope this helps everyone who has requested meal plans.

YOU: I bought your *Butter Busters* cookbook. The one thing missing is a sample of daily menus. If you have a sample weekly menu, I would really like a copy. I am about 15 pounds over what I would like to weigh. Please let me hear from you.
—*R.H. San Angelo, Texas*

ME: You aren't the first person to request sample menus. I'm sending you seven day's worth of recipes. I hope this helps. Good Luck!

YOU: I just bought your cookbook and can't wait to get started. My cholesterol is high, so I want to try this book. There was one thing I noticed that you don't have in the book that I wish you did. I would appreciate meal plans, for say 5-7 days. Could you please send me at least one week of menus on how you eat and what you cook? I want to stay in the 10% fat or less range a day.
—*D.B. Tyler, Texas*
P.S. I walk two miles four times a week, so as you can see I am exercising.

ME: (I sent this lady seven days of menus.) I'm glad you are excited about using the book. You will notice in the front of the *BUTTER BUSTERS* on pages XV-XVIII I've listed my personal favorites. This might help you decide what to cook as well as the following meal plans.

The reason I did not put meal plans in *BUTTER BUSTERS* was because I didn't want to make it look like some kind of diet. I don't consider low-fat eating a "diet," because I still eat all the foods that I always have, just converted to low-fat. I guess some folks would rather have it spelled out, but I would rather decide for myself what to cook, so it is hard for me to understand this concept. However, since this book is called, *I'M LISTENING!*, I feel it is my duty to give my readers what they want. For this reason I will list seven day's worth of menus from *BUTTER BUSTERS THE COOK-BOOK* (with page numbers from the 7th edition) plus a bonus Picnic Meal Plan, too! If the calories are less than you would like to eat, simply add another piece of bread, fruit, or extra vegetable to one or more of your meals. If you want less calories, simply leave off a dessert. I would not recommend going under 1200 calories a day (even if you are trying to lose weight). Instead, watch the fat gram count. You will notice how low-fat the meals are, but just look how much you get to eat. The reason the calorie counts aren't too high, is because they are such low-fat. Remember 1 fat gram equals 9 calories, and 1 gram of carbohydrate or protein equals only 4 calories. That is the real key to eating a lot more food if you don't each much fat. These meal plans are only guidelines for those who want it "all spelled out for them." I hope you will mix and match, and even add your own ideas. The most important thing about weight loss is to eat enough calories to keep your metabolic rate elevated by constantly fueling your body (with enough calories) and exercising aerobically 4-5 times a week to burn the fat on your body. If you have an earlier edition of the book, your page numbers will differ. If that's the case, simply use the index in the back of the book to locate the recipe.

Happy Healthy Cooking!

Pam Mycoskie

7 DAYS OF MEAL PLANS
Plus a Bonus Low-Fat Picnic

Note: The following meal plans are VERY low in fat as well as calories. The reason is because most of my readers requesting Meal Plans are trying to lose weight. If you wish to add a little more fat to your day, please do so with healthy choices (such as olive oil on your salad).

SUNDAY

	Calories (All Sugar)	Calories (½ Sweet 'N Low)	Fat Grams
Breakfast:			
Whole Wheat Pancakes with Maple or Cinnamon Syrup (page 159)	95 calories	80 calories	0.4 fat grams
Blender Fruit Smoothie (page 464)	128 calories		0.5 fat grams

Lunch:

I made the lunch a larger meal than usual, because many people eat their main meal for Sunday at lunchtime.

Country Chicken with Creamy Gravy (page 262)	230 calories		3 fat grams
Sweet Potato Fruit Salad (page 132)	127 calories		0.6 fat grams
Broccoli and Cheese Rice Casserole (page 188)	172 calories		0.9 fat grams
On the Double Dinner Rolls (page 166)	118 calories		0.4 fat grams
Cherry Cheesecake Delight (page 413)	82 calories	63 calories	0.01 fat grams

Dinner:

Chicken Tortilla Soup (page 334) (This recipe is new in the 7th edition).	137 calories		1.7 fat grams
Jalapeño Corn Bread (page 170)	103 calories		0.8 fat grams
Quick Cobbler (page 440)	204 calories	138 calories	0.3 fat grams

TOTAL FOR DAY:
1,396 calories (all sugar)
1,296 calories (made with Sweet 'N Low)
8.5 fat grams

MONDAY

	Calories (All Sugar)	Calories (½ Sweet 'N Low)	Fat Grams
Breakfast:			
Yummy Oatmeal Apple Squares (page 156)	85 calories	70 calories	0.5 fat grams
Lunch:			
Mexican Pita Pockets (page 239)	229 calories		1.6 fat grams
(Tortilla soup leftover from Sunday)	137 calories		1.7 fat grams
Dinner:			
Pam's Special Hawaiian Chicken (page 263)	360 calories	353 calories	3.4 fat grams
Layered Twenty-Four Hour Salad (page 143)	89 calories		0.1 fat grams
Artichokes Au Gratin (p. 199)	87 calories		0.4 fat grams
Pam's Best Beer Bread (page 163)	94 calories	78 calories	0.2 fat grams
Chocolate Meringue Pie (page 450)	228 calories	232 calories	0.8 fat grams

TOTAL FOR THE DAY:
1,369 calories (all sugar)
1,275 calories (made with Sweet 'N Low)
8.7 fat grams

TUESDAY

	Calories (All Sugar)	Calories (½ Sweet 'N Low)	Fat Grams

Breakfast:

Fruit Smoothie (page 464)	128 calories		0.5 fat grams
Broccoli and Cheese Omelet (page 154)	123 calories		0.3 fat grams

Lunch:

Spicy Chicken Salad (page 139)	158 calories		2 fat grams
Pam's Best Beer Bread (page 163)	94 calories	78 calories	0.2 fat grams
3 Orange Slice Candy Cookies (page 392)	132 calories	108 calories	0.3 fat grams

Dinner:

Pasta Pizza (page 235)	124 calories		0.8 fat grams
Light Spinach Dip (page 120) with Vegetables for dipping	120 calories		0.4 fat grams
Romaine Lettuce Salad with Dorcas Pohl's Honey Mustard Dressing (page 146)	56 calories	50 calories	0.3 fat grams
Honey Baked Onions (page 192)	148 calories		0.5 fat grams
Tangy Italian Cheese Bread (page 169)	113 calories		1 fat gram
Banana Pudding Cake (page 370)	186 calories	158 calories	2 fat grams

TOTAL FOR THE DAY:
1,382 calories (all sugar)
1,308 calories (made with Sweet 'N Low)
8.3 fat grams

WEDNESDAY

	Calories (All Sugar)	Calories (½ Sweet 'N Low)	Fat Grams

Breakfast:

Two Carrot-Pineapple Muffins
(page 180)...212 calories..........164 calories ....1.0 fat grams

Lunch:

Macaroni and Bean Bake (page 203)..........155 calories ....0.7 fat grams
Pam's Best Beer Bread (page 163) ....94 calories..........78 calories ....0.2 fat grams
Dump Cake (page 425) ....120 calories..........111 calories ....1.5 fat grams

Dinner:

Sweet Chicken and Rice (page 257) ....331 calories..........260 calories ....1.9 fat grams
Westport Room Salad (page 144) ....54 calories ....0.2 fat grams
Broccoli Soufflé (page 189)...........................64 calories ....0.3 fat grams
Streamlined Batter Bread (page 165)..........124 calories..........119 calories ....0.5 fat grams
Pam's Famous No-Guilt Mud Pie
(page 438)...248 calories..........218 calories ....0.7 fat grams

TOTAL FOR THE DAY:
1,402 calories (all sugar)
1,223 calories (made with Sweet 'N Low)
7.0 fat grams

THURSDAY

	Calories (All Sugar)	Calories (½ Sweet 'N Low)	Fat Grams

Breakfast:

Mexican Eggs Olé (page 151) ....146 calories ....1 fat gram
Fresh Fruit (orange, apple, or banana)..........100 calories ....0 fat gram

Lunch:

Very Basic Tuna Salad sandwich
(includes bread on analysis) (page 136) ......200 calories ....1.4 fat grams
(1-oz.) Frito Lay Baked Tostito Chips ....110 calories ....1 fat gram
Two Molasses Oat Bran Cookies(page 395)......96 calories ....80 calories ....0.6 fat grams

Dinner:

Fresh Mushroom Soup
with Mozzarella Cheese (page 330)................33 calories ....0.8 fat grams
Italian Turkey Cutlets (page 243) ....277 calories ....2.5 fat grams
Creamy Scalloped Potatoes (page 214) ......149 calories ....0.2 fat grams
Hawaiian Sweet Bread (page 164)................131 calories ....121 calories ....0.4 fat grams
Cherry Crunch (page 425) ....105 calories ....84 calories ....0.1 fat grams

TOTAL FOR THE DAY:
1,347 calories (all sugar)
1,300 calories (made with Sweet 'N Low)
8 fat grams

FRIDAY

	Calories (All Sugar)	Calories (½ Sweet 'N Low)	Fat Grams
Breakfast:			
(Two) Oat and Raisin Bran Muffins (page 181)	158 calories	146 calories	1 fat gram
1 medium piece fresh fruit	100 calories		0 fat grams
Lunch:			
Quick Spicy Chile (page 243)			
(with beans)	216 calories		2 fat grams
(without beans)	178 calories		1.9 fat grams
Green Chile Cheese Corn Bread (page 170)	95 calories	89 calories	0.4 fat grams
Strawberries Romanoff (page 423)	192 calories	170 calories	1.7 fat grams
Dinner:			
Chicken Tetrazzini (page 251)	125 calories		1 fat gram
Apple and Orange Slaw (page 132)	90 calories	80 calories	0.2 fat grams
Jalapeño Cheese Spinach Casserole (page 194)	42 calories		0.3 fat grams
Cheese Bread (page 169)	113 calories	111 calories	0.6 fat grams
Banana Pudding Cake (page 370)	186 calories	158 calories	2 fat grams

TOTAL FOR THE DAY:
1,317 calories (1279 without beans in chile and all sugar)
1,237 calories (made with Sweet 'N Low and beans in chile)
9.1 fat grams

SATURDAY

	Calories (All Sugar)	Calories (½ Sweet 'N Low)	Fat Grams
Breakfast:			
Apple Sour Cream Coffee Cake (page 377)	100 calories	85 calories	0.2 fat grams
Lunch:			
Mexican Spaghetti (page 266)	158 calories		2 fat grams
(1-oz.) Frito brand or Smart Temptations Low-Fat Tortilla Chips (or homemade chips on page 121)	110 calories		1 fat gram
Best Pound Cake (page 357)	269 calories	217 calories	0.3 fat grams
Dinner:			
Calamari and Shrimp with Linguine (page 291)	189 calories		1.9 fat grams
Italian Minestrone Soup (page 329)	151 calories		0.6 fat grams
Artichoke Salad with Caper Dressing (page 145)	76 calories		0.6 fat grams
Tangy Italian Cheese Bread (page 169)	113 calories		1 fat gram
Hot Fudge Pudding Cake (page 358)	137 calories	124 calories	0.5 fat grams

TOTAL FOR THE DAY:
1,303 calories (all sugar)
1,223 calories (made with Sweet 'N Low)
8.1 fat grams

A LOW-FAT PICNIC

	Calories (All Sugar)	Calories (½ Sweet 'N Low)	Fat Grams
Mock Deviled Eggs (page 127)	19 calories		0.1 fat grams
Sweet Pickle Potato Salad (page 142)	162 calories		0.9 fat grams
Oven Baked Fried Chicken (259)	238 calories		3.5 fat grams
Calico Cole Slaw (page 144)	33 calories	28 calories	0.1 fat grams
Easy Fudge Brownies (page 409)	83 calories		1.3 fat grams

TOTALS:
535 calories (all sugar)
447 calories (made with Sweet 'N Low)
5.9 fat grams

I hope you will enjoy these sample menus from *BUTTER BUSTERS THE COOKBOOK*.

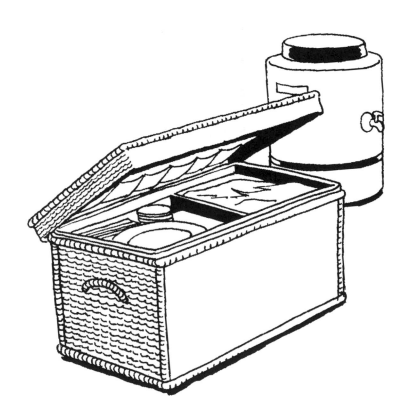

NOTES

THE
COOKBOOK

Equivalent Weights and Measures

Dry Measures	Liquid Measures
3 tsp. = 1 Tbs.	½ fluid ounce
6 tsp. = 2 Tbs.	1 fluid ounce
4 Tbs. = ¼ cup	2 fluid ounces
5 ⅓ Tbs. = ⅓ cup	2.7 fluid ounces
8 Tbs. = ½ cup	4 fluid ounces
12 Tbs. = ¾ cup	6 fluid ounces
16 Tbs. = 1 cup	8 fluid ounces
2 cups = 1 pint	16 fluid ounces
4 cups = 1 quart	32 fluid ounces
4 quarts = 1 gallon	128 fluid ounces

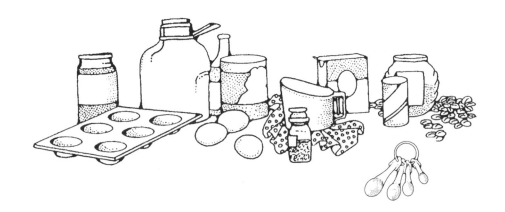

COOKBOOK GUIDELINES

Emergency Substitutions

If You Don't Have	Substitute
1 cup cake flour	1 cup minus 2 Tbs. all-purpose flour
1 cup self-rising flour	1 cup all-purpose flour, ½ tsp. baking soda, 1 ½ tsp. baking powder, and ½ tsp. lite salt
1 Tbs. cornstarch	2 Tbs. all-purpose flour
1 tsp. baking powder	¼ tsp. baking soda plus ½ cup buttermilk or sour milk (to replace ½ cup of the liquid in the recipe)
1 pkg. active dry yeast	1 cake compressed yeast
1 cup granulated sugar	1 cup brown sugar or 2 cups sifted powdered sugar
1 sq. (1 ounce) unsweetened chocolate *We would substitute this for fat purposes anyway.	3 Tbs. unsweetened cocoa plus 1 Tbs. liquid Butter Buds
1 cup buttermilk	1 Tbs. lemon juice or vinegar plus skim milk to make 1 cup
2 cups tomato sauce	¾ cup tomato paste plus 1 cup water
1 clove garlic	⅛ tsp. garlic powder or ⅛ tsp. minced dried garlic or ½ tsp. minced garlic in a jar
1 small onion	1 tsp. onion powder or 1 Tbs. minced dried onion, rehydrated
1 tsp. dry mustard	1 Tbs. prepared mustard
1 tsp. grated lemon peel	½ tsp. lemon extract

Refrigerator Storage

Dairy Products	Storage Time	Handling Suggestions
Liquid Butter Buds	3 days	store in container with a lid (airtight)
Egg Beaters	7 days	store in carton
Hard cheeses (unopened)	3-6 months	store in original wrapping
Hard cheeses (opened)	3-4 weeks	repackage in moisture-proof wrap
Soft cheeses (ricotta and cottage)	7 days past sell-by date	store tightly covered
Cream cheese	2 weeks past sell-by date	store tightly covered
Milk	5 days past sell-by date	store covered
Yogurt	7-10 days past sell-by date	store covered
Eggs (in shell)	4-5 weeks	store covered small ends down

Meat, Poultry, and Fish	Storage Time	Handling Suggestions
Flank steak	2-3 days	store in original wrapping
Ground turkey and chicken	1-2 days	store in original wrapping
Luncheon meats (sliced turkey and chicken)	4-6 days	store tightly wrapped after opening
Chicken	1-2 days	store in original wrapping
Turkey	2 days	store in original wrapping
Fish (store-bought or fresh-caught)	1-2 days	store tightly wrapped

COOKBOOK GUIDELINES

How to Analyze the Analyses

The nutritional analysis on all recipes is current with the information available in June 1995. Products change and so do their ingredients, so you must always read the labels. You will find when you look through the recipes that you are given a choice of fat-free substitutions in place of butter, oil, or margarine. You have the option of using Liquid Butter Buds, Fleischmann's Fat-Free Spread, Promise Ultra Fat-Free Margarine, or in some cases (except baking) fat-free chicken broth. You can see by the following chart there is a slight difference in nutritional information (especially calories and sodium content). Please take this into account when preparing your recipes.

Fat-Free Substitutions				
Nutrient	Campbell's Healthy Request Fat-Free Chicken broth	Promise Fat-Free Margarine	Liquid Butter Buds (made from mix)	Fleischmann's Fat-Free Spread (squeeze bottle)
	1 oz. (2 Tbs.)	1 oz. (2 Tbs.)	1 oz. (2 Tbs.)	1 oz. (2 Tbs.)
Calories	2	10	12	10
Fat	0	0	0	0
Protein	0.3 g	0	0	0
Carbohydrate	0.1 g	0	4 g	2 g
Cholesterol	0.2 g	0	0.2 g	0
Sodium	58 mg	180 mg	140mg	250 mg
Fiber	0	0	0	0

What about sodium?

I would like to inform each of you that using fresh vegetables instead of the canned variety will cut down on the sodium content considerably in the recipes. Many times canned mushrooms were used for convenience sake. If you are on a sodium restricted diet due to high blood pressure, substituting fresh mushrooms in the recipes when "canned" is listed would be advantageous. It is a good idea to rinse and drain all canned vegetables before eating to cut down on the sodium content. I always use sodium reduced chicken broth, soy sauce, and Worcestershire sauce in my recipes. You will notice that I always list the "lite" salt as optional. I recommend Papa Dash Lite Salt. It has the best flavor of any lite salt or salt substitute on the market. Always prepare food first without salt, adding it only when necessary. It is a fallacy that salt is necessary in baked goods for proper baking to occur. It is only NECESSARY in yeast breads. Even then, you don't need to use that much, and Papa Dash Lite Salt works great. In most cases salt is merely a flavor enhancer. Omit salt unless you find it necessary and you will cut down the sodium content in the recipes dramatically.

The following chart shows how you can cut down the sodium content by using Papa Dash Lite Salt in your recipes.

Papa Dash Lite Salt	¼ tsp.	90 mg. sodium
Morton Lite Salt	¼ tsp.	275 mg. sodium
Plain Table Salt	¼ tsp.	595 mg. sodium

IF YOU DO FIND SALT NECESSARY IN YOUR RECIPES, PLEASE CHOOSE PAPA DASH LITE SALT AND YOU WILL BE MAKING A WISE CHOICE!!

Sugar Substitutes—A sweet thought!

You will notice that all recipes containing sugar include the option of using Sweet 'N Low for one half of the sugar. In some cases this can make a considerable difference in caloric content. One cup of granulated sugar, for instance, contains 753 calories. On the other hand, one cup of brown sugar contains 793 calories. With 469 calories, powdered sugar contains the least amount of calories per cup. Even though MY PRIMARY CONCERN IS FAT, there are some people who need to monitor their sugar consumption (especially diabetics). It is for this reason, the option was included. The recipes include analysis using both methods for your convenience. The choice is up to you. The following chart will help you modify your own personal recipes using sugar substitutions. You will notice in the analysis that the only numbers affected by sugar substitutes are the calories and carbohydrates. In some cases the difference is quite vast, while in other cases it might only amount to a couple of calories difference per serving. At any rate, you now have an option and THE CHOICE IS YOURS!!!

Granulated Sugar OR Sweet 'N Low					
Granulated Sugar	¼ cup	⅓ cup	½ cup	¾ cup	1 cup
Sweet 'N Low Packets	3 packets	4 packets	6 packets	9 packets	12 packets
Sweet 'N Low Bulk	1 tsp.	1 ¼ tsp.	2 tsp.	3 tsp.	4 tsp.
Brown Sugar OR Sweet 'N Low Brown					
Brown Sugar	¼ cup	⅓ cup	½ cup	¾ cup	1 cup
Sweet 'N Low Brown	1 tsp.	1 ¼ tsp.	2 tsp.	3 tsp.	4 tsp.

Recipe Analyses

The recipes were computer-analyzed by the Department of CLINICAL Nutrition at the University of Texas Southwestern Medical Center at Dallas under the direction of Jo Ann S. Carson, M.S., R.D., L.D., Associate Professor and Director of the Coordinated Program in Clinical Dietetics.

Note: I would like to personally thank Jo Ann for the many hours she spent on this project using her spare time at home (on weekends). I could have never made my deadline had it not been for her generous help. Thanks a bunch, Jo Ann!

The analysis of the recipes is accurate to the best of my knowledge. Computer software programs can differ. If you find a discrepancy in nutrients per serving when using your own computer program, please realize this could be the reason.

Each recipe has a nutrient breakdown per serving. The nutrients include grams of fat, carbohydrate, protein, and fiber. Calories are listed along with % of calories from fat in each serving. Cholesterol and sodium content are listed in milligrams.

I use name brands in most of my recipes and the analysis was computed with the products listed. If you choose to use another brand, please check the label for nutritional information to compare fat, calories, sodium, cholesterol, carbohydrate, and fiber content for the most accurate substitution. Optional ingredients are not included in the analysis. If two choices are given in a recipe (for instance Betty Crocker "Light" cake mix and Pillsbury Lovin' Lites cake mix), the analysis was calculated according to the first product given. These options simply give you more freedom and variety in cooking to help fit your individual needs.

Suggested Nutrient Intake per Day:

Fat: 30% or less of total caloric intake (10% - 20% for weight loss)

Calories: Approximately your desired weight x 15 (not less than 1200 calories a day for a woman or 1,400 calories a day for a man)

Carbohydrate: At least 50% of total caloric intake

Protein: 20% of total caloric intake (or less)

Cholesterol: less than 300 mg.

Sodium: 2,400 mg. or less (unless you are on a sodium restricted diet)

Fiber: 25-30 grams a day (or more)

To find the percentage of calories from fat in a recipe, multiply the grams of fat by 9 (the number of calories per gram of fat) to get fat calories per serving. Next divide this quantity by the total calories and you will find what percentage of fat contributes to the calories in one serving.

To calculate the calories contributed by carbohydrate and protein, multiply grams of carbohydrate or protein per serving by 4 (the number of calories per one gram of carbohydrate or protein). Divide the quantity by total calories per serving.

For Example:
How to calculate the distribution of a 2,000 calorie diet:

50% carbohydrates = 1,000 calories ÷ 4 = 250 grams of carbohydrate

20% protein = 400 calories ÷ 4 = 100 grams of protein

30% fat = 600 calories ÷ 9 = 67 grams of fat
Or
20% fat = 400 calories ÷ 9 = 44 grams of fat
Or
10% fat = 200 calories ÷ 9 = 22 grams of fat

When you lower the percentage of fat in your diet from 30% to 20% or 10%, you can add more carbohydrate calories in their place. Remember fat calories are fattening, while carbohydrate calories are not (in reasonable amounts). The majority of fat calories you consume go straight to your fat stores. The carbohydrate calories are usually burned off immediately, or stored temporarily in the form of glycogen, and then burned for energy to make room for the next day's intake.

I hope this information makes all of the analyses in the book easier to understand.

Good Luck!
Pam

MAKING BREAD THE OLD-FASHIONED WAY
VS.
MAKING BREAD IN A BREAD MACHINE

I wish I could tell you the old way is better, but I'm afraid I would be telling you a fib. I'm sure there are plenty of folks out there who might disagree with me, but I certainly have enjoyed my bread machines. Yes, you heard me right, I actually own three different bread machines. You see, about a year and a half ago I wrote *BUTTER BUSTERS THE BREAD BOOK*. While I was working on the book, I needed to bake a lot of bread to test my recipes. With three machines I could bake about nine loaves a day. I really enjoyed testing and especially EATING all of that bread. I did run into a problem though. Originally I started out with all three machines in the kitchen. Well, bread machines use a lot of energy. I kept shorting out the electrical outlets. Finally I realized that I would have to separate my machines if I ever wanted to get anything done. You see, they would short out right in the middle of the bread making or baking process. It was VERY FRUSTRATING! I finally figured out if I put one in my bathroom, one in the laundry room, and one in the dining room, I could still use my kitchen for all my other cooking and testing of regular recipes for other books. You probably think all I ever do is cook. Well, I do that quite a bit, I must say! Just ask my kid's friends! They really do act surprised when they come over to visit that Mrs. Mycoskie really does cook all the time and spend half her life in the kitchen. I wonder just WHO they thought wrote my books, anyway! I haven't published *BUTTER BUSTERS THE BREAD BOOK* yet, because I was more anxious to publish this book and my next one, *THE BUTTER BUSTERS COOKNOTES* for *KIDS IN THE KITCHEN*. I hope to have that book out in early 1996. Even though it is directed at, and written for, kids (easy to understand and follow), the more than 100 new quick and easy recipes are some of my all time favorites! I think adults will enjoy reading and using this book as much as their kids (especially if they are a Mom or Dad themselves)! I think all parents will be able to identify with

what I have to say. After all, although our children might not realize it, WE WERE ONCE KIDS OURSELVES!! In other words, I've been there and done that....if you know what I mean!

I spent a few months cooking and experimenting with all kinds of new ideas. I even invited kids into my home to help me cook, taste, and (in some cases) help develop some of the great-tasting recipes included in the book. There will be a "Fast Food Restaurant Guide for Kids" (and adults who eat like them). There is even a chapter called "Cheat Sheet for Kid Cooks." It was written so children of all ages can participate. There are really easy "Beginner Recipes" (for children 4-10), "Intermediate Recipes" (for children 10-16), and

Roxie, Tyler, Blake, and Paige Madearis Studio ©
February 1995

even an "Advanced Recipes" section for teenagers and adults. Most adults know their way around a kitchen and ALL teenagers THINK they do! Just ask them! The advanced recipes may prove to be quite a challenge to some of our teenagers who think they know it all! Seriously, none of the recipes are difficult. My daughter Paige, who is 15, can make every recipe in the book. Tyler, who is 11, can make most of them, and Blake, who is almost 19, can't make any of them (however that is probably NOT what HE would tell you). Ha Ha! Well, I better stop talking or I'm going to give it all away! At any rate, watch for *THE BUTTER BUSTERS COOK-NOTES for KIDS IN THE KITCHEN* to hit the book stores in the near future!

Jeremy, Chase, Carter, and Collin

Back to the bread thing.....Like I said (before I went off on a tangent), bread machines are wonderful! They take all the guess work out of making perfect homemade bread. Not only do they save you hours in preparation time, the mess they eliminate (in my opinion) is their greatest attribute of

Bobby Brentlinger, Collin Ashworth, Chase Ellis, Jeremy Stewart, and Carter Ellis
January   1995

all! If you don't have a bread machine, I would consider asking for one this Christmas. If you love homemade bread (and who doesn't?) you owe it to yourself to get a bread machine. We are all busy these days and many folks don't have time to cook at all (much less bake homemade bread). Most bread machines are simple enough for children to operate (if they can read directions). Never mind on that one. Have you ever seen a four year old play a video game? I swear, I just don't know how they know how to play those games without reading directions. However, on the other hand, I CAN READ DIRECTIONS and it hasn't helped me figure them out.

If you do happen to own a machine, then simply follow the instructions in your owner's manual. I have listed ingredients for three different size loaves. All machines are a little different, but you shouldn't have any trouble with the recipes, since I have made them in three different kinds of machines myself. I own a Dak Turbo (my personal favorite), Welbilt, and Hitachi. Two of mine make large loaves and one makes a smaller loaf. One of my machines has a "Quick Bread Cycle." Bread machines get more sophisticated every day, so I would hate to recommend any particular brand or model, because they change so quickly. You just need to concentrate on what the most important features are to you personally. However, I would suggest buying a machine with a viewing window. That way you can see all the amazing things it can do and appreciate the fact that the mess and work are on the inside and you're not! Good luck, and I hope you will enjoy the various bread recipes I've included in this book (no matter how you choose to make them)!

In case you don't own a Bread Machine and would like to make the recipes in this book using the manual method, these directions are for

YOU!

MANUAL METHOD FOR MAKING BREAD

Step 1.
Pick a spot in the kitchen where you have plenty of counter space and can really spread out your supplies. You will need a large, heavy bowl (about 4 quarts) for mixing by hand or with a mixer. Make sure your counter is a comfortable height for you to work. Your counter needs to be at a height that allows your arms to be fully extended with your palms resting on it. Your back will thank you when you start kneading the dough.

Helpful Hint:
You can always use your kitchen table. That way, you won't have to stand up the whole time.

Step 2.
Pour ¼ cup warm water into your bowl. Next add a package of yeast and stir until it is dissolved. Use 120 to 130 degrees for all liquids. Stir in other warm liquids, Liquid Butter Buds (made from mix and hot water), or Fleischmann's Fat-Free Margarine (at room temperature), salt, sugar, or honey. Keep stirring until mixture is well blended.

Helpful Hint:
All of the recipes have liquid included, so when you make the recipe, simply subtract ¼ cup from the water or other liquid listed in the Bread Machine Recipe. For example: In the recipe for "Zulema's Favorite Sweet Bread" on page 362, the large loaf calls for ½ cup water. Therefore, you just add ¼ cup water, because you already added ¼ cup when you dissolved your yeast. I would always go by the water or liquid in the "large loaf" column, because if you are going to the time and trouble of making bread by hand, I'm sure you will be making the large loaf recipe, right?

Step 3.
Stir in the sifted flour and other dry ingredients about one cup at a time. Beat until dough is very smooth and stretchy (or elastic). Dough will be stiff. Mix at least 5-10 minutes.

Step 4.
Spread some flour on the counter and place the dough on the floured surface. Stick your hands in the flour and cover them well. This will allow you to work with the dough without getting all sticky.

Step 5.
Start kneading! This is the MOST IMPORTANT STEP because this is how the gluten forms "it's net" that "holds in" the bubbles coming from the yeast. These bubbles are what make your bread light and airy. Fold the dough in half. Push down and away from you. Turn it around and fold in half again. Don't be afraid to push really hard. The harder you work the dough, the better the texture

your bread will have. This will also help with the rising process. Push, turn, and fold it over again and again. If your dough is too sticky, add a little flour. The temperature of your kitchen will affect the amount of water or flour you need. If it is too dry, sprinkle a few drops of water over the dough and continue kneading.

Helpful Hint:

Kneading really isn't as hard as it seems, you just need to put your weight into it. To test if you have kneaded it long enough, after 10-15 minutes of kneading try pushing your clean hand against it. If it doesn't stick to your hand then it isn't too wet, and you know it is probably ready. Check to see if it is smooth and elastic (springy and flexible).

Step 6.

Put your dough in the same big bowl that has been washed and sprayed with I Can't Believe It's Not Butter! cooking spray. Spray a tad on the top of the dough. Cover with a clean dishcloth. Pick a nice warm place with no drafts (this is very important) and let the dough rise until it doubles in size (about 1 ½ hours).

Helpful Hint:

You can use the oven (not turned on of course) for the rising process because it is warm, dark, and draft-free.

Step 7.

Take your dough out of the bowl and punch it down. This simply means to knead it for a couple of minutes. At this time, you can add any cheese, herbs, or other ingredients to the dough. Divide the dough in two portions and shape into loaf size. Place each into a loaf pan that has been sprayed with a cooking spray (about 8 X 4 X 2-inch) or place formed loaves on a cookie sheet that has been sprayed with cooking spray. Most of the large recipes for bread machines will make two manual loaves of bread. Cover the loaf pans or cookie sheets with a dish towel and put them back in a warm place to double in size again. This will take about 45 minutes.

Step 8.

AND FINALLY... Place the loaf pans into a 350°F. preheated oven and bake until brown (40-45 minutes). Remove the pans. Tap on the bread and if you hear a hollow sound, this means it's done! Now for the best part....Eat it while it's warm with jelly, jam, or the low or non-fat margarine of your choice!

BEST HELPFUL HINT OF ALL:

Ask for a Bread Machine for Christmas so you will have more time to do all the other things you need to do like......clean the house.....pick up the kids.....go to work....pick up kids......go to the mall.....pick up kids.....go to the grocery store.....pick up kids.....cook the rest of your dinner..... pick up kids.....READ THIS BOOK.......Sure! Just TEASING!! BREAD MACHINES REALLY ARE GREAT FUN for the whole family!

**Paige and Courtney Ellis
Trying out the "Manual Method"
May 1991**

NOTES

SIPS

AND

DIPS

MOCK PIÑA COLADA
(A Pam Original)

1 cup Danon Light Piña Colada-flavored fat-free and sugar-free yogurt
1 cup vanilla flavored fat-free and sugar-free yogurt
¼ cup thawed frozen unsweetened pineapple juice concentrate
¾ tsp. coconut extract
¼ tsp. rum extract
1-2 cups ice cubes
1 cup Vanilla Guilt Free (fat-free and sugar-free) ice cream
4 thin lime slices for garnish

In a blender, combine both yogurts, pineapple juice concentrate, coconut and rum extracts adding a few ice cubes. Process until ice is coarsely chopped. Continue adding ice and processing until smooth and creamy. Add 1 cup Guilt Free Ice Cream (sugar-free and fat-free) and process until smooth. Garnish with lime slice on glass if desired.

Note: If you can't find the Piña Colada flavor yogurt in your area, you can use 2 cups vanilla yogurt. You might want to add a little more coconut and rum extract to add flavor.

Yields: 4 (1 cup servings)

Per Serving:

Fat:	0.2 g	Calories:	133	Protein:	9 g
Cholesterol:	5 mg	2% Calories from Fat		Carbohydrate:	24 g
Fiber:	0 g			Sodium:	122 mg

SIPS AND DIPS

FROSTY ORANGE DREAM DRINK
(A Pam Original)

2 cups skim milk
2 (6-oz.) cans frozen orange juice concentrate
2 tsp. vanilla
1 cup powdered sugar (or ½ cup powdered sugar and 6 packets Sweet 'N Low)
12 ice cubes

Place all of the ingredients and process until smooth and creamy.

Yields: 6 (1-cup servings)

Per Serving: All sugar

Fat:	0.3 g	Calories:	201	Protein:	4 g
Cholesterol:	2 mg	1 % Calories from Fat		Carbohydrate:	46 g
Fiber:	< 1 g			Sodium:	44 mg

Per Serving: ½ Sweet 'N Low

Fat:	0.3 g	Calories:	166	Protein:	4 g
Cholesterol:	2 mg	1 % Calories from Fat		Carbohydrate:	37 g
Fiber:	> 1 g			Sodium:	44 mg

PAM'S SECRET MOCK GUACAMOLE DIP
(A Pam Original)

2 cups cooked green split peas, drained and chilled (Prepare as directed on bag.)
1 Tbs. chopped onion
2 Tbs. lime juice
1 tsp. minced garlic (comes in a jar)
1 small tomato with seeds removed
1 (4-oz.) can chopped green chilies (drained)
Tabasco to taste
green food coloring
½ cup picante sauce
¼ tsp. garlic powder
½ tsp. ground cumin
¼ cup Kraft Free fat-free Miracle Whip or Kraft Free fat-free mayonnaise substitute

Cook your split peas (as directed on package) ahead of time and chill in the refrigerator 45-60 minutes. You can even cook them 1-3 days before you plan to use them to make the dip and store in the refrigerator.

Place all of the ingredients except Tabasco and green food coloring in the blender. Process until smooth. If the color isn't green enough, simply add a drop or two of green food coloring. Add Tabasco to suit your own taste. This can be used as a dip with baked Tostito Chips or with any of your favorite Mexican dishes. Olé!

Note: I have served this at parties and no one could tell the difference! In fact, they questioned the fact that Pam Mycoskie (the low-fat queen) was serving a dip so high in fat! I laughed and told them it was fat-free! They couldn't believe it. I really did hate to tell them how I made it. (I don't really care for peas and thought it would turn them off to my great-tasting dip.) Some things are best left unsaid!

Well, for all of you that wanted to know my secret, now you do!

Yields: 2 cups—8 (¼ cup servings)

Per Serving:

Fat:	0.30 g	Calories:	77	Protein:	5 g
Cholesterol:	0 mg	4% Calories from Fat		Carbohydrate:	15 g
Fiber:	1 g			Sodium:	458 mg

MOM'S ZUCCHINI BREAD APPETIZER

Margie Esposito
Coral Springs, Florida

3 cups thinly sliced zucchini (about 4 small)
1 cup Pioneer Low-Fat Biscuit and Baking Mix
½ cup chopped onion
½ cup Alpine Lace Fat-Free Parmesan Cheese (or Weight Watchers' brand)
2 Tbs. chopped parsley
½ tsp. Papa Dash "Lite" salt
½ tsp. seasoned salt
½ tsp. dried oregano
½ tsp. minced garlic (comes in a jar) dash of pepper
½ cup Liquid Butter Buds (made from the mix)
1 cup Egg Beaters
6 slices Borden Fat-Free "Sharp Cheddar" Cheese or another fat-free cheese of your choice
    (each slice cut in half)

Turn the oven on and set the temperature at 375 degrees. Mix together all ingredients (except cheese slices) and spread in a 13 X 9-inch pan that has been sprayed with Pam Cooking Spray. Bake at 375° F. for about 15 minutes. Remove, and add cheese slices on top. Return to oven and bake 10-15 minutes longer (or until golden brown). Cut into 24 squares and serve warm.

Note: This recipe was given to me by my dear friend Margie Esposito. Margie was one of the testimonials in my infomercial. She lives in Coral Springs, Florida with her husband Bill and their two children, Jessica and Billy. Margie teaches the low-fat lifestyle (as a result of her own and Bill's success with "The *Butter Busters* Low-Fat System") in her own hometown. Read more about Margie and Bill in "MY READERS INSPIRE ME" on page 486.

Yields: Serves 24

Per Serving:

Fat:	0.1g	Calories: 48		Protein:	4 g
Cholesterol:	2 mg	2% Calories from Fat		Carbohydrate:	9 g
Fiber:	<1 g			Sodium:	258 mg

TEXAS TRASH
(A High-Fat Snack Pam Modified To Low-Fat)

2 cups Wheat Chex cereal
2 cups Corn Chex cereal
2 cups Cheerios
4 cups Rice Chex cereal
4 cups fat-free pretzel sticks or small knots
¼ cup apple juice
½ cup Worcestershire Sauce (low-sodium)
1 tsp. garlic powder
2 tsp. onion powder
"I Can't Believe It's Not Butter!" Spray (You can find this great product in the refrigerated section of your grocery store with the margarine.)

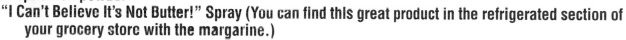

Turn the oven on and set the temperature at 225 °F. Combine dry cereals and pretzels in a large bowl or pot. Combine apple juice, Worcestershire Sauce and seasonings. Toss with cereal mixture. Spray a couple of large cookie sheets (or shallow pans) with I.C.B.I.N.B. Cooking Spray. Bake at 225° F. for 40-45 minutes (stirring every 15 minutes). Cool and store in airtight containers.

Note: Baking times may vary according to your oven. Check for doneness when you remove to stir mixture every 15 minutes.

Yields: 14 (1-cup servings)

Per Serving:

Fat:	0.4 g	Calories:	127	Protein:	3 g
Cholesterol:	0 mg	3% Calories from Fat		Carbohydrate:	28 g
Fiber:	1 g			Sodium:	318 mg

MEXICAN DEVILED EGGS
(A Pam Original)

1 dozen eggs, boiled, peeled and sliced in half (discard yolks because
    that is where all the fat is: 6 fat grams per yolk)
1 (8-oz.) carton Egg Beaters egg substitute (or other fat-free brand)
¼ cup Kraft FREE Miracle Whip (fat-free)
½ tsp. chopped jalapeño pepper (comes in a jar)
1-2 tsp. cumin seasoning (it's a Mexican seasoning)
    * Start with 1 tsp. and add to suit your taste
1 Tbs. yellow mustard
¼ -½ tsp. cayenne pepper (to suit your taste)
¼ tsp. Papa Dash "Lite" Salt (optional)
paprika (for sprinkling on top)

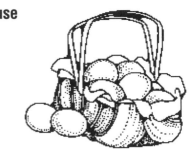

In an (8-inch) non-stick skillet that has been sprayed with a cooking spray, pour in the Egg Beaters. Cover tightly; cook over low heat 10 minutes or until just set. Remove from heat; let stand, covered for ten minutes. Remove from heat and cool completely. Chop finely and place in a medium-sized bowl. Add all of the rest of the ingredients, except the cooked egg whites. Blend well with a fork. When you add the seasonings, add a little at a time. Everyone's taste is a little different, and some folks like these spicier than others. Using a small spoon, stuff the cooked egg whites with the Egg Beater mixture. Sprinkle paprika on top and refrigerate until ready to serve. We like our food spicy here in Texas, even our deviled eggs!

Yields: 24 Mexican Deviled Eggs (Serving Size-2)

Per Serving:

Fat:	0.1 g	Calories: 31		Protein:	5 g
Cholesterol:	0 mg	2% Calories from Fat		Carbohydrate:	2 g
Fiber:	0 g			Sodium:	162 mg

SIPS AND DIPS

BREAD
AND
BREAKFAST

MOLASSES OATMEAL BREAD
(Pam Modified to Low-Fat)

2 cups boiling water
1 cup Quick Oats
#1—½ cup molasses or
#2—½ cup Aunt Jemima "Lite" Maple Syrup and ½ cup brown sugar or
#3—½ cup maple syrup and ¼ cup brown sugar and 1 tsp Sweet 'N Low Brown Sugar
1 tsp. Papa Dash Lite Salt
1 Tbs. Fleischmann's Fat Free Squeeze Margarine
½ cup warm water
1 pkg. dried yeast
4 ½ cups bread flour or all-purpose

In a large bowl, mix boiling water and oats. Let stand one hour. Add molasses (or maple syrup), lite salt, and margarine to oats and mix well. In a small bowl, dissolve yeast in ½ cup warm water stirring until dissolved. Add to oatmeal mixture.

Stir in flour. Beat well. Cover with a cloth and let dough rise in a warm place about 1 hour. (No kneading required). Spray 2 (9 X 5-inch) loaf pans with a non-stick cooking spray. Spoon dough evenly into the two pans. Let rise again for 45-60 minutes. Heat oven to 350°F. Bake loaves 45 minutes (or until golden, and when tapped lightly with fingers on top it makes a hollow sound). Remove from pans and cool on a wire rack.

Yields: Serves 24 (two loaves—12 slices per loaf)

Per Slice: Molasses Method #1

Fat:	0.5 g	Calories:	117	Protein:	3 g
Cholesterol:	0 mg	4% Calories from Fat		Carbohydrate:	25 g
Fiber:	1 g			Sodium:	23 mg

Per Slice: Maple Syrup and Brown Sugar Method #2

Fat:	0.5 g	Calories:	133	Protein:	3 g
Cholesterol:	0 mg	3% Calories from Fat		Carbohydrate:	42 g
Fiber:	1 g			Sodium:	34 mg

Per Slice: Maple Syrup with ½ Sweet 'N Low Method #3

Fat:	0.5 g	Calories:	107	Protein:	3 g
Cholesterol:	0 mg	3% Calories from Fat		Carbohydrate:	38 g
Fiber:	1 g			Sodium:	34 mg

OPRYSHEK'S FRENCH BREAD

The recipe was given to me by a dear man, John Opryshek, who owned and operated Opryshek's Coffee Etc. (a coffee and gourmet food shop) with his wife, Betty, in Arlington, Texas for several years, but has since retired. They were kind enough to sell my books in their shop when I first wrote _BUTTER BUSTERS_ (and published it myself in March 1992). He didn't even make a profit, but sold them to help me get started. I love his recipe for French Bread and I'm sure you will too!
P.S. John tells me he got the recipe from a man named James Beard.

5-6 cups bread flour
1 Tbs. Papa Dash "Lite" Salt
1 ½ pkg. yeast
1-2 Tbs. sugar
1 ½ cups cold water
1 Tbs. cornmeal
2 egg whites

John and Betty Opryshek
Arlington, Texas

Olan Mills ©

Do not preheat oven. Combine yeast with ¼ cup warm water. Add sugar and 1¼ cups cold water slowly. Combine sugar/yeast mixture with bread flour and salt. Knead for 1 minute. Cover and let rise 2 hours. Remove dough and form 2 loaves. Place them on a cookie sheet that has been sprayed with Pam Cooking Spray. Slash the tops with a knife. Brush with egg whites and sprinkle a little cornmeal on top of each loaf. Place bread in a cold oven and turn temperature at 400 degrees. Bake bread 35-40 minutes. This is a great recipe the kids can make. It doesn't require a bread machine, but will work in one. Just add the ingredients according to manufacturer's directions.

Yields: 2 loaves

Per One Ounce Slice:

Fat:	0.2 g	Calories: 58		Protein:	2 g
Cholesterol:	0 mg	4% Calories from Fat		Carbohydrate:	11 g
Fiber:	< 1 g			Sodium:	56 mg

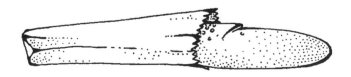

PUMPERNICKEL QUICK BREAD OR MUFFINS
(A Pam Original)

1 cup bread flour
1 cup rye flour
⅓ cup brown sugar (or 3 Tbs. brown sugar and ¾ tsp. Sweet 'N Low Brown Sugar)
2 Tbs. unsweetened cocoa
½ tsp. Papa Dash Lite Salt
½ cup raisins (optional)
½ tsp. caraway seed
1 ¼ cups fat-free buttermilk (This is made by pouring 1 Tbs. plus 1 tsp. lemon juice OR vinegar
   into a glass measure and adding enough skim milk to make 1 ¼ cups total liquid.)
¼ cup Fleischmann's Fat-Free Squeeze Margarine
1 Tbs. molasses
¼ cup Egg Beaters

Turn the oven on and set the temperature at 350 degrees (If baking the traditional way). If using a bread machine, simply place all of the dry ingredients into the bread machine canister. Next add all the liquids (including the margarine). Set your machine on the "Quick Bread Cycle." If making the traditional way, simply measure all of the dry ingredients into a large bowl. Add liquids and stir until just moistened. Pour into one (4 X 6-inch) large loaf pan, two (3X 5-inch) loaf pans, or 12 muffin cups.

Oven Method:
Spray the loaf pans or muffin cups with a non-stick cooking spray. Pour the batter in pans (fill ½-¾ full for muffins). **Bake at 400° F. 15-20 minutes for muffins and 350° F. 45-50 minutes for loaves.**

Yields: 12 muffins, 1 large, or two small loaves (1 oz.) per serving for sliced bread *Serving size for muffins would be 1 muffin.

Per Serving: Muffins

Fat:	0.4 g	Calories: 112		Protein:	3 g
Cholesterol:	0 mg	3% Calories from Fat		Carbohydrate:	24 g
Fiber:	2 g			Sodium:	80 mg

Per Serving: Muffins w/ ½ Sweet 'N Low

Fat:	0.4 g	Calories: 104		Protein:	3 g
Cholesterol:	0 mg	3% Calories from Fat		Carbohydrate:	22 g
Fiber:	2 g			Sodium:	80 mg

Per Serving: Slice of Bread

Fat:	0.3 g	Calories: 75		Protein:	2 g
Cholesterol:	0 mg	3% Calories from Fat		Carbohydrate:	16 g
Fiber:	1 g			Sodium:	53 mg

Per Serving: Slice of Bread w/ ½ Sweet 'N Low

Fat:	0.3 g	Calories: 69		Protein:	2 g
Cholesterol:	0 mg	3% Calories from Fat		Carbohydrate:	15 g
Fiber:	1 g			Sodium:	53 mg

ZULEMA'S FAVORITE SWEET BREAD

(I named this for Zulema, because she really loved this bread when I was developing recipes for my *BUTTER BUSTERS THE BREAD BOOK*.)

Ingredients:	Small	Medium	Large
skim milk	½ cup	¾ cup	1 cup
Fleischmann's Fat-Free Margarine or Liquid Butter Buds (made from mix)	1 Tbs.	1½ Tbs.	2 Tbs.
Egg Beaters	¼ cup	¼ cup	½ cup
Papa Dash "Lite" Salt	½ tsp.	½ tsp.	¾ tsp.
sugar	3 Tbs.	¼ cup	½ cup
bread flour	1½ cups	2 cups	3 cups
yeast	1 tsp.	1½ tsp.	2½ tsp.

*Add ingredients according to manufacturer's instructions.

The shape of your bread will depend on the type of Bread Machine you own. I have a Dak, Welbilt and Hitachi. When I was writing the Bread Book, I needed three machines to test all the bread I was baking. I usually made nine loaves a day! We were eating bread for breakfast, lunch, and dinner. I love bread and so does my family! I make homemade bread 3-4 times a week!

Note: This is a high-rising bread. For that reason, do not increase the yeast or decrease the salt. If you change the amounts I suggested, your bread might rise too much!

Madearis Studio ©

Pam and Zulema

Yields Small loaf (1 lb.) • Medium Loaf (1 ½ lb.) • Large Loaf (2 lb.)

Per 1 oz. Serving:

Fat:	0.3 g	Calories:	73	Protein:	3 g
Cholesterol:	0 mg	4% Calories from Fat		Carbohydrate:	15 g
Fiber:	<1 g			Sodium:	47 mg

PLEASE AND THANK YOU BLUEBERRY MUFFINS
(A Pam Original)

1 cup Fleischmann's Fat-Free Squeeze Margarine
1 cup brown sugar (or ½ cup brown sugar and 2 tsp. Sweet 'N Low Brown)
1 cup granulated sugar (or ½ cup sugar and 6 packets Sweet 'N Low)
2 tsp. vanilla extract
¾ cup Egg Beaters
1 cup Land O Lakes NO-FAT sour cream
1 tsp. baking powder
1 tsp. soda
3 cups all-purpose flour
1 (15-oz.) can "Thank You" brand rinsed and drained Blueberries (or other brand)

Turn the oven and set the temperature at 400 degrees. Cream together the margarine and both sugars, add the Egg Beaters and vanilla blending well. Add the sifted dry ingredients alternately with the sour cream. Gently fold in the blueberries. Spray muffin tins with "I Can't Believe It's Not Butter!" cooking spray and fill each cup ½-¾ full. Bake at 400° F. 12-16 minutes (depending on your oven and how many you are baking at a time) *Check them after 12 minutes, and go from there.

Note: This recipe started out as a cookie recipe that I was modifying to low-fat. The dough was just too runny, and I didn't want to add more flour, because the batter tasted so good. I looked in my pantry to see if I could get any ideas what to do with the batter. Sitting on the shelf right in front of me was a can of "Thank You" brand blueberries. I have tried for months to come up with a home-made blueberry muffin recipe that tastes as good as the Krusteaz brand fat-free mix that you buy in the store. They really are hard to beat, but I thought that I would give it one last try. Well, my whole family loved them and said they were the best they had ever had. I said, "Thank You" and they said, "Please" make some more tomorrow. And that is why I decided to call them my "PLEASE AND THANK YOU BLUEBERRY MUFFINS." Now, aren't you glad I shared that little tid-bit with you?

Yields: 3 dozen muffins

Per Muffin: All sugar		
Fat: 0.1 g	Calories: 97	Protein: 2 g
Cholesterol: 0 mg	1% Calories from Fat	Carbohydrate: 22 g
Fiber: < 1 g		Sodium: 105 mg

Per Muffin: ½ Sweet 'N Low		
Fat: 0.1 g	Calories: 76	Protein: 2 g
Cholesterol: 0 mg	1% Calories from Fat	Carbohydrate: 17 g
Fiber: <1 g		Sodium: 105 mg

EASY FOCACCIA BREAD
(Pam Modified to Low-fat)
(Pronounced Fo-ca-she-ah)

GARLIC

1 (16-oz.) pkg. "Original" Pillsbury Hot Roll Mix
½ cup wheat germ (optional)
1 Tbs. chopped fresh basil or 1 tsp. dried basil
1 Tbs. fresh chopped oregano or 1 tsp. dried oregano
1 ½ tsp. minced garlic (comes in a jar) or ½ tsp. garlic powder
1 ¼ cups hot water
¼ cup Egg Beaters
2 Tbs. Fleischmann's Fat-Free Spread (squeeze bottle)
1 medium onion, thinly sliced (about 1 cup)
Pam Olive Oil Cooking Spray

Turn the oven on and set the temperature at 375 degrees. Lightly spray 2 large baking sheets with Pam Olive Oil Cooking Spray. Prepare hot roll mix according to directions, stirring in the wheat germ, basil, oregano, minced garlic, water, Egg Beaters, and margarine. In a non-stick skillet sprayed with Pam Olive Oil Cooking Spray, sauté sliced onions about 2-3 minutes or until softened. Divide dough in half. Pat dough out into 8-inch circles on prepared baking sheets. Lightly press cooked onions on top of loaves. Sprinkle with a little additional wheat germ if desired. Bake 20-25 minutes at 375°F., or until golden brown.

> Yields: Serves 12 (⅙ of a loaf per serving)
> 2 (8-inch) round loaves

Per Serving:

Fat:	1.9 g	Calories: 134	Protein:	4 g
Cholesterol:	0 mg	13% Calories from Fat	Carbohydrate:	24 g
Fiber:	< 1 g		Sodium:	239 mg

BREAD AND BREAKFAST

DELL'S FAVORITE OREGANO CHEESE BREAD
(A Pam Original)

**Dell Ellis
Arlington, Texas**

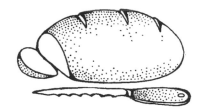

This recipe is for all of you that own a Bread Machine. I actually wrote *BUTTER BUSTERS THE BREAD BOOK*, but haven't published it yet. I have over 150 great low-fat recipes for bread. Maybe I'll publish it sometime. Until then, I'm including a couple of my favorites in this book.

Ingredients:	Small	Medium	Large
water	⅝ cup	1 cup +1 ½ Tbs.	1 ¼ cups
Fleischmann's Fat-Free Margarine	2Tbs.	2 ½ Tbs.	¼ cup
Papa Dash "Lite" Salt	1 tsp.	1 ⅓ tsp.	2 tsp.
Alpine Lace Fat-Free Parmesan Cheese	2 Tbs.	3 Tbs.	¼ cup
oregano	1 ½ tsp.	2 tsp.	1 Tbs.
bread flour	1 ½ cups	2 cups	3 cups
non-fat dry milk	2 ½ Tbs.	3 Tbs.	⅓ cup
yeast	1 tsp.	1 ½ tsp.	2 ½ tsp.

Add ingredients according to the directions that came with your machine. The small is for a machine that makes a 1-lb. loaf. The medium list of ingredients makes a medium-sized loaf (1 ½ lb.). The large indicates ingredients to make a 2 lb. loaf. All bread machines are different. Check out your machine's capacity and make your bread accordingly. Note: I personally like this recipe best with a touch of sugar. I usually add 1, 2, or 3 tsp. depending on the size of the loaf I am making.

Yields: small loaf: (1 lb.) • medium loaf (1 ½ lb.) • large loaf: (2 lb.)

Per 1 oz. Serving:

Fat:	0.2 g	Calories:	55	Protein:	2 g
Cholesterol:	0 mg	4% Calories from Fat		Carbohydrate:	11 g
Fiber:	< 1 g			Sodium:	49 mg

JALAPEÑO AND SUN DRIED TOMATO CORNBREAD
(A High-Fat Recipe Pam Modified to Low-Fat)

½ cup hot water
¼ cup sun dried tomato bits
1 cup all-purpose flour
1 cup yellow cornmeal
¼ cup sugar (or 2 Tbs. sugar and 1 ½ packets Sweet 'N Low)
1 tsp. baking soda
¾ tsp. Papa Dash "Lite" salt
1 cup nonfat buttermilk (check substitutions on page 336 for non-fat buttermilk)
2 Tbs. Fleischmann's Fat-Free Squeeze Margarine
½ cup Egg Beaters
1 cup fresh corn (about 2 ears) or 1 cup canned corn (rinsed and drained)
½ cup sliced green onions
3 Tbs. minced jalapeño pepper
½ tsp. minced garlic (comes in a jar)
Pam Cooking Spray

Turn the oven on and set the temperature at 375 degrees. Combine tomato bits with hot water in a bowl. Let stand about 10 minutes. Drain and set aside. Combine flour, cornmeal, sugar, soda, and salt in a large bowl. Make a well in the center of the mixture. Combine buttermilk, margarine and Egg Beaters. Add tomato bits and corn, onions, jalapeño, and minced garlic mixing well. Add to dry ingredients stirring until just moistened.

Spoon batter into a 9-inch square baking pan that has been sprayed with Pam Cooking Spray. Bake at 375° F. for 30 minutes or until a toothpick inserted in center comes out clean. Cool 10 minutes on wire rack.

Yields: Serves 16 (2¼ - inch square per serving)

Per 2 ¼-inch Square:

Fat:	0.4 g	Calories: 94		Protein:	3.3 g
Cholesterol:	0 mg	4% Calories from Fat		Carbohydrate:	20 g
Fiber:	1 g			Sodium:	150 mg

BREAD AND BREAKFAST

BACON AND CHEESE BEER BATTER MUFFINS
(A Pam Original)

1 can non-alcoholic beer or "Lite" beer
3 cups Pioneer Low-Fat Biscuit and Baking Mix
¼-⅓ cup sugar
1 cup Polly O Free (fat-free) or 1 cup Lifetime by Lifeline fat-free cheese
 (any flavor) *The Mild Mexican Fat-Free Lifetime cheese is good in this recipe.
4 Tbs. Bac-O's imitation bacon bits

Turn the oven on and set the temperature at 350 degrees. Mix everything together (except bacon bits). Pour into muffin cups that have been sprayed with Pam Cooking Spray. Sprinkle ½ tsp. Bac-O's on top of each muffin. Bake at 375° F. 25-30 minutes.

Option: You can make these plain without cheese or Bac-O's and they are still great!

Yields: 21 muffins

Per Muffin: with Bac-O's and cheese

Fat:	0.8 g	Calories: 113		Protein:	4 g
Cholesterol:	0 mg	6% Calories from Fat		Carbohydrate:	26 g
Fiber:	<1 g			Sodium:	413 mg

Per Muffin: plain

Fat:	0.3 g	Calories: 100		Protein:	2 g
Cholesterol:	0 mg	2% Calories from Fat		Carbohydrate:	26 g
Fiber:	<1 g			Sodium:	292 mg

APPLE RAISIN GRANOLA BARS
(A Pam Original)

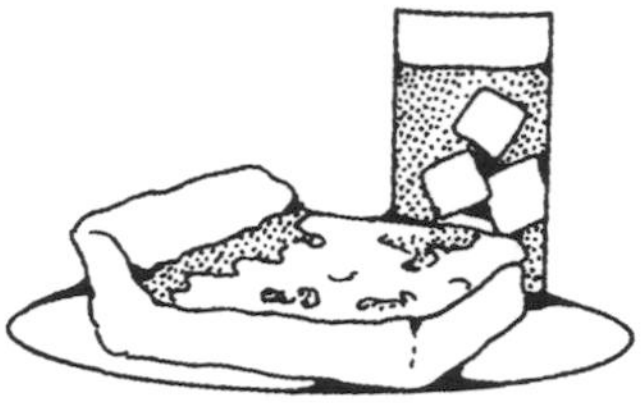

¾ cup flour (you can use whole wheat)
½ tsp. baking soda
½ tsp. cinnamon
¼ tsp. Papa Dash "Lite" Salt
¼ cup Fleischmann's Fat-Free Squeeze Margarine
    or Promise Ultra Fat-Free Margarine
½ cup brown sugar (or ¼ cup brown sugar and 1 tsp. Sweet 'N Low Brown)
¼ Egg Beaters
1 tsp. vanilla extract
1 cup Quick Oats instant oatmeal
2 cups Kellogg's Apple Raisin Crisp Cereal (fat-free)
¼ cup oat bran

Turn the oven on and set the temperature at 350 degrees. Spray a 9 X 13-inch baking dish or pan with Pam Cooking Spray. In a small bowl, stir together flour, baking soda, cinnamon, and lite salt. In a large bowl, beat together brown sugar, margarine, Egg Beaters, and vanilla with an electric mixer on medium speed until smooth. Beat in flour mixture until soft dough forms. Fold oatmeal, cereal, and oat bran into dough. Spread dough in prepared baking dish. Bake 20-25 minutes, or until top is golden brown and a toothpick inserted comes out clean. Remove pan to a rack and cut into 30 bars immediately and let cool to harden. Store in an airtight container.

Option: If your kids don't like raisins, you can use plain cornflakes cereal or wheat flakes cereal in place of the Apple Raisin Crisp Cereal.

Yields: 30 bars

Per Bar: All sugar

Fat:	0.3 g	Calories:	48	Protein:	1 g
Cholesterol:	0 mg	5% Calories from Fat		Carbohydrate:	11 g
Fiber:	1 g			Sodium:	61 mg

Per Bar: ½ Sweet 'N Low

Fat:	0.3 g	Calories:	41	Protein:	1 g
Cholesterol:	0 mg	5% Calories from Fat		Carbohydrate:	9 g
Fiber:	1 g			Sodium:	61 mg

BREAD AND BREAKFAST

MORN'N HONEY PANCAKES
(A High-Fat Recipe Pam Modified to Low-Fat)

3 Tbs. honey
½ cup Egg Beaters
¼ cup Fleischmann's Fat-Free Spread (squeeze bottle)
1 cup skim milk
2 cups Pioneer Low-Fat Biscuit and Baking Mix

Combine honey, Egg Beaters and margarine. Add the other ingredients mixing until smooth and the lumps disappear. Spray a griddle or large non-stick skillet with Pam Cooking Spray. Preheat the griddle to 325 degrees, or turn the heat to medium-high. Drop batter by ¼-cupfuls onto prepared hot skillet. Cook about 1¼ minutes (until bubbles form). Flip and cook another minute or so. Serve with warm honey and sliced bananas or the syrup or topping of your choice. I like to slice a banana and heat it with honey to top my pancakes. This recipe got it's name, because when the kids come in for breakfast I say, "Morn'n Honey."

Yields. 12 (4-inch) pancakes

Per Pancake:

Fat:	0.4 g	Calories: 130	Protein:	4 g
Cholesterol:	0 mg	2% Calories from Fat	Carbohydrate:	33 g
Fiber:	<1 g		Sodium:	407 mg

MIKE'S MOCK EGG MCMUFFINS
(A High-Fat Recipe Pam Modified To Low-fat)

4 English muffins or hamburger buns *I use hamburger buns (low-fat or Wonder "Light" Buns).
1 (8-oz.) carton (1 cup) Egg Beaters
Pam Cooking Spray
4 slices Borden "Sharp" flavor fat-free cheese
4 Tbs. imitation bacon Bac-O's (1 fat gram for two Tbs.) OR 4 slices Decker brand low-fat
  Canadian style bacon

Turn the oven on and set the temperature at 350 degrees. Using a biscuit cutter (or you can make a circle free-hand with a knife) cut out a circle to make a well being careful not to go all the way through. Cut center out of the top buns (the fatter ones) or the top half of each of the four English muffins. Lift the circle out with a fork and discard or eat. Place bun halves on a cookie sheet that has been sprayed with Pam Cooking Spray.

Pour ¼ cup Egg Beaters in each well. Bake at 350° F. about 10-15 minutes or until Egg Beaters are set. Wrap the other half of the buns or English muffins in foil and heat in oven while you are cooking the tops. Top each with a slice of cheese and sprinkle Bac-O's over cheese. Return to oven 2-4 more minutes. Put buns together to make sandwiches and enjoy. These are a great quick breakfast or snack when you are in a hurry!

Variation: Instead of the Bac-O's you can top the cooked Egg Beater with a slice of low-fat Canadian bacon under the cheese. Four slices of Decker brand Canadian style bacon are only 1.4 fat grams. This would be 0.3 fat grams per serving.

Yields: 4 Mock Egg McMuffins

Per sandwich: using Bac-O's

Fat:	1.5 g	Calories:	201	Protein:	16 g
Cholesterol:	0 mg	7% Calories from Fat		Carbohydrate:	30 g
Fiber:	< 1g			Sodium:	784 mg

Per sandwich: using Canadian style bacon

Fat:	0.3 g	Calories:	204	Protein:	18 g
Cholesterol:	5 mg	6% Calories from Fat		Carbohydrate:	29g
Fiber:	< 1 g			Sodium:	829 mg

BREAD AND BREAKFAST

HOT
OR
COLD

CHEESE BEER SOUP
(A Very High-fat Recipe Pam Modified to Low-fat)

½ cup finely chopped onion
1 large carrot, chopped finely (about ½ cup)
1 large stalk celery, chopped finely (about ½ cup)
3 (15 ½-oz.) cans Healthy Request Fat-Free Chicken Broth (low-sodium)
1 tsp. Butter Buds Sprinkles
½ cup all-purpose flour
2 cups grated fat-free cheddar cheese or 2 cups cubed Healthy Choice fat-free
   "Velveeta" style cheese (your choice)
2 Tbs. Alpine Lace Fat-Free Parmesan cheese
1 ½ tsp. spicy-brown mustard
1 (12-oz.) flat "Lite" beer *You can use the non-alcoholic version if you desire.
Pinch of cayenne pepper
Papa Dash Lite salt to taste (optional)

In a large saucepan, combine ½ cup chicken broth, chopped onions, chopped celery, and grated carrots. Cook until vegetables are limp. Stir in flour and Butter Buds Sprinkles until moistened. Add the rest of the chicken broth and stir with a wire whisk to blend until smooth. Cook and stir until mixture boils (about 3-6 minutes). Gradually stir in both cheeses cooking until melted (do not boil, once you add the cheese). Add mustard, cayenne pepper, and beer. Cook until well blended and heated through.

Note: If your soups starts to separate after adding beer, purée small amounts in an electric blender and return to pot and heat before serving.

Option: You can make this soup without the beer if desired. Substitiute 1½ cups evaporated skimmed milk or regular skim milk in place of the beer.

Yields: 6 (1-cup servings)

Per Cup:

Fat:	0.2 g	Calories: 121	Protein:	14 g
Cholesterol:	2 mg	1% Calories from Fat	Carbohydrate:	13 g
Fiber:	1 g		Sodium:	1148 mg

HOT OR COLD

CREAMY CLAM AND POTATO CHOWDER
(A Pam Original)

3 Tbs. Liquid Butter Buds (made from the mix)
3 Tbs. Healthy Request Fat-Free Chicken Broth
1 cup chopped celery
½ cup chopped onion
1 (8-oz.) can "Bits and Pieces" mushrooms, drained and rinsed well
4 cups boiled new potatoes, peeled and chopped (*You can use drained canned potatoes, but be sure and rinse well.)
½ tsp. Papa Dash Lite Salt (optional)
¼ tsp. dried thyme
¼ tsp. ground black pepper
4 (16 ½-oz.) cans minced clams, drained (reserving juice for later)
½ cup all-purpose flour
1 (10 ½-oz.) can Campbell's Healthy Request 99% fat-free Cream of Chicken Soup
6 cups skim milk

Sauté celery and onion in Liquid Butter Buds, reserved clam juice, and chicken broth until vegetables are tender. Add thyme, lite salt (optional), and pepper. Gradually add skim milk and Cream of Chicken Soup. Pour ¼ cup milk mixture into a glass measure. Add flour to glass measure blending with a wire whisk until smooth. Return thickened milk mixture to pot and continue to cook over low heat. Cook until thickened. Add drained clams, mushrooms, and potatoes. DO NOT BOIL! Simmer on low heat until ready to serve. You can garnish with a few oyster crackers sprinkled on top if desired. (*Oyster crackers contain about 1 fat gram for 10 pieces.)

Yields: 12 (1-cup servings)

Per 1-cup Serving:

Fat:	1.7 g	Calories:	213	Protein:	19 g
Cholesterol:	55 mg	8% Calories from Fat		Carbohydrate:	29 g
Fiber:	1 g			Sodium:	1134 mg

HOT OR COLD

CHAR'S LOOSE CHILI
(A Char Doehler Original)

Char Doehler
Granbury, Texas

1 lb. Broken Arrow Ranch Brand ground venison (11 fat grams a pound), Vermillion Valley Low-Fat Ground Beef (16 fat grams a pound), or The Turkey Store Extra Lean Turkey Breast Meat (6 fat grams a pound)
3 (15-oz.) cans Mexican Style Chili Beans, undrained
2 cans (28 ½-oz.) cans Hunts "Light" Fat-Free Spaghetti sauce (or other fat-free brand)
2 (10-oz.) cans Ro-Tel Diced Tomatoes and Green Chilies, undrained

Cook and drain the meat. In a large pot, combine all of the ingredients and heat about 30 minutes. This recipe is quick and good. It really is easy enough for a child to make. It resembles soup because it is not as thick as chili. I guess that is why Mom calls it "Loose Chili."
This is great served with my Jalapeño & Tomato Cornbread on page 366.

Yields: 14 (1-cup servings)

Per Serving: made with venison

Fat: 1.8 g	Calories: 213	Protein: 18 g
Cholesterol: 29 mg	7% Calories from Fat	Carbohydrate: 30 g
Fiber: 6 g		Sodium: 649 mg

Per Serving: made with Vermillion Valley Low-Fat Beef

Fat: 2.1 g	Calories: 209	Protein: 16 g
Cholesterol: 16 mg	9% Calories from Fat	Carbohydrate: 31 g
Fiber: 6 g		Sodium: 700 mg

Per Serving: made with Extra Lean Turkey Breast Meat

Fat: 1.5 g	Calories: 205	Protein: 17 g
Cholesterol: 15 mg	6% Calories from Fat	Carbohydrate: 30 g
Fiber: 6 g		Sodium: 657 mg

Please note: One day when I was making my Mom's "Loose Chili" I didn't have enough of the Mexican Style Chili Beans, so I made some substitutions and ended up with a recipe I call **"A Blast From the Past Bean Soup."** If you are from Texas (especially the Dallas/Ft. Worth area) you will probably remember a restaurant called "Jamie's." It was a (kind of fancy) hamburger restaurant with little flags on the tables. You raised your flag if you needed your waitress or were ready to order. Anyway, they had this Bean Soup they served as an appetizer with chips (for dipping). Mike and I used to eat there all the time in the early '70s when we first got married and lived in Dallas.

When I made the changes in Mom's recipe, and tasted my new creation, I couldn't believe my tastebuds! It tasted just like "Jamie's Bean Soup." It was like de-ja-vu. Mike was on the phone in the next room and Paige was in the kitchen with me (watching as I went nuts about the soup). I think she figured that I was finally flipping out. (After all, I had been cooking like crazy and staying up every night for the past four weeks until 3:00 or 4:00 in the morning trying to finish this book.)

I told her not to say anything, but I was going to ask Dad to taste it when he got off the phone. When Mike walked in I could hardly contain myself. I just knew he was going to agree with me! I said, "Mike, I have something that I would like you to taste. Tell me if it resembles anything you have ever eaten." Paige stood by watching (as she rolled her eyes). He took one bite and started laughing. He said, "I know exactly what it tastes like but I'm not going to give you the satisfaction of telling you." (Of course, he was just kidding.) As Paige stood there watching us I could tell what she was thinking. (Wow, they are both going nuts!) He turned to her and said, "It tastes just like the Bean Soup at Jamie's Restaurant." I couldn't believe it and Paige REALLY COULDN'T BELIEVE IT!

That restaurant closed down over 15 years ago, yet Mike and I both remembered just how their Bean Soup tasted. We used to go there a lot to eat, because it was inexpensive and really good, too! Even though this recipe is almost exactly like Mom's "Loose Chili," I just had to add my version of "Jamie's Bean Soup" A BLAST-FROM-THE-PAST BEAN SOUP!

HOT OR COLD

A "BLAST FROM THE PAST" BEAN SOUP
(Pam's Version of "Jamie's Bean Soup")

2 (15-oz.) cans of Mexican Style Beans in Chile Sauce (any brand), undrained
1 (10-oz.) can "Old El Paso" brand Mild Enchilada Sauce
1 (15-oz.) can Ranch Style Pinto Beans, rinsed and drained
1 (15.5-oz.) "Green Giant" brand Light Kidney Beans, rinsed and drained
2 (27 ½-oz.) jars of Ragu "Light" Pasta Sauce (Tomato and Herb flavor)
2 (10-oz.) cans of Ro-Tel Diced Tomatoes & Green Chilies, undrained
1 lb. "The Turkey Store" Extra Lean ground turkey breast (6 fat grams a pound) cooked and drained

Lightly spray "I Can't Believe It's Not Butter!" cooking spray in a non-stick large pot. Cook the turkey about 5 minutes. There won't be any grease. Pour in all of the ingredients and cook on low about 30 minutes. If you remember "Jamie's Bean Soup," let me know if you agree with Mike and me on this recipe!

Note: Serve it with baked Frito-Lay Tostito Chips for dipping!

Yields: 14 (1-cup) servings

Per Serving: one cup

Fat:	1.2 g	Calories:	231	Protein:	17 g
Cholesterol:	14 mg	5% Calories from Fat		Carbohydrate:	38 g
Fiber:	6 g			Sodium:	718 mg

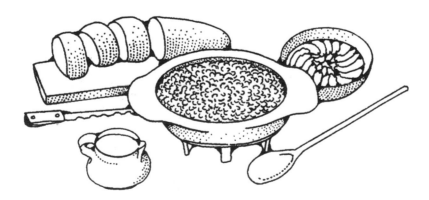

PAM'S BEST VEGETABLE BEEF SOUP
(A Pam Original)

2 lbs. Vermillion Valley Low-Fat Stew
    Meat or Broken Arrow Ranch Brand
    "chunk style" venison
1 large onion, chopped
1 tsp. minced garlic (comes in a jar)
2 cups chopped carrots
2 cups chopped celery
12 New Potatoes quartered with peel on
½ cup Healthy Request fat-free chicken
    broth (for sautéing vegetables)
1 (46-oz.) can Tangy V-8 Juice
1 (16-oz.) can green beans, rinsed well and
    drained (or you can use 2 cups frozen)
1 (17-oz.) can whole kernel corn, rinsed well
    and drained (or you can use 2 cups frozen)
2 (14 ½-oz.) cans (Del Monte or other brand)
    diced tomatoes and juice

2 whole bay leaves
½ tsp. ground black pepper
½ tsp. celery salt
½ tsp garlic powder
1 tsp. crushed basil
1 tsp. thyme
1 cup uncooked noodles
    (shells or other shape)
2 Tbs. low-sodium Worcestershire Sauce
3 (15 ½-oz.) cans low-fat beef broth or one
    large (46-oz.) can low-fat beef broth
    (Skim off any fat floating on top when
    you open the can.)
¼ cup red cooking wine

Using a large pot or Dutch Oven (another name for a big pot with a lid), brown the meat chunks and chopped onion in chicken broth. Add the remaining ingredients (except noodles) and bring to a boil. Reduce heat to simmer, and cover cooking about 30 minutes (or until vegetables are tender). Add the noodles and simmer 15-20 more minutes. If you like it spicy, you can add a chopped de-seeded Jalapeño pepper (when you add the other ingredients) for a little more zing! We like our food spicy in Texas!

Super Slicer Time Saver:
This soup is really quick and easy if you happen to own the "Super Slicer" (a device to chop and cut vegetables quickly). My son, Tyler, gave me one for my birthday! It is wonderful. If you want to order your own, call: (800) 652-4433.

Yields: 24 (1-cup servings)

Per Serving:

Fat:	0.8g	Calories:	136	Protein:	11 g
Cholesterol:	21 mg	5% Calories from Fat		Carbohydrate:	23 g
Fiber:	2 g			Sodium:	623 mg

ITALIAN TOMATO SOUP

4 cups tomato juice or 2 cups tomato juice and 2 cups Campbell's Healthy Request Fat-Free Chicken Broth
4 cups (15 ½-oz.) canned whole tomatoes, crushed (the quick method) or 8-10 tomatoes, peeled, cored, and chopped (making 4 cups) *To peel tomatoes, cut a shallow X-shaped slash on the bottom of each tomato. Drop them into a pot of boiling water for about 5-10 seconds. Use a slotted spoon and transfer the hot tomatoes to ice cold water immediately. Let stand 1 minute. When tomatoes are cool enough to handle, use a paring knife to pull off the skin.
8-10 washed basil leaves (to suit your individual taste)
1 cup (8-oz.) Pet evaporated canned skimmed milk
½ cup Liquid Butter Buds (made from the mix)
Papa Dash "Lite" salt to taste
¼ tsp. cracked ground pepper

Combine tomatoes, tomato juice and chicken broth (if using) in a saucepan. Simmer 30 minutes. Pour tomato mixture into a blender and pureé, along with the basil leaves, in small batches. Return to sauce pan and add evaporated skim milk and Liquid Butter Buds. Add salt and pepper to taste.

Note: The sodium content will differ if you use fresh tomatoes instead of the canned variety.

Yields: Serves 8 (1 ½ cups servings)

Per Serving: made with canned tomatoes

Fat:	0.2 g	Calories:	64	Protein:	4 g
Cholesterol:	3 mg	3% Calories from Fat		Carbohydrate:	13 g
Fiber:	1 g			Sodium:	645 mg

Per Serving: made with fresh tomatoes

Fat:	0.5 g	Calories:	79	Protein:	4 g
Cholesterol:	3 mg	6% Calories from Fat		Carbohydrate:	16 g
Fiber:	2 g				
Sodium:	567 mg				

BROCCOLI CHEESE SOUP
(A High-fat Recipe Pam Modified to Low-fat)

½ cup chopped onion
2 (16-oz.) cans Healthy Request Fat-Free Chicken Broth
½ cup all-purpose flour
3 (10-oz.) pkg. frozen chopped broccoli, thawed and well drained
1 tsp. low-sodium Worcestershire sauce
16 ounces Healthy Choice fat-free "Velveeta Style" cheese cut in cubes (½ of a 2 lb. box)
    or 2 (8-oz.) pkg. Lifetime by LIFELINE Food Co. fat-free "Mild Mexican" flavor cheese, cubed
    or grated (for a spicy cheese flavor)
2 cups skim milk or 2 (8-oz.) cans Pet evaporated skimmed milk (fat-free)

In a large pot or kettle, cook the chopped onion in ¼ cup of the chicken broth until tender. Stir in flour using a wire whisk (if you have one). Gradually stir in the rest of the chicken broth (1 ½ cups), broccoli, and Worcestershire. Over medium heat, cook and stir until thickened and broccoli is tender (about 10 minutes). Add cheese and skim milk (or evaporated skimmed milk). Cook and stir until cheese melts. DO NOT BOIL!

HOT OR COLD

Yields: 8 (generous 1 cup servings)

Per Serving:

Fat:	0.5 g	Calories:	139	Protein:	22 g
Cholesterol:	0 mg	3% Calories from Fat		Carbohydrate:	18 g
Fiber:	3 g			Sodium:	921 mg

TEXAS STYLE PASTA SALAD
(A High-fat Recipe Pam Modified to Low-fat)

<u>Salad:</u>
1 (8-oz.) pkg. rotini noodles (plain or tricolor)
½ lb. ground turkey (white meat, skinless)
¼ cup chopped onions
¼ cup Healthy Request Fat-Free Chicken Broth
1 (1 ¼-oz.) pkg. taco seasoning mix ("light" if you can find it)
1 (15-oz.) can kidney, pinto or black beans (drained and rinsed well)
1 (8-oz.) can whole kernel corn (drained and rinsed well)
2 medium tomatoes, chopped finely
1 small green pepper, chopped (optional)
1 cup grated Polly-O Free Mozzarella Cheese (or other fat-free cheese of your choice) *Lifetime
    by Lifeline Cheese Company offers a Mild Mexican Cheese flavor that is fat-free. This is
    delicious grated and used in place of mozzarella cheese.

<u>Dressing</u>:
1 (10-oz.) can RO-TEL Diced Tomatoes and Green Chilies, rinsed and drained
½ cup Fat-Free Italian Salad Dressing (your choice)
2 tsp. sodium-free herb seasoning (your choice)

Prepare noodles according to package directions. Drain. Brown the ground turkey and chopped onion in ¼ cup chicken broth in a non-stick skillet. Add the taco seasoning mix and cook 2-3 minutes longer. Cool completely. In a large bowl, combine all of the salad ingredients with the ground turkey and mix well. Add the noodles. In a small bowl, combine the dressing ingredients and pour over salad and mix gently to coat. Refrigerate until ready to serve.

Yields: 8 (1 cup servings)

Per Serving:

Fat:	1.2g	Calories:	256	Protein:	17 g
Cholesterol:	9 mg	4% Calories from Fat		Carbohydrate:	46 g
Fiber:	4 g			Sodium:	942 mg

HOT OR COLD

PAM'S CREAMY CAESAR FAT-FREE SALAD DRESSING
(A Pam Original)

1 cup Kraft Free Miracle Whip (or Kraft Free mayonnaise substitute)
1 cup Land O Lakes No-Fat Sour Cream
¼ cup lemon juice
¾ cup water
1 Tbs. minced garlic (comes in a jar)
1 Tbs. caper juice
1 Tbs. anchovy paste (This comes in a tube found in the spice section of the grocery store or in the canned seafood section.)
¼-½ tsp. ground fresh black pepper
1 tsp. Worcestershire Sauce (reduced sodium)
¼ cup red wine vinegar
¼ tsp. dry mustard
¼ cup Egg Beaters
2 Tbs. Alpine Lace Fat-Free Parmesan Cheese
1 Tbs. Dijon Mustard

Place all of the ingredients in a large bowl and blend with a wire whisk until smooth. Refrigerate at least one hour. This will keep a week in the refrigerator. This is my family's favorite Caesar Dressing!

Yields: about 4 ½ cups (24—3 Tbs. per serving)

Per Serving:

Fat:	0 g	Calories:	26	Protein:	1 g
Cholesterol:	0 mg	0% Calories from Fat		Carbohydrate:	3 g
Fiber:	0 g			Sodium:	257 mg

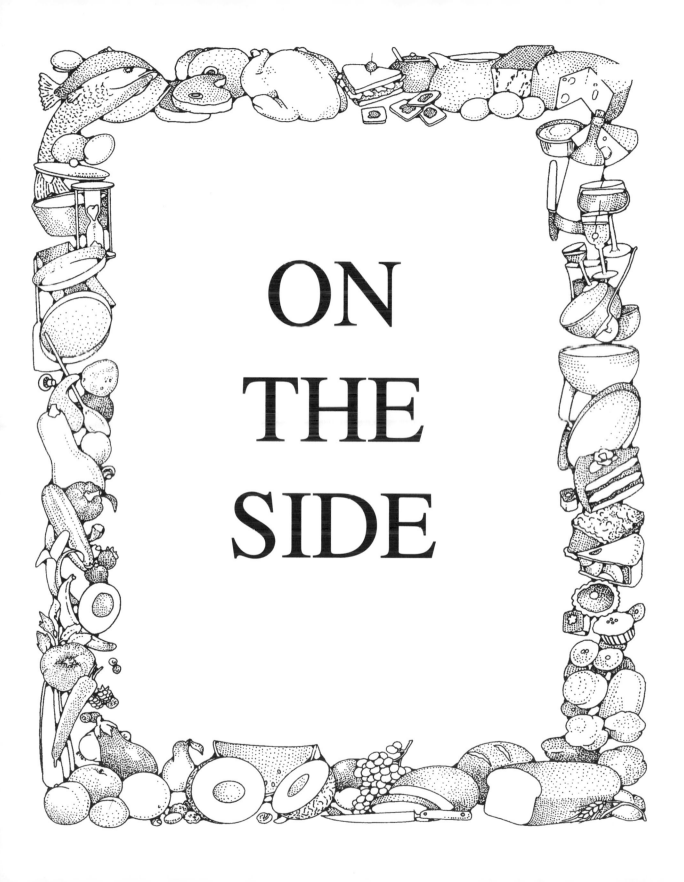

ON
THE
SIDE

CHEESE STUFFED POTATO BALLS
(A High-Fat Recipe Pam Modified To Low-Fat)

4 medium potatoes (baked or boiled and peeled) or a box of instant mashed potatoes (any brand)
1 (8-oz.) pkg. Lifetime by Lifeline fat-free cheese (Mild Mexican, Jalapeño, Jack,
**   Onion and Chives, or Sharp Cheddar) or other fat-free cheese of your choice**
½ cup crushed cornflakes (Kellogg's brand comes already crushed in a box
**   or crush your own with a rolling pin)**
½ cup Liquid Butter Buds (made from the mix)

Turn the oven on and set the temperature at 325 degrees. Mash potatoes, adding a little skim milk, with a hand mixer until smooth. Don't add too much milk, because you want them kind of stiff (not runny). If you are using instant potatoes, prepare as directed on box, omitting margarine. Use the directions on the box that serve 6. Prepare mashed potatoes in advance and let cool (you might even put them in the refrigerator about 15 minutes). Pour ½ cup crushed cornflakes on a small plate. Pour ½ cup Liquid Butter Buds on another small plate. Cut the cheese into 1-inch cubes. Form about ¼ cup mashed potatoes into a ball around a cube of cheese. Roll the ball in cornflakes crumbs, then in the Liquid Butter Buds. Place on a cookie sheet that has been sprayed with Pam Cooking Spray. Bake 20-30 minutes (check them after 20) at 325° F. or until golden brown. The balls can be prepared in advance and refrigerated until ready to use.

** You can make these ahead and freeze.

Yields: 12 Mashed Potato Balls

Per Ball:

Fat:	0.1 g	Calories:	90	Protein:	6 g
Cholesterol:	0 mg	1% Calories from Fat		Carbohydrate:	17 g
Fiber:	1 g			Sodium:	363 mg

NOT FRIED GREEN STICKS
(A High-Fat Recipe Pam Modified to Low-Fat)

3 medium zucchini
¼ cup Egg Beaters
2 Tbs. Land O Lakes NO-FAT Sour Cream
1 tsp. lemon juice
½ cup crushed Pepperidge Farms Herb Seasoned Stuffing mix
4 Tbs. Weight Watcher's Fat-Free Parmesan Cheese
"I Can't It's Not Butter!" Cooking Spray (or other brand)

Turn the oven on and set the temperature at 450 degrees. Cut each zucchini lengthwise in half. Next, cut each half into four strips (or as I call them green sticks). Blend the Egg Beaters, sour cream and lemon juice in a shallow bowl. Place the stuffing mix in a zip-lock baggie and roll over with a rolling pin to crush. Place ½ cup of the crushed mix on a large plate adding the Parmesan cheese and mixing well. Spray a baking pan with cooking spray. Dip each zucchini stick into the Egg Beaters mixture and then gently coat with the stuffing mixture. Place the zucchini sticks on the prepared baking pan and **lightly** spray them with the fat-free cooking spray. Bake for 10-15 minutes. Serve with fat-free Ranch Dressing or Ragu "Light" fat-free spaghetti sauce (heated) for dipping.

Yields: Serves 4 (6 sticks per serving)

Per Serving:

Fat:	0.4 g	Calories: 60		Protein:	5 g
Cholesterol:	2 mg	5% Calories from Fat		Carbohydrate:	10 g
Fiber:	1 g			Sodium:	152 mg

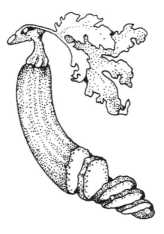

SWEET AND DELICIOUS CARROTS
(This Recipe Is Very Rich In Beta Carotene)

2 cups cleaned and (½-inch) sliced carrots (about ¾ lb.)
2 cups (½-inch) peeled, cubed sweet potatoes (about ¾ lb.)
1 (20-oz.) can unsweetened pineapple chunks, undrained
¼ cup water
2 Tbs. brown sugar (or ½ tsp. Sweet 'N Low Brown)
1 Tbs. cornstarch
2 tsp. low-sodium soy sauce
1 tsp. vinegar
½ tsp. grated orange peel
¼ cup golden raisins (optional)

Place carrots in a vegetable steamer; cover and steam over boiling water about 2 minutes. Add sweet potato; cover and steam an additional 8 minutes or until crisp-tender. Set aside.

Drain pineapple, reserving ½ cup of the juice. Use the rest of the juice in a fruit smoothie or another recipe. Combine ½ cup pineapple juice, water, and brown sugar, cornstarch, soy sauce, vinegar, and grated orange peel. Place over medium heat and bring to a boil, stirring constantly. Add pineapple and raisins and cook one minute. Combine vegetables and pineapple mixture in a large bowl. Stir gently.

Yields: Serves 6 (1 cup a serving)

Per Serving: all sugar

Fat:	0.4 g	Calories:	164	Protein:	2 g
Cholesterol:	0 mg	2% Calories from Fat		Carbohydrate:	40 g
Fiber:	4 g			Sodium:	84 mg

Per Serving: ½ Sweet 'N Low

Fat:	0.4 g	Calories:	149	Protein:	2 g
Cholesterol:	0 mg	2% Calories from Fat		Carbohydrate:	36 g
Fiber:	4 g			Sodium:	84 mg

ON THE SIDE

ALL SHOOK UP NOT FRIED ONION RINGS (OR SPICY FRIES)
(A High-fat Recipe Pam Modified to Low-fat)

1 large jumbo-sized sweet onion, cut into ¼-inch thick slices
½ cup beaten Egg Beaters (or 2 beaten egg whites)

Seasoning Mix:
1 tsp. Papa Dash "Lite" salt
1 tsp. pepper
1 tsp. chile powder
½-1 tsp. cayenne red pepper (depending how spicy you like them)
1 cup all-purpose flour

Turn the oven on and set the temperature at 425 degrees. Spray a cookie sheet with Pam Cooking Spray and set aside. Steam onion rings over boiling water (in a double boiler) about 5 minutes. Remove from steamer and immediately place in ice cold plain club soda water. Remove after 2 minutes and drain well. Pour beaten Egg Beaters in a shallow dish. Combine all the seasonings in a large zip-lock plastic baggie. Dip the onion rings in the Egg Beaters and coat well. Shake off the excess. Place the onion rings (one at a time) in the baggie and shake until well-coated. Place on the prepared cookie sheet and bake at 425° F. 10 minutes. Remove from oven and turn with a spatula. Return to oven 10-15 minutes longer or until lightly browned and crispy. Eat and enjoy dipped in ketchup or plain.

Note: You can chop these up and use them on top of casseroles or any time you would normally use those high-fat onion rings that come in a can!

SPICY FRY VARIATION: This recipe also works well to coat potatoes for spicy oven baked fries. Replace the onion with 2 medium-sized baking potatoes. Boil the potatoes until they are partially cooked (about 15-20 minutes). Cool until you can handle easily. Peel the potatoes and slice (lengthwise) into six pieces. Cut each piece into french fry sized sticks. Soak the fries in ice cold soda water about ten minutes. Dip in Egg Beaters (shake off the excess) and place in seasoning bag to shake and coat well. Follow the baking instructions above.

Yields: Serves 4

Per Serving: Onion Rings		
Fat: 0.6 g	Calories: 154	Protein: 7 g
Cholesterol: 0 mg	3% Calories from Fat	Carbohydrate: 30 g
Fiber: 2 g		Sodium: 140 mg

Per Serving: Spicy Fries		
Fat: 0.5 g	Calories: 192	Protein: 8 g
Cholesterol: 0 mg	3% Calories from Fat	Carbohydrate: 39 g
Fiber: 2 g		Sodium: 142 mg

ON THE SIDE

GARLIC MASHED POTATOES
(A High-fat Recipe Pam Modified to Low-fat)

3 lbs. all-purpose potatoes (6-9 potatoes), peeled and cut into chunks
6 cloves garlic, peeled (or 3 tsp. minced garlic in jar)
1 tsp. Papa Dash Lite Salt (optional)
¾ - 1 ¼ cups Healthy Request Fat-Free Chicken Broth, heated
3-4 Tbs. Land O Lakes No-Fat Sour Cream
fresh ground pepper to taste
pinch of nutmeg (optional)

GARLIC

Place potato chunks and peeled garlic cloves into a large Dutch Oven or pot and cover with cold water. Add ½ tsp. Lite Salt (optional) and bring to a boil. Cook, covered, over medium heat until the potatoes are tender. (about 15-20 minutes). Drain the potatoes and return them to the pan. Discard the garlic cloves. Shake the pan over low heat to dry the potatoes slightly. Remove the pan from the heat.

Mash the potatoes with a potato masher or a hand-held electric mixer. Add enough hot chicken broth to make a smooth creamy texture (don't add too much). Stir in the sour cream, lite salt (optional), ground pepper to taste, and pinch of nutmeg (if desired). Serve warm.

Option: You can also add ½-1 cup grated fat-free cheese stirred into the potatoes before serving.

Yields: Serves 8 (¾ cup per serving)

Per Serving:

Fat:	0.1 g	Calories: 111		Protein:	3 g
Cholesterol:	0 mg	1% Calories from Fat		Carbohydrate:	25 g
Fiber:	2 g			Sodium:	55 mg

ON THE SIDE

FETTUCCINE IN A FLASH
(A Pam Original)

1 cup Frigo or Polly-O FREE brand fat-free ricotta cheese (or other fat-free brand)
1 tsp. olive oil
½ cup Alpine Lace Fat-Free Parmesan Cheese
¼-½ cup skim milk (or evaporated skimmed milk)
½ tsp. minced garlic (comes in a jar)
1 pinch of nutmeg (about ⅛ tsp.)
¼ tsp. fresh ground black pepper
1 (8-oz.) pkg. fettuccine (no yolk) noodles
1 (6-oz.) pkg. Alpine Lace "Garlic & Herbs" Fat-Free flavored Cream Cheese

Bring a large pot of water to a boil for the pasta. In a food processor or blender, process the Ricotta cheese until smooth. Add the Parmesan Cheese, skim milk (starting with ¼ cup and adding more if too thick), "Garlic & Herb" cream cheese, Egg Beaters, garlic, nutmeg, salt, and pepper. Process until very smooth and creamy. Cook the fettuccine as directed on package. Drain and put back in the pan. Add the cheese sauce and mix. The heat from the pasta and the pan is enough to warm the sauce.

Yields: Serves 4 (1 cup per serving)

Per Serving:

Fat:	2.1 g	Calories: 335		Protein:	24 g
Cholesterol:	18 mg	6% Calories from Fat		Carbohydrate:	51 g
Fiber:	1 g			Sodium:	405 mg

THE
BIG
DEAL

MIKE'S FAVORITE FIESTA CASSEROLE
(A High-fat Recipe Pam Modified to Low-fat)

1 lb. "The Turkey Store" Extra Lean ground white meat turkey (6 fat grams per pound), ground low-fat beef, or ground venison
1 cup chopped onion
½ cup Healthy Request Fat-Free Chicken Broth
1 ½-2 tsp. ground cumin
1 ½ tsp. dried oregano
½ tsp. garlic powder
¼ tsp. Papa Dash Lite Salt (optional)
¼ tsp. ground pepper
1 (16-oz.) Old El Paso Fat-Free Refried Beans (or other brand)
½ cup picante sauce
2 (4-oz.) cans whole green chilies, drained and cut lengthwise into quarters
2 cups (one 8-oz. bag) grated Polly-O Free Mozzarella (fat-free)
1 cup frozen (thawed and drained) whole kernel corn or 1 (15 ½-oz.) canned corn (rinsed well and drained)
⅓ cup all-purpose flour
¼ tsp. Papa Dash Lite Salt (optional)
1 ¼ cups skim milk
⅛ tsp. Tabasco Sauce
½ cup Egg Beaters
2 egg whites

Turn the oven on and set the temperature at 350 degrees. Pour ½ cup chicken broth into a non-stick skillet and cook the ground turkey and chopped onion over medium-high heat until browned. Remove the turkey and onions from heat and place in a large bowl adding the cumin, oregano, garlic powder, pepper, salt (optional), picante sauce, and refried beans. Stir and set aside.

Spray a 9½ X 11-inch casserole dish with "I Can't Believe It's Not Butter!" Cooking Spray. Arrange half of the green chile strips in the bottom of the dish. Top with ½ of the cheese. Spoon the meat and bean mixture over the green chilies and spread evenly. Leave a ¼-inch border around the edge of the dish. Top with corn. Arrange the remaining chile strips over the corn. Top with the remaining 1-cup grated cheese.

Combine flour and lite salt (optional) in a medium-sized bowl. Add milk and Tabasco and stir with a wire whisk until blended. Beat the Egg Beaters and egg whites slightly and add to milk mixture stirring well to blend. Pour over the casserole. Bake at 350° F. for 45 minutes to 1 hour or until set and lightly browned. Remove from oven and let set about 5 minutes before cutting to serve.
Note: the high sodium count comes from canned ingredients and cheese.

Yields: Serves 8 (3 ½-inch square per serving)

Per Serving:

Fat:	1.1 g	Calories: 217	Protein:	27 g
Cholesterol:	26 mg	4% Calories from Fat	Carbohydrate:	26 g
Fiber:	4 g		Sodium:	1122 mg

THE BIG DEAL

PRESSED-FOR-TIME SKILLET DINNER
(A High-fat Recipe Pam Modified to Low-fat)

1 lb. The Turkey Store "Extra Lean Ground Breast" turkey (6 fat grams a pound),
(Maverick Natural Lite low-fat ground beef, ground venison, or Vermillion low-fat ground
beef)
2 cups (4-oz.) uncooked "No yolks" noodles
1 cup frozen whole kernel corn (or canned rinsed well and drained)
1 cup chopped green onions

<u>Sauce</u>:
1 cup water
½ cup thick and chunky salsa (Frito-Lay's salsa is good)
2 (8-oz.) cans no-salt-added tomato sauce

Brown turkey or ground beef in a non-stick skillet. If it is too dry (for lack of fat) add a little fat-free chicken broth to cook the turkey or meat. Drain fat, and wipe out the skillet with a paper towel. Return turkey to skillet and add all of the remaining ingredients (including noodles). Bring to a boil. Reduce heat to low; cover and simmer 10-12 minutes or until noodles are of desired doneness.

Note: Check the "Resource Guide" pages 539-540 for ordering information concerning venison and low-fat beef products.

Yields: 6 (1-cup servings)

Per Serving:

Fat:	1.1 g	Calories:	199	Protein:	21 g
Cholesterol:	33 mg	5% Calories from Fat		Carbohydrate:	27 g
Fiber:	4 g			Sodium:	127 mg

THE BIG DEAL

CHRIS AND BILL'S SUPER STROGANOFF

2 lbs. ground white meat skinless chicken
3 medium onions, chopped
2 (16-oz.) cans straw mushrooms, drained
1 (16-oz.) Land O Lakes No-Fat Sour Cream
2 (12-oz.) bags "No Yolk" egg noodle substitute
½ tsp. Papa Dash "Lite" salt
⅛-¼ tsp. white pepper
⅛-¼ tsp. lemon pepper
1 Tbs. paprika
3 Tbs. beef bouillon
1 Tbs. Worcestershire Sauce (low-sodium)
4 Tbs. Low-Fat Cultured Buttermilk Powder (for extra flavor and thickness)
    (Saco Brand - 0.7 fat grams per cup reconstituted)
½ cup water
Garlic Oil Cooking Spray
Garlic Oil (drops) (fat-free) (spice section of the grocery store)

Chris and Bill Beauchamp
Greentown, Pennsylvania

Boil "No Yolk" noodles according to directions on the package in a large pot. Spray a large skillet with Garlic Oil Cooking Spray. Put a couple of drops (Garlic Oil) in the pan for added flavor. Brown the ground chicken and chopped onions. Add the rest of the seasonings and water. Stir until well mixed. Add the sour cream stirring constantly. Fold in the drained straw mushrooms. Strain and rinse noodles. Spoon the noodles into a large serving bowl or 9 ½ X 13-inch baking dish. Pour sauce over noodles and toss gently.

Option: This recipe could be made with ground turkey, ground venison, or ground low-fat beef if desired. You can also add 1 (10½ oz.) can Campbell's Healthy Request 99% fat-free Cream of Mushroom Soup for extra richness. This would only add 0.3 fat grams per serving.

Note: Chris first wrote me a letter on December 7, 1993. (See her letter on page 484.) I wrote her back and over the past year and a half we have become good friends. We write each other about once a month. Chris was one of the Testimonials in my Infomercial. It was so exciting to finally meet my "Pen Pal." Chris is a darling woman who lives in Greentown, Pennsylvania with her dear husband, Bill, and their three boys Beau, Bryan, and Paul.

THE BIG DEAL

Yields: Serves 9

Per Serving:

Fat:	2.5 g	Calories:	485	Protein:	41 g
Cholesterol:	24 mg	5% Calories from Fat		Carbohydrate:	73 g
Fiber:	6 g			Sodium:	584 mg

MICROWAVE SWEET AND SPICY CHICKEN STRIPS
(A High-fat Recipe Pam Modified to Low-fat)

2 lbs. plain ButterBall skinless white meat chicken breasts (1 fat gram per 4 ounces)
1 envelope Lipton "Golden Onion Recipe" soup mix
⅓ cup honey
¼ cup water
¼ cup frozen concentrated orange juice, partially thawed
¼ cup cooking sherry
1 Tbs. prepared mustard
2 tsp. sodium reduced soy sauce
¼ tsp. ground ginger
3 dashes hot pepper sauce

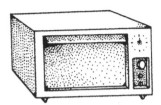

Rinse and drain the chicken. Cut chicken breasts into bite-sized strips. In a 13 X 9-inch casserole dish that has been sprayed with Pam Cooking Spray, blend the remaining ingredients. Add the chicken strips and coat well. Heat uncovered at HIGH (full power), basting and rearranging chicken occasionally 20 minutes or until chicken is done and sauce is thickened. Let stand uncovered 5 minutes. These Chicken Strips make a great snack or appetizer. They can also be served over fluffy rice as a meal.

> Yields: 48 chicken strips—Serves 12 as an appetizer (4 chicken strips per serving)
> Serves 6 as an entree over rice.

Per Serving: Appetizer

Fat:	0.7 g	Calories:	127	Protein:	17 g
Cholesterol:	16 mg	5% Calories from Fat		Carbohydrate:	13 g
Fiber:	<1 g			Sodium:	97 mg

Entree: Per Serving

Fat:	1.5 g	Calories:	254	Protein:	34 g
Cholesterol:	32mg	5% Calories from Fat		Carbohydrate:	26 g
Fiber:	<1 g			Sodium:	190 mg

THE BIG DEAL

CHICKEN A LA QUEEN
(A High-fat Recipe Pam Modified to Low-fat)

1 cup Land O Lakes NO-FAT fat-free sour cream
3 Tbs. all-purpose flour
2 Tbs. cooking sherry (optional)
1 (16 oz.) bag frozen vegetable mix (carrots, broccoli, water chestnuts,
　　and red peppers or your choice of vegetables)
3 boneless and skinless chicken breast halves, cooked and cut in bite-sized pieces
　　*You could also use canned cooked chicken
1 (10 ¾-oz.) can Campbell's Healthy Request 99% fat-free Cream of Chicken Soup
1 (10 ½-oz.) can condensed chicken broth
6 fat-free English Muffins (any brand) (split and toasted)

In a small bowl, stir together sour cream and flour. Set aside. In a 4-qt. saucepan, combine frozen vegetables, chicken, and chicken broth. Cook over medium-high heat until vegetables are crispy tender (about 5 minutes). Reduce to medium heat. Add sour cream mixture and Cream of Chicken Soup. Continue cooking, stirring constantly, until mixture thickens and just starts to come to a boil (1-2 minutes). Remove from heat and stir in lite salt and pepper if desired. Serve over hot toasted English Muffins.

Yields: Serves 6 (1 cup servings)

Per Serving:

Fat:	1.5 g	Calories:	190	Protein:	17g
Cholesterol:	13 mg	9% Calories from Fat		Carbohydrate:	29 g
Fiber:	2 g			Sodium:	439 mg

THE BIG DEAL

RECIPES

QUICK SKILLET CHICKEN DIJON WITH VEGETABLES
(A High-fat Recipe Pam Modified to Low-fat)

4 boneless and skinless chicken breast halves
¼ cup Healthy Request Fat-Free Chicken Broth
1 ¼ cups water
2-3 Tbs. Dijon mustard
¼ tsp. Papa Dash Lite Salt (optional)
⅛ tsp. ground black pepper
1 cup instant brown rice (or 1 ½ cups white rice cooked in 1 ½ cups water instead of 1 ¼ cups water)
2 cups frozen broccoli, carrots, water chestnuts, and red pepper (from 16-oz. pkg.), thawed
½ cup grated Polly-O Free Mozzarella cheese (fat-free) (or other fat-free cheese of your choice)

Spray a non-stick skillet with a non-stick cooking spray. Heat to medium heat until quite hot. Add chicken and chicken broth and cook 2-3 minutes on each side until browned. Remove chicken from skillet. Add water, mustard, lite salt, pepper and bring to a boil. Stir in the rice and vegetables. Return to a boil. Place chicken pieces over rice and vegetables. Reduce heat to low; cover and simmer 10-12 minutes or until most of the liquid is absorbed and the chicken is fork tender and juices run clear. Sprinkle with cheese; cover and let stand 3-4 minutes.

Yields: Serves 4 (chicken breast half plus rice and vegetables)

Per Serving:

Fat:	1.4 g	Calories:	209	Protein:	26 g
Cholesterol:	18 mg	6% Calories from Fat		Carbohydrate:	24 g
Fiber:	2 g			Sodium:	439 mg

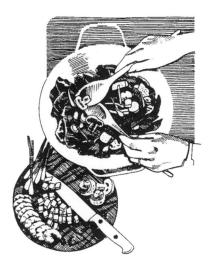

COUNTRY STYLE CHICKEN 'N DUMPLINGS
(A High-fat Recipe Pam Modified to Low-fat)

Chicken:
3 (15 ½-oz.) cans Healthy Request Fat-Free Chicken Broth
1 small onion, chopped
1 carrot, chopped
1 stalk celery, chopped
½ tsp. Papa Dash lite Salt (optional)
¼ tsp. pepper
4 boneless and skinless chicken breast halves, cut into large bite-sized pieces

Dumplings:
2 cups cake flour or all-purpose flour
1 ½ tsp. baking powder
½ tsp. Papa Dash Lite Salt
2 Tbs. Fleischmann's Lower Fat Margarine
⅓ cup skim milk
¼ cup Egg Beaters
1 (10 ¾-oz.) can Campbell's Healthy Request 99% fat-free Cream of Chicken Soup
1 Tbs. fresh chopped parsley (optional)

In a Dutch oven, combine chicken broth, onions carrots, celery, pepper, and salt (optional). Bring to a boil. Add chicken and continue to boil. Reduce heat. Remove chicken and set aside. With slotted spoon, remove vegetables and place in a blender. Pureé and return to broth in Dutch oven.

Dumplings:
Lightly spoon flour into measuring cup and level off with knife. In a medium bowl, combine flour, baking powder, and lite salt. Mix well. With a pastry blender or two knives, cut margarine into flour mixture. Add milk and ¼ cup Egg Beaters stirring until soft dough ball forms.

Turn dough onto well-floured surface. Gently knead dough in floured surface 2-3 minutes, kneading in enough flour until no longer sticky. Roll out to a ⅛-inch thickness. Cut into 3 X 1-inch strips.

Bring broth in Dutch oven to a boil. Add dumplings. Reduce heat; cover and simmer 25-30 minutes or until dumplings are tender and thoroughly cooked. Gently stir in Cream of Chicken Soup and chicken. Cook until heated through. Top with chopped parsley if desired.

Note: My Dad used to love Chicken 'N Dumplings. I never really cared for them as a child, but I sure like them now. This is an old southern recipe. If you have your own family favorite, simply modify it to low-fat using my guidelines!

Yields: Serves 6 (1½ cups per serving)

Per Serving:

Fat:	3.3 g	Calories:	258	Protein:	21 g
Cholesterol:	17 mg	12% Calories from Fat		Carbohydrate:	36 g
Fiber:	2 g			Sodium:	730 mg

THE BIG DEAL

POUR-IT-ON MEXICAN CHICKEN
(A High-fat Recipe Pam Modified to Low-fat)

1 (16-oz.) pkg. ButterBall brand "Mesquite" flavor Seasoned skinless and boneless chicken breasts (1 fat gram per breast)
1 (8-oz.) can tomato sauce
1 (4-oz.) can chopped green chilies (drained)
1-2 tsp. chile powder
½ tsp. minced garlic (comes in a jar)
½ tsp. ground cinnamon
1-2 Tbs. honey
2 cups water
1 box Uncle Ben's Hearty Soups mix "Black Beans & Rice"

Spray a 9 ½ X 11-inch glass casserole dish with Pam Cooking Spray. Pour everything into the dish and stir to mix. Cover with foil and bake at 375° F. for 40-45 minutes. Remove and serve at once.

Yields: Serves 4 (1 chicken breast and ¾ cup beans and rice)

Per Serving:

Fat:	2.3 g	Calories:	302	Protein:	33 g
Cholesterol:	25 mg	7% Calories from Fat		Carbohydrate:	38 g
Fiber:	2 g			Sodium:	673 mg

THE BIG DEAL

CHINESE SPAGHETTI
(A High-fat Recipe Pam Modified to Low-fat)

1 (8-oz.) pkg. uncooked vermicelli, fettuccine, linguini, or spaghetti
¾ cup Land O Lakes No-Fat Sour Cream
1 (1.5-oz.) stir-fry seasoning mix (any brand)
½ cup Healthy Request Fat-Free Chicken Broth
1 (16-oz.) pkg. "Teriyaki" ButterBall brand Seasoned Chicken Breasts
**   (1 fat gram a breast)**
1 tsp. minced garlic (comes in a jar)
4 cups broccoli/cole slaw mix (comes in a bag from the produce section)
1 medium red pepper, cut into thin strips

Cook pasta according to package directions. Rinse with hot water and drain. Meanwhile, in a small bowl, combine sour cream and the stir-fry seasoning mix until well blended and set aside. In a wok or large non-stick skillet heat a little chicken broth adding chicken (cut into strips) and minced garlic. Keep adding broth as it cooks down. Cook over medium heat, stirring constantly, until chicken is no longer pink. Add broccoli/cole slaw mix and red pepper while stirring constantly, until vegetables are crispy tender (1-2 minutes). Reduce heat to low, and stir in sour cream mixture. Continue cooking until heated through. Add pasta and toss to coat. This is quick and tasty!

Note: You can make this dish with Vermillion Valley Low-Fat Beef. One pound of low-fat tenderloin beef would be 8 fat grams. This would be 1.3 fat grams per serving (for the beef).

Yields: Serves 6 (1 cup per serving)

Per Serving:

Fat:	1.6 g	Calories: 267		Protein:	25 g
Cholesterol:	16 mg	5% Calories from Fat		Carbohydrate:	40 g
Fiber:	4 g			Sodium:	511 mg

NAN NAW'S SWISS BLISS
(My Mom Has Made This For Years!)
(Pam Modified to Low-fat)

**Char Doehler
Granbury, Texas**

2 lbs. Vermillion Valley Low-Fat Beef (tenderloin, sirloin, or roast) (6-oz. serving is only
   3 fat grams and 168 calories) *This would be 5.3 fat grams total and 890 calories total
   (for the whole recipe). Mail order (800)365-BEEF (2333). It is wonderful!!!
1 envelope onion soup mix (from a 2-oz.) box of Lipton's Recipe Secrets Onion soup mix
2 (8-oz.) cans sliced or button mushrooms, drained or 1 pound fresh mushrooms rinsed
   and sliced
1 green pepper, sliced
1 (14.5-oz.) can Hunt's Choice-Cut Diced Tomatoes,
   drained (save juice for sauce) torn apart

Sauce:
¼ tsp. Papa Dash "Lite" salt
¼ tsp. ground pepper
½ cup A-1 Sauce
juice from canned tomatoes
1 Tbs. cornstarch

Spray a large piece of foil with Pam Cooking Spray. Place foil on cookie sheet or in a large casserole dish. Place meat, mushrooms, tomatoes, and sliced green pepper on foil. Sprinkle onion soup mix over meat and vegetables. Stir together the sauce ingredients and pour over top. Seal the foil. Bake 1 hour at 325° F. This is just delicious served over rice or all by itself. It is so quick and easy. Your family or friends will think you slaved in the kitchen all day with this one. It's also good served with "CHEESE STUFFED POTATO BALLS" on page 385.

THE BIG DEAL

Yields: Serves 6 (4-oz. meat per serving plus vegetables)

Per Serving:

Fat:	1.8 g	Calories: 186		Protein:	33 g
Cholesterol:	83 mg	9% Calories from Fat		Carbohydrate:	9 g
Fiber:	1 g			Sodium:	731 mg

VICKI'S NO-PEEK BEEF BURGUNDY
(Pam Modified to Low-fat)

**Vicki Milling Tanner
Roswell, Georgia**

2 lbs. Vermillion Valley Low-Fat Stew Beef Chunks (This would be 5.3 fat grams for two pounds)
1 envelope onion soup mix (from a 2-oz.) box of Lipton's Recipe Secrets Onion soup mix
2 (8-oz.) cans sliced or button mushrooms (drained), or 4 cups fresh mushrooms, rinsed and sliced
1 cup red cooking wine (Burgundy)
4 cups prepared rice (white or brown) *Use Liquid Butter Buds (made from the mix) to prepare
    your rice instead of butter. Check the instructions on the box to make 8-½ cup servings.
    OR 4 cups prepared "No Yolks" egg noodles substitute (Broad brand)

Spray a large baking dish with Pam Cooking Spray. Mix all the ingredients together and place in the baking dish. Cover with foil and bake at 300° F. 1 ½ hours. NO PEEKING!!! Serve over ½ cup prepared rice or noodles for a real taste treat!

It tastes delicious and everyone will think you really fussed over this. Be ready with your recipe cards. Everyone will want a copy of this one!

I got this recipe from one of my best friends, Vicki Tanner. Vicki was my Maid of Honor and gave me this recipe (at my Mom's recipe shower; see page 39) when I got married in 1970. It is actually her Mom's (Helen Milling) recipe! It's always a "hit" and so easy to make! It tastes rich and fancy (a good company dish)! I was so excited when I found the Vermillion Low-Fat Beef so I could start making one of my favorites more often (and not worry about the high fat content of regular beef).

Yields: Serves 6 (4-oz. meat per serving plus vegetables and rice)

Per Serving:

Fat:	1.4 g	Calories:	217	Protein:	26 g
Cholesterol:	62 mg	6% Calories from Fat		Carbohydrate:	25 g
Fiber:	<1 g			Sodium:	674 mg

THE BIG DEAL

CAJUN MEAT LOAF
(A High-fat Recipe Pam Modified to Low-fat)

Meat Loaf:
1 ½ lb. Broken Arrow Ranch Brand ground venison, ground white meat turkey, or low-fat ground beef
½ tsp. dry mustard
⅛ tsp. black pepper
½ cup finely chopped red onion (or regular onion)
¾ cup crushed Pepperidge Farms Herb Seasoned Stuffing Mix
1 can (5-oz.) evaporated skimmed milk
1 Tbs. cornstarch
½ cup Egg Beaters, beaten

Cajun Sauce:
1 green pepper, seeded, cored, and chopped
1 small onion, chopped
1 (4-oz.) sliced mushrooms (drained and rinsed well)
¼ cup Healthy Request Fat-Free Chicken Broth
1 ½ cups sodium reduced tomato juice (or regular tomato juice)
1 Tbs. cornstarch
Dash of Tabasco Sauce
½ tsp. dried thyme

Turn the oven on and set the temperature at 350 degrees. In a large bowl, combine all of the meat loaf ingredients and mix well. Place in a large loaf pan or a ring (like an angel food cake) pan that has been sprayed with a non-stick cooking spray. Smooth top with a fork. Bake at 350° F. about 45 minutes or until done. Venison, low-fat beef, and turkey all cook faster than regular ground beef, so check after 30 minutes.

While the meat loaf is baking prepare the Cajun Sauce. Pour the chicken broth in a non-stick skillet. Add the chopped green pepper and onion. Sauté until onion is soft, but not browned. Add mushrooms and cook about a minute. Remove from heat. In a small bowl, mix the cornstarch with a little tomato juice. Add the remaining tomato juice to the skillet with the green peppers and onions. Return to heat and bring to a boil. Add the cornstarch mixture, stirring well. Add the Tabasco and thyme. Boil and stir 1-2 minutes or until thickened. Serve meat loaf with sauce.

Option: This is great served over steamed rice. Simply place ½ cup steamed rice on a plate, place a slice of meat loaf on top of rice and pour sauce over both.

Note: I usually double the sauce recipe so I will have some for leftovers.

Yields: Serves 8

Per Serving:

Fat:	3.4 g	Calories:	193	Protein:	26 g
Cholesterol:	80 mg	16% Calories from Fat		Carbohydrate:	13 g
Fiber:	1 g			Sodium:	205 mg

THE BIG DEAL

CHEESEBURGER PIE
(A Pam Original)

1 lb. Maverick Ranch Natural Lite low-fat ground beef, or ground venison, or Vermillion Valley low-fat ground beef
¾ cup chopped onion
1 bottle (18-oz.) barbecue sauce
2 cups shredded Polly-O Free fat-free mozzarella or fat-free Cheddar (your choice)
2 cups Pioneer Low-Fat Biscuit and Baking Mix
1 cup skim milk
½ cup Egg Beaters

Turn the oven on and set the temperature at 400 degrees. Place ground beef and chopped onion in a glass bowl. Cover with waxed paper and microwave on high about 4-5 minutes. Remove and stir. Heat longer if needed until the pink is gone. Drain meat and onion in a colander and pat with paper towels to remove any grease. Wipe out the bowl with a paper towel and place meat and onion back in it. Pour in barbecue sauce and mix well. Spoon meat mixture into a 13 X 9-inch casserole dish that has been sprayed lightly with Pam Cooking Spray. Sprinkle shredded cheese over meat. In a medium bowl combine Pioneer Biscuit Mix, skim milk, and Egg Beaters stirring until well blended. Pour over meat and cheese mixture. Bake at 400° F. 25-30 minutes or until crust is light golden brown. My kids like this with ketchup. Oven baked french fries are a great addition to this dish. This is quick and easy!

Note: Use no-salt added sauce to cut down on sodium. If you use plain white meat skinless turkey in place of meat, you will save about 2 fat grams per serving.

Yields: Serves 10

Per Serving:

Fat:	1.9 g	Calories:	255	Protein:	19 g
Cholesterol:	22 mg	6% Calories from Fat		Carbohydrate:	44 g
Fiber:	1 g				

THE BIG DEAL

STUFFED MEAT POCKETS
(A High-fat Recipe Pam Modified to Low-fat)

Meat Pocket Patties:
1 lb. Vermillion Valley Low-Fat Ground Beef,
    ground venison, or Maverick Ranch
    Natural Lite low-fat ground beef
1 (15 ½-oz.) can tomato sauce (only use 2 Tbs.
    for patties saving rest for the sauce)
¼ cup Egg Beaters
½ cup crushed Pepperidge Farms Herb
    Seasoned Stuffing (plus 2 Tbs. for stuffing)
2 Tbs. red cooking wine
½ tsp. onion powder

Stuffing:
2 Tbs. Egg Beaters
2 Tbs. seasoned stuffing, crushed
½ cup chopped fresh mushrooms or 1 (4-oz.)
    can "Bits and Pieces" mushrooms,
    rinsed well and drained (optional-my kids
    do not like mushrooms)
½ cup grated Polly-O Free fat-free
    Mozzarella cheese
¼ cup Alpine Lace Fat-Free Parmesan Cheese
¼ tsp. dried basil
⅛ tsp. dried thyme
⅛ tsp. dried oregano
¼ tsp. Papa Dash "Lite" salt (optional)

Pockets:
In a large bowl, mix together ground meat or venison, 2 Tbs. of the tomato sauce, crushed stuffing mix, Egg Beaters, cooking wine, and onion powder. Divide mixture into 8 equal parts and flatten into patties.

Stuffing:
In a medium bowl, combine all of the stuffing ingredients and blend well. Spoon a little filling on one side of half of the meat patties. Place the other halves on top to make 4 stuffed pockets. Press firmly around the edges to form a seal. Spray a large non-stick skillet with Pam Cooking Spray and heat skillet over medium-high heat, browning patties on both sides. Do not overcook! Venison and low-fat beef cook faster than regular ground beef because of the low fat content.

Sauce:
1 (15 ½-oz.) can tomato sauce with 2 Tbs.
    missing (used in patties)
¼ tsp. crushed dried basil
⅛ tsp. dried thyme
⅛ tsp. dried oregano
⅛ tsp. ground black pepper
1 tsp. cornstarch
1 Tbs. water

Sauce:
Mix together 1 cup tomato sauce, basil, thyme, oregano, and pepper. Add sauce mixture to skillet with meat patties. Reduce heat, cover, and simmer for 15 minutes. Blend cornstarch and water. Add to skillet, and cook stirring until thick. Add remaining tomato sauce if more sauce in desired.

Yields: Serves 4

Per Serving:

Fat:	4.7 g	Calories:	200	Protein:	30 g
Cholesterol:	60 mg	9% Calories from Fat		Carbohydrate:	17 g
Fiber:	2 g			Sodium:	473 mg

THE BIG DEAL

MARINATED PORK TENDERLOIN
(Or Marinated Low-Fat Eye of Round Roast)
(A High-fat Recipe Pam Modified to Low-fat)

1 (2- lb.) boneless pork tenderloin (*This would be 32.8 fat grams) or 2 lb. Vermillion Valley Low-Fat Beef Eye of Round Roast (This would only be 12 fat grams.) or a 2 lb. Maverick Ranch Natural Lite Low-Fat Beef Eye of Round Roast. (*This would be about 15 fat grams.)
½ cup red wine
1 Tbs. chopped fresh rosemary or 1 tsp. dried rosemary leaves, crushed
1 medium-sized onion, sliced
1 tsp. Papa Dash Lite Salt (optional for rubbing on roast before baking)
1 garlic clove, cut in half
1 pound green beans (fresh or frozen)
1 (17-oz.) can whole kernel corn, drained and rinsed well
1 (3-oz.) jar capers, drained
2-3 Tbs. Liquid Butter Buds (made from the mix)

The day before:
Trim any fat from the roast. In a large zip-lock baggie, combine rosemary, wine, onion, and garlic. Place roast in baggie with seasonings and seal. Put the baggie in a bowl or dish and place in the refrigerator (a minimum of 4 hours). Occasionally turn the roast.

The next day (or at least 4 hours later):
Remove the roast from marinade, **but do not discard the marinade!** Rub the roast with 1 tsp. Papa Dash Lite Salt if desired. Place roast on rack in a small roasting pan. Add marinade and 1 cup of water. Roast at 325° F. for about 1 hour or until meat thermometer reaches 160 degrees F. (28-33 minutes per pound). *If using low-fat beef, the cooking time will be cut in half.

Meanwhile, in a 10-inch non-stick skillet over high heat, (in ½-inch boiling water) heat green beans to boiling. Reduce heat to low; cover and simmer 5-10 minutes until beans are tender crisp. Drain and cool. Slice the beans diagonally. In the same skillet, mix beans, corn, capers, 2-3 Tbs. Liquid Butter Buds and ½ tsp. Papa Dash Lite Salt. Set aside.

When roast is done, place on a warm platter. Remove rack from roasting pan; add 3/4 cup water. Over medium heat, bring to a boil stirring to loosen brown bits. Skim fat by placing an ice cube on top. The fat will congeal around the ice cube for easy removal. Pour gravy into gravy boat. Heat beans mixture over medium heat until hot. Spoon onto platter with roast. Serve with gravy.

Note: You can cut the fat in the recipe by using Vermillion Low-Fat Beef or other low-fat beef.

THE BIG DEAL

Yields: Serves 8 (3-oz. pork tenderloin per serving plus vegetables)

Per Serving:

Fat:	4.7 g	Calories:	218	Protein:	27 g
Cholesterol:	79 mg	19% Calories from Fat		Carbohydrate:	18 g
Fiber:	2 g			Sodium:	587 mg

SPICY CAJUN JAMBALAYA
(A High-fat Recipe Pam Modified to Low-fat)

¼ cup Healthy Request Fat-Free Chicken Broth
1 medium onion, chopped finely
1 medium green pepper, seeded and chopped finely
1 (14.5-oz.) can stewed tomatoes (Cajun OR Italian flavored stewed tomatoes by Del Monte are
   both good in this recipe.)
1 (12-oz.) pkg. frozen ready-to-cook shrimp, thawed and drained
4-oz. (cubed) Healthy Choice Low-Fat "Polska Kielbasa" Sausage (*This would be about ⅓ of one
   of the long sausages that comes in a 14-oz. package.) *This would be 3 fat grams.
1 tsp. dried Italian seasoning
¼ tsp. Tabasco Sauce
4 cups cooked white or brown rice as directed on the package using Liquid Butter Buds (made
   from the mix) and Papa Dash Lite salt in preparation

Heat the chicken broth in a large non-stick skillet or Dutch oven over medium-high heat. Add the chopped onion and green pepper cooking until tender crisp. Stir in all of the rest of the ingredients (except rice). Bring to a boil. Reduce heat and simmer about 5 minutes or until shrimp turn pink, stirring occasionally. Stir in cooked rice and continue cooking until most of the liquid is absorbed and rice is thoroughly heated.

Yields: 6 (1 ⅓ cup) Servings

Per Serving:

Fat:	1.5 g	Calories: 239		Protein:	17 g
Cholesterol:	100 mg	6% Calories from Fat		Carbohydrate:	38 g
Fiber:	1 g			Sodium:	601 mg

THE BIG DEAL

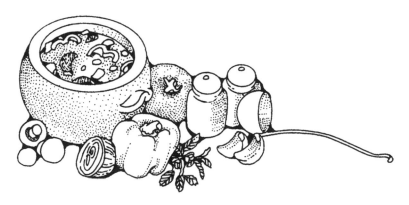

PAM'S FAVORITE QUICK MEAL
(A Pam Original)

1 ½ cups uncooked instant white or brown rice
1 ½ cups whole kernel frozen corn or 1 (15 ½-oz.) can whole kernel corn (rinsed and drained)
1 cup chopped red or green bell pepper (optional if I have on hand)
1 (15-oz.) can black beans (rinsed well and drained)
1 (4-oz.) can chopped green chilies, drained
¼ cup Guiltless Gourmet Fat-Free Spicy Black Bean Dip (or Tostito brand Fat-Free Black Bean Dip)

Sauce:
1 cup water
1 jar (11 ½-oz.) thick and chunky salsa (I use Frito-Lay's Tostito brand)
1 (8-oz.) can no-salt added tomato sauce

Combine sauce ingredients in a large non-stick skillet and mix well. Bring to a boil. Stir in all the rest of the ingredients and reduce heat to low. Cover and simmer about 10 minutes (or until rice is cooked and vegetables are tender).

Pam's Personal Option:
I like to eat this in a bowl with chopped Romaine lettuce and tomatoes. I usually sprinkle about 1 Tbs. Polly-O fat-free mozzarella on top. I eat my quick meal with Frito-Lay's Baked Low-Fat Tostito Chips or El Paco brand fat-free flour tortillas. This is quick, easy, filling, and cheap (but very rich in vitamins, protein, and fiber)! I eat this meal at least once a week!

Yields: 6 (1-cup servings)

Per Serving:

Fat:	0.8 g	Calories:	316	Protein:	11 g
Cholesterol:	0 mg	2% Calories from Fat		Carbohydrate:	67 g
Fiber:	6 g			Sodium:	373 mg

THE BIG DEAL

VEGGIE LASAGNA
(A High-fat Recipe Pam Modified to Low-fat)

1 (8-oz.) pkg. Pasta DeFino brand "No Boil" lasagna noodles
½ cup cooking sherry or unsweetened apple juice
1 medium onion, finely chopped
8-oz. fresh mushrooms (or 1 8-oz. can sliced mushrooms, rinsed and drained)
2 large zucchini, coarsely grated (about 4 cups)
1 medium red pepper, seeded and chopped
1 medium green pepper, seeded and chopped
2 cups chopped fresh spinach, rinsed and drained or 1 (10-oz. box) frozen spinach, thawed
1 (32-oz.) jar Ragu Light "Tomato and Herb" flavor fat-free pasta sauce
1 (15-oz.) Polly-O Free brand fat-free Ricotta (or other brand)
2 cups grated Polly-O Free (fat-free) Mozzarella Cheese (divided use)
½ cup Egg Beaters, beaten
½ cup Alpine Lace Fat-Free Parmesan Cheese

Turn the oven on and set temperature at 375 degrees. Spray a 13 X 9-inch (3-qt.) baking dish with a non-stick cooking spray.

In a large non-stick skillet sprayed with a non-stick cooking spray (over medium-high heat) bring the cooking sherry to a boil. Add the onion and cook 3-5 minutes. Add mushrooms, zucchini, red and green chopped peppers and cook 5 more minutes. Add more cooking sherry if needed. Add spinach and pasta sauce. Cook about 5 minutes over low heat. Remove from heat and set aside. In a medium bowl, combine ricotta, 1 cup grated mozzarella, ¼ cup Parmesan cheese and ½ cup Egg Beaters. Mix well. Pour enough of the pasta sauce in the bottom of the prepared pan or dish to cover. Layer part (about ⅓) of the lasagna noodles over the sauce. Spread ⅓ of the ricotta cheese mixture and ⅓ of the vegetable mixture. Repeat layering two more times ending with pasta sauce on top. Sprinkle the remaining 1 cup grated mozzarella and the remaining ¼ cup Alpine Lace Fat-Free Parmesan cheese on top. Cover dish tightly with foil (that has been sprayed with non-stick cooking spray to prevent sticking to the melted cheese).

Bake at 375° F. 40-45 minutes or until bubbly around the edges. Remove foil and bake about 5 more minutes or until top is golden brown. Let set in the pan about 5 minutes before cutting to serve.

Yields: 10 (1 ¼ cups per serving)

Per Serving:

Fat:	0.5 g	Calories:	187	Protein:	17 g
Cholesterol:	4 mg	3% Calories from Fat		Carbohydrate:	26 g
Fiber:	4 g			Sodium:	730 mg

THE BIG DEAL

TEXAS STYLE BEANS AND RICE
(A Pam Original)

1 cup uncooked rice (Minute brand white or brown)
½ cup Healthy Request Fat-Free Chicken Broth
1 red pepper, chopped
1 green pepper, chopped
2 cans (15 ½-oz.) pinto beans, rinsed well and drained
2 (15-oz.) cans black beans, rinsed well and drained
2 (10-oz.) pkg. frozen corn, thawed (you can used canned corn,
   but be sure to rinse well and drain)
2 tsp. chili powder
1 (4-oz.) can chopped green chilies
¼ tsp. Papa Dash "Lite" Salt (optional)
¼ tsp. pepper
2-3 Tbs. chopped fresh cilantro (optional) or parsley

Cook rice as directed on package omitting butter. Meanwhile in a non-stick skillet over medium-low heat, heat chicken broth and add chopped peppers. Cook until tender (about 5 minutes). Add pinto and black beans, chopped green chilies, corn, and chile powder. Cook until heated through. Stir in rice, seasonings, and chopped cilantro or parsley. This takes about 25 minutes. It's a great quick dinner filled with vitamins, protein, and fiber.

Note: For all of you who aren't from the South, cilantro, also known as chinese parsley, is used in Mexican cooking and gives a very distinctive flavor. It has a lemony taste. The seeds of the plant are known as coriander. You might have heard of that because it is used in a variety of foods from baked goods to pickles.

Yields: Serves 8 (1½ cups per serving)

Per Serving:

Fat:	1.2 g	Calories:	245	Protein:	12 g
Cholesterol:	0 mg	4% Calories from Fat		Carbohydrate:	49 g
Fiber:	5 g			Sodium:	432 mg

THE BIG DEAL

MOCK MONTE CRISTO SANDWICHES
(A High-fat Recipe Pam Modified to Low-fat)

2 cups Rice Krispie Cereal (crushed to 1 ½ cups)
½ cup Egg Beaters (or 4 egg whites slightly beaten)
½ cup skim milk
1 Tbs. powdered sugar
8 slices English muffin bread or other firm white bread
4 oz. thinly slice Healthy Choice low-fat ham (or other brand)
4 slices Borden Fat-Free Swiss Cheese (or other brand)
4 oz. ButterBall Fat-Free Roasted Turkey Breast slices (or other fat-free brand)
¼ cup Land-O-Lakes NO-FAT Sour Cream (optional)
4 Tbs. Strawberry Preserves or spreadable fruit (optional)

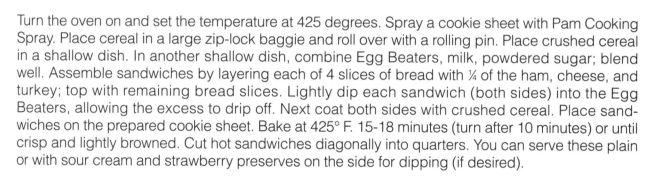

Turn the oven on and set the temperature at 425 degrees. Spray a cookie sheet with Pam Cooking Spray. Place cereal in a large zip-lock baggie and roll over with a rolling pin. Place crushed cereal in a shallow dish. In another shallow dish, combine Egg Beaters, milk, powdered sugar; blend well. Assemble sandwiches by layering each of 4 slices of bread with ¼ of the ham, cheese, and turkey; top with remaining bread slices. Lightly dip each sandwich (both sides) into the Egg Beaters, allowing the excess to drip off. Next coat both sides with crushed cereal. Place sandwiches on the prepared cookie sheet. Bake at 425° F. 15-18 minutes (turn after 10 minutes) or until crisp and lightly browned. Cut hot sandwiches diagonally into quarters. You can serve these plain or with sour cream and strawberry preserves on the side for dipping (if desired).

Note: The Monte Cristo sandwich has been around a long time, but is usually a high-fat "fried" sandwich. I first tasted one in California in the early '70s (before I realized I had a cholesterol problem). A traditional Monte Cristo Sandwich fried in butter, with eggs, high-fat luncheon meats and high-fat Swiss cheese could contain as much as 60 or 70 fat grams. With my recipe, you can still have the great taste without all the fat!

Yields: 4 sandwiches

Per Sandwich:

Fat:	3.7 g	Calories:	323	Protein:	26 g
Cholesterol:	27 mg	11% Calories from Fat		Carbohydrate:	46 g
Fiber:	<1 g			Sodium:	988 mg

THE BIG DEAL

MEAT *of* WHEAT CHILI BURGERS
(A Recipe Pam Modified to Even Lower-Fat)

6 MEAT *of* WHEAT burgers
1 green pepper, chopped
¼ cup Healthy Request Fat-Free Chicken Broth (in place of oil)
1 large onion, chopped
3 cloves garlic, minced or 1 ½ tsp. minced garlic (in a jar)
1 (15-oz.) can kidney beans, undrained
1 (15-oz.) can pinto beans, undrained
2 Tbs. chopped green chilies
1 Tbs. chili powder
¼ tsp. cayenne pepper
1 tsp. cumin
1 (15-oz.) can stewed tomatoes, undrained and cut up
6 Wonder low-fat hamburger buns
6 Tbs. Polly-O-FREE fat-free grated mozzarella cheese (or other fat-free cheese of your choice)

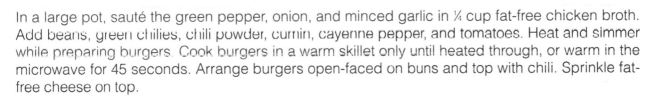

In a large pot, sauté the green pepper, onion, and minced garlic in ¼ cup fat-free chicken broth. Add beans, green chilies, chili powder, cumin, cayenne pepper, and tomatoes. Heat and simmer while preparing burgers. Cook burgers in a warm skillet only until heated through, or warm in the microwave for 45 seconds. Arrange burgers open-faced on buns and top with chili. Sprinkle fat-free cheese on top.

Note: The original recipe is from the MEAT *of* WHEAT booklet that comes with the products. MEAT *of* WHEAT is an all vegetable and wheat product that is very low in fat. One patty contains 1.2 fat grams. They are made from wheat gluten, rice, sprouted beans, onions, carrots, mushrooms, tamari, bean flour, canola oil, xanthan gum, spices and natural seasonings. This is perfect for the vegetarian or anyone else who enjoys a great burger. For ordering information call: (800) 488-9283. The MEAT *of* WHEAT Products are manufactured by White Wave, Inc.

THE BIG DEAL

Yields: Serves 6

Per Serving:

Fat:	3.7 g	Calories:	475	Protein:	46 g
Cholesterol:	0 mg	7% Calories from Fat		Carbohydrate:	70 g
Fiber:	7 g			Sodium:	1012 mg

SWEET
TREATS

PAM'S SPECIAL CHOCOLATE CHIP COOKIES
(It's Hard to Believe They're Low-fat)
(A Pam Original)

¾ cup Fleischmann's Lower Fat margarine (4.5 fat grams per Tbs.)
1 cup brown sugar (or ½ cup brown sugar and 2 tsp. Sweet 'N Low Brown)
1 (14-oz.) can reduced fat "Eagle Brand" Sweetened Condensed Milk
1 tsp. vanilla extract
4 cups Pioneer Low-Fat Biscuit and Baking Mix
½ cup Nestlé brand Mini Morsels Chocolate Chips

Turn the oven on and set the temperature at 375 degrees. In a large bowl, cream together margarine, brown sugar, Eagle Brand Milk, and vanilla extract. Stir in the biscuit mix blending well. Stir in ½ cup Mini Morsels. Chill dough 5-10 minutes. Spray a cookie sheet with a cooking spray and drop dough by teaspoonfuls onto the prepared cookie sheet about 2-inches apart. Bake at 375° F. 8-12 minutes, or until golden brown.

Note: I worked on recipes a long time to come up with a really good low-fat chocolate chip cookie. I love these and hope you will too!

Yields: 6 dozen cookies

	Per Cookie: All sugar		
Fat: 1.5 g	Calories: 71	Protein:	1 g
Cholesterol: 0 mg	17% Calories from Fat	Carbohydrate:	15 g
Fiber: 0 g		Sodium:	134 mg

	Per Cookie: ½ Sweet 'N Low		
Fat: 1.5 g	Calories: 66	Protein:	1 g
Cholesterol: 0 mg	17% Calories from Fat	Carbohydrate:	14 g
Fiber: 0 g		Sodium:	134 mg

PERFECT PEANUT BUTTER COOKIES
(A High-fat Recipe Pam Modified to Low-fat)

**½ cup Fleischmann's Fat-Free Squeeze Margarine
   or ½ cup Promise Ultra Fat-Free Margarine
½ cup Skippy brand reduced fat peanut butter (6 fat grams per Tbs.)
1 ¼ cups brown sugar (or ¾ cup brown sugar and 2 tsp. Sweet 'N Low Brown)
½ cup sugar (or ¼ cup sugar and 3 packets Sweet 'N Low)
3 Tbs. skim milk
1 Tbs. vanilla extract
¼ cup Egg Beaters
1 ¾-2 cups all-purpose flour (start with 1 ¾ and add more if the dough is too sticky)
¾ tsp. baking soda
1 Tbs. sugar (for dipping fork when flattening cookies)**

Turn the oven on and set the temperature at 325° or 375° F. (For a harder crunchy cookie, bake at 325° F. For a softer chewy cookie bake at 375°F.) Combine first 6 ingredients in a large bowl. Beat at medium speed until well-blended. Add ¼ cup Egg Beaters and beat until blended. Combine baking soda and flour adding to creamed mixture at low speed. Mix until blended. Chill dough in the refrigerator about 10-15 minutes. Remove from fridge and drop the dough by teaspoonfuls 2 inches apart on a cookie sheet that has been sprayed with Pam Cooking Spray. Between cookies, dip the teaspoon in flour to prevent sticking. Flatten cookies with a fork making a crisscross pattern. Dip the fork in sugar between cookies to prevent sticking. Bake the cookies at 325° F. 12-15 minutes (for a crunchier cookie) or at 375° F. 7-10 minutes for a softer chewy cookie. Cool 2-3 minutes on baking sheet before removing to cool.

Yields: 4 dozen cookies

Per Cookie: All Sugar

Fat:	1 g	Calories:	66	Protein:	1 g
Cholesterol:	0 mg	14% Calories from Fat		Carbohydrate:	13 g
Fiber:	<1 g			Sodium:	58 mg

Per Cookie: Sweet 'N Low

Fat:	1 g	Calories:	54	Protein:	1 g
Cholesterol:	0 mg	16% Calories from Fat		Carbohydrate:	10 g
Fiber:	<1 g			Sodium:	58 mg

SWEET TREATS

OATMEAL COOKIES IN A FLASH
(A Pam Original)

¾ cup Fleischmann's Lower Fat Margarine
1 cup packed brown sugar (or ½ cup brown sugar and 1 tsp. Sweet 'N Low Brown)
1 (14-oz.) can reduced fat "Eagle Brand" Sweetened Condensed milk
1 tsp. cinnamon
1 tsp. allspice
½ tsp. nutmeg
2 tsp. vanilla extract
3 cups Pioneer Low-Fat Biscuit and Baking Mix
1 cup Quick Oats Oatmeal
1 cup raisins (optional)

Turn the oven on and set the temperature at 375 degrees. In a large bowl, cream together margarine, brown sugar, Eagle Brand milk, cinnamon, allspice, nutmeg, and vanilla extract. Stir in the biscuit mix and oatmeal. In a small saucepan, cover raisins with water and boil until they are puffed up. Drain raisins and fold into dough. Chill dough 5-10 minutes. Spray a cookie sheet with a non-stick cooking spray and drop dough by teaspoonfuls onto the prepared cookie sheet 2-inches apart. Bake at 375° F. 8-10 minutes or until set and golden brown.

Yields: 6 dozen cookies

Per Cookie: All Sugar

Fat:	1.1 g	Calories: 60		Protein:	1 g
Cholesterol:	0 mg	16% Calories from Fat		Carbohydrate:	13 g
Fiber:	<1 g			Sodium:	105 mg

Per Cookie: ½ Sweet 'N Low

Fat:	1.1 g	Calories: 54		Protein:	1 g
Cholesterol:	0 mg	18% Calories from Fat		Carbohydrate:	11 g
Fiber:	<1 g			Sodium:	105 mg

SWEET TREATS

CHOCOLATE CREAM CHEESE FUDGE BARS
(A Pam Original)

Cake:
1 (1 lb. 2.25-oz.) box Chocolate Betty Crocker "Light" or Lovin' Lites low-fat cake mix
1 cup Fleischmann's Fat-Free Squeeze Margarine
¼ cup Egg Beaters
1 tsp. vanilla

Topping:
½ jar Mrs. Richardson's or Smucker's Fat-Free Fudge Topping
2 cups Cool Whip "Light" topping (16 fat grams)

Cream Cheese Filling:
1 (8-oz.) pkg. Philadelphia Free fat-free cream cheese, softened
½ cup Egg Beaters
2 cups sifted powdered sugar (or 1 cup powdered sugar and 12 packets Sweet 'N Low)
1 tsp. vanilla

Cake:

Turn the oven on and set the temperature at 325 degrees. Spray a 9 ½ X 13-inch baking dish or pan with Pam Cooking Spray. Blend the cake ingredients together with a hand mixer, beating until smooth. Spread the batter in the prepared dish.

Cream Cheese Filling:

Beat the cream cheese together with the powdered sugar, Egg Beaters, and vanilla. Spoon cream cheese mixture over cake batter. Swirl by taking a butter knife (not sharp) and cutting through the two mixtures to give a swirled affect. Bake at 325° F. 45-50 minutes. It should be more like a cheesecake texture than a regular cake texture. It will be more moist. Cool. To speed up this process, you can stick the cake in the freezer about 15 minutes.

Topping:

Spread ½ jar (about 1 cup) of the fudge topping over the cake. Spoon 2 cups "Light" Cool Whip on top and refrigerate until ready to serve.

Option: You can always use 1 cup Mrs. Richardson's or Smucker's Fat-Free Caramel or Butterscotch topping instead of the Fudge topping for a variation. I love to make it with ½ cup Fudge and ½ cup Caramel mixed together.

Yields: Serves 24

Per Bar: All Sugar					
Fat:	2.4 g	Calories:	226	Protein:	4.5 g
Cholesterol:	0 mg	9% Calories from Fat		Carbohydrate:	45 g
Fiber:	1.3 g			Sodium:	405 mg

Per Bar: ½ Sweet 'N Low					
Fat:	2.4 g	Calories:	204	Protein:	4.5 g
Cholesterol:	0 mg	10% Calories from Fat		Carbohydrate:	38 g
Fiber:	1.3 g			Sodium:	405 mg

SWEET AND TART LEMON BARS
(A High-fat Recipe Pam Modified to Low-fat)

Crust:
½ cup powdered sugar
¼ cup Fleischmann's Lower Fat Margarine
1 cup all-purpose flour
¾ cup wheat germ (optional)
2 tsp. grated lemon peel

Filling:
¾ cup Egg Beaters and 2 egg whites
2 cups granulated sugar (or 1 cup sugar and 12 packets Swee 'N Low)
⅓ cup lemon juice (fresh is best)
¼ cup all-purpose flour
1 tsp. baking powder
1 tsp. grated lemon peel
1 Tbs. powdered sugar for dusting

Turn the oven on and set the temperature at 350 degrees. Lightly spray a 13 X 9-inch baking pan with a non-stick cooking spray.

Crust:
Beat the powdered sugar and margarine until well blended. Add the flour, wheat germ and lemon peel. Mix thoroughly. Mixture will be crumbly. If crust is too dry, add a little Fleischmann's Fat-Free Squeeze Margarine. Press crust mixture into the bottom of the prepared pan. Bake at 350° F. 12-15 minutes or until golden brown.

Filling:
In a medium-sized bowl, combine Egg Beaters, egg whites, and sugar beating until thick and light lemon colored (about 3 minutes). Add lemon juice, flour, baking powder and lemon peel, stirring until just blended. Pour over crust. Bake at 350° F. 20-25 minutes or until edges are light golden brown and filling is set. Cool completely. Sprinkle or sift powdered sugar over top. Cut into bars.

Yields: 24

Per Bar: All Sugar		
Fat: 0.8 g	Calories: 112	Protein: 2 g
Cholesterol: 0 mg	6% Calories from Fat	Carbohydrate: 25 g
Fiber: <1 g		Sodium: 31 mg

Per Bar: ½ Sweet 'N Low		
Fat: 0.8 g	Calories: 82	Protein: 2 g
Cholesterol: 0 mg	8% Calories from Fat	Carbohydrate: 17 g
Fiber: <1 g		Sodium: 31 mg

SWEET TREATS

FANTASTIC FROSTED BROWNIES
(A High-fat Recipe Pam Modified to Low-fat)

<u>Brownies:</u>
½ cup Fleischmann's Fat-Free Squeeze Margarine
1 cup sugar (or ½ cup sugar and 6 packets Sweet 'N Low)
1 tsp. vanilla
½ cup Egg Beaters
½ cup all-purpose flour
⅓ cup Hershey Cocoa
¼ tsp. baking powder
¼ tsp. Papa Dash "Lite" salt
½ cup Grape Nuts Cereal (optional)

<u>Frosting:</u>
3 Tbs. Fleischmann's Lower-Fat Margarine
3 Tbs. Hershey's Cocoa
1 Tbs. light corn syrup
½ tsp. vanilla
1 cup powdered sugar (do not use Sweet 'N Low in frosting)

<u>Brownies:</u>
Blend margarine, sugar and vanilla in a large bowl. Add Egg Beaters (using a wooden spoon) and
beat well. Combine flour, cocoa, baking powder, and salt; gradually blend into margarine/sugar mixture. Stir in Grape Nuts Cereal. Spread in a 9-inch baking pan that has been sprayed with Pam Cooking Spray. Bake at 350° F. for 20-25 minutes or until brownies start to pull away from the edges of the pan. Meanwhile prepare frosting while brownies are baking.

<u>Frosting:</u>
Cream margarine, cocoa, corn syrup and vanilla in a small mixing bowl. Add powdered sugar. Beat to spreading consistency. Add more skim milk if too dry and a little more powdered sugar if too runny. Yields: 1 cup frosting

SWEET TREATS

Note: You will only need ½ of the frosting for this recipe. Use the rest to make Graham Cracker Icing Sandwich Cookies with low-fat graham crackers. Just spread about 1 Tbs. frosting on ½ of a graham cracker and place the over half on top to make a sandwich. My Mom used to make these all the time when I was a kid. We always knew if she had baked a cake that day when we came home from school and found Graham Cracker Icing Sandwich Cookies in the fridge. I think she always made a little extra frosting on purpose because she knew how much my brother, Dad and I loved those special little treats. It's funny how we grow up and do the same things for our families that our parents did for us, isn't it?

Yields: 20 Frosted Brownies

Per Frosted Brownie: All Sugar		
Fat: 0.7 g	Calories: 79	Protein: 1 g
Cholesterol: 0 mg	7% Calories from Fat	Carbohydrate: 18 g
Fiber: 1 g		Sodium: 79 mg

Per Frosted Brownie: ½ Sweet 'N Low		
Fat: 0.7 g	Calories: 68	Protein: 1 g
Cholesterol: 0 mg	9% Calories from Fat	Carbohydrate: 17 g
Fiber: 1 g		Sodium: 79 mg

PUMPKIN PIE CAKE SQUARES
(A High-fat Recipe Pam Modified to Low-fat)

1 (1 lb. 4.5-oz.) box Betty Crocker "light" yellow cake mix
½ cup Fleischmann's Fat-Free Squeeze Margarine
1 ¼ cups Egg Beaters (divided use)
4 tsp. cinnamon (divided use)
2 tsp. nutmeg (divided use)
1 (1 lb. 14-oz.) can solid-pack pumpkin
1 ¾ cups sugar (divided use) (or 1 cup sugar and 9 packets Sweet 'N Low mixed together)
½ tsp. Papa Dash Lite Salt
1 tsp. ground ginger
½ tsp. ground cloves
1 cup evaporated skimmed milk
¼ cup Promise Ultra Fat-Free Margarine

Crust:
Turn the oven on and set at 350 degrees. Measure out 1 cup of the cake mix and set aside. Combine the remaining mix with ½ cup Fleischmann's fat-free margarine, ¼ cup Egg Beaters, 1 tsp. nutmeg, and 1 tsp. cinnamon. Mix well and pour into a 13 X 9-inch baking dish that has been sprayed with a non-stick cooking spray.

Filling:
In a large bowl, combine pumpkin, ¾ cup Egg Beaters, 1 ½ cups of the sugar, 2 tsp. cinnamon, remaining 1 tsp. nutmeg, lite salt, ginger, cloves and evaporated skimmed milk. Mix well with a hand blender or wire whisk. Pour over unbaked crust.

Topping:
Combine reserved cake mix with the remaining 1 tsp. cinnamon, remaining ¼ cup sugar, and ¼ cup Promise Ultra fat-Free Margarine. Using two knives or a pastry blender, cut the margarine into the other ingredients until crumbly. Sprinkle over pumpkin filling. Bake at 350° F. 45-50 minutes or until a knife inserted in center comes out clean. Cool and cut into squares. You can top these with a dollop of Cool Whip "Light" or other light whipped topping if desired.

Yields: Serves 24

Per Serving: All Sugar		
Fat: 1.5 g	Calories: 176	Protein: 3 g
Cholesterol: 0 mg	8% Calories from Fat	Carbohydrate: 37 g
Fiber: 2 g		Sodium: 235 mg

Per Serving: ½ Sweet 'N Low		
Fat: 1.5 g	Calories: 153	Protein: 3 g
Cholesterol: 0 mg	9% Calories from Fat	Carbohydrate: 32 g
Fiber: 2 g		Sodium: 235 mg

SWEET TREATS

MIKE'S MILLION DOLLAR POUND CAKE
(My Husband's Favorite)

1 cup Fleischmann's Fat-Free Squeeze Margarine
½ cup Philadelphia Free (fat-free) Cream Cheese
4 cups sifted powdered sugar (or 3 cups powdered sugar
   and 12 packets Sweet 'N Low)
½ cup Egg Beaters
3 egg whites
½ tsp. cream of tartar
1 Tbs. vanilla extract
2 tsp. almond extract
¼ cup cornstarch
3 ½ cups self-rising flour
1 cup skim milk

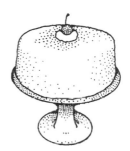

Turn the oven on and set at 325 degrees. In a large bowl, cream together margarine, powdered sugar, Egg Beaters, almond extract, vanilla extract and cream cheese. Beat with a hand mixer until smooth. In a separate bowl, beat the egg whites with cream of tartar until stiff. Set aside.

Mix the cornstarch and flour together. Add a little skim milk to the batter and then some of the flour mixture beating after each addition. Alternate the milk and flour until it is all gone. Fold in the beaten egg whites. This recipe makes enough batter for one bundt cake and 6-8 cupcakes (depending on the size of your muffin cups). Bake at 325° F. 50-60 minutes. Bake the cupcakes at 350° F. 15-20 minutes. This cake is so rich-tasting, that it really doesn't even need frosting!

Option #1: You can spoon Cherry Pie Filling over the cake and garnish with Cool Whip "Light" if you desire.
Option #2: You can make a vanilla or chocolate glaze and spoon over cooled cake.
Option #3: You can eat it plain. Mine doesn't usually last long enough to frost, once they smell it baking!

Note: I made the recipe larger than I needed on purpose. I used to make it for parties and the kids would want a piece before I was ready to serve it. I decided to make the recipe larger so it would also make a few cupcakes (to hold the kids over) until the cake was served. This way, you have some cupcakes for the kids (or your husband in my case), and you don't have to cut the cake until YOU are ready!

Note: Mike really doesn't like it as well made with Sweet 'N Low. I like it both ways!

Yields: Serves 20 • 1 bundt cake (serves 12) plus 6-8 cupcakes

Per Serving: All Sugar

Fat:	0.3 g	Calories:	204	Protein:	5 g
Cholesterol:	2 mg	1% Calories from Fat		Carbohydrate:	44 g
Fiber:	<1 g			Sodium:	470 mg

Per Serving: ½ Sweet 'N Low

Fat:	0.3 g	Calories:	183	Protein:	5 g
Cholesterol:	2 mg	1% Calories from Fat		Carbohydrate:	38 g
Fiber:	<1 g			Sodium:	470 mg

BANANA BASH SMASH SURPRISE CAKE
(A Pam Original)

<u>Bottom of the Bash:</u>
1 (1 lb. 2.25-oz.) Betty Crocker "Light" yellow cake mix
  (or other low-fat cake mix)
⅓ cup water
1 tsp. vanilla
½ cup Fleischmann's Fat-Free Spread (squeeze bottle)
¾ cup Egg Beaters

<u>Banana Smash:</u>
2 very ripe bananas
1-2 Tbs, skim milk
1 ½ cups powdered sugar, sifted (or 1 cup powdered sugar and 6 packets Sweet 'N Low)
1 tsp. vanilla
¼ cup Fleischmann's Fat-Free Spread

<u>Creamy "Cool" Filling:</u>
1 (3.4-oz.) pkg. instant vanilla pudding (regular or sugar-free)
1 ¾ cups skim milk
1 tsp. vanilla

<u>Surprise:</u>
40 Keebler Reduced Fat Vanilla Wafers (This would be 17.5 fat grams) *Actually most of the fat in the recipe is in the cookies-Surprise!!

<u>The Icing on the cake (so to speak):</u>
1 (7.5-oz.) box Betty Crocker Fat-Free Fluffy Frosting prepared with ½ cup hot water (You will only need ½ of the frosting which is 1½ cups) *Save the rest in the refrigerator to make Graham Cracker Icing Sandwiches or use as a topping for another dessert.

<u>Bottom of the Bash:</u>
Turn the oven on and set the temperature at 350°F. Spray a 9 ½ X 13-inch baking pan or dish with Pam Cooking Spray. Blend the cake ingredients together with a hand mixer until smooth. Pour into prepared pan.

<u>Banana Smash:</u>
In a medium-sized bowl, mash the banana. With a hand mixer, beat in the sifted powdered sugar, evaporated skimmed milk, margarine, and vanilla. Beat until smooth. Using a one-fourth cup measure, drop the banana mixture over the cake mixture. Swirl the two mixtures together using a knife to cut through the batter. Bake at 350° F. 40-45 minutes or until toothpick inserted comes out clean. Cool completely.

Creamy "Cool" Filling:

Prepare pudding using 1¾ cups skim milk and vanilla, beating until thickened. Spread pudding over cooled cake.

Surprise:

Place 40 reduced fat Vanilla Wafers on top of pudding. (8 lengthwise and 5 across)

Icing on the Cake:

Spread 1½ cups Betty Crocker Fat-Free Fluffy Frosting over the top of the vanilla wafers covering well. This is one of my favorites. I made it up as I was experimenting with another cake recipe that didn't turn out the way I wanted. I love bananas, so I just changed things around and came up with this creation. I hope you enjoy it as much as I did making it up!

Yields: Serves 24

Per Serving: All Sugar

Fat:	2.1 g	Calories: 200		Protein:	3 g
Cholesterol:	0 mg	9% Calories from Fat		Carbohydrate:	42 g
Fiber:	<1 g			Sodium:	289 mg

Per Serving: ½ Sweet 'N Low

Fat:	2.1 g	Calories: 180		Protein:	3 g
Cholesterol:	0 mg	10% Calories from Fat		Carbohydrate:	37 g
Fiber:	<1 g			Sodium:	289 mg

SWEET TREATS

CARAMEL APPLE CAKE
(A Pam Original)

Cake:
1 (1 lb. 2.25-oz.) Betty Crocker "Light" or Pillsbury Lovin' Lites yellow low-fat cake mix
⅓ cup water
¾ cup Fleischmann's Fat-Free Spread (squeeze bottle)
1 tsp. vanilla
¾ cup Egg Beaters
3 cups peeled and finely chopped apples (Granny Smith or Red Delicious)

Caramel Filling:
½ cup brown sugar (or ¼ cup brown sugar and 1 tsp. Sweet 'N Low Brown)
¼ cup sugar (or 2 Tbs. sugar and 1 ½ packets Sweet 'N Low)
¼ cup Fleischmann's Fat-Free Spread
1 tsp. vanilla

Topping:
1 cup Mrs. Richardson's or Smucker's Fat-Free Caramel Topping
2 cups miniature marshmallows

Cake:
Turn the oven on and set the temperature at 350°F. Spray a 9½ X 13-inch dish with a non-stick cooking spray. In a large bowl combine cake ingredients (except chopped apples). Blend with a hand mixer until smooth. Fold finely chopped apples into batter. Pour into the prepared 9½ X 13-inch baking dish.

Caramel Filling:
In a medium-sized bowl combine both sugars, margarine, and vanilla. Pour over cake batter and cut through batter with a butter knife swirling both mixtures together. Bake at 350° F. 35 minutes. Remove from oven and pour 1 cup caramel topping on top. Sprinkle 2 cups miniature marshmallows over top and return to oven for 5 more minutes or until marshmallows start to melt and turn golden brown. This is really delicious served warm.

Option: You can omit the apples and have a plain caramel cake. My husband Mike liked the cake better without the apples, but he doesn't like apples very much. Everyone else that tried it like the apples in the cake. The apples add no fat and very few calories, so it's just a matter of your own personal taste!

Yields: Serves 24

Per Serving: All Sugar

Fat:	1.3 g	Calories: 175	Protein:	2 g
Cholesterol:	0 mg	7% Calories from Fat	Carbohydrate:	39 g
Fiber:	1 g		Sodium:	267 mg

Per Serving: ½ Sweet 'N Low

Fat:	1.3 g	Calories: 163	Protein:	2 g
Cholesterol:	0 mg	7% Calories from Fat	Carbohydrate:	36 g
Fiber:	1 g		Sodium:	267 mg

CUP OF COFFEE CHOCOLATE CAKE
(A Pam Original)

Cake:
2 cups sugar (or 1 cup sugar and 12 packets Sweet 'N Low)
½ cup Fleischmann's Fat-Free Spread (squeeze bottle)
½ cup Egg Beaters
¾ cup cocoa
2-3 drops red food coloring
1 tsp. baking powder
½ tsp. Papa Dash "Lite" salt
2 tsp. baking soda dissolved in 1 cup fat-free buttermilk (You can make your own fat-free buttermilk by combining (1 cup skim milk and 2 tsp. vinegar or lemon juice; let set for 5 minutes)
1 tsp. vanilla
2 cups all-purpose flour
1 cup hot coffee (I use Amaretto or Irish Cream favored, non-alcoholic coffee for added flavor.)

Frosting:
1 cup Betty Crocker Fat-Free Fluffy Frosting mix (prepared)
½ cup Mrs. Richardson's fat-free fudge topping

Cake:
Preheat the oven to 350°F. Cream together everthing except flour, milk and coffee. Add the flour and milk alternating a little at a time. Beat until smooth. Stir in coffee. Pour the batter into a 9-inch pan that has been sprayed with Pam Cooking Spray. Bake 30-35 minutes. Frost or eat plain.

Frosting:
Combine prepared frosting and ½ cup fudge topping. Spread evenly over cake. You can also swirl the two together, giving it a black and white effect.

Yields: Serves 16

Per Serving Unfrosted: All Sugar

Fat:	0.8 g	Calories:	178	Protein:	4 g
Cholesterol:	0 mg	4% Calories from Fat		Carbohydrate:	41 g
Fiber:	2 g			Sodium:	260 mg

Per Serving Unfrosted: ½ Sweet 'N Low

Fat:	0.8 g	Calories:	132	Protein:	4 g
Cholesterol:	0 mg	5% Calories from Fat		Carbohydrate:	29 g
Fiber:	2 g			Sodium:	260 mg

Per Serving Frosted: All Sugar

Fat:	0.8g	Calories:	218	Protein:	4 g
Cholesterol:	0 mg	3% Calories from Fat		Carbohydrate:	50 g
Fiber:	2 g			Sodium:	293 mg

Per Serving Frosted: ½ Sweet 'N Low

Fat:	0.8g	Calories:	172	Protein:	4 g
Cholesterol:	0 mg	3% Calories from Fat		Carbohydrate:	39 g
Fiber:	2 g			Sodium:	293 mg

SWEET TREATS

CHOCOLATE CHIP CREAM CHEESE CUPCAKES
(A Pam Original)

Filling:
1 (8-oz.) pkg. Philadelphia Free fat-free cream cheese
¼ cup Egg Beaters
⅓ cup sugar (or 1 heaping Tbs. sugar and
    2 packets Sweet 'N Low)
½ cup Hershey's Mini chocolate chips

Frosting:
1 ¼ cups Betty Crocker Vanilla prepared Low-Fat
    Frosting (0.5 fat grams per 2 Tbs.)

Chocolate Batter:
1 ½ cups all-purpose flour
1 cup sugar (or ½ cup sugar and 6
    packets Sweet 'N Low)
¼ cup cocoa
1 tsp. baking soda
⅛ tsp. Papa Dash "Lite" salt
1 cup water
⅓ cup Fleischmann's Fat-Free Squeeze Margarine
1 Tbs. vinegar
1 tsp. vanilla

Turn the oven on and set the temperature at 350 degrees. Spray a muffin tin with Pam Cooking Spray.

Filling:
In a medium-sized bowl, blend together cream cheese, Egg Beaters, and ⅓ cup sugar, mixing well. Stir in mini chocolate chips. Set aside.

Chocolate Batter:
In a large bowl, mix together all ingredients. Stir at slow speed for about 2 minutes, or until batter is smooth. Fill the baking cups one-third full with chocolate batter. Top each with one heaping teaspoon of the cream cheese mixture. Bake at 350 F. 40-45 minutes. Cool completely. Top each cupcake with 1 Tbs. frosting.

Note: This is a great recipe for kid's parties. You might make them in the mini cupcake tins to eliminate the "half-eaten cupcake" syndrome!

Yields: 18 cupcakes or 50 mini cupcakes

Per Cupcake: All Sugar

Fat:	2.2 g	Calories: 145		Protein:	49 g
Cholesterol:	2 mg	14% Calories from Fat		Carbohydrate:	29 g
Fiber:	1 g			Sodium:	191 mg

Per Cupcake: ½ Sweet 'N Low

Fat:	2.2 g	Calories: 114		Protein:	49 g
Cholesterol:	2 mg	17% Calories from Fat		Carbohydrate:	20 g
Fiber:	1 g			Sodium:	191 mg

Per Mini Cupcake: All Sugar

Fat:	0.8 g	Calories: 52		Protein:	1 g
Cholesterol:	1 mg	14% Calories from Fat		Carbohydrate:	10 g
Fiber:	<1 g			Sodium:	69 mg

Per Mini Cupcake: ½ Sweet 'N Low

Fat:	0.8 g	Calories: 41		Protein:	1 g
Cholesterol:	1 mg	17% Calories from Fat		Carbohydrate:	7 g
Fiber:	<1 g			Sodium:	69 mg

SWEET TREATS

PIE CRUSTS
(A Low-Fat Challenge)

I receive letters with requests for low-fat pie crusts quite frequently. After experimenting with all kinds of ingredients, I found quite a few that work well and are low-fat, too! The following recipes are some of my favorites you might consider trying. I hope with these new options, you will be able to find one your family likes, too. Good Luck!

MY BASIC PASTRY PIE CRUST

1 ¼ cups all-purpose flour
¼-½ tsp. Papa dash "Lite" Salt
2 Tbs. sugar (or 1 Tsp. Sugar and 1 ½ packets of Sweet 'N Low)
3 Tbs. Fleischmann's Lower-Fat margarine (4.5 fat grams per Tbs.)
4-5 Tbs. ice cold water
1-3 Tbs. flour or cornstarch for rolling dough

Optional: ½-1 cup dried beans to fill pie in foil lined mold to prevent shrinkage. This is not necessary if you are making a pie where the filling bakes in the crust.

Preheat the oven to 475°F. for a baked pie crust shell. Check with your pie recipe if you are making this crust to be filled as it bakes (as in a Pumpkin Pie). Times and temperatures will vary. Mix together all of the ingredients except the water. Stir with a fork to mix and use a pastry cutter or two knives to cut the margarine into the flour and sugar mixture. Add the ice water and shape into a ball. DO NOT OVERWORK THE DOUGH! Place the flattened circle in between two pieces of waxed paper coated with a little flour or cornstarch (to prevent sticking). Roll the pastry into a circle large enough to cover a 9-inch pie plate. Spray the pan or plate with a little cooking spray. Arrange the crust in pan. Cut the edges off with a knife, leaving a 1-inch overhang. Turn the overhang under and crimp with your thumb and index finger all around the edge. Prick the bottom and sides of the crust (if it is for a pre-baked pie crust) with a fork. Place a piece of foil over the crust and form to fit the pie. Fill the foil with 1 cup of dried beans (they act as a weight so the crust doesn't shrink) and bake about 6 minutes. Remove foil and beans and return to oven for about 4-5 more minutes or until golden brown. Cool before adding the filling. If you are making a pie where the filling bakes in the crust, simply preheat the oven to 350°F. and bake pie the amount of time that your recipe calls for (usually about 45 minutes). To prevent the edges of the crust from becoming too brown, cut a 3-inch wide strip of foil (the length of your pie) and wrap the foil strip around the edge like a shield. Remove the foil for the last 5 minutes.

Note: Double this recipe for a two-crust pie!

Yields: Serves 8

Per Serving:

Fat:	1.8 g	Calories: 91	Protein:	2 g
Cholesterol:	0 mg	17% Calories from Fat	Carbohydrate:	18 g
Fiber:	<1 g		Sodium:	45 mg

BASIC GRAHAM CRACKER CRUST

12 full-sized (or 2 cups crushed) Keebler Low-Fat Cinnamon Crisp Graham Crackers
2 Tbs. sugar (or 1 Tbs. sugar and 1 ½ packets Sweet 'N Low)
2-3 Tbs. Fleischmann's Fat-Free Squeeze Margarine or Liquid Butter Buds (made from the mix)
   ***Both are fat-free.**

Crush the graham crackers by using a rolling pin to roll over the graham crackers sealed in a Zip-Lock Baggie (or roll over crackers placed on a piece of waxed paper on your counter). In a medium-sized bowl, combine all of the ingredients and mix well with a fork until just moistened. If it is too dry, add a little more margarine. If it is too runny or sticky, add a little more cookie crumbs. Press into a prepared pie pan or plate that has been sprayed with "I Can't Believe It's Not Butter!" spray. Use the crust as your recipe directs.

Note: You can use SnackWell's fat-free Cinnamon Graham Snacks and make the crust fat-free.

Note: You can make this a **chocolate crust** by substituting 3 Tbs. powdered sugar for the regular sugar and adding ½ cup Nestles Quick powder mix. If it is too dry, add a little more fat-free margarine.

Yields: Serves 8

Per Serving:

Fat:	1 g	Calories: 93		Protein:	1 g
Cholesterol:	0 mg	% Calories from Fat		Carbohydrate:	29 g
Fiber:	1 g			Sodium:	170 mg

VANILLA WAFER CRUST

1 ½ cups crushed Keebler Reduced Fat Vanilla Wafers (about 32 cookies)
2 Tbs. Fleischmann's Fat-Free Spread (squeeze bottle)

Heat oven to 350° F. Spray a pie pan with Pam Cooking Spray. Combine crumbs and margarine in an 8 or 9-inch pan. Pat mixture evenly on bottom and sides of pan. Bake 8-10 minutes until edge is slightly browned. Cool on a wire rack.

Yields: Serves 8

Per Serving:

Fat:	1.7 g	Calories: 66		Protein:	1 g
Cholesterol:	0 mg	23% Calories from Fat		Carbohydrate:	13 g
Fiber:	<1 g			Sodium:	101 mg

SWEET TREATS

PHYLLO PIE CRUST

Pam Cooking Spray or I Can't Believe It's Not Butter! Cooking Spray
5 or 6 Phyllo pastry sheets

I have had wonderful results using Phyllo pastry sheets. You can find them in the freezer section or cold department (by frozen pie crusts) of your grocery store. **Five or six sheets are less than 2.5 fat grams.** You might want to lay the sheets on a damp towel to keep them moist and supple as you work with them. I suggest you spray the pastry sheets with a little non-stick cooking spray and **layer in a pie plate, tucking the edges under and molding to fit the pan. Bake at 375° F. for 5-7 minutes.** Cool and fill as directed by your recipe. If you are making a pie that bakes in the crust, simply follow the recipe directions. **You will find baking instructions on the box of Phyllo Sheets, as well.** I think you will like the taste and texture of this pie crust.

Yields: Serves 8		

		Per Serving:			
Fat:	0.3 g	Calories: 50	Protein:	2 g
Cholesterol:	0 mg	4% Calories from Fat	Carbohydrate:	11 g
Fiber:	<1 g		Sodium:	63 mg

GRANOLA PIE CRUST

2 cups fat free granola (Health Valley or Back to Nature brand)
1 Tbs. apple juice or apple juice concentrate
1 Tbs. honey
1 egg white or 2 Tbs. Egg Beaters egg substitute

Simply place 2 cups fat-free granola in a food processor and grind about 2-3 minutes. Add one tablespoon apple juice or apple juice concentrate (for more flavor), 1 tablespoon honey, and one egg white or (2 Tbs. Egg Beaters egg substitute). Process until all ingredients are blended. Remove and press into a 9-inch pie plate sprayed lightly with Pam Spray. Bake 12-15 minutes at 325° F. Cool and fill as your recipe directs.

Note: The only fat is the natural fat found within the grains of the cereal. Since the cereal nutritional information lists ½ cup per serving it could contain 0.49 fat grams per serving (or less) and still be considered fat-free. For that reason if you take 0.49 X 4 (2 cups)= 1.96 fat grams. This would amount to 0.2 fat grams per serving.

Yields: Serves 8		

		Per Serving:			
Fat:	0.2 g	Calories: 50	Protein:	1 g
Cholesterol:	0 mg	4% Calories from Fat	Carbohydrate:	13 g
Fiber:	1 g		Sodium:	14 mg

SWEET TREATS

PRETZEL PIE CRUST

2 cups crushed fat-free pretzels (about 8-oz.)
1 Tbs. sugar (or 1 ½ packets Sweet 'N Low)
½ cup Liquid Butter Buds (made from the mix) or Fleischmann's Fat-Free Squeeze Margarine

Simply crush fat-free pretzels with a rolling pin to equal two cups. Add 1 Tbs. sugar (or Sweet 'N Low), and ½ cup liquid Butter Buds (made from mix) or Fleischmann's Fat-Free Margarine. This will provide a crust for a 9 1/2 X 13-inch dish. I use this crust recipe in "Paige's Party Pie" on page 472 in the "Kids In The Kitchen" section of this book.

Yields: Serves 24

Per Serving:

Fat:	0 g	Calories:	41	Protein:	1 g
Cholesterol:	0 mg	0% Calories from Fat		Carbohydrate:	9 g
Fiber:	<1 g			Sodium:	137 mg

MERINGUE PIE CRUST

4 egg whites
4 Tbs. Maple Syrup
1 tsp. Lemon juice
¼ tsp. cream of tartar

Beat the egg whites until bubbly. Add the syrup, lemon juice, and cream of tartar. Beat on high about 5 minutes until peaks form, but not too dry. Spread the meringue in two pie plates that have been sprayed lightly with Pam Spray, and bake at 275° F. 8-10 minutes or until lightly browned. Turn the oven off and leave the meringue crusts in the oven for about one hour. Remove and use at once by filling, or store in an air tight container for later use. My family really likes this crisp and crunchy (but light) crust.

Note: If you let the filling set in the crust, it will get soggy. **Fill just before serving!**

Yields: 2 pie crusts-serves 16

Per Serving:

Fat:	0 g	Calories:	17	Protein:	1 g
Cholesterol:	0 mg	0% Calories from Fat		Carbohydrate:	3 g
Fiber:	0 g			Sodium:	14 mg

SWEET TREATS

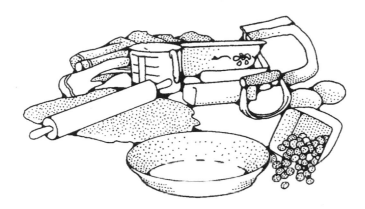

ATTENTION READERS:

There is a new low-fat product called MRS. BATEMAN'S Baking Butter. It is a fat substitute that can be used in place of butter, oil, margarine, or lard in making pie crusts. It contains a very small amount of butter, which explains the rich buttery taste and is primarily maltodextrin (a carbohydrate) derived from corn, potatoes, and rice. It contains a mere 13 fat grams a cup and 35 mg. of cholesterol compared to 184 fat grams found in one cup of butter (not to mention 496 mg. of cholesterol). You can use it by substituting the exact same amount of Baking Butter in place of the fat called for in your recipe. There is no need to adjust the ingredients. MRS. BATEMAN'S Baking Butter is available in some Sam's Clubs and Albertson's stores across the country. It is also available by mail order. Call: (800) 574-6822 for ordering information. This product can be used for cooking and baking, but is especially good in pastries, such as pie crusts.

SWEET TREATS

CHOCOLATE CHIP COOKIE DOUGH PIE
(A Pam Original)

Basic Pastry Crust:
1 ¼ cups all-purpose flour
2 Tbs. sugar
¼ tsp. Papa Dash Lite Salt
3 Tbs. cold Fleischmann's Lower Fat
    Margarine (4.5 fat grams a Tbs.)
4-5 Tbs. ice water

Note: This pie gets its name because it
    tastes like cookie dough-Yum!

Filling:
½ cup Egg Beaters
1 cup Fleischmann's Fat-Free
    Squeeze Margarine
½ cup all-purpose flour
½ cup sugar (or ¼ cup sugar and
    3 packets Sweet 'N Low)
½ cup brown sugar (or ¼ cup packed brown
    sugar and ½ tsp. Sweet 'N Low Brown)
1 tsp. vanilla extract
1 cup Grape Nuts Cereal
¼ cup Mini Chocolate Chips

Crust:
Turn the oven on and set the temperature at 325°F. Mix together all of the crust ingredients except ice water. Cut the margarine into the flour/sugar mixture with a pastry blender or two knives until just mixed. Add ice water and blend, but do not overwork. Mold into a ball and place, flattened, between two pieces of waxed paper (sprinkled with flour) on your counter. Sprinkle a couple of drops of water underneath the waxed paper to prevent the dough from sliding around when you are rolling out the dough. Roll dough into a circle larger than your 9-inch pie plate. Leaving the top piece of waxed paper on the crust fold in half, then into fourths. Remove the bottom piece of waxed paper and place the ¼ folded-over-dough into the pie plate. Unfold to cover the plate. Trim any excess around the edge leaving a ½-1-inch overhang. Fold under the excess and crimp with your thumb and index finger all around the top edge. Place the pie shell in the refrigerator until ready to fill.

Pie Filling:
In a large bowl, beat the Egg Beaters with margarine until foamy. Add flour, sugar, brown sugar, and vanilla. Beat until well-blended. Stir in Grape Nuts Cereal and Mini Chocolate Chips. Pour into pie shell. Place a strip of foil 3-inches x 12-inches molded around the top edge of the pie crust, careful not to disturb the filling. This will act as a shield so the crust won't get too brown. Remove the foil during the last 5-10 minutes of baking time. Bake 50-60 minutes. Check your pie after 40 minutes. Remove the foil at this time and continue baking until done. Remove from oven and serve warm with Guilt Free Vanilla (sugar-free and fat-free which would add no fat) ice cream if you desire. You can also top each piece with 1 Tbs. "Light" Cool Whip if you like. This would add ½ fat gram per serving.

Yields: Serves 8		

		Per Serving: All Sugar			
Fat:	3.9 g	Calories:	319	Protein:	7 g
Cholesterol:	0 mg	11% Calories from Fat		Carbohydrate:	64 g
Fiber:	2 g			Sodium:	413 mg

		Per Serving: ½ Sweet 'N Low			
Fat:	3.9 g	Calories:	265	Protein:	7 g
Cholesterol:	0 mg	13% Calories from Fat		Carbohydrate:	58 g
Fiber:	2 g			Sodium:	413 mg

SWEET TREATS

PEANUT BUTTER SUNDAE PIE
(A High-fat Recipe Pam Modified to Low-fat)
(A Real Taste Treat!)

Crust:
3 Tbs. corn syrup
2 Tbs. packed brown sugar
10 marshmallows
1 tsp. Butter Buds Sprinkles
3 cups Rice Krispie Cereal

Sauce:
2 Tbs. Peter Pan "Smart Choice" reduced fat peanut butter
¾ cup Mrs. Richardson's Fat-Free Fudge Sauce
3 Tbs. corn syrup

1 Qt. Yarnells Guilt Free (fat-free and sugar-free) Vanilla Ice Cream

Combine the 3 Tbs. corn syrup, brown sugar, marshmallows, and Butter Buds Sprinkles in a medium-sized saucepan. Cook over low heat, stirring occasionally, until marshmallows melt or heat mixture on high about two minutes in the microwave or until marshmallows melt. Remove from heat. Add Rice Krispie Cereal, stirring until well-coated. Spray a little Pam Cooking Spray on your fingers to prevent sticking as you handle the crust. Press evenly in a 9-inch pie pan that has been sprayed with Pam Cooking Spray. Stir together peanut butter, fudge sauce, and 3 Tbs. corn syrup. Spread half the peanut butter mixture over the crust. Freeze until firm. Allow ice cream to soften slightly. Spoon into frozen piecrust, spreading evenly. Freeze until firm. Let pie stand at room temperature about ten minutes before cutting. Warm remaining peanut butter mixture and drizzle over the top as you serve. Serve with 1 Tbs. "Light" Cool Whip on top and you will only add ½ of a fat gram. This is a real taste treat!

Yields: Serves 8

Per Serving:

Fat:	1.5 g	Calories:	265	Protein:	7 g
Cholesterol:	5 mg	10% Calories from Fat		Carbohydrate:	56 g
Fiber:	1 g			Sodium:	283 mg

SWEET TREATS

CHOCOLATE BROWNIE PIE
(A Pam Original)

Crust:
⅓ cup hot water
2 tsp. instant coffee granules, divided use
½ (1 lb. 2.25-oz.) box Betty Crocker "Light" brownie mix or Lovin' Lites brownie mix (about 2 cups)
1 tsp. vanilla, divided
½ cup Egg Beaters

Filling and Topping:
1 Tbs. hot water
1 tsp. instant coffee granules
¾ cup plus 2 Tbs. skim milk
1 tsp. vanilla
1 (3.9-oz.) pkg. chocolate flavored fat-free instant pudding (regular or sugar free)
1 (7.2-oz.) box Betty Crocker Fat-Free Fluffy Frosting Mix (prepared as directed on package with ½ cup hot water)
2 Tbs. Mini Chocolate Chips

Crust:
Turn the oven on and set the temperature at 325 degrees. Combine ⅓ cup hot water with 2 tsp. coffee granules in a medium bowl and stir well. Add 2 cups brownie mix, 1 tsp. vanilla and Egg Beaters stirring until well blended. Spoon mixture into a 9-inch square baking dish sprayed with Pam Cooking Spray. Bake at 325° F. for 20-25 minutes. Let crust cool completely.

Filling and topping:
Combine 1 Tbs. hot water and 1 tsp. instant coffee granules. Add skim milk, 1 tsp. vanilla, and pudding mix beating until thickened (about 2-3 minutes). Prepare frosting mix using ½ cup hot water and beat until stiff peaks form. Fold 1 ½ cups prepared frosting (about ½ of the frosting) into the pudding mixture. Spread over cooled crust. Place in the refrigerator about 15 minutes. Remove and top with remaining Fluffy Frosting. Sprinkle 2 Tbs. Mini Chocolate Chips over the top. Refrigerate until ready to serve.

Yields: Serves 12

Per Serving: using regular pudding

Fat:	2.5 g	Calories:	200	Protein:	3.3 g
Cholesterol:	0 mg	15% Calories from Fat		Carbohydrate:	46 g
Fiber:	.6 g			Sodium:	332 mg

Per Serving: using Sugar Free Pudding

Fat:	2.5 g	Calories:	182	Protein:	3.3 g
Cholesterol:	0 mg	16% Calories from Fat		Carbohydrate:	40 g
Fiber:	.6 g			Sodium:	167 mg

SWEET TREATS

MOM'S BLUEBERRY DELIGHT
(Pam Modified to Low-fat)

**Char Doehler
Granbury, Texas**

Crust:
24 full-sized Keebler Low-Fat Cinnamon Crisp Graham Crackers (crushed with a rolling pin)
¼ cup sugar (or 2 Tbs. sugar and 1 ½ packets Sweet 'N Low
5-6 Tbs. Liquid Butter Buds (made from the mix) or Fleishmann's Fat-Free Spread

Filling:
½ cup Egg Beaters
1 (8-oz.) pkg. Philadelphia Free fat-free cream cheese
½ cup sugar (or ¼ cup sugar and 3 packets Sweet 'N Low)

Topping:
¼ tsp. almond extract
1 (21-oz.) can "Light" Blueberry Pie Filling (can use cherry or other flavor)
1 packet Sweet 'N Low
½ cup Cool Whip "Light" Topping
1 cup Betty Crocker Fat-Free Fluffing Frosting (comes in a box you mix with hot water)
   *The box makes 3 cups, but it will save in the refrigerator several days.

Turn the oven on and set the temperature at 350 degrees. Mix the graham cracker crumbs, ¼ cup sugar, and Liquid Butter Buds. Press into the bottom of a 9 ½ X 11-inch glass casserole dish that has been sprayed with Pam Cooking Spray. Save 2-3 Tbs. of the graham cracker mixture for the topping.

Beat Egg Beaters, cream cheese, and ½ cup sugar together. Pour over crust and bake at 350° F. for 15 minutes. Cool. Mix ½ tsp. almond extract and 1 packet Sweet 'N Low with the Blueberry Pie Filling in a small bowl. Spread over cooled filling. Mix ½ cup "Light" Cool Whip with 1 cup Betty Crocker (prepared) Fat-free Fluffy Frosting. Spread over Blueberry layer. Sprinkle reserved 2-3 Tbs. graham cracker crumbs on top.

Note: You can reduce the fat by using SnackWell's Cinnamon Graham Snacks in place of the low-fat graham crackers.

Yields: Serves 20

Per Serving: All Sugar

Fat:	0.9 g	Calories: 146	Protein:	3 g
Cholesterol:	2 mg	6% Calories from Fat	Carbohydrate:	30 g
Fiber:	1 g		Sodium:	213 mg

Per Serving: ½ Sweet 'N Low

Fat:	0.9 g	Calories: 131	Protein:	3 g
Cholesterol:	2 mg	6% Calories from Fat	Carbohydrate:	26 g
Fiber:	1 g		Sodium:	213 mg

SWEET TREATS

PAM'S SWEET PIZZA
(A High-fat Recipe Pam Modified to Low-fat)

Crust:
1 pkg. Betty Crocker or Lovin' Lites low-fat
    yellow cake mix
¼ cup water
¼ cup brown sugar (or 2 Tbs. brown sugar
and ½ tsp. Sweet 'N Low Brown)
¼ cup Fleischmann's Fat-Free Squeeze
    Margarine or ¼ cup Promise Ultra
    Fat-Free Margarine
½ cup Egg Beaters
½ cup Grape Nuts Cereal

Glaze:
½ cup orange juice
½ cup sugar (or ¼ cup sugar and
    3 packets Sweet 'N Low)
¼ cup water
1 Tbs. cornstarch
2 Tbs. lemon juice

Filling:
1 (8-oz.) pkg. Philadelphia Free fat-free
    cream cheese
2 cups Betty Crocker Fat-Free Frosting mix
    (prepared as directed on box) *You will
    have one cup left to use for another time. It
    will keep in the refrigerator about three days.

Topping:
1 (20-oz.) can drained chunk pineapple
1 (21-oz.) Lite Cherry pie Filling (mixed with
    2 packets Sweet 'N Low and ½ tsp.
    almond extract)
20 green grapes
*You can use any kind of fruit you like (bananas,
    cantaloupe, strawberries, Kiwi, etc.)
1 (15-oz.) can drained blueberries

Crust: Blend first 6 ingredients together and press into a pizza pan that has been sprayed with Pam Cooking Spray. Bake at 350° F. about 15-20 minutes or until light brown. (This recipe makes two crusts.)

Filling: Prepare frosting mix as directed on package. Beat cream cheese and fold into 2 cups of the prepared frosting. (You will have enough to cover two pizzas.)

Topping: Ring the outside of the pizzas with blueberries (1 can does two pizzas), second row-pineapple chunks, third ring pie filling cherries, and grapes with cherries again in the middle or blueberries (use you own imagination). You can even do a face with fruit or any way you want to do it. Place both pizzas in the refrigerator while you make the glaze.

Glaze: Mix and boil the glaze ingredients about 1-2 minutes or until thickened. Stir cornstarch in with a wire whisk. If the cornstarch clumps together, use an electric hand mixer to blend (be careful if it is still hot) or put in blender (to mix ingredients well) before you cook it. Cool well by placing in the refrigerator about 15 minutes. Remove pizzas from refrigerator and spoon glaze over fruit. Chill until ready to serve.

Note: These freeze well. Place in freezer until frozen. Remove and wrap in Saran Wrap and then foil. They will keep months in the fridge. They are great to have on hand when unexpected company arrives!

SWEET TREATS

PAM'S SWEET PIZZA (cont.)

Yields: 24-30 servings (two pizzas - each pizza serves 12-15)

Per Serving: All Sugar

Fat:	1.3 g	Calories:	204	Protein:	3 g
Cholesterol:	2 mg	6% Calories from Fat		Carbohydrate:	44 g
Fiber:	1 g			Sodium:	258 mg

Per Serving: ½ Sweet 'N Low

Fat:	1.3 g	Calories:	194	Protein:	3 g
Cholesterol:	2 mg	6% Calories from Fat		Carbohydrate:	40 g
Fiber:	1 g			Sodium:	258 mg

CHOCOLATE CHIP COOKIE ICE CREAM SUNDAES
(A High-fat Recipe Pam Modified to Low-fat)

1 package Betty Crocker Fat-Free Fluffy Frosting Mix
1 tsp. vanilla
½ tsp. almond extract (optional)
¾ cup Quick Oats oatmeal
1 ½ cups crushed Keebler brand low-fat graham crackers (This would be 9 whole crackers.)
½ cup mini chocolate chips
1 cup Mrs. Richardson's fat-free fudge topping or Smucker's fat-free fudge topping
1 Qt. Yarnell's Guilt Free Vanilla (sugar and fat-free) ice cream (or other brand) (¼ cup per sundae)

Turn the oven on and set temperature at 350 degrees. In a large mixing bowl, prepare frosting mix according to package directions. Stir in vanilla and almond extract. Fold in oatmeal, graham cracker crumbs, and mini chocolate chips. Spoon batter into a 9-inch square glass dish that has been sprayed lightly with Pam Spray. Bake at 350° F. for 30 minutes or until light brown. Remove from oven and cool about 10 minutes. Meanwhile, heat the fudge sauce (in a glass bowl) in the microwave about one minute (or on top of stove in a saucepan). Cut cake into squares and top each serving with a 1/4-cup scoop of fat-free ice cream and top with 1 Tbs. hot fudge sauce.

Note: You can reduce the fat by using SnackWell's Fat-Free Cinnamon Graham Snacks.

Note: You can add a squirt of Redi Wip "Light" topping or "Light" Cool Whip if desired.

Yields: 16 servings

Per Serving:

Fat:	2.8 g	Calories:	233	Protein:	4 g
Cholesterol:	3 mg	11% Calories from Fat		Carbohydrate:	46 g
Fiber:	2 g			Sodium:	167 mg

SWEET TREATS

RICH AND GOOEY BANANA SUNDAES
(A Pam Original Taste Treat!)

⅔ cup Smucker's Butterscotch (or Caramel) Fat-Free dessert topping
2 Tbs. water*
½ tsp. rum extract
⅛ tsp. cinnamon
4 firm ripe medium-sized bananas
3 cups Guilt Free Praline flavored OR Vanilla Yarnell's Guilt Free (fat-free and sugar-free) ice cream (your choice)
2 Tbs. fat-free granola (any brand)

In a large skillet, combine dessert topping, water, rum extract, and cinnamon. Cook over medium heat, stirring frequently, until well mixed and hot. Cut bananas lengthwise, then crosswise into thirds. Stir bananas into the topping mixture. Cook stirring gently, until bananas are thoroughly heated.

Scoop ½ cup fat-free ice cream into dessert goblets or dishes. Spoon bananas and sauce over the ice cream. Sprinkle 1 tsp. fat free granola on top of each sundae. Enjoy!!

* Some butterscotch toppings may require 1-3 Tbs. more water to reach desired consistency.

Note: You can mix and match any topping and flavor of ice cream that appeals to you. I just gave you a couple of suggestions that I happen to like myself.

Yields: Serves 6 (1/2 cup ice cream plus toppings)

Per Serving:

Fat:	0.4 g	Calories:	250	Protein:	9 g
Cholesterol:	5 mg	1% Calories from Fat		Carbohydrate:	24 g
Fiber:	5 g			Sodium:	122 mg

NOTES

KIDS ARE PEOPLE TOO!

OUR CHILDREN—THE FUTURE!

I don't know about you, but I want my own children to grow up healthy and not be forced to contend with cholesterol and weight related problems so many of us adults have had to deal with (myself included). If children develop good healthy eating habits while they are young, they won't HAVE to change their lifestyles when they grow up. The kids today are really bright. They learn how to work computers in kindergarten. I just learned last year (and it wasn't easy). As a matter of fact, I wrote *BUTTER BUSTERS* on a word processor. You see, I didn't grow up around computers, so I had to learn something that I was unfamiliar with. That is my point. Let's not make it hard on our kids. Let's teach them healthy eating and exercise habits from the beginning so they won't have to learn later in life when they are forced to because of health problems.

Even though our kids can work computers and videogames without directions (amazing to me), these activities, unfortunately, make them much less active than we were. When I was a kid, I couldn't wait to go outside and play as soon as I got home from school. In the summer we played outside all day long. Today, many of the children come home to an empty house (because both parents work) and it is up to them to choose a healthy snack before they settle down in front of the T.V. to watch cartoons or play video games. Hey, I can say this, because I have children, too. I'm not always home when Tyler rolls in, and yes, he does like to watch T.V. and play video games. I know the problems you face, because I face them, too. Lack of physical activity along with high-fat/ high-sugar snacks (on a regular basis) can't help but lead to problems. That is why it is so important to teach our children good healthy habits from the beginning. Try to stock your pantry with tasty low-fat snacks your children will WANT TO EAT. Give them a variety of healthy choices. This way it will appear to them that THEY are the one deciding what to eat. As for exercise, you can't force physical activity on your children. It just doesn't work and usually leads to resentment. Most kids are involved in sports at school, or otherwise, so this isn't a problem for everyone. However, there are a lot of inactive children. It has been found that kids who watch T.V. three to four hours a day are 4 times as likely to have high cholesterol as kids who watch less than two hours. As most of us know, a sedentary lifestyle can result in obesity. When do you think most people develop those sedentary habits? In childhood for the most part. Most overweight children grow into obese adults. As a matter of fact, obesity in children between the ages of six and eleven has increased by almost 60%. For our teenagers the obesity rate has gone up about 40%. This means we are raising 20 million obese children right here in the United States. It's true, we do have a problem. However, the solution is not putting your child on a diet, forcing them to attend an exercise class, or sending them to "Fat Farm Camp." Yes, many children attend weight-loss camps every summer. I'm not knocking them, nor am I trying to make a joke. I'm just trying to prove my point. Prevention is the key to success!! Let's set a positive example for our children by our own healthy lifestyles. I know it may be necessary to place SOME children on restrictive eating plans (for health purposes), but please don't put your child on a diet because YOU ARE EMBARRASSED if they are a little heavy. Even though it may be necessary (in some cases), most of the time it can be avoided. Dieting is usually ineffective because most diets rely on food deprivation and that just doesn't work for very long. Kids will be kids. If you think they won't "cheat" when you're not around, then I have some swamp land in Florida you might be interested in buying. Seriously, dieting can be down right dangerous to the health of our children. I'm not only talking physically (as in disrupting their natural growth patterns), but emotionally as well. Eating disorders in teenagers, such as anorexia, bulimia, and compulsive overeating are more common than not. There is a good chance that children pressured by their parents to diet or lose weight may be emotionally scarred for life. I know, as a parent, we would never want to hurt or harm our children (in any way) because we love them. Don't inflict YOUR attitude about weight and dieting on your children. It will cause nothing but tension in your household, and nine times out of ten, they will end up eating more food (just to spite you). Instead, try emphasizing health, more energy, and feeling great as the benefits of a healthy lifestyle.

**Pam and Paige
February 1985**

Because I am interested in teaching our children about healthy nutrition, I've decided to make it a little easier to understand. Besides, I think my way makes more sense! For this reason, I have come up with my own healthy food guide. I call it THE BUTTER BUSTERS HEALTHY SAVE YOUR HEART FOOD GUIDE.

Over the years, most of us grew up learning about nutrition through "The Four Basic Food Groups." They included Milk and Milk Products, Meat and Protein Foods, Vegetables and Fruits, and the Bread and Cereal Group. They had another food category that was referred to as "other foods," but it was not considered one of "The Basic Four." It consisted of all high-fat and high-sugar products with little or no nutritional value. The Milk Group (recommended 3 servings a day for children, 4 servings a day for adolescents, and 2 servings for adults) included milk, cottage cheese, yogurt, cheese and ice cream. The Meat Group (with 2 servings recommended a day) consisted of meats, fish, poultry, eggs, cheese, beans or peas, nuts, seeds, and peanut butter. The Vegetable and Fruit Group (which recommended four servings daily) included a citrus fruit, other fruit or vegetable high in vitamin C, and a deep-green or yellow-orange vegetable for vitamin A. The "other foods" category consisted of high calorie foods with limited or no nutritional value, like fats, oils, alcohol, salad dressings, sweets, and high-fat snacks. It was recommended that these foods only be eaten in moderation. As the saying goes, "We've come a long way baby!" (I guess!) Let me explain myself.

**Pam and Paige
February 1995**

In 1993, the United States Department of Agriculture decided we, as Americans, needed to update our Food Guide for healthy eating. Everyone in the field of nutrition was really excited about the new guidelines because they thought it would make it easier on the American people. Don't ask me how they came up with the pyramid idea. It was confusing to some and well-accepted by others. At least it was a vast improvement over "The Basic Four," but in my opinion, still lacks some important details and pertinent information. The Food Guide Pyramid allows 2-3 servings of protein a day and the worst part is they don't distinguish between red meats, poultry, fish, beans, eggs, and nuts. It also suggests several servings of milk, yogurt, and cheese. That is fine if the people using this guide choose low or non-fat dairy products, but could prove disastrous if they consume this many servings in high-fat varieties. Believe me, I am not knocking the importance of calcium in our diets. I am just as concerned about osteoporosis as the next forty-five year old, pre-menopausal woman! I'm just saying that it is "too bad" that low or non-fat products couldn't have been suggested. There are a lot of people in the world that take important information, such as this, at face value. Those are the poor souls that I am concerned about. Like I said, the Food Pyramid is better, but why they put beans with the meats, recommending limited consumption, is beyond me. Everything you read tells you the many health benefits of beans and legumes. **That is my biggest complaint and one I truly do not understand.**

Next enters the folks from Europe who think they have this "health thing" all figured out. Pour olive oil on everything before you eat it, drink only red wine to wash it all down, and you will live to be 120 years old. Does "The Mediterranean Diet" or "The French Paradox" sound familiar? If not, I will try to explain why they are trying to challenge the U.S. Department of Agriculture's Food Guide Pyramid to a duel. Their premise is they do not think dietary fat is a problem. In fact, they feel a moderate amount is actually good for you! The Mediterranean Pyramid actually has some good points. It recommends plenty of breads, pasta, rice, beans, fruits, and vegetables. They suggest some fish, a little cheese, and some poultry. However, they suggest a tremendous amount of olive oil in the diet. Even though it isn't actually listed "on the pyramid," they highly recommend a glass of wine daily. Milk is nowhere to be found on the pyramid of our European friends. Meat is in the tip of the pyramid and only recommended a couple of times a month. They actually give sweets a bigger bill than red meat, pork, or veal. The U.S. Government's Food Guide Pyramid, in contrast, allows two or three servings a day of protein foods but doesn't distinguish between red meats, beans, eggs, poultry, and nuts, **which I personally feel is a major mistake.** The U.S. Government's Pyramid also includes several servings of milk, yogurt, and cheese (not stressing low or non-fat). However, "The Mediterranean Diet" has sparked quite a bit of interest recently. You might have seen "The French Paradox" segment on "60 Minutes" a few years ago. In the 1950s it was discovered that middle-aged men living in Greece and Crete had a 90% lower risk of heart disease compared to American counterparts. The reason it was so interesting was because the men were obtaining 40% of their calories from fat. "The Mediterranean Diet" advocates a very small amount of red meat (which happens to be the major source of protein and fat in the diets of most Americans). In Greece and Crete the main source of protein comes from beans, nuts, yogurt, cheese, and fish. And of course, the primary source of fat, is olive oil. "The Mediterranean Diet" advocates insist that the olive oil is responsible for the low heart disease rates. I agree, to a certain extent, that if you must use an oil, I, too, would recommend olive or canola (both monounsaturated fats) over a polyunsaturated or saturated fat. We all know that saturated fats (such as coconut and the other tropical oils) and animal products (which contain cholesterol) are the major dietary culprit in coronary artery disease (CAD). Most experts feel monounsaturated fats help reduce oxidation of LDL (the "bad" cholesterol) in our blood. LDL oxidation initiates the build-up of plaque (or fatty deposits) in the coronary arteries which increases the risk of a heart attack. Some even feel monounsaturated fats help diabetics by reducing their insulin requirements thus improving glucose metabolism. On the other hand, when the American Heart Association met in 1994 they found no major difference in monounsaturated and polyunsaturated fats and the effect they had on cholesterol and other fats. That theory seems to change with the seasons. **The bottom line is that monounsaturated fats or even polyunsaturated fats are ALWAYS better choices than saturated fats!** The exception, of course, would be if the polyunsaturated fat has been transformed into a trans fatty acid as a result of hydrogenation (a manmade process). However, there are lots of other ways to decrease your consumption of saturated fats than to increase the amount of monounsaturated fats you consume in your diet.

Remember that all fats are 100% fat, and if you are trying to lose or control your weight, you would be wise to steer clear of any kind of fat. I know, we need 5% fat in our diet to perform our bodily functions. I've heard that story, too. Fine, I say, you will consume that much fat in your diet naturally (as in grains, vegetables, etc.) even if you are on a very-low fat diet. AS LONG AS YOU EAT FOOD, YOU WILL CONSUME SOME FAT, I PROMISE!

Tyler and Pam
May 1994

This brings us to the third and final Pyramid. You might not have heard of this one, because it's not exactly "official." This is the pyramid that bothers me the most, because it is the one that concerns our children. I call it the "The Kid's T.V. Guide to Good Eating Pyramid." The problem involves the hours between 6:30-11:30 A.M. (especially Saturdays) when our little cherubs are camped out in front of their favorite shows. Have you sat down with your kids recently to watch T.V. on Saturday morning? Well, I hadn't either until about a week ago. I decided I wanted to spend some quality time with Tyler, and that was the only way I had a chance of bonding with him on that particular morning. So, I figured what the heck, and settled down next to him in Paige's Rainbow Bright sleeping bag (from long ago) that I happened to find in the bottom of the linen closet. Well, if you haven't watched T.V. on Saturday morning lately, I suggest you make an effort to catch a few cartoons in the near future. As we flipped through "Ninja Turtles," "The Little Mermaid," "Power Rangers," and "Saved by the Bell" (my personal favorite), I was amazed at what I saw in a matter of minutes. So, that is how my kids knew about every kind of fun fruit, fruit roll-up, string fruit, etc., etc. in the grocery stores before they ever showed up in my Sunday coupon clippings or appeared on the shelves of our local supermarket. I swear, my kids have given me advance warning (on more than one occasion) to be on the look-out for a number of "kid's fun to eat foods" before they have ever been manufactured. I think they advertise some of that stuff before they even make it just to drive us poor, eager-to-please parents a little crazy!

On Saturday mornings they have a commercial (on the average) every five minutes (I started timing them after the first two). I didn't see anything that resembled fruits or vegetables (except the fruit flavored fun-to-eat-food) that we all have grown to know and buy (if our kids happen to be with us). WE CAN'T SEEM TO GET PAST THAT AISLE FAST ENOUGH BEFORE THEY SCREAM "BUY ME!" TO OUR CHILDREN. I think you know what I am talking about! The only dairy product I caught sight of was the milk they poured on the thirty-five different kinds of sugar-coated cereal and the milk used to make a popular brand of

Tyler and Roxie
February 1995

candy bar (that uses the word milk in its name). What I did see was candy, cereal, soft drinks, cakes, cereal, cookies, pastries, and more cereal, whipped toppings, chips, cereal, and a variety of puddings (I did see milk in this one) and gelatin desserts. No wonder my kids always get so hungry for junk food on Saturday mornings while they watch T.V. I did too! The sad thing about this whole problem is most young children really don't know the difference between a cartoon and a commercial, since many of the advertisements are in "cartoon form." I'm sure there are MANY parents who think food advertisements aimed at young children should be eliminated. Don't hold your breath on this one. My suggestion would be to encourage your kids to tune into the PBS channel or watch a movie on video or go outside to play. Aside from the commercials on Saturday mornings, hours of sitting in front of the T.V. have been associated with obesity and high cholesterol in children. Somehow, after my morning of T.V. with Tyler, I can understand how that could happen!

LETS GET TO THE "HEART" OF THE MATTER!

THREE DIFFERENT OPINIONS OF HEALTHY EATING:
Everyone has a right to their own opinion!

The U.S. Agricultural Food Guide Pyramid

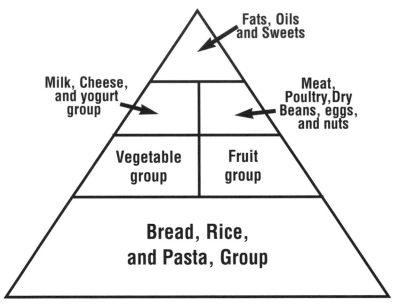

#1 The U.S. Agricultural Food Guide Pyramid

Even though the American Heart Association recommends a diet that contains no more than 30% fat, the

40% Fat
20% Protein
40% Carbohydrate

U. S. Food Guide Pyramid does not designate low-fat products in the various categories. For that reason, anyone using this chart as a guide (who didn't understand hidden fat in foods) could think they were eating a healthy diet while consuming 40-50% fat in their diet. They might also limit healthy foods (such as beans) because they are listed with the meat products. It indicates using fats and oils sparingly, but does not warn against saturated fats or cholesterol containing products. The bottom half of the chart is fine (except the beans should be included in the vegetable section). I think this chart has possibilities, but needs to be more specific for the normal every day lay-person who has not educated in the field of nutrition (which is less than 1% of the entire population).

The Mediterranean Diet Pyramid

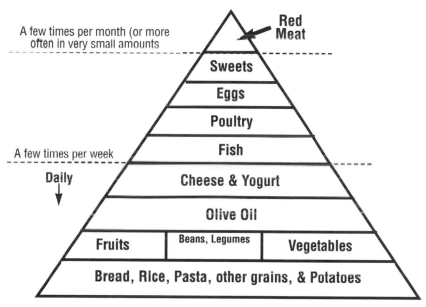

A few times per month (or more often in very small amounts

Red Meat

Sweets

Eggs

Poultry

Fish

A few times per week

Daily

Cheese & Yogurt

Olive Oil

Fruits | Beans, Legumes | Vegetables

Bread, Rice, Pasta, other grains, & Potatoes

#2 The Mediterranean Diet Pyramid

30% Fat
20% Protein
50% Carbohydrate

I actually prefer this Food Guide Pyramid over the U.S. model (in several categories) for several reasons. I think the top of the pyramid is realistic. I don't agree with the size (or %) of the chart given to olive oil, however, at least they have been specific letting the consumer know that this is a "safe oil" to use regarding your heart health. I think leaving off milk and dairy products (except cheese) must have been an oversight. How could anyone ignore milk completely regarding nutrition and do so intentionally? I like the idea that they suggest regular exercise, but have trouble relating to a source that advocates moderate alcohol consumption as part of a healthy diet. Do they consider wine (just because it comes from grapes) a part of the fruit section or what?

The Kid's T.V. Guide to Good Eating Pyramid

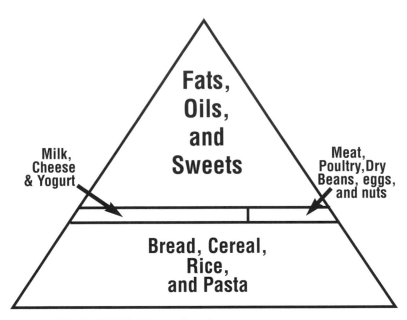

#3 The Kid's T.V. Guide to Good Eating Pyramid

This is the pyramid that really scares me. If our children can be influenced by T.V. (and we know they can), the future adults of our

70% Fat
10% Protein
20% Carbohydrate

country (meaning the kids of today) might be in big trouble (especially if they watch a lot of television). I fear it has a cumulative effect. Let's hope they learn otherwise in school, and most of all they learn from their parents' example of healthy living not to believe everything they happen to see on Saturday mornings between the hours of 6:30-11:30 A.M. I can see it now in the T.V. Guide Program next to the name of the program: "Teenage Mutant Ninja Turtles" 9:00 A.M. WARNING: Watching this program may be hazardous to your health due to commercials containing food suggestions and recommendations that may be detrimental to your health! View at your own risk! I'm just sure! A nice thought, but I wouldn't count on it!

EVERYONE HAS A RIGHT TO THEIR OWN OPINION!

I have my own version of a Healthy Food Guide, and it isn't shaped like a pyramid. I hope this doesn't offend anyone, but I never did understand how or why they came up with the "Pyramid" concept. I am a firm believer in visuals (to make a point), and somehow I just don't see the connection between a pyramid and healthy food suggestions. If you think about it, a pyramid is actually a place to store dead bodies. Pretty scary, huh? I hate to think there might be any connection between the two. Why didn't they just use tombstones? I know this is getting kind of morbid, and I won't say anything else about their choice of healthy food symbols. However, that is exactly why I chose the shape of a heart (for obvious reasons) to represent the BUTTER BUSTERS "SAVE YOUR HEART" FOOD GUIDE. Anyway, it makes a lot more sense to me. Eat these foods and your hearts will be healthy! It doesn't take a rocket scientist to figure out what I am trying to say. So without further ado, I give you ....drum roll please!

THE BUTTER BUSTERS
"SAVE YOUR HEART" FOOD GUIDE

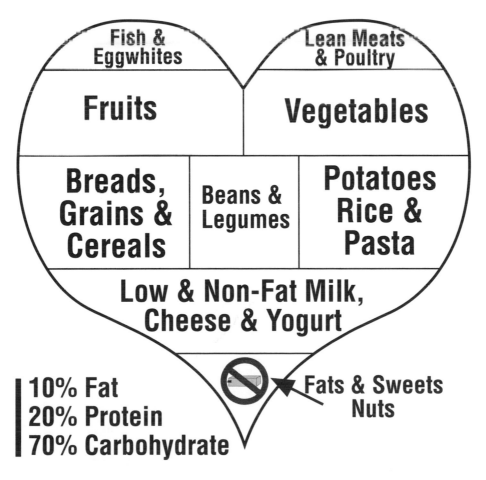

Fish & Eggwhites

Lean Meats & Poultry

Fruits

Vegetables

Breads, Grains & Cereals

Beans & Legumes

Potatoes Rice & Pasta

Low & Non-Fat Milk, Cheese & Yogurt

Fats & Sweets Nuts

10% Fat
20% Protein
70% Carbohydrate

As you can see, my guidelines of 10% fat, 20% protein, and 70% carbohydrates **are what most nutrition experts recommend.** There are plenty of ways to acquire protein in your diet without eating fat-laden products. Therefore I have placed the meat, poultry, fish, and egg whites at the top of the heart. It is also possible to eat low-fat beef, white meat poultry (without skin), low-fat fish (depending on preparation) and to use egg whites in place of whole eggs. The protein is in the white of the egg and the yolks contain fat and cholesterol (which we try to avoid). The other small (10%) section is the fats and sweets. A little goes a long way (in both cases), so don't over-do either one. Besides, there are so many GREAT fat substitutes on the market that you won't miss a thing in taste! The majority of my "Save Your Heart" Food Guide includes fruits and vegetables (rich in vitamins, minerals, and the antioxidants) and the grain products that provide fiber, vitamins, and minerals so important in the nourishment of our bodies. I've included beans, peas, and legumes in this section because they are a wonderful source of protein, and very low in fat.

In the remaining 10% sector you'll find milk, cheese, and yogurt (the dairy products). These foods are rich in calcium that is so important in the prevention of osteoporosis. There is no reason to use whole-milk highly saturated dairy products (after the age of two). Fat SHOULD NEVER be restricted in the diet of your baby before age two (unless they have some very unusual circumstance and your physician recommends this method of treatment). All babies (and children for that matter) need fat in their diets to grow and develop normally. After age two children only need about 30% fat until their teenage years. After the age of 16, it would depend on your family history and hereditary risk factors to determine the need to restrict your child's fat consumption. If your child is of normal weight (for their height and frame size) and is relatively active (with no hereditary or lifestyle risk factors), then 30% fat should be no problem. The American Heart Association recommends no more than 30% total fat (with 10% or less coming from saturated sources) for healthy adults wishing to maintain their weight, with no hereditary or other risk factors.

I personally recommend between 10-20% total fat if you are trying to lose weight or have a weight/fat related problem concerning your health. Even if you are not overweight but have diabetes, heart disease or high cholesterol, you should still consider cutting the fat in your diet.

Saturated fats and cholesterol containing products have been proven detrimental to your heart - health. You would be wise to limit these products as much as possible. As long as you can eat all the foods you love and are used to eating (using low-fat substitutions), you won't be missing out on anything. Always choose low or non-fat dairy products when possible! YOUR HEART WILL THANK YOUR FOR IT!

Moving on now, I want everyone reading this book to realize that even though I make jokes about some of these points, I really do think there are some major problems when it comes to informing the general public of increased risks concerning various diseases resulting from a high-fat diet. I've said this in my workshops, and I really do feel this way. I have no patience with food manufacturers using label deceptions to sell their products. It's one thing if a person needs to drop twenty or thirty pounds for their high school reunion, but quite another when a heart attack survivor purchases turkey bacon because the front of the package states that the product is 80% fat-free (according to weight, but they don't tell you that part), when in all reality the darn stuff is 78% fat. This could be a "life or death" situation for some people. No, I'm not saying that one package of turkey bacon will cause a cardiac arrest. WHAT I AM TALKING ABOUT IS THE GENERAL LACK OF ACCURATE NUTRITIONAL INFORMATION ON ALL FOODS! Now, THAT should be mandatory! In my opinion, and I admit it is my own, I consider intentional labeling deceptions a crime, and I will continue to inform the consumers how to effectively read food labels and to make wise healthy choices (as long as they will listen to me). I guess the reason I feel so strongly about this matter is

**Pam explaining labels
October 1994**

because, at age forty, I discovered my cholesterol was 242. I didn't have any warning or even a clue there might be a problem. The only risk factor I knew of was my brother Tom died at age 19, unexpectedly, due to a heart-related problem. My parents were told his heart had "just stopped." Even the autopsy report was inconclusive. At the time we were all watching calories. We had no idea that fat in foods could be a problem. We thought it was the bread and potatoes that were

**Low-fat workshop
October 1994**

making us fat, not the sour cream, cheese, or bacon bits. After all, they were such rich sources of protein (or so we thought). Little did we know that the fat MADE us fat and probably contributed to the majority of heart and cholesterol problems, too. It sure took a while, but I'm glad they figured it out in my lifetime, how about you? Since we know what causes the problems, why do so many people continue to ignore the warnings and eat extremely high-fat diets? Maybe they want to find out what the inside of a pyramid looks like!

Even though I may jest about these matters, it doesn't mean that I am not very concerned. If I just preached, listed statistics, and yelled at you, no one would listen, so instead I appeal to your humorous side, hoping you will sense my serious undertones. So, please remember as I talk about our kids and their "Saturday Morning Line-Up of Dietary Disasters" that informing the general public of the disease risks associated with a high-fat diet is of major concern to me. It is for this reason, I continue so passionately with my work. I simply want to teach others what I have learned and only ask one thing in return. I ask that you pass on (if only to one person) what you have learned. A good friend of mine, Nina Burgett, once said this to me and I have carried it within my heart, but would like to share it with each of you: "When the student is ready, the teacher will appear." This means that you cannot expect to learn until you are honestly ready (and through your faith a teacher will be provided). YOU might even be someone's teacher. If you feel someone reaching out who might need answers, take the time to listen. It may be the most rewarding experience of your life. I have found if you just take the time "to listen," it's amazing how much YOU can learn. The gift of really listening to someone in need means more than anything you can offer..... and it doesn't cost a penny!

**Pam and Laura Reeves
October 1994**

You see we are all students AND teachers. Think of it as a chain reaction. Pass on what you learn to help other people. If we all continue to give and receive information from others, maybe our future generations will learn to live and work together in harmony towards the ultimate goal of good health!

As for listening to our children.....well that is one of the greatest gifts of all.....in THEIR opinion. Do you have any idea how much honor you show your child by asking for THEIR opinion or just listening to what THEY have to say? Just ask THEM if you don't believe me, but be prepared for what they have to say. I know how hard it is to stop what you are doing (especially if you are really busy) to listen to your child relay the play by play action of a football game that occurred during recess at school that day. I'm warning you now, if you never take the time to listen, chances are

Blake and Pam
Halloween   1981

they will eventually lose interest in telling you anything at all. I have found, through experience, if your child makes the effort to tell you something (no matter what it may be) it is important to him or he would have never brought it up in the first place. Don't be afraid to ask for their opinion and admit you don't know everything (even though we like to pretend that we do). Honor your child with respect and tell him how proud you are of him (instead of just thinking it). Look for the good qualities in your children and compliment them even if you have to search, instead of always pointing out their mistakes (as if YOU were per-fect). Try spending a day on your knees to see what it feels like to

Blake, Pam, and Roxie
Christmas 1994

always have to look up to people and always feeling "looked down upon." Give your child the unconditional love and respect you would like in return. Chances are, you will get it. Always trust your child until they give you a reason not to. Don't expect your children to act like an adult. I know a lot of adults that act like children, and they seem to get away with it. Respect your child's privacy and chances are they will WANT to share more with you. Don't ever embarrasses your child in front of their peers. Nothing is more humiliating than to look stupid in front of your friends (no matter what your age). Don't always ask for more information than they offer about their friends, their day at school, etc. Chances are they will be a lot more willing to fill you in if they feel it was THEIR idea.

And last but not least, tell your child every single day that you love him, even if you don't love the way he acted. Don't ever let your children think you love them because of how they look, or how good they are at sports, or how smart they are in school. This makes a child feel like he must per-form or look a certain way, for acceptance. Don't ever make your child feel like he has to "do some-thing" to make you love him. That is what I mean by unconditional love. Once I asked a little boy why he loved his Mom so much, and do you know what he said to me? He said, "I love her because she is my Mom." That is unconditional love. You should never make your child feel like he has to "be a certain way" to make you love him. The less pressure and restrictions you put on your

**Pam, Tyler, Paige, and Blake
Halloween 1984**

child, the more responsible he will become (because he thinks YOU trust him). The love and understanding you show your child today will give him the confidence and self esteem he needs to make it on his own tomorrow. Take the time to listen when they are children, and they will want to talk and listen to you someday (even when they are busy with their own families). Someday YOU will have all the time in the world to listen, because you have nothing else to do, but will they make the effort (or just be TOO busy) to come and visit you? There is a good chance their decision will depend on how they were treated WHEN YOU were busy (and they had all the time in the world). Treat your children today the way that you would like to be treated when you are old and all alone. Take the time to listen. Someday they may return the favor..... Now, if I could only do and say everything I preach....Hey! No one is perfect!!!

**Tyler, Blake, Paige, and Pam
December 1994**

You have all heard the saying, "a picture is worth a thousand words." Well, it's a good thing because looking at these two photos of Blake, and wondering how on Earth the years flew by so quickly, has left, even me, speechless...temporarily! Share a special time with your child every single day, for the time will come too quickly, when they are all grown up and out of the house, leaving only precious photos you have pasted in an album to keep you company when you miss them more than you ever thought you could. **Trust me on this one!**

**May 1982
Blake - age 6**

Thirteen years of memories fall between these two photos...and I'm so glad that I have those special moments recorded on film so I can remember each and every one of them...forever!

**May 1995
Blake - age 18**

MY SON GROWS UP

My hands were busy through the day,
I didn't have much time to play
The little games you asked me to.
But when you'd bring your teddy bear
And ask me please to share
Your fun,
I'd say, "A little later, son."
I'd tuck you in all safe at night
And hear your prayers, turn out the light,
Then tiptoe softly to the door...
I wish I'd stayed a minute more.
For life is short, the years rush past...
A little boy grows up so fast
No longer is he at your side,
His precious secrets to confide
The teddy bears are put away,
There are no longer games to play.
No good-night kiss, no prayers to hear...
That all belongs to yesteryear.
My hands, once busy,
Now are still
The days are long
And hard to fill.
I wish I could
Go back and do
The little things
You asked me to.

                    -author unknown-

Blake - age 8
1984

photo by Polly Waites ©

Blake - age 18
1994

KIDS IN THE KITCHEN!

KIDS IN PAM'S KITCHEN!

The following recipes are taken from my new book, *KIDS IN THE KITCHEN* due out in 1996. It is a low-fat cookbook written for kids. The book will contain over 100 kid-tested recipes that are easy enough for children of all ages to prepare. They have been tasted and (and in some cases prepared) by a special group of 25 children ranging from 4-19 years of age. (Talk about fun!) The book will also contain an extensive "Fast Food Restaurant Guide" as well as all kinds of tips and information regarding children's health, fitness, and nutrition. Watch for *THE BUTTER BUSTER'S COOKNOTES* for *KIDS IN THE KITCHEN* in the near future! Until then, please enjoy a few of my own kid's favorites!

Official Testers: Jeremy Stewart, Chase Ellis, Carter Ellis, and Collin Ashworth

"Show me how you do that Jeremy," asks Chase Ellis.

Collin Ashworth perfects the technique.

At last..........we get to eat! Yum!

PITA PIZZAS
(A High-Fat Recipe Pam Modified To Low-Fat)

½ lb. ground vension or low-fat hamburger (Vermillion Valley or Maverick Natural Lite)
8 (4-inch) pocket (pita) breads (fat-free)
½ cup Ragu "Light" pasta sauce (fat-free)
½ cup Polly-O fat-free mozzarella cheese (grated)
¼ cup Alpine Lace Fat-Free Parmesan Cheese

Heat oven to 350° F. Place ground meat in a bowl and cover with waxed paper. Microwave about 3-5 minutes on high. Stir and heat a little longer until cooked and no pink remains. Remove meat and place in colander to drain. Place pocket breads on a cookie sheet that has been sprayed with Pam Spray. Top each with a tablespoon of pasta sauce and three tablespoons cooked ground beef. Sprinkle each with 1 tablespoon grated fat-free mozzarella cheese and ½ tablespoon Alpine Lace Fat-Free Parmesan Cheese. Bake at 350° F. for 5-8 minutes or until cheese is melted.

Note: Check "Resource Guide" for information regarding low-fat beef options.

Serves: Yields 8 Pizzas

Per Serving:

Fat:	1.1 g	Calories: 131		Protein:	12 g
Cholesterol:	25 mg	8% Calories from Fat		Carbohydrate:	17 g
Fiber:	1 g			Sodium:	286 mg

Tyler age 3

TYLER'S FAST AND EASY JAIL BIRD HOT DOGS
(A Pam and Tyler Original)
(Tyler makes these himself....quite often!!)

1 package Oscar Mayer FREE Hot Dogs (fat-free)
1 package Pillsbury soft Breadsticks (8 to a pack) (You will only need ½ of the package.)
    ***You use ½ breadstick per hot dog.**
4 slices Borden "Sharp" flavor fat-free cheese (optional)

Turn the oven on and set the temperature at 350° F. Remove the hot dogs from the package and slice down the middle (but not all the way through). Cut each cheese slice into four strips. Place two strips of cheese inside each hot dog. Remove the breadsticks from the package. Unroll one strip of the dough and cut it in half. Using ½ of a breadstick, roll it around the cheese-stuffed hot dog to resemble stripes (like jail bars). Pinch the dough together on each end so it sticks to the hot dog while baking. Repeat process on the rest of the hot dogs. Place Jail Bird Hot Dogs on a cookie sheet that has been sprayed with Pam Cooking Spray. Bake 12-15 minutes at 350° F. or until golden brown. These can be picked up to eat and dipped in mustard or ketchup if desired.

Note: Tyler loves to impress his friends with his cooking skills by serving these for breakfast or lunch. He likes them better without cheese, but most of his friends prefer the cheese added.

Variation: If you like the taste of bacon, sprinkle a few (¼ tsp.) imitation bacon BACO-O Bits over the cheese before wrapping with breadsticks.

Yields: Serves 8

Per Serving:

Fat:	1.3 g	Calories: 95		Protein:	8 g
Cholesterol:	15 mg	12% Calories from Fat		Carbohydrate:	11 g
Fiber:	<1 g			Sodium:	678 mg

Chris Siglin, Tyler, Joe Siglin
June 1994

LAZY DAY LASAGNA
(A Pam Original)

1 lb. Vermillion Valley or Maverick Natural Lite low-fat ground beef or ground venison
¾ cup water
1 32-oz. jar Ragu "Light," Hunts "Light," or Healthy Choice spaghetti sauce (all are fat-free)
1 8-oz. box Pasta DeFino brand "No Boil" lasagna noodles
2 cups Frigo fat-free ricotta cheese (or other brand)
2 Egg Beaters (½ cup)
½ cup Alpine Lace fat-free Parmesan Cheese (located in the deli dept.)
16-oz. grated Polly-O Free fat-free mozzarella (or other brand)

Turn your oven on and set the temperature at 375 degrees. Place the ground beef or venison in a medium sized glass bowl. Cover with a sheet of waxed paper. Microwave on high 3-4 minutes. Remove and stir. Cook longer (if still pink) if needed. Drain meat in colander or mesh sieve (ask your Mom or Dad if you don't know what this is). You can also pour the meat on a paper towel and sop up any grease with another paper towel. (In other words, kind of dry off the meat.) Wipe bowl with a paper towel and return meat to the bowl. In a separate bowl combine ½ cup Egg Beaters, 2 cups ricotta, half of the fat-free Parmesan cheese (¼ cup), and ½ (8-oz.) of the grated fat-free mozzarella cheese. Stir together and set aside. Add the ¼ cup water and 32-oz. fat-free spaghetti sauce to the cooked meat. Spray Pam spray (low-fat cooking spray) in a 9 x 13-inch (or close to that size) glass dish. Pour about 1 cup of the meat sauce into the bottom of the dish. Place a few lasagna noodles over the sauce to cover it. Spread ½ of the ricotta cheese mixture over the noodles. Sprinkle a little of the remaining mozzarella cheese over that. Repeat layers until you end up with meat sauce on top. Sprinkle the remaining mozzarella and Parmesan cheese on top. Cover the Lasagna with foil and bake 45-60 minutes. Remove foil and let stand 15 minutes before serving.

Note: You can use ground white turkey meat in place of low-fat beef and reduce the fat content even lower.

Yields: Serves 12

Per Serving:

Fat:	1.6 g	Calories:	222	Protein:	25 g
Cholesterol:	20 mg	7% Calories from Fat		Carbohydrate:	26 g
Fiber:	2 g			Sodium:	886 mg

GRAB-IT-QUICK GARLIC CHEESE BREAD
(A Pam Original)

8 THICK slices of French bread
8 Tbs. Polly-O Free fat-free mozzarella cheese, grated
8 tsp. Alpine Lace Fat-Free Parmesan Cheese
garlic powder to taste
Butter Buds Sprinkles to taste
Pam "Olive Oil" flavor Cooking Spray

Turn the oven on and set the temperature knob on "Broil." LIGHTLY spray the front and back of each piece of bread with "Olive Oil" Pam Cooking Spray. Sprinkle a little garlic powder and Butter Buds Sprinkles on both sides. Place the bread on the cookie sheet and place the cookie sheet on the top rack in the oven. Leave the oven door ajar and watch the bread closely. It doesn't take long!! Remove when lightly browned and carefully turn the bread over with a spatula. Sprinkle 1 Tbs. Polly-O Free mozzarella cheese on the top of each slice of bread. Sprinkle 1 tsp. of Alpine Lace Fat-Free Parmesan cheese on top. Return to the oven and cook until cheese melts! Serve immediately, but you better "Grab it Quick." This bread got it's name because it doesn't last long in our house. If you don't "grab it quick," you won't get any!

Yields: Serves 8

Per Serving:

Fat:	0.9 g	Calories:	105	Protein:	5 g
Cholesterol:	8 mg	8% Calories from Fat		Carbohydrate:	19 g
Fiber:	<1 g			Sodium:	301 mg

Paige   age 5

...........with her masterpiece

PICK YOUR FAVORITE PUDDING COOKIES
(A High-Fat Recipe Pam Modified To Low-Fat)

½ cup Fleischmann's Lower-Fat Margarine
½ cup Egg Beaters
6 Tbs. water
2 pkg. (4-serving size) JELL-O Fat-Free Instant Pudding (any flavor)
2 cups Pioneer Low-Fat Biscuit and Baking Mix
2 Tbs. sugar (optional for sprinkling on top)

Turn the oven on and set temperature at 375 degrees. Blend margarine, Egg Beaters, and water in a medium-sized bowl with a hand mixer. Stir in pudding mix and Pioneer Biscuit mix and stir until well blended. Chill dough in refrigerator about 5-10 minutes. Drop dough by teaspoonful onto a cookie sheet that has been sprayed with Pam Cooking Spray about 2 inches apart. Bake at 375° F. for about 12 minutes or until lightly browned. Remove from oven and sprinkle sugar on tops immediately (if desired). Remove from cookie sheets and cool.

Yields: 4 dozen cookies

Per Serving:

Fat:	0.9 g	Calories: 46	Protein:	1 g
Cholesterol:	0 mg	15% Calories from Fat	Carbohydrate:	10 g
Fiber:	<1 g		Sodium:	129 mg

Blake age 6

PAIGE'S FAVORITE PEANUT BUTTER KISSES
(A High-Fat Recipe Pam Modified To Low-Fat)

1 ¾ cups all purpose flour
½ cup sugar (or ¼ cup sugar and 3 packets Sweet 'N Low)
½ cup brown sugar (or ¼ cup brown sugar and 1 tsp. Sweet 'N Low Brown)
2 Tbs. sugar (for rolling dough)
1 tsp. baking soda
½ tsp. Papa Dash Lite Salt
½ cup Fleischmann's Fat-Free Squeeze Margarine or Promise Ultra Fat-Free Margarine
½ cup Peter Pan "Smart Choice" reduced fat peanut butter (6 fat grams per Tbs.)
¼ cup Egg Beaters
2 Tbs. skim milk
1 tsp. vanilla extract
48 chocolate Hershey Kisses (unwrapped)

Turn the oven on and set the temperature at 325 degrees. In a large mixing bowl, combine all the ingredients except the Hershey Kisses and 2 Tbs. sugar (for rolling dough). Blend well at low speed or stir by hand until dough is well blended. Place dough in the refrigerator about 10-15 minutes.

Pour 2 Tbs. sugar on a small plate. Using a rounded teaspoon scoop out the dough and shape into small balls. (Coat your fingers with flour to prevent the dough from sticking to your hands.) Roll balls in sugar to coat.

Place about 2-inches apart on a cookie sheet that has been sprayed with Pam Cooking Spray. Bake 10 minutes. Remove from oven and push a Hershey Kiss into each cookie, pressing down firmly so cookie cracks around the edge. Return to oven and bake 3 more minutes.
Note: Paige LOVES these cookies!

Yields: 48 cookies

Per Serving: All sugar

Fat:	2.5 g	Calories: 77	Protein:	2 g
Cholesterol:	1 mg	28% Calories from Fat	Carbohydrate:	13 g
Fiber:	<1 g		Sodium:	70mg

Per Serving: ½ Sweet 'N Low

Fat:	2.5 g	Calories: 73	Protein:	2 g
Cholesterol:	1 mg	30% Calories from Fat	Carbohydrate:	11g
Fiber:	<1 g		Sodium:	70 mg

BLAKE'S GIVE ME SMORE NO-BAKE CAKE
(A Pam Original)

24 whole Keebler brand low-fat graham crackers (10.6 fat grams)
2 (3.4-oz.) boxes vanilla instant pudding (can use sugar-free)
1 box Betty Crocker Fat-Free White Fluffy Frosting Mix
2 ¾ cups skim milk
1 cup Mrs. Richardson's or Smucker's fat-free fudge topping
2 packets Sweet 'N Low

Crust:
Spray a 9 x 13-inch pan or dish with Pam Cooking Spray. Place 7 ½ of the graham crackers in the bottom of the pan.

Filling:
Make frosting as directed on the package and set aside. Blend pudding with the milk until thickened and fold in ½ of the frosting mix (1 ½ cups). Pour ½ of the pudding mixture over the crackers and spread evenly. Repeat with graham cracker layer and pudding ending with graham crackers on top. Set uncovered in refrigerator for two hours.

Topping:
Blend 1 cup Mrs. Richardson's fat-free fudge topping with two packets of Sweet 'N Low. Spread over the crackers. Top with the remaining 1 ½ cups Betty Crocker fat-free frosting.

Yields: Serves 24

Per Serving:

Fat:	0.5 g	Calories:	134	Protein:	3 g
Cholesterol:	0 mg	3% Calories from Fat		Carbohydrate:	31 g
Fiber:	1 g			Sodium:	175 mg

Blake   age 2

CRUNCHY MUNCHIES
(A High-Fat Recipe Pam Modified To Low-Fat)

1 cup Rold Gold fat-free pretzel sticks or Tiny Twists
½ cup Corn Pops Cereal
1 Tbs. Fleischmann's Fat-Free Spread (squeeze bottle)
1 Tbs. sugar (or 1 ½ packets Sweet 'N Low)
6 cups air-popped popcorn
1 cup honey flavored Teddy Grahams
½ cup raisins
ground cinnamon to taste

In a large bowl, combine pretzels and Corn Pops Cereal. Pour Fleischmann's Fat-Free Squeeze margarine over mixture. Sprinkle with sugar and toss gently to coat. Add the popcorn and Teddy Grahams. Sprinkle lightly with cinnamon. Toss gently. Bake at 225° F. for 30-45 minutes. Cool. Add raisins and store in an airtight container.

Note: You can use Orville Redenbacher Smart Pop microwave popcorn to save time. It will add less than 1 fat gram per serving.

Yields: 9 (1-cup) servings

Per Serving:

Fat:	0.4 g	Calories:109	Protein:	3 g
Cholesterol:	0 mg	3 % Calories from Fat	Carbohydrate:	22 g
Fiber:	2 g		Sodium:	210 mg

Tyler   age 3

PAIGE'S PARTY PIE
(A Pam and Paige Original)

Crust:
2 cups finely crushed fat-free pretzels (about 8 oz.)
3 Tbs. sugar (or 1 ½ Tbs. sugar and 2 packets Sweet 'N Low)
½ cup Fleischmann's Fat-Free Squeeze Margarine or
    ½ cup Liquid Butter Buds (made from the mix)

Paige's 3rd Birthday

Filling:
¼ cup cold water
1 envelope unflavored gelatin
1 (8-oz.) pkg. Philadelphia Free fat-free cream cheese (softened)
1 cup sugar (or ½ cup sugar and 6 packets Sweet 'N Low)
1 (8-oz.) carton "Light" Cool Whip

Topping:
1 (6-oz.) pkg. strawberry gelatin (JELL-O)
1 ½ cups boiling water
2 (10-oz.) pkg. frozen strawberries in lite syrup, partially thawed and broken apart

Crust:
Turn the oven on and set the temperature at 400 degrees. Spray a 13 x 9-inch glass baking dish with Pam Cooking Spray. Place about 1/2 bag (8-oz.) pretzels in a large zip-lock plastic bag and roll over with a rolling pin until crushed. Repeat with more pretzels. Measure two cups and place in a medium-sized bowl. Add the sugar and margarine and mix well with a fork (or your fingers). The dough will be crumbly. Coat your fingers with a little flour and it will prevent the dough from sticking to your fingers. Press into bottom of baking dish. Bake 8-10 minutes at 400° F. Cool.

Filling:
Meanwhile, in a small saucepan, or 2-cup glass microwave-safe measuring cup, sprinkle unflavored gelatin over 1/4 cup cold water. Let stand 3 minutes. Heat over low heat or microwave on HIGH 30-40 seconds, until gelatin is dissolved. Cool slightly. In a medium-sized bowl, beat cream cheese and 1 cup sugar until well blended. Beat in gelatin mixture. Place bowl in freezer for 5 minutes. Remove from freezer and beat at high speed for 2 minutes. Fold in the whipped topping. Spread mixture evenly over the cooled crust. Refrigerate while making the topping.

Topping:

In a medium bowl, combine strawberry gelatin and 1 ½ cups boiling water. Stir until gelatin is dissolved. Add frozen strawberries. Stir to separate strawberries and thicken gelatin slightly. Pour evenly over cream cheese layer. Refrigerate 1 hour to set. This recipe might look like a lot of trouble, but Paige insists it is well worth the effort! This is one of her favorites and SHE CAN MAKE IT HERFELF!

Yields: Serves 24

Per Serving: All sugar

Fat:	1.2 g	Calories:	159	Protein:	3 g
Cholesterol:	2 mg	7% Calories from Fat		Carbohydrate:	33 g
Fiber:	1 g			Sodium:	235 mg

Per Serving: 1/2 Sweet 'N Low

Fat:	1.2 g	Calories:	141	Protein:	3 g
Cholesterol:	2 mg	7% Calories from Fat		Carbohydrate:	28 g
Fiber:	1 g			Sodium:	235 mg

Paige age 2

cookie dough........Yum!!

STRAWBERRY DREAM DRINK
(A Pam Original)

1 (10-oz.) can frozen Bacardi "Strawberry Daiquiri Mixer" (contains no alcohol)
1 cup skim milk
1 tsp. vanilla
6-12 ice cubes
1 cup vanilla Guilt Free brand (sugar and fat-free) ice cream
¼ cup powdered sugar (or 3 packets Sweet 'N Low)

Place all of the ingredients (except ice cream) in the blender and process until smooth. Add ice cream and continue to blend until smooth and creamy. My kids and their friends love these!

Option: You can use the Banana Daiquiri or Piña Colada Daiquiri mixers in place of the Strawberry Daiquiri Mixer if you desire.

Yields: 6 (1 cup servings)

Per Serving: All Sugar

Fat:	0.1 g	Calories:	179	Protein:	3 g
Cholesterol:	2 mg	0% Calories from Fat		Carbohydrate:	42 g
Fiber:	0 g			Sodium:	45 mg

Per Serving: ½ Sweet 'N Low

Fat:	0.1 g	Calories:	162	Protein:	3 g
Cholesterol:	2 mg	0% Calories from Fat		Carbohydrate:	38 g
Fiber:	0 g			Sodium:	45 mg

Paige age 11   Tyler   age 7

Tyler, Paige, and Jessica Dodson
July 1989

Paige creating a "Masterpiece"

February 1984

Paige with her cousins
Katy - age 5   Paige - age 4   Jordan - age 4

MY READERS
INSPIRE ME!

In December 1994, I had the opportunity to meet the people in this picture. They were flown to Los Angeles, California to give their testimonies for my "BUTTER BUSTERS LOW-FAT SYSTEM" Infomercial. A few months earlier, when I was in L.A. meeting with my producers about the show, they asked if I had any letters from my readers who had lowered their cholesterol, or lost a large amount of weight as a result of using my cookbook. You will notice as you read the letters in this chapter, there are several folks that have done "just that." This picture was taken during the filming of

Back Row: Jimmy Allison, Doug Miller, Sharon Smith, Al Corley, Betty Corley, and Bill Esposito
Front Row: Susan Allison, Carole Robinson, Chris Beauchamp, Pam, Char Doehler, and Cindy Cochran

the show. The whole experience was exciting and fun, but THE BEST PART for me was finally meeting the wonderful people who had shared their stories and taken the time to write me a letter. As the time approached to leave Texas and go to L.A. to film the show, I realized that I was very nervous. I must be honest and tell you that it wasn't "filming the show" that had me worried. I knew that part was in God's hands and He would take care of me. No, I was worried about something else. I was so sure the testimonial people would be disappointed when they met me. After all they were coming to Hollywood "to meet a star" or so they thought, and all they were going to find was a housewife and Mom who happened to write a cookbook (not too glamorous)!! Those fears evaporated into thin air the minute I saw their smiling faces. They didn't care what I looked like or how I talked. I could sense their warmth and affection as soon as we met. There was no awkward "lack of conversation" as we dug into our low-fat lunch on the soundstage at the studio. We couldn't talk fast enough. It was obvious to anyone watching we shared a real bond and genuine interest in what each other had to say. The only bad part was the time went too quickly. We posed for some quick pictures, and then they were swept away for make-up. After my rehearsal was finished, I found my way back to "The Green Room" where they were all waiting to film their segments. Since only one person was filmed at a time, that left me in the room with the rest to visit and share. We had the opportunity to spend about two hours together so we really got to know each other. Every time one person came back another left. No one wanted to miss anything, so we were constantly telling each person (when they returned) what we had talked about when they were gone. We talked and laughed, we talked and cried, we talked and talked, and talked some more. We had so much to share with each other. We talked about our children, our families, new products, recipes, restaurants, exercise, eating disorders, body fat, weight loss, cholesterol, health, dreams, fears, love, and people. But most of all we listened.......to what each other had to say! The time came too quickly to say goodbye until the next day, when my segment would be filmed. They all headed "out on the town" to celebrate, and I ventured back to my hotel to try and get a little rest before my wake-up call at 5:30 A.M. I had to be at the studio by 7:00A.M. I was so excited after meeting everyone that I couldn't even think about going to bed. Besides my husband Mike and daughter Paige arrived from Texas at the hotel about 11:00 P.M. I couldn't wait to tell them all about my day. I finally fell asleep about 2:30 A.M. (That was the last number I remember seeing on the alarm clock, anyway.) I guess I did sleep, because when my call came at 5:30 A.M. it woke me up. Great, I thought. I was getting ready for one of the longest and hardest days of my life with less than three hours of sleep. I wasn't really that worried, however, because I knew God would give me the direction and strength I needed. Some of the testimonials were able to stay for the morning filming and some had to get back home. After all, Christmas was in two weeks and it was a very difficult time to be away. I knew this better than anyone. I had been in L.A. all week and felt terrible about the holiday activities I was missing at home. I

Mrs. Cheryl Wright's 5th Grade Class
Dunn Elementary   December 1994

hated being away from my family at such a special time. I did manage to make it back home in time to help with Tyler's school Christmas party. Thank goodness!

After wrapping the show at 2:00 A.M. (19 hours later), I knew it was God's strength who helped me through it! There was no way I could have lasted that long with less than three hours of sleep without His help!

The next day was a breeze with only a few things to wrap up before heading home to Texas. That is until that night while I was talking on the phone to my husband. My bed started shaking and my clothes in the closet were swaying back and forth. I couldn't imagine what was happening as I screamed to Mike that my bed was shaking. It was then it hit me that I was in an earthquake (all alone on the 17th floor of my hotel). The next thing I knew they were showing people on T.V. running out of malls and theaters. It only lasted a few seconds, but it was enough to start me packing my suitcase. Even though I was exhausted, it was a little hard falling asleep not knowing if I would be waking up the next day!!

To put it lightly the infomercial was "a real experience" filled with excitement, hard work, and lots of fun, but the best part and the memory I will treasure forever (even more than the earthquake) was meeting and getting to see the people I had only known through letters. I'm sure our friendship will continue to grow as we stay in touch. My future project will be figuring out how and when we can all get together for a "Butter Busters Reunion." I would love to fly them all to Texas to appear on my T.V. show and re-hash our L.A. experience.

Since I have been home, I often think about that afternoon in L.A. I'll never forget each of them telling me in detail how my book had changed their lives. I just can't express how it makes me feel to think my book actually made a difference to these people. What they didn't realize was just how much their letters meant to me, and how their words had influenced and inspired me to write this book. I told them they had each made a difference in my life, too! I wanted them to know how much they meant to me. I went on and on and on...but no one said a word. They were all LISTENING!

I hope you will enjoy reading the book as much as I've enjoyed writing it. I don't think I have ever had so much fun working on a project. I never really considered it work, but truly a labor of love! As you read through the letters you will notice some include names and not just initials. Those are the letters from the testimonials. They gave me permission to use their full names. I've also included pictures taken when we were together. You will notice Margie is not in the group shot. I didn't realize she was missing until I had the film developed. As it turned out, she was doing "her segment" for the infomercial when the picture was taken. However, you will find Margie's picture with her letter. Because these people mean so much to me and were responsible for the inspiration to write this book, I would like to dedicate this very special chapter, "MY READERS INSPIRE ME!" to my dear friends: Margie and Bill Esposito from Coral Springs, Florida, Susan and Jimmy Allison from Blacksburg, South Carolina, Betty and Al Corley from Odenville, Alabama, Carole Robinson from Tunkhannuck, Pennsylvania, Sharon Smith and Doug Miller from Poteau, Oklahoma, Chris and Bill Beauchamp (Bill couldn't make the trip to L.A.) from Greentown, Pennsylvania, Cindy Cochran from Dallas, Texas, and of course my Mom, Char Doehler from Granbury, Texas (she is the one in the jacket next to me) and the one I am the most proud of!!

The following are letters from some of my readers that have, in most cases, lost quite a bit of weight, lowered their cholesterol, or even changed their life-style as a result of reading and using *BUTTER BUSTERS THE COOKBOOK*. I wrote to all of these folks to thank them, but have not included my responses in this section. I just wanted to share their testimonials. Their words have been VERY inspirational to me, and I feel they will be an inspiration to you, too!

NOTE: The following letters were copied without editing. I didn't want to change a word of what they had to say (or how they said it)!

March 22, 1994
Dear Pam: I love the book. I never put it away. It stays on my kitchen counter. I started eating low-fat and fat-free on January 28, 1994 and as of today I have lost 20 pounds. I am thrilled! After my

second child, I was carrying a lot of extra weight. Since I am still nursing, most diets would not work for me. Eating this way is so easy and delicious and healthier for me and my baby. Thank you for the best cookbook ever!   —*C.B. Lawerenceville, Virginia*

July 30, 1994
Dear Ms. Mycoskie: My name is B.H. and I'm writing this letter to let you know how much my family and friends are enjoying *BUTTER BUSTERS*. Let me start at the beginning.

My daughter-in-law's father is a doctor. In November 1993 he had bypass surgery. He was told, of course, to watch his fat intake. By luck, he discovered your cookbook. He so enjoyed the recipes he called my daughter-in-law about it, who was just pregnant and was having major gall bladder problems at the time. She was hospitalized for 5 days, and when she was told to eat no fat, she bought a book. I read the book and I was really impressed so I bought one too.

My other son and his wife are always watching their diets so they bought a book. My sister, who lives in Ft. Lauderdale, has always said she wouldn't do low-fat because the food was awful, was really surprised and she bought one.

My niece, who was visiting from Ohio and had just finished the Opti Fast program (and looked great wanted to stay that way), enjoyed our dinners, so she bought one.

Back to my daughter-in-law. Her mother lives in Chicago, came for a couple of weeks to help with the new baby, and she bought one after trying the food my daughter-in-law had cooked and frozen before the birth of her baby.

I am sure several friends have also purchased the book because we all talk about it. We are really convinced that eating healthy is absolutely necessary for good health. I just wanted to share this story with you and say a big thank you!   —*B.H. Wellington, Florida*

July 15, 1994
Dear Pam: I am writing to tell you how grateful I am to you for writing such a terrific book. Last Christmas I had transient ischemic attack (a temporary stroke) and fortunately had no disablement. After a week in the hospital I vowed to change my lifestyle and particularly my diet. The doctors told me to "watch my diet" but gave no specifics or requirements to lose weight. Most of all they didn't tell me how to lose weight, and then your book comes in.

My wife and I were shopping for diet recipe books at Borders Bookstore where they had a large display with your books. By using your recipe book since Christmas I have lost 52 pounds and my overall health has improved with it. My blood pressure and cholesterol have both never been better. I exercise mostly by walking a brisk 1-2 miles a day. I can't thank you enough for helping me, but I hope you just might come out with a new book soon. My wife has learned how to substitute low fat in cooking and more companies are coming out with low fat foods. I'm a walking/talking ad for your book and have been responsible for many sales because people who knew me fifty pounds ago are astonished at my weight loss, but are amazed when I tell them how easy it was with *BUTTER BUSTERS*! Again, thank you for taking the time to create one of the best diet books ever! —*T.D. Lancaster, Pennsylvania*

February 21, 1994
Dear Pam: I've never written a letter like this before, but I love your cookbook. Last summer my husband (at 50 years old!) had open heart surgery-triple by-pass! Needless to say I've changed my cooking habits. He's your basic meat and potatoes real food type. He was convinced that any substitutions for the regular fat-filled ingredients made the food taste wrong. Some of his comments about recipes I've made from your book: "Do you have any more of these?" "Are you sure I can eat this?" I've been collecting low-fat cookbooks since July and yours is my favorite. The only one I felt the urge to write about!! I just bought another one for a friend of mine cause I kept telling her about it. I do feel I need to buy stock in the Butter Buds company though. I had some of it on my kitchen shelf but rarely used it. Now it's a staple on my grocery list every week or so. Thanks for all the wonderful recipes and great ideas! Happy cooking! —*K.S. Clackamas, Oregon*

January 10, 1994
Dear Pam: I hope you don't mind if I call you Pam, but I feel as if I know you. The first part of August, 1993, I decided it was time to permanently do something about my weight and my health. I had been reading different ways to go about it and decided that cutting out fat would be the direction to take. Well, it worked. Combined with walking every day, I have lost approximately 45 pounds. I have dropped from a size 22 to 13/14. I had been looking for a cookbook for a long time that had easy recipes my whole family would eat and other information also. Wow! When I found yours, that was it! We have been eating several things made from it and still have many more to try. Your advice and hints in the front of the book have also been an inspiration to me. I really do miss walking, though, now that the snow is on the ground. I do exercise regularly to a video tape, though. I feel good and look great! I had my gallbladder out December 1 and I still have been exercising and still feeling great.

There are several favorites in your book. My son is crazy about the "Cream Cheese Cake Bars." I have even had people ask me how to make them. We all adore the "Quick Cobbler." Although, I must confess, I use a can of peaches instead of the pie filling and it is still great. I use "Paige's Pretzel" recipe for pizza with fat-free cheese and sauce so our pizza is practically fat-free! I feel guilty eating it. Also, I have found the Healthy Choice ground beef is extremely good. In fact, that is all we eat as far as ground beef goes. I made taco salad again and again. It is practically fat-free. I just felt I had to write and thank you for a normal cookbook. NONE of the "far out foods" that normal people don't eat. Thanks again! —*P.D. Elmore, Ohio*

February 8, 1994

Dear Pam: As a result of your wonderful cookbook I have changed my buying, eating, and cooking habits and have lost 35 pounds since November 3, 1993. I went to have my physical and my cholesterol had climbed to 257, blood sugar 127 and weight over 200 pounds. The doctor gave me a low-fat diet along with a diabetic diet. I left his office and went to Sam's Club to look around (as I felt very low and doubtful about these diet plans). I love books and the first book I saw was your cookbook. It is excellent. I took it to my doctor's office the next visit and he agreed it was a very well written, informative book. Believe it or not I have read and studied every single page. I try to walk two miles each day during my lunch hour, as I work full time, and I drink 8 or more glasses of water each day. I don't feel hungry all the time like I did, and I have such fun with your recipes.

I used to cook a lot and enjoyed having guests over for my "fat" meals—no longer. I was featured in our local newspaper last year as "one of the best cooks in the country." Now, I cook, but YOUR cookbook is in front of me! Thank you for writing this great book. Just wanted to let you know what it has meant, and still means, to me. I am going to lose 25 more pounds so I will probably wear your book out. Several friends have purchased the book after I told them about it. Good luck and be proud that you have contributed something to society that will greatly improve people's health. Sincerely, —*E.K. Franklin, North Carolina*

December 7, 1993

Dear Ms. Mycoskie: On October 24, 1993 my husband and I started this new way of eating fat-free to help ourselves become healthy and slim forever. The only thing I was lacking in my kitchen was a good cookbook with great recipes. My husband found your book at one of our favorite stores in Scranton and he got so excited that he bought it for me as a surprise.

We absolutely love your book. All the information is very useful and helpful in understanding in lay terms about lean muscle mass, fat grams, LDL, HDL and aerobic exercising. These tips are just great by themselves, but a person needs the recipes too in order to create great meals for the entire family.

My two sons are eating no-fat or low-fat now and for the most part they do stick with it. One is 21 and the other is 17. They certainly are aware of what is good and what foods to avoid. All of us have been successful in los-

Chris and Pam

ing weight. Of course, my husband and I really need to lose weight for our health. I have never been successful. I have led a life as a fat child, teenager, young adult, and now middle-aged. Enough is enough! We can all live with this new way of life and be healthy. I have lost 24 pounds in five weeks and I truly do not feel deprived at all. Best of all, I have no ice cream or chocolate cravings (two of my biggest desires) at all because we are now eating healthier.

I needed to thank you for your cooking inspirations. I am trying several new recipes this weekend plus a few during the week. Thanks for making my life and my family's lives more aware of the foods we eat and a better way of preparing them! Getting slimmer every day...
Sincerely, —*Chris Beauchamp*
Greentown, Pennsylvania

P.S. Hooray for Butter Buds!

January 11, 1995
Chris has written me faithfully over a year now. We write back and forth about once a month. I can't tell you how much I look forward to her letters. I joked with her in California (when we finally got to meet) because we know everything about each other's lives after writing each other for so long. I actually have a very prized possession in my filing cabinet and one that means a great deal to me. It is the Chris Beauchamp file. You see, she even has her own file and it is filled with stories about our children, questions, stories about our husbands, comments, ideas, dreams, suggestions, plans, secrets, recipes, and anything else you could ever imagine two forty-something year old women (with birthdays one day apart) would discuss in great detail. It's Chris' letters I turn to when I GET DOWN because SHE is one of the most positive and upbeat people I have ever known. I will treasure her letters forever! At last count, I had 15. I'm expecting a new one any day now!!

May 24, 1993
Dear Pam: I wanted to drop you a note for several reasons. #1 Your cookbook is great and all the recipes I've tried are great and tasty. Thank you. Your cookbook has been a life saver since I started my low-fat diet. I've lost 25 pounds since February and I have 75 more to lose, and KEEP OFF forever! #2 The best chips I've found are "Smart Temptations." Again, thanks so much for what you have done with this book. Sincerely, — *S.S. Ft. Worth, Texas*

May 9, 1994
Dear Pam:
Thank you, thank you, thank you for taking the time to compile and print *BUTTER BUSTERS THE COOKBOOK!* For the first time ever, I have hope! I have been overweight for many years and have felt "imprisoned" by my weight and eating habits problem. I've hated myself. I could never stay on strict diets because I always felt hungry as well as deprived. Since purchasing *BUTTER BUSTERS* and following your suggestions (as well as your recipes), I have lost 18 pounds and my husband

has lost 28 pounds. We eat a lot, it's true! It was fat that has made us fat; not the food itself. I ride my bike everyday and feel great. People are asking us what diet we're on and we just tell them it's not a diet, but a lifestyle change of enjoying food without the fat! We've told all our friends and relatives about your cookbook. I've already bought a second copy for myself since the first one is getting worn out! Please keep me on your mailing list! —*Margie and Bill Esposito* *Coral Springs, Florida*

(The following is a second letter from Margie dated two months later!)

Bill, Pam, and Margie

July 30, 1994
Dear Pam: My husband and I wish to thank you for publishing the *BUTTER BUSTERS COOKBOOK*. By applying the principles taught in your book, as well as implementing many of your recipes, we have both lost a substantial amount of weight. My husband has lost 50 pounds and I have lost 30 pounds. My cholesterol level dropped from 212 to 138! We've told a lot of our friends about your book, so don't be surprised if you notice an increase of sales. We are looking forward to obtaining your new book, *BUTTER BUSTERS TOO!* Do you know when it is scheduled to be released in bookstores?

I like to cook and I've learned how to modify a lot of my own recipes to low-fat as well (thanks to your ideas).

I had planned on requesting a substitution for sweetened condensed milk, but I saw your substitution in the video series workbook. Thanks again for the great cookbook. We're so glad that you published this for us! Sincerely, —*Margie and Bill Esposito* *Coral Springs, Florida*

NOTE: As of March 1995, Margie has maintained her **40 pound weight loss**. She has started her own business called "Health For Life", Inc. and teaches workshops all over Florida as a result of her own success. For more information concerning Margie's workshops, write to her at: 934 N. University Drive, Suite 121, Coral Springs, FL 33071. I am so proud of her. She is an inspiration to me!

January 22, 1993
Dear Pam: Thank you! Thank you! Thank you! At last, a cookbook I can open to any page and not feel guilty!

For forty years I have battled the bulge and the bulge always won. A lifetime of yo-yo dieting left me discouraged and 80 pounds overweight. After the holidays, my husband (who wants to lose 60 pounds) and I decided we needed to do "something" about our diet. As luck would have it, we picked up a copy of *BUTTER BUSTERS*. After reading the first few pages (in the bookstore), we were hooked.

It has only been three weeks, but I am happy to report that my husband and I have lost 8 1/2 and 7 pounds, respectively. Each evening we walk 2 miles in 30 minutes.....quite a feat since we both lead very sedentary lives. Not once have we felt hunger pains, and we have come to the conclusion that this is a lifestyle we can follow.

Must sign off now. "Blueberry Upside Down Cake" is ready to come out of the oven (yum!) Sincerely, — *C.B. Charleston, South Carolina*

January 12, 1994
Dear Pam: My husband is a heart by-pass patient here at the Cleveland Clinic. While he is here I have been staying at the Cleveland Clinic Guesthouse and attending classes on nutrition, etc. Since I have used your cookbook for a year, I decided to take it with me so I can share it with others who are now going to have to change their ways of cooking.

These ladies (from all over the U.S.), can hardly believe the recipes are so-o-o good. I keep telling them "Trust me they are." "Your husband will love all of the food you prepare from this book!"

The nutritionist, on the cardiology floor and who conducts the classes, said she can't wait to get a copy. She will start using it at home as well in all her future classes at the Cleveland Clinic.

I just thought you might like to know how one satisfied person can be your best "Cheerleader." Several ladies have already found the book and can hardly wait to get their husbands home and start some happy and good cooking. Sincerely, —*J.C. Madison, Ohio*

August 22, 1994
Dear Pam: I just had to write to tell you how thrilled I am with your *BUTTER BUSTERS COOKBOOK*. I have been using the recipes for about six weeks now and have lost about 15 pounds and I don't know how many inches. I have tried just about every diet in the world with no success and have finally found a healthy and delicious way of eating (not dieting) that I feel I can live with for the rest of my life. I have not always had an overweight problem. Like many others, until I had three babies, I was very thin and could not seem to gain weight. I actually envied fat people, because they could lose weight. Ha Ha! I hope you don't mind, but I have been in contact with QVC Shopping Network's Vendor Relations Department to suggest that they carry this book for sale to their viewers. They were very nice and suggested that if you haven't done so yet, you should con-

tact them. I have never done anything like this before, but I am just so thrilled with your recipes that I want to share them with everyone I meet. Please send me information on your video series and workbook called "Butter Busters-The Low-Fat System." Once again, I thank you from the bottom of my heart. I still have about fifty pounds to go, but for the first time in my life, I know I will make it. Please know that anytime you need an endorsement I will praise you and your book to the skies! Regards, —A.S. South Ozone Park, New York

November 20, 1992
Dear Pam: Your talk at the luncheon benefiting "The Friends of the Arlington Public Library" yesterday was entertaining and enlightening. I, along with the audience, enjoyed hearing how you came to write your book, *BUTTER BUSTERS*, and its success. I know that I have served your delicious recipes to my family and friends and have given your books as gifts. I admire your pluck in taking control of your life (I dropped my cholesterol 75 points and I do attribute much of it to information and knowledge gained from your book), and persistence in overcoming obstacles to publish it yourself. Too often we think things come so easily when there is really a lot of hard work involved. Thank you for sharing your special story. Sometimes it is impossible to know how many people you have helped and lives you may have improved because you have taken the time to share with others! I wish you success in the future. Who knows where *BUTTER BUSTERS* may take you! I enjoyed visiting with you at lunch. Sincerely, —M.K. Arlington, Texas

February 21, 1994
Dear Pam: I really enjoyed meeting you. My mom and daughter were so impressed! They have been telling everyone they talk to about it. My mom went to Florida and took my aunt her autographed copy of
. She loved it! While my Mom was there, they saw you on "The Ricki Lake Show." They made several of your recipes during her visit and they were a hit, of course!

Did you know there was an article in the *The Detroit News* about low-fat desserts while you were here? If you don't have a copy and would like one, let me know. Your "Chocolate Buttermallow Cake" won the contest! A lot of my patients read the article and mentioned it in class. On February 15th, we had our Cardiac Rehab Banquet in celebration of National

Low-fat cakes: Rising to the occasion

We baked five chocolate cakes from different recipes and put them to a blind taste test. One was sinfully rich, but the other four used low-fat recipes. On a 5-point rating scale (with 5 being the highest), with one-twelfth of a cake as a serving size, here's how the cakes rose to the occasion in the eyes of our judges:

DESSERT	STRATEGY FOR REDUCING FAT	CALORIES	FAT (GRAMS)	OVERALL RATING	COMMENTS
Chocolate Domingo Cake, from *The Cake Bible*, Rose Levy Beranbaum	None	285	17.3	2	Dry, heavy, not chocolaty
Shirley's Chocolate Cake, from food scientist Shirley Corriher	Reduces flour, adds pureed sweet potato, uses egg whites and no-fat sour cream	139	1.9	1.25	Moist, chewy, gummy
Chocolate Buttermallow Cake, from *Butter Busters* cookbook by Pam Mycoskie	Uses Butter Buds, low-fat buttermilk and Egg Beaters	197	0.4	3.62	Good flavor and texture
Chocolate Cloud Cake, from Los Angeles Times foodstylist Donna Deane	Replaces butter with pureed prunes	257	2.0	2.5	Good flavor, tastes like it's not all the way done
Betty Crocker SuperMoist Light Cake Mix	Uses egg whites or egg substitutes	190	3.0	3	Crumbly texture, "I think I am going to eat the whole thing"

The Detroit News **January 1994**

Cardiac Rehabilitation week, and I had several patients make the cake for our dessert. People couldn't believe it was low-fat!

I wanted to ask your permission to use recommendations on eating out in restaurants in our cardiac education program for our patients. I would like to give them a handout using this information. The majority of our patients have purchased your book, but for those who haven't, I want to make sure they have the information they need. Yours truly, —*M.C., R.N. Garden City, Michigan*

April 19, 1994
Dear Pam: I, like you, am a mother and very busy. Unlike you, I am overweight and not in good shape. But, that is changing. With thanks to you! I never believed that counting fat grams would teach me a healthy lifestyle. I have been through many different diet programs, bought many different recipe books, all to no avail. Who actually eats lamb and raspberry sauce? Not me, and certainly not my family. My family eats things like your "My Mom's Noodle Casserole" and "Basic Macaroni and Cheese." Butter Buds are miracle workers. I actually want to eat baked potatoes again. Look in my fridge and pantry and you will find many of the items suggested in your book in the "Shopping Guide." Well, thanks to you, I have lost 17 pounds (23 more to go). Three friends have purchased your book after seeing mine. Just please, keep me posted about anything new! Sincerely, —*C.H. Cicero, Illinois*

January 28, 1994
Dear Pam: I bought your new and revised *BUTTER BUSTERS COOKBOOK* and have read every page (and so has my husband)! We couldn't be happier with your recipes and have really enjoyed getting back in the kitchen after years of frozen diet dinners.

Since starting to eat low-fat my husband (he is 56) has lost 47 pounds and I have lost 28 pounds (I am 53). It's so easy to change the way we eat using the recipes in your book! I've even taken a lot of your suggestions and changed a bunch of our favorite recipes to low-fat as well. I'm planning a low-fat dinner party for our anniversary in March! We both started exercising too. We bought a treadmill and stair climber we both use religiously (thanks to your suggestions).

You have probably added a lot of years to our lives and we just can't thank you enough for taking the time to help others. I noticed you wrote the book in memory of your brother. My brother died suddenly at a very young age too. As a matter of fact, that is why I bought your book in the first place (when I saw that in the front). When people do things out of love they always turn out good. It's so nice to see that your efforts putting a cookbook together can make people happy and healthy! Let me know when you write another book! Fondly, —*R.A. Ardmore, Oklahoma*

March 15, 1994
Dear Pam: I just wanted to let you know how wonderful your *BUTTER BUSTERS COOKBOOK* is! I changed my lifestyle to low-fat about six months ago and have had much success. Like you, my cholesterol was high (242), and in six months, I dropped my cholesterol to 172 and dropped 25 pounds seemingly effortlessly. I enjoy cooking, but I was finding myself getting stuck in a "food rut" always making the same things and feeling somewhat confined food-wise until I discovered your cookbook through a woman who brought it to our office and raved about it! I feel like I've found a gold mine!

Thank you so much for all your research and writing a book that is easy to understand and extremely user-friendly. I have asked my local grocery store to order several of the products you recommended and have found your recommendations very helpful and most importantly, TASTE-FUL!! Thank you for sharing your knowledge and insights. I wish you much continued success!!
Very Sincerely, —*R.R.S. Omaha, Nebraska*

June 4, 1994
Dear Mrs. Mycoskie: I just wanted to write and say Thank you! Your wonderful book, *BUTTER BUSTERS,* has been a cornerstone in my weight loss program. After 26 years of constant dieting and a record high of 285 pounds, I have lost fifty pounds and continue to lose.

It has been a slow process, but with counseling, exercise, and learning to substitute low fat foods, it has been a freeing experience. I no longer count calories. I am a nurse practitioner and over the years have read countless books.

Your book helped me substitute foods I had never considered so that I can continue to eat the foods I love and still become more healthy. Again, thank you so much!—*S.J. Orem, Utah*

June 24, 1994
Dear Pam: Next to my *BIBLE, BUTTER BUSTERS* is my "book." I have tried every diet for years and lost some weight, but it always came back. This time I've lost more already than I ever did before!

I have lost 40 pounds so far and I have 60 more to go. My husband has been on it with me and he has lost 55 and reached his goal weight. He looks like a different person. I am a nurse and I really need to be down to my ideal weight. We started our diet February 7, 1994. I fell and hurt my ankle and could not exercise for six weeks. If I hadn't fallen, I think I would have had 10 more pounds off because I couldn't exercise for a while. I stayed on the low-fat eating and did not gain a pound back!

Of all the literature I have on diets, weight, and exercise, YOURS IS #1. I love the list of products you tell us about. I live by your book and the weight is falling off! Thank you! Thank you! God Bless

You! —*L.C. Tuscoloosa, Alabama*
P.S. Write another book and please send me your Low-Fat System workbook and videos! BUST-ING THE FAT REALLY WORKS!

March 3, 1994
Dear Pam: Thank you so much for the pictures and the card you sent myself and the girls I work with. It will be a wonderful before and after picture!!! We have been doing a fantastic job sticking to our new food program. We have combined your recipes and ways of eating with Richard Simmons "Sweatin' To the Oldies." The combo seems to be working well, as between the girls at work (3) and myself and one staff person, we have lost a combined weight of ....drum roll, please.....40+ pounds so far!!!!! And that is only from February 6 to February 28!!!!!

Never in all my years of "dieting" have I lost so much weight and ate so well. I'm not a complete witch because I have to constantly deprive myself, either. On the contrary, I have eaten brownies, milkshakes, lasagna, pizza (which is my client's favorite), and with few modifications, almost anything I want!

I have read several "low-fat recipe books," but yours is the only one that has real, basic, and fast recipes. So, from me and the girls, THANK YOU! We will keep in touch every month or two with an update. In the meantime, we wish you and your family all the best.
God Bless! —*C.W. (C., H., and K.) Vancouver, Washington*

March 14, 1995
Dear Pam:
I hope I have not been too forward by mailing you a letter at your husband's work. I just wanted to take a quick minute of your time to send my thanks for a fantastic cookbook (*BUTTER BUSTERS*). I have been battling the bulge for most of my life. My weight yo-yos by at least 100 lbs. or more. I have clothes that range from size 7 to 24. My husband and I have been changing the way we live and eat and I found myself serving baked chicken and potatoes most of the week. I bought several cookbooks and was very frustrated by the fat content in most of the meals. I just couldn't bring myself to eat 20 grams of fat in the last meal of the day, which most celebrity cookbooks have in all their main meals. I could not believe no matter how hard I tried I could not find a diet cookbook that was low in fat. Then I saw your cookbook at Sam's Club and when I opened it and saw that most of the recipes have less than 5 grams of fat I thought for sure they would be bland and tasteless, but I bought the cook anyway.

I HAVE NEVER BEEN MORE PROUD THAN I AM WHEN I COOK ONE OF YOUR RECIPES. THEY ARE WONDERFUL AND WILL HELP MY QUEST TO EAT BETTER FOREVER.

I have everyone in my office trying everything I make and they are sold on you also. I just wanted to say thanks for helping my new nutritional awareness become better tasting and exciting. I look forward to every trip to the grocery store, because now I buy food that helps me on my quest to lose weight and feel great. I hope there is some way you can let me know when the next book comes out. Thanks again, —*Teresa McKeen Furquay-Varina, N.C.*

March 3, 1994
Dear Pam: I enjoyed your book. Lost 30 pounds in 8 weeks.
Thank you, —*D.S. North Kingston, Rhode Island*

October 14, 1994
Dear Pam: I received your cookbook as a Christmas gift last year from my husband. I love to cook for people and I love to eat; (food is entertainment for my face) however, I also want to cook and eat healthy.

Pam, the reason for my letter is twofold. First, I wanted to let you know how much I enjoy your book and I recommended it to many people. I also love to bake, and your recipes have enabled me to bake healthy and share it with my friends, family, and co-workers.

I am in the process of fulfilling a lifelong dream by purchasing a nutritional/fitness center. It is called Inches-A-Weigh and is located in Bedford. It will enable me to work one on one with women, produce healthy, low fat menu plans, and I will also have exercise equipment. It will truly be a "full service" center. My personal goal is to help women lose their weight, improve their health and self-esteem, and provide the skills and motivation to change their lifestyle forever. I am 43 years old and have also tried every diet invented until I met my husband and he proved to me that eating

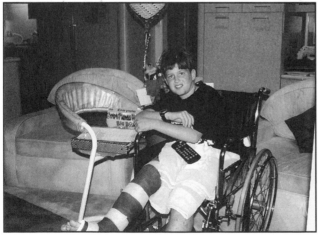

Tyler   August 1994

healthy and exercising can be a fun challenge and I now know what it is like to feel wonderful about myself. Health is wealth. We will be selling some supplements and food products; however, I want people to learn how to eat healthy (not "diet") while they are losing weight. I would be honored if you would consider allowing me to sell your cookbook as part of my program. Not only are the recipes wonderful, the information prefacing the Cookbook is fantastic and a great motivator.

I have worked part time for a weight loss center as a counselor, and I believe they have good products, but I saw many, many returning clients who did not know how to eat/cook correctly after they lost the weight, so they considered themselves failures.

I am planning to take over the center January 1, 1995 and I truly feel that an important part of improving one's lifestyle is to make it fun and exciting. Your book will enable my clients to cook healthy for themselves and their families, while learning how to make the new lifestyle a permanent one. I look forward to hearing from you. Sincerely, —*E.B. Bedford, Texas*

Tyler's "Get well Cookies" from Mom
Low-Fat (of course)

August 10, 1994

Dear Pam: I want to thank you for your *BUTTER BUSTERS COOKBOOK*. In August of 1993 I was diagnosed with an incurable disease. By March of 1994 the disease had invaded my pancreas which caused severe pain. No medication could be given to help with the pain. My doctor knowing that fat triggered pain in the pancreas put me on a diet consisting of 10 grams of fat per day. I could not have anything that was not cooked or of soft consistency. It was up to me to find the recipes to use. I discovered *BUTTER BUSTERS* at the Sam's Club in Fairbanks. Since then I have not only lost 32 pounds, but am pain free and I strongly feel that if it wasn't for your wonderful recipes I wouldn't be feeling the best I have in months. I will never be cured of the disease, but your recipes have made it easier to live with. I no longer consider myself to be on a diet. I think of it as a change of lifestyle. Thank you again.
Sincerely, —*K.M. North Pole, Alaska*

(This letter is from the same dear woman. We have actually become pen pals.)

September 4, 1994

Dear Pam: First of all I want to thank you for the tapes and workbook. It helped me understand the process better and also helped my husband see how much he can do to lower his cholesterol.

I was sorry to hear about your son, Tyler, breaking his leg. I hope he's adjusting to the cast and has accepted the fact that he may need some help for awhile. It can be really tough on kids. I know from experience.... my oldest had a cast from ankle to hip for 8 weeks when he was a sophomore. It was tough on him. He was a basketball player and couldn't play that season.

I feel like I know you from your tapes, so I thought I would share some information about myself. I am 46 years old and have been married for 26 years. We have two sons. J. is 25, married and teaches high school (physics and chemistry) in Sandy, Oregon. J. is 21 and is still trying to find himself. He lives in Costa Mesa, California with his girlfriend. I have worked for Fairbanks School District as an Administrative Secretary for 17 years. We first came to Fairbanks with the military. We liked it so much we decided to stay. Alaska is not for everyone! It gets down to -60 degrees below zero during the winter and can get up to 100 degrees during the summer. The summers of course are the best time of the year! We have 24 hours of daylight and everyone uses it to the fullest! During the winter we have only about 4 hours of daylight (like dusk). So you have to keep your spirits up by being active and not becoming a couch potato because of the weather. Some people find this very hard to do.

I haven't had too much trouble finding the ingredients for your recipes. I had to order my Butter Buds from New Jersey, but they now carry them in the stores. I haven't been able to get Fat-Free Parmesan cheese anywhere. Eventually they'll get it in, just may take a year or two. Ha. I have people at the different stores checking to see if they can get it in. Doesn't hurt to ask is my motto.

I've had fun buying a new wardrobe because of my weight loss. I went from a size 14 to an 8. I want to maintain where I am right now. I'm still losing a pound here and there, but am slowing down now. I want to be slim but have to stay healthy at the same time. I will not let this disease take me over. I am going to control it!!

I wanted to send you something "Alaskan" to show my appreciation for the tapes and workbook you gave me. I hope you like it and enjoy it. Thanks again, —*K.M. North Pole, Alaska*

NOTE: (She sent me a beautiful birchwood wooden bowl filled with spiced teas and an assortment of jelly. What a sweetheart she is. I hope I make it to Alaska some day to meet her in person.)

January 1994
HI Pam: My name is Sharon Smith and I am from a small town named Heavener, Oklahoma. I recently purchased your book *BUTTER BUSTERS* and I think it's terrific! You have given me many

new ideas that I never dreamed possible. I had no idea that you could substitute Butter Buds for oil in recipes. That was a huge fat saver. I have been on a low-fat "Lifestyle" for approximately 2 1/2 months now and have lost approximately 16 pounds. I originally started out with a book called *The T-Factor Diet.* Now I am using a combination of both books. I have enjoyed all of your recipes that I have tried so far. I work a full time job at a vo-tech and therefore I don't have a great deal of time to dedicate to cooking. But your recipes have proven to be quick and easy and I might add delicious! I would like to tell you how I use

Doug, Pam, and Sharon

"Lean Eye of the Round" beef in many of my recipes. Like ground turkey, my butcher is more than happy to either ground it up or cut it into steaks, or any other way I request. It is not as low in fat as ground turkey; but it makes a great substitute for high fat beef. According to the T-Factor book it only has 4.2 grams of fat for a 3 1/2 oz. serving. This is a huge savings over hamburger or even

ground chuck. It costs a little more here. It is between 2.88 lb and 3.29 a lb, but is well worth it in my opinion once you see the difference in portion size. I would love to see more "beef recipes" in your hopefully next cookbook. Your cookbook has opened so many doors to low-fat eating! I have recommended your book to all of my friends and they couldn't wait to get to the store to purchase one. Thank you for a terrific cookbook, what you have done has definitely made a difference in Heavener, Oklahoma! Sincerely, —*Sharon Smith Heavener, Oklahoma*
(Sharon and Doug now live in Poteau, Oklahoma)

October 13, 1994
Dear Pam: I've just come home from a family reunion get-together. "The Basic Vanilla Non-Fat Frozen Yogurt" (from your book) was a big hit! Your cookbook was often the topic of conversation. I've talked about your book so much that now my mom, sister-in-law, three aunts, a good friend, and co-worker now have and use your *BUTTER BUSTERS COOKBOOK.*

The main thing that makes your cookbook unique, is that it contains "every day people food" and not recipes that call for ingredients that need to be bought in a specialty shop. I personally liked the special hints for modification and substituting, so I can make my own favorite recipes low-fat.

Within three months my cholesterol was lowered 26 points. My husband's was lowered 13 points, but his triglycerides were down to 170. Three months ago they were 512! His family asks how our "diet" is going. I always correct them and say we are not dieting. We have made a lifestyle change.

I do have one suggestion. How about a newsletter with all the new product updates? Well, I better get busy. I'm making your "Layered Bean Dip" for supper. My husband also wants some "Orange Slice Candy Oatmeal Cookies!" Thanks for your help! —*T.W. Leeds, Alabama*

September 16, 1993
Dear Pam: I am writing to tell you how thrilled I am with your cookbook. I began in April just cutting fat from my diet and yet NOT dieting. I have lost 20 lbs. and am still losing. I was doing most of the things you recommended in your book but I didn't have many recipes (especially for cakes and goodies). With your book I have been able to make it through birthdays and cookouts and other special occasions and continue my slow but regular weight loss. I am telling all my friends (fat people have fat friends) about your book and even giving them samples of your recipes. I have sold several books for you! It is easy to do when you yourself are sold on a product. I especially enjoyed the front of your book. You have written it in such plain simple terms that it was easy to understand. I especially like the fact that you name stores and brands which I have not seen in any other book. One thing I recommend using along with your book is *The Complete Up To Date Fat Book* by Karen J. Bellerson. I am sure you must be familiar with that book. Between your book and that book, I can tell how much fat is in every meal I cook.

I had not tried Butter Buds until your book and now I use them all the time. (The "Quick Cobbler" is wonderful.) There are so many recipes that call for butter (like Stovetop Stuffing) that do not need butter at all but is included in the directions. I am learning to eat all the time the way I should. My sister has always been about 110 lbs. and I used to make fun of her for the way she would eat. Well, we are the same height but I reached 160 this past Spring. (I don't tease her anymore!) I even made my own honey mustard dressing and took it to the restaurant we like (T.K. Tripps) and compared it to theirs and no one could tell the difference. I spoke with the manager about how they should offer items like you have in your book. He said the more people speak up about it, the sooner that will happen. Anyway, I could talk about it for hours. (My friends tease ME about all the fat free stuff.) Just THANK YOU, THANK YOU, THANK YOU!!!!!
Sincerely, —*B.S. Midlothian, Virginia*

September 1994
Dear Pam: I am writing a short note because it sounds like your free time is extremely limited. I'm an elementary teacher, married five years, and until I was given a copy of your cookbook, I was a "non-cook, chef, or baker" and "non-grocery shopper."

My husband and I both struggle with our weight. At this point, we both have forty pounds to lose-eighty collectively. My cholesterol is very high (like my Mom's—who has never been overweight, but works extremely hard to keep it that way).

A few months ago, my husband, (a process engineer for a truck lift making company) was loaned a copy of your book by a co-worker. My husband was the sole chef of the household back then. Soon (at my request) he bought a copy for me and I've been cooking, grocery shopping, losing weight, and feeling better ever since.

I think I thought that by avoiding the whole cooking issue, I would be better off because food seemed to be the problem. Thank you for making cooking an easy, healthy, productive process for me. This may sound crazy, but I was thinking about not having children because I didn't want to pass on our eating habits and weight problems to our children. I think your cookbook may even have some influence on changing my decision about children (some day). Thanks a bunch!
—*M.M. Arvada, Colorado*

July 13, 1994
To Whom It may Concern: If at all possible I'd like this letter to be given to Pam Mycoskie so that she may read it also. I know you must receive thousands of letters and you can't read them all, but I hope you can read this one.

My life has changed for the better the day I bought *BUTTER BUSTERS THE COOKBOOK*. It was a Mother's Day gift to myself. The best gift I could have given myself. I have been trying to lose weight and get fit by going to the gym, and this was helping, but slowly. When I started to read your cookbook I decided I could change my life and eventually my family's.

It has worked. I've trimmed down and I'm not even on a diet. My husband said to me the other day, "I've never seen you eat so much." I just smiled. I've learned from you how to eat better and how to bake the goodies I love. And what to eat. I've even turned a few friends on to your cookbook by baking them some "too good to be low-fat cookies" (that's what I call them) from your cookbook. They could not believe how good they were and yes they too now own and use your cookbook. I could keep going because of how happy this book has made me, but I'll wrap by saying thank you!

Also I'd like to let you know that my husband and I (my family too) have eaten venison since we've been married (which is nine years). I interchange with chicken and now turkey. Just to let you know I have many many recipes for venison. And now I can make them even more low-fat than ever before because of my new knowledge on fat free cooking.

I'd love to share some of my recipes for venison with you. Let me know if you are interested. Thank you again   —*D.M. Wyandotte, Michigan*

October 12, 1994
Dear Pam: I just want you to know how much I am enjoying your cookbook. It is playing a major role in ensuring my family's health.

Three years ago I started eating Lean Cuisine to lose some weight. I was 22 years old and weighed 250 pounds. The first year went okay, but little did I know how much better it would get. I soon discovered low-fat and non-fat cooking. I read everything about low-fat that I can find. Now I know how to cook low-fat, eat low-fat. I even survived the cravings I had while I

Susan, Pam, and Jimmy

carried my second baby. I only gained 22 pounds with her and did step aerobics and walking the whole time. I had my ups and downs and it has not been easy at times, but I am a totally different person today. I am now 25 years old and weigh 137 lbs. I feel much better and cannot wait for my class reunion.

With your wonderful cookbook I can give my family a variety of great tasting low-fat meals. Keep up the good work and God Bless you and your family.—*Susan Allison Blacksburg, South Carolina*

P.S. Without the Lord's strength I could not have made it.

NOTE: As of March 1995, Susan has lost well over 100 pounds. She has been asked to speak at her church and to other groups as a result of her inspirational story. I think it is wonderful that she has chosen to share her story with others who might need help!

December 16, 1992
Dear Pam: Here we are!! Another holiday season is upon all of us. We know you are busy with shopping and all the preparations for family and friends. Here's wishing you and your family the merriest of Christmases.

I would like to thank you for helping us with our fund-raising projects at Arlington Court Reporting College. We raised about $170.00, and I can assure you it will be put to good use. We are all waiting anxiously for your next book to appear on the book stands. I will be one of the first ones in line to buy it.

Last month I went to visit my parents for Thanksgiving. My parents are Cubans and they have a lot of fat in their diet. They try to eat healthy, but like most of us are not aware of just how much fat they eat. I, of course, took my "Food Bible" with me. My parents wrote me and wanted us to send them three books. I just mailed them. So, now your cookbook is being praised in the Cuban community in Miami, Florida. I wonder if you would be interested in having your book translated in Spanish. I know there is a market for it. My mother would bless you, because it is more difficult for her to read it in English.

I just received a note in my mailbox at work from my friend, B. She said that she feels that your cookbook is like the "Second Coming." Shy says she has to watch herself because she finds herself actually preaching about it to her co-workers until their eyes start to glaze. She is now wearing her old uniforms that were in the back of her closet which she thought she would never wear again, and, of course, there is a new man in her life. She says that, of course, she has you to thank for that too.

In closing, thank you and keep up the good work. May the spirit of Christmas sweep down upon your home and all of your loved ones during the holidays, and we hope the New Year brings you the best life has to offer. FELIZ NAVIDAD,   —N.V. Bedford, Texas

January 15, 1994
Dear Pam: Thank you so much for the cookbook! I've tried all kinds of diets most of my life- I'm 76- but it took my teen-age grandson to educate me (and most of our family) to the fact that the only way to get rid of fat is just not to eat it!

I found your book at Sam's Club while Christmas shopping and bought several as gifts and kept one for myself. It has been a Godsend! It is fine to know that you shouldn't eat fat- but your book tells you how to make the process pleasant!

I particularly like the little comments about fats and carbos scattered throughout the book but I guess I am most impressed with the "Shopping Guide" and "New Products" sections. Thanks so much for the research—I would never have found many of the new products without it.

Again, thanks for your research and for helping so many of us to live longer!
Sincerely, —*F.A. Mesquite, Texas*

September 27, 1994
Dear Pam: Thank you so very much for writing and publishing your *BUTTER BUSTERS COOK-BOOK.* I received it from my mom two weeks ago and I have used it every day since then. I have never been much of a cook so I didn't feel a lot of self esteem in the kitchen until I got your book. Now I feel like a gourmet cook and my husband loves the dishes that I prepare. He has battled with a 300+ cholesterol problem for 2 or 3 years now and his doctor kept telling him to eat low-fat. My problem was that I didn't know how to cook low-fat until your wonderful book came along. I've learned more from your book in 2 weeks than I learned in a Nutrition class for one whole semester in college.

I don't know how much weight we will lose, but I already feel much healthier by eating low-fat. For five years I've abused diet pills trying to lose weight and in between I had two children. I hope this system of low-fat cooking will help. I'd love to have a healthy alternative to diet pills.

Thank you again for taking the time to write this book. You may have saved my husband from a heart attack by changing my cooking style. Please write another book with more great recipes. THANKS A MILLION! Sincerely, —*J.C. Lake City, Florida*

October 20, 1994
Dear Pam: I'm wondering if you are going to put out another *BUTTER BUSTERS COOKBOOK*? I have the cookbook plus I have the 3 tapes and workbook. I've shown several people the materials and they were so impressed that they went out and got their own. In fact, I got my mother one for Mother's Day this year. She loves it! It's the BEST cookbook ever!

I've lost a total of 17 pounds since April just by cutting down on my fat and walking. Of course I used the *BUTTER BUSTERS COOKBOOK* to help me out. I really do hope you come out with a *BUTTER BUSTERS II*. Keep up the good work! Thanks! —*B.W. Napoleon, Ohio*

October 29, 1994
Dear Mrs. Mycoskie: My husband and I would like to thank you for writing such a wonderful book. We have changed our way of eating because the *BUTTER BUSTERS COOKBOOK* explained exactly how to lose weight while eating just about everything we love. My husband has tried every

diet in the world (or so it seems) and has always lost the weight he wanted but put it back on (shock !!). He heard about your book from a family friend who has changed her way of eating and kept off the weight she lost for the last six months. For yo-yo dieters, as you know, continued success is very important. The best thing about your book was your explaining of fat, fat calories, and the metabolism of the human body. I have been trying for years to get my husband to believe eating just one meal a day was not the way to lose weight and keep it off, but once I read and explained your section on the body's need for constant "healthy" fuel, he understood better. He was discouraged for awhile because the weight wasn't dropping off quickly as with the other diets, but when he hit the one month mark and he tried on a suit we had ordered a month prior to his following the book, and the suit was huge forcing us to purchase another size DOWN. He was thrilled. He has lost a solid 9 pounds and his body shape has changed. He has not starved and as a matter of fact he often pushes his plate away because he is comfortably full (a first for him).

I have taken favorite recipes and changed them to low-fat and healthy. We made an entire turkey meal that was not only low fat, but very tasty. My kids did not even miss the dark turkey meat and they even enjoyed the fat-free gravy. It was so easy to make the meal healthy.

Recently we went to a family get together and we were asked to bring a dessert. I made the "Quick Cobbler" with apples and the "Low-fat Rice Krispie Treats." I told no one except my husband and waited until everyone had eaten. Not one person could tell the cobbler was low-fat and the fact that I made the Rice Krispie Treats without butter and they still tasted so good was amazing to everyone. We told everyone that we made fat-free garlic bread, they couldn't believe it was possible until we told them about Butter Buds.

I must admit that learning to cook over again is a challenge, but a fun challenge. The food chains don't make finding low-fat and no-fat foods very easy. It takes time, but in the end it is worth it. My husband and I both feel uncomfortable if we eat outside of the "diet" and have learned how to ask "How was this prepared?" or "Do you have fat-free salad dressing?" If he cheats one day the next two days he makes sure he eats correctly. (My husband is a fireman and the firehouse is the worst place to be on any kind of diet or watching your fat intake.) I am very proud of him. He takes his no-fat salad dressing and his Butter Buds and if he can his Egg Beaters too. Did you know if you mix fresh veggies with onions, mushrooms and Egg Beaters, you have the best omelet? My husband likes feeling good physically and loves to see the change he has gone through.

I wish we had found your book years ago. We could have saved ourselves a lot of aggravation. We will continue to tell people about your book and look forward to another book of recipes. Thank you for sharing your life with us and thanks so much for the book. Sincerely, —*K.S. Chicago, Illinois*

October 18, 1994
Dear Pam: Thank you so much for the *BUTTER BUSTERS* cookbooks! My husband and I have been using your cookbook and information since February 1994. Al lost about 60 pounds and is in

much better health! (He does not even snore anymore.) I have lost 43 pounds and feel better getting back into the sizes I used wear.

We came to your book signing at Books A Million in Birmingham last February. I was delighted to find that you are what you preach. Your enthusiasm and energy inspired us. We took both editions of your cookbook on a 29th anniversary weekend to the beach. We read and walked and enjoyed working on the new eating ideas together. Our children (ages 23 and 17) like the home cooking and don't even miss all the hamburger. I am having trouble losing the

Betty, Pam, and Al

last 15 pounds. I keep bouncing between -45 and -40 pounds lost. Please send the information on your video and workbook. I really need your help to finish getting this last bit off. Thank goodness this is not a "diet" but a way of life to keep us healthy! Keep up the good work!
Sincerely, —*Betty and Al Corley Odenville, Alabama*

October 31, 1994
Dear Pam: I'm a 33 year old mother of three that has been battling a weight problem my whole life. I remember as a child being considered chubby. I have an older sister who is petite and a younger sister who is tall and slim. I have never been an obese person, but usually am anywhere between 20-40 pounds overweight.

In November of 1993 I weighed 162 pounds. I am 5'4" tall. That is the heaviest I have ever been (except when I was pregnant). I started working November 22, 1993 at Wallmart. Within 2 weeks I was promoted to department manager and in about 2 months I dropped 16 pounds. That was due to the physical work involved. I was happy at 146 pounds for a while, but still was 20 pounds overweight. I tried starving, Slim Fast, exercising a few times a week, but nothing would budge my

weight or size. Sometimes I would lose a pound or two, but would soon it would come right back on like it had before. In April of '94, I was promoted to support manager(which requires nice clothes). I found some very nice summer outfits in size large or 11/12. I would look in the mirror and say, "If I could only lose 20 pounds I would be so much happier." My mother came to visit in July and I rented a video camera. When I saw myself on that tape that was the final straw. At work we had received a big shipment of books and yours was one of them. I skimmed through it and thought, what the heck, I'll give it a try.

Carole and Pam

Well today, 3 months later, I weigh 128 pounds and wear a size 7/8 most of the time. And the best part of it all is I eat more than I ever did. I eat breakfast, lunch, and dinner and snacks in between. Your recipes are fantastic! The best part about your book isn't just the recipes, but the way you explain everything. It is so easy to understand. I have completely changed the way I eat but can eat the same things other people eat just by simple substitutions and modifications. I have a very busy schedule and have not found the time to join an aerobics class yet, but I exercise 10 minutes in the morning and 10 minutes at night.

I thank God every day that I found your book. I have told several people about it and consider it my bible. Thanks for keeping it simple and making it easy.
—*Carole Robinson Tunkhannock, Pennsylvania*

January 10, 1995
Dear, dear Pam!
Thank you so much for changing my life forever! Your *BUTTER BUSTERS* book opened my eyes to a new world! I never knew there were so many low-fat and non-fat delicious foods out there! In exactly one year I have lost 54 pounds!! And the great thing is–I never wanted for anything! I never felt like I was on a diet!! I am 5 feet tall and weighed 194 when I started watching my fat gram intake. I'm wearing size 10 jeans now and just for kicks I'll put on my size 18 jeans once in a while. I just can't believe that I was ever that big! Thank you so much, you are a miracle-worker!! Gratefully,
—*Julie Wooten Arlington, Texas*

Julie Wooten

January 24, 1995
Dear Mrs. Mycoskie,
As a writer for *MUSCLE & FITNESS* magazine, I am often called upon to review nutritional cookbooks. Some are based on healthy principles, but lack important ingredients—like taste and practicality.

Photo by Randy Reid ©
Les Maness

Perhaps that's why I found *BUTTER BUSTERS* so appetizing. *BUTTER BUSTERS* teaches you how to shop 'til you drop—fat. It offers technical nutritional information in a lite easy manner. And best of all, it thoroughly explains how to cook up a healthy lifestyle.

So, when people ask me for a low-fat cookbook recommendation I simply say, "If other nutritional cookbooks have left a bad taste in your mouth, try *BUTTER BUSTERS.* You'll discover so much flavor, you'll feel guilty. And you'll see results so quickly, you can't help but stay pumped up!" Stay Healthy!
—*Les Maness, Phoenix, Arizona*

Note: I don't have a letter from Cindy Cochran. She lives in Dallas, and just called me up one day to tell me how *BUTTER BUSTERS* had changed her life. Cindy has lost over 100 pounds and has kept it off for more than two years. She is a wonderful person and a real friend. Even though we live quite near each other (35-40 minutes away), I don't see her often enough. We are both busy working mothers, with very active kids, so we don't have a lot of extra time (to say the least). I feel very blessed that our paths crossed and honored to know such a positive upbeat person as Cindy! I thank her for the love and support she has given me over the past two years that we have known each other. She is an inspiration to me!

Cindy Cochran

January 22, 1995
Dear Pam:
My Sloppy Joe Casserole is in the oven and I wanted to let you know HOW WONDERFUL *BUTTER BUSTERS* truly is! I have tried many low-fat cookbooks, and most are gathering dust on my shelf, as the recipes tasted "low-fat," and were very unsatisfying. Your cookbook, however, is SO FULL of wonderful tasting recipes, that I cook from it most every evening. I've yet to cook something that my husband did not want to add to our list of "regulars." Thanks so much for taking the time to prepare this book! Although we have a ways to go, at least we eat healthier at home!
Sincerely, —*J.T. Chattanooga, Tennessee*

January 24, 1995
Dear Pam,
After losing 90 pounds, I automatically assumed I'd have to give up flavor forever. Imagine how excited I was to discover your inspirational and educational cookbook!

Pam, you took all the guess work out of planning and measuring. You introduced me to healthy, tasty alternatives I didn't know were possible. And ultimately, the principles you taught allowed me to enjoy results so profound, I was asked to share my success story with the seven and a half million readers of *Muscle and Fitness Magazine*. I can't thank you enough!
Sincerely, —*Linda Thornhill Tempe, Arizona*

Note: At the age of 28 and 216 pounds (a size 22 1/2), Linda decided she was ready to do something positive for herself. Featured in *MUSCLE & FITNESS* magazine because of her success story, Linda is a perfect example of a woman "on a mission." She kept with it and, because of her determination, is now a healthy, happy, and quite petite young woman. At 126 pounds (and a size 5) you should see her now. What a beautiful lady on the outside as well as the inside! Thank you for your letter, Linda. I'm so proud of you and what you have accomplished. I'm so glad my book has helped make it a little easier to cook the foods you enjoy! Please stay in touch!

Photo by Les Maness©

Linda Thornhill

January 24, 1995
Dear Pam:
I am writing this letter to let you know that you have made a believer out of me and I have passed on the good news to many others and will continue to do so.

Two years ago my husband was diagnosed with Multiple Sclerosis. Recently, while reading one of the MS newsletters, they made mention of a book a physician had on the market regarding low-fat diets and people with MS. I purchased the book and read it from front to back. The first half of the book dealt with specifics on MS, the second half of the book was on nutrition, which foods to eat, which foods not to eat and foods to limit as well as hundreds of recipes for low-fat cooking.

Well, the race was on! As I began cooking low-fat we found the meals were wonderful, we were not snacking as we had previously done and we (especially my husband) began losing weight. One day a fellow in my husband's office mentioned another cookbook which was "low-fat." That evening my husband and I went to check it out. Most of the recipes were 9 grams of fat, 12 grams of fat, etc. I said, "this is not low-fat," thus we began looking closely at other cookbooks and came across your *BUTTER BUSTERS*. When I saw on the cover that most recipes were under 5 grams, of fat, I opened it up and began checking out the recipes; just briefly thumbing through, I found some that sounded very tasty, so I bought it (by the way, the saleslady told us it was the 2nd best selling cookbook in the store, second only to Oprah's!). I was excited that I felt I had made a good choice, took it home and read it from front to back.

Pam, I cannot say enough good things about your cookbook. It is the best collection of tasty, nutritious meals I have seen. I began bringing my book to work with me on a daily basis. I read through it to find a recipe for dinner, and mark my choice with a Post-it Tape Flag. As I make recipes, I write comments next to them so we know which ones we have tried and what we thought of them. People in my husband's office began noticing his weight loss and asked what he was doing. He told them we were cooking low-fat and gave them the name of your cookbook. Within a matter of weeks, people in my husband's office, people in my office, my relatives, my husband's relatives - everyone I talked to was hearing about *BUTTER BUSTERS* and Pam Mycoskie! People laughed and some would ask, "Do you know this woman"? My reply was, (of course), that I personally had never met you but that through your cookbook, we had become good friends. Just yesterday two additional people in my husband's office got the name of your book to go buy it, and this morning I was speaking with a woman in my office discussing low-fat cooking and I told her about your book, and in fact, had it with me so I showed it to her. She is going after work to buy her own copy!

You have simplified my meal planning and cooking through the ease with which you put your recipes together. As I told my friend, "for example," I said, "Pam has a recipe in her book for Mexican Spaghetti that is out of this world. I throw together (after coming home from work!) your 'On the Double Dinner Rolls,' mix up the 'Mexican Spaghetti' and get it to baking, put together a fresh fruit salad and there's dinner! So simple and so delicious and so healthy!"

I was hesitant to write to you as I'm sure you get hundreds or thousands of letters, But I do hope you read mine as I would really like for you to know how excited I am about your *BUTTER BUSTERS*. I wanted you to know that from passing on the good news to others, I have probably sold another 50 or so copies and I am hoping that you have another cookbook in the works. I will watch for one - just in case and I will continue to pass on the news about your *BUTTER BUSTERS!*

By the way, my husband (who will turn 50 in February) stands 5' 11" and now weighs about 150 lbs. When he began eating low-fat, he weighed approximately 194 lbs. I am almost 48 years old, I stand 5' 1" and now weigh 117 lbs. I began at 132 lbs. I continue to exercise and eat low-fat and am hoping to get down to 110 lbs. We began eating low-fat back in May and the good news is that neither one of us has gained so much as a pound since that time. We have truly learned that it is not a "diet." We simply eat low-fat. Thank you for you and your book.
Sincerely, —*S.R. Port Neches, Texas*

January 25, 1995
Dear Pam:
I am writing to thank you for *BUTTER BUSTERS*. As a professional trainer I recommend your book to all of my clients. I think everyone should have a copy of *BUTTER BUSTERS*, because it is the best book I have found that explains how to make the transition to a low-fat lifestyle, by giving excellent, easy to understand information and recipes that anyone can follow. Also, I appreciate the nutritional breakdown given with each recipe. Exercise combined with a low-fat lifestyle is the way to go!
Sincerely, —*Kathy M. Pichnarcik, S.M.A., O.A. Phoenix, Arizona, Western Regional Bodybuilding Champion*

Photo by Les Maness©

Kathy Pichnarcik

Note: Kathy was featured in the June 1994 issue of *MUSCLE & FITNESS* magazine. If you locate a back copy it is on page 19. She has a very inspirational story. Kathy virtually went from an invalid (confined to bed) to the "Ms. Western Regional Bodybuilding Champion." Kathy attributes her recovery to proper nutrition, exercise, and adequate rest. She is a true inspiration to all of us. With such determination, Kathy has overcome numerous obstacles, and shown the world what can happen to a beautiful young woman who refuses to give up no matter what the odds! Thank you, Kathy, for your letter. I wish you continued success!

January 20, 1995
Dear Pam:
My name is D W. and a friend of mine has your book, *BUTTER BUSTERS*, and she let me read it, and I found it to be a very good book. I'd like to take a minute and tell you that May 3, 1993, I weighed 218 lbs. I am the mother of two girls. At 34 years young, with a birth defect that had affected my life even more than being fat, I started drinking 3-4 quarts of water a day, also went on a low-fat high-carbohydrate diet. If I wanted to snack after 5:00 p.m., it was something fat-free or I just drank more water to stay full. I started an exercise program. I mean a good one (Tony Little) the best money a person can spend and it has been great. I've lost 72 lbs. and 53 inches. I went from a 20 1/2 pants to a size 10 etc., and it's almost been two years now and boy do I look great! As I was reading all the food substitutions in your book, I noticed you listed every product that I use, and let me tell you I live on pasta. I find it good to eat every 2-3 hours (lots of small meals so your body will know that it's always going to have more food). There is no reason to go into the starvation mode, which then helps you to always burn fat (that ugly "F" word). I want to thank you for writing a book like this, and I do hope to buy it soon when I have the money. All my friends say I look better than they have ever seen me look and they say I even have a glow about me. My two daughters are happy because they can reach completely aroung my waist now. A large part of my appreciation goes to Tony Little, a wonderful person who truly cares about people as you do.

You see, Tony Little shows you how to properly exercise because if you're not exercising properly, then you could also hurt yourself. Check into the Tony Little tapes. Thank you very much Pam for your time reading this letter and <u>please</u> do respond and let me know what you think. Thanks again, — *D.W. Stockton, California (Or should I say the NEW D.W.)*

Note: The following letter is from the same person.

February 1, 1995
Dear Pam,
I just wanted to thank you for the *BUTTER BUSTERS* book. That was so sweet of you and so unexpected, it surprised me and touched my heart (the book and your kindness) that it almost made me cry (happy tears of course). I can't express what it meant to me! Thank you so much. It's people like Tony Little and yourself that keep me motivated. I've enclosed before and after pictures of myself and whenever I'm feeling down (because I'm at a standstill), I either look at my after picture, or listen to Tony Little, and now my new book, or look at your picture and any of those things will cheer me up. I also read on your card that I didn't say what kind of birth defect I have. Well, I have 1 finger on each hand and on my feet I have 1 toe on each foot and it's the baby toe. So imagine 1 toe on each foot supporting 218-220 lbs. I suffer from foot problems and swollen ankles. My balance is not too great and I have fallen 2 times and broken my foot. I could never walk long (like at Disneyland) and since I've lost 72 pounds and 53 inches I have taken my girls to Marine World and walked all over the place with no problem. Isn't that great? That's why the doctors said if I didn't lose weight I would probably end up in a wheel chair the rest of my life. Well, I changed that quick. I will watch for your book, *I'M LISTENING!* and your infomercial. You can tell that you truly do care about people. I want to wish you great success in all your goals. Well, I don't want to keep you too long as busy as you are. I just wanted to thank you again for my book and I hope you have a good day!
—D. W. Stockton, California

P.S. I will keep your card handy in case I need to be cheered up!

January 27, 1995
Dear Pam:
Thank you so much for *BUTTER BUSTERS*, it is truly a special book. I am 32 years old, married, a mother of two very energetic preschool boys, and I have been an aerobics instructor and personal trainer for over a decade.

My early years in the fitness world seemed to revolve around an eating program that involved "dieting" and "deprivation." Fortunately, through a lot of reading and searching, my nutritional standards and habits have evolved into one of regular healthy and low-fat eating. This program, combined with my exercise regimen, has allowed me to maintain a lean body by eating well without depriving myself of the foods I enjoy. *BUTTER BUSTERS* has played an important role for me as I use it and refer to it on a regular basis. My favorites are the turkey lasagna and the rich fudge brownies.

Photo by Les Maness©

Shana Hill

Thanks to your wonderful and informative book, my family, friends, and I are all enjoying great healthy low-fat eating. It is nice to have a great cookbook that is also a motivational book to refer to all of my students and clients. I hope there will be a *Butter Busters Cookbook II!*
Yours Healthfully,   —*Shana Hill, Scottsdale, Arizona*

P.S. People tell me that we look alike - I think it must be not only our common physical appearance, but also the vibrance we get from our healthy lifestyles - don't you agree?

February 26, 1995
Dear Pam,

I will try to make this as brief as possible, for I know you must be very busy. My daughter is 2 ½ yrs old. She almost died this past May. After much testing (which has been done on her most of her life) they have given her a diagnosis of Intestinal Lymphangiectasia. Without going into a lot of detail, this basically means that she has to be on a low-fat (2 grams per 100 calories), high protein diet or she will die.

When she was first diagnosed I was beside myself on how to cook. Being from the South, fried food has been a way of life. She finally got to the point where she wouldn't eat because her foods were the same thing over and over. I went to the library to see if any of the cookbooks could help. I tried the Weight Watchers and the one the Heart Society puts out, but still most of their recipes contained too much fat or were too exotic. I ran across yours and I praise God!

Thank you for teaching me how to cook. Your explanation in the front has been very helpful in changing some old recipes into new ones! Casey is doing well and the whole family is happy with my new cooking! It was very hard eating in front of her and she always wants to eat what we do, so this has made our life much, much easier.

Casey Simpson

As a note, there are only 16 other known cases of what Casey has. I have written the few that returned my letters, and told them about your cookbook. One resides in England and I am not sure she can get it there, but if she is interested I will be willing to get her one.

Thank you again, and may God bless you and your efforts at helping others.
Sincerely,   —*Shawnee Simpson, Columbia, S.C.*

March 27, 1995
Dear Pam:

I am writing in regard to your *BUTTER BUSTERS* Cookbook, seventh edition. After my husband's recent angioplasties and change in diet, we purchased your cookbook. We are most pleased with it, and find it better, easier to read, and more informative than any low-fat, no-fat cookbook that we have purchased. In fact, we have used it so much and praised it to so many friends, that I believe at least twenty others have also purchased the cookbook.

Please continue with a new *BUTTER BUSTERS,* with additional recipes. I will be the first to purchase it. By the way, my husband's cholesterol has dropped from 278 to 190 in only three months! Thanks *BUTTER BUSTERS*! Sincerely—J.B. Mansfield, Pennsylvania

Dear Mrs. Mycoskie,

I'm writing to say thank you so much for the *BUTTER BUSTERS* Cookbook. It's opened a whole new world for me. This past Christmas I knew things had to change. After 10½ years of marriage I had gained approximately 100 lbs! Mostly because we've moved quite a bit from state to state, from a very small town to Orlando, Florida was the biggest culture shock. My lifestyle changed drastically from walking daily to staying home <u>all</u> the time. Not driving and not working outside the home and fear of the unknown made me a couch potato! I was miserable and homesick. I used food for a good time. Believe me, I had one good time after another. I accept the blame because it was my own pity for myself that held the fork. But no more, I wanted my life back.

At Christmas I asked for an exercise bike. First time I rode only two miles, and it was a struggle. Slowly I increased it, and now I ride 20 miles at a time. On Valentine's Day I asked my husband to skip the flowers and chocolates and get me a "Sweatin to the Oldies" tape by Richard Simmons. He got one for me. Since then I've gotten all four Sweatin tapes and two other workout tapes that I rotate. Two have weight segments and floor exercises.

During all this time I've read up on nutrition and cutting fat from my diet. I started making changes. Like I no longer skip meals. The quantity I've eaten in the last 4 months is more that I've eaten in 10 years! I've lost approximately 40 lbs. At the rate of 2 lbs. a week, I should reach my goal weight just before Christmas this year. I finally feel in control.

My biggest problem was that I was eating everything over and over because I knew they were low-fat. When my oldest sister Bev told me about your book I checked it out. I was thrilled to actually find recipes for food I used to cook like Jambalaya, Tamale Pie, Dump Cake and Chocolate Pudding Cake. I can't thank you enough! My husband and son appreciate it, too. They've lost weight since my changes have been made. My husband has gone from 242 to 225 and my son went from 145 to 135 and is now right in his target weight range. None of us have missed the goodies of the past, because we can still eat them made LOW-FAT!

I'm currently planning meals for next week and am making out a list. I'm most interested in your video series and workbook. How do I obtain them? Thank you for all the work and time in compiling the Cookbook. It's the best purchase I've ever made. Sincerely,—*J. H. Winfield, West Virginia*

This is my Mom, Char Doehler. They used to call her "Big Mama." After losing over 50 pounds and lowering her cholesterol to a safe range, she truly is a walking example of what I teach. Mom is my cheerleader and has always given me the love and support that have meant so much in my life.

Mom's Birthday 1989

September 1989

Char and Pam   Christmas 1994

Pam and Char   February 1995

She has stood beside me through the good times and the hard times. She has never given up on me no matter what others may think or say. The thing I appreciate most about my Mom is that she REALLY LISTENS to me and provides positive feedback when I need it the most. At 75 years young, she is an inspiration to all of us! I love you Mom more than words can express!

YOUR
RESOURCE GUIDE

NAME BRAND
LOW-FAT SHOPPING LIST

BREADS AND BAKERY ITEMS
- Wonder low-fat buns and breads
- Hostess Lights Snackcakes (all varieties)
- Entenmanns fat-free bakery items
- Health Valley fat-free muffins and cookies
- Greenfield Healthy Food "Homestyle Brownies" (fat-free)
- Greenfield Healthy Foods "Blondie" Chocolate Chip Bars (fat-free)
- Mission "Light" flour tortillas
- Mission and El Paco corn tortillas
- El Paco fat-free flour tortillas
- Pepperidge Farm's Cubed Style Seasoned or Country Style Stuffing (Low-Fat)
  These can be used as croutons or breading (for crust) when crushed.
- La Madaline fresh breads and Caesar croutons
- Wolfermans brand fat-free or low-fat English muffins and crumpets
- Lenders' bagels
- Quaker Oats fat-free corn and rice cakes
- FI-BAR low-fat snack bars (all varieties)
- Power Munch fat-free turnovers (All flavors)
- Kabuli Gourmet Natural Pizza Bread (fat-free ready to serve crust)
- Boboli low-fat pizza crust shells

SALAD DRESSINGS AND CONDIMENTS
- Kraft fat-free salad dressings (Peppercorn Ranch and Honey Dijon are my favorites)
- Kraft Fat-Free Miracle Whip and mayonnaise substitute
- Kraft fat-free tartar sauce
- Weight Watchers' fat-free mayonnaise substitute
- SmartBeat fat-free mayonnaise substitute
- Wish-bone Healthy Sensations fat-free salad dressings (Honey Dijon is my favorite)
- Seven Seas FREE fat-free salad dressings (Red Wine Vinegar is my favorite)
- Hidden Valley fat-free salad dressings (Honey Dijon and Creamy Parmesan are my favorites)
- Pfeiffer fat-free salad dressings (the Ranch is good)
- Good Season's fat-free salad dressing mixes (all varieties)
- Weight Watchers' fat-free salad dressings (also come in individual packets)
- Marie's fat-free salad dressings (found in the produce section)
- Pritikin fat-free salad dressings (very low sodium)
- Walden Farms fat-free salad dressings (in the produce section)

- Hidden Valley fat-free dressing and dip mixes
- BAC-O'S imitation bacon chips and bits (2 Tbs. are only one fat gram)
- Peter Pan "Smart Choice" reduced fat peanut butter (6 fat grams per Tbs.)
  *Regular peanut butter is 13 fat grams per Tbs.
- Papa Dash Lite Salt (1/4 tsp. only 90mg sodium) (Regular salt is 595 mg. sodium per
  1/4 tsp.) *This is a great sodium substitute with no bitter aftertaste.

*Watch for your own store brands. They are always cheaper and usually just as good!

SOUPS AND SAUCES
- Hunts "Light" fat-free pasta sauces
- Ragu "Light" fat-free pasta sauces (The "Garden Harvest" and "Tomato & Herb" varieties are good.)
- Healthy Choice fat-free soups and sauces
- Weight Watchers' low-fat canned soups and sauces
- Weight Watchers' low-fat soup mixes
- Campbell's "Healthy Request" fat-free soups and sauces
- Progresso "Healthy Classics" soups (all varieties)
- Health Valley fat-free soups, sauces and Chile
- Uncle Ben's Hearty Soup mixes ("Black Bean and Rice" is really good.)
- Pritikin fat-free soups and sauces
- K.C. Masterpiece Original Barbecue Sauce (also Dijon flavor)
- Campbell's low-fat dry soup mixes
- Pioneer fat-free gravy mixes (brown gravy and country white gravy)
- McCormick low-fat sauce mixes
- McCormick "Light" low-fat taco mix

*Use the mixes in moderation due to the high sodium content (in most cases). Always prepare the mixes with low or fat-free ingredients (such as skim milk, Egg Beaters, and liquid Butter Buds).

CANNED FRUITS AND VEGETABLES
- Green Giant low-fat and fat-free beans (all varieties)
- Rosarita fat-free refried beans
- Old El Paso fat-free refried beans
- Lucky Leaf "Lite" pie fillings (use Sweet'N Low to sweeten)
- Comstock "Light" pie fillings (use Sweet'N Low to sweeten)
- Lucky Leaf applesauce (fat substitute)
- Sunsweet prunes (can be pureéd and used as a fat substitute) *You can also use baby food prunes or other baby food fruits as a fat substitution.

*Most fruits and vegetables are fat-free. Shop for the low sodium varieties. Always rinse your canned vegetables to reduce the sodium content.

CEREALS AND GRANOLA BARS
- Grape-Nuts Cereal
- Back to Nature "No-Fat Added" low-fat granola (only natural fat found in the grains)
- Health Valley Fat-Free Granola and Granola Bars
- 3-Minute Quick Oats Oatmeal
- Kellogg's Low-Fat Granola and Granola Bars
- FI-BAR Low-Fat Snack Bars
- SNACKWELLS fat-free breakfast bars
- Quaker low-fat granola bars (2 fat grams per bar)
- Quaker fat-free corn and rice cakes (other brands are fine)
- Auburn Farms fat-free toaster pastries

*Most cereals are low in fat or fat-free (except regular granola). Watch for sugar and sodium content, however.

SPICE AND BAKING SECTION
- Butter Buds Sprinkles
- Butter Buds Mix (Fat-Free) (Look for a box containing 8 packets to be mixed with hot water.)
- Molly McButter fat-free sprinkle -on seasonings
- McCormick's "Best O Butter" fat-free sprinkle- on seasonings
- "Spike" fat-free sprinkle-on seasoning
- Sweet'N Low (bulk, liquid, or packets to be used in baking)
- Sweet'N Low Brown (brown sugar substitute to be used in baking)
- Necta Sweet (saccharin based sugar substitute in tablet form used for baking)
- Hershey's Syrup
- Hershey's cocoa (low-fat)
- Nestlé's cocoa (low-fat)
- Nestlé's fat-free and sugar free cocoa mix
- Carnation fat-free and sugar free cocoa mix
- Swiss Miss fat-free and sugar free cocoa mix
- Pet "Light" evaporated canned skimmed milk (fat-free)
- Eagle Brand low-fat condensed sweetened milk (1.5 fat grams per 2 Tbs.)
- Dream Whip low-fat topping mix (does contain saturated fat, but a very small amount- less than 1 fat gram and 6 calories per Tbs.)
- Estée brand sugar free whipped topping mix (does contain saturated fat, but a very small amount - less than 1 fat gram and 4 calories per Tbs.)
- JELL-O Brand "Light" pudding and dessert mixes
- Nabisco's brand "Royal Lite Cheesecake" mix (sugar-free and low-fat)
- Betty Crocker "Light" cake, brownie, and muffin mixes (low-fat)
- Martha White's low-fat muffin mixes
- Krusteaz fat-free muffin mixes (The blueberry mix is great!)
- Pillsbury Lovin' Lites low-fat cake, brownie, and muffin mixes

- Sans Sucre de Paris "Cheesecake Mousse" mix (sugar-free and low-fat)
- Saco Cultured Buttermilk Blend mix (low-fat)
- Betty Crocker Fat-Free White Fluffy Frosting Mix *I use this in place of Cool Whip
- "Light" or Dream Whip as a topping as well as for a frosting. It has a marshmallow consistency, but tastes great chilled.
- Carnation instant non-fat powdered milk
- Fat-Free Coffee Mate (check the label-not all fat-free)
- Mid-America instant non-fat powdered milk
- Weight Watchers' low-fat cooking spray
- Wesson "Light" low-fat cooking spray
- Pam low-fat cooking spray (regular and olive oil)
- I Can't Believe It's Not Butter! cooking spray
- Karo Syrup (fat substitute)
- Argo Cornstarch (a non-fat thickener for sauces and gravies)
- Kellogg's crushed corn flakes (fat-free coating or breading mix for crusts)
- Nabisco fat-free cracker crumbs or cracker meal (used for coating or breading)
- HOUSE-AUTRY chicken breading (for crispy baked chicken)
- McCormick extracts (coconut, walnut, butter) *These are great to use when you want the flavor of high-fat foods (but not the fat)!
- ENER-G Egg Replacers (usually found in Health Food Stores) This is a dry mix (when added to water) equivalent to 162 eggs. ($4.69)
- Marshmallows
- Kraft Marshmallow Cream
- "Quick Loaf" by Daily Bread Company (fat-free bread mixes) These come in many varieties and are delicious (especially the "Garlic and Herb").
- Howard's garlic oil and onion oil (fat-free drops to add flavor) *This also comes in a spray.
- Miller's fat-free soup base (beef and chicken)
- Pillsbury Hot Roll Mix (fat-free)
- Pioneer Low-Fat Biscuit Mix (The box used to read No-Fat.) With the new labeling laws, it must read low-fat because there is 0.49 fat grams (less than one) per serving. This is a great product and VERY LOW-FAT!
- Papa Dash "Lite" Salt

REFRIGERATED DAIRY PRODUCTS

CHEESE
- Alpine Lace fat-free cheeses (Swiss, American, mozzarella, Cheddar and a variety of other choices)
- Alpine Lace reduced-fat cheese products (all varieties)
- POLLY-O FREE fat-free mozzarella (This is the BEST fat-free mozzarella cheese on the market!) This cheese comes in the block (16-oz.) and grated (8-oz.) varieties.
- POLLY-O "Lite" mozzarella and "Lite" string cheese sticks (2.5 fat grams an ounce)

- POLLY-O FREE fat-free string cheese sticks
- Lifetime by Lifeline low and fat-free cheeses (all varieties) I love their "Mild Mexican" fat-free variety! I also love their low-fat (3 fat grams an ounce) Cheddar.
- Jarlsberg "Lite" reduced fat Swiss cheese (3.5 fat grams per ounce)
- Kraft FREE American slices cheese
- Kraft "Healthy Favorites" fat-free cheeses (all varieties)
- Borden fat-free cheese slices (all varieties) I really like their "Sharp Cheddar" flavor.
- Healthy Choice fat-free cheese products (all varieties including string cheese)
- Healthy Choice Velvetta style fat-free cheese (This is a great product for making Rotel Cheese Dip!)
- Sargento "Light" low-fat mozzarella and Cheddar (grated)
- Frigo brand low-fat cheeses (mozzarella and Cheddar)
- Sorrento low-fat cheeses (mozzarella and Cheddar)
- SmartBeat fat-free cheese slices
- Weight Watchers' fat-free and low-fat cheeses (all varieties)
- Precious "Lite" low-fat cheeses

*Watch for your own store brands!

CREAM CHEESE AND CHEESE SPREADS
- Philadelphia FREE fat-free cream cheese
- Healthy Choice fat-free cream cheese
- Weight Watchers' cream cheese spread (low-fat)
- Alpine Lace Fat-Free cream cheese spreads (French Onion, Garden Vegetable, Garlic & Herb, Horseradish, Cheddar, and Mexican Nacho)

*Watch for your own store brands!

PARMESAN CHEESE
- Alpine Lace fat-free fresh Parmesan *This is a wonderful NEW product found in the "Deli" section of your grocery store!
- Emperial "Lite" low-fat Parmesan cheese
- Kraft FREE Parmesan cheese
- Weight Watchers' fat-free Parmesan cheese

RICOTTA AND COTTAGE CHEESE
- Frigo "Light" fat-free Ricotta
- Precious fat-free Ricotta
- POLLY-O FREE fat-free Ricotta
- Sargenta low-fat Ricotta
- Sorrento fat-free Ricotta
- Weight Watchers' fat-free cottage cheese
- Borden Lite Line fat-free cottage cheese

- Light n' Lively fat-free cottage cheese
- Oak Farms non-fat cottage cheese

SOUR CREAM
- Land O Lakes NO-FAT sour cream and fat-free dips
- Light n' Lively fat-free sour cream
- Oak Farms NO-FAT sour cream
- Breakstone's fat-free sour cream
- Real Dairy (Naturally Yours) NO-FAT sour cream
- Schepps NO-FAT sour cream
- Hall's fat-free dips (all varieties)

*There are new fat-free sour creams hitting the market every day!

EGG SUBSTITUTES
- Egg Beaters (fat-free) *frozen and refrigerator sections
- Better'N Eggs (fat-free) *frozen and refrigerator sections
- Quick Eggs (fat-free) *refrigerator section
- The Right Egg (fat-free) *refrigerator section
- Second Nature egg substitutes (fat-free) *refrigerator section
- Morningstar Scramblers egg substitutes (fat-free)* refrigerator section

*All egg substitutes ARE NOT fat-free. Read the labels!

MARGARINE
- Promise Ultra Fat-Free Margarine (no trans-fatty acids) (fat-free)
- I Can't Believe It's Not Butter! Spray (4 sprays = 1 fat gram)
- SmartBeat Trans Fat-Free Margarine (no trans-fatty acids) (2 fat grams a Tbs.) (0.5 g Polyunsaturated and 1.5g monounsaturated)
- SmartBeat FAT-FREE margarine
- Promise Ultra low-fat margarine (4.0 fat grams a Tbs.)
- Weight Watchers' "Extra Light" low-fat margarine (4.0 fat grams a Tbs.)
- Blue Bonnet Lower-Fat margarine (4.5 fat grams per Tbs.)
- Fleishmann's Lower-Fat margarine (4.5 fat grams a Tbs.)
- Fleishmann's Fat-Free Spread This comes in a squeeze bottle.
- MRS. BATEMAN'S Baking Butter (fat substitute - 13 fat grams per cup)

*Watch for new low and fat-free margarines!

YOGURT
- Dannon plain and flavored "Light" fat-free yogurts (all flavors)
- Weight Watchers' Ultimate 90 non-fat flavored yogurts
- Weight Watchers' plain non-fat yogurt
- Yoplait fat-free yogurts (all flavors)
- T.C.B.Y. non-fat flavored yogurts

*Watch for your own store brands!

REFRIGERATOR SECTION
- Weight Watchers' low-fat biscuits
- Pillsbury brand Hearty Grain low-fat biscuits
- Pillsbury Soft canned Breadsticks (2.5 fat grams per breadstick) (also make great low-fat cinnamon rolls-recipe in "A Change for the Better" chapter of this book!)
- Pillsbury Crusty French Loaf (1 fat gram per serving-loaf serves 5)
- Apollo Fillo pastry sheets (makes great low-fat pie crust)
- Carnation liquid flavored Coffee-Mate (fat-free) (many flavors)
- Mocha Mix fat-free non-dairy creamer
- Fit 'n Free fat-free microwavable pizza (some grocery stores and mail order)
- Green Giant low-fat Harvest Burgers (all varieties)
- Morningstar Farms Garden Vege-Patties (low-fat)
- Midland Harvest Burgers (low-fat) (all varieties)
- Broken Arrow Ranch Brand venison (regular grind, Chile grind, and chunks) (11 fat grams a pound)
- Natural Touch fat-free Vegan Burgers
- Aunt Jemima low-fat pancakes and waffles
- Kellogg's fat-free waffles (Eggo brand)
- Bakers' Best low-fat giant soft pretzels (microwaveable)
- Simply Potatoes shredded hashbrown potatoes (fat-free)
- SUPERPRETZEL brand low-fat microwaveable soft giant pretzels
- Contadina "Light" pasta sauces (not all fat-free) Read labels!
- JELL-O brand fat-free pudding snacks
- Hershey's brand fat-free pudding snacks
- Swiss Miss fat-free pudding snacks
- Reddi Wip "Lite" whipped topping (low-fat) (made with soybean and cottonseed oil)
- Weight Watchers' frozen low-fat frozen foods (all varieties)
- Lean Cuisine low-fat frozen foods (all varieties)
- Healthy Choice low-fat frozen foods (all varieties)

LUNCHEON MEATS AND FRANKS
- ButterBall brand fat-free turkey breast and other low-fat luncheon meats
- Decker low-fat Canadian style bacon (4 slices are only 1.5 fat grams)
- Louis Rich fat-free turkey breast and other low-fat luncheon meats
- Healthy Choice "Light" low-fat luncheon meats
- Hafina Lean & Low 97% fat-free ham and other luncheon meats
- Dak low-fat luncheon meats
- Oscar Mayer fat-free franks
- Oscar Mayer fat-free bologna and other luncheon meats
- Peter Eckrich Deli "Lite" luncheon meats (low-fat)
- Wilson "Continental Deli" low-fat luncheon meats
- Hillshire Farms low-fat luncheon meats

- Hormel Light and Lean 97% fat-free franks (1 fat gram a frank)
- Healthy Choice 97% fat-free franks (1.5 fat grams a frank)
- Healthy Choice low-fat sausage

*Watch for other brands of low and fat-free luncheon meats. Remember if a product is 0.49 fat grams per serving, it can be considered fat-free. If you use 6 or 7 slices of luncheon meat on a sandwich (at 0.49 fat grams a slice), this would be about 3 fat grams.

FREEZER SECTION (FROZEN DESSERTS AND SNACKS)
- Yarnell's '"GUILT-FREE" fat-free and sugar-free ice cream (all flavors) THIS IS THE BEST FAT-FREE ICE CREAM ON THE MARKET!!
- Yarnell's "GUILT-FREE" fat-free and sugar-free frozen yogurt (all flavors) THIS IS THE BEST FAT-FREE FROZEN YOGURT ON THE MARKET!!
  *Yarnell's also carries a wide range of other low and fat-free frozen desserts!
- Blue Bell Extra Light frozen desserts (fat-free)
- Blue Bell Free frozen desserts (sugar and fat-free)
- Blue Bell fat-free frozen yogurt
- Weight Watchers' frozen dessert bars (low-fat)
- Simple Pleasures fat-free frozen dessert
- Borden fat-free frozen dessert (very good) (all varieties)
- Kemps fat-free frozen yogurt (all varieties)
- Dole Fruit 'N Juice bars (fat-free) (all flavors)
- Welch's fruit juice bars
- Freezer Pleezer fat-free fudge bars
- Blue Bunny fat-free frozen yogurts (all varieties)
- T.C.B.Y. low-fat frozen yogurts
- Healthy Choice low-fat frozen yogurt
- Dannon "Light" frozen yogurts
- Dreyer's fat-free frozen yogurts (all varieties)
- Crowley fat-free frozen yogurts
- Weight Watchers' Grand Collection fat-free frozen dessert
- Mrs Butter-worths low-fat cinnamon sweet rolls and glaze (frozen - you bake them yourself) (less than 1 fat gram)
- Rich's Enriched Homestyle roll dough (1 fat gram per roll - you bake them yourself)
- Sara Lee Free and "Light" frozen desserts (all varieties)
- Weight Watchers' low-fat desserts (all varieties)

*Watch for your own store brands!

DESSERT AND ICE CREAM TOPPINGS
- Smucker's Sundae fat-free syrups (caramel and butterscotch)
- Smuckers "Light" hot fudge topping (fat-free)

- Mrs. Richardson's fat-free toppings (caramel and hot fudge)
- Braum's Light Fudge Topping (fat-free) (only at Braum's Ice Cream Stores)
- Hershey's fat-free chocolate syrup
- I Can't Believe it's Yogurt fat-free and sugar-free fudge topping (only at I.C.B. I. Y. shops)
- Kraft Marshmallow Cream (fat-free)
- Betty Crocker Fat-Free Fluffy White Frosting mix (I use this in place of whipped topping)

*Many stores have their own brand of fat-free toppings! In most cases they are just as good and much cheaper! Most ice cream and yogurt stores carry their own brand of fat-free toppings as well.

COOKIES AND CRACKERS
- Keebler "Elfin Delights" low-fat cookies (many varieties)
- Keebler fat-free "Elfin Delights" Devil's Food Cookies
- Sunshine Oh! Berry Fat-Free Strawberry Wafers
- SNACKWELLS low and fat-free cookies and crackers (all varieties)
- Greenfield Healthy Foods "Homestyle Brownies" (fat-free) (Delicious!)
- Venus brand fat-free crackers (all varieties)
- Nabisco fat-free Fig Newtons
- Nabisco fat-free saltine crackers
- Health Valley fat-free cookies and crackers
- Frookie brand fat-free cookies and crackers
- Honey Maid low-fat graham crackers
- Sunshine low-fat graham crackers
- Nabisco low-fat graham crackers
- Keebler low-fat graham crackers
- Keebler reduced-fat Vanilla Wafers
- Burns & Ricker Fat-Free Party Mix (mixed crackers, pretzels, bagel chips, and snacks) *This product is kind of like Do Dads snack mix, but this one is fat-free and yummy! They also make fat-free Bagel Crisps and Fat-Free Mini Crispini (bite-sized flatbreads).

*Watch for new low and fat-free cookies and crackers!

CHIPS, PRETZELS, POPCORN, AND DIPS
- Frito Lay Baked Tostitos (1 fat gram per ounce) My favorite! *Watch for more low and non-fat Frito-Lay products in the future. You can recognize them by their new green band with a sun icon and the logo, "Taste The Fun, Not The Fat."
- El Paco's brand "Indulge Snacks" low-fat tortilla chips
- Amazing Taste baked NO-FAT tortilla chips
- El Galindo low-fat tortilla chips
- Planter's Reduced Fat Honey Roasted Peanuts, Cheez Curls, Cheez Balls, and Orchard Crunch Snack Mix

- Vera Cruz Baked Tortilla Rounds tortilla chips
- Childers Natural potato chips (fat-free) (all varieties)
- Louise's fat-free and low-fat potato chips and tortilla chips (all varieties)
- Louise's fat-free caramel corn (delicious!)
- Louise's Low-Fat buttered popcorn (2.5 fat grams per 3 1/2 cups)
- Louise's Low-Fat premium white popcorn (1.5 fat grams per 3 1/2 cups)
- Pacific Snax Lites low-fat rice snacks (all flavors) (1.5 fat grams for 2 cups)
- Houston Foods Co. low-fat caramel corn (1 fat gram per 1 cup)
- Richard Simmon's fat-free caramel popcorn (also offer low-fat Potato Crisps and Snacks)
- Pop Secret By Request popcorn (only 1 fat gram per 3-cup serving)
- Weight Watcher's microwave popcorn (only 1 fat gram per 3 cup serving)
- Orville Redenbacher's Smart-Pop popcorn (only 2.5 fat grams per 8 cups) *Also available in single serving bags.
- Guiltless Gourmet low-fat tortilla chips (all varieties)
- Smart Temptations low-fat tortilla chips
- Betty Crocker's "Pop Chips" low-fat potato chips (three flavors)
- "Nature's Classic" low-fat caramel popcorn (formally called Flavor House Caramel Crunch) I found this at K-Mart stores.
- Pop Weavers 97% Fat-Free caramel popcorn (1 fat gram per ½ cup)
- Pop Weavers Gourmet Light butter flavor low-fat microwave popcorn (2 fat grams for 3 cups)
- Orville Redenbacher's Butter Light microwave popcorn (2 fat grams per 3 cup serving)
- Pop-Rite Light microwave popcorn (2 fat grams for 3 cups)
- Tom Sturgis low-fat Dutch style pretzels
- Wege Dutch style large pretzels (low-fat)
- Mr. Salty fat-free pretzels
- Rold-Gold fat-free pretzels
- Guiltless Gourmet fat-free dips (spicy and mild Black Bean, spicy and mild Pinto Bean, spicy and mild Cheddar Queso)
- Frito Lay brand Tostitos Fat-Free Black Bean Dip

*Watch for new low and fat-free snacks!

BEEF, VENISON, TURKEY, CHICKEN, FISH
(fresh, frozen, and canned)
- ButterBall brand low-fat turkey and chicken
- ButterBall fresh ground all white turkey (4 fat grams per 4-oz. serving)
- ButterBall turkey breast medallions (1 fat gram per 4 pieces)
- ButterBall boneless breast cutlets (0.5 fat grams per cutlet)
- ButterBall turkey breast strips (1 fat gram per 4-oz. serving)
- ButterBall breakfast sausage links (2 fat grams per 2-link serving)
- ButterBall brand chicken breasts (marinated all varieties) (only 4 fat grams a pound) *These are delicious and so easy to pop in the microwave.

- Healthy Choice low-fat ground beef (16 fat grams a pound) (discontinued) Note: I called the company and was told the low-fat beef has been discontinued due to "lack of interest." that is hard for me to believe. Maybe they will reconsider with **enough requests!**
- Herritage Lifestyle Lite beef (low-fat beef) (in some grocery stores)
- Shady Brook ground turkey breast (1 fat gram per 4-oz. serving)
- Vermillion Valley (formally Covington Ranch) low-fat beef (mail order) Check Resource File for ordering information. (6-oz. serving only 3 fat grams) You beef lovers will appreciate this great product!!
- Louis Rich fresh ground turkey
- Louis Rich boneless breast tenderloins
- Laura's Lean Beef (found in grocery stores and mail order)
- Maverick Ranch Natural Lite low-fat beef (some grocery stores and mail order-check "Resource Guide.")
- The Turkey Store Seasoned Cuts (steaks, chops, and filets in three great flavors:Italian, Hickory, and Terriyaki) (99% fat-free)
- The Turkey Store turkey products (ground, skinless and boneless breasts, cutlets, etc.)
- Holley Farms fresh ground chicken
- Texas Western seasoned chicken breasts
- Texas B-B-Q seasoned chicken strips
- Shenandoah ground turkey
- Lake Lanier Farms ground chicken
- Broken Arrow Ranch Brand venison (all varieties)
- Tyson boneless and skinless chicken breast portions
- Tyson Mesquite flavored skinless and boneless chicken breasts portions
- Tyson Lemon Pepper flavored boneless and skinless chicken breast portions
- ButterBall turkey and chicken breast tenders
- Pilgrim's Pride chicken tenders
- The Turkey Store Extra Lean Ground Breast ground turkey (only 6 fat grams a pound)
- The Turkey Store ground turkey (watch the fat grams on this one because it contains skin and is higher in fat)
- Avalon Bay Ocean perch filets (frozen)
- Avalon Bay Ocean orange roughy filets (frozen)
- Delta Pride Farm catfish nuggets and filets (frozen)
- Sea Pack cooked artificial crab and lobster
- Treasure Isle (ready to cook) peeled and deveined shrimp
- Meridian (already cooked) peeled and deveined shrimp
- Tyson canned white meat chicken and turkey
- Starkist chunk light tuna (in spring water)

MISCELLANEOUS (PREPARED BOX MIXES)

- Betty Crocker's brand Potato Shakers (low-fat potato seasoning for oven baked french fries) Do not add oil. Spray lightly with a low-fat cooking spray.
- Pasta DeFino "No Boil" Lasagna and Ribbon Noodles
- Shake 'N Bake Perfect Potatoes "Herb & Garlic" seasoning (low-fat seasoning for oven baked french fries) Do not add oil. Spray lightly with a low-fat cooking spray.
- Uncle Ben's Low-Fat Hearty Soups boxed mixes (Black Bean and Rice is great)
- Betty Crocker Potato Buds Instant mashed potatoes (use skim milk and liquid Butter Buds in preparation)
- Pillsbury Hungry Jack Instant Mashed Potatoes (use skim milk and liquid Butter Buds in preparation)
- Casbah Couscous Pilaf mix (fat-free)
- Rice A Roni low-fat noodle mixes (also low sodium)
- Rice A Roni Low sodium and low-fat rice mixes
- Betty Crocker Hashbrown mix (low-fat)

*There are all kinds of prepared box mixes. You can use these in moderation, but be sure to use fat-free skim milk, Egg Beaters, and Liquid Butter Buds, or other fat-free condiments when making them. Most prepared box mixes contain a lot of sodium. Be sure and read your labels!

FAT-FREE CANDY (or very low-fat)

- gummy bears
- jelly beans
- most hard candy
- red licorice
- candy corn
- gum drops
- orange slices
- raisins (nature's candy)

*Avoid anything chocolate. It contains cocoa butter (a hydrogenated fat). Hydrogenated fats are a form of trans-fatty acids (which can be detrimental to your health)!

HEALTH FOOD STORES

- ENER-G Egg Replacers
- WonderSlim (fat and egg substitute derived from plums) (Natural Food Technologies)
- Mori-Nu Lite low-fat tofu (1 fat gram per serving)
- Just Like Shortenin' (fat substitute derived from plums) (The PlumLife Company)
- Garden Chef Wholesome and Hearty Garden Burgers
- Health Valley products (cookies, muffins, cereals, granola bars, soups, sauces, etc.)
- Guiltless Gourmet low and fat-free chips and dips
- Lifetime by Lifeline low and fat-free cheeses
- WHEAT OF MEAT Products (meat substitutes made from wheat and vegetables) all varieties (White Wave, Inc.)

*Check your local health food store for a large variety of low and fat-free products, as well as other low sodium, wheat free, and other allergy related food substitutes.

NEW PRODUCTS
(manufacturers and ordering information)

You have read about all of the great new low-fat items in the "NEW PRODUCTS" chapter. I've told you how to choose them and use them. Even though, in most cases, I gave you ordering information, I thought it would be easier if you had all the telephone numbers in one place for quick reference. I've listed the manufacturers according to the product they produce. In some instances you will find a manufacturer in more than one section. That is because they make more than one product. I've tried to group the products according to where they are located in most grocery stores. If you don't find a product, ask your grocer. Sometimes they place products where you would least expect to find them. Many of these products can be found in your local supermarket, but if not, I have provided the information you need to order. You might also show this list to your grocer if you are interested in getting the products into your local supermarket! If you have the telephone number to give him, chances are he will make the effort and give it a try!
Good Luck!

Happy Healthy Cooking !
Pam Mycoskie

BAKING AND SPICE SECTION

CUMBERLAND PACKING CORPORATION (800)231-1123
#2 CUMBERLAND ST.
BROOKLYN, NEW YORK 11205
IF CALLING FROM NEW YORK: (800)336-0363
    Butter Buds (sprinkle on variety) (fat-free)
    Butter Buds (the mix to make liquid) (fat-free)
    Sweet'N Low (bulk, liquid, or packets to be used in baking)
    Sweet'N Low Brown (brown sugar substitute to be used in baking)

NECTA SWEET (800)952-5129
    Necta Sweet (saccharin based sugar substitute in tablet form used for baking)

NATURAL FOOD TECHNOLOGIES, INC. (800)497-6595
    Wonderslim (fat-free) *This is a fat and egg substitute to be used in baking.

THE PLUMLIFE COMPANY (203)245-7893
    Just Like Shortenin' (fat-free) *This is a fat and egg substitute to be used in baking.

THE ESTÉE CORPORATION (201)335-1000
    Estée brand sugar free whipped topping mix (does contain saturated fat,
    but a very small amount- less than 1 fat gram and 4 calories per Tbs.)

CONTINENTAL MILLS, INC. (800)457-7744
    Krusteaz fat-free muffin mixes (all varieties)

SACO FOODS, INC. (800)373-SACO(7226)
    Saco Cultured Buttermilk Blend mix (low-fat)

BETTY CROCKER (800)328-6787
    Betty Crocker Fat-Free White Fluffy Frosting Mix *I use this in place of
    Cool Whip "Light" or Dream Whip for a topping as well as frosting.
    It has a marshmallow consistency, but tastes great chilled.

ENER-G FOODS,INC. (800)331-5222
In Washington State (800)325-9788
    ENER-G Egg Replacers This is a fat-free dry powdered egg mix (when added to water)
    equivalent to 162 eggs ($4.69).This product can be found in most health food stores.

DAILY BREAD COMPANY (800)635-5668

"Quick Loaf" by Daily Bread Company (fat-free bread mixes)
This comes in many varieties and is delicious (especially the "Garlic and Herbs").

PILLSBURY, INC. (800)767-4466

Pillsbury hot roll mix (fat-free)
Lovin'Lites low-fat muffin and cake mixes

PIONEER MILLS, INC. (800)235-8186

Pioneer Low-Fat Biscuit and Baking Mix (The box used to read No-Fat.) With the new labeling laws, it must read low-fat because there is 0.5 fat grams (less than one) per serving. This is a great product and VERY LOW-FAT! They also offer two fat-free gravy mixes that are wonderful!

ALBERTO-CULVER USA, INC. (708)450-3000
MELROSE PARK, IL. 60160

Papa Dash "Lite" Salt   Note: This is the best lite salt on the market!

BORDEN, INC. (800)426-7336

Eagle Brand low-fat sweetened condensed milk

REFRIGERATED DAIRY PRODUCTS

CHEESE PRODUCTS

ALPINE LACE BRANDS, INC. (201)378-8600
111 DUNNELL ROAD
MAPLEWOOD, NEW JERSEY 07040

Alpine Lace fat-free cheeses (Swiss, American, mozzarella, Cheddar and a variety of other choices) *The Alpine Lace fat-free Parmesan cheese is the BEST on the market! Look for it in the deli section of your grocery store. Alpine Lace also offers fat-free cream cheese flavored spreads that are great!

POLLIO DAIRY PRODUCTS (800)845-3733
120 MINEOLA BLVD.
MINEOLA, NEW YORK 11501

POLLY-O FREE fat-free mozzarella (This is the BEST fat-free mozzarella cheese on the market!) This cheese comes in the block (16-oz.) and grated (8-oz.) varieties. They also offer POLLY-O "Lite" mozzarella, "Lite" String Cheese sticks (2.5 fat grams an ounce), and POLLY-O FREE fat-free string cheese sticks, as well as fat-free ricotta cheese. All of their products are wonderful! *They also offer Jarlsberg "Lite" reduced fat Swiss cheese (3.5 fat grams per ounce).

LIFELINE FOOD COMPANY, INC. (408)899-5040
426 ORANGE ST.
SAND CITY, CA. 93955
  Lifetime by Lifeline low and non-fat cheese products (all varieties)
  I love their fat-free cheeses (especially the Monterey Jack, Jalapeño Jack, and Mild Mexican flavors). They offer a FANTASTIC low-fat "Mild Cheddar" (only 3 fat grams per ounce) that is the BEST low-fat Cheddar on the market! (Mail order available)

IMPERIA FOODS, INC. (800)526-7333
  Empiria low-fat Parmesan and Romano cheese

WEIGHT WATCHERS' PRODUCTS (800)651-6000
  They offer a variety of cheese products including a fat-free Parmesan cheese that is very good.

KRAFT FOODS, INC. (800)551-5557
  They offer a variety of cheese products including a fat-free Parmesan cheese that is very good.They also offer Philadelphia brand FREE (fat-free) cream cheese.

BORDEN, INC. (800)426-7336
  Borden fat-free cheese slices (all varieties) I really like their "Sharp Cheddar" flavor.
HEALTHY CHOICE (800)323-9980
  Healthy Choice fat-free cheese products (all varieties) I really love their "Velveeta Style" Fat-Free cheese!

SARGENTO FOODS, INC. (800)558-5802
#1 PERSNICKETY PLACE
PLYMOUTH, WISCONSIN 53073
  Sargento "Light" low-fat mozzarella and Cheddar (grated)

STELLER FOODS (800)558-7315
  Frigo brand low-fat cheeses (mozzarella and Cheddar) and fat-free ricotta

SORRENTO CHEESE CO. INC. (800)524-3373
  low and fat-free cheese products including "Precious" Fat-Free Ricotta

SOUR CREAM AND YOGURT

DANNON COMPANY, INC. (800)321-2174
  Dannon "Light" fat-free flavored and plain yogurts (all varieties)

YOPLAIT USA, INC.(800)328-1144
  fat-free flavored yogurts

LAND O LAKES PRODUCTS (800)328-4155
Land O Lakes NO-FAT sour cream (my favorite) and fat-free dips

KRAFT GENERAL FOODS (800)551-5557
Light n' Lively fat-free sour cream
Breakstone Free (fat-free) sour cream

M STAR, INC. (800)441-3321
Real Dairy (Naturally Yours) NO-FAT sour cream

SCHEPPS DAIRY PRODUCTS (800)428-6455
Schepps NO-FAT sour cream

BORDEN FOODS, INC. (800)426 7336
Borden fat-free sour cream and cottage cheese

HALLMAN INTERNATIONAL (800)759-1277
Dill and Spinach Dips (fat-free)
(I love the Spinach dip!)

WEIGHT WATCHER'S (800)333-3000
fat-free flavored yogurts

OAK FARMS (800)938-4848
Oak Farms fat-free sour cream and other low and fat free dairy products

DAISY BRAND, INC. (800)527-0205
Daisy NO FAT sour cream

EGG SUBSTITUTES

NABISCO BRANDS, INC. (800)932-7800
Egg Beaters (fat-free) *frozen and refrigerator sections

WORTHINGTON FOODS, INC.
MORNINGSTAR FARMS (800)243-1810
Better'N Eggs (fat-free) *frozen and refrigerator sections
Scramblers egg substitutes (fat-free)*refrigerator section

M STAR INC. (800)441-3321
Second Nature egg substitutes (fat-free) *refrigerator section

MARGARINE

VADENBURG FOODS (800)735-3610

Promise Ultra fat-free margarine (no trans-fatty acids) (fat-free)
They also offer Promise Ultra margarine (4 fat grams per Tbs.)
I Can't Believe It's Not Butter! cooking spray (4 sprays = 1 fat gram)

DIV. GFA BRANDS, INC. (201) 568-9300
HEART BEAT FOODS
P.O. BOX 397
CRESSKILL, N.J. 07626-0397

SmartBeat Trans Fat-Free margarine (no trans-fatty acids) (2 fat grams a Tbs.) (0.5 gm
polyunsaturated and 1.5gm monounsaturated)*They now offer a fat-free margarine, too.

WEIGHT WATCHER'S (800)333-3000

Weight Watcher's Light margarine (4 fat grams a Tbs.)
Weight Watcher's sodium free light margarine (4 fat grams a Tbs.)

MRS. BATEMAN'S BAKING BUTTER (800) 574-6822

Butter flavored fat substitute (13 fat grams per cup) *You can find this wonderful baking and
cooking product in some Sam's Clubs, King's Soopers, and Albertson's stores, as well as mail
order.

CUMBERLAND PACKING CORPORATION (800)231-1123
IN NEW YORK STATE (800)336-0363

The Butter Buds (mix to make liquid) can be found in the margarine refrigerated section,
spice section, or diet food section in most grocery stores. (also available by mail order)

NABISCO (800)622-4726

Fleischmann's Fat-Free Spread *This comes in a squeeze bottle.
Fleischmann's Lower Fat margarine (4.5 fat grams per Tbs.)
Blue Bonnet Lower-Fat margarine (4.5 fat grams per Tbs.)

REFRIGERATOR SECTION

(MISCELLANEOUS)

PILLSBURY PRODUCTS (800)767-4466
Pillsbury brand Hearty Grain low-fat biscuits
Pillsbury soft canned breadsticks (2.5 fat grams per breadstick) (also make great low-fat cinnamon rolls-recipe in "A Change for the Better" chapter of this book!)
Pillsbury Crusty French Loaf (1 fat gram per serving-loaf serves 5)

ATHENS PASTRIES & FROZEN FOODS, INC. (216)676-8500
CLEVELAND, OHIO 44142-2596
Apollo Fillo pastry sheets (makes great low-fat pie crust)

PIZZA FREE, INC. (800)779-5588
Fit 'n Free fat-free microwaveable pizza (some grocery stores) *mail order

THE PILLSBURY COMPANY (800)998-9996
Green Giant low-fat Harvest Burgers (all varieties)

GFA BRANDS, INC. (800)243-1810
MORNINGSTAR FARMS
Morningstar Farms Garden Vege-Patties (low-fat)

ARCHER DANIELS MIDLAND, CO. (800)835-2867
Midland Harvest Burgers (low-fat) (all varieties)

BROKEN ARROW RANCH (800)962-7264
Broken Arrow Ranch Brand venison (regular grind, chile grind, and chunks) (11 fat grams a pound)

WORTHINGTON FOODS, INC. (800) 243-1810
Natural Touch fat-free Vegan Burgers (This product won the "People's Choice Award" for best taste, when compared with burgers containing fat, in 1994.)

NORTHERN STAR CO. (800)648-7608
Simply Potatoes shredded hash brown potatoes (fat-free)

J & J SNACK FOODS CORPORATION (800)486-9533
SUPERPRETZEL brand low-fat microwaveable soft giant pretzels

BAKERS BEST SNACK FOOD CORPORATION (215)822-3511
1880 NORTH PENN RD.
HATFIELD, PENNSYLVANIA 19440
    Dutch Twist Soft Microwaveable Pretzels (fat-free)

LUNCHEON MEATS AND FRANKS

BUTTERBALL TURKEY COMPANY (800)323-4848
    ButterBall brand fat-free turkey breast and other low-fat luncheon meats

DECKER FOODS, INC. (800)678-1548
    Decker low-fat Canadian style bacon (4 slices are only 1.5 fat grams) and other
    low- fat luncheon meats

LOUIS RICH COMPANY (800)722-1421
    Louis Rich fat-free turkey breast and other low-fat luncheon meats

HEALTHY CHOICE (800)323-9980
    Healthy Choice "Light" low-fat luncheon meats
    Healthy Choice 97% fat-free franks (1.5 fat grams a frank)
    Healthy Choice low-fat sausage

OSCAR MAYER PRODUCTS (800)222-2323
    Oscar Mayer FREE fat-free franks
    Oscar Mayer FREE fat-free bologna
    Oscar Mayer other FREE fat-free luncheon meats

ECKRICH FOODS, INC. (800)325-7424
    Peter Eckrich Deli "Lite" luncheon meats (low-fat)

HORMEL FOODS. INC. (800)523-4635
    Hormel Light and Lean 97% fat-free franks (1 fat gram a frank)
    Chicken by George (marinated low-fat chicken products)

BIL MAR FOODS (800)537-7328
    Mr. Turkey Products (low-fat luncheon meats)

ARMOUR FOOD COMPANY (708)512-1840
DOWNERS GROVE, IL. 60515
    low-fat luncheon meats and other low-fat products

HILLSHIRE FARM (800)543-4465
    low-fat luncheon meats and other low-fat products

FREEZER SECTION

FROZEN DESSERTS AND SNACKS

YARNELL ICE CREAM COMPANY (800)766-2414 OR (800)666-2431
Yarnell's "GUILT-FREE" fat-free and sugar-free ice cream (all flavors) THIS IS THE BEST FAT-FREE ICE CREAM ON THE MARKET!! Yarnell also offers "GUILT-FREE" fat-free and sugar-free frozen yogurt (all flavors). THIS IS THE BEST FAT-FREE FROZEN YOGURT ON THE MARKET!! *Yarnell also carries a wide range of other low and fat-free frozen desserts!

BORDEN, INC. (800)426-7336
Borden fat-free ice cream *This is one of the best!

DANNON COMPANY, INC. (800)321-2174
low-fat frozen yogurt (all varieties)

HEALTHY CHOICE (800)323-9980
low-fat frozen desserts

WEIGHT WATCHERS' (800)333-3000
low and fat-free frozen deserts (all varieties)

BLUE BELL CREAMERIES L.P. (409) 836-7977
BRENHAM, TEXAS 77833
Blue Bell brand low and fat-free frozen yogurts and ice creams (all varieties)
*They also offer sugar-free products.

BRAUMS ICE CREAM AND DAIRY STORES (800)327-6455
low and fat-free ice creams and frozen yogurts (all varieties)

DESSERT AND ICE CREAM TOPPINGS

SMUCKER'S PRODUCTS (216)682-0015
Smucker's Sundae fat-free syrups (caramel and butterscotch)
Smuckers "Light" hot fudge topping (fat-free)

QUAKER COMPANY (800)494-7843
Mrs. Richardson's fat-free toppings (caramel and hot fudge)

BRAUM'S ICE CREAM AND DAIRY STORES (800)327-6455
 Braum's Light Fudge Topping (fat-free) (only at Braum's Ice Cream Stores)

GENERAL MILLS, INC. (800)328-6787
 Betty Crocker Fat-Free Fluffy White Frosting mix (I use this in place of whipped topping)

THE ESTÉE CORPORATION (201)335-1000
 Estée Whipped topping mix (low-fat)

SOUPS AND SAUCES

PIONEER FLOUR MILLS, (210)227-1401
P.O. BOX 118 DEPT. A
SAN ANTONIO, TEXAS 78291
 Pioneer fat-free gravy mixes (brown gravy and country white gravy)

HEALTH VALLEY (800)423-4646
 low and fat-free soups and sauces

HEALTHY CHOICE (800)323-9980
 low and fat-free soups and sauces

VANDENBERG FOODS, INC. (800)328-7248
 Ragu "Light" fat-free pasta sauces (all varieties) *Be sure and read the labels. They aren't all fat-free!

WEIGHT WATCHERS' (800) 333-3000
 low-fat soups and sauces (all varieties)

PRITIKIN PRODUCTS (800)458-5711
 Pritikin low and fat-free soups, sauces, and a variety of other products

CAMPBELL' S HEALTHY REQUEST (800)257-8443
 low-fat soups and sauces

THE HVR COMPANY (800)537-2823
 K.C. Masterpiece fat-free sauces (Original Barbecue and Dijon Mustard flavors are great!)

THE NESTLÉ FOOD COMPANY (818)549-6000
 Contadina low and fat-free sauces (check the labels - not all low-fat)

SALAD DRESSINGS AND CONDIMENTS

KRAFT PRODUCTS (800)551-5557
   low and fat-free salad dressings and condiments

WEIGHT WATCHERS' (800)333-3000
   low and fat-free salad dressings

HIDDEN VALLEY (800) 537-2823
   low and fat-free salad dressings, dip mixes, etc.

HUNT WESSON, INC. (714) 680-1000
P.O. Box 4800
FULLERTON, CA 92634
   Peter Pan "Smart Choice" peanut butter
   lowest fat peanut butter on the market (6 fat grams per Tbs.)

GFA BRANDS, INC. (201) 568-9300
HEART BEAT FOODS
P.O. BOX 397
CRESSLILL. N.J. 07626-0397
   SmartBeat fat-free mayonnaise

THOMAS J. LIPTON, INC. (800)697-7897
   Wish-bone's Healthy Sensations fat-free salad dressings

SEVEN SEAS FOODS, INC. (no telephone number listed)
P.O. BOX 21
GLENVIEW, IL. 60025
   Seven Seas FREE fat-free salad dressings (all varieties)

COOKIES AND CRACKERS

KEEBLER COMPANY (708) 782-2532
#1 HOLLOW TREE LANE
ELMHURST, IL 60126
   Keebler "Elfin Delights" low-fat cookies (many varieties)
   Keebler fat-free "Elfin Delights" devil's food cookies
   Keebler low-fat graham crackers
   Keebler reduced-fat Vanilla Wafers

NABISCO FOODS (800)622-4726
SNACKWELLS low and fat-free cookies and crackers (all varieties)
Nabisco fat-free Fig Newtons, graham crackers, fat-free saltine crackers and a variety of other low and fat-free products
Mr. Phipps low-fat crackers

R.W. FROOKIES, INC. (800)913-3663
Frookie's fat-free cookies and snacks

ENTENMANN'S INC. (800)842-9595
fat-free bakery items (all varieties)

THE GREENFIELD FOOD COMPANY (800)544-2670
Greenfield Healthy Foods "Homestyle Brownies" (fat-free) (Delicious!)
*They also make fat-free "Blondies" with chocolate chips that are great, too!

VENUS WAFERS, INC. (800)545-4538
Venus brand fat-free crackers (all varieties)

MOTHER'S CAKE AND COOKIE COMPANY (800)342-5129
Bakery Wagon fat-free cookies and Mother's fat-free cookies

HEALTH VALLEY (800)423-4846
Health Valley fat-free cookies and crackers

CHIPS, PRETZELS, POPCORN, AND DIPS

FRITO LAY (800)352-4477
Frito Lay "Baked Tostitos" (1 fat gram per ounce) My favorite! *Watch for more low and non-fat Frito-Lay products in the future. You can recognize them by their new green band with a sun icon and the logo, "Taste The Fun, Not The Fat."
Frito Lay brand "Tostitos Fat-Free Black Bean Dip" and other dips are great too.

SMART TEMPTATIONS (708)647-0787
Baked low-fat tortilla chips (really good)

EL PACO (800)225-6915
El Paco's brand "Indulge Snacks" low-fat tortilla chips
EL Paco fat-free flour tortillas

PLANTERS LIFESAVERS, INC. (800)541-1222
Reduced Fat Honey Roasted Peanuts
Reduced Fat Cheez Curls and Cheez Balls

YOUR RESOURCE GUIDE

GATES ENTERPRISES OF DALLAS (800)858-2783
Amazing Taste Baked NO-FAT tortilla chips

EL GALINDO (512)478-5756
El Galindo low-fat tortilla chips

GUILTLESS GOURMET PRODUCTS (512)443-4373
low-fat chips (all varieties)
Guiltless Gourmet fat-free dips (spicy and mild Black Bean, spicy and mild Pinto Bean, spicy and mild Cheddar Queso)

CHILDERS FOOD PRODUCTS (704)377-0800
Childers "Natural" potato chips (fat-free) (all varieties)

ATGTBT, INC. (800)284-8280
Louise's fat-free and low-fat potato chips and tortilla chips (all varieties)
Louise's fat-free caramel corn (delicious!) (THE BEST!)
Louise's low-fat buttered popcorn (2.5 fat grams per 3 1/2 cups)
Louise's low-fat premium white popcorn (1.5 fat grams per 3 1/2 cups)

PACIFIC GRAINS PRODUCTS (800)333-0110
"No Fries" low-fat Potato Snacks (all flavors) (1.5 fat grams for 2 cups)

PACIFIC SNAX PRODUCTS (800)494-4100
low-fat rice chips in all varieties (1 1/2 cups equal 1.5 fat grams)
*The caramel flavor is delicious!

HOUSTON FOODS CO. (800)548-5896
Houston Foods Co. low-fat caramel corn (1 fat gram per cup)

HUNT-WESSON, INC. (714)680-1000
Orville Redenbacher's Smart-Pop (only 2.5 fat grams per 8 cups) *Also available in single serving bags)

G.T. DIRECT (800) 341-6699
P.O Box 3561 (203) 949-0381
Wallingford, Connecticut 06494
Richard Simmon's fat-free caramel popcorn and Richard Simmon's low-fat "Potato Crisps" and other low-fat snacks

GENERAL MILLS (800)328-6787
Betty Crocker's "Pop Chips" low-fat potato chips (three flavors)
FLAVOR HOUSE PRODUCTS, INC. (800)233-5979
"Nature's Classic" low-fat caramel popcorn (formally called Flavor House Caramel Crunch)
I found this at K-Mart stores.

WEAVER POPCORN COMPANY (800)634-8161
Original Weaver Movie Popcorn Butter "Light" (1 fat gram for 3 cups)
Pop Weaver 97% fat-free caramel popcorn (1 fat gram per ½ cup)

BURNS & RICKER, INC. (no telephone number listed)
426 EAGLE ROCK AVE., ROSELAND, N.J. 07068
Burns & Ricker Fat-Free Party Mix (mixed crackers, pretzels, bagel chips, and snacks)
*This product is kind of like Do Dads snack mix, but this one is fat-free and yummy! They also make fat-free Bagel Crisps and Fat-Free Mini Crispini (bite-sized flatbreads).

CEREALS AND GRANOLA BARS

THE ORGANIC MILLING COMPANY (800)638-8686
Back to Nature "No-Fat Added" low-fat granola (only natural fat found in the grains.)

HEALTH VALLEY (800)423-4846
fat-free cereal, granola, and granola bars

NATURAL NECTAR CORP. (no telephone number listed)
CITY OF INDUSTRY, CALIFORNIA 91748
FI-BAR low-fat snack bars (all varieties)

THE QUAKER OATS COMPANY (800)856-5781
low-fat granola and granola bars
Quick Oats oatmeal

POST FOODS, INC. (800)431-7678
Grape-Nuts cereal
KELLOGGS' PRODUCTS (800)962-1413
low and fat-free cereals and a variety of other products

NABISCO FOODS (800) 622-4726
SNACKWELLS fat-free cereal bars (all flavors) (The strawberry flavor is our favorite!)

AUBURN FARMS, INC. (916)565-2800
P.O. BOX 348180
SACRAMENTO, CALIF. 95834
    Fat-Free Toast'N Jammers (kind of like pop tarts),
    Auburn Farms fat-free brownies (all varieties),
    and other fat-free cookies and snacks

BEEF, VENISON, TURKEY, CHICKEN, FISH
(fresh, frozen, and canned)

BUTTERBALL TURKEY CO. (800)323-4848
    low-fat turkey and chicken products (all varieties)

HEALTHY CHOICE PRODUCTS (800)323-9980
    low-fat luncheon meats, hot-dogs, sausage

UNITED HERITAGE CORP. (817)641-3681
    Heritage Lifestyle Lite Beef (low-fat beef) (in some grocery stores)

VERMILLION VALLEY LOW-FAT BEEF (800)365-BEEF(2333)
    Vermillion Valley (formally Covington Ranch) low-fat beef (mail order) (6-oz. serving only
    3 fat grams) You beef lovers will appreciate this great product!! *THIS IS THE BEST AND
    THE LEAST EXPENSIVE!

LAURA'S LOW-FAT BEEF (800)487-5326
    Laura's Lean Beef (found in grocery stores and mail order)
    *This is not as low-fat as Vermillion Valley or Maverick Natural Lite low-fat beef.

MAVERICK RANCH NATURAL LITE BEEF (800)497-2624
    This low-fat beef is available in some grocery stores and mail order (very good!)

JEROME FOODS, INC. (715)537-3131
BARRON, WISCONSIN 54812
    The Turkey Store turkey products (all varieties)
    Extra Lean ground turkey (6 fat grams a pound)

BROKEN ARROW RANCH BRAND (800)962-4263
    Broken Arrow Ranch Brand venison (chunk, chile grind, and ground meat)
    *This is a great low-fat substitute for beef at only 11 fat grams per pound.

ROCCO TURKEY, INC. (800) 233-8757
Shady Brook Farms ground breast of turkey (only 4 fat grams) and other low-fat turkey products

TYSON FOODS, INC. (800)643-3410
Tyson low-fat chicken (marinated and plain)

CUDDY FAMILY FARMS (704)624-2693
MARSHVILLE, N.C. 28103
low-fat turkey products

MISCELLANEOUS
(Prepared box mixes)

SHADE PASTA, INC. (800)662-6451
Pasta DeFino "No Boil" Lasagna and Ribbon noodles

SHAKE & BAKE PRODUCTS (800)431-1003
Shake 'N Bake Perfect Potatoes "Herb & Garlic" (low-fat seasoning for oven baked french fries) Do not add oil. Spray lightly with a low-fat cooking spray.

UNCLE BENS, INC. (800)548-6253
Uncle Ben's low-fat hearty soups boxed mixes (Black Bean and Rice is great)

FANTASTIC FOODS, INC. (707) 778-7801
PETALUMA, CALIF. 94954
Casbah Couscous pilaf mix (fat-free)(all varieties)

GENERAL MILLS, INC. (800)328-6787
Betty Crocker Hashbrown mix (low-fat) Betty Crocker's brand Potato Shakers (low-fat potato seasoning for oven baked french fries) Do not add oil. Spray lightly with a low-fat cooking spray.

HEALTH FOOD STORES
(Check your local health food store for many more!)

ENER-G FOODS, INC. (800)331-5222
In Washington State (800)325-9788
> ENER-G Egg Replacers (powder you mix with water) one box is equivalent to 162 Fat-Free eggs ($4.69).

NATURAL FOOD TECHNOLOGIES, INC. (800)497-6595
> WonderSlim (fat and egg substitute derived from plums)

THE PLUMLIFE COMPANY (203)245-7893
> Just Like Shortenin' (fat substitute derived from plums)

HEALTH VALLEY PRODUCTS (800)423-4040
> low and fat-free soups, sauces, cereals, muffins, cookies, etc.

WHITE WAVE, INC. (800)488-9283
> Meat *of* Wheat Products (meat substitute made from vegetables and wheat) all varieties

FANTASTIC FOODS, INC. (707)778-7801
PETALUMA, CALIF. 94954
> Casbah Couscous Pilaf mix (fat-free) (all varieties)

LIFELINE FOOD COMPANY, INC. (408)899-5040
> low and fat-free cheese products

WHOLESOME AND HEARTY FOODS, INC. (800)636-0109
> Garden Veggie Burgers (fat-free vegetable burgers)

WORTHINGTON FOODS, INC. (800)243-1810
> Natural Touch fat-free Vegan Burgers

MORINGA NUTRITIONAL FOODS, INC. (310) 787-0200
2050 W. 190TH ST.
SUITE 110
TORRANCE, CA 90504
> Mori-Nu Lite tofu (This product is low-fat, dairy-free, and an excellent source of cholesterol-free protein.)

NOTES

A FINAL
THOUGHT
(ENOUGH SAID!)

TAKE TIME OUT TO REALIZE YOU ARE SPECIAL!!

Do you often feel overloaded with too much to do and not enough time in the day? Then you are probably like most of us- human! Even though we would all love to be SUPER WOMAN OR SUPER MAN (by doing it all), most of us realize at some point (usually extreme exhaustion) that it just isn't humanly possible.

Most of us would like to feel special, loved, and happy, right? Did you know that we can only accumulate these treasures through our own self-love? How in the world can you expect others to love and respect you if you don't show them that you deserve that kind of attention? Wait a minute Pam, you say! I thought this book was about answers and now YOU are asking ME the questions? Yes, it is true. I am asking each of you to search within your heart to find your own self-worth. Every living person deserves to be loved and cherished by someone. I only want you to start by accepting yourself just the way you are. This can be very hard to do. Believe me, it took a very long time to finally accept the fact that I, like each of you, am a unique person that was placed here on Earth to receive love, and give it. Remember, like I said earlier in the book, you never REALLY possess love until you give it away. Your love is a wonderful gift to share with others. It's actually easier for most people to give, than to receive. I only ask each of you to save a little for yourself. You really do deserve it!!

A FINAL THOUGHT

As far back as I can remember, I hated being alone! I never knew why, only that it made me feel very uncomfortable. I guess I had always equated being alone with being unchosen. It wasn't until I was on my book tour (promoting *BUTTER BUSTERS THE COOKBOOK*) that I learned time alone can be very rewarding and a learning experience (as strange as that may seem). Once I realized that I wasn't REALLY alone (because God was with me in my heart), the fear of "being by myself" vanished. I must admit my own self-image has never been too great. I'm sure my fear of being alone stemmed from the fact that I didn't really like myself (much less love myself) enough to give it a try. I was uncomfortable without people around to provide distractions. This was the way I coped with "not being chosen," or truly looking at myself in an objective way, most of my adult life. Does this make sense to you? It was only after I realized that God was ALWAYS with me (BECAUSE HE LOVED AND CHERISHED ME) that I was able TO TRULY LOVE MYSELF! I gained great comfort and peace when I lost my fear of solitude. Let me say one thing before I continue. I REALIZE WE ALL COME FROM DIFFERENT SPIRITUAL BACKGROUNDS! I am not trying to convert anyone reading this book to my own personal Christian beliefs. Your ideas may differ from mine, and I can accept that.

You may be Jewish, Morman, Buddhist, or even agnostic or atheist. I am not here to change anyone, but only to share the spiritual experience, and acceptance of myself, that enabled me to conquer fear. When I use the term spiritual, I mean experiencing the feeling of being a part of something larger than myself. This was how I got over being alone. If you can't feel safe enough to let down your emotional barriers and walls, then you will be lonely and fearful. It is only when you truly experience faith and trust that the walls of isolation can disappear. Unfortunately, those same walls you have built around yourself for protection can also isolate you and stunt your personal, emotional, and spiritual growth.

I encourage each of you to learn to love yourself, by tearing down your walls of protection and trusting the higher power, of YOUR OWN CHOICE, to help you feel comfortable with that decision. Through faith you might just find out what a decision like this could mean in your own personal life!

If you are confused and don't know where to turn while searching for the answers, I can only recommend the solution that worked for me: If you find yourself scared to be alone (as I was), please realize by simply asking God into your own heart, YOU WILL NEVER HAVE TO BE ALONE AGAIN! It's a wonderful feeling and relief that can belong to ANYONE, if you only have the desire and the courage to ask! REMEMBER, GOD IS ALWAYS LISTENING!!!

I share because I care!

Fear Not

Fear not those
things which God has sent,
Though troublesome
they seem,
For He knows best
What must be done
To lead you to
your dream.

He'll test your strength
To make you strong,
For what's not used
grows weak,
And strip you of
What pulls you from
The highest goal
you seek.

He'll show you that
Where faith is placed,
A harvest soon is grown,
And what you'll learn
Is that in time
You reap what you
have sown.

For all that's His
Belongs to you
To do with
as you will.
But when you give
it back to Him,
He does your dreams fulfill.

author-unknown

A FINAL THOUGHT

FRIENDS ARE FOREVER!

Pam and Jill
January 24, 1994

This poem was given to me on a bookmark by a very dear friend, Jill Humbracht, when I first began writing *I'M LISTENING!* Jill is included in my "Earth Angel Poem" in the front of the book. I've had the poem taped to the side of my printer next to my computer where I have worked this past year. I look at it every day and think about how much faith I have placed in God concerning the wisdom, strength, and guidance it has taken me to write this book. I know that I am never alone in my venture for He is here with me guiding and directing, always leading the way. I have never feared what has been placed before me (such as deadlines, lack of material, resources, etc.), because from the beginning I realized that I was being led by someone much greater than myself. I believe that God has tested my strength this past year and it has certainly made me stronger in my faith and has also taught me a very valuable lesson. If you only take the time to "Listen" to your heart, the words will always come. God has shown me, by completing this book, that your dreams really can come true if you only have faith in Him. I know that I could have never physically endured these past seven weeks (with less than four hours of sleep a night) had it not been for His strength within me. He guided my fingers as I typed the words, and at times what I had written even surprised me. It was yet another sign that I was not alone. This poem has served as a tremendous inspiration to me and I wanted to share it with each of you. Read the poem out loud and really "listen" to the words. "For all that's His belongs to you, To do with as you will. But when you give it back to Him, He does your dreams fulfill!" It's amazing how much you can really learn, IF you just take the time "To Listen."

P.S. February 3, 1995

As I sit here at my computer writing the last words of *I'M LISTENING!*, I feel kind of sad. This book has been my heart and soul for the past year, and I really am going to miss the work I put into it every day (especially these past seven weeks). I know that I should be happy that it is finished (and I really am), but I've enjoyed it so much that it's kind of like the "let down" after Christmas (I hate to see it go)!

Dad's last Birthday
February 3, 1978

I've been trying to finish it for days, but one thing after another has come up and distracted me from actually completing the book. When I glanced at the calendar today as I was finishing "THE RESOURCE GUIDE" I noticed the date. Today would have been my Dad's 80th Birthday. Dad died in 1978. As a matter of fact this book is in memory of him (notice in the front). I found it rather fitting, for that reason, that this was the day I wrote the final words. Maybe that is why I am a little sad today, too. I miss my Dad so much! He died when Blake was two. Paige and Tyler never knew Gramps, but they have learned to know and love him through the pictures and stories that I have shared. My Dad was a wonderful man and I know he would be very proud of his grandchildren if he were here today!

My father was a major inspiration for this book, because he always had time to "Listen" to me no matter how busy he was! Maybe that is why he was so smart! You know, you really can learn a lot by listening.

I want you all to know how much I appreciate you for sharing your lives with me (through your letters), enabling me to learn so much (through my research), but most of all for allowing me to share my life with each of you! Thanks—for listening to me!!

In His Name,
Pam

Lagniappe
May 1, 1995

The word "Lagniappe" means "something extra" in French. You are probably wondering how I know that. Well, my husband Mike attended Tulane Medical School in New Orleans and it's kind of a New Orleans slang word. "Something Extra" is exactly what this is, too. You won't even find this page in the Table of Contents. I wasn't about to ask Mike to add or change one more thing! You are probably wondering now why I said "Mike" change things. Well, to put it bluntly, my typesetters could only put up with me for so long. Let me go back a bit and try to explain.

The Saga Continues!

On February 3, 1995 I really did write the final words to I'M LISTENING!...sort of. What you may not real ize is just how much work actually goes into a book once it has been written. The actual typesetting process began in November 1994 while I was still writing the book. The rough draft of the typeset manuscript went to Warner Books on March 15th. I knew when I sent it to New York there was still a ton of work to be done, but I had to send them something because we were on a deadline. About two weeks prior to that date I hired two additional typesetters, Stephanie Christian and Michael Hadwin, to finish the job. There were a lot of pictures to be scanned and additional work to be done in order to make the publishing date. On April 1st, I was asked by Warner Books to add 10 additional recipes so the book would contain over 100 instead of just 93 that were already included. That was no problem because I already had the recipes. You see, the original manuscript of I'M LISTENING! contained over 800 pages. I got kind of carried away when I was writing the "Kids Section." For this reason I split the book, including only a short kid's chapter in I'M LISTENING!, and decided to save the rest of the text and recipes for my next book, KIDS IN THE KITCHEN. The kid's recipes had all been tested and analyzed but not yet typeset. So, just when I thought the book was finished, it really wasn't. Along with that "little job" there were still permission letters to be sent, additional photos to be placed, captions to be written, and other corrections and revisions to be made. In other words, a whole lot more to do before the manuscript went back to New York for its final proof reading. There was no way my original typesetter had time to help me out. He had a full time job. My other typesetters, Stephanie and Michael, were a tremendous help, but two people can only do so much.

It was then my husband realized the job could not be completed on time unless HE took action. As you know Mike is an orthopedic surgeon. Well, to put it bluntly, he learned how to be a typesetter real quick. For two weeks Mike spent all of his free time at the BUTTER BUSTERS office helping me get things together. He learned amazing computer skills in less than a day. If

you are wondering why he has his surgery scrub suit on in this picture, it is because he was "on call" the final weekend as we worked around the clock (literally). He went back and forth to the hospital; setting broken arms and repairing (typesetting) the damaged pages of my manuscript, I had managed to mess up as I moved the text around, adding and deleting.

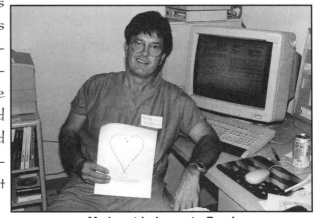
My heart belongs to Pam!

I think it is rather appropriate that he had the scrub suit on in this picture, because in my opinion, this was an emergency! There was no way the job could have been completed without Mike's help!

I've loved Mike since the day I met him (in July 1963), but my love has grown over the years and doubled during the past two weeks! His work has been a labor of love, and even though Mike has no idea this page is in the book (one of my other typesetters added it for me), his love and devotion could not go unnoticed! We even made him a name tag (notice the cardboard name tag paper-clipped to his pocket) that read, "Typesetter Coordinator." I'll never forget just how much Mike gave of his time and love (not to mention sleep) to see me through yet another project. As we celebrate our 25th Anniversary on May 23, 1995, I'll tell him that I love him more today than yesterday, but not as much as tomorrow (like I do every year), but this year those words will mean even more than they ever have before!

Mike, I really do love you "more than all the rice in China" and I thank you from the bottom of my heart for **always** standing beside me through the good times and the bad. Your unconditional love has carried me through on more than one occasion and I look forward to many, many more years of sharing our lives together.

The following poem is actually a song we used to sing in my sorority, Zeta Tau Alpha. I changed the words a bit, but it was the only way I could express just how I feel about Mike. All of my Gamma Psi Zeta sisters from TCU will understand, I'm sure!

GOD GAVE
God gave to the wise men their wisdom.
To the poets, their hopes and their dreams.
To Dad and Mother, He gave each other.
Not a soul was left out, so it seemed.
Now I thought that I'd been forgotten.
That life was an empty affair.
But when God gave me Michael,
It was then that I knew.
That I'd gotten more than my share!
author- unknown

Together Forever!